A VIEW FROM THE CORE

A SYNTHESIS OF OHIO HOPEWELL ARCHAEOLOGY

EDITED BY

PAUL J. PACHECO

THE OHIO ARCHAEOLOGICAL COUNCIL-COLUMBUS, OHIO

*The Ohio Archaeological Council is a private, non-profit corporation registered with the State of Ohio in 1975 as a charitable scientific and educational organization promoting the advancement of archaeology in Ohio. Its members include professional archaeologists, avocational archaeologists, and interested students of Ohio archaeology.

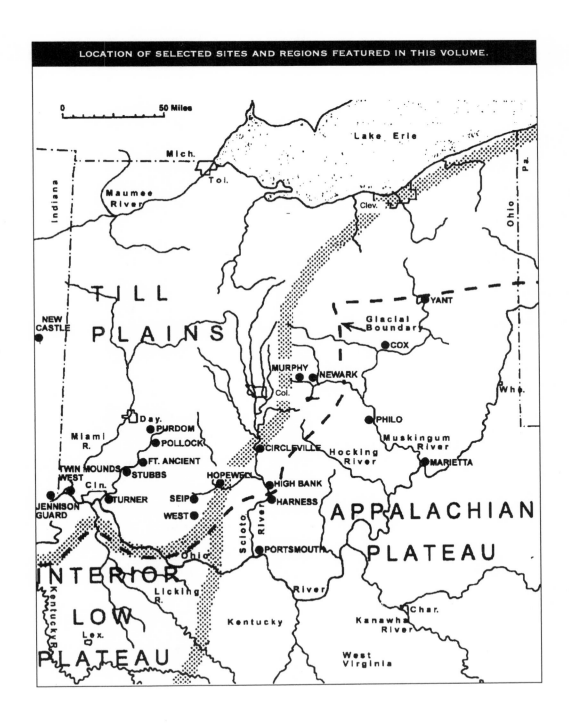

LOCATION OF SELECTED SITES AND REGIONS FEATURED IN THIS VOLUME.

Contents

INTRODUCTION
Paul J. Pacheco VI

SECTION ONE: THE CORE
PART 1; SETTLEMENT, SOCIAL ORGANIZATION, AND SYMBOLISM

1. **THE HOPEWELL HOUSING SHORTAGE IN OHIO, A. D. 1-350**
James B. Griffin 4

2. **OHIO HOPEWELL REGIONAL SETTLEMENT PATTERNS**
Paul J. Pacheco 16

3. **THE OHIO HOPEWELL ECONICHE: HUMAN-LAND INTERACTION IN THE CORE AREA**
Dee Anne Wymer 36

4. **THE 1984 EXCAVATION AT 12D29S: A MIDDLE WOODLAND VILLAGE IN SOUTHEASTERN INDIANA**
Jack K. Blosser 54

5. **REVISING THE OHIO MIDDLE WOODLAND CERAMIC TYPOLOGY: NEW INFORMATION FROM THE TWIN
MOUNDS WEST SITE**
Rebecca A. Hawkins 70

6. **BLADELETS ARE TOOLS TOO: THE PREDOMINANCE OF BLADELETS AMONG FORMAL TOOLS AT OHIO
HOPEWELL SITES**
Robert A. Genheimer 92

7. **FLINT RAW MATERIAL USE IN OHIO HOPEWELL**
Kent D. Vickery 108

8. **SOCIAL IMPLICATIONS OF OHIO HOPEWELL ART**
C. Wesley Cowan 128

9. **A COMMENTARY ON THE CONTEXTS AND CONTENTS OF LARGE TO SMALL OHIO HOPEWELL DEPOSITS**
N'omi B. Greber 150

10. **SOCIAL STRUCTURE AND THE PRAGMATIC MEANING OF MATERIAL CULTURE: OHIO HOPEWELL AS ECCLE-
SIASTIC- COMMUNAL CULT**
A. Martin Byers 174

11. **HOPEWELLIAN GEOMETRY: FORMS AT THE INTERFACE OF TIME AND ETERNITY**
William F. Romain 194

12. **TOWARDS A DEFINITION OF THE OHIO HOPEWELL CORE AND PERIPHERY UTILIZING THE GEOMETRIC
EARTHWORKS**
James A. Marshall 210

PART 2: RESEARCH AT EARTHWORKS AND MOUNDS

13. **THE NEWARK EARTHWORKS AND THE GEOMETRIC ENCLOSURES OF THE SCIOTO VALLEY: CONNECTIONS AND CONJECTURES**
    Bradley T. Lepper 224

14. **THE ENCLOSED HILLTOPS OF SOUTHERN OHIO**
    Robert V. Riordan 242

15. **PREHISTORIC LAND MODIFICATION AT THE FORT ANCIENT HILLTOP ENCLOSURE: A MODEL OF FORMAL AND ACCRETIVE DEVELOPMENT**
    Robert P. Connolly 258

16. **1990 EXCAVATIONS AT CAPITOLIUM MOUND (33WN13), MARIETTA, WASHINGTON COUNTY, OHIO: A WORKING EVALUATION**
    William H. Pickard 274

17. **THE PURDOM MOUND GROUP: THE DAYTON MUSEUM OF NATURAL HISTORY'S EXCAVATION AND A SYNOPSIS OF THE EXCAVATIONS OF ADAMS AND BAILEY**
    J. M. Heilman and Lynn M. Mahoney 286

SECTION TWO: THE PERIPHERY

18. **THE OHIO HOPEWELL CORE AND ITS MANY MARGINS: DECONSTRUCTING UPLAND AND HINTERLAND RELATIONS**
    Mark F. Seeman 304

19. **THE MIDDLE WOODLAND-LATE WOODLAND TRANSITION IN THE CENTRAL MUSKINGUM VALLEY OF EASTERN OHIO: A VIEW FROM THE PHILO ARCHAEOLOGICAL DISTRICT**
    Jeff Carskadden and James Morton 316

20. **THE ADENA/HOPEWELL CONVERGENCE IN EAST CENTRAL INDIANA**
    Donald R. Cochran 340

21. **DECORATED LEATHER OBJECTS FROM THE MOUNT VERNON SITE, A HOPEWELL SITE IN POSEY COUNTY, INDIANA**
    Curtis H. Tomack and Frank N. Burkett 354

22. **PINSON MOUNDS AND THE MIDDLE WOODLAND PERIOD IN THE MIDSOUTH AND LOWER MISSISSIPPI VALLEY**
    Robert C. Mainfort, Jr. 370

SECTION THREE: COMMENTARY

23. **PUTTING AN END TO OHIO HOPEWELL**
    William S. Dancey 394

24. **CORE AND PERIPHERY: THE FINAL CHAPTER ON OHIO HOPEWELL**
    Olaf H. Prufer 406

LIST OF CONTRIBUTORS 426

INTRODUCTION

PAUL J. PACHECO

A View from the Core: A Synthesis of Ohio Hopewell Archaeology is the second book in a series sponsored by the Ohio Archaeological Council to celebrate the rich archaeological heritage of the state of Ohio. The book primarily represents a proceedings volume of the OAC's Second Annual Conference on Ohio Archaeology, held at the Comfort Inn November 19-20, 1993 in Chillicothe, Ohio. While a nominal geographic core and periphery concept was utilized as an organizational framework for both the book and conference, it did not limit the perspectives taken by any of the contributing authors who addressed a variety of topics concerning Ohio Hopewell archaeology. One of our goals at this conference and in creating the volume was to provide a forum for presenting the many diverse approaches and aspects of Ohio Hopewell research. We purposely attempted to cast a wide net.

The "View from the Core" conference, from which the book took its name, was organized into three sessions, a Plenary session held on Friday November 19, a Contributed Papers session, held on Saturday November 20, and a concurrent Poster session that ran for both days. The Plenary session was composed of ten solicited papers aimed at summarizing major aspects of Ohio Hopewell archaeology. The Plenary session was followed by a panel discussion which brought notable comments from Olaf H. Prufer. His participation during this panel discussion was behind the invitation for Prufer to make a contribution to the volume as the discussant. The Contributed Papers session included twelve papers on a variety of topics. The Saturday session followed a 3-hour bus tour of important Hopewell sites in the Chillicothe vicinity, a tour which was attended by almost half of the conference registrants.

Following the panel discussion on Friday was a banquet and Key-Note Address given by Robert C. Mainfort, Jr. Mainfort's entertaining and informative talk concerned Hopewellian manifestations of the Middle South, which included his work at the Pinson Mounds site in Tennessee. A substantive version of Mainfort's presentation is included in the volume for a view of the Middle Woodland period far beyond the Ohio Hopewell core. Mainfort's chapter, and the Mount Vernon Mound chapter by Tomak and Burkett, are the only chapters included in the volume not clearly dealing with Ohio Hopewell (treating the eastern Indiana material presented by Cochran as the western periphery to the Ohio core).

A View from the Core is organized into three sections. The first section focuses on chapters dealing with topics connected to the Ohio Hopewell core, with the southern Ohio "heartland" acting as the geographic center. This section is further divided into two parts, one with twelve chapters concerning settlement, social organization, and symbolism, and the other with five chapters concerning research at earthwork and mound sites. The venerable James B. Griffin opens section One with a look at Ohio Hopewell settlement patterns. The second section of the book focuses on topics dealing with the Ohio Hopewell periphery. The five chapters in this section move from topics clearly marginal to the Ohio core, to topics having little if anything to do with the core (i.e. the Mount Vernon and Middle South chapters). The final section of the book presents commentary and discussion. Two chapters are included in this section; the first by Dancey deals with the important topic of the Ohio Hopewell "collapse", while the second by Prufer is a solicited discussion of the the other chapters that not only critically examines, but summarizes the book. Prufer offers several important insights into Ohio Hopewell archaeology.

The resulting mix is perhaps the most comprehensive summary of Ohio Hopewell / Middle Woodland period archaeology ever assembled. Nineteen of the twenty-three papers (including the Key-Note Address) presented at the 1993 Chillicothe conference are included in the book. Also included are two chapters (Marshall and Tomak & Burkett) that were presented as posters at the conference, one chapter (Byers) that arrived to late to be included on the program, one chapter (Greber) which was presented elsewhere and substituted for the conference paper, and one chapter (Prufer) that was solicited after the conference.

This twenty-four chapter OAC effort might be seen as a "resurgence of the North" after the "revolt of the South", as Griffin had labeled the 1978 Chillicothe Conference in reference to the limited number of papers dealing with Ohio Hopewell presented at that conference. *A View from the Core* reclaims the Hopewellian spotlight for Ohio, representing the first volume dedicated solely to summarizing this important component of Middle Woodland period archaeology in the Eastern Woodlands. The OAC and its membership is to be applauded for the continuing effort to bring Ohio back onto the "archaeological map".

This book is the product of several peoples' efforts, primarily of the volunteer variety. Al Tonetti and Bob Genheimer deserve the most credit for making the OAC series a success. Their tireless work on the OAC Education Committee and as both past and current President of the organization, respectively, is at the "True Core" of this volume. Ohio archaeology owes them a great deal of thanks. Other members of the OAC Education Committee who deserve to be singled out include Marilyn Orr, William Dancey, John Blank, and Kevin Pape. Marilyn's help with the technical editing is appreciated tremendously. William Dancey, having forged through uncharted waters with the first volume, provided answers to the many particular questions that arose during production. John Blank provided equipment, personnel, and the financial support of his Cleveland State University office to help desktop publish the book. The personnel he offered came in the form of Gail Baker, a veteran of the first OAC book in this series. I wish to thank her for the day to day help she provided. I also want to thank Mark Seeman, 1994-95 OAC President, for his help and support during our 1995 publication collapse. His ideas carried the book forward. Kevin Pape offered the services of his Graphics Department at Gray & Pape, Inc., especially Kris Luce and Casey Fagin. They created the beautiful new format for the volume, saving us in our moment of crisis. All of us appreciate their help in creating a volume which captures the spirit of the Ohio Hopewell core. I also want to acknowledge all the authors from the book for their patience and cooperation during what was often an arduous process. I especially appreciate Olaf Prufer's willingness to act as a discussant for the volume. His insights and contributions to Ohio Hopewell archaeology are unmatched. Finally, thanks to all of you who have helped me to see the end of this project; know that you are indeed, appreciated.

Cover and Section Breaks: Wray Figurine, recovered from one of the principal burial mounds at Newark Earthworks, is a possible representation of a Hopewell shaman (see Chapter 13, this volume). Courtesy of the Ohio Historical Society.

Chapter Breaks and Back Cover: Double-headed frog effigy, in copper, recovered from the Rutledge Mound, Licking County, Ohio. Courtesy of the Ohio Historical Society.

SECTION ONE: THE CORE

PART ONE: SETTLEMENT, SOCIAL ORGANIZATION, AND SYMBOLISM

THE HOPEWELL HOUSING
SHORTAGE IN OHIO, A.D. 1-350

JAMES B. GRIFFIN

ABSTRACT

One of the major concerns of individuals during the last 200 years who have studied the remains of the Great Earthwork Builders in southern Ohio has been the identity of the societies who left the remarkable geometric earthworks and burial mounds associated with them. Gerard Fowke and others compiled opinions of the ignorant, the deluded, and just plain dotty. Opinions varied as to the size of the population from many thousands who, in order to construct the earthworks, must have had an agricultural base. In the last 20 to 30 years a considerable number of Ohio professional archaeologists have suggested that Hopewell societies in southern Ohio primarily lived in small groups away from the major earthworks and only occupied the large earthworks during the construction of the burial mounds and other group activities. Some testimonials to habitation debris at the major sites are offered in this paper.

INTRODUCTION

For a long time archaeologists have debated whether there are any village sites associated with the Hopewell mounds and earthworks of southern Ohio. Most of the excavations were concentrated on the burial mounds with scant interest in, or attention to a search for the areas occupied by the people during the mound and earthwork construction. The idea that there were no village sites with similar materials to those in the mounds reached a peak in the late 1920s and early 1930s when it was suggested that what were called Fort Ancient village sites were really those of the Hopewell earthwork builders. Some thirty to forty years later it was suggested that the earthworks enclosed unoccupied ceremonial centers. There can be no consensus about the definition of a village site unless adequate excavation has been made and living areas, workshop areas and other evidence has been secured.

EVIDENCE FOR HOPEWELL VILLAGES IN SOUTHERN OHIO

Turner Site

Lack of village sites is especially true for the Hopewell culture of southern Ohio where only the Turner site near Cincinnati, excavated almost 100 years ago, strongly suggested evidence of living debris. The report on the Turner site was not published for more than thirty years after the major excavations and was remarkably condensed.

Anyone who has read the Turner site report (Willoughby and Hooton 1922) cannot help but be impressed with the evidence for extensive village site occupation under the wall of the Great Embankment, in the large space inside it, and in the debris gathered up with the earth which formed the burial mounds. The collection of pottery from this site is by far the largest of any Ohio Hopewell earthwork site. Prufer's analysis of the Turner collection in the Peabody Museum comprised some 3,385 sherds (Prufer 1968:138). When Griffin and Morgan studied the Turner pottery collection which was shipped by Peabody to the Ohio State Museum in 1943 we had a count of 6,185 sherds carefully identified as to their provenience. We are at a loss to explain this discrepancy. In regard to the rela-

tive scarcity of pottery fragments from Ohio Hopewell mounds excavated by the Columbus archaeologists, the classic comment applies that, "There can be little doubt that if the explorations of the Hopewell, Mound City, Liberty (Harness), and other well-known sites of southern Ohio had been as prolonged and as carefully conducted as these of the Turner Group, an equal number and variety of potsherds would have been found" (Willoughly and Hooton 1922:93). It is certain that pottery sherds were held in low esteem by late nineteenth and early twentieth century Ohio and many other archaeologists, and not enough care was expended in the excavation, cataloging, or conservation of those that were recovered.

When C. L. Metz M.D., who did much of the excavation at the Turner site, presented a model of the Turner site to the Cincinnati Museum in 1911, a pamphlet was issued by the Museum with a brief discussion of the site by Metz. There is also a plan of the site by Metz who identifies a six acre area north of the Great Enclosure and on the edge of the terrace as a village site. This identification does not appear on the plan published by Willoughby and Hooton (1922:plate 1), which was made by professional surveyors in 1887, and somewhat modified when drawn for the publication.

In addition to the probability that the occupational debris incorporated in the Turner site earthworks and mounds is from a "true" village site, Starr (1960) mentions four village areas he believed to be associated with the Turner Earthworks because of the collections made from them. There was also a small nearby cemetery area.

Other Miami Valley Village Sites

Starr (1960) also refers to three Hopewell village sites in Miami Township of Hamilton county and one village in the Whitewater Valley in Colerain Township. A small village site in Crosby Township identified as Paddy's Run produced lamellar blades, Middle Woodland pottery and stemmed points. The Nine Mile site east of Cincinnati has Middle Woodland pottery, lamellar blades, some of them made from Flint Ridge flint. Most of the Nine Mile pottery is tempered with limestone particles.

In Dearborn County, Indiana two local collectors have collected from a site (aka Jennison Guard) with four habitation areas which are almost certainly house areas. Their small excavations have yielded two mica effigy projectile points, Flint Ridge and Harrison County, Indiana (i.e. Wyandotte) chert, lamellar blades, broad stemmed and corner notched points, celts, shell hoes, cut mica fragments, well made polished bone needles, bone fish hooks and antler projectile points. The Middle Woodland pottery is plain and cordmarked with one tetrapod foot (Whitacre and Whitacre 1986).

The Miami Fort Twin Mounds area has produced Middle Woodland pottery along with the other diagnostic indications of village debris. The Headquarters site (Lee and Vickery 1972), on the second terrace of the Great Miami River some forty feet above the stream, is a village with three female burials which had Middle Woodland pottery, a variety of bone tools, and chippage and implements made from local cherts. Some Flint Ridge and Harrison County cherts were also recovered.

Fort Ancient

Fort Ancient in Warren County, Ohio is located on the uplands east of the Little Miami River. It is a major Ohio Hopewell construction and has drawn the attention of archaeologists (I use that appellation loosely) for over a hundred years.

Mound 50, excavated by W.K. Moorehead (1890:36), is likely a Hopewell construction located in the North Enclosure. Debitage was extensive on the surface just inside and outside of the east breach of the wall at the Lebanon-Chillicothe Road, much of it from Flint Ridge and from the Wyandotte deposits in Indiana. A great many chert discs made of both kinds of chert were found in the field north of the fort (Essenpreis and Moseley 1984:26). Projectile points and lamellar blades from within the fort and unfinished pre-platform pipe blocks of Scioto fired clay were found together two feet below the surface of the South Enclosure. Moorehead refers to the considerable amount of aboriginal artifacts collected in and around Fort Ancient, but since the items he illustrates range from Late Archaic to the Anderson phase of Fort Ancient, it is a bit difficult to accurately assess the amount of Hopewellian occupational debris obtained by collectors.

R.G. Morgan and H.H. Ellis excavated at Fort Ancient in 1939-1940, and W.C. Mills in 1908. The following statements by Morgan support the presence there of occupational debris.

The evidence establishing the identity of the builders is to be found not only in the structure of the works themselves but also in the pottery tools, implements and ornaments found in around the fort. One of the villages of this early Indian group was located just east of the eastern walls of the North Fort. Here have been found artifacts and pottery characteristic of the Hopewell Culture as it has been delineated through explorations of other Hopewell Indian sites, such as Mound City, Seip Mound, the Hopewell Group in Ross County and the Tremper Group in Scioto County. Implements, ornaments, or pottery typical of the Hopewell Culture have been found in the mounds, in the interior depressions and in the walls of all three sections of the Fort Ancient Earthworks.

Another feature which links this remarkable structure with the Hopewell Culture is the Parallel Walls which also occur at such Hopewell sites as the Turner Group in Hamilton County, the Newark Earthworks at Newark and several other geometrical works. The use of stone coverings for burial mounds, the presence of a crematory basin in one of the mounds and the artifacts used as offerings to the dead are also indicative of the Hopewell Culture [Morgan 1946:9-10].

Furthermore, the numerous evidences of domestic activities found within the enclosure and adjacent to it, clearly show that the Hopewell people actually lived on the site and did not use it merely for defensive and ceremonial purposes. Rites connected with the Hopewell cult of the dead were carried out within the enclosure as is indicated by the burial mounds with their offerings. The offering of ceremonially "killed" copper objects found near the Parallel Walls also suggest a burial ritual [Morgan 1946:9-15].

Morgan's reference to a village site just east of the eastern walls of Fort Ancient was identified at least partly as the result of one of the tasks performed by a Civilian Conservation Corps camp at Fort Ancient in the early 1930s. When J. B.Griffin studied C. C. Anderson's collection from the lowland village site along the Little Miami River in 1934 he viewed an area about 90 m (100 yards) south of the east-west road through the North Fort and immediately east of the large segmented mounds of the east wall, which had been excavated about .6 m to .9 m (2 to 3 feet) to obtain earth to fill in a shallow ravine about .4 km (a quarter mile) to the east on which to place the park superintendents new residence. It was easy to recognize the bottoms of refuse pits with habitational debris that were distributed over what was then the surface. Some of these were still visible in the fall of 1937 when W. K. Moorehead, H. C. Shetrone, E. Lilly, R. Morgan, and J. B. Griffin visited the location. A small amount of shovel testing convinced them of the presence of Hopewell occupation.

As a result of Richard Morgan's intensive study of Fort Ancient from the museum collections, published accounts and two seasons excavation, the Ohio State Archaeological and Historical Society booklet *Fort Ancient* (Morgan 1946:38-39) has the following statement:

> *An extensive village of the Hopewell peoples, the builders of the Fort Ancient Earthworks, once occupied this site. The exact boundaries of this village site are not known, but it was several acres in extent. Explorations in this area, which was directly east of the great walls, brought to light the characteristic tools, pottery and ornaments of the Hopewell Culture. Among the artifacts found at the village site may be mentioned grooved axes, pestles, plummets, flake knives, prepared cores of Flint Ridge flint, platform pipes, quartz arrow points, flint arrow and spear points, flint disks, gorgets, sheets of mica, cones, ungrooved axes, scrapers, drills, hammerstones, and several types of banded slate ceremonial pieces.*

South of the Twin Mounds the remains of storage pits were discovered with a village. Between Mound 9 and the wall of the enclosure there was a spring in prehistoric times which was surrounded by large slabs of limestone. Excavations in 1941 revealed this spring and a piece of typical Hopewell pottery on some of the flat slabs of stone.

In 1898, a ceremonial offering of copper artifacts and other objects was found in the northeast section of this village. It consisted of fifty-nine copper specimens, forty-four pieces of galena or lead ore and eight fragments of pendants. They were found twelve inches beneath the surface within a space of eighteen by twenty four inches. Over the top of this offering more than one hundred sheets of mica had been placed. All of the copper specimens, as well as the pendants, had been ceremonially "killed" apparently to release their spirits, for they were all battered, and bent to a marked degree. The following types of artifacts, however, could be determined: embossed breast plates, axes, spool-shaped ear ornaments, a reel-shaped gorget and a bracelet.

There is quite a long interlude between Mills' recovery of the 1898 cache, the work in the 1930s, and the discovery of another significant find:

> *A second cache was recently discovered by a local landowner while plowing fields that now overlie the parallel-walled enclosure. It comprised ritual artifacts flaked from exotic stone, including 17 spear points and curved knives of obsidian procured from Yellowstone Park, Wyoming; 11 ceremonial blades, each aproximately 20 cm long of finely crafted Wyandotte chert acquired from southern Indiana; and 5 magnificent blades, each some 7 cm long of clear quartz crystal secured from an unknown locality [Essenpreis and Moseley 1984:26].*

Robert Connolly's report at the 1992 Pittsburgh S. A. A. Meeting stated that the Fort Ancient Earthworks and their immediate environs were loci of habitational activity left by the Hopewellian populations. These included substantial structures, fire pits, limestone pavements, and midden deposits in the area east of the North Enclosure. Additional Hopewell evidence is found in 30 ha or more northeast of Connolly's excavations (Connolly 1992).

Stubbs Mills

In addition to the village site occupation east of, and within, Fort Ancient, a recent examination of Warren County identified about twenty-eight Middle Woodland sites, six of strong Hopewell affliation (Genheimer 1984). Some of these produced only small amounts of materials, but three of them in the Little Miami Valley were of particular importance. These were located in the flood-plain and outwash terraces between South Lebanon and Morrow. Cores and Hopewell lamellar blades of Flint Ridge and Harrison County chert, sheet mica fragments, crystalline quartz, obisidian flakes, and one Knife River chalcedony flake firmly identify the occupation as Hopewell. Ceramic evidence was scanty, but what was recovered corresponded to the pottery from Fort Ancient of Hopewell affiliation. Most of it was grit tempered with plain and cordmarked surface. Only two sherds were decorated: one with rocker-stamping and one with incising. The sites identified east of South Lebanon were probably associated with the construction and ceremonial activities of the Stubbs Earthworks, which were surveyed by Whittlesey (1851). This was a large rectangular enclosure, extending into a larger semi-circle. A purported Serpent Mound west of the Stubbs construction was probably also a Hopewell construction, but is not a serpent mound.

At the Pittsburgh conclave, Genheimer (1992) reported that in the Lower Little Miami Valley the more productive sites were larger than hamlets, and that on some sites debris clusters suggest discrete household units with a small range of domestic activities and not specialized tasks.

Fort Hill

Fort Hill in the eastern part of Highland County, Ohio is on the eastern side of Baker Fork of Brush Creek. It is about 16 km (10 miles) north of Serpent Mound and is an erosional remnant of Paleozoic formations capped by the Berea sandstone. The sandstone provided the stone which was incorporated into the earthworks which stands at an elevation of 391 m (1,283 feet). This stone and earthen wall, about 2.6 km (1.625 miles) long around the brow of the hill, is not continuous, but broken by thirty-three openings of 4.5 to 6 m (fifteen to twenty feet), placed at irregular intervals. There is little evidence of occupation within the enclosure, but to the south of the hill on the valley floor there were two circular earthworks.

Excavations in this area by the Ohio Historical Society from 1952 to 1954 obtained plain and cordmarked pottery, projectile points and other tools fashioned from Flint Ridge and Harrison County, Indiana chert, mica fragments and other indications of Hopewell occupation. The same materials were found in trenches excavated in the general area and within and under one of the circular enclosures on a house floor (Potter and Thomas 1970).

The Boblett and Campbell Sites

The Boblett Group of prehistoric mounds is located upon a secondary terrace east of Donnels Creek, in the west central part of Section Number 3, Bethel Township, Clark County, Ohio on the farm of Mr. K. M. Boblett. About 1.6 km southwest across the valley on a high terrace is the Campbell Group of prehistoric earthworks explored by the Society in 1955. This is a group of six small mounds located in the woods back east from the terrace border. Between the mounds and the terrace edge, Arthur Altick (1940, 1941) indicated a habitation site for approximately 300 m (1,000 feet north-south) and from approximately 15 to 60 m (50 to 200 feet) wide.

The Hopewell Site

The first published identification of a village at the Hopewell site was by Moorehead (1892a, 1892b). Moorehead (1892b:509) noted that after three months of excavation in late 1891: "one hundred acres are enclosed, on which lie twenty-six mounds and an extensive village site." This was further emphasized in the brief report issued thirty years later: "The entire space enclosed (Hopewell earthworks) was occupied as a village site, but the indications are most numerous where the words 'village site' have been placed on the map" (Moorehead 1922:86). He also referred to lumps of galena picked up on the village site and to an ordinary cooking pot about "14 cm" in height and "13 cm" in diameter at the lip. Corroborative evidence was given by Clifford C. Anderson, who had excavated as a part of Moorehead's crew. He told me in 1934 when I was studying his Anderson site material, that there was evidence of habitational debris in the Hopewell site. However very little remains in the Field Museum collections that is attributed in the catalogue to village site materials. Recently, a carefully controlled systematic survey for surface material was done by Seeman with very little to show for it. However, there has been some amount of slope wash from the northern side of the site, it has been extensively cultivated, and many collectors are believed to have picked up whatever may have appeared over the last 100 years. Moorehead (1892b:511) also wrote "Upon the site of their lodges or tepees we have found many ash-pits, fragments of their cooking vessels, broken and unfinished implements, and bones upon which they have carved fanciful designs".

A small 12 m by 12 m (40 feet by 40 feet) habitation area of distinctively Hopewell material in Ross County was identified in 1983. This was surface collected and then partially excavated. Large quantities of fire cracked rock, burnt earth, a large number of pottery fragments with a *Hopewellian Series* cross-hatched rim and a slight under rim channel, *McGraw Cordmarked* and *McGraw Plain* body sherds were recovered. The cooking jars have a slightly everted or vertical rim which was usually plain. Some of these vessels were judged to be

about 45.7 cm (18 inches) in diameter at the rim. Flint Ridge Hopewell bladelets, corner notched points, a large trianguloid knife(?) and other chert tools are identified. While the exact location of this site discovered by Ned and Mark Shaw is not given, it was not near a stream or any of the numerous Hopewell earthworks in Ross County. The author of the report states that there are "numberless similar locations in south central Ohio" (Converse 1984:23).

The Hopeton Works

In his report to the National Park Service in 1976, David Brose wrote: "The Hopeton site has yielded to these recent archaeological investigations nearly the entire range of traditional artifact types associated with the florescence of Ohio Hopewell....The recovery of mica, obsidian, hematite, and exotic ceramics demonstrated the participation of Hopeton in the inter- and intraregional Hopewellian exchange system". His statements were based on his collecting efforts at a number of locations in and near the earthworks, and the observations and collections of Howard Opp of Chillicothe, Don McBeth of Kingston, Louise Stanhope, and Lloyd Overly. It is not known whether the several locations represent roughly contemporaneous small units of the Hopeton builders or temporally distinct family units.

Ginther and Shilder Mounds

In his brief report on the Ginther Mound excavations in Ross County, Ohio on the east side of the Scioto River, Shetrone (1925:164) discloses that under the mound there was village site material, and that the Shilder Mound immediately northwest of the Ginther Mound had nearby:

> ...a number of tipi-[sic] sites and fireplaces. The presence of these was readily noted when the ground was freshly plowed, or in the greater luxurious [sic] of the grain under cultivation. These are characterized by an abundance of burned stone, flint chips, broken pottery ware and fragments of mica. In two of these, beneath the plow lines, were found flake knives of the drab flint, exactly similar

to those taken from the Shilder and the Ginther Mounds. It is everywhere evident, from the remains of tipi [sic] sites and other indications that the entire face of the terrace from the Cedar Banks group southward past the Ginther Works to the Hopeton group was the place of habitation of the people who constructed and utilized these several works.

Feurt Village Site

In W. C. Mills' discussions of finds at The Feurt Village Site in Scioto County across the Scioto River east of the Tremper Mound, the indications of Hopewell village occupation are unmistakable. In speaking of the materials in a local collection of Mr. Charles V. Wertz of Portsmouth he says:

Mr. Wertz also found numerous pieces of copper on some of which an attempt had been made to destroy their identity by hammering the finished products into a mass. The finding of the masses of bent and battered copper implements by Mr. Wertz led him to make the examination to determine, if possible, whether the Feurt people were contemporaneous with the Tremper Mound people across the river.

Only two burials showed friendly contact with some tribe of Hopewell Culture. One of these was a splendid necklace made of shell and copper beads, and the other consisting of bear teeth, and imitation bear teeth made of wood and covered with copper. However, Mr. Wertz found a number of copper pieces corresponding in type of those found in the Tremper Mound which were hammered and bent out of semblance and resembling in many respects the cache of copper implements and ornaments found at Ft. Ancient. The specimens found by Mr. Wertz were taken from the edge of the bank where refuse from the village was dumped... [Mills 1917:308].

Wertz did indeed find a copper reel and some copper beads for they are illustrated in Mills' report. There may have been more in an earlier collection by Wertz or some of the other

collectors in the neighborhood. That the Feurt location had been a favorite one for village occupation for thousands of years is indicated by the grooved axes, tubular cloud blower type pipes, a turkey-tail knife, large Archaic notched knives, and bell shaped pestles illustrated by Mills as coming from the village sites. One group of village residents was a Hopewell group at the time the Tremper Mound was built.

Seip Earthworks

The Seip Earthworks and mounds are located on Paint Creek in Ross County, Ohio. In his report on the excavation of the smaller Seip Mound 2, W.C. Mills made the following pertinent observations:

The flint knives flaked from cores of jasper and chalcedony from the Flint Ridge region were not abundant in the graves, although quite a number were found with the remains, the greater number were found promiscuously throughout the mound, indicating that they were perhaps lost during the construction of the mound. The knives were found abundantly upon the surface in the field surrounding the mound, showing that the implement was much used by the builders of the mound.

Fragments of broken pottery were found in almost every portion of the mound, and in several instances, potsherds of good size, and representing a high type of fictile art, were found in several of the graves, but were not associated with the charred remains.

It seems strange that a people well versed in the fictile art, and able to produce objects in pottery as shown by the discarded sherds; articles requiring great skill and patience to produce the symmetry and grace therein displayed; that these people would not in some way employ this art facility in their mortuary customs [Mills 1909:50-53].

One archaeologist who worked at the Seip village site in the late 1960s stated: "One thing is certain: Seip, at least, was not a 'vacant ceremonial center' (sensu Prufer 1964:71). In addition, investigations and surface survey and collections nearby - outside the embankment - have fairly certainly pinpointed the location of at least one large village site, and it is presently presumed to have been related to the Seip complex, and possibly to other sites in the area as well" (Baby and Langlois 1979:17).

In the report of H. C. Shetrone's excavation of Seip Mound, in the late 1920s is the following statement:

> The entire mound above the stratum of clay over the primary mound was built up of dark brown earth profusely intermixed with humus, charcoal and ashes and quantities of animal bones and other refuse material, including an occasional artifact. In view of the nature of the soil and of the artifacts found in it, this portion of the mound appears to have been removed from the surface of the immediate vicinity upon which its builders of the mound lived [Shetrone and Greenman 1931:359].

There is also a reference to the "pits which contained refuse material, ashes and charcoal" in the level below the floor of the mound and to a number of depressions below the floor (Shetrone and Greenman 1931:304). They also mention additional pits with occupational debris. Following is their description:

> One-hundred and thirty feet from the west end of the mound and about forty feet south of center three small depressions in the floor were filled with charcoal, fragments of pottery and marine shells, mica and flint-flake knives of Flint Ridge material. The exact nature of these deposits is somewhat obscure. They were roughly circular, about a yard in diameter, and from 6 to 10 inches in depth. Probably they were ceremonial in nature, the artifacts contained in them having

been symbolically "killed" by burning or breaking them. A similar deposit containing fragments of obsidian spears occupied an oval area nine by five feet on the floor adjacent to the platforms of burial sixty". There are also references to additional pits with occupational debris [Shetrone and Greenman 1931:367].

In the section on the pottery from the largest Seip Mound they noted, "Quantities of broken pottery were taken from the floor of the mound, from the three refuse pits, the Burnt Offering and the platforms of several burials. The pottery is of the two kinds, commonly distinguished as ceremonial and utility" (Shetrone and Greenman 1931:430). At the end of the section on pottery we are told, "In an excavation in a portion of the great wall of the Seip Group eighty potsherds were found at a depth of two feet in an ash deposit" (Shetrone and Greenman 1931:438). They infer that the pottery was either located on the mound floor as a part of village occupational debris, or carried in and dumped along with other items picked up from village occupation to build up the mound. The broken sherds from the ash deposits included Hopewellian Series rims, cord marked and other "utility" pottery.

Robert Goslin, a staff member of the Ohio State Museum who participated in all four years of Shetrone's excavations at the big Seip (Pricer) Mound, told J. B. Griffin in the late 1930s that there was village site debris under the mound, thrown up into the mound, and under and in the earthwork walls.

In the late 1930s or 1940s, J. B. Griffin saw a large private collection in Dayton of polyhedral Flint Ridge cores from which Hopewell style bladelets had been struck. The cores about the size of a man's fist had come from the field west of the big Seip Mound and embankments according to the collector.

Liberty (Harness) Earthworks and Vicinity

There are few if any references to the presence of occupational debris at the Liberty (Harness) Earthworks in Ross County on the east side of the Scioto River, but the fairly large sherd collection in the Ohio State Museum would seem to have been from village debris picked up and placed in the large mound. A recent study of lithic material (Greber 1983) from the west side of the earthwork enclosure and due south of the great circle and west of the C and O Railroad tracks found that these were lithic processing areas, as well as others on the Robert Harness Farm. This can be interpreted as occupational areas belonging to some of the populations who built the earthworks and mounds. Chert from at least 15 different sources was identified but most of it was from Flint Ridge and other nearby sources. There were no obsidian debitage specimens even though there was a large blade biface in the mound. There were Knife River debitage but no whole specimens from excavations or surface collections.

In the Scioto floodplain, John Blank, in 1964, excavated the Browns Bottom site on an eastern alluvial terrace which had three low rises 91 m long by 32 m (100 yards by 35 yards) wide. In the plowzone were habitational debris of the Hopewell people who presumably built the Harness Earthworks and the Russell Brown Mounds. Seeman and Soday report (1980:97), "The area immediately surrounding the Russell Brown Mounds is one of two areas at the site where prismatic blades were produced in quantity. That many of these blades were actually used in this area is supported by the presence of utilized and broken blades in the charnel houses and in the immediate vicinity of the mounds."

The Marietta Earthworks

In an article intitled "Pyramids at Marietta" Hildreth (1843:243-248) wrote:

> Traces of their hearths may yet be seen by digging away the earth in the inside of the parapets or walls along the borders of which their dwellings would seem to have been erected. Numerous relics of copper and silver have been found in the cinders of these hearths. They are generally in the form of ornaments, rings of copper, or slender bars of copper that had been used as awls. In the mounds

> have been found several curious articles of metal. The bowl of a brass spoon taken from one of the parapets in the northwest corner of the old city at a depth of six feet below the surface. Grit tempered pottery which was fairly hard was found near one of the platform mounds which contrasted with shell tempered pottery found nearer the river, which was stated to be similar to that of contemporary Indians.

These statements by S. P. Hildreth are in letters to Caleb Atwater (1820) that were published in his *Archaeologia Americana.*

In N'omi Greber's excavation of the Library Mound at Marietta, originally called Capitolium, a considerable number of Ohio Hopewell pottery sherds were recovered. It appears that the builders gathered up earth from a habitation area to build the mound. There are no indications of feasting from the items found in the mound.

CONCLUSION

This collection of past references to various debitage items from Hopewell sites in southern Ohio is intended to give pause to what I will call the "Columbus Circle Cabal" conviction that the Ohio Hopewell earthwork sites were not occupied by the builders except on ceremonial occasions and that they were scattered in "hamlets" the rest of the year. Excavations with modern recovery and analytical techniques developed since 1950 could be a great help in rectifying that interpretation.

REFERENCES CITED

Altick, A. R. 1940 The Survey of the Bobblet (sic) Group of Prehistoric Mounds. *Escalade* 34-37. The Springfield Writers Club, Springfield, Ohio.

1941 Exploration of Mound 2 of the Boblett group of Prehistoric Mounds. *Escalade* 25-35. The Springfield Writer's Club, Springfrield, Ohio.

Atwater, C. 1820 Description of the Antiquities Found in the State of Ohio and Other Western States. *Archaeologia Americana* 1:105-267.

Baby, R. S., and S. M. Langlois 1979 Seip Mound State Memorial: Nonmortuary Aspects of Hopewell. In *Hopewell Archaeology: The Chillicothe Conference*, edited by D. S. Brose and N. Greber, pp. 16-18. The Kent State University Press, Kent, Ohio.

Brose, D. S. 1976 *An Historical and Archaeological Evaluation of the Hopeton Works, Ross County, Ohio.* Report on file, Hopewell Culture National Park, Chillicothe, Ohio.

Connolly, R. 1992 The Evidence for Habitation at the Fort Ancient Earthworks. Paper presented at the Annual Meeting of the Society for American Archaeology, Pittsburgh.

Converse, R. N. 1984 An Open Hopewell Site in Ross County, Ohio. *Ohio Archaeologist* 34(2):23.

Essenpreis, P. S. and M. E. Moseley 1984 Fort Ancient: Citadel or Coliseum. *Field Museum of Natural History Bulletin* 55:5-10, 20-26.

Genheimer, R. A. 1984 *A Systematic Examination of Middle Woodland Settlements in Warren County, Ohio.* Report on file, Ohio Historic Preservation Office, Ohio Historical Society, Columbus, Ohio.

1992 The Stubbs Cluster: Hopewellian Site Dynamics along the Middle Reaches of the Little Miami River. Paper presented at the Annual Meeting of the Society for American Archaeology, Pittsburgh.

Greber, N. 1983 Recent excavations at the Edwin Harness Mound, Liberty Works, Ross County, Ohio. *Kirtlandia* 39.

Hildreth, S. P. 1843 Pyramids at Marietta. *American Pioneer, III,* 1:243-248

Lee, A. M., and K. D. Vickery 1972 Salvage Excavations at the Headquarters Site, A Middle Woodland Village Burial Area in Hamilton County, Ohio. *Ohio Archaeologist* 22(1):3-11.

Mills, W. C. 1909 Explorations of the Seip Mound. *Certain Mounds and Village Sites in Ohio* 2(1). The F.J. Heer Printing Co., Columbus, Ohio.

1917 The Feurt Mounds and Village Site. *Ohio Archaeological and Historical Publications* 36: 304-449.

Moorehead, W. K. 1890 *Fort Ancient.* Robert Clarke and Co., Cincinnati.

1892a Recent Archaeological Discoveries in Ohio. *Scientific American Supplement,* XXXIV:13886-13890.

1892b *Primitive Man in Ohio.* Putnam's, New York.

1922 The Hopewell Mound Group of Ohio. *Field Museum of Natural History Publication 211,* 6(5):73-181.

Morgan, R. G. 1946 *Fort Ancient.* Ohio State Archaeological and Historical Society, Columbus.

Potter, M. A., and E. S. Thomas 1970 *Fort Hill.* The Ohio Historical Society, Columbus.

Prufer, O. H. 1964 The Hopewell Complex of Ohio. In *Hopewellian Studies,* edited by J. Caldwell and R. Hall, pp. 35-83. Illinois State Museum, Scientific Papers 12, Springfield.

1968 *Ohio Hopewell Ceramics: an Analysis of the Extant Collections.* Museum of Anthropology, Anthropological Papers 33, University of Michigan, Ann Arbor.

Seeman, M. F. 1979 *The Hopewell Interaction Sphere: The Evidence for Interregional Trade and Structural Complexity.* Indiana Historical Society, Prehistory Research Series 5(2), Indianapolis.

Seeman, M. F. and F. Soday 1980 The Russell Brown Mounds: Three Hopewell Mounds in Ross County, Ohio. *Midcontinental Journal of Archaeology* 5(1):73-116.

Shetrone, H. C. 1925 Exploration of the Ginther Mound. *Ohio Archaeological and Historical Quarterly* 34:154-168.

Shetrone, H. C. and E. F. Greenman 1931 Explorations of the Seip Group of Prehistoric Earthworks. *Ohio Archaeological and Historical Quarterly* 40:343-509.

Starr, F. A. 1960 The Archaeology of Hamilton County, Ohio. *Journal of the Cincinnati Museum of Natural History* 23 (1).

Whitacre, D. and B. Whitacre 1986 The Whitacre Site (12D246). *Ohio Archaeologist* 36:24-34.

Whittlesey, C. 1851 Descriptions of Ancient Works in Ohio. *Contributions to Knowledge* 3(7). Smithsonian Institution, Washington D. C.

Willoughby, C. C. and E. A. Hooton 1922 The Turner Group of Earthworks, Hamilton County, Ohio. *Papers of the Peabody Museum* 8(3).

TWO

OHIO HOPEWELL REGIONAL
SETTLEMENT PATTERNS

PAUL J. PACHECO

ABSTRACT

Olaf Prufer's research in the central Scioto region during the
1960s produced the first empirically grounded inferences
regarding Ohio Hopewell settlement patterns. Prufer argued
that during the Middle Woodland period Ohio Hopewell populations were organized in a pattern of vacant ceremonial centers surrounded by dispersed agricultural hamlets. While much
research supports Prufer's hypothesis, herein called the Vacant
Center Model, the case is far from closed. This paper provides
further discussion of the model and summarizes independent
support for it from Middle Woodland settlement pattern data
collected in the central Muskingum-Licking region.

A View From the Core a Synthesis of Ohio Hopewell Archaeology•edited by Paul J. Pacheco
© Copyright 1996 by The Ohio Archaeological Council• Columbus, Ohio•All Rights Reserved•ISBN 0-9626931-9-7

PAUL J. PACHECO
OHIO HOPEWELL REGIONAL SETTLEMENT PATTERNS

INTRODUCTION

Bruce Smith (1992), in a recent synthesis of Hopewell archaeology, lamented that the Ohio Hopewell domestic sphere continues to be under emphasized as research efforts focus on the more spectacular civic-ceremonial sphere. The efforts of William S. Dancey, Dee Anne Wymer, and myself (members of Griffin's "Columbus Circle Cabal") represent one exception to this pattern. Our research in the central Muskingum - Licking region (Dancey 1991, 1992a, 1992b; Dancey and Pacheco n.d.; Pacheco 1988, 1992, 1993, n.d.; Wymer 1987, n.d.) has produced considerable data which not only support Prufer's model (i.e., Prufer 1964a, 1964b, 1965, 1967), but illustrate its utility as an organizational framework for understanding Ohio Hopewell. Settlement data from this region are summarized later in the paper.

In addition to research conducted by the "Cabal", the Ohio Hopewell settlement pattern problem has received increased attention from other researchers in Ohio over the last decade. At the 1992 Pittsburgh SAA Conference, Dancey and I organized the symposium "Testing the Prufer Model of Ohio Hopewell Settlement Patterns" to bring together some of this research. The papers presented at that symposium, and a few others solicited after the conference, have been collected into a volume entitled *Ohio Hopewell Community Organization*, which is currently in press. While several contributing authors in Ohio Hopewell Community Organization expressed legitimate concerns with the application of the Vacant Center Model to their settlement data, we argued that the regional variability expressed by these data was parsimoniously accommodated by the model, rather than some alternative (Dancey and Pacheco n.d.). Most of the problems expressed about the application of the Vacant Center Model stemmed from what we believe to be several important misconceptions. One goal of the discussions presented in this paper is to identify and clarify these misconceptions.

Before turning to further evaluation of Ohio Hopewell settlement patterns, it is necessary to define the term `Ohio Hopewell' as used herein. Ohio Hopewell refers to those Middle Woodland (circa first century B.C. to fourth century A.D.) populations in the Middle Ohio Valley who participated in a pan-eastern Hopewellian cosmology (Caldwell 1964). In particular, construction and use of earthwork-mound complexes symbolically link Hopewellian populations within the Ohio area. However, all Ohio Hopewell populations were not culturally homogeneous. Evidence is accumulating that settlement systems from geographically separate regions within the Middle Ohio Valley represent independent variants of Ohio Hopewell. Recognizable variants are localized within drainage basins such as the Great and Little Miami in southwestern Ohio, the central Scioto in south-central Ohio, and the central Muskingum-Licking in east-central Ohio (Dancey 1991; Greber and Ruhl 1989; Greber 1991; Hawkins, this volume). The myriad interactions between independent variants, not only defined the core, but in essence were Ohio Hopewell.

The ancestors of Ohio Hopewell populations in the Middle Ohio Valley belong to the loosely defined Early Woodland period/Adena Complex (e.g., Swartz 1971). However, Hopewellian cosmology was not uniformly adopted by all Adena populations throughout the Middle Ohio Valley, especially in areas marginal to the Miami, central Scioto, and central Muskingum-Licking regions. Consequently, typologically Early Woodland /Adena cultures continued to exist in the peripheral areas surrounding the Ohio Hopewell core well into the Middle Woodland period (Clay 1980). In certain peripheral areas, such as northeastern Ohio, local versions of Hopewellian ceremonialism crop-up in otherwise local Middle Woodland societies (see Seeman, this volume). In other areas, such as eastern Indiana and the Philo district, at the southern margin of the central Muskingum Valley, there is a time lag in the replacement of Adena by Hopewell (see Carskadden and Morton n.d.; Cochran, this volume). In other areas, such as northern Kentucky, and possibly the Hocking Valley and western West Virginia, Hopewellian manifestations are very limited or never appeared (Clay 1980; Greber 1991:22). The relationship between Adena and Ohio

Hopewell is thus more than one of simple ancestor-descent; a complex situation of intraregional cultural lag is also involved. This relationship needs to be studied in detail at the level of the individual local regions within the Middle Ohio Valley where Ohio Hopewell did or did not develop. I concur with Gerber's argument that:

> ...different choices were made, deliberately or otherwise, by people living in the various tributaries of Central Ohio during the several centuries centered on the beginning of the calendar change (B.C./A.D.). Some groups, in a relatively restricted area, greatly elaborated upon and possibly changed what had been wide spread, common ritual/ceremonial themes and left behind what we know as Ohio Hopewell [Greber 1991:21].

OHIO HOPEWELL REGIONAL SETTLEMENT PATTERNS

While many researchers have supported the Vacant Center Model, either explicitly (i.e., Brown 1982; Lynott and Monk 1985; Seeman 1981), or implicitly (i.e., Cowan, this volume), others have voiced opposition and expressed alternative views. Opposition to the model has focused on three issues: 1) that Hopewellian material found near earthworks was created by nucleated Hopewell villages; 2) that Hopewellian sites like McGraw were seasonal horticultural camps rather than sedentary farmsteads; and 3) that relatively permanent cultural facilities in earthworks make them no longer `vacant'. Each of these positions will be discussed in the following section.

Griffin (n.d., this volume), in particular, supports a position harkening back to the views of Lewis H. Morgan: that the earthwork centers themselves are the location of substantial nucleated Hopewell villages. Recently, Converse (1993; 1994) has also taken up the banner of Hopewell villages. He concludes that large villages have been ignored by professional archaeologists due to their unfamiliarity with surface collections (Converse 1993:5). Both Griffin and Converse document the existence of Hopewellian sites near earthworks, concluding that some of these represent nucleated villages. Neither author provides an objective standard by which to judge what consti-

tutes a nucleated village. In contrast, the Vacant Center Model provides an objective distinction between villages and hamlets at the level of community residence patterns. In the model, we define nucleated villages as communities in which all members of the group reside in a single location. Dispersed communities represent the opposite type of settlement pattern and are composed of independent households or hamlets scattered about the landscape (Dancey 1991; Pacheco 1993).

The primary issue for Griffin and Converse is how to interpret Hopewell sites near earthworks. Prufer (1964a:70-71, 1964b:58, 1965:128, 1967:289) collectively refers to these debris scatters as specialized camps, created by the members of dispersed hamlets at the time of their episodic use of the centers. Prufer's (1967) survey of the Liberty (Harness) Earthworks documented several scatters in the general vicinity of the earthworks. Some of these sites, like the Russel Brown's Upper Terrace, were interpreted as specialized loci for the production of Hopewellian bladelets (Prufer 1967:288-289). These, and other similar sites, are the same remains that Griffin and Converse maintain represent the location of Hopewell villages. However, it should be noted, that despite 150 years of Ohio archaeology, none of these sites has been shown to have archaeological remains commensurate with the nucleated villages of the later Newtown or Ft. Ancient traditions which are common in this region.

This assertion is consistent with the results of surveys and excavations near central Scioto Ohio Hopewell centers, such as Mound City (Lynott and Monk 1985) Hopewell (Seeman 1981), Seip (Greber n.d.), and High Bank (Prufer, this volume). Each of these studies documented low densities of Ohio Hopewell materials near the earthworks, but none found anything which possibly represented the remains of contemporaneous nucleated villages. In contrast, small, dispersed Ohio Hopewell farmsteads such as McGraw and Murphy abound (Dancey 1991; Prufer 1965). Both Griffin and Converse apparently concede the existence of numerous dispersed Hopewell farmsteads (see Converse 1984; Griffin, this volume), but treat them as components of a greater whole; i.e. as part of a hierarchy.

The nucleated villages position may be based on the mis-conception that the earthworks have to be the product of a large, populous people. This view was often expressed during the nineteenth century:

> Authorities differ regarding matters con-nected with the Mound Builders, but a few facts seem to be fully established by their works. There can be no doubt that they were a numerous people. Works so elabo-rate, so gigantic, could not have been erected by a people insignificant in num-bers [Hill 1881:187-188].

Yet, large Ohio Hopewell populations do not appear to be involved in earthwork constructions (Greber 1979). Greber (n.d.) has shown how complex centers like Seip are the product of long-term activities by relatively small numbers of cooperating households. In other words, Ohio Hopewell earthworks grew sequentially (see Riordan, this volume; Wymer et al. 1992).

Yerkes (1988, 1990, 1994) takes this idea of smaller, `leaner' Hopewell populations to the extreme, expressing an alternative interpretation of Ohio Hopewell settlement patterns which is diametrically opposed to the nucleated vil-lages position. Upon examining microwear polishes from limited samples of Hopewellian bladelets provenienced to several distinct contexts, he notes (1994:124); "We should not be limited by strict adherence to assumptions that the Hopewell lived in sedentary farmsteads and visited vacant ceremonial centers. Their settlement and subsistence sys-tems, like their ritual and economic interactions, were more complicated than that." Surprisingly, he offers a conceptu-ally less complex alternative: a mobile, "semi-sedentary for-ager-farmers" pattern (Yerkes 1994:116). This alternative appears similar to the position for Hopewell settlement pat-terns once advocated by Caldwell (1958).

Yerkes contends that dispersed Ohio Hopewell farmsteads are seasonal camps, rather than sedentary residences:

> What is striking is that the more elaborate "Hopewell phenomena" in Ohio were created by mobile populations that regularly shifted their resi-dences between the earthworks, upland sites, and flood plain and terrace settlements. The aggrada-tion and increased sedentism that occurred among the Illinois Hopewellian societies did not develop to the same degree in Ohio [Yerkes 1994:124].

He apparently concedes that the Hopewellian debris at earthwork centers are the remains of transient social gather-ings, not the remains of nucleated villages. However, he notes that some of these sites may have been occupied for "extended periods of time" (Yerkes 1994:116). Yerkes also concedes the farming orientation of sites like McGraw and Murphy, but differs as to the relative contribution made to the economy by the Hopewell plant complex (for the oppo-site position see Blosser, this volume; Smith 1992; Wymer, this volume). He interprets these sites as warm-season grow-ing camps, which were components of a mobile settlement pattern that included winter dwellings in upland rockshelters. Aside from the non-sequitur committed by the generalization of settlement patterns from microwear analyses, there are several other problems with this alternative view of Ohio Hopewell settlement patterns. Yerkes has yet to address sev-eral independent lines of evidence which support the posi-tion that sites like McGraw and Murphy are sedentary farm-steads (i.e., Dancey 1991, 1992b; Kozarek 1987, n.d.; Pacheco 1993:53-77).

Perhaps the strongest of these positions supporting seden-tism has been developed by Kozarek (1987, n.d.) to inter-pret her work at the Jennison Guard site (aka Whitacre). Her argument is based on analysis of the structure of the archaeological record. Kozarek argues that sedentary resi-dences display systematic evidence of regular maintenance of occupation space, especially refuse dumps or midden deposits. In contrast, seasonal settlements exhibit low degrees of maintenance. Maintained refuse dumps are a cross-cultural indicator of sedentism (Kent 1992). The long-term outcome of systematic maintenance of the occupation space is an archaeological record with clearly defined zones or clusters of features, structures, refuse deposits, and open spaces. Areas used for domestic activities were cleared of debris "predicated on the intended future use of that area" (Kozarek 1987:127). Dancey (1991:66) used this argument at the Murphy site to infer zones of occupation, with the high density debris cluster representing a maintained refuse deposit. Duration of occupation, and its corollary—debris density, may be the most important variable for understanding archaeological patterning at dispersed Hopewell hamlets (Dancey 1992b; Pacheco 1993).

Yerkes also neglects to document upland activities of a sufficient intensity to account for half of his proposed yearly Hopewell settlement pattern. As Seeman (this volume) has shown, the limited available data pertaining to Middle Woodland rockshelter use in Ohio do not support Yerkes' interpretation. In contrast, the Vacant Center Model views the sparse Middle Woodland rockshelter data as evidence of logistical camps. These short-term camps were created by work parties sent out from sedentary hamlets to exploit upland resources (Pacheco 1988:94).

Ultimately, the debate over the degree of sedentism exhibited by Hopewell farmsteads may turn out to be moot. Church and Ericksen (n.d.) have argued for convergence of the two models if the only issue is whether occupants of Ohio Hopewell household clusters are staying in one location throughout the year. As long as these households maintain the dispersed hamlet residence pattern throughout their seasonally scheduled cycle, the Vacant Center Model retains its validity (Pacheco 1988:96).

The third major opposition to the Vacant Center Model was presented first by Baby and Langlois (1979:18) following their excavation of several structures within the Seip Large Circle. They confused the meaning of the term `vacant' by proclaiming "one thing is certain: Seip at least was not a `vacant ceremonial center' (sensu Prufer 1964a:71)". Upon finding cultural features within the earthwork they argue that

Seip was not empty and thus should not be considered `vacant'. Yet prior to this proclamation they argued convincingly that these structures were neither family dwellings nor charnel houses for preparation of the dead. Instead, they suggest that the structures are craft workshops. Their interpretation was based on the lack of domestic debris and cooking features, which they contrasted with the presence of quantities of exotic materials and Hopewellian bladelets, many heavily utilized.

The misconception expressed by Baby and Langlois is that Prufer's `vacant' ceremonial centers meant empty, isolated monuments, lacking evidence of extensive utilization. Quite the contrary, the vacant centers of the model represent multi-purpose localities at which the remains of many different kinds of activities, such as craft production and mortuary ceremonialism, are to be expected (see also Greber 1979, n.d.). Some of the structures associated with these activities may have been relatively permanent features, as those at Seip seem to indicate. Social gatherings for any purpose at the earthworks would have necessarily included many otherwise typical domestic activities. Various interpretations of the Newark Expressway sites (Li.79 #1 and Li.79#2) by Lepper (this volume) and Lepper and Yerkes (n.d.) indicate the pervasiveness of this misconception (see also Yerkes 1994:116). The presence of such camps or even more substantial remains is not evidence to reject the model as long as these are not the remains of nucleated communities. Thus, it is not the lack of occupational debris that makes Ohio Hopewell centers vacant, but the lack of permanent villages. In other words, on occasion, Hopewell `vacant' centers would have been abuzz with activity, while on other occasions they would have sat empty. If the Seip structures are workshops, then they are precisely the type of feature predicted to be at centers by the Vacant Center Model. Brown (1982) concurred with this interpretation, reporting a possible craft structure at Mound City, but not altering his explicit acceptance of the Vacant Center Model.

THE VACANT CENTER SETTLEMENT PATTERN

A static two-dimensional representation of the Vacant Center Model is shown in **Figure 2:1**. The figure graphs a hypothetical dispersed Ohio Hopewell community, with a vacant earthwork center, surrounded by associated hamlets. Specialized camps are shown near the earthwork, although theoretically they can occur anywhere within the spatial boundaries of a community. The static model depicted in **Figure 2:1** has two major limitations. First, it does not include inter-hamlet logistical sites, such as gardens, chert quarries, and hunting camps at upland rockshelters, among others (Kozarek 1987, n.d.; Pacheco 1988). Second, it conflates dynamic processes into a spatial distribution (Dancey and Pacheco n.d.). For example, not depicted is the differential history of community growth, development, success, and failure. Distribution maps created with smaller units of time resolution are one possible solution to this problem (see Pacheco 1993, n.d.).

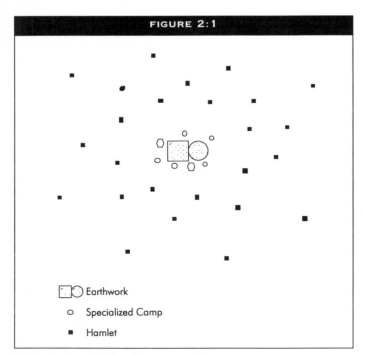

FIGURE 2:1

☐◖○ Earthwork

○ Specialized Camp

■ Hamlet

Generalized model of an Ohio Hopewell Community.

DISPERSED COMMUNITIES AND VACANT CENTERS

Dispersed communities aggregate periodically at vacant ceremonial centers. The gatherings at centers provide a mechanism for group integration, social cohesion, and corporate identity. Vacant centers and mound building are likely to occur in dispersed societies that organize themselves as territorially based descent groups or lineages (Railey 1991). Mounds, in particular, have been suggested as symbols of corporate ownership linked to local territories (Charles and Buikstra 1983). Unpredictable local fluctuations in resource availability require territorially based descent groups to have periodic access to resources controlled by other adjacent or distant territorially based descent groups (Railey 1991:58-59). This access is solidified, formalized, and regulated at vacant centers through such social structures as marriage alliances.

While the emphasis here is upon socially integrating behavior, the model in no way precludes the type of societal competition documented by Seeman (1988), based on the presence of trophy-skull artifacts in Ohio Hopewell burial mounds. Hopewellian marriage alliances may represent attempts by communities to tighten social bonds and dampen conflict, but evidence of underlying intra or intercommunity competition as expressed by violent deaths, should not be unexpected. Seeman (1988) correctly identifies the *Realpolitik* behind models which paint pictures of peaceful, cooperating Hopewellian farming communities. The Vacant Center Model is no exception; integrating features aside, no vacant center can be expected to completely stem the flow of human competition.

Dillehay's (1990, 1992) ethnographic study of the Mapuche provides a working example of the vacant ceremonial center-dispersed agricultural hamlet settlement pattern. The Mapuche dwell in the temperate valleys flowing west into the Pacific Ocean along the face of the southern Andes Mountains. They gather periodically at isolated ceremonial centers for scheduled festivals and religious events. Mapuche centers are designated places on the landscape that include large cleared and maintained dance plazas and associated burial mounds. Dispersed

Mapuche communities are comprised of sedentary, single household residential units, each of which independently engages in a horticultural economy. These households are members of local lineages, which are tied to defined territories. The Mapuche have a total population of some 200,000 individuals, organized into lineage-based dispersed communities with populations ranging between 200 and 3000 members. Groups of three to four contiguous communities, ranging in size from 2000 and 10,000 members, are organized into non-hierarchical *trokinche* units (i.e. peer-polities). Individual *trokinches* interact at designated isolated ceremonial fields which are maintained by members of the group (Dillehay 1992:382).

Mapuche ceremonial centers are periodically cleaned of debris. These clean-up efforts represent ritual cleanings, but are also practical to the extent that dancers' feet are protected from potentially sharp objects. Debris is deposited away from the important ritual spaces, sometimes into associated troughs or ditches. Ritual cleaning may account for the domestic trash located in ditches at Ohio Hopewell centers such as Turner and Seip--trash that Griffin, in particular, attributes to nucleated Hopewell villages.

Trokinches are organized through a web of agnatic and cognatic wife exchanging lineages, lacking any semblance of centralized control mechanisms. The main organizational structure of the individual *trokinche* units is the creation of alliances from these marriages. These kind of interlineage marriage alliances, in particular, provide social mechanisms for dampening intergroup conflicts. Alliances also provide the key structure for regulating access to the resources of other families and communities (Dillehay 1990). As such, Mapuche *trokinche* units constitute non-hierarchical peer groups, "in which anything goes in terms of social and economic transactions between different lineage levels" (Dillehay 1992:387). "Individual lineages and *trokinche* units are uniform in religious rules, household and community patterns, and political relations" (Dillehay 1992:386). Archaeological evidence of Proto-Mapuche culture suggests stability in community organization stretching back at least 400 years:

Participation in group activities (at ceremonial fields) leads to reinforcement of pan-Mapuche social, economic, and religious institutions (e.g. alliances, public ceremony, and ancestral worship). This, in turn, results in the emergence and persistence of lineage-specific historical and social contexts at the same time that it contributes to an uninterrupted development of Mapuche architectural ideology that is etched across the landscape in the form of fields and mounds. The material and spatial continuity of this architecture and of the ceremonial activity associated with it are vital to the social and cultural persistence of lineages because it contributes to the integration and continuity of these institutions [Dillehay 1990:227].

The Mapuche example demonstrates the dynamic relationship between dispersed communities and their use of vacant ceremonial centers as focal points for group interactions. As Dillehay (1990:226) elegantly explains:

Mapuche monuments are permanent ceremonial fields and earthen mounds where public activities are spatially located and anchored, and where kinship and other lineage relations are historically and continuously formed. As viable social places, these monuments do not just emerge temporarily out of a local group, go out of use, collapse, and, after their abandonment, become part of past lineage history. They contribute to local history in a specific spatial and temporal context through the perpetual and intergenerational creation and utility of particular geographical and ceremonial locations.

This example also dispels the argument advanced by Converse (1993:5) that interpretation of the Ohio Hopewell centers as vacant ceremonial centers supported only by dispersed farmsteads constitutes a "paradox of major proportions" and makes Hopewell "unique among cultures of the world". In actuality, many other examples of dispersed farming societies organized around vacant ceremonial centers are known from archaeological and ethnographic records, especially in the New World (e.g., Bullard 1962; Chapman 1981; DeBoer and Blitz 1991; Railey 1991; Willey 1956).

OHIO HOPEWELL SETTLEMENT PATTERNS: EXAMPLES FROM CENTRAL MUSKINGUM- LICKING REGION

The following section presents a summary of Middle Woodland settlement data collected from three sub-regions of the central Muskingum Valley **(Figure 2:2)**. Although data in each sub-region were collected with different methods and goals, the disparities in these techniques will serve to demonstrate the utility of the model. These data represent independent examples of Ohio Hopewell communities, presumably each of which is a component of a peer-polity organized through the Newark Earthworks, in Licking County (Pacheco 1988, 1992, 1993). This central Muskingum-Licking peer-polity included as many as six sub-regions within 30 km of Newark **(Table 2:1)**, providing a settlement system on the order of 2000 square kms, much of which is peripheral uplands.

The occurrence of multiple earthwork-mound centers within sub-regions is probably indicative of time, rather than additional communities. Likewise, the weak negative correlation between the size of subregional earthworks and the distance to Newark (Rs= -.34), probably reflects the relative autonomy of sub-regional Hopewellian communities in the peer-polity. The disparate size contrast between Newark and its sub-regional earthwork counterparts is a classic example of a primate center supported by relatively autonomous social units. Primate centers often occur in regions which interact with an equally or more complex regional counterpart. The large size of primate centers is a reflection of boundary maintenance behavior (Johnson 1981). In this particular case, the spectacular size of the central Muskingum-Licking peer-polity centered at Newark may reflect interaction with the central Scioto peer-polity centered in the Chillicothe area, probably at the Hopewell Earthworks.

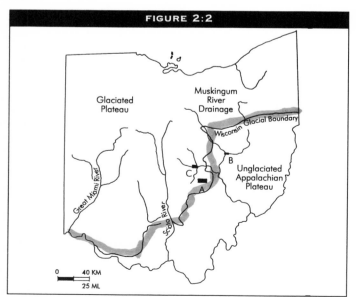

Map of Ohio showing location of sub-regional Hopewell communities in the central Muskingum Licking region: A=Upper Jonathan Creek, B=Dresden, C=Granville.

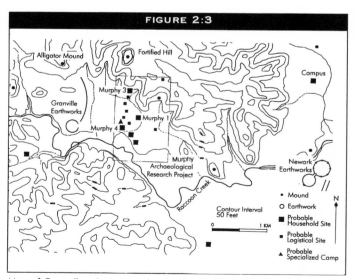

Map of Granville sub- region, showing known Hopewell sites, and all known mounds and earthworks.

TABLE 2:1						
EARTHWORK	OAI #	SHAPE	LOCATION	SIZE (ha)	DIST. TO NEWARK (km)	SUB-REGION
Claypool	33LI46	Circular	Terrace	0.3	22.4	Lower Licking
Larimore	33KN8	Circular	Terrace	1.2	27.4	North Fork
Fort #5	33LI7	Arc	Hilltop	2.0	3.2	Newark
Trinway	33MU573	Circular	Terrace	2.4	30.2	Dresden
Hazlett	33LI18	Trapezoidal	Ridge	2.8	13.3	Flint Ridge
Moore	33LI19	Oval	Hilltop	4.0	8.5	Flint Ridge
Amsterdam	33LI16	Oval	Hilltop	4.3	10.1	Flint Ridge
Granville	None	Circular	Terrace	7.2	4.1	Granville
Heart	33LI6	Heart	Hilltop	7.3	3.9	Granville
Glenford	33PE3	Irregular	Hilltop	10.5	19.1	Jonathan
Yost	33PE5	Elliptical	Ridge	14.7	17.2	Jonathan
Newark	33LI10	Geometrical	Terrace	72.0	NA	Newark

* All earthworks were independently mapped with aerial photography and ground surveys by James Marshall.

Characteristics of central Muskingum-Licking earthworks.

THE GRANVILLE SUB-REGION

From 1983-1993, the Murphy Archaeological Research Project was conducted on the Murphy property east of Granville, in Licking County, Ohio. This area is due west of the Newark Earthworks (Figure 2:3) in the Raccoon Creek Valley. The project was directed by William S. Dancey of The Ohio State University and Paul Hooge of the Licking County Archaeology and Landmarks Society, focusing specifically on understanding the evolution of the Middle Woodland period-Hopewell occupation of the study area. The project included complete excavation of the Murphy site (hereafter referred to as Murphy I), test excavations at Murphy III and Munson Springs, and a systematic surface survey covering 30 ha of the glacial terrace adjacent to Murphy I. The proximity of the Granville Earthworks, Fortified Hill, and Alligator Mound to the project area, lend credence to the interpretation of this sub-region as an Ohio Hopewell community (Pacheco 1992, 1993).

The Murphy I excavation produced the first complete site plan of a Ohio Hopewell household, occupied for potentially several consecutive generations centering around A.D. 150 (Dancey 1991). The site plan reveals zones of systematically maintained spaces for activities such as food processing, one or more dwellings, refuse disposal, and an open yard. Forty-three features were identified in a .6 ha area, twenty of which were pit features, especially earth ovens and at least one cylindrical storage pit. The lack of a clear pattern of postmolds is probably the result of extensive re-building combined with plowzone degradation. A longer duration of occupation, testified to by the high density of debris contained within the refuse dump at the site, can be expected to blur postmold patterns (Dancey 1992b). Wymer's analysis of the carbonized plant remains recovered from the features at this site, and the nearby Campus site, indicated to her a sophisticated gardening system based on plants of the Eastern Agricultural Complex (Wymer 1987, n.d., this volume). Yerkes (1990) identified a generalized

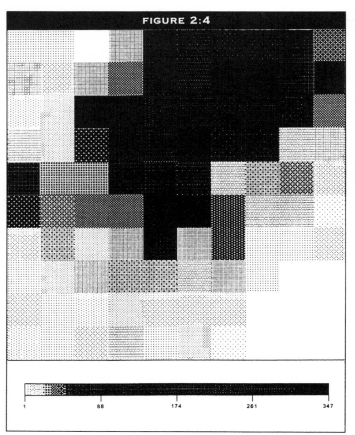

Surface distribution map of all lithics collected at Murphy III, by 4x4 m units.

Surface distribution map of all bladelets collected at Murphy III, by 4x4 m units.

pattern of use-wear on a sample of bladelets and utilized flakes from the site, indicative of domestic activities. Together, these data support interpretation of the site as a sedentary farmstead.

A systematic surface survey of the Murphy I neighborhood was designed to recover evidence of other Hopewell households that may have been components of a dispersed community (Pacheco 1988). Hopewell diagnostics were recovered from eleven concentrations and intercluster space (Pacheco 1993). Six of these concentrations were interpreted as dispersed households (including Murphy I), characterized by similar sizes, assemblages, and site plans, spaced

on average about 400 m apart. The other five locations represent logistical utilization of inter-hamlet space. It is unlikely that more than three of these proposed households were contemporaneous at any given time (Pacheco n.d.).

One large area centering on the Murphy IV cluster, 33LI245, was interpreted as a specialized camp. Approximately 250 Hopewellian bladelets (65 percent of which were manufactured from Wyandotte chert) were recovered from a 4 ha area that includes Murphy IV. Many of these bladelets were heavily utilized.

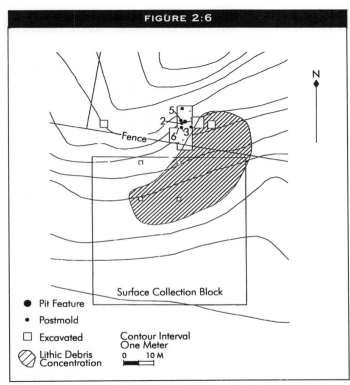

FIGURE 2:6

Surface Collection Block

● Pit Feature
• Postmold
□ Excavated
◿ Lithic Debris Concentration

Contour Interval One Meter

0   10 M

Map showing location of excavated features at Murphy III.

FIGURE 2:7

0 1 2 3 4 5 CM / IN   0   1   2

Photograph of selected Middle Woodland ceramics from Murphy III.
Column one: Turner Simple Stamped B, Turner Simple Stamped Ax2.
Column two: Turner Simple Stamped B, McGraw Cordmarked.
Column three: Murphy Plain rim, Unidentified plain rim-possibly from Turner Simple Stamped A vessel.

Limited excavations were conducted at the Murphy III (33LI311) cluster, located 400 m northwest of Murphy I, in order to test independently the conclusions derived from the surface survey and the Murphy I excavation. A site size of .32 ha was estimated from the surface data and a series of shovel tests. The surface survey indicated a dense concentration of lithic debris along the slope edge **(Figure 2:4)**.

A corresponding pattern in the distribution of the 257 Hopewellian bladelets recovered during the surface collection document this concentration as a systematically maintained refuse deposit **(Figure 2:5)**.Excavations were conducted north of the dense lithic concentration, in an area of pasture **(Figure 2:6)**. Approximately 60 m² have been investigated, focusing on one large contiguous block in the central portion of the site. Seven pit features, and four postmolds, arranged in a

complimentary distribution to the refuse deposit, have been excavated or sampled. Mica fragments were recovered from Features 3 and 5. Feature 3 is a deep earth oven, but Feature 5 is a cylindrical, flat-bottomed pit, 90 cm in diameter and 65 cm deep. Feature 5 has the characteristics of a storage pit. Wymer (personal communication 1990, n.d., this volume) identified squash, hazelnut, and maygrass in flotation samples from Features 3 and 5. Radiocarbon samples from Features 1 and 2, both probably earth ovens, produced third century B.C. dates that may reflect an Early Woodland component at Murphy III, although both features contained Middle Woodland ceramics (see Dancey and Pacheco n.d.:Table 2). Partial overlap of Feature 2 by Feature 5 may account for the Middle Woodland ceramics in Feature 2. Three of the four postmolds are substantial (averaging 25 cm in diameter and 50 cm deep). One postmold (Feature 11) contained a utilized Wyandotte bladelet in its fill.

Excavations from four pit features and the plowzone produced a fragmentary Hopewellian ceramic assemblage **(Table 2:2 and Figure 2:7)**. The plain surface-grit tem-

TABLE 2:2							
TYPE	FEATURE 1	FEATURE 2	FEATURE 3	FEATURE 5	PLOWZONE	TOTALS	%
Murphy Plain	8	13	28	11	6	66	50
McGraw-Cordmarked	2	0	2	10	3	17	13
Turner Simple Stamped A	1	12	4	21	0	38	29
Turner Simple Stamped B	1	2	2	1	3	9	7
Unidentified Plain Rim	0	1	0	0	0	1	1
TOTALS	12	27	36	43	12	131	100

Ceramic assemblage from Murphy III (33LI311).

pered ceramics recovered from Murphy III appear closely affiliated to the type *Murphy Plain* which Dancey (1991) defined based on his analysis of the 858 sherds in the Murphy I assemblage. There is little apparent difference between these plain ceramics and the plain ceramics Seeman (1986) recovered at the Locust site 33MU160, along the Lower Licking River. Seeman noted the poor fit of the types *Adena Plain* and *McGraw Plain* to his plain ceramics, but did not propose a new type as Dancey has done. The relationship between these assemblages and established ceramic series needs to be studied in earnest before further conclusions can be drawn. The assemblage also includes examples of the type *McGraw Cordmarked* and the types *Turner Simple Stamped A and B* . Prufer (1968) suggests that the later type represents imported vessels characterized by hard, fine, sand-tempered pastes, while type A represents local copies of the these imports. The numerous *Turner Simple Stamped A* sherds in Features 2 and 5 may come from a single, thin (average 3.5 mm thick) vessel. The unidentified plain rim sherd in Feature 2 may be a part of this vessel based on similarities in color, hardness, and paste composition. Only two other rim sherds are included in the assemblage, one from a *Murphy Plain* vessel recovered in the plowzone, the other from a plain vessel with a thickened rim strip recovered in Feature 3 that is similar to rims reported from Late Adena sites in the Philo area by Carskadden and Morton (n.d.).

The results of the Murphy III excavations support interpretation of this cluster as a sedentary household like Murphy I. The site contains evidence for the systematic use of space as indicated by the well defined refuse disposal area and the complimentary distribution of features. The lithic, botanical, and ceramic assemblages provide numerous diagnostics relating to the Middle Woodland occupation of the site. The overwhelming balance of evidence collected during the Murphy project supports an interpretation that the local Ohio Hopewell settlement patterning in the Granville sub-region represents a dispersed community.

THE DRESDEN SUB-REGION

Another well-documented community cluster can be identified in northern Muskingum County, near the modern town of Dresden (**Figures 2:8**). This area is about 30 km northwest of Newark, but is linked to the Licking Valley by the abandoned channel of the pre-Illinoian Deep Stage Newark River. At Dresden, the Muskingum flows south into its own deeply incised ancient channel. This area has been studied sporadically over the last two decades by Jeff Carskadden and James Morton, founding members of the Muskingum Valley Archaeological Survey. They have conducted extensive ground surveys in the region in order to identify cultural components from all surface sites. Limited excavations have

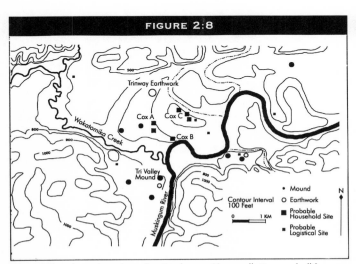

FIGURE 2:8

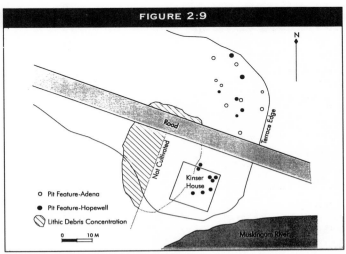

FIGURE 2:9

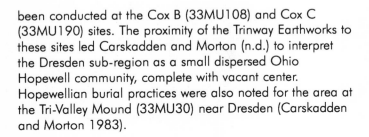

Map of Dresden sub region, showing known Hopewell sites, and all known mounds and earthworks.

Map showing location of features at Cox B.

been conducted at the Cox B (33MU108) and Cox C (33MU190) sites. The proximity of the Trinway Earthworks to these sites led Carskadden and Morton (n.d.) to interpret the Dresden sub-region as a small dispersed Ohio Hopewell community, complete with vacant center. Hopewellian burial practices were also noted for the area at the Tri-Valley Mound (33MU30) near Dresden (Carskadden and Morton 1983).

Morton and Carskadden (1987) have reported their limited excavations at the Cox C site. Test pits in the southern cluster or "hotspot" at the site produced diagnostic Hopewell lithics, ceramics, and pit features. The radiocarbon date they obtained from one of these features of 100 ± 80 B.C. is considered to be to early, although like Murphy III, there is also an Early Woodland component at the site. Several of the over 300 bladelets surface collected at this site were used by Carskadden (1972) in a metric analysis of the Dresden cluster bladelets.

The Cox B site is located 400 m southeast of Cox A (33MU107) along the edge of the terrace nearest the Muskingum River **(Figure 2:9)**. The cultural materials at the site are distributed along the terrace edge, with the highest density located on the southwest slope of the terrace, directly west of

the Kinser House. This concentration probably represents a refuse disposal area. A complimentary distribution of features was noted by Carskadden and Morton north of the road during the early 1980s. Recent extension of Kinser's foundation has produced evidence for eight additional pit features south of the road, all of which appear to relate to the Hopewell occupation of the site based on the associated ceramics. A lengthy description from Carskadden illustrates the nature of the Hopewellian household identified at Cox B:

> This site consists of a single hotspot located on the terrace edge immediately along the bank of the Muskingum River. We excavated approximately 25 plowed out pit features at this location, 15 of which could be located by triangulation. Some of the pits were Adena, but most were Hopewell and contained bladelets and McGraw Cordmarked pottery. Small pieces of mica and a Hopewell platform pipe **(see Figure 2:10)** were surface collected several years before the excavation. A radiocarbon date of A.D. 30 ± 90 was obtained from one of the excavated Hopewell pits. The

excavated material has never been tabulated, but the following was surface collected at the site: 25 generalized Middle Woodland points, 4 Steuben Expanding Stem points, 7 Hopewell cache blade fragments, 19 Hopewell blade cores, and 494 Hopewell parallel-sided prismatic blades [Carskadden, personal communication, 1990 (emphasis added)].

THE UPPER JONATHAN CREEK SUB-REGION

The final example of a sub-regional Ohio Hopewell community is the least well documented of the three examples. This sub-region is focused on the Upper Jonathan Creek Valley, just east of Buckeye Lake, in northern Perry County **(Figure 2:11)**. The

numerous Hopewell sites in this sub-region have all been documented through amateur surface collections. Morton and Pacheco's examination of the Robert Sterling collection in 1989, which focused on the Buckeye Lake region, recorded 98 Hopewell diagnostics to 22 of the localities shown within Figure 2:11 **(see Table 2:3)**. The Gordon 1 site (Sterling code #M6P5H2S) is a typical example of Sterling's collection. Five diagnostic Hopewell artifacts, including the *Snyders* point shown in **Figure 2:12**, were recovered at this site. Sterling noted the approximate size of the surface scatter and recorded all artifacts taken from each location. The sites with Hopewell materials ranged between .5 and 2 ha in size. Although more specific data concerning site structure and artifact assemblages are lacking from this sub-region, the aggregate spatial pattern of the data (combining Sterling's data and other site data recorded in

		TABLE 2:3			
OAI #	STERLING #	BLADELET CORES	BLADELETS	PROJECTILE POINTS	TOTALS
None	M5L15L2S	1	0	0	1
33LI152	M6L10B2S	2	2	3	7
33LI153	M6L10B2S	4	1	0	5
33LI159	M6L10B3S	0	2	2	4
33LI170	M6L10B5S	0	7	1	8
None	M6L11B1S	4	1	0	5
33LI38	M6L11B2S	3	0	0	3
33LI147	M6L12B1S	2	0	1	3
33LI41	M6L12B2S	1	0	0	1
33LI148	M6L12B3S	4	0	1	5
33LI149	M6L17B1S	3	0	0	3
33LI151	M6L17B7S	1	0	0	1
33LI211	M6L18B1S	1	0	0	1
None	M6P1T1S	3	5	0	8
None	M6P5H1S	2	3	4	9
None	M6P5H2S	1	3	1	5
33LPE32	M6PH1S	2	0	1	3
33PE33	M6P6H2S	2	0	3	5
33PE35	M6P13T1S	0	7	4	11
33PE34	M6P13T2S	0	3	1	4
None *	M6P14T1S	1	0	2	3
33PE36	M6P18H1S	0	1	2	3
TOTALS		37	35	26	98
* A 4-hole chlorite gorget was also recovered at this site.					

Middle Woodland Artifacts from Robert Sterling Collection, Johnathan Creek sub-region.

FIGURE 2:10

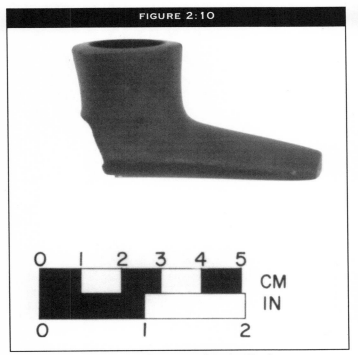

0 1 2 3 4 5 CM
0 1 2 IN

Photgraph of Hopewellian platform pipe collected at Cox B.

FIGURE 2:12

0 1 2 3 4 5 CM
IN

Photograph of Snyders projectile point collected at Gordon 1.

FIGURE 2:11

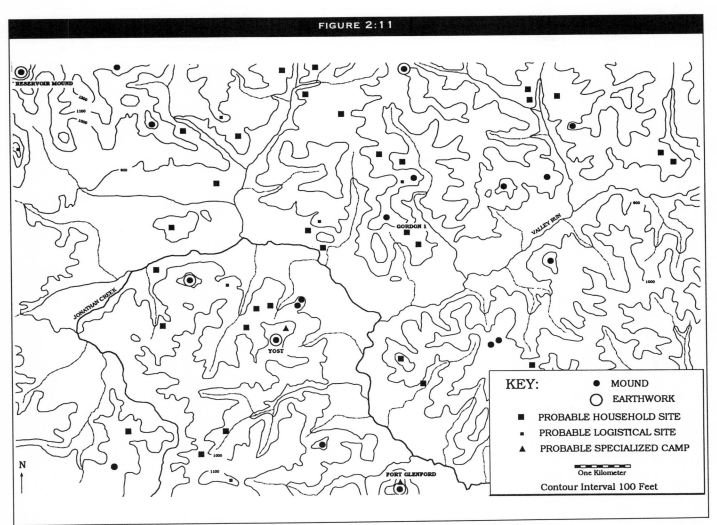

Map of Upper Johnathan Creek sub-region, showing known Hopewell sites, and all known mounds and earthworks.

the Ohio Archaeological Inventory) suggests the applicability of the Vacant Center Model to the Hopewellian community of the Upper Jonathan Creek sub-region. Two primary earthworks, Glenford and Yost, are located within the sub-region while the large Reservoir Mound, of known Hopewellian affiliation, is located along the northwest edge of this community, in the direction of Newark (Pacheco 1992).

CONCLUSIONS

The lack of large sedentary villages associated with Ohio Hopewell earthwork-mound centers has long been a mystery. Examination of alternative models and a set of regional settlement data suggest that the lack of the Hopewell villages is best accounted for by the Vacant Center Model, much as Prufer (1965, 1967) had argued. Small, dispersed, sedentary hamlets surround `vacant' earthwork-mound centers, which were periodically visited by some or all of the group. Vacant centers provided the means of integrating dispersed Ohio Hopewell communities. Although these communities lacked centralized control, they were bound together through kinship and tradition, solidified through mound building and mortuary rituals. This is a pattern of horizontal rather than vertical complexity, probably indicative of tribal as opposed to chiefdom level social organization. Regional variants of Ohio Hopewell are characterized by groups of dispersed communities, each of which maintained its own local ceremonial center. These communities were linked together into peer-polities, possibly formalized in complex earthworks like the Hopewell or Newark sites. The apparent hierarchy created by this social organization is illusory, but is typical of horizontally flat, lineage based tribal organizations composed of equivalent social units (Dancey and Pacheco n.d.). Braun (1991:435) characterizes these non-hierarchical social organizations as examples of the principle of sequential hierarchy, consisting "of a nesting of patterns of interaction and decision making, so that people interact as members of nested categories of social identity."

Vacant centers existed because of the dispersed sedentary communities, but while they were the focal point of community social activities, they were not the focal point of habitation. As such, the Ohio Hopewell settlement pattern is a stable social organi-zation. The Hopewell vacant center pattern lasted until nucleated villages subsumed the need for them. This change in regional scale social organization occurred sometime during the fourth century A.D., and signals the beginning of the Late Woodland period (Dancey 1991, this volume).

ACKNOWLEDGMENTS

I want to thank the following people for their help with this paper, the ideas which it expresses, and the data it presents: William Dancey, Jeff Carskadden, Robert Sterling, James Marshall, James Morton, William Pickard, Dewey Albright, Robert and Mary Kinser, Olaf Prufer, Denice Weinberg, and Dee Anne Wymer. Any errors are my responsibility.

REFERENCES CITED

Baby, R.S., and S.M. Langlois 1979 Seip Mound State Memorial: Nonmortuary Aspects of Hopewell. In *Hopewell Archaeology: the Chillicothe Conference*, edited by D.S. Brose and N. Greber, pp. 16-18. Kent State University Press, Kent, Ohio.

Braun, D.P. 1991 Are There Cross-Cultural Regulations in Tribal Social Practices? In *Between Bands and States*, edited by S.A. Gregg pp. 423-444. Center for Archaeological Investigations, Ocassional Paper No. 9, Southern Illinois University, Carbondale.

Brown, J. 1982 Mound City and the Vacant Ceremonial Center. Paper presented at the Annual Meeting of the Society for American Archaeology, Minneapolis.

Bullard, W. R. 1962 Settlement and Social Structure in the Southern Mayan Lowlands During the Classic Period. In *Ancient Mesoamerica*, edited by J. Graham, pp. 137-145. Peek Publications, Palo Alto, California.

Caldwell, J. R. 1958 *Trend and Tradition in the Prehistory of the Eastern United States*. American Anthropological Association Memoirs 88, Menasha, Wisconsin.

1964 Interaction Spheres in Prehistory. In *Hopewellian Studies*, edited by J. Caldwell and R. Hall, pp. 133-143. Illinois State Museum, Scientific Papers 12, Springfield.

Carskadden J. 1972 An Analysis of Blades from Three Hopewellian Sites in Muskingum County, Ohio. *Ohio Archaeologist* 22(2):8-10.

Carskadden, J. and J. Morton 1983 A Hopewell Mound, Dresden, Ohio. *Ohio Archaeologist* 33(1):44-45.

n.d. Living on the Edge: A Comparison of Adena and Hopewell Communities in the Central Muskingum Valley. In Ohio *Hopewell Community Organization*, edited by W. Dancey and P. Pacheco. Kent State University Press, Kent, Ohio "in press".

Chapman, R. 1981 The Emergence of Formal Disposal Areas and the "Problem" of Megalithic Tombs in Prehistoric Europe. In *The Archaeology of Death*, edited by R. Chapman, I. Kines, and K. Randsborg, pp. 71-81. Cambridge University Press, London.

Charles, D. K. and J. Buikstra 1983 Archaic Mortuary Sites in the Central Mississippi Drainage: Distribution, Structure, and Behavioral Implications. In *Archaic Hunters and Gatherers in the American Midwest*, edited by J. Phillips and J. Brown, pp. 117-145. Academic Press, New York.

Church, F. and A. Ericksen n.d. Beyond the Scioto Valley: Middle Woodland Occupation in the Salt Creek Drainage. In *Ohio Hopewell Community Organization*, edited by W. Dancey and P. Pacheco. Kent State University Press, Kent, Ohio in press.

Clay, R. B. 1980 The Cultural Placement of Fayette Thick Ceramics in Central Kentucky. *Tennessee Anthropologist* 5(2):166-178.

Converse, R. N. 1984 An Open Hopewell Site in Ross County, Ohio. *Ohio Archaeologist* 34(2):23.

1993 The Troyer Site: A Hopewell Habitation Site, and a Secular View of Ohio Hopewell Villages. *Ohio Archaeologist* 43(3):4-12.

1994 The Harness Hopewell Village Sites. *Ohio Archaeologist* 44(1):4-9.

Dancey, W. S. 1991 A Middle Woodland Settlement in Central Ohio: A Preliminary Report on the Murphy Site (33Li212). *Pennsylvania Archaeologist* 61:37-72.

1992a Village Origins in Central Ohio: The Results and Implications of Recent Middle and Late Woodland Research. In *Cultural Variability in Context: Woodland Settlements of the Mid-Ohio Valley*, edited by M. Seeman, pp. 24-29. MCJA Special Papers 7, Kent State University Press, Kent, Ohio.

1992b Small Site Formation Processes and the Hopewell Settlement Problem. Paper presented at the Southeastern Archaeological Conference, Little Rock.

Dancey, W. S. and P. J. Pacheco n.d. The Ohio Hopewell Settlement Problem in Historical Perspective. In *Ohio Hopewell Community Organization*, edited by W. Dancey and P. Pacheco. Kent State University Press, Kent, Ohio "in press".

Deboer, W. E. and J. Blitz 1991 Ceremonial Centers of the Chachi. *Expedition* 33(1):53-62.

Dillehay, T. D. 1990 Mapuche Ceremonial Landscape, Social Recruitment and Resource Rights. *World Archaeology* 22(2):223-241.

1992 Keeping Outsiders Out: Public Ceremony, Resource Rights, and Hierarchy in Historic and Contemporary Mapuche Society. In *Wealth and Hierarchy in the Intermediate Area*, edited by F. Lange, pp. 379-422. Dunbarton Oaks Research Library, Washington, D.C.

Greber, N. 1979 A Comparative Study of Site Morphology and Burial Patterns at the Edwin Harness Mound and Seip Mounds 1 and 2. In *Hopewell Archaeology: the Chillicothe Conference*, edited by D. Brose and N. Greber, pp. 27-38. Kent State University Press, Kent, Ohio.

1991 A Study of Continuity and Contrast Between Central Scioto Adena and Hopewell Sites. *West Virginia Archaeologist* 43(1/2):1-26.

n.d. The Seip Geometric Enclosures and Environs: An Estimate of Possible Changes in Community Patterns Through Time. In *Ohio Hopewell Community Organization*, edited by W. Dancey and P. Pacheco. Kent State University Press, Kent, Ohio "in press".

Greber, N. and K. Ruhl 1989 *The Hopewell Site: A Contemporary Analysis Based on the Work of Charles C. Willoughby*. Westview Press, Boulder, Colorado.

Griffin, J. B. n.d. Interpretations of Ohio Hopewell 1845-1984 and the Recent Emphasis on the Study of Dispersed Hamlets. In *Ohio Hopewell Community Organization*, edited by W. Dancey and P. Pacheco. Kent State University Press, Kent, Ohio "in press".

Hill, N. N. 1881 *History of Coshocton County, Ohio*. A. A. Graham, Newark, Ohio.

Johnson, G.A. 1981 Monitoring Complex System Integration and Boundary Phenomena with Settlement Size Data. In *Archaeological Approaches to the Study of Complexity*, edited by S. E. van der Leeuw, pp. 143-188. Albert Egges van Giffen voor Prae-en Protohistorie, CINGVLA VI, University van Amsterdam, Amsterdam, Denmark.

Kent, S. 1992 Studying Variability in the Archaeological Record: An Ethnoarchaeological Model for Distinguishing Mobility Patterns. *American Antiquity* 57:635-660.

Kozarek, S. E. 1987 *A Hopewellian Homestead in the Ohio River Valley*. Masters thesis, Department of Anthropology, University of Cincinnati, Cincinnati.

n.d. Demonstrating Sedentism in the Archaeological Record: A Hopewellian Homestead in Southwestern Indiana. In *Ohio Hopewell Community Organization*, edited by W. Dancey and P. Pacheco. Kent State University Press, Kent, Ohio "in press".

Lepper, B. T. and R. W. Yerkes n.d. Hopewellian Occupations at the Northern Periphery of the Newark Earthworks: The Newark Expressway Sites Revisited. In *Ohio Hopewell Community Organization*, edited by W. Dancey and P. Pacheco. Kent State University Press, Kent, Ohio "in press".

Lynott, M. J. and S. Monk 1985 *Mound City, Ohio, Archaeological Investigations*. Midwest Archaeological Center, Occasional Studies in Anthropology 12, Lincoln, Nebraska.

Morton, J. and J. Carskadden 1987 Test Excavations at an Early Hopewellian Site near Dresden, Ohio. *Ohio Archaeologist* 37:8-12.

Pacheco, P. J. 1988 Ohio Middle Woodland Settlement Variability in the Upper Licking River Drainage. *Journal of the Steward Anthropological Society* 18(1/2):87-117.

1992 The Legacy of the Moundbuilders: An Overview of Early and Middle Woodland Archaeology in the Licking River Basin. In *Vanishing Heritage: the Story of Archaeology in Licking County, Ohio*, edited by P. Hooge and B. Lepper, pp. 12-31. Licking County Archaeology and Landmarks Society, Granville, Ohio.

1993 *Ohio Hopewell Settlement Patterns: An Application of the Vacant Center Model to Middle Woodland Period Intracommunity Settlement Variability in the Upper Licking River Valley.* Ph.D. dissertation, Department of Anthropology, The Ohio State University. University Microfilms, Ann Arbor.

n.d. Ohio Middle Woodland Intracommunity Settlement Variability: A Case Study from the Licking Valley. In *Ohio Hopewell Community Organization,* edited by W. Dancey and P. Pacheco. Kent State University Press, Kent, Ohio "in press".

Prufer, O. H. 1964a The Hopewell Complex of Ohio. In *Hopewellian Studies,* edited by J. Caldwell and R. Hall, pp. 35-83. Illinois State Museum, Scientific Papers 12, Springfield.

1964b The Hopewell Cult. *Scientific American* 211:90-102.

1965 *The McGraw Site: a Study in Hopewellian Dynamics.* Cleveland Museum of Natural History, Scientific Publications 4(1), Cleveland.

1967 The Scioto Valley Archaeological Survey. In *Studies in Ohio Archaeology,* edited by O. Prufer and D. McKenzie, pp. 267-328. The Press of Western Reserve University, Cleveland.

1968 *Ohio Hopewell Ceramics: an Analysis of the Extant Collections.* Museum of Anthropology, Anthropological Papers 33, University of Michigan, Ann Arbor.

Railey, J. A. 1991 Woodland Settlement Trends and Symbolic Architecture in the Kentucky Bluegrass. In *The Human Landscape in Kentucky's Past,* edited by C. Stout and C. Hensley, pp. 56-77. Kentucky Heritage Council, Frankfort.

Seeman, M. F. 1981 *An Archaeological Survey of the Hopewell Site (33Ro27) and Vicinity, Ross County, Ohio.* Report on file, Ohio Historic Preservation Office, Columbus.

1986 *The Locust Site (33MU160): The 1983 Test Excavation of a Multicomponent Workshop in East Central Ohio.* Kent State Research Papers in Archaeology 7, Kent State University Press, Kent, Ohio.

1988 Ohio Hopewell Trophy-Skull Artifacts as Evidence for Competition in Middle Woodland Societies Circa 50 B.C. - A.D. 350. *American Antiquity* 53:565-577.

Smith, B. D. 1992 Hopewellian Farmers of Eastern North America. In *Rivers of Change: Essays on Early Agriculture in Eastern North America,* by B. Smith, pp. 201-248. Smithsonian Institution Press, Washington D.C.

Swartz, B. K., ed. 1971 *Adena: The Seeking of an Identity.* Ball State University Press, Muncie, Indiana.

Willey, G. R. 1956 Problems Concerning Prehistoric Settlement Patterns in the Maya Lowlands. In *Prehistoric Settlement Patterns in the New World,* edited by G. Willey, pp. 107-114. Viking Fund Publications in Anthropology, No. 23, New York.

Wymer, D. A. 1987 *The Paleoethnobotanical Record of Central Ohio - 100 B.C. to A.D. 800: Subsistence Continuity Amid Cultural Change.* Ph.D. dissertation, Department of Anthropology, The Ohio State University, Columbus. University Microfilms, Ann Arbor.

n.d. Paleoethnobotany in the Licking River Valley, Ohio: Implications for Understanding Ohio Hopewell. In *Ohio Hopewell Community Organization,* edited by W. Dancey and P. Pacheco. Kent State University Press, Kent , Ohio "in press".

Wymer, D. A., B. T. Lepper, and W. T. Pickard 1992 Recent Excavations at the Great Circle, Newark, Ohio. Paper presented at the Midwestern Archaeological Conference, Grand Rapids, Michigan.

Yerkes, R. W. 1988 The Woodland and Mississippian Traditions in the Prehistory of Midwestern North America. *Journal of World Prehistory* 2:307-358.

1990 Using Microwear Analysis to Investigate Domestic Activities and Craft Specialization at the Murphy Site, a Small Hopewell Settlement in Licking County, Ohio. In *The Interpretative Possibilities of Microwear Studies,* edited by K. Knutsson and J. Taffinder, pp. 167-176. Aun 14, Societas Archaeologica Upsaliensi, Uppsala, Sweden.

1994 A Consideration of the Function of Ohio Hopewell Bladelets. *Lithic Technology* 19(2):109-127.

THREE

**THE OHIO HOPEWELL ECONICHE:
HUMAN-LAND INTERACTION
IN THE CORE AREA**

D E E   A N N E   W Y M E R

ABSTRACT

This paper summarizes over a decade of past research into
Ohio Hopewell paleoethnobotany and highlights new analyses
that are currently underway. Several topical areas are
explored, including subsistence data, human-environmental
interactions, ceremonial plant use, and implications for various
theoretical approaches to elucidating the Hopewell phenomenon. Additionally, intraregional similarities and distinctions for
developing paleoethnobotanical data bases for the Ohio core
area will be explored. Results to date indicate a basic similarity among the Ohio river valleys, with Hopewell populations
intensely utilizing cultigens of the Eastern Agricultural Complex,
as well as regional distinctions in the use of gathered non-
cultigen resources.

A View From the Core a Synthesis of Ohio Hopewell Archaeology•edited by Paul J. Pacheco
© Copyright 1996 by The Ohio Archaeological Council• Columbus, Ohio•All Rights Reserved•ISBN 0-9626931-9-7

DEE ANNE WYMER

THE OHIO HOPEWELL ECONICHE: HUMAN-LAND

INTRODUCTION

At the last conference of this nature, held in Chillicothe in 1978, one of the topical papers addressed the known data for Hopewell plant utilization (Ford 1979). The data base was largely from Illinoian sites, and the material from Ohio sites were principally isolated specimens from mound contexts with poor sampling control. At this time Hopewell subsistence was characterized as emphasizing the collection of gathered resources, especially nut masts, with garden products acting merely as supplements to the diet and were thus considered relatively unimportant. Ford stated unequivocally that as of 1978 "...no native cultigens, maygrass (*Phalaris caroliniana*), sumpweed, or sunflower have been found in Ohio Hopewell sites." (Ford 1979:234).

Since 1978 the data base for Ohio Hopewell paleoethnobotany has expanded considerably. Although Ford's original admonishment about sampling size and biases still remains, we now have a much firmer understanding of Ohio Hopewell plant utilization. The goal of this paper is to summarize the available data garnered since 1978. I will also review recent research and offer some new and exciting results from analyses still in progress, addressing the nature of Hopewell subsistence, and discussing the intriguing aspect of the impact of Hopewell populations on their local environment. Due to our widening data base, we now have the ability to explore regional variability among paleoethnobotanical assemblages. Recent investigations have also revealed fascinating glimpses into the ritual use of plants among the Ohio Hopewell populations. Lastly, the raw data and the information generated by our deeper understanding of Hopewell plant utilization has implications for larger theoretical issues.

We now have paleoethnobotanical samples from a variety of contexts, including habitation and ceremonial sites, and from a variety of valley systems **(Table 3:1)**. The most extensive regional data base is for the Licking River Valley, from habitation sites associated with the Newark Earthwork complex. The Murphy site (dating to the second century A.D.), in fact, is the most completely excavated Ohio Hopewell habitation site and the paleoethnobotanical analysis there has been both intensive and

extensive (Dancey 1987, 1991, 1992; Wymer 1987a, 1987b, 1990a). The other three sites from the valley (Murphy III, Campus, and Nu-Way) are in proximity to the Murphy site and represent much smaller samples of Hopewell habitation sites (Wymer 1987b). These sites date to both the earlier, and probably later, portion of the Middle Woodland period.

Research on sites outside the Licking Valley is currently in progress. For example, analysis has just begun on materials from the Jennison Guard (aka Whitacre) site located along the Ohio River. Samples are being analyzed from materials collected during the 1985 University of Cincinnati excavations conducted by Sue Kozarek (1987) and from current excavations by Debbie Whitacre into a well-preserved midden zone. Flotation and macrobotanical samples (items collected by hand during excavation) reveal that preservation of the plant remains at the site is quite remarkable.

An extensive series of flotation samples was collected from the well-known Capitolium Mound, one of the platform mounds of the Marietta Works, during excavations directed by Dr. N'omi Greber in the summer of 1990. I have also examined macrobotanical materials, consisting primarily of wood charcoal collected for radiocarbon dating, from the mound. Consequently, a rich data base is now being established for a wide variety of valleys, and diverse environments, for the Ohio Hopewell "core region."

TABLE 3:1
East-Central Ohio: Licking River Valley Murphy - A.D.-150 18 features; 37 samples:135 liters Murphy III - A.D.-300? 4 features; 9 samples: 25.6 liters Campus - 10 B.C.-3 features; 7 samples: 25 liters Nu-Way - 100 B.C.-2 features; 3 samples:12 liters
SW Ohio River Floodplain Whitacre/Jennison Guard-A.D. 200-work in progress; to date: 6 midden samples: 7.5 liters
Ohio River/Muskingum River Floodplain Marietta Works - Capitolium Mound-A.D. 200-work in progress; to date:15 features; 20 samples: 73.6 liters

Ohio Hopewell Paleoethnobotanical Assemblages: Site and Sample Information

THE PALEOETHNOBOTANICAL DATA
Subsistence - The Habitation Sites

The paleoethnobotanical assemblages from the sites can be used to generate a number of indices for a comparison among the sample population. For example, there is a great degree of variation among the sites in terms of the density of wood charcoal, nutshell, seeds, and cucurbit rind *(Figures 3:1 and 3:2)*. In all cases, wood charcoal densities exceed nutshell quantities; the majority of the sites have yielded moderate to high densities for these two plant classes.

Sample biases and deposition distinctions probably account for the majority of the variability in these assemblages. The sample from the Nu-Way site is a single large pit that contained numerous pottery sherds and had a high organic content. The Jennison Guard values are slightly higher than those at the Licking Valley sites, and may reflect the excellent preservation qualities of the midden at this site. For the numerical indices summarized in this paper, detailed analysis of recently collected midden flotation samples have been utilized from Jennison Guard. However, an initial scan of material collected from the 1985 feature excavations reveals the same plant classes.

One pattern that is quite typical of Ohio Hopewell habitation sites is that carbonized seeds and often cucurbit rind (primarily the rind of the yellow-flowered gourd squash - *Cucurbita pepo* var. *ovifera*) are ubiquitous and are recovered in high densities. Seed density for the majority of the sites range from 20 to 35 seeds per liter, while squash rind quantities tend to vary to a greater degree **(Figure 3:2)**. To place these values in perspective, the wood charcoal and nutshell densities for the Middle Woodland habitation sites are slightly below or comparable to the quantities from several large Late Woodland villages (e.g., Waterplant, Zencor, and Childers) (see Wymer 1990b, 1992, 1993). Seed densities, in fact, are higher for the Ohio Hopewell sites (by twice as much), while the cucurbit rind densities for the Nu-Way and Jennison Guard site are much higher as well (Wymer 1992).

Interesting patterns are revealed when considering individual plant classes. The nut types identified in the sites' samples indicate that a wide variety of taxa had been utilized, including hickory (*Carya* spp.), black walnut (*Juglans nigra*), butternut (*Juglans cinerea*), acorn (*Quercus* spp.), and hazelnut (*Corylus* cf. *americana*) **(Figure 3:3)**. The percentage of the identified fragment counts does vary, with hickory typically the most common. The presence of

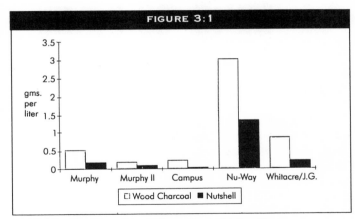

Middle Woodland Sites: Wood Charcoal and Nut Densities

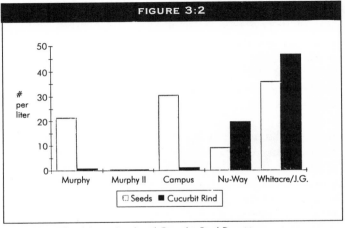

Middle Woodland Sites: Seed and Cucurbit Rind Densities

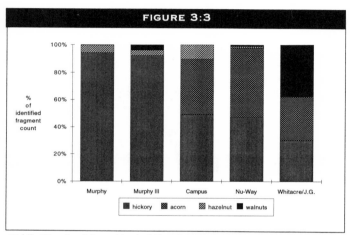

Middle Woodland Sites: Nutshell Taxa Percentages

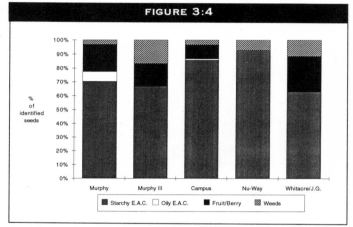

Seed Groups: Economic or Environmental Classes

acorn, hazelnut, and the walnuts (black walnut and butternut combined) shifts in importance from site to site (Figure 3:3). The differences undoubtedly reflect environmental distinctions among the sites' microclimates, as will be discussed below.

The most impressive aspect of the sites' plant assemblages is the diversity of the identified seeds recovered in flotation samples (Figure 3:4). A wide variety of fruit and berry seeds and pits have been identified (ranging from sumac [Rhus], raspberry [Rubus], elderberry [Sambucus], and honey locust [Gleditsia triacanthos] to grape pits [Vitis]) with ubiquitous but low quantities of seeds from ruderal taxa (e.g., panic grass [Panicum], bedstraw [Galium], spurge [Euphorbia], purslane [Portulaca], and tick-trefoil [Desmodium], among others) (Wymer 1987b, 1990a, 1990b, and 1993).

However, the greatest component of the identified seed assemblages from the Middle Woodland sites are cultigens of the Eastern Agricultural Complex (Figures 3:4 and 3:5). Literally, thousands of seeds and achenes of the Complex taxa have been recovered at all of the sites under consideration and constitute from 60 to nearly 90 percent of the identified seeds (values around 80 percent seem to be typical for this time period). The major cultivars are members

of the high-carbohydrate ("starchy") taxa and include maygrass (Phalaris caroliniana), erect knotweed (Polygonum erectum), and goosefoot (Chenopodium spp.). Achenes of domesticated sumpweed or marshelder (Iva annua) and sunflower (Helianthus annuus) are less commonly recovered from the sites, but are often present. Both species have been identified in samples from Murphy (including 154 sumpweed and 11 sunflower achenes and fragments) and from the Campus site (five sumpweed achenes). A single sunflower specimen identified by Wes Cowan was recovered in a sample from the 1984 University of Cincinnati excavations at the Jennison Guard site (Blosser 1989), and I suspect more of the high-fat/oil taxa will appear in samples as analyses progress.

There is a great degree of variation in the prominence of any specific starchy taxon in the sites' seed assemblages (Figure 3:5). At the sites with the best sample sizes and/or preservation — Murphy, Campus, and Jennison Guard — all three species of the starchy Eastern Agricultural Complex (e.g., maygrass, goosefoot, and erect knotweed) are present. Goosefoot was identified in the assemblages from all of the sites and, in fact, confirmed thin-testa (domesticated) goosefoot (Chenopodium berlandieri spp. Jonesianum - [Smith 1985]) was identified at all sites with the exclusion of Murphy III.

FIGURE 3:5

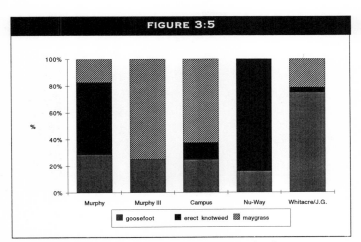

Individual Taxon Percentages of Starchy Eastern Agricultural Complex Totals by Site

SUBSISTENCE - SUMMARY

The data noted above, along with information outlined below, allows us for the first time to address in some detail the nature of Ohio Hopewell subsistence. One of the major concerns, for example, hinges upon exactly how important crop plants had been in their diet; had they been staples or supplements to a largely collected food base? How did gathered resources (e.g., nut masts, roots/tubers, and fruits/berries) fit into the overall subsistence regime? Additionally, more specific research questions focus on the nature of the horticultural system we now designate as the "Eastern Agricultural Complex."

I believe current research indicates that *the Ohio Hopewell had been sophisticated farmers and managers of their environment.* I am using the term "farmers," and the connotation of the term, for a specific reason. The paleoethnobotanical record suggests that these prehistoric populations had been garden horticulturalists — utilizing a diverse array of cultigens (from a warty hard squash to the grain crops of the Eastern Agricultural Complex) in clearings within the deciduous forests. Undoubtedly, the garden "patches" were on a smaller scale than the larger nearly mono-crop maize fields of the Late Prehistoric and Early Historic periods.

TABLE 3:2

Seed Taxa	Site Totals	% of Identified Seeds
Eastern Agricultural Complex:		
goosefoot - total:	- 98 -	46.45
— domesticated form	32	15.17
— weedy form	16	7.58
— indeterminate	50	23.70
maygrass	28	13.27
erect knotweed	2	0.95
— unid. knotweed	3	1.42
Fruit/Berry:		
— honey locust	46	21.80
— hackberry	2	0.95
— sumac	1	0.47
— grape	2	.095
— strawberry	1	0.47
— pokeberry	1	0.47
— elderberry	1	0.47
Weedy/Incidental:		
— bedstraw	16	7.58
— panic grass	3	1.42
— wood sorrel	1	0.47
— Lithospermum	1	0.47
Solanaceae (groundcherry?)	1	0.47
— Solomon's Seal?	1	0.47
— catchfly	1	0.47
Other:		
unidentified small legume	2	0.95
— unidentifiable	52	- -
TOTAL:	263	N = 211

Whitacre/Jennison Guard Site: Seed Assemblage

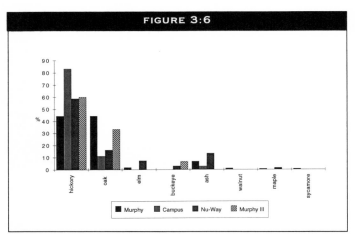

Licking Valley Sites: Identified Wood Fragment Count Percentages

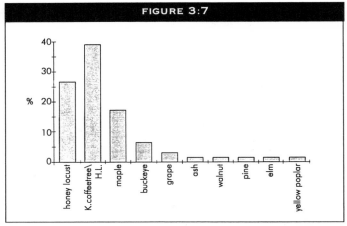

Whitacre/Jennison Guard Site: Identified Wood Fragment Count Percentages

However, based on the density and ubiquity indices of the Middle Woodland paleoethnobotanical assemblages, particularly in comparison with the succeeding large nucleated Late Woodland communities, I would suggest that the cultigens from those gardens were a major, *if not the* major, portion of their diet (see also Smith 1992). Thus, rather than garden products acting merely as supplements to their diet, I would argue that they had been a basic staple (and unfortunately, when the term "garden horticulture" is used, people somehow come away with the impression that this had been an unsophisticated, inefficient, and unproductive technique). Additionally, the Ohio Hopewell populations were utilizing a wide variety of non-agricultural resources; from nut masts to fruits and berries. Interestingly, the density and diversity of nut and fruit/berry taxa at these Middle Woodland habitation sites does not match the values from the well-documented plant assemblages from the nucleated early Late Woodland villages. The botanical materials from the Ohio Hopewell hamlets indicates that they were rather selective about their gathered resources - emphasizing locally available, easily collected and processed, and nutritious nuts, fruits, and tubers. This is in contrast to the Late Woodland sites where every available resource seems to have been intensely utilized, including less desirable plants foods (red oak acorns, upland blueberries, among others - see Wymer 1990b, 1993). This, plus other factors (i.e., wood charcoal

assemblage), suggests that the Ohio Hopewell, although affecting their local environment (see below), had not yet reached the level of impact around their habitation sites as that documented for the nucleated Late Woodland communities (Wymer 1990b, 1992).

INTERREGIONAL COMPARISONS

As the previous data have shown, the most striking aspect of the paleoethnobotanical data is the similarity of the assemblages regardless of location — from the Ohio River flood plain to the small terrace of the Raccoon Creek drainage of the Licking River Valley. The same basic densities and diversity of plant classes, from cultigens to gathered resources, have been documented. The closest similarity is in the garden products — from the quantity and taxa presence of squash rind to the members of the Eastern Agricultural Complex.

Collected resources, despite use of the same basic plant classes (nuts, fruits, among others), do reveal distinctions which may reflect variations in the local environments. Variation exists in the dominance of hickory or walnuts, and more rarely, acorn, in the nutshell assemblage. Fruit and berry seeds and pits reveal a mixture of collected plant materials from re-growth in recently abandoned garden

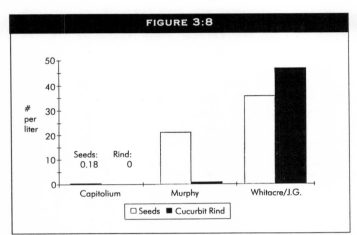

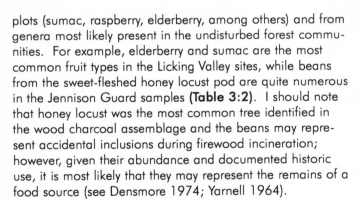

Density Comparisons of Seeds and Cucurbit Rind for Mound and Habitation Contexts

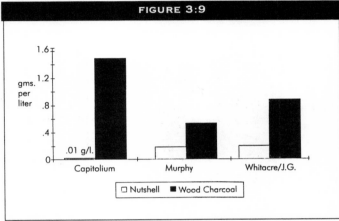

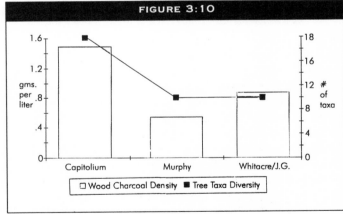

Density Comparisons of Nutshell and Wood Charcoal for Mound and Habitation Contexts

plots (sumac, raspberry, elderberry, among others) and from genera most likely present in the undisturbed forest communities. For example, elderberry and sumac are the most common fruit types in the Licking Valley sites, while beans from the sweet-fleshed honey locust pod are quite numerous in the Jennison Guard samples **(Table 3:2)**. I should note that honey locust was the most common tree identified in the wood charcoal assemblage and the beans may represent accidental inclusions during firewood incineration; however, given their abundance and documented historic use, it is most likely that they may represent the remains of a food source (see Densmore 1974; Yarnell 1964).

Due to the remarkable preservation conditions at Jennison Guard, other more unusual plant specimens have been recovered and identified. For example, a midden flotation sample yielded a single possible gourd rind fragment (*Lagenaria siceria*) and nearly every flotation sample produced fragments of groundnut tubers (*Apios americana*). Numerous complete specimens of groundnut, along with several Liliaceae tubers, are represented in macrobotanical items collected during excavation (many specimens of honey locust beans were also collected).

Distinctions between Mound and Habitation Contexts in the Wood Assemblages

An important distinction between this site and the Licking Valley sites is that a few specimens of maize have been recovered from what appears to be fairly good contexts in the Jennison Guard samples.

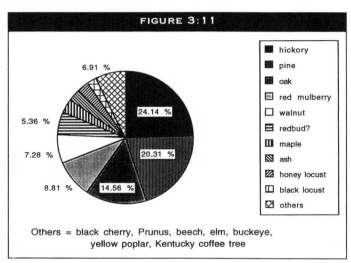

Capitolium Mound Wood Charcoal Assemblage: Percentages of Identified Wood Fragment Counts

To date, I have identified a cob fragment and a nearly complete kernel from the midden context in macrobotanical samples. Wes Cowan also identified seven kernel and two cupule maize fragments in midden samples from the University of Cincinnati 1984 excavations (Blosser 1989). These specimens could easily be contaminates from more recent occupations (a Fort Ancient site lies adjacent to the Middle Woodland occupation area). However, Hopewell maize from the Edwin Harness Mound has been documented (see below; Ford 1987). Verification of the cultivation of this tropical crop at the Jennison Guard site must await until accelerated ^{14}C dating can be done on an actual maize specimen from the site. If these specimens are indeed Middle Woodland in age, this marks a clear distinction with the Licking Valley sites.

The identified wood charcoal assemblage, largely representing firewood utilization with some structural members such as posts (see below), indicates the use of local resources. For example, the wood assemblages from the Licking Valley sites closely mirror the proposed prehistoric forest composition (**Figure 3:6**, essentially an oak-hickory forest with adjacent mesophytic communities) (Wymer 1987b). The

Jennison Guard wood charcoal taxa also apparently reflect the bottomland forests of the Ohio River (**Figure 3:7**). Honey locust is a tree species that is most abundant in bottomland hardwood forests, growing along with mesic oaks, sweetgum, green ash, elms, and maples, among others (Harlow et al. 1979). However, honey locust also tends to be more common in disturbed areas, since this species is shade intolerant. The prevalence of this taxon may reflect the beginning stages of the impact to the local forests through clearance activities by the small communities of Hopewellian horticulturalists. An additional support of this possibility is the presence of a significant quantity (approximately 4 g in two samples to date) of black cherry (*Prunus serotina*) in the hand-collected specimens from the midden. Black cherry is also quite common in more open conditions. Lastly, a large burned post, apparently part of a structure, recently uncovered at the Jennison Guard site represents the utilization of ash (probably black ash - *Fraxinus nigra*).

To summarize, the data base thus far analyzed suggests that there is a greater degree of similarity rather than differences, among the various regions. Moderate to high quantities of all the plant classes, from nutshell to seeds, are typical for the Ohio Hopewell habitation sites. In all cases, the paleoethnobotanical record is dominated by the presence of cultigens, including cucurbits and members of the Eastern Agricultural Complex. The high-carbohydrate taxa, maygrass, erect knotweed, and goosefoot, are consistently the most prevalent component of the seed assemblages, although the importance of any individual taxon may vary.

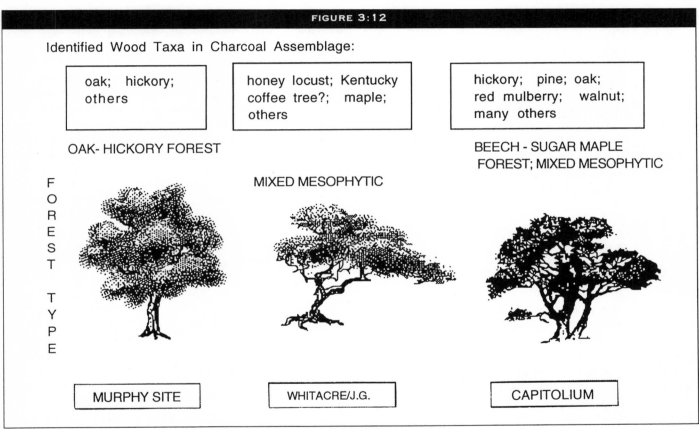

FIGURE 3:12

Identified Wood Taxa in Charcoal Assemblage:

| oak; hickory; others | honey locust; Kentucky coffee tree?; maple; others | hickory; pine; oak; red mulberry; walnut; many others |

OAK- HICKORY FOREST

BEECH - SUGAR MAPLE FOREST; MIXED MESOPHYTIC

MIXED MESOPHYTIC

F O R E S T   T Y P E

MURPHY SITE

WHITACRE/J.G.

CAPITOLIUM

Comparison of Identified Wood Charcoal Assembleges to Probable Prehistoric Forest Composition

The wood charcoal identifications reveal the utilization of arboreal resources from the immediate environment with some slight indication of beginning impact to the local ecosystem (probably due to land clearance activities associated with garden production). The presence and quantity of collected resources (i.e., nut masts, fruits/berries, and other materials such as tubers), although fairly diverse, indicate that at most sites the prehistoric populations had selected a few locally available taxa to emphasize.

Overall the impression is that, regardless of regional environmental distinctions, the impact and modification to the environment by the Ohio Hopewell populations was quite similar. This is also true when comparing the Ohio data to the extensive paleoethnobotanical data base for Middle Woodland sites from other regions (Asch and Asch 1985a and 1985b; Crites 1987; Ford 1985; Fritz 1993; Johannessen 1984; Wymer 1989).

CERMONIAL PLANT USE

An additional aspect of paleoethnobotanical analysis is the exploration of possible ceremonial plant use. Certainly, recent investigations (Connolly, this volume; Greber 1983; Pickard, this volume; Wymer et al. 1992) have illustrated the often extremely complicated use of distinctly colored and textured sediments in mound construction and the elaborate nature of the features within and around the larger Hopewell mounds. Re-examination of earlier excavations supports the implication that intensive and extensive ceremonial activities had taken place at these localities (see, for example, Greber and Ruhl 1989). Is it possible, then, that careful collection and analysis of flotation samples and macrobotanical remains would as well reveal the remnants of a complex utilization of plant material?

N'omi Greber's 1990 excavations at the Capitolium Mound, located within the Marietta Earthwork complex, have provided a detailed flotation record from a ceremonial context. Samples from features, including postmolds and large burned masses with less obvious functions, from several superimposed prepared floors have been analyzed to date, as have burning episodes on top of and within different construction levels of the mound strata.

I have compared the plant assemblages from the two Ohio Hopewell habitations sites with the best preservation and sample size - Murphy and Jennison Guard - to the Capitolium Mound samples. The results are quite intriguing. For example, the greatest density of cucurbit rind and seeds are recovered from the habitation sites (**Figure 3:8**). The same is true for nutshell, but wood charcoal occurs at nearly twice the density as the habitation sites (**Figure 3:9**). The nutshell and carbonized seeds recovered from Capitolium are probably incidental specimens perhaps included within general construction fill (**Table 3:3**), although they may represent food debris from the individuals participating in the mound-building and mound-use activities. In this light it is interesting that a single domesticated goosefoot specimen was recovered from a large shallow pit (Feature 35) built into one of the prepared floors.

The most distinctive signature of the Capitolium Mound samples is not only the density of the wood charcoal but the diversity and taxa of the wood utilized for the various burning episodes (**Figure 3:10**). The large sample from this site suggests this pattern is not due to the sample size effect (**Table 3:1**). Twice as many wood taxa have been identified in the Capitolium samples compared to the habitation sites. An additional wood species, sweetgum (*Liquidamber styraciflua*), was identified in one of the macrobotanical specimens collected for radiocarbon dating. Hickory, pine (*Pinus* spp.) (southern yellow varieties - such as shortleaf pine and Virginia pine), and oak have high ubiquities and form the largest component of the wood charcoal assemblage at Capitolium (**Figure 3:11**). Other taxa, such as red mulberry (*Morus rubra*), honey locust, black locust (*Robinia pseudoacacia*), and mesic genera such as walnut, maple (*Acer*), and ash, are also significant in the wood identification profile. The features with the greatest diversity of taxa, typically including red mulberry and the various locusts, are largely from burned areas associated with the mound floors. In at least one case (Feature 47), a burned mass which appears to have been on the surface of one of the mound fill construction episodes included all of the taxa shown in **Figure 3:11**.

The most impressive aspect of the wood taxa from Capitolium Mounds, however, is not exclusive to the diversity of genera or species (**Figure 3:11**). As I previously noted, the wood charcoal assemblage from habitation sites tends to reflect the forest composition of the local environment. This is not the case with the Capitolium wood charcoal profile. Reconstruction of the Marietta Works environment, from floodplain to uplands, indicates that the terrace on which the earthworks once stood had supported a beech-sugar maple forest (Boetticher 1929; Rypma 1961). More mesic taxa, such as sycamore, elms, ashes, and others would have been found along the lower topography, and more xeric taxa, such as oaks (particularly the red group), hickory, and chestnut would have been found on the uplands overlooking the terrace. Particularly crucial is the evidence that pine, especially members of the southern yellow group, would have been found as scattered individuals or small groups growing in the hinterlands in rocky, dry

TABLE 3:3	
NUT TAXA:	**FRAGMENT COUNT:**
hickory	13
black walnut	5
walnut sp.	1
hazelnut	1
acorn?	1
Juglandaceae	41
	62
SEED TAXA	**COUNT:**
bedstraw	3
sumac	1
panic grass	1
erect knotweed	1
aquatic knotweed	1
knotweed sp.	1
goosefoot (thin testa)	1
Polygonaceae (*Rumex*)	1
unidentifiable	3
	13

Capitolium Mound Nutshell and Seed Assemblage

areas (Boetticher 1929; Rypma 1961). It seems likely, therefore, that a wide variety of species from a wide variety of environments had been deliberately collected and utilized during as yet unspecified ceremonial activities associated with construction and utilization of the Capitolium Mound.

The same pattern occurs at the Connett Mounds, a series of small Late Adena burial mounds associated with the earthworks at the Plains in Athens County. In one of the mounds, an older woman had been cremated with red mulberry and cherry/plum wood (Wymer 1984). Tristine Smart and Richard I. Ford's (1983) analysis of samples from the Edwin Harness Mound also identified a large amount of pine wood from a burned area uncovered on the central floor of the middle structure of the "Big House" (Smart and

Ford 1983:54). Additionally, maize kernel fragments were identified in two features (one a bundle burial) from the Edwin Harness Mound and have been verified as Middle Woodland in age with accelerator radiocarbon dating (Ford 1987). This, along with other research, has indicated that maize, rather than a subsistence item, played a ceremonial role in this and the succeeding early Late Woodland period (Johannessen 1993; Johannessen and Hastorf 1994; Wymer 1994; Riley et al. 1994). Thus, it is apparent that the rich iconography of the Ohio Hopewell is also reflected in their plant use.

HUMAN- LAND IMPACT

The data outlined above, along with research conducted in other regions (e.g., Illinois and the American Bottom - see Smith 1985, 1992), indicates that Hopewellian populations practiced a sophisticated system of agriculture based upon a wide variety of crops and most likely utilizing some form of swidden or garden plot rotation system. The presence of cultigens certainly attests to the clearance of garden plots within rather dense forests. The large quantities of second-growth genera such as hazelnut, sumac, elderberry, honey locust, and raspberries, in the same depositional contexts with garden products, implies human-created patches in differing stages of re-growth in proximity to the habitation sites. The Ohio Hopewell landscape can be envisioned as a series of dispersed hamlets (see Pacheco, this volume), with differing patches of in-use current gardens, recently abandoned plots, and secondary forest re-growth in older cleared areas surrounding the sites. The Ohio Hopewell impact to the environment goes beyond the clearance activities associated with garden plot formation. Reviewing the literature and raw data describing the environment noted by the first European settlers in Ohio, some of the large and elaborate earthwork complexes, like Marietta, must have been constructed within dense forests.

Consequently, regardless of the length of time it took to complete these elaborate geometric enclosures or the number of individuals involved, a rather formidable degree of forest clearance must have taken place before any single segment could be built. And, as new investigations indicate, some of these complexes had been aligned to lunar or solar observations; it then becomes conceivable that these areas must have been kept cleared of significant vegetational re-growth.

A recent phytolith and pollen analysis of a soil sample from excavations conducted by the author, Brad Lepper, and William Pickard at the Great Circle, has produced fascinating results. A sample of what appeared to be the original paleosoil upon which the first stage of construction of the earthwork's embankment occurred, sealed by nearly 3 m of overlying deposits, was carefully collected and submitted to Linda Scott Cummings. She has reported that the sample shows that a mixed grasslands-herbaceous cover had existed at that specific sample locality, with the presence of oak trees somewhere in the general vicinity (Cummings 1993). In contrast, my research indicates that a rather dense white oak forest should have been growing at Newark. It is possible that prolonged human intervention (perhaps through the use of fire) had kept the area purposefully cleared (flecks of charcoal were also present in the same paleosoil sample). Systematic use of fire is a well documented activity of historic Native Americans (see Day 1953).

OTHER THEORETICAL IMPLICATIONS

One of the most significant aspects of this research is that the data, and the interpretations, can be used to address a variety of issues beyond the speciality of paleoethnobotany itself. For example, there have been a series of debates in the literature about the exact nature of Ohio Hopewell settlements. Were the populations sedentary, living in year-round residences, or did they follow the pattern hypothesized for some areas of Illinois and the American Bottom (winter habitations with separate spring through fall hamlets) (Bareis and Porter eds. 1984; Fortier et al. 1984; Fortier et al. 1989)? The extensive use of crops documented at the Ohio sites minimally implies that some members of these

small communities were present during spring garden preparation and planting, most likely conducted summer maintenance of those plots, and certainly participated in fall harvesting activities. Additionally, the presence of mid and late summer ripening taxa such as elderberries, raspberries, and hazelnut (which must be closely monitored to prevent heavy animal predation) supports this inference.

Although winter occupation can never be firmly supported with botanical data, the pattern of plant use documented at Ohio Hopewell sites is characteristic of sedentary populations. At the least, it is difficult to envision the sites' occupants harvesting what must have been fairly large quantities of garden products and then carrying the processed material to some distant winter camp.

Another question involves settlement movement beyond a possible annual cycle. Did the individual hamlets, for whatever reasons (soil exhaustion, animal depletion, among others), periodically relocate (every 20,30,50 years) some distance from the original occupation (see Prufer 1965)? If this is the case, what is the long-term impact to the environment (and how would that affect the human populations)?

Evidence from comparing the Middle Woodland habitation sites to the Late Woodland communities indicates that there had been an on-going subtle evolution of the horticultural system. Sunflower, for example, begins to replace sumpweed throughout the Late Woodland as the primary oil-rich seed crop and goosefoot becomes prominent at the expense of the other starchy Eastern Agricultural Complex members. Firewood analyses also reveals rather extensive impact to the local forests surrounding the Late Woodland sites (with second-growth tree genera often composing a third or more of the entire wood assemblages). Could we as well document these types of subtle paleoethnobotanical changes if the data base included adequately sampled habitation contexts from early through late Middle Woodland period sites? And if this pattern was revealed, what might that imply about 'human to environment' and 'people to people' interaction in increasingly sedentary populations?

CONCLUSION

It is obvious from the above discussion that although much work has been done in the investigation of Ohio Hopewell paleoethnobotany, further research remains. Hopefully, the data outlined in this article, and the theoretical implications noted, will encourage a vigorous interest in exploring subtle patterns of plant use within the Middle Woodland period. Perhaps another Hopewell Core conference in twenty years will find some of the above questions answered - as well as sparking a new set of inquiries.

ACKNOWLEDGMENTS

I would like to thank the many individuals who have graciously acquiesced to my pestering for access to their paleoethnobotanical materials and information about their various projects. This research would not have been possible without the work and input from William S. Dancey and the members of the Licking County Archaeology and Landmarks Society (the Licking County sites), as well as Debbie Whitacre, Tony DeRegnaucourt, and Sue Kozarek for the Jennison Guard site materials. The many conversations and discussions with N'omi Greber and William Pickard have been a special delight that has enriched my research as a paleoethnobotanist and as an archaeologist. Lastly, Paul Pacheco's hard work, insights, and friendship reverberates through much of this Ohio Hopewell paleoethnobotanical odyssey.

REFERENCES CITED

Asch, D.L. and N. Asch 1985a Archeobotany. In *Smiling Dan*, edited by B. Stafford and M. Sant, pp. 327-401. Kampsville Archeological Center, Research Series 2. Center for American Archaeology, Kampsville.

1985b Prehistoric Plant Cultivation in West-Central Illinois. In *Prehistoric Food Production in North America*, edited by R.I. Ford, pp. 149-203. Museum of Anthropology, Anthropological Papers 75, University of Michigan, Ann Arbor.

Bareis, C.J. and J.W. Porter (eds.) 1984 *American Bottom Archaeology: A Summary of the FAI-270 Project Contribution to the Culture History of the Mississippi River Valley*. University of Illinois Press, Urbana.

Blosser, J.K. 1989 *Mica Working at the Jennison Guard Site: A Middle Woodland Village in Southeastern Indiana*. Master's thesis, Department of Anthropology, University of Cincinnati.

Boetticher, A.W. 1929 *A Study of Type Forest Associations of Athens County, Ohio*. Master's thesis, Department of Botany, The Ohio State University, Columbus.

Crites, G. 1987 Human-Plant Mutualism and Niche Expression in the Paleoethnobotanical Record: A Middle Woodland Example. *American Antiquity* 52:725-740.

Cummings, L.S. 1993 *Pollen and Phytolith Analysis of a Single Sample from the Great Circle at Moundbuilders State Memorial, Ohio*. Report on file, Department of Anthropology, Bloomsburg University, Bloomsburg, Pennsylvania.

Dancey, W.S. 1987 The Murphy Site: A Middle Woodland Settlement in Central Ohio. Paper presented at the Annual Meeting of the Society for American Archaeology, Toronto.

1991 A Middle Woodland Settlement in Central Ohio: A Preliminary Report of the Murphy Site (33LI212). *Pennsylvania Archaeologist* 61(2):37-72.

1992 Village Origins in Central Ohio: The Results and Implications of Recent Middle and Late Woodland Research. In *Cultural Variability in Context: Woodland Settlements of the Mid-Ohio Valley*, edited by M.F. Seeman, pp. 24-29. Midcontinental Journal of Archaeology Special Paper 7, Kent State University Press, Kent, Ohio.

Day, G.M. 1953 The Indian as an Ecological Factor in the Northeastern Forest. *Ecology* 34:329-346.

Densmore, F. 1974 *How Indians Use Wild Plant for Food Medicine, and Crafts*. Dover Publications, New York. (Originally published 1928, Bureau of American Ethnology, Washington, D.C.)

Ford, R.I. 1979 Gathering and Gardening: Trends and Consequences of Hopewell Subsistence Strategies. In *Hopewell Archaeology: The Chillicothe Conference*, edited by D.S. Brose and N. Greber, pp. 234-238. Kent State University Press, Kent, Ohio.

1985 Patterns of Prehistoric Food Production in North America. In *Food Production in North America*, edited by R.I. Ford, pp. 341-364. Museum of Anthropology, Anthropological Papers 75. University of Michigan, Ann Arbor.

1987 Dating Early Maize in the Eastern United States. Paper presented at the Annual Meeting of the American Association for the Advancement of Science, Chicago.

Fortier, A.C., T.E. Emerson, and F.A. Finney 1984 Early Woodland and Middle Woodland Periods. In *American Bottom Archaeology: A Summary of the FAI-270 Project Contribution to the Culture History of the Mississippi River Valley*, edited by C.J. Bareis and J.W. Porter, pp. 59-103. University of Illinois Press, Urbana.

Fortier, A.C., T.O. Maher, J.A. Williams, M.C. Meinkoth, K.E. Parker, and L.S. Kelly 1989 *The Holding Site: A Hopewell Community in the American Bottom*, American Bottom Archaeology FAI-270 Reports 19. University of Illinois Press, Urbana.

Fritz, G.J. 1993 Early and Middle Woodland Paleoethnobotany. In *Foraging and Farming in the Eastern Woodlands*, edited by C.M. Scarry, pp. 39-56. University of Florida Press, Gainesville.

Greber, N.B. 1983 *Recent Excavations at the Edwin Harness Mound, Liberty Works, Ross County, Ohio*. Midcontinental Journal of Archaeology Special Papers 5, Kent State University Press, Kent, Ohio.

Greber, N.B. and K.C. Ruhl 1989 *The Hopewell Site: A Contemporary Analysis Based on the Work of Charles C. Willoughby*. Westview Press, Boulder, Colorado.

Harlow, W.M., E.S. Harrar, and F. White 1979 *Textbook of Dendrology*. McGraw-Hill, Chicago.

Johannessen, S. 1984 Paleoethnobotany. In *American Bottom Archaeology: A Summary of the FAI-270 Project Contribution to the Culture History of the Mississippi River Valley*, edited by C.J. Bareis and J.W. Porter, pp. 197-214. University of Illinois Press, Urbana.

1993 Farmers of the Late Woodland. In *Foraging and Farming in the Eastern Woodlands*, edited by C.M. Scarry, pp. 57-77. University of Florida Press, Gainesville.

Johannessen, S. and C.A. Hastorf 1994 Becoming Corn-Eaters in Prehistoric North America. In *Corn and Culture in the Prehistoric New World*, edited by S. Johannessen and C.A. Hastorf, pp. 427-444.

Kozarek, S.E. 1987 *A Hopewellian Homestead in the Ohio River Valley*. Master's thesis, Department of Anthropology, University of Cincinnati.

Prufer, O.H. 1965 *The McGraw Site: A Study in Hopewellian Dynamics*. Cleveland Museum of Natural History, Scientific Publications 4(1), Cleveland.

Riley, T.J., G.R. Walz, C.J. Bareis, A.C. Fortier, and K.C. Parker 1994 Accelerator Mass Spectrometry (AMS) Dates Confirm Early *Zea* Maize in the Mississippi River Valley. *American Antiquity* 59:490-498.

Rypma, R.B. 1961 *The Structure and Pattern of the Primary Forests of Athens and Washington Counties, Ohio*. Ph.D. dissertation, Department of Botany, The Ohio State University, Columbus. University Microfilms, Ann Arbor.

Smart, T.S. and R.E. Ford 1983 Plant Remains. In *Recent Excavations at the Edwin Harness Mound, Liberty Works, Ross County, Ohio*, by N. Greber, pp. 55-58. Midcontinental Journal of Archaeology Special Papers 5, Kent State University Press, Kent, Ohio.

Smith, B.D. 1985 The Role of *Chenopodium* as a Domesticate in Pre-Maize Garden Systems of the Eastern United States. *Southeastern Archaeology* 4:51-72.

1992 Prehistoric Plant Husbandry in Eastern North America. In *The Origins of Agriculture: An International Perspective*, edited by C.W. Cowan and P.J. Watson, pp. 101-119. Smithsonian Institution Press, Washington, D.C.

Wymer, D.A. 1984 *The Archaeobotanical Assemblage from the Connett Mounds #3 and #4, the Wolf Plains Project, Athens County, Ohio*. Report on file, Department of Archaeology, Ohio Historical Society, Columbus, Ohio.

1987a The Middle Woodland - Late Woodland Interface in Central Ohio: Subsistence Continuity Amid Cultural Change. In *Emergent Horticultural Economies of the Eastern Woodlands*, edited by William F. Keegan, pp. 199-214. Center for Archaeological Investigations, Occasional Papers 7, Southern Illinois University, Carbondale.

1987b *The Paleoethnobotanical Record of Central Ohio - 100 B.C. to A.D. 800: Subsistence Continuity Amid Cultural Change*. Ph.D. dissertation, Department of Anthropology, The Ohio State University, Columbus. University Microfilms, Ann Arbor.

1989 The Middle Woodland - Late Woodland Cultural Shift in the Midwest: the Paleoethnobotanical Record. In *Anthropology: Unity in Diversity*, edited by M.H. Sidky, J. Foradas, and P. Pacheco, pp. 34-52. Department of Anthropology, Occasional Papers No. 4, The Ohio State University, Columbus.

1990a The Paleoethnobotany of the Murphy Site. Paper presented at the Annual Meeting of the Eastern States Archaeological Federation, Columbus, Ohio.

1990b Archaeobotany. In *Childers and Woods: Two Late Woodland Sites in the Upper Ohio Valley, Mason County, West Virginia*, edited by M.J. Shott, pp. 402-535. Cultural Resource Assessment Archaeological Report 200, University of Kentucky, Lexington.

1992 Trends and Disparities: The Woodland Paleoethnobotanical Record of the Mid-Ohio Valley. In *Cultural Variability in Context: Woodland Settlements of the Mid-Ohio Valley*, edited by M.F. Seeman, pp. 65-76. Midcontinental Journal of Archaeology Special Papers 7, Kent State University Press, Kent.

1993 Cultural Change and Subsistence: The Middle and Late Woodland Transition in the Mid-Ohio Valley. In *Plant Production and Social Relations in the Eastern Woodlands*, edited by C.M. Scarry, pp. 138-156. University Press of Florida, Gainesville.

1994 The Social Context of Early Maize in the Mid-Ohio Valley. In *Corn and Culture in the Prehistoric New World*, edited by S. Johannessen and C.A. Hastorf, pp. 411-426. Westview Press, Boulder, Colorado.

Wymer, D.A., B.T. Lepper, and W.T. Pickard 1992 Recent Excavations at the Great Circle, Newark, Ohio. Paper presented at the Midwestern Archaeological Conference, Grand Rapids.

Yarnell, R.A. 1964 *Aboriginal Relationships between Culture and Plant Life in the Upper Great Lakes Region*. Museum of Anthropology, Anthropological Papers 23, University of Michigan, Ann Arbor.

FOUR

THE 1984 EXCAVATION AT 12D29s:
A MIDDLE WOODLAND VILLAGE
IN SOUTHEASTERN INDIANA

JACK K. BLOSSER

ABSTRACT

Excavations in 1984 by the author at a single component Middle Woodland habitation site situated on a terrace of the Ohio River in Dearborn County, Indiana were confined to two of four midden concentrations. A limestone concentration and two features were present in one midden area while the other yielded the semi-flexed burial of a 25-30 year old adult male. Recovered were decorated pottery, copper, lithics, and a mica cutout industry including projectile point effigies, one of which resembles a Snyders-like type. Floral and faunal analyses suggest at least a fall through late spring occupation of the site, and possibly some form of year round occupation.

A View From the Core a Synthesis of Ohio Hopewell Archaeology•edited by Paul J. Pacheco
© Copyright 1996 by The Ohio Archaeological Council• Columbus, Ohio•All Rights Reserved•ISBN 0-9626931-9-7

INTRODUCTION

This paper describes the results of the author's 1984 excavation at the Jennison Guard site-south (12D29s, also referred to as the Whitacre Site, 12D246), a Middle Woodland habitation in Dearborn County, Indiana **(Figure 4:1)**. Middle Woodland people at Jennison Guard participated in the Hopewell Interaction Sphere or trade network, as evidenced by the recovery of pottery, copper, Harrison County (Wyandotte), and Flint Ridge chert, and mica. There appears to be a mica working industry at the site, represented by mica effigy cutouts, as well as scrap and cut fragments, all of which were recovered during the excavation (Blosser 1989).

Few Middle Woodland habitation sites are recorded in the Midwest in which exotic raw material industries are apparent, although such industries are well documented within the major Ohio Hopewell ceremonial centers; this pattern also seems to be true for the southwestern Ohio/southeastern Indiana region. Crafting of bladelets is evident for habitation sites such as Denneman (33HA55) in Hamilton County, Ohio (Starr 1960:50) and near the Stubbs Mill Earthwork (e.g., 33WA256) in Warren County, Ohio (Genheimer 1984).

The Jennison Guard site-south is situated on a high flood plain, 1.6 km south of the modern Great Miami River confluence with the Ohio River, and about .5 km northeast of Lawrenceburg in Lawrenceburg Township, Dearborn County, Indiana. The present channel of the Ohio River is approximately 830 m to the southeast. 12D29s lies within the former delta of the Great Miami River. Adjacent to its northern edge is a meander scar that constituted the Great Miami channel before 1847. Prior to that time, the river flowed by Hardinsburg in a loop known as "Horseshoe Bend" (Burress 1970). However, on November 23, 1847, the Great Miami cut a new channel to the east that left Hardinsburg stranded about 3 km away.

A slough-like "trough" immediately southeast of the excavation area is probably an ancient meander channel or outlet for the Great Miami River. Enlargement of this trough has exposed cultural materials and midden deposits along the slope. The site occupation occurred on a level surface and is buried under

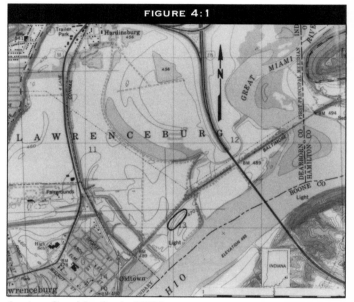

FIGURE 4:1

Jennison Guard Site-South: 12D29s

alluvium. Cultural debris is sparsely distributed over the surface and includes light densities of chert debitage, and low densities of pottery, bone, and shell. Because most of the site lies buried, these sparse amounts of cultural material probably do not accurately reflect the intensity or size of the site occupation. The surface scatter covers an area of approximately .85 hectares.

The entire site complex was originally given a site number of 12D29 and named Jennison Guard in 1934 by Glenn Black to describe a historic site and two prehistoric sites: one a Fort Ancient village with earth mounds, the second is the Ohio Hopewell habitation area this paper discusses. Excavation suggests the four darkened areas visible at the time of excavation represent midden deposits. When the Middle Woodland site was recognized as a distinct site it was given a separate site number of 12D246, and was referred to as the Whitacre site. Adoption of the original 12D29 site number still does not solve the problem of distinguishing the Middle Woodland and Fort Ancient occupations; hence, the letter "s" has been added to the site number to designate that area of the site which is located "south" of the B & O Railroad tracks, which has primarily Hopewell cultural remains.

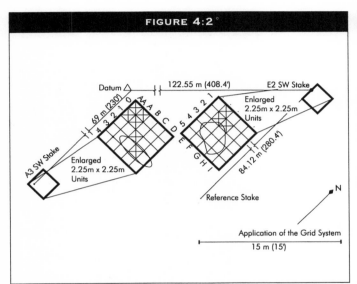

Application of the Grid System

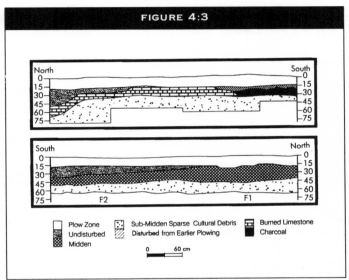

East Profile of Units AA0 and AA1; West Profile of Units F1 and F2

SUMMARY OF EXCAVATION RESULTS AND ANALYSES

The excavations described in this paper at Jennison Guard site-south were completed between June 12 and September 5, 1984. The first objective was to establish a series of excavation units in and around two of the four visible surface stains **(Figure 4:2)**. The first midden area exhibited surface staining over an 11.3 m east/west by 4.6 m north/south area. A block of grid units was superimposed over an area immediately north of and slightly impinging upon the second area of excavation at the second midden stain which measured 10.5 m northwest/southeast and 6.2 m northeast/southwest.

Excavation disclosed three separate periods of site occupation: the earliest episode was rather casual, probably intermittent or sporadic, that left only sparse debris. Later, an intense occupation of the site occurred that resulted in the deposition of midden, features and other activities on a "living floor"-like horizon. A substantially reduced occupation followed, apparently again, intermittent or sporadic.

Three identifiable cultural zones correspond with these different occupational episodes **(Figure 4:3)**. Zone I was recognized as undisturbed non-midden cultural deposits that overlay midden, features, or other evidence of intense occupation, but which underlay the plowzone. This may represent the final Middle Woodland occupation of the site. However, it is possible that only a portion of the site was abandoned, with the inhabitants shifting their activities to another area. Feature 1, a Middle Woodland burial of an adult male (25-30 years at time of death), was intruded into the midden from a ground surface that post-dates the termination of midden deposition at this locus.

Zone II represents midden deposition that underlay the burial in what was referred to as the "F" units. The second midden area in the western portion of the site referred to as the "A" units, provided evidence of a burned limestone layer and a deposit of charcoal. The rocks comprising the limestone layer consisted of 27,964 pieces of burned limestone and a few fire-cracked rocks weighing 267.2 kg. The absence of in situ burning immediately underneath the rock layer suggests redeposition. The size of the exposed limestone layer is 3.35 m long by 2.83 m wide. The associated charcoal layer measures 1.35 m in maximum width and 1.68 m in maximum length.

Two fire features were uncovered immediately below the limestone and charcoal layers in Zone II. Feature 2 measured 1.37 m by 91.4 cm with a depth of 39.6 cm, and demonstrated heavy in situ burning. The feature yielded 574 pieces (21.8 kg) of burned limestone. Feature 3, was uncovered 2 m to the southwest of Feature 2. The maximum width of Feature 3 was 1.18 m with a nearly circular aperture. It was 22.6 cm in depth. The excavated portion of Feature 3 yielded 1,416 pieces (51.5 kg) of limestone. The largest slab of limestone weighed 12.5 kg and was found in the center of the feature. More than 500 g of charcoal were recovered from Feature 3.

Zone III was non-midden cultural deposits that underlay the evidence of intense occupation. This zone apparently represents the initial Middle Woodland use of the landform. As in the case of Zone I, the nature of this occupation may merely have been due to peripheral utilization at a time when other portions of the site were more intensely occupied.

MICA ANALYSIS

Nowhere in the archaeological record of the Ohio Valley has a Middle Woodland habitation site produced sufficient evidence to warrant an interpretation of craft specialization of exotic material for the modification or manufacture of specific materials for mortuary purposes. Evidence from the Jennison Guard-south excavations however, does suggest the modification and manufacture of sheet mica into forms suitable for ceremonial activities or trade.

During the limited excavations of 1984, a total of 611 pieces of mica weighing 47.9 g was recorded. Of that total, 81 percent displayed cut edges. Two mica cutouts of projectile effigies were recovered, including a *Snyders-like* (**Figure 4:4d**) and a possible Middle Woodland corner notched variety (**Figure 4:4c**). Two fragments of cutouts were also recognized: a "wing-like" cutout with scalloped edges (**Figure 4:4a**), probably a stylistic wing, and a fragment of a human leg below the knee (**Figure 4:4b**). The latter artifact may also represent scrap from a previous cutout. Two additional possible projectile cutouts (**Figure 4:4e, f**) were

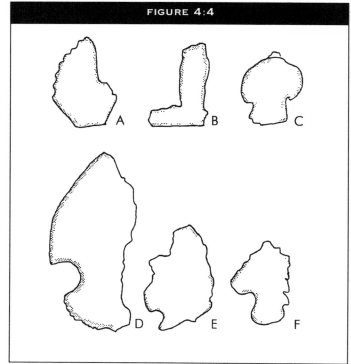

Mica Cutouts with Demarcated Cut Edges

also recorded. These specimens demonstrate cut edges characteristic of other projectile effigies recovered from this site, however, damaged edges prevent definite diagnosis.

Prior to and after the author's excavations in 1984, the Whitacres recovered three additional mica projectile effigies. The first effigy shows similar characteristics to that of a deep corner notched *Cypress Creek* projectile point with slightly excurvate blade edges. A second effigy is similar to a *Ross Barbed* point type. Although fractured, it illustrates a constricted diamond flared base. The third effigy is that of a *Snyders*-like projectile, with a hole punctured through the distal end near the tip.

DISCUSSION

The exchange of trade through the Hopewell Interaction Sphere assumes that certain raw materials were obtained through exchange or direct acquisition for mortuary and social status contexts. This discussion directs attention to the occurrence and distribution of mica at major ceremonial centers in the Midwest, as well as smaller habitation sites, to document the importance of mica at 12D29s.

The major source of mica can be found in the southern Appalachian Mountains (western North Carolina). According to Seeman (1979) muscovite (mica) can be found in northern Ontario, New Hampshire, Maine, South Dakota, North Carolina, Virginia, and Alabama.

Mica cutouts have been recovered in other Ohio Hopewell contexts, predominantly at major mortuary centers including: Hopewell (Moorehead 1922; Shetrone 1926), Mound City (Brown and Baby 1966; Mills 1922; Squier and Davis 1848), Edwin Harness Mound (Mills 1907; Putnam 1886; Squier and Davis 1848), Seip Mound (Mills 1909), Tremper Mound (Mills 1916), and Turner Earthworks (Willoughby and Hooton 1922). Mica cutouts at Middle Woodland habitation sites, on the other hand, have rarely been documented. Cut mica has been uncovered at McGraw (Prufer 1965), Miami Fort (Starr 1963), and the Murphy site (Dancey 1991). Although mica has been found at these sites, cutouts have not been documented at other Middle Woodland habitation sites other than Jennison Guard.

Evidence suggest that a mica cutout industry occurred at 12D29s as indicated by the cut mica fragments, finished cutout artifacts, and the necessary scrap that would accompany the modification and manufacture of such items. Prentice (1983) argues that evidence for the manufacture of trade items will most likely be represented by the occurrence of exotic items at different stages of manufacture, or possibly through unusually large quantities of finished items or waste materials produced from such material. The occurrence of specific tool types asso-ciated with certain manufacturing activities may also signal the presence of local manufacture. Therefore, it is suggested that

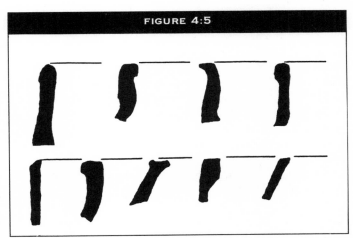

FIGURE 4:5

Twin Mounds Cordmarked Rim Profiles

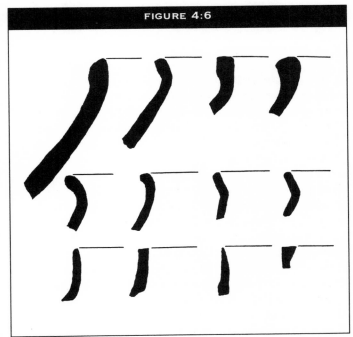

FIGURE 4:6

Twin Mounds Plain Rim Profiles

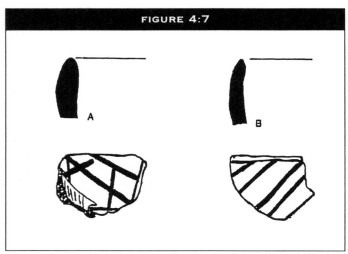

Rim Profiles of Hopewell Crosshatched and Twin Mounds Plain var. Incised

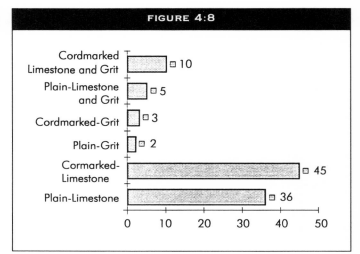

Ceramic Traits: Unit F1, F2, G2 Combined

the Middle Woodland inhabitants at 12D29s obtained mica as a raw material, to manufacture cutouts for inclusion with either social or mortuary activities. Whether or not the artifacts were used within the community is speculative.

It can be hypothesized that the Jennison Guard site-south inhabitants were making mica cutouts for mortuary inclusion. Mica projectiles, however, have not been found elsewhere in the area, and are lacking at Turner, the closest and largest Middle Woodland mortuary site in Hamilton County, Ohio. If the inhabitants manufactured the cutouts for trade, where would the artifacts have been traded? If mica was initially distributed out of the Paint Creek Valley in raw form and received at 12D29s for manufacture, it would have been impractical to have manufactured cutouts for exportation back to the Scioto Valley where the cutout centers are suggested to have occurred (Struever and Houart 1972:69). Yet, it appears that mica was obtained through trade since the amount of mica recovered thus far does not warrant the probability of direct procurement. Likewise, materials including galena, quartz or East Coast items are not present. If one group traveled to the Appalachian region, it would seem illogical to have by-passed a variety of other raw materials. Consequently, trade in this area via other

groups must be considered.

The explanation preferred here considers a trade route up the Tennessee River to the Ohio and Illinois area via the Ohio River. This would have permitted trade to exist in the Havanna and Crab Orchard regions of Illinois without traveling through Ohio. A continuous band of major centers is illustrated by Seeman (1979:260, Figure 1) indicating trade of exotic raw materials extending from the Appalachian quarries northwest to the Illinois Valley. This would have provided a direct line of communication via water-way and overland transportation through southeastern Indiana.

It has been established that mica cutouts were manufactured at Jennison Guard site-south, as indicated by the abundance of cut material when compared to uncut material, and no less than seven mica cutouts and two probable cutouts. There is a good indication that local manufacture existed at one point in time during the occupation of 12D29s.

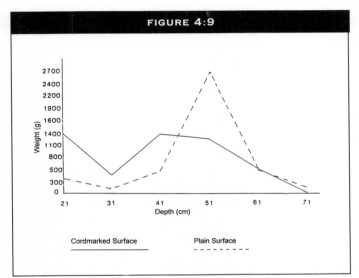

FIGURE 4:9

Cordmarked and Plain Ceramics; All Tempers Combined

CERAMIC ANALYSIS

The ceramic assemblage of 2,219 sherds weighing 11.6 kg recovered during the 1984 excavations consists predominantly of cordmarked and plain sherds with a small percentage of *Hopewellian* and *Southeastern Series*. The *Scioto Series* as described by Prufer (1965) does not fit the ceramic assemblage from the site. The author, with the help of Dr. James B. Griffin, observed enough comparative differences to believe this assemblage is not typical *McGraw-Scioto Series* ceramics. Due to the ceramic differences between southcentral Ohio and southeastern Indiana, Rebecca Hawkins Bennett (1986) has formed a revised *Miami Series* which includes *Twin Mounds Plain*, *Twin Mounds Plain* var. *Incised*, and *Twin Mounds Cordmarked*. These three types were used in describing the assemblage.

The cordmarked rim sherds **(Figure 4:5)** demonstrate thickened, flattened and sometimes rounded lips; only five illustrate thinning. The majority display cordmarking up to the lip. One rim is flared, one is indented in cross-section, and three rim sherds from one vessel are angular. The plain rim

sherds are shown in **Figure 4:6**. Rims demonstrating a flared morphology generally display a rounded lip, with an occasional flattened lip. Rims displaying a straight form generally display a flat lip with an occasional angular orientation. Overall, plain rims demonstrate less rim thickening, with an occasional thinned rim. Only one incised rim sherd was recovered **(Figure 4:7)**. This rim was vertical yet slightly constricted inward. The lip was rounded and thinned with a smoothed over lip fold. Within the *Hopewellian Series*, three cross-hatched rim sherds were recovered; no punctates are recorded. Two cross-hatched rims demonstrate partial horizontal lines or incisions at the base of the rim **(Figure 4:7)**.

Two tetrapodal supports were recovered. During the analyses, 19 body sherds, all grit tempered, were found to be associated with the tetrapodal supports. The presence of these supports which were made from non-local clay and molded into the body, and the recovery of *Hopewellian Series* ceramics may indicate trade between groups.

Plain wares were more popular during the earliest occupation episode and cordmarked wares were dominant during the latter part of the occupation **(Figure 4:8)**. Limestone tempering is found within 80 percent of the total assemblage, with limestone and grit comprising 15 percent, and grit tempering being the least dominant with only 5 percent of the total ceramic assemblage. At Jennison Guard, approximately 58 percent of the identified sherds are cordmarked, while 42 percent are plain when expressed by weight **(Figure 4:9)**. A ceramic surface treatment/tempering breakdown includes: cordmarked limestone temper (45 percent), plain limestone temper (36 percent), cordmarked limestone and grit (10 percent), plain limestone and grit (5 percent), cordmarked grit (3 percent), and plain grit (2 percent).

ARTIFACT ANALYSIS

The analysis of artifacts is important as it represents the activities associated with raw materials that do not normally preserve. As illustrated by the presence of specific artifacts, it was determined that woodworking, hide and leather preparation, plant food preparation, and leather manufacturing occurred at 12D29s.

When incorporating Winters' (1969) functional categories it is found that general utility tools represent 61.5 percent of the overall tool assemblage and include: 88 bladelets of Ohio Flint Ridge, Harrison County, and Upper Mercer chert; three bifacial blades, one of which is typed as *Snyders* (Scully 1951); and two hafted scrapers. Weapons consisting of hunting and fishing equipment represent 13.4 percent of the assemblage and include: 12 segmented bifaces, four projectiles similar to *Steuben Expanding Stemmed* (Morse 1963), one forked spatula, and one antler projectile. Fabricating and processing tools encompassing 11.2 percent of the tool assemblage include: nine awls, one stone drill, one flensing tool, one antler punch, and three beaver incisors. Ornaments represent 8.6 percent of the assemblage. They include five drilled raccoon and fox canines, and four antler and bone pins. Woodworking tools include a single celt and adze (1.4 percent). Within the miscellaneous category, two antler tools, a turtle carapace container, five bone tools, and two pieces of copper are recorded (3.9 percent). One of the copper artifacts appears to have been cold-hammered.

FAUNAL ANALYSIS

The faunal remains recovered from the 1984 excavation and submitted for analysis provide useful information regarding Ohio Hopewell subsistence strategies. A total of 2,461 burned and unburned bone is recorded, 384 of which have been identified (Table 4:1). Mammals dominate the recovered faunal assemblage, accounting for 90 percent of the total estimated weight. Large mammals affect the data considerably. A single elk represents 33.6 percent of the total meat yield, followed by an estimated 26.5 percent representation from four deer. One black bear (?) represents 24.4 percent of the meat yield.

Aquatic food resources such as fish, beaver, frog, painted turtle, box turtle, soft shell turtle, snapping turtle, and snake comprise an edible meat yield estimate of 39.9 kg (9.1 percent of the total yield).

The avian assemblage (n=45) represents nine identified specimens including owl (n=1), turkey (n=2), bobwhite (n=1), teal (n=1), duck (n=2), and Canada Goose (n=2). Turkey comprised 2.6 percent of the total meat yield, followed by two Canada geese (1.1 percent) and two ducks (.4 percent).

FLORAL ANALYSIS

Floral recovery through the use of 1/4" field screens and water separation has provided environmental and subsistence information (Table 4:2). Approximately 40 percent of the floated remains were submitted for analysis. The most abundant edible plant remains recovered include hickory (*Carya* spp.), of which three varieties are recorded from midden context: *C. glabra, C. tomentosa,* and *C. ovata.* A total of 97 hickory nut shell fragments, weighing 10.5 g, represents 45.7 percent of the assemblage by number. Black Walnut (*Juglans nigra*) fragments were much less abundant. Only six fragments (2.8 percent) are noted, along with eight fragments of acorn shell and meat (3.7 percent). Only one hazelnut *Corylus americana* fragment (.5 percent) was recovered from flotation. Underground plant foods such as ground nut (*Apios americans*), tubers and bulbs including wild onion (*Allium cernum*) were recorded. The combined weight of these specimens is 44.7 grams. Twenty (9.4 percent) ground nut fragments weighing 2.8 g were identified as were eleven (5.1 percent) tuber fragments weighing 2.1 g, ten (4.7 percent) bulbs which weigh .6 g, and three (1.5 percent) wild onion bulbs that weigh 1.5 grams. Other plant foods recorded may have been supplemental and include three (1.5 percent) grape (*Vitis* spp.) seeds, one (.5 percent) wild bean (*Strophostyles* spp.), five hackberry (2.4 percent) (*Celtis occidentalis*) seeds and one honey locust (.5 percent) (*Gleditsia trianathos*). One probable knotweed seed (*Polygonum erectum*) was recovered from the midden in addition to the plant remains mentioned above.

IDENTIFIED FAUNAL REMAINS	COUNT	MNI	KC MEAT YIELD 1	% 2	(P1) F1	BURNED
Mammalian:						
Whitetail deer (*Odocoileus virginianus*)	191	4	116.8	26.6	0.070	46
Elk (*Cervus elaphus canadensis*)	1	1	147.7	33.6	0.113	
Black bear (*Ursus americanus*) (?)	1	1	107.2	24.4	0.060	
Raccoon (*Procyon lotor*)	1	1	7.5	1.7	—-	
Dog (*Canis familiaris*)	39	4	—-	—-	—-	
Beaver (*Castor canadensis*)	5	1	14.3	3.3	0.001	3
Gray squirrel (*Sciurus carolinenesis*)	4	1	0.4	—-	—-	3
Cottontail rabbit (*Sylvilagus floridanus*)	6	2	1.2	0.3	—-	11
Rice rat (*Oryzomys palustris*)	2	1	—-	—-	—-	
Vole (*Microtus spp.*)	2	2	—-	—-	—-	
Chipmunk (*Tamias striatus*)	6	1	—-	—-	—-	
Identified Mammal	258					54
Unidentified Mammal	1263					*741
Combined Total	1845	19	395.1	90.0		795
Avian:						
Owl (Order Strigiformes)	1	1	—-	—-	—-	2
Turkey (*Meleagris gallopavo*)	21	2	11.6	2.6	0.001	1
Bobwhite (*Colinus virginianus*)	1	1	0.1	—-	—-	1
Blue-winged Teal (*Anas discors*)	3	1	0.3		—-	2
Mallard (*Anas platyrhynchos*)	14	2	1.8	0.4	—-	
Canada Goose (*Branta canadensis*)	5	2	5.0	1.1	—-	
Identified Bird	45					5
Unidentified Bird	279					92
Combined Total	324	9	18.6	4.3		97
Reptilian:						
Box turtle (*Terrapene carolina*)	8	1	0.1		—-	1
Softshell turtle (*Trionyx spiniferus spiniferus*)	4	1	0.5		—-	
Painted/Map turtle (*Chrysems picta*)	1	1	0.1		—-	
Snapping turtle (*Chelydra serpentina*)	2	1	0.2	0.3	—-	
Snake (Family Colubridae)	1	1	—-	—-	—-	1
Identified Reptile	16					2
Unidentified Reptile	16					1
Combined Total	32	5	1.9	0.4		3
Amphibian:						
Frog (*Rana spp.*)	1	1	—-	—-		
Frog/Toad	1	—	—-	—-	—-	
Unidentified Amphibian	1					
Combined Total	3	1				
Fish:						
Redhorse Suckers (*Moxostoma spp.*)	31	3	6.8	1.5	—-	1
Channel Catfish (*Ictalurus punctatus*)	16	2	4.5	1.0	—-	4
Drumfish (*Aplodinotus grunniens*)	14	5	11.4	2.6	0.001	
Suckers (*Catostomus spp.*)	3	—	—-	—-	—-	
Garfish (*Lepisosteus osseus*)	1	1	1.0	0.2	—-	
Identified Fish	65					5
Unidentified Fish	192					1
Combined Total	257	11	23.7	5.4		6

1 Kilocalories
2 Percent of meat yield
* Unidentified includes 31 (3 burned) small mammal, and 2 (1 burned) small rodent

Results of Faunal Analysis at 12D29s

TABLE 4:2		
PLANT NAME	**NO/%**	**WEIGHT**
Hickory nut (*Carya* spp.)	97/45	10.5 g
Groundnut (*Apios americana*)	20/9.4	2.8 g
Goosefoot (*Chenopodium berlandieri*)	20*/9.4	.1 g
Tubers	11/5.1	2.1 g
Bulbs	10/4.7	.6 g
Maize ** (*Zea mays*)	9/4.3	1.2 g
Acorn (*Quercus* spp.)	8/3.7	.1 g
Black Walnut (*Juglans nigra*)	6/2.8	.4 g
Hackberry (*Celtis occidentalis*)	5/2.4	.4 g
Rhizomes	4/1.9	.1 g
Grape (*Vitis* spp.)	3/1.8	.2 g
Wild Onion (*Allium cernuum*)	3/1.8	1.5 g
Wild Bean (*Strophostyles* spp.)	1/0.5	.2 g
Sunflower (*Helianthus annus*)	1/0.5	.2 g
Knotweed (*Polygonum erectum*)	1/0.5	.1 g
Honey Locust (*Gleditsia tricanthos*)	1/0.5	.1 g
Hazelnut (*Corylus americana*)	1/0.5	.1 g
Copperlear (*Acalypha* spp.)	1/0.5	.1 g
Carpetweed (*Portulaca* spp.)	1/0.5	.1 g
Grass (*Gramineae*)	1/0.5	.1 g
Unidentified seeds	8/3.7	.2 g
Total:	212/100.0	20.4 g

* 13 specimens are domesticates
** 7 kernels, 2 are cupules

Results of Floral Analysis at 12D29s

CULTIVATED PLANT REMAINS

At 12D29s, cultivated plant remains are comprised of goosefoot (*Chenopodium berlanderi*), sunflower (*Helianthus annus*), and maize (*Zea mays*). Fall annuals such as goosefoot rank second to nuts, yet are one of the most frequently recovered seeds from Middle Woodland sites in Ohio (see Wymer, this volume). Ford (1979) reports Twin Mounds in Ohio, Piesker, Macoupin, and Scoville sites in Illinois, and the Young site in Missouri as having goosefoot in the floral assemblage. Wymer (1992) and Hooge and Wymer (1992) discuss recent evidence and interpretations of Ohio Hopewell cultigens in great detail.

A single sunflower seed was recovered from the lower midden level. Evidence for sunflower cultivation is uncommon in Ohio, although the presence of sunflower within Illinois Middle Woodland sites is discussed by Ford (1979:234) and Asch et al. (1979:83).

The recovered maize has given rise to questions concerning probable intrusion or contamination. Five kernels and two cupules recovered from undisturbed midden context were examined. Due to the large size of these specimens, it is possible the maize could be an intruded eight-row northern flint variety of corn. However, due to the fact that other kernel and cupule fragments have been found within other midden areas at Jennison Guard, additional analysis and radiocarbon dating is necessary before discounting this particular cultigen.

This analysis has illustrated that the inhabitants of this site utilized an array of food resources from three major localities; the forest edge, forest, and aquatic environments, all of which were present at or adjacent to the site. The 1985 excavation conducted by Kozarek (1987) supported the original findings of the 1984 excavation. While a definite seasonal occupation is present during the fall through spring months, evidence also suggests some form of activity, possibly habitation, occurring during the late spring to fall months. It is therefore within reason to argue that based upon prevailing subsistence strategies, the site may have supported a sedentary population on a year-round basis.

CHRONOLOGICAL ASSESSMENT

Three charcoal radiocarbon samples were collected from the 1984 excavations at 12D29s and include two samples from midden context and one from Feature 3 (fire hearth). The first sample was collected from the top of Zone II to estimate the latest uncontaminated midden deposition and to approximate when the site was abandoned. This sample yielded a date of 1660 B.P. ± 70 years (Wis-1745) (ca. A.D. 290). The second sample was collected at the base of the midden which was determined to be the occupants living floor. An earlier date of 1800 B.P. ± 70 years (Wis-1744) (ca. A.D. 150) at this level suggest the midden was not contaminated. A third radiocarbon date of 1810 B.P. ± 70 years (WIS-1746) (ca. A.D. 140) from the charcoal collected from Feature 3 is consistent with the latter assay.

The Whitacres, owners of the site, have one radiocarbon date assayed from a burned black ash log, 2 m in length. The sample was presented to Beta Analytic, Inc. for dating because the feature was recovered directly underneath a midden deposit and represented the initial period just before midden deposition in that specific area. A date of 1660 B.P. ± 70 years (Beta 67622) was obtained (Whitacre, personal communication, 1993), which corresponds to the latest date recovered from the 1984 excavations. This suggests the midden deposition excavated by the Whitacres postdates the midden deposition uncovered from earlier excavations.

SUMMARY AND CONCLUSION

Presented in this paper have been the results of a sixteen week excavation at the Jennison Guard site-south, 12D29s, a Middle Woodland habitation site located on the flood plain of the Ohio River near its confluence with the Great Miami River. Of particular interest is the recovery of mica artifacts in specific states of manufacture; cut and uncut scraps, scraps illustrating cutout by-products, fragmentary portions of cutouts, as well as finished specimens.

Through various analyses of this site excavation, it is possible to provide a limited interpretation concerning the activities occurring at Jennison Guard. This is limited in the sense that the 1984 excavations were preliminary investigations oriented toward the initial examination of the Middle Woodland habitation site. This investigation has provided a foundation and comparative reference for future excavations.

From the evidence presented, the occupants of this site may have sustained habitation or associated activities throughout the year. Hunting and gathering appear to be primary subsistence activities during the fall and winter months. Additional evidence supports the idea that the occupants performed activities at this site during the spring and summer. Consequently, the site may have been occupied on a year-round basis. The presence of mica remains also indicates the inhabitants were capable of initiating and carrying out the local manufacture of mica into cutouts for trade or use in the local community.

ACKNOWLEDGMENTS

The writer wishes to thank Dr. Kent D. Vickery, Department of Anthropology, University of Cincinnati for much needed advice and assistance with the 1984 excavation and initial manuscript. Robert and Debbie Whitacre deserve special thanks for bringing the site to the attention of the University of Cincinnati in hopes of preserving the site. Gratefully acknowledged is the assistance of many field and lab volunteers without whose help this manuscript could not have been undertaken. These volunteers are; The Central Ohio Valley Archaeological Society, Jerry, Mark, Greg and Lisa Alford, Michele Rives, Ann Alexis, Jeff Cavanaugh, Diane Webster, Bill and Sue Kozarek, Barbara Kuroff, Steve Stadelman, Ella Kullenburg, Debbie Gibbons, Robert Genheimer and Ted Sunderhaus. A special thanks to Don Bier and Jody Bennett who helped with the figures. Dr. Wes Cowan (CMNH) identified plant remains while the faunal remains were identified by Emanuel Breitburg.

The radiocarbon dates were submitted to the Radiocarbon Lab of the Center for Climatic Research, University of Wisconsin-Madison, and supported by the Climate Dynamics Program, National Science Foundation under grant number ATM82-19079.

REFERENCES CITED

Asch, D. L., K. B. Farnsworth, and N. B. Asch 1979 Woodland Subsistence and Settlement in West Central Illinois. In *Hopewell Archaeology: The Chillicothe Conference*, edited by D. S. Brose and N. Greber, pp 80-85. Kent State University Press, Kent, Ohio.

Bennett, R. H. 1986 *The Twin Mounds Village and Hopewell in Southwestern Ohio: A Ceramic Identity Crisis*. Master's thesis, Department of Anthropology, University of Cincinnati.

Blosser, J. 1989 *Mica Working at the Jennison Guard Site: A Middle Woodland Village in Southeastern Indiana*. Masters thesis, Department of Anthropology, University of Cincinnati.

Brown, J. and R. S. Baby 1966 *Mound City Revisited*. Report on file, Department of Archaeology, Ohio Historical Center, Columbus, Ohio.

Burress, M. B. 1970 *It Happened Round North Bend, A History of Miami Township And Its Borders*. Self-published, Cincinnati.

Dancey, W. S. 1991 A Middle Woodland Settlement in Central Ohio: A Preliminary Report on the Murphy Site (33Li212). *Pennsylvania Archaeologist* 61(2):37-72.

Ford, R. I. 1979 Gathering and Gardening: Trends and Consequences of Subsistence Strategies. In *Hopewell Archaeology: The Chillicothe Conference*, edited by D. S. Brose and N. Greber, pp 234-238. Kent State University Press, Kent, Ohio.

Genheimer, R. 1984 *A Systematic Examination of Middle Woodland Settlements in Warren County, Ohio*. Report on file, Ohio Historic Preservation Office, Ohio Historical Society, Columbus, Ohio.

Hooge, P. E., and D. A. Wymer 1992 Licking County's First Farmers. In *Vanishing Heritage*, edited by P. E. Hooge and B. T. Lepper, pp 51-57. Licking County Archaeology and Landmarks Society, Granville, Ohio.

Kozarek, S. E. 1987 *A Hopewellian Homestead in the Ohio River Valley*. Master's thesis, Department of Anthropology, University of Cincinnati.

Mills, W. C. 1907 Explorations of the Edwin Harness Mound. Reprinted 1907 in Mills, *Certain Mounds and Village Sites* 1(4).

   1909 Explorations of the Seip Mound. *Ohio Archaeological and Historical Pubilications*. 18:269-321.

   1916 Exploration of the Tremper Mound. *Ohio Archaeological and Historical Publications*. 25: 262-398.

   1922 Exploration of the Mound City Group. *Ohio Archaeological and Historical Quarterly*. 31: 423-584.

Moorehead, W. K. 1922 The Hopewell Mound Group of Ohio. *Field Museum of Natural History Publication* 211 6(5):73-181.

Morse, D. F. 1963 *The Steuben Village and Mounds: A Multicomponent Late Hopewell Site in Illinois*. Museum of Anthropology, Anthropological Papers, University of Michigan, Ann Arbor.

Prentice, G. 1983 Cottage Industries: Concept and Implications. *Midcontinental Journal of Archaeology*. 10(1):107-122.

Prufer, O. 1965 *The McGraw Site: A Study in Hopewellian Dynamics*. Cleveland Museum of Natural History, Scientific Publications, 4(1), Cleveland.

Putnam, F. W. 1886 Explorations in Ohio: The Marriott Mound No. 1 and its Contents, *Annual Reports*, Peabody Museum, Harvard University, Cambridge.

Scully, E. 1951 *Some Central Mississippi Valley Projectile Points*. Report on file, Museum of Anthropology, University of Michigan, Ann Arbor.

Seeman, M. 1979 *The Hopewell Interaction Sphere: Evidence for Interregional Trade and Structural Complexity*. Indiana Historical Society, Prehistory Research Series, 5(2), Indianapolis.

Shetrone, H. C. 1926 Explorations of the Hopewell Group of Prehistoric Earthworks. *Ohio Archaeological and Historical Quarterly,* 40:343-509.

Squier, E. G. and E. H. Davis 1848 *Ancient Monuments of the Mississippi Valley.* Contributions to Knowledge. Smithsonian Institution, Vol. 1, Washington, D.C.

Starr, S. F. 1960 The Archaeology of Hamilton County, Ohio. *Journal of the Cincinnati Museum of Natural History,* 23(1).

1963 Prehistoric Miami Fort. *Bulletin of the Historical and Philosophical Society of Ohio,* 21(1):14-21.

Struever, S., and G. L. Houart 1972 An Analysis of the Hopewell Interaction Sphere. In *Social Exchange and Interaction,* edited by E. Wilmsen, pp. 47-79. Museum of Anthropology, Anthropological Papers, University of Michigan, Ann Arbor.

Willoughby, C. C. and E. A. Hooton 1922 The Turner Group of Earthworks, Hamilton County, Ohio. *Papers of the Peabody Museum* 8(3).

Winters, H. D. 1969 *The Riverton Culture: A Second Millenium Occupation in the Central Wabash Valley.* Illinois State Museum, Reports of Investigations No. 13, Springfield, Illinois.

Wymer, D. A. 1992 Trends and Disparities: The Woodland Paleoethnobotanical Record of the Middle Ohio Valley. In *Cultural Variability in Context,* edited by M. Seeman, pp. 65-76. Midcontinental Journal of Archaeology Special Paper 7, Kent State University Press, Kent, Ohio.

FIVE

REVISING THE OHIO MIDDLE WOODLAND CERAMIC TYPOLOGY: NEW INFORMATION FROM THE TWIN MOUNDS WEST SITE

REBECCA A. HAWKINS

ABSTRACT

The Twin Mounds West site (33HA24-WHA) is a stratified Middle Woodland habitation site in extreme southwestern Ohio. Since 1974, Twin Mounds Village, along with about a hundred other sites, has been protected within Hamilton County's Shawnee Lookout Park, Ohio's first designated National Register Archaeological District. Partially excavated in 1969 and 1970, this domestic site revealed at least three distinct stratigraphic levels, the post mold pattern of a 90 m^2 house, carbonized maize cupules, numerous pit and thermal features, an extensive lithic artifact assemblage, and over 13,000 ceramic sherds. The Ohio Flint Ridge bladelets, fragments of mica, fossilized shark tooth, and diagnostic pottery types recovered clearly indicate the site's Hopewellian affinities. This chapter focuses on Twin Mounds West ceramic data to revise the Ohio Middle Woodland ceramic typology. Also presented are the results of the comprehensive ceramic analyses, and a discussion of the site and its research significance within the context of our present knowledge of Ohio Hopewell in the lower Great and Little Miami Valleys.

A View From the Core a Synthesis of Ohio Hopewell Archaeology • edited by Paul J. Pacheco
© Copyright 1996 by The Ohio Archaeological Council • Columbus, Ohio • All Rights Reserved • ISBN 0-9626931-9-7

Rebecca A. Hawkins

Revising the Ohio Middle Woodland Ceramic Typology:

Introduction

For well over a century, studies of material culture have contributed to currently accepted archaeological interpretations of the Hopewell phenomenon in Ohio's Middle Woodland period. As a class of material culture, ceramics have figured regularly in these investigations. However, the traditional classificatory scheme developed for Ohio Hopewell ceramics 30 years ago needs revising (Prufer 1968; Prufer and McKenzie 1965). In this chapter, I use the results of ceramic analyses from the Twin Mounds West site to propose a complete modification of the traditional typology. As it presently exists, the traditional typology may, in fact, be clouding our view of the Ohio Hopewell phenomenon, whether we stand at its geographic "core" in the Scioto Valley or on its periphery. Close examination of the Twin Mounds West ceramic assemblage reveals the kinds of variation and interpretive potential that can be found in ceramic collections. In addition to its contributions to ceramic studies, the Twin Mounds West site provides a rare opportunity to examine a non-earthwork, stratified, Middle Woodland occupation site. Its investigation also highlights a geographic area, the lower Great Miami River Valley, that historically has received little attention in Ohio Hopewell studies.

The Twin Mounds West Site

The Ohio Hopewell Phenomenon in the Lower Great Miami Valley

The lower Great Miami Valley (**Figure 5:1**) is the region that surrounds the confluences of the Great Miami River with the Whitewater and the Ohio Rivers in southwestern Ohio and southeastern Indiana. Beyond the confluences, the region stretches for perhaps 20 to 40 km in all directions, especially along the valleys of the Miami, Ohio, and Whitewater Rivers. This region is delineated for heuristic purposes strictly on the basis of presently available archaeological data. In actuality, the phenomena discussed in this chapter may cover a larger or smaller area when examined at different points in time. The lower Great Miami Valley does not contain earthworks as complex as, for example,

those in the lower reaches of the Little Miami Valley 35 km to the east. However, Middle Woodland period residents of the lower Great Miami Valley clearly participated in the "Hopewell Interaction Sphere." Numerous mounds — some containing elaborately appointed burials, several hilltop enclosures, and other earthworks dot the region. Additional sites have yielded abundant "diagnostic" items such as Hopewell bladelets, as well as other chipped stone artifacts manufactured from "exotic" raw materials (e.g., Ohio Flint Ridge and Wyandotte cherts, and obsidian), ornaments of copper, shell, and freshwater pearls, fossilized shark teeth, mica cutouts, and ceramic sherds bearing characteristic Ohio Hopewell motifs (e.g., Blosser, this volume; Fischer 1974; Hawkins 1986; Seeman 1979; Squier and Davis 1848). Yet, although non-earthwork sites that have yielded Hopewell artifacts are not uncommon in this region, few have been examined systematically. As a result, archaeologists do not have a complete picture of subsistence practices, settlement patterning, social organization, or exchange networks for the Middle Woodland period in the lower Great Miami Valley.

Site Description

The Twin Mounds West site is a stratified, Middle Woodland residential site located on an upland ridge that overlooks the confluences and broad alluvial terraces of the Great Miami, Whitewater, and Ohio Rivers. The Middle Woodland hilltop enclosure Miami Fort is located about 500 m away at the ridge's southern terminus. Small streams fed by springs and runoff have dissected the ridgetop into lobes of flat land. These areas were cultivated by Euroamerican farmers from the late 1800s until 1965, when the Hamilton County Park District acquired several hundred acres of property that included Miami Fort, Twin Mounds West, and more than a hundred other recorded sites. Now known as Shawnee Lookout Park, the preserve became Ohio's first National Register Archaeological District in 1974 (Hawkins 1986:48). The Twin Mounds West site formerly was known as the "Western Habitation Area of the Twin Mounds Village." It is one of two separate sites (the "Western" and "Eastern" habitation areas that once were lumped together as a single site

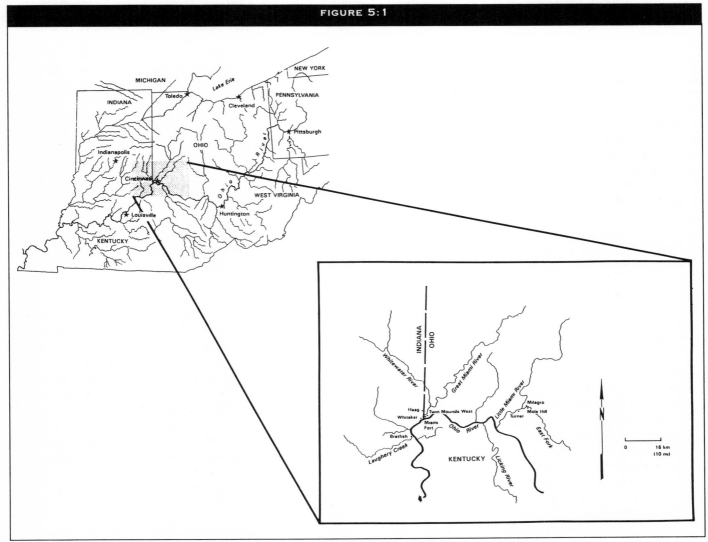

Locations of the lower Great Miami River Valley and selected archaeological sites (inset map) within the Middle Ohio Valley.

(Twin Mounds Village) named for two basally conjoined mounds located nearby. The site's original name notwithstanding, available evidence suggests that each of three strata defined at the Twin Mounds West site represents the remains of a household or hamlet, rather than a village (sensu Dancey 1992). Indeed, excavation of the middle stratum exposed the post mold pattern of a 90 m^2 house, presumable the home of an extended family.

The horizontal extent of the circa 85,200 ft^2 (7,919.34 m^2) lithic and ceramic scatter reported on the surface of the Twin Mounds West site was used to define site boundaries in 1968-1970; no field work has been performed at the site since then. Within this scatter, 13 units 10 x 10 ft (9.3 m^2) in size and a 1,000 ft^2 (93 m^2) block where the house pattern was discovered were excavated by University of Cincinnati Field Schools from 1968 through 1970 under the direction of W. Frederick Fischer (**Figure 5:2**). The 2,300 ft^2 (213.8 m^2) excavated square area represents about 2.7 percent of the recorded square area of the surface scatter.

Stratigraphy

Fischer's reports (1968, 1969, 1970) and extensive field notes (on file, Department of Anthropology, University of Cincinnati) from the 1968 through 1970 field seasons indicate that plowzone extended to a depth of .6 ft (18.3 cm) and that cultural material was encountered up to an average depth of about 1.4 ft (42.7 cm) below surface. During the excavations, Fischer recorded his observations of thin lenses of compacted soil and fire-cracked rock that suggested "living floors" to him. Fischer's observations, other details recorded in numerous excavation unit profile and plan view drawings, and, especially, information regarding the varying depths at which different features first were detected during excavation, all strongly suggest that three primary, distinct depositional horizons were encountered. The three horizons consist of features, artifacts, and other prehistoric occupational debris in a matrix of silty clay. Each horizon appears to have formed as result of natural and cultural processes relating to either a separate prehistoric occupation of the site or a series of such occupations

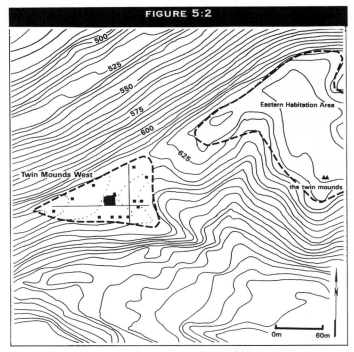

FIGURE 5:2

Plan view of the Twin Mounds West Site. The small black squares represent excavation units and the large black square represents the block excavation around the Middle Woodland house.

that were closely grouped in time (e.g., annual or seasonal re-occupations of the site). These separate occupational episodes or groups of occupational episodes have been labeled, from most recent to oldest, Occupation A, Occupation B, and Occupation C. Fortuitously, the levels by which the Twin Mounds West site was excavated closely paralleled the three depositional soil horizons.

In the 1,000 ft^2 block excavation, the three horizons are particularly distinct stratigraphically. The development of Horizon III (ca. 15-18 cm thick), which contained Occupation C, was terminated and the formation of Horizon II began with the construction of a 90 m^2 house during Occupation B. The aggradation of Horizon II (circa 6-9 cm thick) ended and the development of Horizon I (up to circa 15 cm thick) began during Occupation A with the

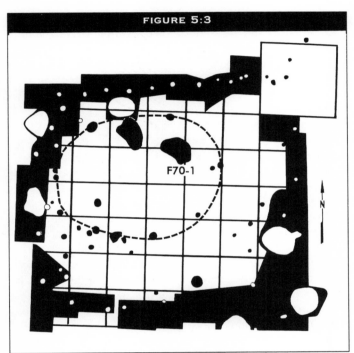

FIGURE 5:3

F70-1

Plan view of the Middle Woodland house at the Twin Mounds West site. Postmolds and the ellipse of features in the excavation trench are shown in white. Postmolds in the "inner ring" are linked by dashed line. Postmolds and features in the interior of the house are shown in black. Gridded excavation units in the house's interior are 5 feet (1.5m) on a side.

construction of an elliptical arrangement of thermal features, some of which were surrounded by postmolds, perhaps from structures such as windbreaks or racks **(Figure 5:3)**. Evidence is lacking of the site's occupation after the Middle Woodland period until it was timbered and cultivated over a millennium later by Euroamerican settlers in the nineteenth and twentieth centuries (Hawkins 1986). Presumably, the three separate prehistoric occupations were separated either by intervals of abandonment or intervals of extremely unintensive and sporadic prehistoric occupation. During these intervals, few or no archaeological remains accumulated and soil accreted over earlier deposits.

MIDDLE WOODLAND HOUSE

The postmold outline of Occupation B's house was roughly square with rounded corners (circa 32 ft [9.8 m] east-west by 30 ft [9.2 cm] north-south) and had an interior floor area of almost 960 ft (90 m²). A small amount of daub (.5 kg) was recovered, some fragments of which exhibit wattle-like impressions. Stratigraphically, only one hearth, **(labeled 70-1 in Figure 5:3)**, appears to have been contemporaneous with the structure. The postmold pattern suggests that there may have been a doorway protected with a windbreak in the house's northwest corner. The profusion of postmolds along the house's west wall may be indicative of reinforcing or rebuilding, interior structural supports, the remains of a loft or bench, or even overlap with the remains of another structure. **Figure 5:3** also illustrates what may have been an inner ring of interior support posts in the house. These inner postmolds, apparently first observed in excavation at a higher level than the outer postmolds, were larger in diameter and extended deeper into the ridgetop sediments than the outer postmolds (Fischer 1970). Alternatively, the inner ring may represent a separate structure.

FEATURES AND SUBSISTENCE DATA

In addition to the house, 12 other features were discovered at the site. Fischer reports that nine of these were hearths and three were small, basin-shaped pits, a few of which contained small numbers of ceramic sherds (Fischer 1969, 1970). Unfortunately, flotation was not employed during the field investigations. Further, the faunal remains recovered during excavation never have been analyzed systematically. As a result, very little in the way of direct subsistence data exists. Ford, who examined the botanical remains encountered in excavation, has identified fragments of carbonized maize (*Zea mays*) from undisturbed contexts (1979:234-235), including one provenience inside of and apparently contemporaneous with the occupation of the house. Ford also reports black walnut (*Juglans nigra*), hickory (*Carya* sp.), goosefoot (probably *Chenopodium bushianum*), and a member of the Legume family (Leguminosae).

MIDDLE WOODLAND TIME FRAME

Samples from the site destined for radiocarbon dating were lost in the early 1970s, making it difficult to estimate the ages of the different strata. However, ceramics from Twin Mounds West closely resemble those from the Whitacre site (also known as Jennison Guard - south) and from Miami Fort. These latter two sites both have yielded radiocarbon dates from the first through the third centuries A.D. suggesting a similar age for Twin Mounds West. Other artifacts also corroborate this estimate. Although no other class of materials from the Twin Mounds West site has been as intensively and systematically analyzed as the ceramic assemblage, analyses of small samples of lithic artifacts have identified bladelets and various Middle Woodland point forms, as well as numerous other chipped stone artifacts made of non-local materials such as Ohio Flint Ridge and Wyandotte cherts (Kaltenthaler 1992). Additional artifacts that typically are considered diagnostic of involvement in the Hopewell Interaction Sphere have been recovered from all levels at the Twin Mounds West site. These artifacts include numerous potsherds bearing Ohio Hopewell motifs, a fossilized shark's tooth, and sheet mica fragments (Hawkins 1986). Reports that a broken Paleoindian point and a Mississippian effigy pipe were recovered from the house both are false; the point was misidentified and the pipe, a modern fake, was a prop used in an elaborate (and well-recorded) practical joke perpetrated during the excavations.

THE TWIN MOUNDS WEST CERAMIC ASSEMBLAGE-ANALYSES

The curated ceramic assemblage from the Twin Mounds West site weighs 19.4 kg and numbers over 13,000 sherds. This assemblage, in terms of sherd counts per excavated site area, rivals that of any other published Ohio Middle Woodland site; the McGraw site comes closest, with a reported yield of 9,950 sherds (Prufer and McKenzie 1965). Such a large sample lent itself well to various distributional and exploratory statistical analyses (Hawkins 1986). All of the Twin Mounds West site ceramics, regardless of size or condition, were analyzed. This approach was adopted because the assemblage was dominated by small sherds and because even the smallest sheds can still provide valuable information about paste and temper. Sherds were both weighed and counted (Shephard 1980; Sollheim 1960); because of the problem of differential breakage, weight is both a more reliable indicator of the number of vessels in an assemblage and a more accurate inter-site comparative index than count (Hawkins 1986). Counts, because they provide no intuitive concept of, and represent no invariant standard for, sherd size, are inappropriate for use in statistical calculations or intersite comparisons.

In addition to weights and counts, a conservative estimate of the minimum-number-of-vessels (MNV) represented in the assemblages also was calculated. Objective criteria, such as paste composition, firing characteristics, surface treatment, rim profiles, and orifice diameter measurements, were used to minimize the chance of counting more than once a vessel represented by multiple sherds. Like sherd weights, minimum-number-of-vessel estimates provide standardized measure for quantitative comparison. Because sherds are fragments of whole pots, minimum-number-of-vessel estimates sometimes can reflect more realistically even than weights the proportions of different ceramic types in an assemblage, particularly of types represented by only a few sherds. Subsequently, the Twin Mounds West ceramics were compared with those from other Ohio and Indiana sites in the lower Great Miami Valley, including Haag, Whitacre, the "eastern habitation area" of Twin Mounds Village, the basally conjoined Twin Mounds, Headquarters, Miami Fort, and Lynch. The Twin Mounds West site ceramic assemblage also was compared with Middle Woodland sherds excavated from the stratified Bratfish site, which is located about 15 km to the southwest, at the confluence of Laughery Creek and the Ohio River, and with several sites with Middle Woodland components near the confluence of the Little Miami River and its East Fork 50 km to the east (Hawkins and Walley 1993).

VERTICAL AND HORIZONTAL DISTRIBUTION

The majority of the assemblage (68.2 percent, 13,203.1 g) was excavated from Levels 1 and 2, which contained the two most recent occupations, including the one responsible for the construction of the house (Occupation B). While one-third of the assemblage (33.9 percent, 6,562.8 g) was excavated from the plowzone (i.e., Level 1 of Occupation A), most (66.1 percent, 12,796.6 g) was excavated in a controlled fashion from subplowzone contexts. Less than 5 percent of the assemblage (968 g) was recovered from feature contexts. More pottery was recovered per square area from those 13 excavation units surrounding the house block than from the house block itself. Still, no significant differences were found in assemblage composition between the house block and surrounding excavation units when temper, surface treatment, vessel size, and wall thickness were compared level-by-level.

THE TRADITIONAL OHIO HOPEWELL CERAMIC TYPOLOGY

The Four Series Approach

Thirty years ago, Prufer examined the extant collections of Hopewell ceramics from Ohio sites and, drawing on a similar study by Griffin (1945), devised four ceramic series: *Scioto, Hopewellian, Southeastern,* and *Miami.* The *Scioto Series* consisted of two types: *McGraw Plain* and *McGraw Cordmarked. Scioto Series* ceramics were thought to be all those Middle Woodland ceramics in Ohio that were the products of "a fundamentally local tradition" (Prufer and McKenzie 1965:18-19). This local tradition, called the *Scioto Tradition,* was viewed as a continuous cultural sequence that evolved from an *Adena Phase* (Early Woodland period) through a *Hopewellian Phase* (Middle Woodland period) and into a *Peters Phase* (Late Woodland period). The *Scioto Tradition,* whose characteristics were extrapolated from a very few sites in the Scioto River Valley of southcentral Ohio, was presumed to apply to archaeological phenomena throughout the entire middle and upper Ohio Valley.

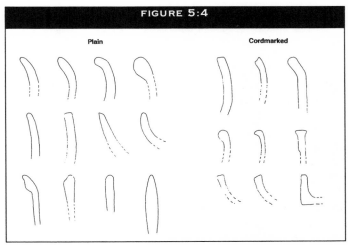

FIGURE 5:4

Plain   Cordmarked

Rim profiles of selected plain and cordmarked sherds. Sample pooled from the Miami and Kope Series, all excavation levels included. Vessel interiors are to the right.

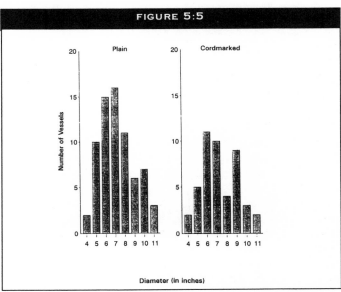

FIGURE 5:5

Histogram of vessel diameters, Sample pooled from the Miami and Kope Series, all excavation levels included.

Hopewellian Series ceramics were thought to represent "elements of the extraneous *Hopewellian Tradition*," which, it was believed at the time, "intrudes into the *Scioto Tradition* and thus defines its middle phase" (Prufer and McKenzie 1965:19, italics original) and "which is characterized by a series of traits and trait clusters of largely "ceremonial" significance" (Prufer and McKenzie 1965:18, punctuation original). Indeed, it was felt that "the Hopewellian intrusion remained essentially restricted to certain ceremonial aspects" of the Middle Woodland lifeway, particularly those involving mortuary ritual (Prufer 1965:128). The third of the four series was created to hold "a few ceramic elements that can be grouped under the general and vague heading of *Southeastern Series*" and that were considered to have somehow invaded Ohio in the Middle Woodland period in the wake of the phenomenon known as Hopewell, but from the Southeast and not from Illinois (Prufer and McKenzie 1965:19).

The *Miami Series* was created as a more localized counterpart to the state-wide *Hopewellian* and *Southeastern Series* (Prufer 1968:7). Originally the *Miami Series* was established provisionally on the basis of 15 sherds to catalog two decorative Middle Woodland ceramic surface treatments (embossing and "hemiconical punctations," i.e., fingernail impressions). The majority of the sherds (n=13) were found at the Turner Earthworks complex in the lower Little Miami Valley. Prufer (1968:7) felt that these sherds simply did not fit into other established Ohio Middle Woodland ceramic series, primarily on the basis of surface treatment. Prufer believed Turner to be a late Hopewell site and perceived close similarities between the *Miami Series* sherds from Turner and late Middle Woodland period *Weaver* ceramics from Illinois (1968:106). As a result, Prufer assumed that the *Miami Series* represented particular ceramic designs that not only seemed to be closely associated with a specific geographic area (southwestern Ohio), but also quite late (after circa A.D. 400-450) in the Ohio Hopewell chronology (Prufer 1968:148, 151; Prufer and McKenzie 1965:39). Others, however, had long recognized that embossed and fingernail-impressed surface treatments also were quite common among various Kentucky and Illinois Early Woodland and early Middle Woodland ceramics (e.g., Griffin 1952:97-101; Haag 1940).

Interpretive Conventions of the Four Series Approach

It was the intention of the architects of the traditional classificatory scheme to predispose the four ceramic series to reflect certain untested assumptions about Middle Woodland period chronology, cultural evolution, ceremonial behavior, and economic and social relationships that, in turn, were "based to a considerable extent upon ceramic evidence" (Prufer and McKenzie 1965:18). The respective ceramic series were designed in keeping with the double tradition concept and expected to reflect a distinct division between local "secular habitation" and "alien" "ceremonial-mortuary" behaviors. The *Hopewellian* and *Southeastern Series* were created to accommodate ceramics whose function was presumed to be of "ceremonial significance" (Prufer and McKenzie 1965:18). Those surface treatments shared by Illinois and Ohio Hopewell ceramics (e.g., rocker stamping, brushing, burnishing or polishing, rims with cross-hatched incising and punctations) that were thought to imply a relationship between the two areas, and to indicate participation in the Hopewell Interaction Sphere, were assigned to the *Hopewellian Series*.

Those surface treatments and vessel appendages that appeared to be influenced directly by, or have their actual origin in, Middle Woodland ceramic industries operating south of the Ohio River (simple, check, and complicated stamping, tetrapods) were thought to signify some form of contact with the greater Southeast and thus were assigned to the *Southeastern Series*. Griffin (personal communication, 1993) believes, however, that, almost without exception, all vessels represented in Ohio Hopewell contexts were made within Ohio or immediately adjoining areas and that a vanishingly small number of vessels acquired from well outside the Ohio Valley are present. Certain stamped and footed ceramic types from Adena sites in neighboring Kentucky, most of which lies within the Ohio Valley watershed, were acknowledged as regional antecedents of considerable antiquity for the *Southeastern Series*. Ceramic types with similar surface treatments that were found further south in sites contemporary with Ohio Hopewell sites strengthened the impression of an ongoing "Southeastern connection." Interestingly, still other Kentucky Adena ceramic types were thought to be ancestral to the *Scioto Series's McGraw Plain* and *McGraw Cordmarked* types, and similar plain-surfaced and cordmarked ceramic types also were legion throughout the Southeast (Prufer and McKenzie 1965:42). Yet, while a relationship between *Southeastern Series* ceramics from Ohio sites and similar types found south of the Ohio River supposedly denoted an ongoing "Southeastern connection," the same relationship was not posited for *Scioto Series* ceramics. Instead, *Scioto Series* ceramics were considered to be the *sui generis* products of the "local tradition" (Prufer and McKenzie 1965:18).

TAXONOMIC INCONSISTENCIES IN THE FOUR SERIES APPROACH

As it was initially developed, Prufer's four-series typology was not internally consistent in regard to the criteria used to define its taxa. In some cases, characteristics of paste were more important than surface treatment, as when sand-tempered cordmarked sherds were placed in the *Southeastern Series*. In other cases, surface treatment was weighted over even obvious variations in paste (Prufer 1968), with suites of types grouped together in particular series partly on the basis of their presumed relationships with types in other areas outside Ohio. The four-series approach also was burdened with unwarranted assumptions regarding the use of vessels in domestic vs. funeral activities, regional variation in participation in an "alien" and "extraneous" Hopewell ceremonial-mortuary cult introduced from Illinois, and the intentions of the prehistoric potters themselves. It was stated that the series' component types "not only are presumed to have classificatory significance for the archaeologist, but also are believed to correspond in some measure to prehistoric cultural reality; they are considered to have temporal, spatial, and possibly functional significance" (Prufer and McKenzie 1965:19).

Further, the four series have, at least in southwestern Ohio and southeastern Indiana, been found to be neither mutually exclusive nor able to accommodate the full range of ceramic variation. This study, therefore, suggests a revision of the original typology for classifying Ohio Hopewell pottery (Prufer 1968; Prufer and McKenzie 1965) to accommodate new findings **(Table 5:1)**. The particular impetus for revising the typology was provided by the variety of Middle Woodland ceramics found at the Twin Mounds West site. Examination of this site's ceramics first prompted a revision of the *Miami Series* (Hawkins 1986).

TABLE 5:1		
TYPE		**MNV**
Twin Mounds Plain		111
Twin Mounds Cordmarked		50
(plain and cordmarked subtypes)		
var. Incised	11	
var. Fingernail Impressed	1	
var. Pinched	1	
var. Punctated	4	
var. Cordmarked lip	4	
var. Interior/Exterior Cordmarked	6	
Twin Mounds Textile Impressed		1
Twin Mounds Polished and Embossed		3
"Hopewell rims"		2
Plain Rocker Stamped		2
Plain Long Rocker Stamped		7
Dentate Rocker Stamped		2
Simple Stamped		5
Totals	27	183

Arrangement of the types within the revised Miami Series

REVISING THE TRADITIONAL CERAMIC TYPOLOGY

The Revised Miami Series

The revised *Miami Series* is not meant to be confined either to the terminus or any other portion of the Middle Woodland period. Neither is it meant to embody ideas about vessel function or about relationships with ceramics from Illinois, the Southeast, or elsewhere. In keeping with accepted principles of archaeological typology in general (Adams and Adams 1991; Dunnell 1971; Sullivan and Rozen 1985), and ceramic typology in particular (Colton 1943; Rice 1987:274-288; Shephard 1980:309-314), the revised *Miami Series* is predicated strictly on technological criteria. Accordingly, the defining characteristic of the revised *Miami Series* is its low-fired, burned limestone-tempered, Kope Formation clay paste. On the basis of macroscopic and microscopic examination, the clays in the paste of *Miami Series* ceramics match the blue-gray Kope Formation clays from southwestern Ohio and adjacent areas, as do, for that matter, the clays for later Fort Ancient ceramic pastes (Matson 1989; Tankersley and Meinhart 1982). Given their abundance and accessibility, Kope clays most likely made up the bulk of the pastes in all the prehistoric ceramic industries in the area. Additional analysis is necessary to corroborate this hypothesis, however, as some non-Kope clays may also have been used.

The various types of the *Miami Series* described in this chapter have been found, so far, most commonly in the lower Great Miami Valley. However, it is not intended that the new *Miami Series* be equated exclusively with ceramics in this particular geographic region. Some *Miami Series* vessels made in the Great Miami Valley may have been transported to other areas, or *Miami Series* vessels may have been made in other parts of the Middle Ohio Valley where Kope clay and limestone also were available. Further, lower Great Miami Valley potters also produced non-*Miami Series* vessels, both during the Middle Woodland period and other periods.

FUNDAMENTAL BREAKS WITH THE TRADITIONAL CERAMIC TYPOLOGY

To avoid the problems outlined above, the revised *Miami Series* has been modified systematically to include types that are objectively defined, mutually exclusive, and able to accommodate the full range of ceramic variation. In addition, the revised *Miami Series* has been expanded to include types representing all the surface treatments that occur on limestone-tempered Kope clay paste, including smoothed-plain and smoothed-cordmarked types. This expansion, by incorporating what often are considered "utilitarian" ceramics together with varieties bearing surface treatments frequently assumed to represent "ceremonial" wares, constitutes the first of two fundamental breaks with traditional Ohio Hopewell ceramic classification.

The revised *Miami Series* (**Table 5:1**), which represent over half of the ceramics found at Twin Mounds West and other lower Great Miami River Valley sites of the Middle Woodland period, have been named *Twin Mounds Plain* and *Twin Mounds Cordmarked*, types analogous to the *Scioto Series'* McGraw Plain and McGraw Cordmarked types. The revised *Miami Series* now also includes the type *Twin Mounds Textile Impressed*, which has been created provisionally to classify sherds from a few vessels that bear the imprint of a twined fabric. As well, the revised *Miami Series* includes several varieties (subtypes), hierarchically arranged within the *Twin Mounds Plain* and *Twin Mounds Cordmarked* types, that encompass additional surface treatments: *Twin Mounds Incised, Twin Mounds Fingernail Impressed, Twin Mounds Pinched, Twin Mounds Punctated, Twin Mounds Cordmarked Lip,* and *Twin Mounds Interior- Exterior Cordmarked.* Among the "decorative" types included within the revised *Miami Series* is *Twin Mounds Polished and Embossed,* which bears a ring of bosses around a straight, vertical rim (i.e., one morphologically analogous to a crosshatched *Hopewellian Series* rim) above a polished body. Polishing is a surface treatment noted for Prufer's *Hopewellian Series.* Interestingly, two additional surface treatments have been found to co-occur with polishing and embossing among the sherds at Twin Mounds West, both of which, in the old typological scheme, would have fallen into separate series: brushing (*Hopewell Series*) and simple stamping (*Southeastern Series*).

In the second fundamental break with traditional Ohio Hopewell ceramic classification, therefore, the *Miami Series* now also includes other surface treatments and appendages that formerly would have been consigned to the *Hopewellian* and *Southeastern Series*. For example, when they occur on limestone-tempered Kope clay paste, tetrapods are now classified as belonging to *Miami Series* vessels, crosshatched *Hopewellian Series* rims are classified as *Miami Series Hopewell Rims*, rocker-stamped sherds are classified as *Miami Series Plain Rocked, Plain Long Rocked,* and *Dentate Long Rocked*, and simple stamped sherds are classified as *Miami Series Simple Stamped*. The revised *Miami Series* is recommended as a model for the revision of the *Scioto Series* and the creation of new series as needed to replace the old *Hopewellian* and *Southeastern Series*.

THE PRINCIPLE OF ANALOGOUS POTTERY TYPES AND THE ABANDONMENT OF THE TRADITIONAL CERAMIC TYPOLOGY

Understanding the importance of the Principle of Analogous Pottery Types (i.e., that similar surface treatments occur on different ceramic pastes [Colton 1943]) is useful for advancing ceramic studies in the Middle Ohio Valley. For example, some of the newly re-classified *Miami Series* types bear surface treatments that formerly would have been placed in the old *Hopewellian* and *Southeastern Series*. However, clear examples also exist at Twin Mounds West of sherds made of what obviously are not *Miami Series* pastes (Hawkins 1986) with surface treatments that conventionally also would have been classed as *Hopewellian* (e.g., rocker stamping) or *Southeastern* (e.g., check stamping) motifs. The newly reclassified *Miami Series* sherds with *Hopewellian* and *Southeastern Series* motifs probably arose from Middle Woodland potters in the lower Great Miami Valley applying those motifs to locally-made vessels. However, whether the non-*Miami Series* sherds with analogous surface treatments occur at Twin Mounds West (1) because their parent vessels were acquired from outside the immediate region or (2)

because local potters experimented with other clay and temper combinations, and perhaps different firing methods, warrants further investigation.

In order for such investigations to proceed, however, the appropriate series designation of these non-*Miami Series* sherds at Twin Mounds West (and of all Ohio Middle Woodland pottery elsewhere) must be ascertained systematically on technological grounds: paste characteristics (clay + temper) and manufacturing techniques. Accurate paste distinctions should be founded on compositional (mineralogical and chemical) analyses (e.g., Bishop et al. 1982; Isphording 1972; Matson 1989), which will enable objective examination of ceramic assemblage variation. Such confirmations of the distinctiveness of the *Miami Series* paste presently are underway. This approach allows greater recognition of ceramic variation and facilitates both intra-site and inter-site comparisons. Indeed, determining paste composition holds perhaps the brightest hope for sorting out locally-made vessels from vessels acquired from groups outside the local area, thereby providing insight into the production and exchange of Ohio Hopewell ceramics, as the Twin Mounds West site example shows.

CHARACTERISTICS OF THE TWIN MOUNDS WEST CERAMIC ASSEMBLAGE

Following is a brief outline of the series identified at Twin Mounds West. The minimum-number-of-vessels (MNV) estimate is used as an expedient index for comparing frequencies of types within series and of series within the overall assemblage. A total of 183 (62 percent) vessels of the 295 excavated from Twin Mounds West belongs to the *Miami Series* (Tables 5:1 and 5:2). Another 59 (20 percent) of the 295 vessels belong to a series whose paste, tempered with grit (i.e., non-limestone crushed rock), also appears to contain Kope clay (provisionally labeled the *Kope Series.*) *Kope Series* types observed at Twin Mounds West are analogous to those of the *Miami Series* in terms of surface treatment (Table 5:2). Another seven vessels (2.4 percent) of the 295 appear to be made of Kope clay, as well, but their paste is tempered with both limestone and grit (provisionally labeled *Unnamed Local Series*). The minuscule sample of *Unnamed Local Series* types includes only plain, cord-marked, rocker stamped (zoned dentate long rocker), and simple stamped surface treatments **(Table 5:2)**. Vessels from all of the Kope clay paste series are built by coiling and paddling.

A total of 46 (15.6 percent) of the 295 vessels belong to at least another seven series whose pastes are composed of clays that do not appear, on the basis of preliminary analysis, to be Kope Formation clays **(Table 5:3)**. These vessels are tempered in whole or in part with sand or with crushed sherds. Types from these unknown series that were observed at Twin Mounds West are similar to those of the *Miami Series*. However, not all *Miami Series* types are represented by analogous types in these seven unknown series, which also include check and linear check stamped sherds, types not found in the recovered sample of *Miami Series* sherds. No obvious exceptions to the coiling-and-paddling construction technique were detected among the several non-Kope clay series, although sample sizes are small for these sherds.

KOPE CLAY PASTES

The Kope Formation clay from which the *Miami Series* vessels were made is fine to medium- grained and generally appears moderately well mixed. *Miami Series* sherds in the Twin Mounds West assemblage fall into medium gray to gray-brown, medium brown, and buff color categories (after Bennett 1974:103). Core colors typically are darker and grayer than surface colors. By and large, the Twin Mounds West site ceramics are not as soft or friable as earlier Woodland ceramics, but not as hard as shell tempered Fort Ancient ceramics. The grit-tempered *Kope Series* and the limestone and grit-tempered *Unnamed Local Series* mimic the *Miami Series* in terms of clay and firing characteristics. The *Kope Series* appears to have been used from perhaps as early as the Early Woodland period through Late Woodland times in this portion of the Middle Ohio Valley. In contrast, the *Miami Series* and perhaps the *Unnamed*

Local Series seem to have been restricted to the Middle Woodland period.

The limestone temper in the *Miami Series* sherds apparently was burned before being crushed and added to the clay. Burned Limestone is easier to pulverize than unburned limestone. In all three of the Kope clay-based series (*Miami, Kope, Unnamed Local*), temper particles range in size from 1.5 to 3 millimeters and average 2 millimeters. Temper densities range from low (2 percent) to low-medium (10 percent) and average 5 percent (after Bennett 1974:105). Proportions of grit and limestone tempers in *Unnamed Local Series* sherds are about even. In general, at Twin Mounds West, the smaller the vessel, the finer the temper and, often, the finer the temper, the more densely it appears to be distributed; however, in terms of a ratio by weight or volume of temper to clay, this appearance may be deceiving.

In the Middle Ohio Valley, such a preponderance of limestone tempering appears to be confined primarily to the Middle Woodland period, yet the exact time depth and duration of the use of limestone in that area currently is not known; it is not common after circa A.D. 600. Although limestone is abundant in the Middle Ohio Valley, both preceding Early Woodland and succeeding Late Woodland pottery in this area tends to be tempered exclusively with non-limestone rock (Hawkins 1992; Riggs 1989). By all accounts, this overwhelming predominance of limestone among Middle Woodland tempering agents also appears to be a localized phenomenon in the Middle Ohio Valley region, in that it is represented most conspicuously in the lower Great Miami Valley and, to some extent, the lower Little Miami Valley. In nearby areas, such as the upper Great Miami Valley and much of the Little Miami Valley, limestone-tempered pottery generally is in the minority, although it may be more common in these immediately surrounding areas than in more distant parts of the region (Hawkins and Walley 1993). However, limestone-temper is characteristic of some early pottery types in Illinois and Kentucky (Griffin 1952, 1974; Haag 1939, 1940). Among the major earthwork complexes of Ohio, only Tremper, Mound City, and Turner, according to Prufer (1968), are

TABLE 5:2

| Analogous Types | SERIES | | | | | |
| | Miami | | Kope | | Unnamed Local MNV | |
	MNV	% of column total	MNV	% of column total	MNV	Totals
Plain	111	(60.66)	30	(50.85)	2	143
Cordmarked	50	(27.32)	14	(23.73)	2	66
Textile Impressed	1	(0.55)	1	(1.69)	0	2
Polished and Embossed	3	(1.64)	0	(0)	0	3
Rocker Stamped	13	(7.10)	7	(11.86)	1	21
Simple Stamped	5	(2.73)	5	(8.470	2	12
Check Stamped	0	(0)	2	(3.39)	0	2
MNV Totals	183		59		7	249

Minimum numbers of vessels compared for analogous types among the three series made of Kope clay. The type Rocker Stamped includes miscellaneous "Hopewell rims."

TABLE 5:3

Analogous Types	Unk. I	Unk. II	Unk. III	Unk. IV	Unk. V	Unk. VI	Unk. VII	Unk. Totals
Plain	2	2	2	1	1	5	0	13
Cordmarked	3	3	0	0	0	4	0	10
Textile Impressed	0	0	0	0	0	0	0	0
Polished and Embossed	0	0	0	0	2	0	0	2
Rocker Stamped	1	1	0	0	0	0	0	2
Simple Stamped	4	8	0	0	0	2	0	14
Check Stamped	0	3	1	0	0	0	1	5
MNV Totals	10	17	3	1	3	11	1	46

Minimum numbers of vessels compared for analogous types among the seven Unknown Series made of non-Kope clays and sand or crushed sherd tempers (I=sand/limestone, II=sand/grit, III=sand/crushed sherd, IV=grit/crushed sherd, V=crushed sherd, VI=sand, and VII=sand/grit/crushed sherd). The type Rocker Stamped includes miscellaneous "Hopewell rims."

characterized by an appreciable amount of limestone-tempered ceramics. However, proportions of any traits in the ceramic collections maintained for these sites is likely to be wholly unrepresentative of the original ceramic populations, because both recovery and curation biases are known to have affected the assemblages.

NON-KOPE CLAY PASTES

Sherds from the vessels that appear, upon preliminary analyses, to be made from non-Kope clay pastes readily stand out in the assemblage. These sherds occur at less than 5 percent of the assemblage in each level (as measured by weight or MNV). The non-Kope pastes are distinctive from those of other Twin Mounds West site vessels not only because of their temper. The non-Kope pastes also are routinely harder, denser, and better fired. Non-temper particle sizes in the pastes tend to be smaller and more uniform, and the pastes tend to be more thoroughly mixed (i.e., the paste appears uncontorted and homogeneous, with an even distribution of temper throughout the paste). Colors also are conspicuously different from those of Kope-paste sherds (e.g., orange, very light gray, very dark gray to black), and core colors tend to more often match surface colors, probably indicating more thorough firing. Even if Kope clay is a constituent in some of these pastes, then different manufacturing and firing technologies clearly were used to produce them. All of the apparently non-Kope paste sherds are tempered with either sand, crushed sherds, or a mixture of these two agents, sometimes coupled with limestone and grit. Grit, limestone, and sherd temper particles in the non-Kope pastes range from 1 to 2.5 mm and average 1.7 millimeters. Sand temper particles range from less than 1 to 1.5 millimeters and average 1 mm. Densities are low-medium (10 percent) to medium (20 percent). Admixtures of more than one kind of temper are generally in roughly equal proportions.

VESSEL MORPHOLOGY

In the Twin Mounds West assemblage, vessel morphology, regardless of series, is one of gentle curvature: rounded to slightly flattened bases, rounded shoulders, smoothly excurving or recurving necks, straight to gently flaring rims. No conoidal or subconoidal bases are known. A minuscule number of tetrapods have been identified (n=1 *Miami Series*, n=2 *Kope Series*, n=1 *Unknown Series I*). Although bowls occur in all series in the assemblage, they appear to comprise no more than 10 to 20 percent of all the vessels (n=295); other than a single, shallow, flat-bottomed "pan"-like vessel, no other forms are known at this time. The sample size of Twin Mounds West vessels with rims that were intact enough to provide representative profiles is small to moderate (n=120, or 40.7 percent). The weak trend through time from flared to more vertical rims on plain and cordmarked vessels that is suggested by **Figure 5:4** is interesting, but it may be meaningless, given that sample sizes per level are small. The more vertical rims may be a harbinger of later *Newtown Phase* types, although, with the exception of a single specimen, no sharply angled sherds are known from Twin Mounds West.

The wall thicknesses of *Miami Series* body sherds (all types) range between 4.2 and 11.4 mm and have a mean of 6.2 millimeters. Sherds from the other series present at the site fall within this range, although the grit-tempered *Kope Series* exhibits a very weak trend toward slightly thicker vessels. Thickness is probably more closely correlated with vessel size than series at Twin Mounds West, with smaller vessels having thinner walls and larger vessels having thicker walls. The diameters of a sample of 71 plain and 46 cordmarked vessels pooled from the *Miami* and *Kope Series*, as shown in **Figure 5:5**, indicate that medium-sized pots, those with diameters of 15 to 23 cm, were most common at Twin Mounds West. Although the proveniences of the 117 rims graphed in **Figure 5:5** suggest a weak trend toward slightly larger vessels through time, the sample size of measured rims in any given level may be to small to reflect reliably any changes in vessel size.

SURFACE TREATMENTS

The exteriors of the *Miami Series Twin Mounds Plain* sherds are smoothed to a soft matte sheen, but not polished. *Twin Mounds Plain* sherds generally appear smoother than plain sherds in other series. The crushed, burned limestone temper found in the *Miami Series* tends to be a rounder, and perhaps softer, particle than the grit found in the *Kope Series* and *Unnamed Local Series* and less densely distributed than the sand found in the unknown series. These characteristics may have enabled potters to achieve a smoother surface on limestone-tempered vessels. However, differences in post-depositional preservation also may have led to the appearance of a smoother surface on *Miami Series* sherds: the carbonates in the limestone seem to have helped *Miami Series* sherds fare better in the acidic soils at Twin Mounds West compared to sherds lacking limestone temper.

The cordmarking on *Twin Mounds Cordmarked* sherds is lightly smoothed, with cord impressions less than 2 mm deep. Cordmarking typically was accomplished with both S and Z twist, two-ply cords, although S twist predominates (circa 80 percent, by weight) in all levels. Cord impressions usually are narrow (2 mm) and are placed touching one another. Some cord impressions are superimposed, giving a cross-hatched appearance that may or may not have been deliberate. A few body and neck sherds exhibit cord impressions that meet at angles between 45 and 90 degrees. Cordmarking on *Kope Series* and *Unnamed Local Series* sherds is similar, while cordmarking on sherds belonging to the seven unknown series exhibits more variation both in cord width and cord spacing. The interior surfaces of some plain and cordmarked sherds (circa 25 percent, by weight) appear smudged, although they may have been blackened during use or after deposition rather than during firing. The interiors of about 15 to 20 percent (by weight) of these sherds also bear traces of charred organic debris, suggesting that they failed during cooking.

The provisional varieties (subtypes) created within the *Miami Series* plain and cordmarked types accommodate the range of other surface treatments observed on otherwise plain or cordmarked sherds: single or multiple linear incisions (*Twin Mounds Incised*); annular rows of fingernail impressions or pinched projections made when the potter indented a fingernail in the pliable clay (*Twin Mounds Fingernail Impressed*) or pinched it between thumb and forefinger (*Twin Mounds Pinched*); round, rectangular, triangular, and wedge-shaped punctations, some of which co-occur (*Twin Mounds Punctate*); cordmarking on lips (*Twin Mounds Cordmarked Lip*); and cordmarking on both the interior and exterior of the rim and neck areas of the same vessel (*Twin Mounds Interior-Exterior Cordmarked*). Sample sizes for these provisional varieties currently are very small **(Tables 5:1 and 5:4)**. Perhaps eventually we may find that a number of these design elements are temporally sensitive or, on the other hand, that they are simply occasional embellishments on *Twin Mounds Plain* and *Cordmarked* vessels, rendering subtypes fairly meaningless.

Textile Impressed sherds from Twin Mounds West represent two vessels (n=1 *Miami Series*, n=1 *Kope Series*). Unlike the other ceramic types discussed, which were recovered from throughout the excavated levels, both textile impressed examples came from excavation Level 3 (Occupation C), suggesting, perhaps, that this surface treatment was a minor constituent of the site's assemblage only during the early phases of its occupation (Hawkins 1986). The surface treatment of the textile impressed sherds exhibits the lightly smoothed but

TABLE 5:4		
	SERIES	
Analogous Types	**Miami**	**Kope**
Incised	11	8
Fingernail Impressed	1	15
Pinched	1	3
Punctated	4	8
Totals	17	34

Comparison of minimum numbers of vessels represented by varieties within plain and cordmarked types in the Miami and Kope Series.

clear impressions of a coarsely-twined (2-ply, S twist) fragment of a mat, basket, net, or other fabric. *Twin Mounds Polished and Embossed* sherds from Twin Mounds West represent only three vessels. The sherds bear between one and three bosses in a single ring around the neck. The bosses were raised on the vessel's exterior by punching a small cylindrical object, such as a reed or bone, into the vessel's neck from the inside. The surface was polished after the neck was embossed. The site also yielded two other vessel fragments composed of refitted rim and body sherds of an analogous polished and embossed type in *Unknown Series V*. The body of one of these two vessels exhibits slightly smoothed-over simple stamping over a polished surface. The other vessel exhibits brushing over a polished surface. All of the site's polished and embossed vessels are thin-walled (4-5 mm) and small (10-12 cm in diameter).

Regardless of series, the surface treatments for Twin Mounds West sherds that bear "Hopewell rim" treatments and various kinds of rocker stamping (i.e., motifs from the old *Hopewellianian Series*), and simple or check stamping (i.e., motifs from the old *Southeastern Series*) generally duplicate those that have been described elsewhere (Prufer 1968; Prufer and McKenzie 1965). However, no clear distinction between analogous types of *Turner A and B Simple Stamped* could be discerned among Twin Mounds West sherds of any series. Of note, the interiors of about 10 percent of the vessels bearing *Hopewellian* and *Southeastern Series* motifs are encrusted with charred organic debris, suggesting that these vessels also failed during cooking.

THE PRINCIPLE OF ANALOGOUS POTTERY TYPES AND THE ANALYSIS OF CERAMICS FROM THE TWIN MOUNDS WEST SITE

Stratigraphic Variation

In addition to solving a thorny taxonomic problem — how to organize ceramic data in a consistent and orderly fashion — employment of the Principle of Analogous Pottery Types also provided a way to capture and evaluate variation in paste and surface treatment in the Twin Mounds Westt assemblage,

both diachronically and synchronically. After the ceramics were classified according to series and type, the data were examined stratigraphically. No obvious differences in at least the raw material aspects of ceramic technology were detected among the three occupations (**Figure 5:6**). Rather, assemblage-wide patterns in paste (clay + temper) reveal that the frequencies of the different series do not vary significantly among the levels and that *Miami Series* sherds regularly occur in significantly greater amounts (70 percent). The grit-tempered *Kope Series* routinely occurs as less than 20 percent of the assemblage; all other series together make up less than 10 percent of the assemblage at any level.

Interestingly, however, although no technological change in terms of paste is suggested, the stratigraphic distinctiveness of the three occupational horizons at Twin Mounds West is mirrored by statistically significant variation among certain ceramic surface treatments (**Figure 5:7**). Whether this variation is stylistic or technological is unknown. An examination of surface treatment trends in the *Miami Series* reveals that, through time, the percentage of cordmarked surfaces increases, while the percentage of plain surfaces decreases. These changing frequencies of plain vs. cordmarked surface treatments are not duplicated exactly in the *Kope Series*, where cordmarked surfaces apparently were consistently more common than plain. Sample sizes for the *Kope Series* also are considerably smaller.

At least three alternative explanations may account for this variation: (1) stylistic preferences for plain vs. cordmarked surface treatments changed during the intervals when the site was not occupied, (2) paddling with a cord-wrapped paddle gained favor as a manufacturing method, or (3) stylistic and technological changes were minimal but different kinds of vessels simply were used and discarded during each occupation in the areas excavated. If these differences do indeed represent a temporal trend, instead of changes in site function or discard practices, then perhaps the trend supports Prufer's (1968) opinion that plain surfaces predominate earlier in the Middle Woodland period, while cordmarked surfaces predominate later (Prufer and McKenzie 1965). Further studies of Middle Woodland ceramics in the region may suggest which of these alternatives is the most likely.

FIGURE 5:6

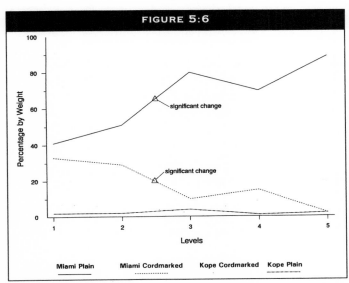

Trends in ceramic series frequency through time at the Twin Mounds West site, as measured by weight.

FIGURE 5:7

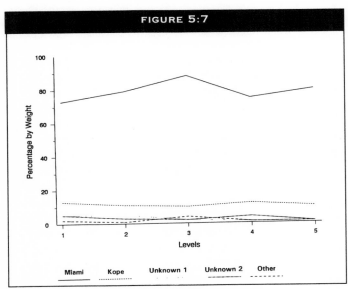

Trends in ceramic type frequency throught time at the Twin Mounds West site, as measured by weight. Statistically significant differences, as evaluated with the Z test (A/2=.05 [Zar 1984:296-298]), exist between Level 2 (Occupation B) and Level 3 (Occupation C).

ASSEMBLAGE-WIDE VARIATION

Additional research also may reveal whether another, apparently stylistic, sort of variation is confirmed in other regional Middle Woodland ceramic assemblages. At Twin Mounds West, *Kope Series* plain and cordmarked types appear to be embellished with incisions, pinching, punctations, and especially, fingernail impressions, more often than analogous *Miami Series* **(Table 5:4)**. These several surface treatments are found on *Kope Series* sherds representing 34 different vessels and on *Miami Series* sherds representing only 17 different vessels. If minimum-number-of-vessel estimates are accurate, then of the 44 *Kope Series* plain and cordmarked vessels, 77.3 percent are embellished with incisions, pinching, punctations, and fingernail impressions, while of the 161 *Miami Series* plain and cordmarked vessels, only 10.6 percent are similarly treated. These surface treatments seem to be about equally common in the various excavation levels (by weight and MNV). The frequencies of occurrence of other types in the *Kope Series* are very similar to those of analogous types in the *Miami Series*. Sample sizes are too small to compare type frequencies in either the *Unnamed Local Series* or the seven unknown series with those of the *Miami Series*.

Comparisons of other analogous types among the series recovered at Twin Mounds West also produce some interesting results. Over half (13 of 23, 56.5 percent) of the Twin Mounds West vessels that exhibit "Hopewellian" motifs (i.e., cross-hatched Hopewell Rims and rocker stamping) are classed in the *Miami Series* and slightly more than one-third (34.8 percent) fall in the *Kope Series* (n=7) and *Unnamed Local Series* (n=1). In other words, a total of 21 of the 23 "Hopewellian" motif vessels (or 91.3 percent) are made of Kope clay pastes (Table 5.5). In contrast, of the 33 vessels bearing "Southeastern" motifs (i.e., simple and check stamping), less that half (42.4 percent) are made of Kope clay pastes (*Miami Series* n=5, 15.2 percent; *Kope Series* n=7, 21.2 percent; *Unnamed Local Series* n=2, 6.1 percent), while over half (n=19, 57.6 percent) appear to be made of non-Kope clay pastes **(Table 5:5)**. Variation in the frequencies of occurrence of these "Hopewellian" and "Southeastern" motifs on Kope clay vs. non-Kope clay pastes certainly also is worthy of further investigation.

		TABLE 5:5				
Analogous Types	Non-Kope Totals	Percent	Kope Totals	Percent	Totals MNV	Total Percent
Plain	13	4.41	143	48.47	156	52.88
Cordmarked	10	3.39	66	22.37	76	25.76
Textile Impressed	0	0	2	0.68	2	0.68
Polished and Embossed	2	0.68	3	1.02	5	1.69
Rocker Stamped	2	0.68	21	7.12	23	7.80
Simple Stamped	14	4.75	12	4.07	26	8.81
Check Stamped	5	1.69	2	0.68	7	2.37
Totals	46	15.59	249	84.41	295	100.00

Minimum numbers of vessels compared for analogous types between series not made of Kope clay and series made of Kope clay. Percents are based on the total MNV (n=295).

It is hoped that further studies of Middle Woodland ceramics in the lower Great Miami Valley can investigate whether different series were preferred for different functions, in that alternative clay and temper combinations may have been better suited to certain tasks because of their abilities to withstand specific stresses (e.g., DeBoer and Lathrap 1979; Henrickson and McDonald 1983; Teltser 1993). More research may likewise help to support or reject the hypothesis that the *Kope Series* and its suite of surface embellishments on plain and cordmarked vessels are conservative holdovers from Early Woodland styles (e.g., *Wright* ceramics from Kentucky) that persist at a low frequency throughout much of the Middle Woodland period in southwestern Ohio and southeastern Indiana. Additional investigations also might reveal why (at least at Twin Mounds West) the "Southeastern" motifs, simple and check stamping, common among Early Woodland ceramics in neighboring Kentucky, seem to occur more frequently on non-Kope (possibly non-local) pastes, especially given that plain, cordmarked, embossed, and textile impressed types likely represent local continuations of an earlier Woodland ceramic tradition heavily influenced by ceramic industries south of the Ohio River. Indeed, it would be interesting to know the frequencies at which "Hopewellian" and "Southeastern" motifs occur on Kope vs. non-Kope clay vessels from other Middle Woodland sites in the region. Perhaps such future studies also will be able to provide additional information regarding whether or not the small number of non-Kope clay sherds at Twin Mounds West are likely to represent vessels acquired through exchange with non-local groups or experimentation with different ceramic technologies; a preliminary experiment has suggested that the sand in several sand-tempered sherds from Twin Mounds West did not come from the immediate area (Klein 1971). Until more research is undertaken, the ceramics from Twin Mounds West will remain a tantalizing harbinger of what it may be possible to learn about Middle Woodland ceramic industries and, by extension, Middle Woodland lifeways.

CONCLUSIONS

The Twin Mounds West site provides a rare opportunity to investigate a non-earthwork, stratified, Middle Woodland occupation site and to expand the information available on non-Scioto Valley Middle Woodland manifestations. Examination of this site's ceramics reveals that the traditional classificatory scheme devised for Ohio Hopewell ceramics is much like the old "reduction sequence" typology for chipped stone artifacts: its categories are laden with meaning, they are not mutually exclusive, and they do not account for the full range of variation manifested by Middle Woodland ceramics. To move beyond these problems, I have advocated the following measures: (1) the *Scioto, Hopewellian, Southeastern,* and *Miami Series* should be abandoned, (2) new ceramic series should be defined strictly on technological grounds, and (3) the Principle of Analogous Pottery Types should be employed to construct series that will serve as meaningful units of comparative analysis. Such an approach has been followed rigorously across the United States for decades, and it is time for the Ohio Valley to catch up with modern principles of ceramic taxonomy and analysis.

As chronicled earlier in this chapter, the *Miami Series,* once composed primarily of a few "aberrant" sherds from the Turner Earthworks, was revised in light of new data from the Twin Mounds West site to address the deficits inherent in the old typology. In its new form, the revised *Miami Series* provides a model for the effective modification and creation of other ceramic series devoid of pre-assigned implications about Middle Woodland behavior and designed to capture rather than subsume important technological and stylistic variation. Employment of the new approach will thereby encourage the development and testing of hypotheses regarding the nature of ceramic technology and production and the role of ceramics in ritual vs. secular contexts and in exchange. Gaining a better understanding of ceramic production, use, and exchange promises to shed light on Middle Woodland subsistence, social organization, and socioeconomic relationships among different regional Middle Woodland groups and doubtless will help us in better comprehending the dynamics of the "Hopewell Interaction Sphere."

ACKNOWLEDGMENTS

I would like to thank Alan P. Sullivan, III for reading a draft of this chapter; his experience in both typological theory and ceramic analysis resulted in excellent suggestions that led to its improvement. I also thank Scott A. Walley and Bart H. Ruter for reading and commenting on an earlier version. I further thank Paul J. Pacheco for his valuable editorial assistance. Unfortunately, any errors remaining cannot be pinned on any of these good people and must remain my responsibility.

REFERENCES CITED

Adams, C. and E. Adams 1991 *Archaeological Typology and Practical Reason*. Cambridge University Press, Cambridge.

Bennett, M.A. 1974 *Basic Ceramic Analysis*. Contributions in Anthropology 6(1). Eastern New Mexico University, Portales, New Mexico.

Bishop, R.L., R.L. Rands, and G.R. Holley 1982 Ceramic Compositional Analysis in Archaeological Perspective. In *Advances in Archaeological Method and Theory*, edited by M.B. Schiffer, 5:275-330. Academic Press, New York.

Colton, H.S. 1943 The Principle of Analogous Pottery Types. *American Anthropologist 45(2): 316-320.*

Dancey, W.S. 1992 Village Origins in Central Ohio: The Results and Implications of Recent Middle and Late Woodland Research. In *Cultural Variability in Context: Woodland Settlements of the Mid-Ohio Valley* edited by M.F. Seeman, pp. 24-29. MCJA Special Paper 7, Kent State University Press, Kent, Ohio.

DeBoer, W.R. and D. Lathrap 1979 The Making and Breaking of Shipibo-Conibo Ceramics. In *Ethnoarchaeology: Implications of Ethnography for Archaeology*, edited by C. Kramer, pp. 102-138. Columbia University Press, New York.

Dunnell, R. 1971 *Systematics in Prehistory*. Free Press, New York.

Fischer, F.W. 1968 *A Survey of the Archaeological Remains of Shawnee Lookout Park*. Report on file, Department of Anthropology, University of Cincinnati.

1969 *Preliminary Report on the University of Cincinnati Archaeological Investigations, 1969*. Part I (of one). Report on file, Department of Anthropology, University of Cincinnati.

1970 *Preliminary Report on the University of Cincinnati Archaeological Investigations, 1970*. Report on file, Department of Anthropology, University of Cincinnati.

1974 *Early and Middle Woodland Settlement, Subsistence, and Population in the Central Ohio Valley*. Ph.D. dissertation, Department of Anthropology, Washington University, St. Louis. University Microfilms, Ann Arbor.

Ford, R.I. 1979 Gathering and Gardening: Trends and Consequences of Hopewell Subsistence Strategies. In *Hopewellian Archaeology: The Chillicothe Conference*, edited by D.S. Brose and N. Greber, pp. 234-238. Kent State University Press, Kent, Ohio.

Griffin, J.B. 1945 The Ceramic Affiliations of the Ohio Valley Adena Culture. In *The Adena People*, edited by W.S. Webb and C.E. Snow, pp. 220-246. University of Tennessee Press, Knoxville.

1952 Some Early and Middle Woodland Pottery Types in Illinois. In *Hopewellian Communities in Illinois*, edited by R. Duel, Illinois State Museum, Scientific Papers, 5(3):93-129. Springfield, Illinois.

1974 Forward. In *The Adena People*, edited by W.S. Webb and C.E. Snow, pp. v-xviii. University of Tennessee Press, Knoxville.

Haag, W.G. 1939 Untitled. *Southeastern Archaeological Conference Newsletter*, 1(1). Lexington, Kentucky.

1940 A Description of the Wright Site Pottery. In *The Wright Mounds*, by W.S. Webb. University of Kentucky Reports in Anthropology and Archaeology 5(1):75-82. Lexington, Kentucky.

Hawkins, R.A. 1986 *The Twin Mounds Village and Hopewell in Southeastern Ohio: A Ceramic Identity Crisis*. Masters thesis, Department of Anthropology, University of Cincinnati.

1992 Subsistence Inferences from Woodland and Mississippian Ceramics: the Central Ohio Valley circa 1000 B.C. - A.D. 1200. In *Research in Economic Anthropology, Supplement 6, Long Term Subsistence Change in Prehistoric North America*, edited by D.R. Croes, R.A. Hawkins, and B.L. Isaac, pp. 47-76. JAI Press, Greenwich.

Hawkins, R.A. and S.A. Walley 1993 *Phases I and II Archaeological Research for the Proposed I-275 Ramp and Related East Miami Business Center in South Milford, Clermont County, Ohio.* Report on file, Ohio Historic Preservation Office, Columbus, Ohio.

Henrickson, E.F. and M.M.A. McDonald 1983 Ceramic Form and Function: An Ethnographic Search and an Archaeological Application. *American Anthropologist* 85(3):630-643.

Isphording, W.C. 1974 Combined Thermal and X-ray Diffraction Technique for Identification of Ceramic Ware Temper and Paste Materials. *American Antiquity* 39(3):477-483.

Kaltenthaler, L. 1992 *Analysis of the Chert Debitage and Tools from the Twin Mounds Village Site.* Masters thesis, Department of Anthropology, University of Cincinnati.

Klein, H. 1971 *Report on Simple Stamped Sandstone (sic) Tempered Pottery from Twin Mounds - A Hamilton County Hopewellian Site.* Report on file, Department of Anthropology, University of Cincinnati.

Matson, F.R. 1989 Shell-Tempered Pottery and the Fort Ancient Potter. In *Pottery Technology: Ideas and Approaches*, edited by G. Bronitsky, pp. 15-31. Westview Press, Boulder, Colorado.

Prufer, O.H. 1965 *The McGraw Site: A Study in Hopewellian Dynamics.* Cleveland Museum of Natural History, Scientific Publications 4(1). Cleveland.

1968 *Ohio Hopewellian Ceramics: An Analysis of the Extant Collections.* Museum of Anthropology, Anthropological Papers No. 33, University of Michigan, Ann Arbor.

Prufer, O.H. and D.H. McKenzie 1965 Ceramics. In *The McGraw Site: A Study in Hopewellian Dynamics*, by O.H. Prufer. Cleveland Museum of Natural History, Scientific Publications 4(1):16-57.

Rice, P.M. 1987 *Pottery Analysis: A Sourcebook.* University of Chicago Press, Chicago.

Riggs, R.E. 1989 New Stratigraphic Sequences from the Lower Little Miami Valley. *West Virginia Archaeologist* 38(2):1-21.

Seeman, M.F. 1979 *The Hopewellian Interaction Sphere: Evidence for Interregional Trade and Structural Complexity.* Indiana Historical Society, Prehistory Research Series 5(2), Indianapolis.

Shepard, A.O. 1980 *Ceramics for the Archaeologist.* Carnegie Institution of Washington, Publication 609, Washington, D.C. (Reprint of the 5th edition, 1965).

Sollheim, W.G. II 1960 The Use of Sherd Weights and Counts in the Handling of Archaeological Data. *Current Anthropology* 1(4):325-329.

Squier, E.G. and W.H. Davis 1848 *Ancient Monuments of the Mississippi Valley.* Smithsonian Contributions to Knowledge 1. Washington, D.C.

Sullivan, A.P. III and K.C. Rozen 1985 Debitage Analysis and Archaeological Interpretation. *American Antiquity* 50:755-799.

Tankersley, K. and J. Meinhart 1982 Physical and Structural Properties of Ceramic Material Utilized by a Fort Ancient Group. *Midcontinental Journal of Archaeology* 7:225-243.

Teltser, P.A. 1993 An Analytic Strategy for Studying Assemblage-Scale Ceramic Variation: A Case Study from Southeast Missouri. *American Antiquity* 58(2):530-543.

Zar, J.H. 1984 *Biostatistical Analysis.* 2nd edition. Prentice-Hall, Englewood Cliffs, New Jersey.

SIX

BLADELETS ARE TOOLS TOO: THE PREDOMINANCE OF BLADELETS AMONG FORMAL TOOLS AT OHIO HOPEWELL SITES

ROBERT A. GENHEIMER

ABSTRACT

Collections from Middle Woodland sites in the vicinity of Stubbs Earthwork in Warren County, Ohio include large numbers of bladelets, which most likely represent utilitarian cutting, scraping, and piercing tools. Bladelets may also have been involved in craft production. Since the frequency of utilization of blades from southwestern Ohio and southeastern Indiana is very high, bladelets appear to constitute a systematically manufactured, standardized tool. Compared to other formal tool types (e.g., projectile points, drills, bifaces, scrapers, and gravers/perforators), bladelets constitute the most abundant formal tool type at Ohio Valley Middle Woodland sites. Stubbs Cluster bladelets exhibit use/retouch along the lateral blade edges, both proximal and distal ends, tip use, and notching. Bladelets were utilized for a wide variety of tasks, which cannot be duplicated for any other traditionally recognized formal tool type. It is argued that during the Middle Woodland period the blade industry provided a standardized tool type that took the place of or obviated the use of a number of formal tools.

A View From the Core a Synthesis of Ohio Hopewell Archaeology•edited by Paul J. Pacheco
© Copyright 1996 by The Ohio Archaeological Council• Columbus, Ohio•All Rights Reserved•ISBN 0-9626931-9-7

ROBERT A. GENHEIMER

BLADELETS ARE TOOLS TOO: THE PREDOMINANCE OF BLADELETS

INTRODUCTION

Bladelets constitute the most distinctive and frequently encountered artifact type at Ohio Valley Middle Woodland sites. Bladelets occur in small numbers at many localities, but literally hundreds or thousands have been recovered from sites such as the Liberty Earthworks [n=1,620] in the Scioto Valley of southern Ohio (Greber et al. 1981), the Murphy Cluster [n=1,100+] in central Ohio (Dancey 1991; Pacheco 1993), the Dresden Cluster [n=1,700+] in east-central Ohio (Carskadden 1972; Carskadden and Morton n.d.), and the Stubbs Cluster [n=1,785] in south-western Ohio (Genheimer 1992). Outside Ohio, the Mann site [n=3,000+] in southern Indiana (Kellar 1979) and the Twenhafel site [n=1,500] along the Mississippi River in southern Illinois (Hofman 1987) have also produced large quantities of bladelets.

While bladelets are recovered in quantity at Ohio Hopewell sites, formal tools, such as projectile points, bifaces, drills, scrapers, gravers/perforators, and spokeshaves are found in relatively small numbers. When bladelets are recognized as tools at Middle Woodland sites, in most instances they comprise the majority formal tool type. The scarcity of non-blade tools and the corresponding abundance of blade tools at many Middle Woodland sites suggest that blades may have been duplicating a number of tasks formerly delegated to non-blade tools. During the Middle Woodland period, therefore, the blade industry provided the means of production of a standardized tool that may have taken the place of additional formal tool types.

In this paper, the use of bladelets as tools is examined and more specific bladelet use patterns at the Stubbs Cluster are detailed. The frequency of blade and non-blade tools are then discussed for Stubbs Cluster and a number of Hopewell sites in south-central and southwestern Ohio, and southern Indiana. The probable uses of bladelets are presented as well as their potential for replacing non-blade tools.

BLADELETS AS TOOLS

Much of the uncertainty concerning the prehistoric use of Hopewellian bladelets can be attributed, until recently, to a lack of systematic microwear studies. Early reports on Hopewellian sites (Ford et al. 1955:147; Fowler 1952:156; McGregor 1952:63, 1958:125-127; Mills 1906:87, 1907:103, 1921:137, 140-141; Neumann and Fowler 1952:240; Willoughby and Hooton 1922:89; Witthoft 1952:473, 1957:20) simply identified bladelets as "knives", inferring a function that was never documented; indeed, through time, bladelets became commonly referred to as "flake knives" or "ribbon knives". Pi-Sunyer (1965:61-63) made a valid argument for the use of the term "blade" instead of a variety of functional terms in use at that time, but bladelets continued to be referred to as "flake knives" (Griffin et al. 1970:Plates 22a, 78b, and 115a; Struever 1968:294) or "uniface flake knives" (Fischer 1974:148) into the mid-1970s.

Although the term "blade" is non-committal with respect to how the artifact was used, the adoption of use-neutral terms has not prevented investigators from assigning functions to them. Initially, function was based on the context of discovery and association of the bladelets with other artifact types. Bladelets have been found in association with human burials both in Ohio Hopewell (Mills 1907:69-70; Willoughby and Hooton 1922:26) and Illinois Hopewell sites (Griffin et al. 1970:Plates 22a, 42a, 51a, 78b, and 115a; Montet-White 1968:95; Neumann and Fowler 1952:Plates LXIX and LXXII). It was assumed that bladelets served as funeral offerings or perhaps "status markers" (Hofman 1987:91) in those instances. Montet-White (1968:95) hypothesized that bladelets were utilized for manufacturing bone artifacts because both bone tools and blades are found in association with burials in Illinois mounds. She further suggested that blades were used in the manufacture of bone awls and points, all three having been present in tool kits associated with Illinois Hopewellian and Baehr Series pottery (Montet-White 1968:169). Montet-White made these arguments even though she reported that blades from burial sites typically do not show visible traces of wear (Montet-White 1968:93).

Similar funerary associations have been noted by Baby and Langlois (1979:18) at Seip Mound, where deposits of mica and shells in conjunction with "utilized and modified flakes and bladelets" suggested to them that mound structures may have served as specialized workshops.

Although it is possible that some bladelets may have been the "implements of craftsmen" (Hofman 1987:91) for the manufacture of bone, antler, and shell tools, the large number of bladelets (many of which show visible signs of use and/or retouch) found within midden or trash pits, as well as on the surface of Ohio Hopewell sites, suggests that many were manufactured and utilized for more secular tasks. Yerkes (1990:171) has pointed out that "most agree that ... bladelets were cutting tools," but there exists a wide range of opinions on just what exactly was being cut. Suggested utilitarian uses include the cutting of plant materials (Montet-White 1968:95; Ken Tankersley, personal communication, 1984), the butchering of animal parts (Fischer 1971:7-8, 1974:148; Hofman 1987:91; Montet-White 1968:95; Struever 1968:294) and the cutting of meat (Ford and Webb 1956:82; Montet-White 1968:169), the processing of skins (Ford and Webb 1956:82; Hofman 1987:91), hides, and pelts (Montet-White 1968:95), and the working of soft wood (Ford and Webb 1956:82). Numerous craft production tasks have also been hypothesized, including the cutting or engraving of designs on mica (Mills 1907:173; Potter 1968:42), bone (Potter 1968:42; White 1963:48), leather (Potter 1968:42), and wood (White 1963:48). Others have indicated in a more general fashion that bladelets were utilized as specialized tools in the manufacture of bone (Hofman 1987:91; Montet-White 1968:95, 169), antler, shell, and wooden tools and utensils (Hofman 1987:91). Hofman (1987:91) argued that bone tools and weapons, such as projectile points, carapace bowls, atlatl hooks, awls, and batons may have been produced using the aid of bladelets.

Morrow (1987:139) indicated that Hopewellian bladelets were "common, utilitarian, cutting and scraping tools," an opinion that is shared by many other investigators (McNerney 1987:78; Montet-White 1968:169; Yerkes 1990:173). In perhaps the most systematic microwear analysis of Ohio Hopewell bladelets to date, Yerkes (1990:173) demonstrated that bladelets were standardized, but not specialized, tools in his study of the lithic assemblage of the Murphy site. Yerkes reported that bladelets were utilized for 12 different tasks, "primarily cutting and engraving, but also for scraping" (Yerkes 1990:173). These tasks include cutting meat; cutting, scraping, and piercing flesh and dry hide; cutting, scraping, boring, and engraving bone or antler; sawing, whittling, and engraving wood; cutting plant material; and engraving or incising stone (Yerkes 1990:172). Both utilitarian and craft production (e.g., engraving or incising) tasks were suggested.

Odell (1985a:323) reported similar findings in his use-wear study of blades from Smiling Dan, a Middle Woodland settlement in west-central Illinois. A distinction was made between retouched and unretouched blades. Retouched blades "were employed primarily for cutting, shaving, and drilling, with secondary usage as scrapers and projectile tips" (Odell 1985a:323). They were used primarily on hard materials and secondarily on substances of medium resistance. Unretouched blades were dominated by a single activity — cutting (Odell 1994:105), and "were employed primarily as knives, though they also served frequently as projectile points and scraping tools" (Odell 1985a:323). They were apparently utilized on a variety of surfaces for woodworking, butchering, and hide scraping tasks. But, although Odell defines a "basic multifunctionality" for blades, he proposes that they served different functions in different contexts. Noting different use-wear patterns on domestic versus ceremonial assemblages at Napoleon Hollow sites in Illinois, Odell (1994:115) states that blades from mortuary sites are functionally specific (e.g., cutting and scraping of soft surfaces) and ritually charged. Conversely, he argues that blades from domestic sites had no ritual connotation, and hence were utilized for a variety of tasks.

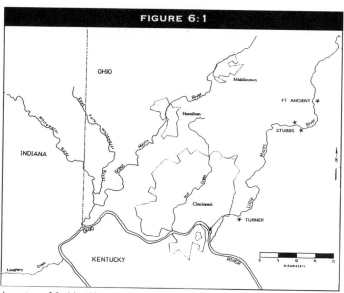

Location of Stubbs Cluster in southwest Ohio (Both north and south subclusters are indicated. Stubbs Earthwork is in the south subcluster).

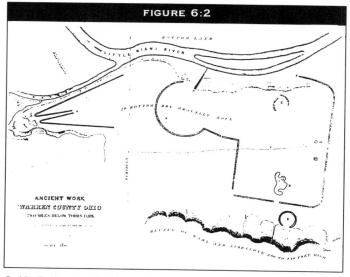

Stubbs Earthwork, 33WA1, as depicted by Whittlesey (1851:Plate II).

STUBBS CLUSTER

The Stubbs Cluster is a concentration of 28 archaeological sites with Middle Woodland components located along the middle reaches of the Little Miami River in Warren County, Ohio. Located only 7 km downstream from the Fort Ancient State Memorial and 30 to 35 km from the Turner and Milford Works, the cluster represents a major corporate center of the Middle Woodland period **(Figure 6:1)**. The focus of the cluster is Stubbs Earthwork, a large rectangular enclosure with an adjoining semicircle situated on a bluff overlooking the river **(Figure 6:2)**. A nearby series of connected embankments was purported by many to represent a serpent effigy, and has come to be referred to as the Warren County Serpent Mound. Each of the earthworks has been destroyed through graveling operations, and the cluster's numerous debris scatters have only recently been discovered by the archaeological community.

In 1979 and 1980, the cluster area was subjected to intensive archaeological survey, and in the summer of 1983 systematic controlled collections were undertaken at three (sites 33WA256, 317, and 362) of the most significant site locations. In all, nearly 9,700 fragments of cultural debris were recovered including more than 1,800 Middle Woodland artifacts. Eleven of the Middle Woodland sites are located north of the river and east of South Lebanon in what is referred to as the north subcluster **(Figure 6:3)**. However, more than 84 percent of all diagnostic Middle Woodland artifacts were recovered at 17 sites in the south subcluster, approximately 1.2 km west of Morrow, Ohio. It is in the south subcluster, that both the geometric earthwork and the "serpent mound" were located.

The most frequently recovered cultural diagnostic at Stubbs Cluster is the Hopewellian bladelet. The 1,785 bladelet and bladelet fragments recovered at the Cluster constitute the largest surface assemblage of blades in Ohio. Blades were found at 24 of the 28 debris scatters, but at 15 of the sites less than 10 blades each were recovered. The vast majority

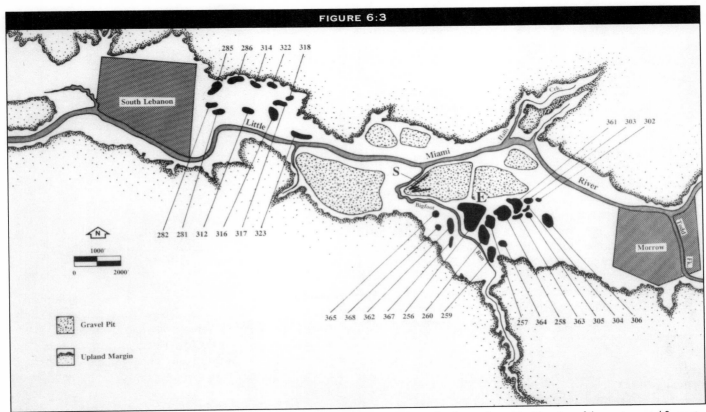

Identified Middle Woodland sites between South Lebanon and Morrow, Warren County, Ohio. S indicates the original location of the controversial Serpent Mound. E indicates the general location of Stubbs Earthwork.

of the bladelets, more than 85 percent, were collected from four large sites (33WA256, 257, 258, and 260) near the former geometric earthwork. Few complete bladelets were recovered, most likely due to a combination of prehistoric utilization resulting in breakage, post-depositional disturbances (particularly cultivation), and amateur collection of whole items. Medial segments (bladelet segments with no platform end or termination) dominated, accounting for nearly half the collection. Of the remaining sections, proximal segments outnumber distal segments by a wide margin.

For the purposes of this study, a total of 374 bladelets and bladelet segments gathered during the systematic surface collection of sites 33WA256, 317, and 362 were utilized. Most, a total of 315, were collected from site 33WA256, the location nearest the former Stubbs Earthwork. More than 40 percent of the blades were manufactured of Wyandotte flint which outcrops in southern Indiana. More than one-fifth were made of Flint Ridge chalcedony from central Ohio. Approximately 15 percent had been flaked from Knox flint, a raw material native to eastern Tennessee.

Metrically, the Stubbs bladelet population exhibits some similarities to other Ohio and nearby samples, and although statistically significant differences can be calculated for mean blade width and thickness among the samples, the Stubbs bladelets share the characteristics of what Greber et al. (1981:524) termed an "Ohio bladelet industry" (vs. a distinct Illinois industry). This Ohio industry relied on high-quality, and often exotic, flint types, and consistent core preparation and detachment procedures to produce highly standardized tools.

BLADELET USE AT THE CLUSTER

During the analysis of Stubbs Cluster bladelets, the presence/absence of use-wear/retouch was recorded along all bladelet and bladelet fragments from systematic controlled collection. Use-wear was defined by the presence of use-damage along any blade edge. The presence of even, discontinuous, but intentional scars from use was deemed sufficient for inclusion in the category. Often, use-wear resulted in visible (microscopic) polish. All attempts were made to exclude scarring resulting from plowing, handling, or other post-depositional damage (see Odell 1985b).

Retouch was defined by the presence of intentional and regular flaking, bevelling, or notching along any blade edge. Retouched blades were included within the utilized category, although it is possible, that retouched examples were not subsequently utilized. Keeley (1978:164) has argued that on a retouched edge it is extremely difficult and often impossible to distinguish between utilization damage scars and retouch patterns. One can readily distinguish a retouched edge from a utilized edge, but once an edge is retouched, utilization is difficult to recognize. Retouch may also have little to do with use, particularly in attempts to blunt a working blade. Semenov (1973:64-66) argues that continuous retouch was used to blunt part of a blade edge in the Paleolithic period as a means of supporting the index finger. Bordaz (1970:57) also cites the example of "backed blades", where an edge has been purposely blunted by abrupt percussion or retouch. Thus, retouch can have occurred either to intentionally blunt an edge or to straighten, sharpen, or strengthen it.

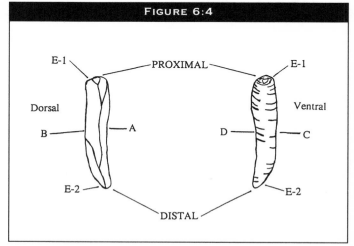

FIGURE 6:4

Location of bladelet use-wear (based on Bennett 1981:Figure 4).

Each use/retouch location of Stubbs Cluster bladelets was assigned an alpha or alpha-numeric code designation, following Bennett (1981). While holding a bladelet with the proximal end up, the following six blade margins were examined: A, right dorsal; B, left dorsal; C, right ventral; D, left ventral; E1, proximal margin; and, E2, distal margin **(Figure 6:4)**.

There is no doubt that Stubbs Cluster bladelets were utilized substantially. An analysis of systematic controlled collection data indicates that approximately 94 percent and 94.2 percent of bladelets at 33WA256 and 33WA362, respectively, exhibit use-damage on at least one blade locus **(Tables 6:1 and 6:2)**. At use-locus A (right dorsal) alone, 75 percent of the bladelets at 33WA362 and 69.2 percent at 33WA256 display use damage. Bennett (1981) had observed a 71.3 percent proportion of utilization for use-locus A among his larger sample of Stubbs Cluster bladelets. In both studies, use-locus A exhibits the highest frequency of use-wear occurrence. In general, use-wear occurrence decreases in frequency with successive alpha designations. At 33WA256, use-damage is 56.2 percent at use-locus B, 48.9 percent at use-locus C, 39 percent at use-locus D, and 7.6 percent at use-locus E1. Use-wear along the distal end (E2) is 20 per-

TABLE 6:1

	Wyandotte						OFR [a]					
	Com [c]	Pro [d]	Med [e]	Dis [f]	All	%	Com	Pro	Med	Dis	All	%
No.	3	43	66	26	138	n/a	4	25	28	13	70	n/a
A	2	32	43	20	97	70.3	2	18	17	8	45	64.3
B	2	28	38	17	85	61.3	2	12	10	6	30	42.9
C	1	27	25	17	70	50.7	2	10	10	5	27	38.6
D	1	16	30	14	69	50.0	1	7	8	6	22	31.4
E1	-	1	6	1	8	5.8	-	1	3	2	6	8.6
E2	-	6	5	14	28	18.1	1	5	3	10	19	27.1
TUL [g]	6	110	147	83	346	n/a	8	53	51	37	149	n/a
ULO [h]	-	-	5	-	5	3.6	-	1	5	-	6	8.6
UL1	1	7	18	2	28	20.3	2	8	7	2	19	27.1
UL2	1	16	14	7	38	27.5	1	10	9	2	22	31.4
UL3	1	11	18	5	35	25.4	-	1	3	5	9	12.9
UL4	-	7	8	8	23	16.7	1	4	3	4	12	17.1
UL5	-	2	3	4	9	6.5	-	-	1	-	1	1.4
UL6	-	-	-	-	-	-	-	1	-	-	1	1.4
DOR [i]	4	66	86	51	207	58.5	5	35	30	24	94	63.1
VEN [j]	2	43	55	31	139	39.3	3	17	18	11	49	32.9
MUL [k]	2.00	2.56	2.23	3.19	2.57	n/a	2.00	2.12	1.82	2.85	2.13	n/a

	Knox [b]						All					
	Com	Pro	Med	Dis	All	%	Com	Pro	Med	Dis	All	%
No.	1	14	25	8	48	n/a	8	99	153	55	315	n/a
A	1	13	16	7	37	77.1	5	74	99	40	218	69.2
B	1	8	16	7	32	66.7	5	57	80	35	177	56.2
C	1	6	15	6	28	58.3	4	56	63	31	154	48.9
D	1	5	12	4	22	45.8	3	34	59	27	123	39.0
E1	-	-	3	1	4	8.3	-	2	16	6	24	7.6
E2	-	2	2	5	9	18.8	1	16	14	32	63	20.0
TUL	4	34	64	30	132	n/a	18	239	331	171	759	n/a
ULO	-	-	3	-	3	6.3	-	4	14	1	19	6.0
UL1	-	2	4	-	6	12.5	3	18	40	4	65	20.6
UL2	-	6	3	-	9	18.8	2	36	40	10	88	27.9
UL3	-	5	8	4	17	35.4	1	21	32	16	70	22.2
UL4	1	-	5	2	8	16.7	2	15	20	16	53	16.8
UL5	-	1	2	2	5	10.4	-	4	7	7	18	5.7
UL6	-	-	-	-	-	———	-	1	-	-	1	0.3
DOR	2	23	34	19	78	59.1	11	147	193	107	358	47.2
VEN	2	11	27	10	50	37.9	7	90	122	58	277	36.5
MUL	4.00	2.43	2.56	3.75	2.75	n/a	2.25	2.41	2.16	3.11	2.41	n/a

a Ohio Flint Ridge / b Knox type 2/3 (Genheimer 1992:90-91) / c complete / d proximal / e medial / f distal / g total modified use-loci / h cumulative number use-loci / i dorsal / j ventral / k mean number of modified use-loci per segment

Bladelet Use-Wear, Systematic Controlled Collection, 33WA256.

TABLE 6:2

	Wyandotte Com[c]	Pro[d]	Med[e]	Dis[f]	All	%	OFR[a] Com	Pro	Med	Dis	All	%
No.	-	6	13	3	22	n/a	1	3	5	2	11	n/a
A	-	3	10	2	15	68.2	-	1	3	2	6	54.5
B	-	2	8	1	11	50.0	-	1	1	1	3	27.3
C	-	4	8	2	14	63.6	-	1	1	-	2	18.2
D	-	-	5	1	6	27.3	-	-	-	-	-	——
E_1	-	-	1	-	1	4.5	-	-	-	-	-	——
E_2	-	-	-	2	2	9.1	1	-	-	2	3	27.3
TUL[g]	n/a	9	32	8	49	n/a	1	3	5	5	14	n/a
ULO[h]	-	1	1	-	2	9.1	-	1	-	-	1	9.1
UL1	-	1	2	1	4	18.2	1	1	3	-	4	36.4
UL2	-	1	3	-	4	18.2	-	1	1	1	3	27.3
UL3	-	2	5	1	8	36.4	-	-	-	1	1	9.1
UL4	-	-	2	1	3	13.6	-	-	-	-	-	——
DOR[i]	0	5	18	5	28	57.1	1	2	4	5	12	85.7
VEN[j]	0	4	13	3	20	40.8	0	1	1	0	2	14.3
MUL[k]	n/a	1.50	2.46	2.67	2.23	n/a	1.00	1.00	1.00	2.50	1.27	n/a

	Knox b Com	Pro	Med	Dis	All	%	All Com	Pro	Med	Dis	All	%
No.	-	4	2	2	8	n/a	1	15	27	9	52	n/a
A	-	4	2	2	8	n/a	-	10	22	7	39	75.0
B	-	3	2	2	7	87.5	-	6	17	5	28	53.8
C	-	1	1	2	4	50.0	-	7	14	5	26	50.0
D	-	1	1	-	2	25.0	-	2	10	2	14	26.9
E_1	-	-	-	-	-	——	-	-	1	-	1	1.9
E_2	-	-	-	-	-	——	1	-	1	5	7	13.5
TUL	n/a	9	6	6	21	n/a	1	25	65	24	115	n/a
ULO	-	-	-	-	-	——	-	2	1	-	3	5.8
UL1	-	1	-	-	1	12.5	1	4	5	1	11	21.2
UL2	-	2	1	-	3	37.5	-	4	8	2	14	26.9
UL3	-	-	-	2	2	25.0	-	3	6	5	14	26.9
UL4	-	1	1	-	2	25.0	-	1	6	1	8	15.4
DOR	0	7	4	4	15	71.4	1	16	40	17	74	64.3
VEN	0	2	2	2	6	28.6	0	9	24	7	40	34.8
MUL	n/a	2.25	3.00	3.00	2.63	n/a	1.00	1.67	2.41	2.67	2.21	n/a

[a] Ohio Flint Ridge / [b] Knox type 2/3 (Genheimer 1992:90-91) / [c] complete / [d] proximal / [e] medial / [f] distal / [g] total modified use-loci / [h] cumulative number use-loci / [i] dorsal / [j] ventral / [k] mean number of modified use-loci per segment

Bladelet Use-Wear, Systematic Controlled Collection, 33WA362.

cent. Lateral retouch or use-damage is noted on 88.5 percent of the bladelets at 33WA362 and 93 percent at 33WA256. Assuming that all E2 use-wear is dorsal, then 60.6 percent of all use-damage at 33WA256 and 65.2 percent of all wear at 33WA362 is on the dorsal surface. End-damage is common at 33WA256, occurring on 27.6 percent of all blades. End-damage occurs on only 8 specimens (15.4 percent) at 33WA362.

Where sufficient numbers of bladelets exist, distal segments exhibit the highest mean number of modified use-loci per bladelet segment at systematically examined sites (Tables 6:1 and 6:2). The mean number of modified use-loci per distal segment at 33WA256 is 3.11, the highest value of any segment. This holds true for both Wyandotte (3.19) and Ohio Flint Ridge (2.85) materials, although Wyandotte bladelets were apparently utilized to a greater extent than Ohio Flint Ridge specimens. While medial and proximal segments peak at two modified use-loci per segment, distal segments peak at four modified use-loci. Medial segments are most often the least utilized segment, undoubtedly because they offer the smallest edge area upon which to identify use-damage. Similar values at 33WA362 reveal a mean number of modified use-loci per distal bladelet segments of 2.67. Increased modification of use-locus E2 at both 33WA256 and 33WA362 is at least partially responsible for this accelerated use-damage. Approximately 58.2 percent of distal segments at 33WA256 and 55.6 percent of distal segments at 33WA362 display use-damage at the E2 use-locus. Prior to bladelet breakage into segments, the extreme distal end of the bladelet apparently offered one of the most advantageous locations for retouch. Because maximum blade thickness occurred at the distal end, these segments were more susceptible to retouch, particularly steep-edged pressure flaking.

In an effort to determine the types of retouch, each of the bladelets from systematic controlled collection was subjected to low power (7x - 30x) microscopic examination. For the purposes of this study, both simple retouch and systematic retouch were recognized. Simple retouch is defined as the intentional, but irregular placement of scars along either a lateral edge or

end. Systematic retouch is the intentional, but regular placement of scars along either a lateral edge or end, often increasing the edge angle where the retouch is unifacial.

The examination of bladelets from 33WA256 reveals that 105 (33.3 percent) were systematically retouched and 9 (2.9 percent) were simply retouched. Eighteen (5.7 percent) of the systematically retouched specimens were notched (four of them double-notched). In addition, six bladelets exhibit indications of having been hafted immediately above the proximal end. Hafting is suggested by rough retouch or notching at similar positions on opposite blade margins. One bladelet is best described as bipolar. A total of 181 (57.5 percent) bladelets exhibit use-wear only. Somewhat lower frequencies of bladelet modification are noted at 33WA362. Eleven (21.2 percent) were systematically retouched, three (5.8 percent) were simply retouched, one (1.9 percent) exhibits tip utilization, and one (1.9 percent) was clearly notched. Two (3.8 percent) blades also exhibit evidence of possible hafting.

Pacheco and Pickard (1992:Figure 5) identified a probable hafted bladelet from the Dow Chemical #2 site in Licking County, Ohio, and Odell (1994:Figure 2) described several probable hafted blades from Smiling Dan and Napoleon Hollow, both Illinois Hopewell sites. Such limited evidence of possible hafting led Pacheco and Pickard (1992:14) to propose that formal hafting is a relatively rare phenomenon among Ohio blade industry tools. Greber et al. (1981:524) reported that "there is no solid evidence to determine whether or not the bladelets were hafted" at Liberty Earthworks, but they believed the relatively short length of identified retouch suggested that hafting was not necessary. Their markedly low incidence of use-wear, however, demands caution in applying such logic.

There is considerable variation in bladelet use-wear frequencies among Middle Woodland sites (Table 6:3), and although some may be explained by varying methods of use/retouch identification, the data suggest that site context and the geographical location of sites may also be important factors. Sites along the Scioto River (McGraw and

TABLE 6:3				
Site	Site Type	Count	Use/Retouch	Percent
Murphy[a]	hab/indus[l]	231	42	18.2
Liberty[b]	earthwork	1620	303	18.7
McGraw[c]	habitation	233	45	19.3
Icehouse[d]	habitation	375[o]	93	24.8
		37[p]	16	43.2
Twenhafel[e]	reg tr center[m]	244	90	36.9
Consol[f]	habitation	148	67	45.3
Ft. Ancient[g]	hab/earthwork[n]	252	200	79.0
Smiling Dan[h]	habitation	174	155	89.1
Stubbs[i]	earthwork	663	621	93.7
33WA256[i]	earthwork	361	344	95.3
33WA317[i]	surface	42	40	95.2
33WA256 SCC[i]	earthwork	315	296	94.0
33WA362 SCC[i]	surface	52	49	94.2
12D29S[k]	habitation	112	112	100.0

[a] Dancey (1991:60)
[b] Greber et al. (1981:523)
[c] Pi-Sunyer (1965:79-80)
[d] Chapman (1973:93)
[e] Hofman (1987:114)
[f] McNerney (1987:78-80)
[g] Connolly (1991:Table 8)
[h] Odell (1985a:302, retouched and unretouched combined)
[i] Bennett (1981)
[j] Genheimer (1992)
[k] Kozarek (1987:81)
[l] habitation/industrial
[m] regional transaction center
[n] habitation/earthwork
[o] local chert
[p] Ohio Flint Ridge

Bladelet Use-Wear/Retouch at Various Hopewell Sites.

Liberty Earthworks) and Raccoon Creek (Murphy) in central Ohio tend to cluster just below a maximum of 20 percent use-wear. Evidence of use-wear was so infrequent at the McGraw site that Pi-Sunyer (1965:79) remarked that "the majority of McGraw blades and blade fragments were either never used or employed in tasks that failed to damage the working edges of the artifacts." The low use frequencies at the Murphy site may be at least partially explained by the potential industrial nature (i.e., manufacturing rather than use) of the site. Significant blade core reduction took place, and it is possible that many of the blades represent reduction waste rather than tools. The relatively low use-wear frequencies are most noticeable, however, in the Liberty Earthworks sample. At this site grouping that appears most similar to the Stubbs Cluster, fewer than one-fifth of all bladelets and bladelet fragments exhibited edge-damage (Greber et al. 1981:523). Again, the low use-wear frequencies may be explained by the on-site manufacture of blades.

Just as the central Ohio bladelet assemblages cluster at relatively low use frequencies, Little Miami and Great Miami River Valley sites in southwest Ohio and southeast Indiana exhibit consistently high frequencies of edge-wear and retouch. Use-wear frequencies range from 79 percent at Fort Ancient [Northeast] (Connolly 1991:Table 8), more than 94 percent at Stubbs Cluster (Genheimer 1992:154), to 100 percent at the Jennison Guard site (Kozarek 1987:81) near the mouth of the Great Miami River. The reason for this significantly greater utilization has not been determined, but is possibly associated with site function or differential access to high quality raw materials.

In summary, use-wear frequencies approaching 100 percent and multiple use locations suggest that the Stubbs Cluster bladelets were subjected to extensive and intensive use. Because microwear analysis was not conducted on Stubbs Cluster specimens, the precise tasks represented by use were not ascertained, but based on use-wear studies by Yerkes (1990) and Odell (1985a; 1994), it can be reasonably assumed that Stubbs Cluster bladelets were utilized for cutting, shaving, engraving, and scraping tasks. Although Odell

Site	Blades	%	Non-Blade	Bf[a]	pp[b]	TP[c]	SE[d]	SC[e]	Mf[f]
256	722	83.8	140	57	4	40	15	14	10
257	329	93.5	23	9	1	10	3	—	1
258	356	96.0	15	2	1	8	—	3	1
260	120	87.6	17	3	1	—	5	2	6
317	58	72.5	22	13	2	3	2	—	2
361	38	92.7	3	2	—	—	1	—	—
362	52	83.9	10	7	1	—	—	—	2
363	41	91.1	4	2	2	—	—	—	—
365	15	75.0	5	2	—	2	—	—	1
TOT	1731	87.9	239	97	12	63	26	19	23

TABLE 6:4

[a] biface

[b] projectile point (Middle Woodland)

[c] tip use

[d] steep edge scraper

[e] unifacial scraper

[f] miscellaneous flint tools including graver/perforators, drills, and spokeshaves

Blades and Non-Blade Tools at Select Stubbs Cluster Sites.

(1994:113) argues that blades from ceremonial or mortuary context are more functionally specific (i.e., utilized in the production of craft items for the deceased), debris analysis from Stubbs Cluster sites supports at least partial domestic use of the corporate center. What is important to this examination is the range of precise tasks identified in the Murphy, Smiling Dan, and Napoleon Hollow site studies. Yerkes (1990) indicates that bladelets were utilized in both plant and animal food processing, hide preparation, and possibly some craft specialization involving the engraving or incising of stone, bone, and wooden artifacts. In essence then, bladelets may represent either a general purpose or functionally specific utilitarian tool in a highly standardized form.

BLADE AND NON-BLADE TOOLS AT HOPEWELL SITES

Both excavated and surface-collected Ohio Valley Middle Woodland sites typically yield relatively few traditionally recognized formal tool types (e.g., bifaces, projectile points, scrapers, graver/perforators, spokeshaves, and drills). Dancey (1991:52) reported a paucity of formal tool types at the Murphy site and noted similar frequencies of non-flake and non-blade tools at the McGraw site, where only 65 formal tools were identified from among nearly 2,000 lithic items (Pi-Sunyer 1965). And of nearly 27,000 fragments of lithic debris at the Jennison Guard site, only 79 non-blade formal tools were identified (Kozarek 1987). As expected from those observations, formal tool types at Stubbs Cluster sites comprise only minor percentages (4 percent and 4.2 percent of the total at 33WA256 and 362, respectively, and 12.8 percent at 33WA317) of the total lithic assemblage. It should be noted that the low recovery of lithic tools at the Stubbs Cluster is at least partially accounted for by the fact that the entire sample was surface collected. Amateur collection likely focused on the acquisition of complete projectile points, "late stage" bifaces, and drills. These items are notably lacking in the recovered assemblages. There is no evidence, however, to suggest that other tools, such as biface fragments and scrapers, were collected in like manner.

When one includes bladelets as a formal tool category, and it is argued here that bladelets do constitute a systematically manufactured tool, it can be demonstrated that bladelets comprise the majority formal tool type at Stubbs Cluster and other Ohio Valley Middle Woodland sites. At Stubbs, nine sites, each with 15 or more blades, were chosen for examination of blade and non-blade frequencies (Table 6:4). These include the three systematically collected sites and six other south subcluster debris scatters. In all cases, bladelets vastly outnumber non-blade tools. As a percentage of total formal tools, bladelets range from 72.5 percent at 33WA317 to as high as 96 percent at 33WA258. The mean percentage for all nine sites was calculated at 87.5 percent. To express the preponderance of bladelets in another fashion, more than five times as many blades as all other tool types combined were recovered from sites 33WA256 and 362. The ratio of bladelets to other formal tool types is as high as 23.7:1 at 33WA258.

Non-blade tools at Stubbs Cluster sites include bifaces, Middle Woodland projectile points, drills, steep-edge end-scrapers, unifacial scrapers, spokeshaves, graver/perforators, and additional tools exhibiting tip use. Bifaces were the most frequently encountered, but tools with tip use were collected in moderate numbers as well. The relatively low number of non-blade tools may actually be inflated, because, with the exception of the projectile points, none of these non-blade tools could definitely be assigned to the Middle Woodland period. It can be safely assumed, however, based upon the extremely low percentages of non-Hopewell artifacts at the sites, that many if not most of the tools originated during the Middle Woodland occupation.

Similar ratios of bladelets to non-blade tools are obtained at other Ohio Hopewell sites. At the Jennison Guard site, 58.6 percent of chipped stone tools are bladelets (Kozarek 1987); at Fort Ancient [Northeast], 85.7 percent of lithic tools are bladelets (Connolly 1991:Table 2); and at the McGraw site, bladelets comprise as many as 78.2 percent of the lithic tools (Pi-Sunyer 1965). A percentage of approximately 38 percent can be calculated for the Murphy site, but Dancey (1991:52,55) indicated that only two formal (non-bladelet) tools were recovered from Middle Woodland

context, and that many of the bifaces on the site may be discards from production failure. This bladelet dominance is not restricted to the Ohio Valley; McNerney (1987:83) indicated that bladelets make up 56 percent of the chipped stone tool assemblage at the Middle Woodland Consol site in southern Illinois.

CONCLUSIONS

These data clearly indicate that bladelets constitute the most frequently recovered tool type at Ohio Hopewell sites. This is not surprising in light of the fact that they were utilized for such a variety of cutting and scraping tasks. Edge-damage studies of bladelets from Stubbs Cluster sites illustrate that in addition to use and retouch along the lateral blade edges, both proximal and distal ends were frequently utilized and retouched as well. Tip use, notching, and possible hafting also have been identified. Bladelets therefore functioned as light duty knives (hafted and/or unhafted), scrapers (both steep edge and low angle), and possibly as graver/perforators and spokeshaves.

Yerkes (1990) and Odell (1985a) demonstrate that bladelets were utilized for a wide variety of tasks, a range that cannot be duplicated for any one of the non-blade formal tool types. It seems likely then, based upon the diverse use of bladelets and the frequencies of blade and non-blade tools at Middle Woodland sites, that bladelets were substituting for other tool types. This should not imply that bifacial reduction had ceased; there is considerable evidence that non-blade tools were being produced, and that blade and non-blade tools were being utilized for similar tasks (see Odell 1994:106-107). It is the multifuctionality of blades, and their ability to perform a variety of domestic or ritual tasks that allowed them to replace bifacial specimens and dominate the lithic tool assemblage. It can be argued, then, that during the Middle Woodland period, the blade industry provided the means of production of a standardized tool type that took the place of or obviated the use of a number of traditionally recognized formal tool categories. This may at least partially explain the low frequencies of non-blade tools at investigated Middle Woodland sites.

REFERENCES CITED

Baby, R. S., and S. M. Langlois 1979 Seip Mound State Memorial: Nonmortuary Aspects of Hopewell. In *Hopewell Archaeology: The Chillicothe Conference*, edited by D. S. Brose and N. Greber, pp. 16-18. Kent State University Press, Kent, Ohio.

Bennett, P. M. 1981 *Metric and Morphological Analysis of Selected Hopewell Blade Collections from Southwestern Ohio*. Report on file, Department of Anthropology, University of Cincinnati.

Bordaz, J. 1970 *Tools of the Old and New Stone Age*. American Museum of Natural History, The Natural History Press, Garden City, New York.

Carskadden, J. 1972 An Analysis of Blades from Three Hopewellian Sites in Muskingum County, Ohio. *Ohio Archaeologist* 22(2):8-10.

Carskadden, J. and J. Morton n.d. Living on the Edge: A Comparison of Adena and Hopewell Communities in the Central Muskingum of Eastern Ohio. In *Ohio Hopewell Community Organization*, edited by W. S. Dancey and P. J. Pacheco. Kent State University Press, Kent, Ohio "in press."

Chapman, J. 1973 *The Icehouse Bottom Site, 40MR23*. Department of Anthropology, Report of Investigations No. 13. University of Tennessee, Knoxville.

Connolly, R. P 1991 *Prehistoric Site Structure at the Fort Ancient State Memorial: New Evidence from Lithic Analysis*. Master's thesis, Department of Anthropology, University of Cincinnati.

Dancey, W. S. 1991 A Middle Woodland Settlement in Central Ohio: A Preliminary Report on the Murphy Site (33LI212). *Pennsylvania Archaeologist* 61(2):37-72.

Fischer, F. W. 1971 *Preliminary Report on the University of Cincinnati Archaeological Investigations at Miami Fort, 1970*. Report on file, Department of Anthropology, University of Cincinnati.

1974 *Early and Middle Woodland Settlement, Subsistence, and Population in the Central Ohio Valley*. Ph.D. dissertation, Department of Anthropology, Washington University, St. Louis. University Microfilms, Ann Arbor.

Ford, J. A. and C. H. Webb 1956 *Poverty Point, A Late Archaic Site in Louisiana*. Anthropological Papers 46(1). American Museum of Natural History, New York.

Ford, J. A., P. Phillips and W. D. Haag 1955 *The Jaketown Site in West-central Mississippi*. Anthropological Papers 45(1). American Museum of Natural History, New York.

Fowler, M. L. 1952 The Clear Lake Site: Hopewellian Occupation. In *Hopewellian Communities in Illinois*, edited by T. Deuel, pp.131-174. Illinois State Museum, Scientific Papers No. 5, Springfield, Illinois.

Genheimer, R. A. 1992 *Bladelets at the Stubbs Earthwork Cluster: An Examination of Middle Woodland Settlement in the Little Miami River Valley*. Master's thesis, Department of Anthropology, University of Cincinnati.

Greber, N. B., R. S. Davis and A. S. DuFresne 1981 The Micro Component of the Ohio Hopewell Lithic Technology: Bladelets. *Annals of the New York Academy of Sciences* 376:489-528.

Griffin, J. B., R. E. Flanders and P. F. Titterington 1970 *The Burial Complexes of the Knight and Norton Mounds in Illinois and Michigan*. Museum of Anthropology, Memoirs No. 2, University of Michigan, Ann Arbor.

Hofman, J. L. 1987 Hopewell Blades from Twenhafel: Distinguishing Local and Foreign Core Technology. In *The Organization of Core Technology*, edited by J. K. Johnson and C. A. Morrow, pp. 87-117. Westview Press, Boulder, Colorado.

Keeley, L. H. 1978 Microwear Polishes on Flint: Some Experimental Results. In *Lithics and Subsistence: The Analysis of Stone Tool Use in Prehistoric Economies*, edited by D. D. Davis, pp. 163-178. Vanderbilt University Publications in Anthropology, No. 20, Nashville, Tennessee.

Kellar, J. H. 1979 The Mann Site and "Hopewell" in the Lower Wabash-Ohio Valley. In *Hopewell Archaeology: The Chillicothe Conference*, edited by D. S. Brose and N. Greber, pp. 100-107. Kent State University Press, Kent, Ohio.

Kozarek, S. E. 1987 *A Hopewellian Homestead in the Ohio River Valley*. Masters thesis, Department of Anthropology, University of Cincinnati.

McGregor, J. C. 1952 The Havana Site. In *Hopewellian Communities in Illinois*, edited by T. Deuel, pp.43-91. Illinois State Museum, Scientific Papers No. 5, Springfield, Illinois.

1958 *The Pool and Irving Villages: A Study of Hopewell Occupation in the Illinois River Valley*. University of Illinois Press, Urbana, Illinois.

McNerney, M. J. 1987 Crab Orchard Core Technology at the Consol Site, Jackson County, Illinois. In *The Organization of Core Technology*, edited by J. K. Johnson and C. A. Morrow, pp. 63-85. Westview Press, Boulder, Colorado.

Mills, W. C. 1906 Explorations of the Baum Prehistoric Village Site. *Ohio Archaeological and Historical Publications* 15:45-136.

1907 Explorations of the Edwin Harness Mound. *Ohio Archaeological and Historical Publications* 16:113-193.

1921 Flint Ridge. *Ohio Archaeological and Historical Publications* 30:90-161.

Montet-White, A. 1968 *Lithic Industries of the Illinois Valley in the Early and Middle Woodland Period*. Museum of Anthropology, Anthropological Papers No. 35, University of Michigan, Ann Arbor, Michigan.

Morrow, C. A. 1987 Blades and Cobden Chert: A Technological Argument for the Role as Markers of Regional Identification During the Hopewell Period in Illinois. In *The Organization of Core Technology*, edited by J. K. Johnson and C. A. Morrow, pp. 119-149. Westview Press, Boulder, Colorado.

Neumann, G. K. and M. L. Fowler 1952 Hopewellian Sites in the Wabash Valley. In *Hopewellian Communities in Illinois*, edited by T. Deuel, pp.175-248. Illinois State Museum, Scientific Papers No. 5, Springfield, Illinois.

Odell, G. H. 1985a Microwear Analysis of Middle Woodland Lithics. In *Smiling Dan: Structure and Function at a Middle Woodland Settlement in the Illinois Valley*, edited by B. D. Stafford and M. B. Sant, pp. 298-326. Kampsville Archeological Center, Research Series, Vol. 2, Center for American Archaeology, Kampsville, Illinois.

1985b Small Sites Archaeology and Use-Wear on Surface-Collected Artifacts. *Midcontinental Journal of Archaeology* 10(1):21-48.

1994 The Role of Stone Bladelets in Middle Woodland Society. *American Antiquity* 59(1):102-120.

Pacheco, P. J. 1993 *Ohio Hopewell Settlement Patterns: An Application of the Vacant Center Model to Middle Woodland Period Intracommunity Settlement Variability in the Upper Licking River Valley*. Ph.D. dissertation, Department of Anthropology, The Ohio State University, Columbus. University Microfilms, Ann Arbor.

Pacheco, P. J., and W. H. Pickard 1992 A Laterally Hafted Ohio Hopewell Bladelet From Dow Chemical #2 (33LI302). *Ohio Archaeologist* 42(2):13-15.

Pi-Sunyer, Oriol 1965 The Flint Industry. In *The McGraw Site: A Study in Hopewellian Dynamics*, edited by O. H. Prufer, pp. 60-89. Cleveland Museum of Natural History, Scientific Publications 4(1), Cleveland.

Potter, M. A. 1968 *Ohio's Prehistoric People*. The Ohio Historical Society, Columbus.

Semenov, S. A. 1973 *Prehistoric Technology: An Experimental Study of the Oldest Tools and Artefacts from Traces of Manufacture and Wear.* Translated, and with a preface by M. W. Thompson. Harper and Row, New York.

Struever, S. 1968 Woodland Subsistence-Settlement Systems in the Lower Illinois Valley. In *New Perspectives in Archeology*, edited by S. R. Binford and L. R. Binford, pp.285-312. University of New Mexico, Aldine Publishing Company, Chicago.

White, A. M. 1963 Analytical Description of the Chipped-stone Industry from Snyders Site, Calhoun County, Illinois. In *Miscellaneous Studies in Typology and Classification*, edited by A. M. White, L. R. Binford, and M. L. Papworth, pp. 1-70. Museum of Anthropology, Anthropological Papers No. 19, University of Michigan, Ann Arbor, Michigan.

Whittlesey, C. 1851 *Descriptions of Ancient Works in Ohio.* Smithsonian Contributions to Knowledge 3(7). Washington, D. C.

Willoughby, C. C., and E. A. Hooton 1922 The Turner Group of Earthworks, Hamilton County, Ohio. *Papers of the Peabody Museum* 8(3).

Witthoft, J. 1952 A Paleo-Indian Site in Eastern Pennsylvania: An Early Hunting Culture. *Proceedings of the American Philosophical Society* 96(4):464-495.

1957 The Art of Flint Chipping: The Human Factor in Flint Technology. *Ohio Archaeologist* 7(1):17-20, 35.

Yerkes, R. W. 1990 Using Microwear Analysis to Investigate Domestic Activities and Craft Specialization at the Murphy Site, a Small Hopewell Settlement in Licking County, Ohio. In *The Interpretative Possibilities of Microwear Studies*, edited by B. Graslund, H. Knutsson, K. Knutsson, and J. Taffinder, pp. 167-176. Aun 14, Societas Archaeologica Upsaliensis, Uppsala, Sweden.

SEVEN

FLINT RAW MATERIAL USE IN
OHIO HOPEWELL

KENT D. VICKERY

ABSTRACT

Two Hopewell sites each in the Scioto, Great Miami, and Little
Miami Valleys in Ohio and Indiana are compared with respect
to the occurrence and relative abundance of different varieties of
flint. Presented and evaluated for their pertinence to these
assemblages are four models: the "political," in which flint and
other raw materials were received as tribute; the "ceremonial,"
in which flint was brought to various sites and deposited as offerings while perhaps being used in ceremonies and ritual observances; the "economic," in which flint was acquired as part of a
"procurement strategy" embedded in a Hopewell Interaction
Sphere, and the "social," in which flint was serendipitously transported by groups traveling to and from Hopewell villages and
centers. Implications for cultural complexity based on a comparison of these models are explored.

A View From the Core a Synthesis of Ohio Hopewell Archaeology•edited by Paul J. Pacheco
© Copyright 1996 by The Ohio Archaeological Council• Columbus, Ohio
All Rights Reserved•ISBN 0-9626931-9-7

KENT D. VICKERY

FLINT RAW MATERIAL USE IN OHIO HOPEWELL

INTRODUCTION

This study examines varieties of flint from six Hopewell sites in Ohio and Indiana (**see Figure 7:1 for locations of sites and flint variety source areas**) and compares them with respect to the utilization of this raw material. The six collections represent samples of much larger assemblages of flint artifacts and debris from each of the sites—two in the Scioto Valley, two in the Little Miami Valley, and two in the Great Miami Valley.

While numerous aspects of the analysis could be pursued, this study focuses on kinds and relative abundances of currently identifiable flint varieties present at each site, then attempts to account for how the material reached them. This attempt considers various models that bear on broader issues of social interaction and cultural complexity.

THE DATA

The Scioto Valley Hopewell sites selected for this study are the Mound City Group (Mills 1922), 33RO32, and the Edwin Harness Mound, 33RO22, and vicinity (Greber 1977, 1983; Greber et al. 1981; Mills 1907), both in Ross County, Ohio. Both collections were examined by Vickery (1983a, 1983b). Mound City is a ceremonial complex consisting of 23 mounds surrounded by an earthwork and a series of borrow pits enclosing 5.26 ha (13 acres) on a high terrace adjacent to and west of the Scioto River near present-day Chillicothe. The embankment assumes the form of a square with rounded corners. The sample from Mound City consists of 860 items gained from the 1963-1964 excavations by James Brown, Raymond Baby, and Richard Faust (Brown and Baby 1966). A total of 709 items is reported on in the present paper, which excludes questionable identifications.

The Edwin Harness Mound is part of a ceremonial earthwork and mound complex—the Harness or Liberty Group—consisting of a square, one large and one small circle, and 14 mounds encompassing ca. 40.47 ha (100 acres) on a terrace overlooking the Scioto River. The sample consists of

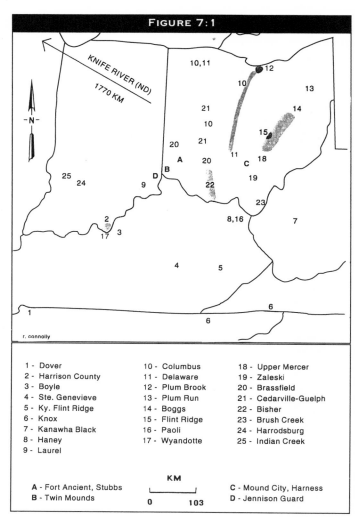

Locations of Hopewell sites and flint variety source areas.

127 items recovered during the 1976 field season of excavation at the Edwin Harness Mound, 1,180 bladelets and bladelet cores surface collected by Robert Harness in the vicinity of the mound, and surface collections including artifacts and debitage from Robert Harness' Sites 18 and 25 in the mound vicinity, consisting of 627 and 720 items, respectively. Questionable identifications were eliminated from the total of 2,654 items, yielding a sample of 2,643.

The Little Miami Valley Hopewell sites whose flint assemblages were selected for examination are Fort Ancient (Connolly 1991; Essenpreis and Moseley 1984; Moorehead 1890, 1908), 33WA2, and three sites of the Stubbs Earthwork National Register District: the 5.26 ha (13 acre) Stubbs Mill Blade site, 33WA256, the 1.35 ha (3.35 acre) Hayner #3 site, 33WA317, and the .745 ha (1.84 acre) Smith site, 33WA362 (Genheimer 1984, 1992). All are located in Warren County in southwestern Ohio.

Fort Ancient is a hilltop enclosure encompassing 51 ha (126 acres) at the edge of an escarpment 80 m above the Little Miami River. Enclosing civic/ceremonial space are 5.7 km of embankment walls roughly assuming the form of a figure eight with 72 openings. Two conical mounds were located just outside the northeast section (Connolly 1991). The sample of 637 items (604 of which are reported on in the present paper) was submitted to the writer by Pat Essenpreis, who surface collected and excavated it in 1985. The Stubbs Earthwork sites are habitation loci with evidence of workshop activity perhaps associated with a nearby earthwork ceremonial complex. They are located on both sides of the Little Miami River on alluvial flood plain deposits and elevated outwash terraces (Genheimer 1984). The sample of 2,936 items from all three sites was analyzed by Genheimer (1984, 1992).

The Great Miami Valley Hopewell sites used for this study are the Twin Mounds Village (Bennett 1986; Fischer 1974; Kaltenthaler 1992), 33HA24-WHA, in Hamilton County, Ohio, in the extreme southwest corner of the state, and the Jennison Guard site (Blosser 1986; Kozarek 1987; Whitacre 1986), 12D29s (or 12D246 [DeRegnaucourt and Whitacre 1993]) in Dearborn County, Indiana. Both are multi-component sites with adjacent Late Archaic and Fort Ancient occupations, respectively. The site designations 33HA24-WHA ("Western Habitation Area") and 12D29s ("South") have been adopted in an effort to specifically identify the Hopewell components of each.

The Twin Mounds Village is a habitation site with at least one house located on a ridgetop, approximately 62 m above the valley floor and the present-day confluences of the Whitewater and Great Miami Rivers and of the Great Miami and Ohio Rivers. This .56 ha (1.38 acre) site is in proximity to two burial mounds of demonstrable Hopewell affiliation, conjoined at their bases—the "Twin Mounds" (Bennett 1986). The Twin Mounds sample of 3,501 items was analyzed by Kaltenthaler (1992).

The Jennison Guard site is situated on the flood plain of the Ohio River west of its confluence with the Great Miami River. Its surface exposed area is ca. .85 ha (2.1 acres); however, a portion of the site is buried under alluvial deposits and its total extent has yet to be determined (Blosser 1986:29-30). It is a habitation site with evidence of workshop activity in at least mica and Harrison County flint. The data on the Jennison Guard collection derive primarily from Kozarek (1987), supplemented by observations from Blosser (1986) and Whitacre and Whitacre (1986). The combined Jennison Guard sample consists of 21,587 items.

The data base is thus comprised of 31,980 flint specimens from the six Hopewell sites selected for comparison. It should be emphasized that this is a small sample that includes many items unidentified as to flint variety. Flint raw material identification is a dynamic undertaking requiring reexamination of previously analyzed collections as the discovery of new sources of flint proceeds and samples for comparative purposes are made available to researchers. However, some (perhaps much) of the flint raw material occurring in Midwestern archaeological contexts was transported by natural means, such as glacial and stream action, and redeposited some distance away from its areas of outcrop. Such redeposited material became locally available in gravel deposits and along stream banks; hence, efforts to source it are irrelevant to the investigation of intentional human transport. It is recognized by hard, often glossy cortex or cortical remnants on knapped specimens. Although completely decorticated items are ambiguous, soft cortex would not have withstood the abuses of glaciers and streams, and must have been obtained from, or very near, their area(s) of outcrop by human agency, then perhaps transported some distance away to become part of an archaeological assemblage.

METHODS

Each of the collections was analyzed somewhat differently. Common to all was the 10X binocular examination of archaeological specimens and their comparison with samples from known and documented outcrops in order to effect an identification on visual grounds alone. Access to such comparative collections, however, varied from researcher to researcher, perhaps resulting in the non-representation of certain varieties at sites where they likely occurred.

If careful observations are made when analyzing a collection and records kept as to the characteristics of unidentified varieties that nevertheless recur in the flint assemblage, it may be possible to "identify" them after the fact when documented comparative specimens become available. It was in this fashion that the writer was able to track Knox flint in the Mound City and Harness assemblages and a subvariety of Haney flint at Fort Ancient. No comparative samples of either were available to the author when the analyses were undertaken. By the same token, Kaltenthaler (1992, Table 3) was able to confirm the presence of Knox in the Twin Mounds collection after personally examining comparative specimens following completion of her analysis.

In most of these studies, a division of the respective collections into artifacts, debitage, and bladelets was undertaken, the latter including bladelet cores, "bladelet-like" flakes, and any other items judged to have been related to a bladelet industry. No flint artifacts were included in the Stubbs and Jennison Guard analyses while Kaltenthaler included some bladelet-like flakes in debitage, relegated retouched flakes to artifacts rather than debitage, and did not segregate bladelet cores from bipolar, flake, and unclassified cores.

A key to the identification of the varieties of flint represented in the samples is offered in an Appendix. Modeled after those in common use in biology, the key presents the user with opposed pairs of statements or combinations of distinctly different traits that lead to other such sets in the key until an identification is achieved.

The first major division is fossiliferous versus non-fossiliferous flint. Some varieties, however, have subvarieties with and without fossils (e.g., Plum Brook) or have such low fossil densities that any particular archaeological specimen may lack them (e.g., Knox, Laurel). These are present in both major divisions of the key. By the same token, some varieties have banded and non-banded subvarieties (Bisher, Knox, Laurel, Paoli) while one (Kentucky Flint Ridge) occurs as either medium or coarse grained material, the latter having been the most abundantly represented in the samples. Similarly, Zaleski is presented in the key under both white inclusions present and absent. Most archaeological specimens lacked them or had so few that they were confidently distinguished from Upper Mercer, the flint variety that Zaleski most closely resembles, but which has more white inclusions.

While all of the flint varieties identified in the samples are documented in the geological literature, the particular specimens used for comparative purposes were obtained from a limited number of outcrops; hence, it is doubtful they represent the range of variation actually present in prehistorically accessible exposures in the entire area of their occurrence. It is for this reason that archaeological specimens may be present in collections whose characteristics do not correspond with the descriptions in the Appendix, even though geologically referable to some or all of these varieties. Particularly small specimens (e.g., microdebitage) may pose identification problems in lacking some characteristic(s) visible only in larger pieces; for example, banding where bands tend to be widely spaced or fossils where fossil density is low.

Color was not often sufficiently uniform within a particular variety to reliably serve as a basis for initiating pathways in the key. Nevertheless, color plates of some of the flint varieties present in the samples may be found in Converse (1994), where Brush Creek is represented as "Crooksville"; Brassfield as "Brush Creek"; Cedarville- Guelph as "Logan County"; Plum Brook as "Pipe Creek," and Upper Mercer as "Coshocton" and "Nellie," and in Fogelman (1983). While a literature search of archaeological and geological references to the identified varieties is beyond the scope of the present paper, photomicrographs of several may be found in Stout and Schoenlaub (1945) and Vento (1982), the latter of whom also provides petrographic descriptions. Stout and Schoenlaub (1945) and Luedtke (1992) also may be consulted for chemical analyses of several flint varieties while Stout and Schoenlaub (1945) and Carlson (1991) give specific locations of outcrops in Ohio.

Butler and May (1984), Vehik (1985), and Luedtke (1978, 1979, 1992) may be consulted for various sourcing techniques that include neutron activation analysis, thin section petrography, and scanning electron microscopy. Approaches such as these are often designed to yield "signature" trace element and other chemical/mineralogical compositions of samples. Although destructive in varying degrees, they potentially offer promise of more accurate identifications than those achieved in the present study.

RESULTS

A total of 26 distinct varieties of flint from six states is represented among the six Ohio Hopewell sites in the Scioto, Little Miami, and Great Miami River Valleys **(see Table 7:1)**. Outcropping in Indiana are Harrison County, Harrodsburg, Indian Creek, Laurel, and Wyandotte; in Kentucky are Boyle, Haney, Kentucky Flint Ridge, Paoli, and Ste. Genevieve; in North Dakota, Knife River; in Kentucky and Ohio, Brassfield; in Ohio, Bisher, Boggs, Brush Creek, Cedarville-Guelph, Columbus, Delaware, Flint Ridge, Plum Brook, Plum Run, Upper Mercer, and Zaleski; in Tennessee, Dover and Knox, and in West Virginia, Kanawha Black. No flint varieties known to outcrop in Illinois were identified in the samples; however, numerous burned fragments of blades identified as Burlington flint are reported by Holzapfel (1994) in a deposit near the Harness Earthworks and DeRegnaucourt and Whitacre (1993) identified a biface from Jennison Guard as Burlington/Crescent flint. The latter also report one biface of Plum Run flint, as well as eight bifaces and two "quarry blanks" of Harrison County flint from Jennison Guard.

Very few varieties of flint occur at all six sites. Among the 26, only Harrison County, Flint Ridge and Upper Mercer are represented in all collections, while only Stubbs lacks Delaware and Cedarville-Guelph in the samples examined. Unique to Twin Mounds are Laurel, Indian Creek, Harrodsburg, and Wyandotte, all of which occur at varying distances to the west of the site in Indiana.

In the Scioto Valley, the Mound City and Harness sites are somewhat similar with respect to the flint varieties present in the collections. For example, essentially "local" flint raw material that could have been obtained short distances away or in the immediate vicinity of the earthwork complexes is present at both, while most of the non-local, "exotic" varieties that are a virtual hallmark of Hopewell also occur at both sites. They include Harrison County, Knife River, Knox, and Plum Run. The most striking difference between Mound City and Harness is the abundance of Harrison County at the former—where it accounts for more than 30 percent of the sample—in comparison to Harness, where only two items of this distinctive southern Indiana flint were found. By contrast, nearly 25 percent of the Harness collection was comprised of Flint Ridge flint while this variety accounted for only 7 percent of the Mound City sample. Mound City also had a greater variety of different kinds of flint, including Ste. Genevieve, Boyle, and Kentucky Flint Ridge from Kentucky and one biface of Dover from Tennessee. The Harness sample is unrepresented by any Kentucky varieties and lacks Dover. There seems to have been a stronger southern and southeastern "connection" at Mound City than at Harness and the abundance of Harrison County flint so far away from its source area is remarkable.

The Little Miami River sites of Fort Ancient and Stubbs are somewhat similar both to each other and to the Scioto River sites, with Harrison County and Flint Ridge dominating both assemblages. More than one-third of the Stubbs sample is comprised of Harrison County flint. The only other identified varieties to exceed one percent of the total are Upper Mercer and Knox at Stubbs and Haney at Fort Ancient. The 46 pieces of Haney flint were not identified as such when

TABLE 7:1																
SITE	MOUND CITY								HARNESS							
FLINT VARIETY	DEBITAGE		ARTIFACT		BLADES		TOTAL		DEBITAGE		ARTIFACT		BLADES		TOTAL	
	N	%	N	%	N	%	N	%	N	%	N	%	N	%	N	%
Harrison County *	91	21.4	11	20	107	46.7	209	29.45		.07			1	.084	2	.076
Flint Ridge	31	7.29	5	9.09	12	5.24	48	6.77	1,162	81.8	7	21.21	1,121	94.2	2,290	86.6
Laurel																
Delaware	55	12.94	8	14.54	19	8.29	82	11.56	26	1.83	5	15.15	22	1.85	53	2.01
Cedarville-Guelph	30	7.06	2	3.64			32	4.51	4	.28	1	3.03			5	.19
Knox	12	2.82	1	1.82	22	9.61	35	4.94	16	1.13			1	.08	17	.64
Upper Mercer	11	2.59	4	7.27	4	1.75	19	2.68	5	.35	2	6.06	1	.08	8	.30
Ste. Genevieve	17	4.0	1	1.81	4	1.75	22	3.10								
Boyle					2	.87	2	.28								
Brassfield									2	.14					2	.08
Brush Creek	18	4.24	2	3.64	2	.87	22	3.10	16	1.13	3	9.09	2	.168	21	.80
Haney																
Zaleski	4	.94	2	3.64	1	.44	7	.80	9	.63	2	6.06	2	.17	13	.49
Knife River	5	1			4	1.75	9	1.27	3	.21					3	.11
Bisher	2	.47					2	.28	1	.07	1	3.03			2	.08
KY Flint Ridge	1	.24					1	.14								
Paoli																
Columbus									3	.21					3	.11
Indian Creek																
Plum Run	1	.24	1	1.82			2	.28	1	.07					1	.04
Plum Brook									1	.07	1	3.03			2	.08
Boggs	1	.24					1	.14								
Harrodsburg																
Dover			1	1.82			1	.14								
Kanawha Black									1	.07					1	.04
Wyandotte *																
Unknown	146	34.35	17	30.91	52	22.7	215	30.32	169	11.90	11	33.33	40	3.36	220	8.32
Combined Total	425	100	55	100	229	100	709	100	1,420	100	33	100	1190	100	2,643	100

Frequency Distribution of Flint Varieties Among Hopewell Sites.

SITE	FORT ANCIENT								STUBBS					
TABLE 7:1 CONTINUED														
FLINT VARIETY	DEBITAGE		ARTIFACT		BLADES		TOTAL		DEBITAGE		BLADES		TOTAL	
	N	%	N	%	N	%	N	%	N	%	N	%	N	%
Harrison County *	58	12.98	1	10	22	14.97	81	13.41	827	32.28	160	42.78	987	33.62
Flint Ridge	72	16.11	2	20	33	22.45	107	17.72	303	11.83	86	22.96	389	13.25
Laurel														
Delaware			1	10			1	.17						
Cedarville-Guelph	3	.67	1	10			4	.66						
Knox	4	.90			1	.68	5	.83			65	17.38	65	2.21
Upper Mercer	1	.22					1	.17	46	1.80	4	1.07	50	1.70
Ste. Genevieve			1	10	2	1.36	3	.50						
Boyle											1	.27	1	.03
Brassfield														
Brush Creek	2	.45					2	.33						
Haney	23	5.15			23	15.67	46	7.62						
Zaleski	1	.22					1	.17						
Knife River					1	.68	1	.17	2	.08	1	.27	3	.10
Bisher														
KY Flint Ridge									1	.31			1	.03
Paoli									2	.08			2	.07
Columbus														
Indian Creek														
Plum Run	1	.22					1	.17						
Plum Brook														
Boggs														
Harrodsburg														
Dover			1	10			1	.17						
Kanawha Black									1	.04			1	.03
Wyandotte *														
Unknown	282	63.09	3	30	65	44.22	350	57.95	1,380	53.86	57	15.24	1,437	48.94
Combined Total	447	100	10	100	147	100	604	100	2,562	100	374	100	2,936	100

Frequency Distribution of Flint Varieties Among Hopewell Sites.

TABLE 7:1 CONTINUED

SITE	JENNISON GUARD						TWIN MOUNDS								TOTAL ALL SITES	
FLINT VARIETY	DEBITAGE		BLADES		TOTAL		DEBITAGE		ARTIFACTS		BLADES		TOTAL			
	N	%	N	%	N	%	N	%	N	%	N	%	N	%	N	%
Harrison County *	19,290	90.35	91	38.40	19,381	89.78	1,138	38.09	88	33.98	34	13.39	1,260	35.39	21,920	68.54
Flint Ridge	17	.08	133	56.12	150	.70	14	.47			2	.79	16	.46	3,000	9.38
Laurel	90	.42			90	.42	520	17.40	53	20.46	79	31.10	652	18.62	742	2.32
Delaware	35	.16			35	.16	63	2.11	4	1.54	1	.39	68	1.94	239	.75
Cedarville-Guelph	4	.02			4	.02	97	3.25	7	2.70	6	2.36	110	3.14	155	.49
Knox							2	.07					2	.06	124	.39
Upper Mercer			1	.42	1	.01					1	.39	1	.03	80	.25
Ste. Genevieve	2	.01			2	.01	21	.70	7	2.70	5	1.97	33	.94	60	.19
Boyle							50	1.67	6	2.32	1	.39	57	1.63	60	.19
Brassfield							53	1.77	2	.77	1	.39	56	1.6	58	.18
Brush Creek	2	.01			2	.01	8	.27					8	.23	55	.17
Haney															46	.14
Zaleski															21	.07
Knife River															16	.05
Bisher	3	.01			3	.01	7	.23	1	.39			8	.23	15	.05
KY Flint Ridge							10	.34			1	.39	11	.31	13	.04
Paoli	1	.01			1	.01	2	.07	1	.39			3	.09	6	.02
Columbus							3	.10					3	.09	6	.02
Indian Creek							5	.17					5	.14	5	.02
Plum Run															4	.01
Plum Brook															2	.01
Boggs									1	.39			1	.03	2	.01
Harrodsburg							2	.07					2	.06	2	.01
Dover															2	.01
Kanawha Black															2	.01
Wyandotte *							1	.03					1	.03	1	.003
Unknown	1,906	8.93	12	5.06	1,918	8.89	992	33.20	88	34.36	120	48.43	1,204	34.39	5,344	16.7
Combined Total	21,350	100	237	100	21,587	100	2,602	100	259	100	254	100	3,501	100	31,980	100

*Wyandotte and Harrison County flint are distinguishable. The former is very dark gray, not mottled microscopically, does not weather to a lighter color, and contains micrite (Kenneth B. Tankersley, personal communication). Harrison County flint is light blue-gray, mottled microscopically, weathers to a lighter color and lacks micrite inclusions.

the Fort Ancient analysis was undertaken; rather, they were part of a bewildering array of unknown flint, doubtless exotic to the area, that was nevertheless represented by many items in the collection resulting in the identification of fewer than half of the total specimens. This particular "subvariety" of Haney is now known to have come from the Upper Newman Formation and outcrops in Box/Echo Canyon in Carter County, Kentucky, where ongoing research by Matt Maley (personal communication, 1995) has resulted in the identification of more than 40 different flint varieties or subvarieties in a small area with a very complex lithology. Yet to be determined is the assignment of "Carter County" or "Carter Cave" flint (Converse 1992, 1994:188-189; Fowke 1928) to Haney (Upper Newman) or Paoli (Lower Newman), the latter of which is known to outcrop only 200 m away from Carter Caves State Park (Matt Maley, personal communication, 1995), presumably the locale for which the variety was named. The Knife River bladelet from Fort Ancient was not present in the sample examined; rather, it was observed in a collection curated at the Ohio Historical Center and was probably found in 1939.

In the Great Miami Valley, the Jennison Guard and Twin Mounds sites are heavily dominated by Harrison County flint, which accounts for 35 percent of the Twin Mounds collection and nearly 90 percent of the Jennison Guard sample. Flint Ridge is correspondingly low, comprising less than 1 percent of the total at both sites. At Jennison Guard, no flint variety apart from Harrison County comprises even 1 percent of the total while Twin Mounds has the greatest number of flint varieties among the six sites, five of which—apart from Harrison County—exceed 1 percent of the total. Accounting for 18 percent of the total is Laurel, which occurs such a short distance away to the west that it can be considered local. Delaware and Cedarville-Guelph were locally available as glacial- or stream-deposited material from the north and east. Boyle is one of the very few Kentucky flint varieties to be present at any site in quantities greater than 1 percent while Brassfield outcrops both to the north and east of the Twin Mounds Village.

With respect to flint raw material representation, the Great Miami River sites seem to be similar to each other while both are more dissimilar to the Little Miami and Scioto River sites than the Little Miami and Scioto River sites are to each other. Likely, this is due at least in part to their proximity to the Ohio River and the role that this corridor of movement of raw materials, goods, and people doubtless played. Nevertheless, Jennison Guard and Stubbs appear to have been functionally similar in exhibiting specialized activities that included mica working at both, the reduction of Harrison County flint at Jennison Guard, and bladelet production at Stubbs. No such "household industries" are evident at Twin Mounds, where the assemblage is dominated by domestic/habitation activities.

Noteworthy is a striking difference between the flint assemblages of the Great Miami River Hopewell sites and those of at least Late Archaic sites in the southwestern Ohio/southeastern Indiana/northern Kentucky region. In the latter region many of the exotic varieties are absent while Kentucky varieties are heavily represented. These include St. Louis, which is unrepresented by even a single positive identification in the nearly 32,000 pieces of flint from the six Hopewell sites; Kentucky Flint Ridge, which is represented by only two pieces of debitage in the Scioto and Little Miami Valley sites, and Paoli, which is represented by only six items at three sites that do not include either Mound City or Harness. Even though the particular flint varieties vary somewhat from site to site, Ohio Hopewell flint raw material assemblages appear to be rather distinctive in comparison to those of other culture periods.

A surprising number of different flint varieties could have found their way into the areas where the six Ohio Hopewell sites are located by natural agencies that include glaciers and ancient and modern rivers. Near the Great Miami River Valley, for example, the northward flowing Kentucky Licking River cuts through outcrops of several varieties to the south and deposits them at its confluence with the Ohio where they become available in stream beds and gravel bars locally and downriver. Similarly, glaciers and southward flowing rivers and streams have brought flint that outcrops

	TABLE 7:2									
Collecting Locale	Scioto River		Mound City		Harness		Little Miami River		Licking River	
Flint Variety	N	%	N	%	N	%	N	%	N	%
Delaware	46	46	22	53.66	8	14.81	2	7.69		
Delaware?			3	7.32			1	3.85		
Cedar-Guelph	8	8	4	9.38	4	7.34	2	7.69		
Cedar-Guelph?			1	2.44						
Bisher	3	3								
Columbus	1	1					1	3.85		
Brassfield	1	1								
Upper Mercer	1	1								
Brush Creek			1	2.44	2	3.70				
Brush Creek?							1	3.85		
Plum Brook							1	3.85		
Boyle									102	25.56
Paoli									25	6.27
St. Louis									7	1.75
KY Flint Ridge									2	.50
Haney									1	.25
Unknown	40	40	10	10	40	74.07	18	69.23	262	65.66
Total	100	100	41	100	54	100	26	100	399	100

Non-Artifactual Flint Pebbles from Rivers and Sites.

far to the north and northeast into the area directly or into the Ohio River upstream from the Great Miami Valley, to which it is carried by the Ohio. The Ohio River itself has been responsible for the redeposition of flint varieties outcropping far to the east, including Kanawha Black. To the north and northeast of the southwestern Ohio tri-state region—in both the Little Miami and Scioto drainages—varieties such as Brush Creek, Zaleski and Kanawha Black may have been carried into the area by the ancient westward and northward flowing Teays River.

It is for these reasons that caution must be exercised in regarding many flint varieties as humanly-transported "exotic" material. Collecting unmodified flint pebbles and cobbles aids the archaeologist in gaining an understanding of which flint varieties can occur locally and recording cortical remnants on archaeological specimens as either hard or soft may serve as a basis for distinguishing redeposited from outcrop material.

Presented in **Table 7:2** are the results of flint pebble/cobble collecting activities at gravel bars on the Scioto and Kentucky Licking Rivers, the latter near its confluence with the Ohio River and therefore contributing pebble/cobble flint for

TABLE 7:3							
Site Origin	Mound City	Harness	Fort Ancient	Jennison Guard	Stubbs	Twin Mounds	Total
Unknown-Not necessarily exotic	95	63	74	965		1,193	2,390
Unknown exotic	59		206	953		11	1,229
Unknown exotic?	61	157	70				288
Total Unknown	215	220	350	1,918	1,437	1,204	5,344
% of Site Totals	30.32	8.33	57.95	8.88	48.94	34.39	28.93

Presumed Origin of Unidentified Flint from Hopewell Sites.

potential exploitation on the part of the Twin Mounds and Jennison Guard site inhabitants. Also identified are flint varieties from a similar collection along the Little Miami River near Fort Ancient and unmodified pebbles from the Mound City and Harness excavations and surface collections.

The representation of unidentified flint varies from more than 8 percent at Harness and Jennison Guard to nearly 58 percent at Fort Ancient. An effort was made to judge, on admittedly subjective grounds, the exotic versus local origin of flint of unknown varieties for several of the collections. Treating Kozarek's (1987) "Unknown I" and "Unknown II" as exotic and her "Unknown" as not necessarily exotic, these results are presented in **Table 7:3,** based on a total sample of 9,251 specimens.

Flint that outcrops to the west of any of the Ohio Hopewell sites treated in this study cannot have been brought into the area by a natural agency. Its presence in archaeological contexts represents intentional procurement and transportation.

INTERPRETIVE MODELS

Data have been presented relating to the occurrence of different kinds of flint in various proportions at each of six Ohio Hopewell sites selected for such an examination. The data will now be transcended in an effort to account for how the flint got to the various sites in which we find it in archaeological contexts.

Various models may be found in the literature on Hopewell archaeology that implicitly or explicitly account for such transportation and ultimate deposition. Four such models will be explored. The first may be labeled the "political" model. It assumes that flint as raw material and finished products was received as "tribute" by chiefs at the major Ohio Hopewell centers with the authority—if not the power—to demand that these goods be brought to them to dispose of as they pleased. In recognizing that "political leaders" in Ohio Hopewell society played an important role in acquiring flint and perhaps other exotica, this "coercive" model assumes the highest level of cultural complexity among the four.

The second model may be called the "economic" one. It views exotic flint as having "circulated" in a Hopewell Interaction Sphere (Seeman 1979; Struever 1964; Struever and Houart 1972). This model also assumes a rather complex society in which chiefs—in "big man" fashion—exercised control over what came into the major centers and what left them by having made arrangements and agreements in advance as to what goods and/or services would be exchanged. The possibility of gift giving and/or a form of "potlatch" among important personages involving flint and likely other raw materials and finished artifacts may also be attributed to this "economic" model.

A third model is the "ceremonial" one. It assumes that flint as raw material and/or finished objects was brought to the major centers and deposited as "offerings" or entered one or more ritual contexts where it was used in various ceremonies. While this model does not necessarily presuppose a chiefdom-level society, it does assume great reverence in which recently departed ancestors were held, thereby implying relatively high social standing for those few with whom non-local flint and other exotica were deposited on the occasion of their death.

Yet a fourth model may be labeled the "social" one. It assumes the least cultural complexity in recognizing that flint may have been brought to the major Ohio Hopewell centers as a strictly voluntary undertaking. Resident earthwork complex/ceremonial center "overseers"—who were not necessarily chiefs—did not know in advance who was going to show up when, bringing what exotica, craft products, food and other items to be exchanged, given away, etc. The social model has been the most neglected, yet the flint raw material data suggest that it merits more serious consideration than it has heretofore received. Accordingly, this model is pursued by presenting a scenario based on ideas initially expressed by James Brown (personal communication, 1981). Flint at the various Ohio Hopewell sites will then be returned to, to explore how well its occurrence fits with this and other models.

On the basis of her study of various sites, Greber (1976) concluded that Ohio Hopewell social organization featured, at perhaps each major center, a "dominant group" of co-residing, collaborating people with claims to a traditional (i.e., hereditary) hold over an area. They were doubtfully chiefs because, as Brown has pointed out, instances of multiple status burials at Hopewell, Mound City and Seip are those of individuals believed to have been contemporaries. For example, 7,000 plus discs of Harrison County flint (Greber and Ruhl 1989:69-70) recovered by Moorehead (1922) from Mound 2 of the Hopewell Group were surrounded by five burials. Several hundred pounds of obsidian debitage were deposited in a grave near two cremated burials on the floor of Mound 11 of the same group (Greber and Ruhl 1989:192). An extensive deposit of copper objects occurred above two burials in Altar 1 in the Central Mound of Mound 25, Hopewell Group (Greber and Ruhl 1989:76) and massive quantities of mica in Mound 13 at Mound City (Mills 1922) were associated with four cremated individuals. The question is thus begged as to how a society can have more than one chief at the same time. It is, however, acknowledged that single chiefs could have existed and that one or more status burials in proximity to them were simply close relatives (e.g., siblings).

The members of these "dominant groups" served as resident "overseers" of various centers who supervised earthwork and mound construction following a preconceived plan and who acted as caretakers of the facility after it was completed. The construction projects were accomplished by Hopewellians from various parts of at least the Midwest and Midsouth, and perhaps beyond, who traveled as single families or as small groups of a few families to the major centers, such as those in the Paint Creek Valley, stopping along the way at smaller centers and villages to feast and trade. When they arrived at the major center, they participated in the construction of the mounds and earthworks for a few days as a strictly voluntary undertaking. Likely, they observed mortuary ceremonies while there, engaged in crafting activities, storytelling, mate selection, and more trading and feasting.

These families had brought with them some exotica from their homelands in the form of local flint, decorated pottery, and mica or some other indigenous minerals or metals. Both raw materials (e.g., quartz, mica, flint, copper) and finished products (e.g., pottery vessels, mica cutouts, copper artifacts) were deposited at the ceremonial centers as "offerings" or worked into various craft items and traded, given away to other families and groups who also had made the pilgrimage, or taken home with them. The dominant groups acted as coordinators of these various activities, accommodating the "spring break" visitors by assigning them places to sleep and to practice their crafts.

This pattern was apparently duplicated on a smaller scale at other Ohio Hopewell sites. While the "heartland" mound and earthwork complexes in the Paint Creek Valley were "first order" centers of major importance and renown, "second order" sites such as Stubbs and hilltop enclosures such as Fort Ancient represent smaller scale versions of these larger centers where earthwork and mound construction was also carried out. Villages with one or more associated mounds represent "third order" Hopewell sites, while "fourth order" hinterland villages lacking earthwork or mound construction perhaps complete the "hierarchy" of site types that is typically found in the Ohio Valley. Being located in proximity to the Twin Mounds, the village of that name is a third order site, while Jennison Guard, with mounds in the area that are not clearly associated with the habitation, is perhaps a fourth order site.

At these and other third and fourth order sites, trace amounts of exotica are found that were probably given as gifts or exchanged for food and lodging. They include 1 to 3 percent Southeastern Series pottery, bladelets (usually of Harrison County or Flint Ridge flint; occasionally of Knox), at least some mica and, more rarely, a little obsidian and copper. Trading and feasting likely occurred at second order centers with less impressive mounds and earthworks than those of the major Scioto Valley centers. These apparently represent smaller scale versions of the latter where people were trying to imitate what was going on in the Paint Creek Valley. Clearly, though, the Chillicothe vicinity was the

"mecca" to which many groups trekked for perhaps the same reason we visit Disneyland, Myrtle Beach and the World's Fair—this was "where it was happening" for Hopewell. People availed themselves of the opportunity to participate—voluntarily—in the "Hopewell phenomenon" in the heartland and to leave their mark (as did the people of Cincinnati in 1987 who paid $25 for a brick with their name on it to be included in a pavement at Sawyer Point along the Ohio River).

Was flint raw material acquired as part of a "procurement strategy" embedded in a Hopewell Interaction Sphere, its transportation to at least first and second order sites "directed" or "arranged" by persons of authority in exchange for certain goods and/or services? Or was the transportation of such flint exotica serendipitous on the part of groups traveling to and from these centers?

The occurrence and condition of various flint varieties at the six Ohio Hopewell sites perhaps provide a clue. For the most part, varieties that could be considered local are represented by debitage in sufficient quantity to reasonably infer their primary utilization for the manufacture of items that were mainly utilitarian and bifacial. On the other hand, most of the exotic varieties were committed to the production of unifacial items such as bladelets. Some are also represented by bifacial artifacts such as cache blades (Plum Run) and projectile points (Dover). On-site crafting actitivies involving flint are documented for many Ohio Hopewell centers such as Seip, Fort Ancient, and Stubbs.

The "political model" that assumes the importation of flint as tribute is attended by the implication that it was demanded by chiefs. This model is disfavored on the grounds that a more homogeneous representation of flint raw material would be expected than what is observed. While deposits such as the 7,000 plus discs of Harrison County flint from Mound 2 of the Hopewell Group, 100 plus obsidian bifaces and several hundred pounds of obsidian debitage from the Central Mound of Mound 25 and Mound 11, respectively, of the Hopewell Group (Greber and Ruhl 1989:78, 192, Table 3.1), and sheets of mica occurring over nearly 40 square meters of floor area in Moorehead Mound 17 (Greber and Ruhl 1989:257) may represent "tribute," it seems unlikely that procurement in this manner satisfactorily accounts for the tiny quantities of numerous exotic flint varieties that occur at the various Ohio Hopewell sites. Furthermore, the disposal of large amounts of valued raw materials and/or finished artifacts is a common way of preventing "wealth" to accumulate in the hands of a few individuals as a basis for social distinction among essentially egalitarian societies, where the practice serves as a "leveling mechanism." Acknowledging that access to stores of raw materials was likely socially restricted and that the dominant group at each major center probably held such positions through hereditary claims, the practice of disposing of their "accumulated wealth" upon death seems inconsistent with a system of social ranking characteristically associated with chiefdoms.

There is little doubt that ceremonies and ritual observances, some associated with mortuary activity, occurred at various Ohio Hopewell sites, and that flint played a role in such activities. The inclusion of discs or preforms, cores, bladelets and well made bifaces of exotic flint with burials may be in accord with the "ceremonial" model. However, the abundant evidence of on-site uniface and biface production, along with the occurrence of debitage in areas away from burials and civic/ceremonial space precludes the idea that all flint coming into the various Ohio Hopewell sites was destined to become "offerings" or played a role in ritual/ceremonial observances. Furthermore, skepticism that deposits such as the 7,000 plus discs of Harrison County flint at the Hopewell site represent "offerings" seems justified.

Elements of the "economic" model in which Hopewell Interaction Sphere goods, including flint, were exchanged or traded for other goods and/or services may be invoked to account for some of the raw material that occurs in abundance at the major Ohio Hopewell centers. These are represented by deposits such as the Harrison County flint discs; the massive numbers of mica sheets at Mound 17 of the Hopewell site and Mound 13 at Mound City; the obsidian bifaces and debitage in Mounds 25 and 11, respectively, at

the Hopewell site; and the large number of copper nuggets, fragments, and artifacts in the Central Mound of Mound 25 at Hopewell (Greber and Ruhl 1989, Table 3.1). The possibility can be entertained that deposits such as these represent raw material brought to various sites under the auspices of the resident dominant groups.   The purpose may have been to supply those visitors whose native flint and other raw materials had been depleted on their treks to these and perhaps other nearby Hopewell centers. If so, the implication is that some kind of "arrangement"—likely of an economic nature—had been made for their importation.

The exotic flint that occurs at the various sites only in trace amounts seems to fit the social model much better than either the political or economic ones, while the ceremonial model is not necessarily eliminated from consideration. Trace amounts of Boyle, Bisher, Kentucky Flint Ridge, Knox and Plum Run at Mound City; Brassfield, Bisher, Knox, Plum Brook and Plum Run at Harness; Dover, Knox, Plum Run, Ste. Genevieve, Upper Mercer and Zaleski at Fort Ancient; Boyle, Kentucky Flint Ridge and Paoli at Stubbs; Knox, Ste. Genevieve and Upper Mercer at Jennison Guard; and Harrodsburg, Indian Creek and Upper Mercer at Twin Mounds likely represent treks of Hopewellian families or small groups from distant homelands.

While the small amount of Knox flint at Fort Ancient suggests its visitation in the manner described above, the larger quantity of this variety at nearby Stubbs suggests at least greater access to this high-grade material. This might have occurred if bladelet makers carrying cores of it had visited the site or resident bladelet makers had been supplied with sufficient raw material from which to fashion bladelets for exportation to the Scioto River Hopewell centers. Knife River flint, which is absent only in the Jennison Guard sample, most likely represents material taken back to local homelands by visitors to the major centers, such as those in the Scioto River Valley, into which it may have been imported directly overland from the west.

By contrast, Harrison County flint dominates the collections at Stubbs, Jennison Guard, and Twin Mounds, with the latter two having been located closer to the source area of this raw material than the other four sites included in this study. The quite impressive abundance of Harrison County flint at Jennison Guard, in particular, where no clearly associated mound or earthwork existed that might have served as a repository for blanks, preforms or finished artifacts, suggests the exportation of bifaces of this relatively high-grade material. The acquisition directly or through trade of Harrison County flint and its on-site "processing" for shipment to the Scioto Valley Hopewell centers as a prearranged undertaking are likely possibilities.

Among villages along the routes from the source areas of flint, minerals, metals, and perhaps other raw materials to the Scioto Valley, such processing likely involved rendering them more suitable for transport (for example, creating blanks from tabular chunks or pebble/cobble material), refining them (for example, converting blanks into preforms), or producing finished items. Similarly, mica working industries are evident at at least Jennison Guard and Stubbs, but the number of finished cutouts found upon excavation is not commensurate with the relatively abundant debris resulting from their manufacture. Perhaps they too were exported to the Paint Creek Valley and vicinity.

It is unknown exactly what was offered in exchange for the services rendered by these second, third, and fourth order sites in "household" or "cottage industry" fashion. Given the virtually ubiquitous presence of Flint Ridge bladelets at hinterland Ohio Hopewell farmsteads such as Jennison Guard and Twin Mounds, where their on-site production is indicated by bladelet core nuclei, it is plausible that itinerant blademakers were dispatched to them by dominant groups at the first order centers near the source area of Flint Ridge flint. Such craftsworkers may have traveled from site to site with a supply of Flint Ridge, Knox, Knife River and perhaps other flint, making blades locally in exchange for food, durable goods, and raw material in fulfillment of obligations incurred for the particular services rendered by each.

CONCLUSION

The presence and condition of flint raw material at each of six Hopewell sites in the Scioto, Little Miami, and Great Miami Valleys inspired consideration of four scenarios modeling the way or ways in which the different flint varieties reached their destinations.

The coercive "political" model was disfavored on the grounds of a lack of evidence for cultural complexity of the magnitude of a chiefdom. Elements of the "ceremonial" model can be invoked to account for some of the caches and deposits of flint that occur at certain sites while the "economic" model perhaps best accommodates abundances of some raw materials at the major Ohio Hopewell centers, such as the deposit of thousands of Harrison County discs at the Hopewell site.

The scenario that perhaps best models the *variety* of flint that occurs in varying quantities among Ohio Hopewell sites—often in trace amounts—is the "social" one that entertains the plausibility of small groups of Hopewellians having traveled to the Paint Creek Valley "mecca," bringing with them flint from their various homelands that was left at villages along the way—and at the major centers—in a context of gift giving, trading, feasting, mate selection, storytelling, and recreation. This scenario views Hopewell not as a ponderous, coercive phenomenon under the thumb of a chiefly elite. Rather, Hopewell was a social "happening" participated in voluntarily by tribal level culture-bearers.

ACKNOWLEDGMENTS

The data organization efforts of Andrea Henn are gratefully acknowledged, as are the contributions of Jim Brown, who shared his thoughts on Ohio Hopewell, and Bob Connolly his data on the Fort Ancient site. The writer also wishes to thank Barry Isaac for his critical comments on the manuscript, but retains sole responsibility for the ideas expressed in this paper. Assistance with manuscript preparation by Patricia Tench, Kenneth Henn, and Joyce Sanders is appreciated.

REFERENCES CITED

Bennett, R. A. H. 1986 *The Twin Mounds Village and Hopewell in Southwestern Ohio: A Ceramic Identity Crisis*. Master's thesis, Department of Anthropology, University of Cincinnati, Ohio.

Blosser, J. K. 1986 *Mica Working at the Jennison Guard Site: A Middle Woodland Village in Southeastern Indiana*. Master's thesis, Department of Anthropology, University of Cincinnati, Ohio.

Brown, J. A., and R. S. Baby 1966 *Mound City Revisited*. Report on file, Department of Archaeology, Ohio Historical Society, Columbus, Ohio.

Butler, B. M., and E. E. May, eds. 1984 *Prehistoric Chert Exploitation: Studies from the Midcontinent*. Center for Archaeological Investigations, Occasional Paper No. 2, Southern Illinois University, Carbondale.

Carlson, E. H. 1991 *Minerals of Ohio*. Division of Geological Survey, Ohio Department of Natural Resources, Bulletin 69. Columbus, Ohio.

Connolly, R. P. 1991 *Prehistoric Site Structure at the Fort Ancient State Memorial: New Evidence From Lithic Analysis*. Master's thesis, Department of Anthropology, University of Cincinnati, Ohio.

Converse, R. N. 1992 Carter Cave Flint. *Ohio Archaeologist* 42:28.

1994 *Ohio Flint Types* (Revised). Archaeological Society of Ohio, Rushville.

DeRegnaucourt, T., and D. S. Whitacre 1993 The Whitacre Site (12D246): A Middle Woodland Habitation Site in Southeast Indiana. Ms. accompanying Poster presented at the Ohio Archaeological Council's 2nd Annual Conference, Chillicothe, Ohio.

Essenpreis, P. S., and M. E. Moseley 1984 Fort Ancient: Citadel or Coliseum? *Field Museum of Natural History Bulletin* 55(6):5-10, 20-26.

Fischer, F.W.1974 *Early and Middle Woodland Settlement, Subsistence and Population in the Central Ohio Valley*. Ph.D. dissertation, Department of Anthropology, Washington University, St. Louis. University Microfilms, Ann Arbor.

Fogelman, G. L. 1983 *Lithics Book*. The Pennsylvania Artifact Series, Booklet No. 34. Fogelman Publishing Co., Turbotville, Pennsylvania.

Fowke, G. 1928 Archeological Investigations—II. *Bureau of American Ethnology Annual Report* 44:399-540.

Genheimer, R. A. 1984 *A Systematic Examination of Middle Woodland Settlements in Warren County, Ohio*. Report on file, Ohio Historic Preservation Office, Ohio Historical Society, Columbus, Ohio.

1992 *Bladelets at the Stubbs Earthwork Cluster: An Examination of Middle Woodland Settlement in the Little Miami River Valley*. Master's thesis, Department of Anthropology, University of Cincinnati, Ohio.

Greber, N. B. 1976 *Within Ohio Hopewell: Analysis of Burial Patterns from Several Classic Sites*. Ph.D. dissertation, Department of Anthropology, Case Western Reserve University, Cleveland, Ohio. University Microfilms, Ann Arbor.

1977 Revisiting a Classic Hopewell Site for Modern Salvage: Ohio Archaeologists at the Edwin Harness Mound. *Ohio Archaeologist* 27:10-12.

1983 *Recent Excavations at the Edwin Harness Mound, Liberty Works, Ross County, Ohio*. Midcontinental Journal of Archaeology, Special Paper No. 5. Kent, Ohio.

Greber, N. B., R. S. Davis, and A. S. DuFresne 1981 The Micro Component of the Ohio Hopewell Lithic Technology: Bladelets. *Annals of the New York Academy of Sciences* 376:489-528.

Greber, N. B., and K. C. Ruhl 1989 *The Hopewell Site: A Contemporary Analysis Based on the Work of Charles C. Willoughby*. Westview Press. Boulder, Colorado.

Holzapfel, E. 1994 The Harness Hopewell Cache. *Ohio Archaeologist* 44:10-11.

Kaltenthaler, L. A. 1992 *Analysis of the Chert Debitage and Tools from the Twin Mounds Village Site.* Master's thesis, Department of Anthropology, University of Cincinnati, Ohio.

Kozarek, S. E. 1987 *A Hopewellian Homestead in the Ohio River Valley.* Master's thesis, Department of Anthropology, University of Cincinnati, Ohio.

Luedtke, B. E. 1978 Chert Sources and Trace-Element Analysis. *American Antiquity* 43:413-423.

    1979 The Identification of Sources of Chert Artifacts. *American Antiquity* 44:744-757.

    1992 *An Archaeologist's Guide to Chert and Flint.* Institute of Archaeology, Archaeological Research Tools 7, University of California, Los Angeles.

Mills, W. C. 1907 The Exploration of the Edwin Harness Mound. *Ohio Archaeological and Historical Publications* 16:113-193.

    1922 Exploration of the Mound City Group. *Ohio Archaeological and Historical Quarterly* 31(4):422-584.

Moorehead, W. K. 1890 *Fort Ancient.* Robert Clarke & Co. Cincinnati, Ohio.

    1908 Fort *Ancient, Part II.* Phillips Academy. Andover, Massachusetts.

    1922 The Hopewell Mound Group of Ohio. *Field Museum of Natural History, Anthropological Series, Publication 211,* 6(5):73-181.

Seeman, M. F. 1979 *The Hopewell Interaction Sphere: The Evidence for Interregional Trade and Structural Complexity.* Indiana Historical Society, Prehistory Research Series 5(2), Indianapolis.

Stout, W., and R. A. Schoenlaub 1945 *The Occurrence of Flint in Ohio.* Division of Geological Survey, Fourth Series,Bulletin 46. Ohio Department of Natural Resources, Columbus, Ohio.

Struever, S. 1964 The Hopewell Interaction Sphere in Riverine-Western Great Lakes Culture History. In *Hopewellian Studies,* edited by J. R. Caldwell and R. L. Hall, pp. 85-108. Illinois State Museum, Scientific Papers, Vol. 12. Springfield, Illinois.

Struever, S., and G. L. Houart 1972 An Analysis of the Hopewell Interaction Sphere. In *Social Exchange and Interaction,* edited by E. N. Wilmsen, pp. 47-79. Anthropological Papers No. 46. Museum of Anthropology, University of Michigan, Ann Arbor.

Vehik, S. C., ed. 1985 *Lithic Resource Procurement: Proceedings from the Second Conference on Prehistoric Chert Exploitation.* Center for Archaeological Investigations, Occasional Paper No. 4. Southern Illinois University, Carbondale.

Vento, F. J. 1982 Flaked Stone Raw Materials. In *The Prehistory of the Paintsville Reservoir, Johnson and Morgan Counties, Kentucky,* edited by J. M. Adovasio, pp. 705-721. Department of Anthropology, Ethnology Monographs No. 6. University of Pittsburgh, Pennsylvania.

Vickery, K. D. 1983a Harness and Mound City: A Flint Raw Material Comparison. Paper presented at the Annual Meeting of the Society for American Archaeology, Pittsburgh, Pennsylvania.

    1983b The Flint Sources. In *Recent Excavations at the Edwin Harness Mound, Liberty Works, Ross County, Ohio,* edited by N.B. Greber, pp. 73-85. Midcontinental Journal of Archaeology, Special Paper No. 5. Kent, Ohio.

Whitacre, D., and R. Whitacre 1986 The Whitacre Site (12D246). *Ohio Archaeologist* 36:24-36.

Key to the Identification of Flint Varieties from Hopewell Sites

1. A. Fossiliferous; medium grained 2
    B. Non-fossiliferous 12
2. A. Banded 3
    B. Not banded 4
3. A. White to tan; weathers yellowish; fossil density very low .... LAUREL
    B. Tan to gray to brown to very dark brown; pitted; sponge fragments
       and spicules rare; does not discolor with weathering .... KNOX
4. A. Mottled 5
    B. Not mottled 7
5. A. Conglomeratic; white to gray with medium to large milky white to brownish red inclusions .... HARRODSBURG
    B. Not conglomeratic 6
6. A. Fossil density very low; white to light bluish gray; weathers yellowish .... LAUREL
    B. Fossil density low to moderate; creamy white to tan to light brown .... PLUMBROOK
7. A. Pitted; tan to gray to brown to very dark brown; sponge fragments and
       spicules rare; does not discolor with weathering .... KNOX
    B. Not pitted 8
8. A. Ostracods (tiny white lenticular fossils) present 9
    B. Ostracods absent 10
9. A. Light gray spots rare; tan .... INDIAN CREEK
    B. Light gray spots absent; tan to grayish brown .... DELAWARE
10 A. Gray to black; iron pyrite rare; lustre non-vitreous; orange ferruginous patina .... BOGGS
    B. White 11
11. A. Fossil density low to moderate; fossils medium to large in size; white to creamy white .... BRASSFIELD
    B. Fossil density moderate to high; fossils very small; white to bluish white,
       occasionally tinged with tan to ochreous yellow to red, light blue, green;
       does not discolor with weathering; black and/or reddish specks common .... BOYLE
12. A. Banded 13
    B. Not banded 16
13. A. Coarse grained; light to purplish tan .... BISHER
    B. Not coarse grained 14
14. A. Medium grained; white to light bluish gray; weathers yellowish .... LAUREL
    B. Fine grained 15
15. A. Pitted; tan to gray to brown to very dark brown; does not discolor with weathering .... KNOX
    B. Not pitted; light blue to grayish blue, red to reddish brown; muscovite
       and red specks common; black specks rare .... PAOLI
16. A. Coarse grained 17
    B. Medium grained 21
    C. Fine grained 25
17. A. Mottled; light and medium brown .... COLUMBUS
    B. Not mottled 18
18. A. Spotted; gray spots in pinkish tan matrix, red specks abundant .... CEDARVILLE - GUELPH
    B. Not spotted 19
19. A. Black .... KANAWHA BLACK
    B. Not black 20
20. A. Light to purplish tan .... BISHER
    B. Yellow to brown to red to gray; muscovite abundant .... KENTUCKY FLINT RIDGE
21. A. Not mottled; medium gray .... KENTUCKY FLINT RIDGE
    B. Mottled 22

22. A. Inclusions present; light bluish gray to dark gray, occasionally tinged
with tan; iron pyrite and milky white quartz inclusions rare to moderate;
thin greenish rust patina .... PLUM BROOK
    B. Inclusions absent 23
23. A. White to light blue gray; weathers yellowish .... LAUREL
    B. Not white 24
24. A. Adjacent color differences subtle; tan and brown; slightly opaque surface film;
orange spots rare .... BRUSH CREEK
    B. Adjacent color differences distinct; light to medium tan to gray; weathers
to dark tan to brownish gray to gray; orange spots absent .... DOVER
25. A. Mottled; white to tan to brown to orange to red, light to dark gray, green;
milky white and quartz crystal inclusions rare .... PLUM RUN
    B. Not mottled 26
26. A. Oolitic; light gray to grayish blue, occasionally tinged with red to reddish brown .... HANEY
    B. Not oolitic 27
27. A. Pitted; tan to gray to brown to very dark brown; does not discolor with weathering .... KNOX
    B. Not pitted 28
28. A. White inclusions present 29
    B. White inclusions absent 30
29. A. Thin white streaks and splotches abundant; bluish black to black, white to
light to dark gray .... UPPER MERCER
    B. Thin white streaks and splotches rare or absent; brownish black to black .... ZALESKI
30. A. Multiple colors/range of colors 31
    B. Uniform color 32
31. A. Light blue to grayish blue, light red to reddish brown; muscovite and red
specks abundant; black specks rare .... PAOLI
    B. Entire color range, often variegated; lustre waxy .... FLINT RIDGE
32. A. Iron pyrite inclusions rare 33
    B. Iron pyrite inclusions absent 35
33. A. Black specks absent; light to dark bluish gray; weathers to light gray; buff
to reddish brown cortex .... HARRISON COUNTY
    B. Black specks present 34
34. A. Light to dark blue; no film or discoloration with weathering; reddish brown cortex .... STE. GENEVIEVE
    B. Very dark gray; light to medium gray cortex .... WYANDOTTE
35. A. Large opaque inclusions present; light to dark brown; greasy or chalky white cortex .... KNIFE RIVER
    B. Large opaque inclusions absent; brownish black to black .... ZALESKI

EIGHT

SOCIAL IMPLICATIONS OF OHIO HOPEWELL ART

C . WESLEY COWAN

ABSTRACT

The complex artwork of Ohio Hopewell has excited the imagination of archaeologists since the 19th century discoveries of
Squier and Davis. Manufactured from a variety of local and
exotic materials, and present in a bewildering array of forms
and shapes — both geometric and zoo- and anthropomorphic
— Ohio Hopewell artwork presents an analytical challenge to
anyone interested in interpreting its meaning. Rather than
attempt to unlock the rich emic and cosmological symbolism
these objects represent, this paper examines their potential for
deciphering the role they played in sacred and secular contexts. In this sense Ohio Hopewell art has meaning which can
be "understood" today, in spite of the fact that it is impossible
to know its precise original connotation.

A View From the Core a Synthesis of Ohio Hopewell Archaeology•edited by Paul J. Pacheco
© Copyright 1996 by The Ohio Archaeological Council• Columbus, Ohio•All Rights Reserved•ISBN 0-9626931-9-7

C. Wesley Cowan

Social Implications of Ohio Hopewell Art

Introduction

The complex artwork for which Ohio Hopewell is so justly famous, is a corpus of rich, but largely uninterpretable emic symbolism. Copper falcons, zoomorphic effigy pipes, mica-cutouts, and a host of copper, bone, and stone objects obviously conveyed information far beyond their aesthetic values. Few would argue that these objects of material culture did not also transmit information about their owners and their position within Hopewellian society. In this sense, the spectacular, and often bewildering array of forms functioned as a form of social "advertising" (see Braun 1977 for a good discussion of this position), a visual display of one's place and probably role, within a larger group. It is this ability of Hopewell material culture to symbol — to transmit information about its owner (sensu Wobst 1977) — that is the subject of this paper.

Theoretical background

We would all agree that material culture has the ability to emit information. Several landmark examinations of stylistic behaviors have discussed the role of symbolic messaging in both the ethnographic present (Wobst 1977) and prehistory (Braun 1977; Plog 1980). These studies argue that items of personal adornment, dress, and decoration communicate information about their owners. This information may include not only the identity of the owner, but also his or her social group membership, status, wealth, religious beliefs, and political ideology (Braun 1977:118).

Each of these studies builds upon a model first proposed for archaeologists by Wobst (1977). Wobst argues that "....stylistic messaging defines mutually expectable behavior and makes subsequent interaction more predictable and less stressful....Thus, an important function of stylistic messaging derives from the fact that it makes social intercourse more predictable: it reduces the stress inherent in first or intermittent encounters, and it broadcasts the potential advantages or disadvantages to be realized from more intimate encounter, before such encounter has taken place" (Wobst 1977:327).

Two important aspects of Wobst's model of stylistic variability in artifacts relate to who is the potential receiver of the information, and the visibility of the artifacts themselves. Wobst argues that stylistic messaging works best when the receiver is socially "...not too close - since the message usually would be known... or could be more easily transmitted ... and not too distant since decoding or encountering the message could not be assured" (Wobst 1977:323-24). Thus transmission of information through material culture works best when the target group is socially intermediate to one's nuclear family, and more distant members of a social network.

The visibility of artifacts is also extremely important in Wobst's model. The more an object is seen, or able to be seen because of its size, or it's context of use, the more chance it has for transmitting information about its owner. But, the information content of an artifact can be maximized only if the object sends an invariate message. This argues for standardization of form or symbolic content, otherwise the object could send multiple, and thus untranslatable messages.

In addition, the more social contexts an artifact enters into, the more chance it has for emitting a message about it's owner. If objects are not visible for others to see, there is little chance that they will be suitable for sending a message to be received by a socially relevant person.

Ohio hopewell

With this abbreviated version of the information exchange model in mind, let us now turn to a specific archaeological example — Ohio Hopewell — and examine the spectacular symbols which have made these peoples so widely known.

The societies we know as Ohio Hopewell are best known through their geometric earthworks and burial mounds and the objects the mounds contain. Less well known is the everyday existence of the Hopewell. In spite of nearly 150 years of research, until comparatively recently, information about Ohio Hopewell was limited to a single report documenting the material culture from the McGraw site in Ross County (Prufer 1964). More recent are tantalizing unpublished manuscripts (e.g., Fisher 1971), articles (Dancey 1991) and several

Master's theses and dissertations (Blosser 1986; Connolly 1991; Genheimer 1992; Kozarek 1987; Pacheco 1993). These have begun to fill in the gaps in our knowledge about Ohio Hopewell material culture, settlement variation and subsistence practices. Our understanding of non-mortuary manifestations of Ohio Hopewell is still in its infancy, however (see Smith 1992 for an excellent review of these data).

In part, this is due to a historical accident. For years, archaeologists assumed they would find large, "village" type habitation sites for Ohio Hopewell populations. After all, many reasoned, there *must* have been a substantial population to build the earthworks, and they had to live *somewhere* (see Prufer 1964). In fact, there are no large villages. Instead, Ohio Hopewell populations continued the earlier Adena settlement pattern of scattered household clusters, composed of families presumably related consanguineously or through marriage. The archaeological visibility of these clusters is often limited to a light scattering of artifacts, which are easily passed over by the researcher who suspects there must be something more tangible to discover.

These individual scattered household clusters, or hamlets, were almost certainly linked through some larger kinship network, whether through clans or simple lineages. If this assumption is correct, then these corporate relationships carried with them proscriptive descent and marriage rules, and rules of mutual obligation, and provided the framework for a complex web of social interactions.

Periodically the scattered household clusters were probably drawn together to fulfill mutual lineage or clan ritual obligations. Whether world renewal observations, or rites of passage, such ceremonies served to integrate a dispersed population by providing a link between the past and the present. It was at the monumental earthworks that the interplay of status, kinship, and cosmology was played out, and provided the social occasion where elaborate art and other exotica was displayed. Not only did the art serve to reinforce society-wide beliefs, but much of the material worn as part of elaborate costumes probably communicated information about the status of their owners, or the status of their clan or lineage.

Major Ohio Hopewell ceremonies and observances took place in sacred precincts — spots on the landscape that were ritually charged with supernatural powers, or otherwise figured prominently in the cosmology of the Hopewell. These sacred precincts were marked as such through the construction of earthen embankments **(Figure 8:1)**. But these embankments did more than enclose sanctified ground; their geometry and the precision with which they were made implies that they too were a reflection of cosmological beliefs.

Our knowledge of the history of the construction of the individual geometric works is frustratingly incomplete. Few remain intact after more than 150 years of intensive cultivation, and when excavations have taken place within their encircling walls, they have produced evidence of construction episodes, but comparatively little material with which these episodes may be dated (Connolly 1994). Judging by experimental work in Mesoamerica and elsewhere in the American Midwest, however, two things are clear: neither a great length of time, nor a large labor force was necessary for their construction (Erasmus 1965; Walthall 1979, 1980).

Recent excavations at Fort Ancient State Memorial in Warren County have disclosed substantial residential zones within and outside of the wall of this immense enclosure (Connolly 1994). Because of the limited scope of these investigations, it is not possible to characterize the nature of the Middle Woodland occupations at the site. Cultural materials recovered from the various trenches and test pits, however, suggest a wide range of domestic activities took place at the earthwork, and the presence of both structures and extramural pit features indicate more than simply casual use of the earthwork locale. None of these lines of evidence contradict the model proposed here: periodic use of the earthwork for world renewal rituals would result in the same archaeological signature.

Many of these enclosures also contain burial mounds that were invariably erected over the site of a former structure. Whether simple, as in those found at Mound City, or complex, multi-roomed affairs like those at Seip, Harness and probably Mound 25 at the Hopewell site, the purpose of

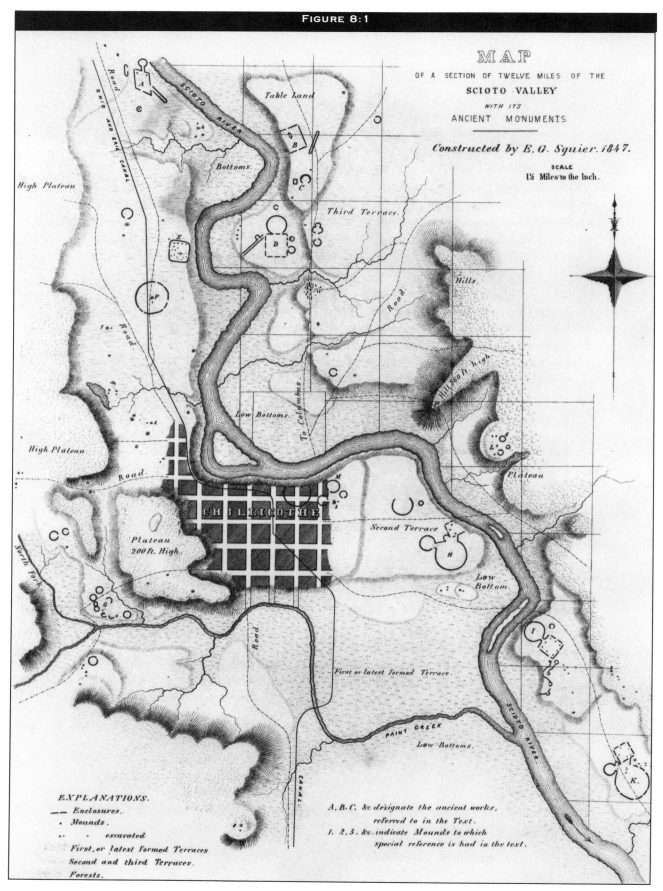

Geometric earthworks in the vicinity of Chillicothe, Ohio. From Squier and Davis, 1848.

these structures was the same: to serve as repositories of the bones and earthly possessions of honored members of the lineages or clans (Brown 1979).

Greber's recent excavation of the so-called "Great House" beneath the Harness Mound, revealed the structure to be a complex of symbols itself. Uses of special colors, trees, and directions were made; debris recovered from the floor and subfloor pits also strongly suggest that the "Great House" was the scene for activities that cannot exclusively be tied to mortuary ritual (Greber 1983).

It should be noted that not all Ohio Hopewell burial mounds are located within the interiors of earthworks (Seeman and Soday 1980). Isolated burial mounds are common in most of the major subareas of Middle Woodland occupation in Ohio, though they are invariably small, and do not contain the same range of material for which the larger tumuli associated with the geometric works are known.

The relationship of these mounds with the earthworks is not at all clear, but probably reflects chronological variation within Ohio Hopewell. While acknowledging the importance of isolated mounds in interpreting Middle Woodland in Ohio, this paper focuses on mortuary data associated with mound burials within the walls of earthworks. As an internal chronology for the Middle Woodland period in Ohio is worked out, it should be possible to delineate change and continuity in the use of material culture as sources of social information.

OHIO HOPEWELL MATERIAL CULTURE AS SOURCES OF SOCIAL INFORMATION

If, as Wobst and others have suggested, material culture functions as a source of information about its owner, an examination of the diverse remains found in individual graves and deposits inside Ohio Hopewell great houses and other mortuary structures may provide useful information about Hopewell society, even though we may not be able to decipher the exact meaning of the symbols. Remembering that the most efficient way to emit a message is

through some simple, invariate format, and that there is a hierarchy of social relationships (i.e., individual, family, lineage or clan) in Ohio Hopewell society, it is possible to identify at least three distinct classes of material culture. First, there are those objects whose meaning was probably known to very few individuals, perhaps only to their owners and their immediate family or associates in a sodality. These items were probably of little importance in communicating a message about their owners. Secondly, there were objects whose meaning was probably known to a wider group of individuals, probably the lineage or clan, and were considered clan or lineage property. Finally, there were those privately owned objects whose meaning was widely recognized by all members of Ohio Hopewell society, and which were sources of clear and unambiguous information about their owners. This classification admittedly glosses over the obvious role that the elaborate paraphernalia played in communicating information about the social position of their owners or a corporate group. As valuable commodities meant to be displayed on important social occasions, much Ohio Hopewell material culture served to validate the status of their owners within a larger social milieu. In this sense, many finely crafted goods, often made of exotic raw materials, also functioned as sources of individual "wealth." And, in a larger, corporate sense, the collective accumulation of wealth also served as a measure of success of the lineage or clan.

In a similar vein, some Ohio Hopewell symbols probably emitted different messages depending on the context of their use. I do not explore the possibility that some objects cross-cut the tri-partite classification proposed here, but acknowledge the multiple meanings inherent in some symbols. Still, as a starting point for deciphering complex Ohio Hopewell artifacts, I believe the methodology outlined here is a useful construct.

ITEMS OF MATERIAL CULTURE EMITTING FEW SOCIAL MESSAGES

By far the majority of the objects found in graves and caches within Ohio Hopewell great houses probably can be considered personal property, whose ultimate meaning may have been known only to their owners. Some were probably personal charms or magic that were used to mediate between their owners and the supernatural. Others may have been totems, received by an individual through some fast-induced vision or similar supernatural experience. Many of the objects, and the meaning they conveyed, may have been closely guarded, and kept secreted away from other individuals. Others probably had more visual roles as parts of costumes worn on important social occasions where public display validated both the status of the individual and the corporate group. Even in these highly public contexts, however, the personal powers of the objects were unlikely to be known to those who viewed them.

Perhaps no other type of Ohio Hopewell artifact better fits this class than the zoomorphic platform pipe (**Figure 8:2**). Archaeologists, and art historians have long marveled over these masterpieces of stone carving. By far the majority are carved from a soft, oolitic limestone which outcrops in the hills overlooking the mouth of the Scioto River. This Ohio "pipe-stone" is extremely soft when it is mined, and can be easily carved. As it becomes exposed to the air it becomes harder and progressively more difficult to work. Judging by the extent of the pipestone deposit, and its use by later Fort Ancient populations, there was no shortage of the stone to work.

Despite its relative natural abundance and the ease with which pipestone can be worked, platform pipes within Ohio Hopewell are not ubiquitous artifacts. Although a number of examples have been found elsewhere (Seeman 1979:329-331) the vast majority are the product of two sites: Mound City and Tremper. In both cases, large caches of pipes were found as part of "offerings" or "gifts" to deceased ancestors made on the floor of a former great house.

The size of these pipes, the diversity of animals represented, and the context in which the pipes were disposed, suggest pipes were the personal property of individual lineage or clan members. I do not mean to imply that symbolic content of the carvings on the pipes was not known in terms of some general Hopewellian cosmology. Indeed, the animals depicted were almost certainly important in Hopewellian myths and legends defining the role of humans and animals

on the earth. On the other hand, the animal probably had a special and extremely powerful meaning to its owner — a representation of a personal protector, or some other supernatural totem — gained through a vision or some other experience. These totems were very much personal property, and, if the Ohio Hopewell were like many ethnographically documented societies, the pipes were believed to contain spirits themselves (cf. West 1934).

In this sense, the platform pipes, though they are arguably the best known kind of Ohio Hopewell art, convey relatively little information about the workings of the society who made them. Needless to say, their rarity suggests that comparatively few individuals probably possessed them; like all such esoteric Ohio Hopewell artifacts, the pipes were also social markers, not only identifying their owners, but also validating their status within society at large. But on a *personal* level, the messages they emitted were not simple and unambiguous because they had multiple meanings — meanings known primarily to their owners. And their relative size — most are only a few centimeters in length and height — argues against the pipes as being a highly visible symbol.

In addition to the pipes, there are a plethora of other symbols whose full meaning was probably largely hidden to other members of society as a whole. Items such as "boat-stones" (**Figure 8:3**), fossil sharks' teeth, carved shell and bone pendants, tubes (**Figure 8:4**), and plaques, were likely personal charms, totems, or contents of individual medicine bundles. While the meanings of the animals and scenes portrayed on these fossils, exotic stones and carvings undoubtedly figured in the cosmology and mythology of the Ohio Hopewell, and hence were easily recognizable by all members of society, like the pipes, the *special powers* they possessed were known only to their owners.

As alluded to at the beginning of this section, many of these personal symbols are found in both graves and in mass "offerings". Their placement within individual graves, often in position on the body suggesting they might have been part of costumes, offers fairly unambiguous evidence of their status as items of "personal property." But the same

FIGURE 8:2

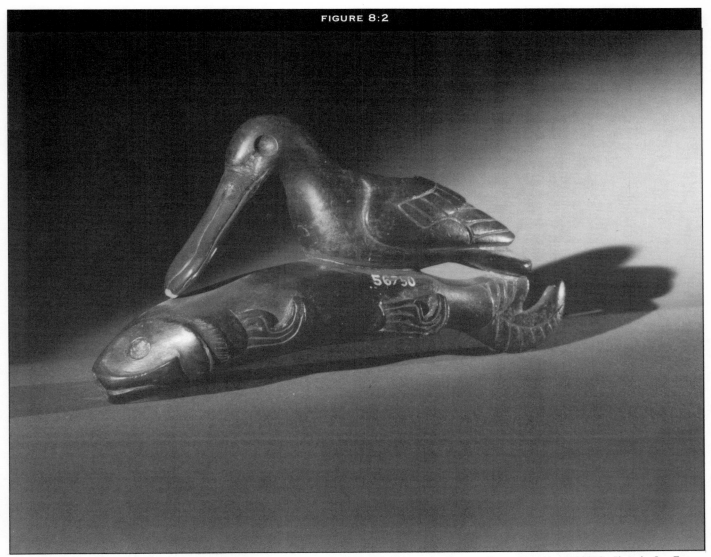

Platform pipe depicting a roseate spoonbill perched atop a minnow. Hopewell site. Field Museum, Chicago, Illinois, Neg. No. A110058. Photo by Ron Testa.

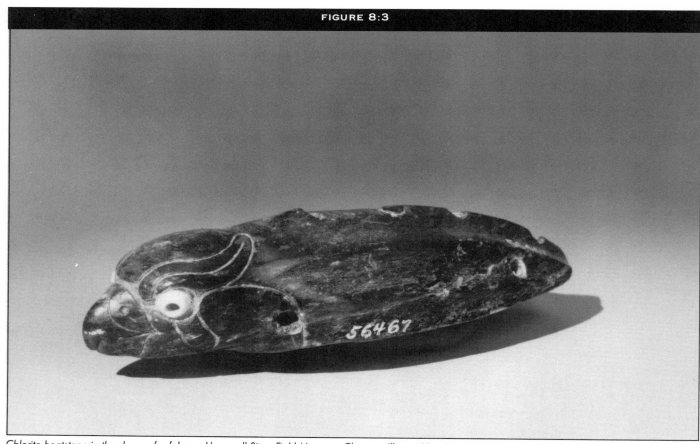

FIGURE 8:3

Chlorite boatstone in the shape of a falcon. Hopewell Site. Field Museum, Chicago, Illinois, Neg. No. A110042. Photo by Ron Testa.

kinds of objects were also placed in what were likely dedicatory gifts made at the time of the death of a great clan or lineage elder, or on some other corporate ritual occasion. The caches of diverse objects found on the floor of Mound 17 at the Hopewell site, for example, primarily contain symbolically-laden objects such as pendants, bars, cones, and both stone, bone and metal animal and human effigies **(Figure 8:4)**. Each of these objects should be considered the special property of an individual, as were the large group (circa 50) of stone celts included in the "offering." These former objects, relatively invariate in shape, probably emitted another, distinctly different message, and are discussed in another section of this paper.

OBJECTS WHOSE MEANING WAS KNOWN TO THE LINEAGE OR CLAN

In our building-block scheme of the organization of Ohio Hopewell society, individuals were members of families first, and a lineage or clan which cross-cut immediate family or lineage ties, next. Typically, such suprafamilial organizations own and use objects in secret ceremonies and/or in public displays (Jonaitis 1986). These objects are considered property of the clan and are held in trust by an important person (or persons). Frequently this important paraphernalia consists of heirlooms, each with its own unique history, and life.

Human femurs with zoomorphic and anthropomorphic incised decorations. Hopewell Site. Field Museum, Chicago, Illinois, Neg. No. A110035. Photo by Ron Testa.

This concept of clan property was played out to its fullest on the Northwest Coast of North America, where important boxes, feast bowls, screens and other totems were kept hidden away within the confines of the house or clan leader's living space until needed for public displays (Jonaitis 1986, 1988). The artwork held by the clan was explicitly not considered sacred or otherworldly, but was an expression of the social order and relationships between people (Jonaitis 1986:12). Clan and house symbols were obtained during mythic times by founding ancestors, and communicated clan or family history, status and destiny. This information was known best to the clan members, a wider circle than the individual or family, but still a circumscribed group of individuals.

Both on the Northwest Coast, in other societies, and probably among the Ohio Hopewell, such important symbols were the property of the lineage or clan, and may have been stored in a corporate place like the great house where they were brought to public light when needed. On the other hand, their presentation and manipulation was probably the exclusive privilege of a clan or lineage elder (or elders) who acquired this right through great deeds or inheritance from a founding ancestor. In either case, these meta-symbols were identified with socially prominent individuals who enjoyed special access not afforded other kinspersons.

Are there objects from Ohio Hopewell mounds that functioned as symbols of some suprafamilial sodalities, and how might these be recognized? First, objects that were not the property of individuals, but were heirlooms of some larger social group might not be expected to be found within an individual grave. Such items might instead be found in a distinctly different context. In the case of the Ohio Hopewell, the "caches" or "offerings" of objects found in many of the major mounds contain items that clearly fall into such a category. These include the so-called "great pipes" found at Seip, much of the copper sheet art from Mound 25 at Hopewell, the remarkable effigies from Altar 1, Mound 4 at Turner, and some of the stupendous non-utilitarian copper celts from the Scioto and Paint Creek mounds.

These items are large, spectacular objects that were meant for public display and use at important social functions. Whether the display was for a circumscribed group of lineage or clan members or for the wider public, the information transmitted by these objects could be interpreted by more than a single individual. Many of these may have been heirlooms that served to remind the corporate group of its shared history or origins. Some were likely integral parts of ceremonies that validated a corporate identity.

The steatite "great pipes", from the Seip Mound, for example, (Shetrone and Greenman 1931:416-417) were probably not smoked by a single individual, but by a larger group of kin (**Figure 8:5**). They are distinctly different from the small platform pipe which were made from a local stone and used by individuals. The great pipes were not made by Hopewell craftspersons, but by their contemporaries in the lower Tennessee-Cumberland drainages of southeastern Tennessee and northeastern Alabama (see Webb 1939; Webb and DeJarnette 1942). At least three of the five pipes from Seip show evidence of multiple repairs, suggesting they were carefully curated heirlooms.

The context in which they were found — all were interred in a low mound covering a group of burials at the entrance to the great house — implies they were not the property of an individual. Shetrone and Greenman (1931:374) make it clear that these pipes ".....were unaccompanied by human or other remains. Apparently they were intentionally placed in the position in which they were found as offerings or symbols of guardianship, subsequent to the sealing of the great communal sepulchre."

Mound 25 at the Hopewell site contained at least one cache of objects that also seems to fit the bill of suprafamilial property. Like the great pipes at Seip, one of the two large accumulations of copper artifacts discovered in Mound 25 was buried above the floor of the great house and not associated with any human remains. From Moorehead's (1922:109-110; see also Greber and Ruhl 1989:) description, it is also clear that this cache was located atop a mound inside the great house.

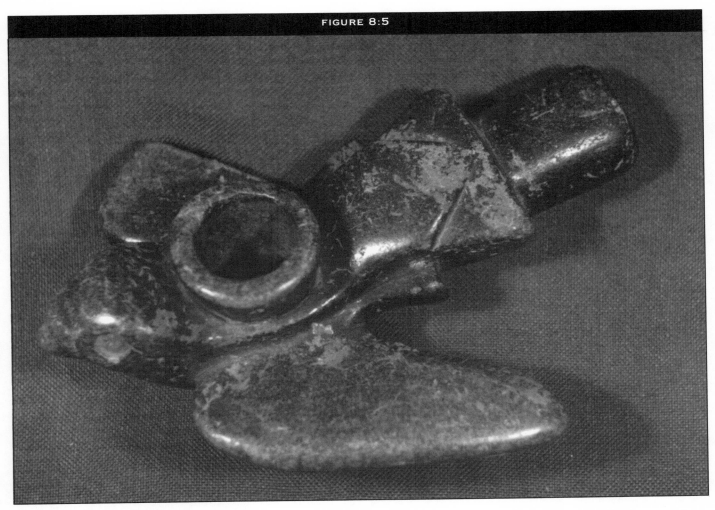

FIGURE 8:5

Steatite "great pipe" from Seip Mound.

"Near the center of the section, 4 feet from the base line, were found one hundred twenty pieces of sheet copper. They were all laid out flat, and occupied a space 3 feet by 2 feet wide, with layers of bark above and below. There were no skeletal remains connected with this deposit, nor was any altar found near it."

It also is apparent that at least some of these copper cutouts were affixed to a long wooden object, possibly a collapsed box or plaque (Moorehead 1922:109) that would have allowed these symbols to be displayed. These symbols represent a great diversity of forms and creatures — serpents, fish, birds, and mammals, and are figured in realistic or stylized format **(Figures 8:6 and 8:7)**.

A similar diversity of symbolism characterized the contents of Altar 1 of Mound 1 of the Turner Works. Here a mica rattlesnake, a three-dimensional carved *piasa* or *uktena* figurine, and an amphibian-like representation were found mixed together with other objects. Like the copper "offering" of varied symbols found in Mound 25 at Hopewell, and the great pipes at Seip, these effigies represent more than simply personal property of an individual artisan. These objects were clan or lineage heirlooms that were held in trust for use by the clan at important functions. This is not to suggest that these sacred heirlooms did not also convey information about the power and status of the lineage or clan. Indeed, their display on important occasions served to identify the corporate group, and much like the crest symbols of some Northwest Coast groups provided visual verification of the clan's prestige and personal history.

ITEMS WHOSE MEANING WAS KNOWN TO SOCIETY AS A WHOLE

In addition to the array of personal symbols that were owned and manipulated by individuals, or those of symbolic significance to the clan or lineage, there is another class of Ohio Hopewell symbols. By virtue of their standard shape and position in which they were worn on the body or otherwise displayed at public ceremonies, these symbols emitted an unambiguous message about the social position of their owners.

FIGURE 8:6

Copper cutouts. Hopewell Site. Field Museum, Chicago, Illinois, Neg. No. A78501. Photo by Ron Testa.

This information was interpretable by the widest range of Hopewellians. Like many of the other symbols discussed above, the objects are also found with graves or in caches that may have been dedicatory gifts to deceased individuals. Included in this group are copper plaques, ear spools, probably most copper and many stone celts, drilled bear's teeth, and *Ross Barbed* blades of obsidian and Knife River chalcedony. [1]

So-called copper "serpent." Hopewell Site. Field Museum, Chicago, Illinois, Neg. No. A312446. Photo by Ron Testa.

FIGURE 8:8

So-called "breastplates." Hopewell Site. Field Museum, Chicago, Illinois, Neg. No. A11003.

Although often termed "breast plates", the rectangular copper plaques found in all major Ohio Hopewell mounds are just as often found underneath the head or pelvis of inhumations (**Figure 8:8**). Many have preserved traces of fabric, and some have even been described as being found "wrapped" in fabric (Moorehead 1922; Mills 1926; Shetrone and Greenman 1931). Judging from the diversity of these associations, it is safe to assert that the copper plaque was probably meant to be sewn onto a fabric costume; some may have been wrapped in fabric for storage.

Recent analysis of these copper-preserved fabrics reveal that some were portions of tunics manufactured of an extremely fine, white fiber that would have required hundreds, if not thousands of hours to construct (Church 1988:11). Multicolored stamped designs were found on some. Like the *Chilkat* blanket of the Northwest Coast, the Hopewell tunics represent labor intensive investments that were not meant to be worn on a daily basis. Shining copper plates on the chest, or back of the head and waist simply added to the overall visual impact of the robes and, ultimately, the physical appearance of their owners.

Earspools of hammered copper, whether plain, or covered with silver foil or sheets of meteoritic iron, are all of the same basic form (**Figure 8:9**). They are also found in some of the same contexts as the plates: either in graves at the sides of the head, or held in the hands of the deceased, or in "offerings" mixed with other objects.

Whether grizzly or black bear, the perforated canines of these creatures also conveyed a standard message, and were worn in an extremely visible position on the body (**Figure 8:10**). When they have been found with primary inhumations, they most often occur in groups of four, rarely six, and almost always at the neck. Imitation bear teeth of marine shell, cannel coal, and deer bone were also part of Hopewell costume, but these replica teeth are *never* found at the neck, occurring instead at the waist, wrists, or even feet.

Two other objects of display — *Ross Barbed* spears (**Figure 8:11**) and copper celts — were not items of apparel per se, but were nonetheless important visual symbols. Both are sometimes found with individual burials, but are more often found overlying burial groups or as parts of special "offerings" in "altars" or caches.[2] Two of these caches, both discovered at Hopewell, are especially informative.

FIGURE 8:9

Copper Earspools. Hopewell Site. Field Museum, Chicago, Illinois, Neg. No. A31246.

The great cache of artifacts associated with burials 260 and 261 in Mound 25 at Hopewell contained almost 70 celts and adzes (63 of copper, one of stone) and at least 90 copper plates, along with a large number of other objects (Moorehead 1922:110; Greber and Ruhl 1989:90-100). While it is possible this massive accumulation of wealth was the personal property of the two individuals which it overlay, it is much more parsimonious to suggest this trove represents individual gifts of members of a common social group. Unlike the platform pipe, with their myriad animals, though variable in size, all copper and stone celts or adzes are basically similar in shape. As such, the message they emitted was relatively invariate. Size of the individual celts varied, however, and those made of copper probably were considered important "valuables" since they could be taken apart and turned into smaller objects.

FIGURE 8:10

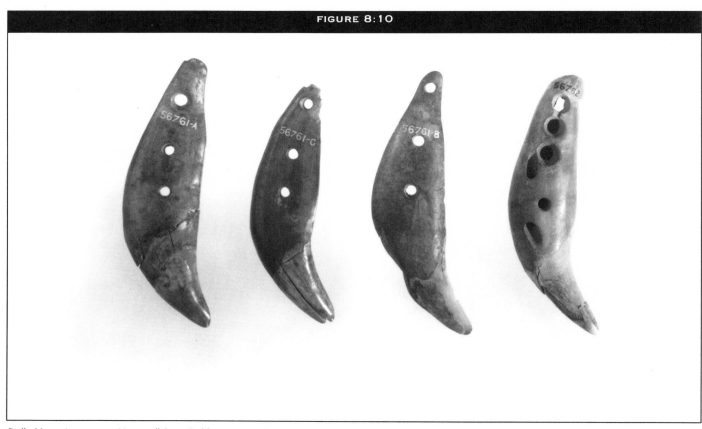

Drilled bears's canines. Hopewell Site. Field Museum, Chicago, Illinois, Neg. No. A110101. Photo by Ron Testa.

In a similar vein, the more than 50 stone celts from one of the two "offerings" found in Mound 17 may also represent symbols recognized by society as a whole. While not necessarily constructed of "exotic" raw materials, the celts nonetheless are more or less uniform in shape, and were probably personal symbols of individual Hopewell kinspersons. Interestingly, two of the celts from this "offering" had been "killed", presumably at the time of their deposition.

The role of the celt as a society-wide symbol is also reinforced by the occurrence of a large, finely-made cannel coal specimen recovered from burial 22 in Mound 25 at the Hopewell site (Mills 1926:196, Figure 44). Unlike the hard-stone axes from Mound 17, which could have been put to potential use,

the cannel coal axe from the Mound 25 burial was non-utilitarian. Like the other copper and stone axes, this specimen probably functioned as a prestige marker.

DISCUSSION

The symbolic content of Ohio Hopewell art will never be known from an emic standpoint. Ethnographic analogies between historically recorded societies in the east, and the prehistoric Ohio Hopewell of 1900 years ago can provide perhaps a glimpse at interpreting some of the animal forms depicted, but by and large specific aspects of Ohio Hopewell myth and cosmology will always remain unknown and unverifiable.

Ross Barbed obsidian spears. Hopewell Site. Field Museum, Chicago, Illinois, Neg. No. A90845.

On the other hand, if we view this complex of symbols as a means of communication — or more specifically objects of material culture as transmitters of information — then the complexity can be reduced to a few categories. These range from objects whose message was not meant to be transmitted to anyone beyond the immediate circle of family, to objects whose message could be received and translated by anyone in Ohio Hopewell society.

The former messages were uninterpretable to most Hopewellians because they had the potential to emit multiple meanings. The latter were simple and invariate — they dealt not with myth or the order of the cosmos but with concrete social relationships. They communicated information about one's prestige or rank within a lineage or clan system.

We saw that there are other symbols whose meaning was known to a wider, but still circumscribed group of kin. These objects were not charms which protected their owner from malevolent spirits, nor were they crass examples of wealth or personal power like the copper plate. These were objects whose meaning was shrouded in the mythology of the lineage or clan and whose very existence depended upon their maintenance as property of the broader social group. They were maintained as heirlooms, which validated the position of the social group — until some powerful event transpired which dictated their removal from use. Whether burial of the objects was triggered by the death of a particularly important elder or some other calamitous social event, these sacred heirlooms were deposited within the sanctified confines of the "Great House".

Finally, I have suggested that a smaller group of objects, whose standardized shape transmitted unambiguous social messages, was also in use. These objects — copper plates, earspools, axes, drilled bear's teeth and large blades made of obsidian and Knife River chalcedony — served to validate one's status within a lineage or clan. Although they were the personal property of their owner, their meaning was not hidden in personal belief or myth. Their meaning was clear to anyone who viewed the object. These were objects whose high visibility and invariant message served to communicate information between social equals at times of potential stress, when disparate lineages or clans came to sacred precincts to fulfill mutual ritual obligations.

NOTES

1. While "Ross Barbed" is a term first proposed by Griffin (1965) to identify the large stemmed and notched bifaces found in the Ross County area of the Central Scioto Valley, for this paper I use the term to denote any of the forms of large Ohio Hopewell bifaces made of obsidian or chalcedony.

2. Since most Ohio Hopewell burials were cremated, this statement applies only to those relatively few in-the-flesh inhumations found at Hopewell, Turner, and Seip.

REFERENCES CITED

Blosser, J. K. 1986 *Mica Working at the Jennison Guard Site: A Middle Woodland Village in Southeastern Indiana*. Master's thesis, Department of Anthropology, University of Cincinnati.

Braun, D. P. 1977 *Middle Woodland — (Early) Late Woodland Social Change in the Prehistoric Central Midwestern U.S.* Ph.D. dissertation, Department of Anthropology, University of Michigan, Ann Arbor. University Microfilms, Ann Arbor.

Brown, J. A. 1979 Charnel Houses and Mortuary Crypts: Disposal of the Dead in the Middle Woodland Period. In *Hopewell Archaeology: The Chillicothe Conference*, edited by D. S. Brose and N. Greber, pp.211-219. Kent State University Press, Kent, Ohio.

Church, F. 1988 Textiles as Markers of Ohio Hopewell Social Identities. *Midcontinental Journal of Archaeology* 9(1):1-25.

Connolly, R.P. 1991 *Prehistoric Site Structure at the Fort Ancient State Memorial: New Evidence from Lithic Analysis*. Master's thesis, Department of Anthropology, University of Cincinnati.

1994 The Built Environment of Hilltop Enclosures. Paper presented at the combined Annual Meetings of the Southeastern Archaeological Conference and the 39th Midwest Archaeological Conference, Lexington, Kentucky.

Dancey, W. S. 1991 A Middle Woodland Settlement in Central Ohio: A Preliminary Report on the Murphy Site (33LI212). *Pennsylvania Archaeologist* 61(2):32-72.

Erasmus, C. J. 1965 Monument Building: Some Field Experiments. *Southwestern Journal of Anthropology* 6:65-70.

Fischer, F. 1971 *Preliminary Report on the University of Cincinnati Archaeological Investigations at Miami Fort, 1970*. Report on file, Department of Anthropology, University of Cincinnati.

Genheimer, R. A. 1992 *Bladelets at the Stubbs Earthwork Cluster: An Examination of Middle Woodland Settlement in the Little Miami River Valley*. Master's thesis, Department of Anthropology, University of Cincinnati.

Greber, N. B. 1983 *Recent Excavations at the Edwin Harness Mound, Liberty Works, Ross County, Ohio*. Midcontinental Journal of Archaeology Special Paper No. 5. Kent State University Press, Kent, Ohio.

Greber, N. B. and K. C. Ruhl 1989 *The Hopewell Site: A Contemporary Analysis Based on the Work of Charles C. Willoughby*. Westview Press, Boulder, Colorado.

Griffin, J. B. 1965 Hopewell and the Dark Black Glass. In *Papers in Honor of Emerson F. Greenman*, edited by J. E. Fitting. *Michigan Archaeologist*, 11:115-155.

Jonaitis, A. 1986 *Art of the Northern Tlingit*. University of Seattle Press, Seattle, Washington.

1988 *From the Land of the Totem Poles*. The University of Washington Press, Washington.

Kozarek, S. E. 1987 *A Hopewellian Homestead in the Ohio River Valley*. Master's thesis, Department of Anthropology, University of Cincinnati.

Mills, W. C. 1926 *Certain Mounds and Village Sites in Ohio*. Ohio Archaeological and Historical Society, Columbus, Ohio.

Moorehead, W. K. 1922 The Hopewell Mound Group of Ohio. *Field Museum of Natural History Publication 211 Anthropological Series*, 6(5):73-181.

Pacheco, P. J. 1993 *Ohio Hopewell Settlement Patterns: An Application of the Vacant Center Model to Middle Woodland Period Intracommunity Settlement Variability in the Upper Licking River Valley*. Ph.D. dissertation, Department of Anthropology, The Ohio State University, Columbus, Ohio. University Microfilms, Ann Arbor.

Plog, S. 1980 *Stylistic Variation in Prehistoric Ceramics*. Cambridge University Press, Cambridge, England.

Prufer, O. 1964 The Hopewell Complex of Ohio. In *Hopewellian Studies*, edited by J. R. Caldwell and R. L. Hall, pp. 35-84. Illinois State Museum Scientific Papers 12, Springfield, Illinois.

Seeman, M. F. 1979 *The Hopewell Interaction Sphere: The Evidence for Interregional Trade and Structural Complexity.* Indiana Historical Society, Prehistory Research Series 5(2). Indianapolis, Indiana.

Seeman, M. F. and F. Soday 1980 The Russell Brown Mounds: Three Hopewell Mounds in Ross County, Ohio. *Midcontinental Journal of Archaeology* 5(1):73-116.

Shetrone, H. C. and E. F. Greenman 1931 Exploration of the Seip Group of Prehistoric Earthworks. *Ohio Archaeological and Historical Quarterly* 40: 343-509.

Smith, B. D. 1992 Hopewellian Farmers of Eastern North America. In *Rivers of Change: Essays on Early Agriculture in Eastern North America*, pp. 201-248. Smithsonian Institution Press, Washington, D. C.

Walthall, J. A. 1979 Hopewell and the Southern Heartland. In *Hopewell Archaeology: The Chillicothe Conference*, edited by D. S. Brose and N. Greber, pp. 200-208. Kent State University Press, Kent, Ohio.

1980 *Prehistoric Indians of the Southeast: Archaeology of Alabama and the Middle South*. University of Alabama Press, Tuscaloosa.

Webb, W. S. 1939 An Archeological Survey of the Wheeler Basin on the Tennessee River in Northern Alabama. *Bureau of American Ethnology Bulletin* 122.

Webb, W. S. and D. L. DeJarnette 1942 An Archeological Survey of the Pickwick Basin in the Adjacent Portions of the States of Alabama, Mississippi and Tennessee. *Bureau of American Ethnology Bulletin* 129.

West, G. A. 1934 Tobacco, Pipes and Smoking Customs of the American Indians. *Bulletin of the Public Museum of the City of Milwaukee*, Vol.17, parts I and II.

Wobst, M. 1977 Stylistic Behavior and Information Exchange. In *Papers for the Director: Research Essays in Honor of James B. Griffin*, edited by C. E. Cleland, pp. 317-42. Anthropological Papers No. 61, Museum of Anthropology. University of Michigan, Ann Arbor.

NINE

A COMMENTARY ON THE CONTEXTS AND CONTENTS OF LARGE TO SMALL OHIO HOPEWELL DEPOSITS

N'OMI B. GREBER

ABSTRACT

Deposits of both common and unusual artifacts are a hallmark
of Ohio Hopewell. Based on their contents and physical contexts, a suggested set of groupings of such deposits is presented.
It is also suggested that, in general, the number of participants
in the activities that precipitated the placement of a deposit
varies inversely with the number of occurrences of the particular
type of deposit. The existence of a shared cross regional calendrical cycle is proposed as a mechanism for spacing the events
associated with the placement of some groupings.

A View From the Core a Synthesis of Ohio Hopewell Archaeology•edited by Paul J. Pacheco
© Copyright 1996 by The Ohio Archaeological Council• Columbus, Ohio•All Rights Reserved•ISBN 0-9626931-9-7

INTRODUCTION

The homelands of Ohio Hopewell peoples lie in the river valleys formed by tributaries of the Ohio, from the Great and Little Miamis on the west, through Brush Creek and the Scioto, to the Muskingum on the east. Although the boundaries between local polities are not yet completely defined, we can recognize general regions (Greber 1993). We, as did some 19th century researchers, also see a unity in the culture shared across these valleys (e.g., Putnam 1882). In this essay, sharing the opinion that there is an Ohio Hopewell world view, I review some cultural customs found across regions. Ohio Hopewell peoples apparently also shared cultural values with politically and economically separate peoples who lived in other scattered locations of east-

ern North America. These values fostered the use of exotic materials and particular artifact or architectural forms as social symbols. At least some Ohio sites were major collection points of such objects and materials. Deposits of dozens, hundreds, to thousands of objects have captured the interest of both scholars and the general public **(Figure 9:1)**. Although in some studies the quantities of materials have been regarded as sources for eventual disbursal, both the objects and their contexts more logically fit an "acquisition" rather than a "distribution" model (e.g., Seeman 1977). In an effort to understand the motivations and mechanisms that resulted in the acquisition of such huge quantities of goods, I consider here the place of large deposits within the total spectrum of Ohio Hopewell deposits, from large to small.

FIGURE 9:1

More than eight thousand flint discs had been placed in two sand separated layers in the center of the Great Flint Mound (Mound 2) at the Hopewell Site. This photograph was taken at the site in Warren K. Moorehead's 1892 field camp (Moorehead 1922:Plate XLII).

Deposits have a symbolic aspect related to a Hopewellian world view. They also had economic, social, and other implications for the sponsoring societies. To gain some insight into their place within societies, I will present some thoughts on tentative groupings of deposits and suggest some possible cultural interpretations of these groupings. I do not consider, nor should the reader, that these groupings are "types" in the technical sense, as the word is customarily used in ceramic studies. Rather, they are a first attempt to distinguish some order in a complicated data set. My suggested groupings are based primarily on deposit contents and physical location. Although I have not formalized the data base into exact counts, it appears that some types are more numerous than others. As a preliminary observation, I suggest that the more rare types were associated with events involving a high percentage of the supporting population while more common ceremonies/rituals were each carried on by a few participants **(Figure 9:2)**. In group activities, individual roles could vary with respect to the degree of responsibility and the nature of participation. Each event might have different sponsors, actual actors, and audience. I further suggest that some portion of these events were scheduled according to a shared cross regional calendrical cycle.

For purposes of illustrating these points I have chosen representative deposits from the regions. They come from the Turner Group in the southwest, Tremper in the south, West Mound between these two, Central Scioto sites, and Eagle Mound from the Newark Group in the northeast (see front plate). These deposits share attributes also seen in wooden structures and associated features, mound strata, and enclosure walls. They reflect the ethos of the Hopewell world view in a planned landscape. Each was formally arranged as part of the activities taking place about a prepared floor within a physically bounded space. Deposits occur on the floor itself, in a pit cut through the floor, within a receptacle built into or onto such a floor, or on a stratum of a mound constructed over an individual feature or a set of features associated with the floor. The great majority of the deposits are not directly associated with a human interment. Published reports too often have had relatively limited basic information, particularly about the organic materials and fragmentary objects which form a significant part of deposit contents. Fortunately, archived records and collections can, in some instances, provide additional data.

SMALL SCALE FEATURES ON PREPARED FLOORS

The floors that are one of the main features of a bounded space are generally cleared or constructed. In the former, the top soil is removed to expose the harder sub-soils which serve as a floor. More formal construction entails the use of clays, gravels, and/or stones to build up a floor, usually upon a surface that has been cleared or otherwise prepared. Either type of floor can be ten to hundreds of feet across. On many floors, deposits of materials and/or artifacts are among the remains from the various activities that took place. What was apparently the most common type of deposit is frequently not well recorded in excavation records, and given cursory, if any, description in early site reports. These are low volume collections arranged in thin strata on the floor. Such features appear to contain remains from a small fire. At times uncharred materials occur among the burned ones. Probably these objects were associated with actions accompanying the actual fire making. It is highly likely that the fires were laid directly on the floors relatively near, but not necessarily congruent with the

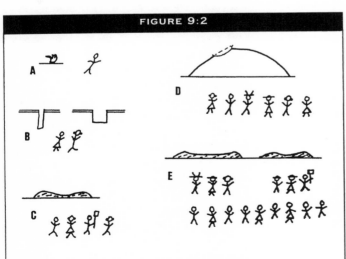

FIGURE 9:2

A symbolic representation of the estimated relative number of individuals taking part in the placement of the various types of deposits. Groupings include deposits arranged A: directly on the floor; B: in pits; C: in ritual basins; D: on sub-mounds, and the most rare, E: paired deposits associated with paired ritual basins.

deposit areas. The remnant floor at the base of the Edwin Harness Mound held such deposits. Apparently similar features are known from all the regions.

As can be seen in the plan of the Harness floor remnant, burned areas were common (Greber 1983:Figure 2.6). With two exceptions, the burning was at most 1 to 2 cm deep and was apparently the results of a one time firing. Two or three shallow fires were probably directly associated with ritual or ceremonial fires at tombs, a particular aspect of this site (Greber 1979b, Mills 1907). In numbers of other burned areas, ash and any other burned materials had been cleared away by either earlier excavators or Hopewellian caretakers — only the reddened floor remained. In six patches on the least archaeologically disturbed floor areas, a 2 cm or less lens of ash and charcoal covered by thinner lens of sands, gravels, or clay still remained. In seven other patches, artifacts were found amidst the redeposited charred materials. Recording the stratigraphy of these features does present a challenge to field archaeologists. When fine screening and flotation are used for recovery, the list of materials from such a deposit can be relatively long. For example, Harness Feature 44, contained broken bladelets, worked fish vertebra, turtle shell fragments, burnt canines and other small beads, and mica fragments. However, the total volume is small. The lithic, faunal and floral remains suggest small scale activities associated with a fire on which the equivalent of an elaborate neck-piece or perhaps a piece of decorated fabric was placed. Some shell fragments, possibly marine, may occur in similar features, but mica is the major exotic material found. In my tallies to date, no copper is in these shallow features.

In some instances, pottery sherds are included. At Seip-Pricer, sherds were mixed with bits of mica, bladelets, and about 18 fragments of obsidian tools in a floor deposit extending about 1.5 by 2.7 meters. Possibly, as in the larger Feature 16 at Edwin Harness, there were discrete deposits. The artifact collection is small but the obsidian is noteworthy. In what was probably a relatively small, separate section of the Seip-Pricer Great House, a mass of charred grass containing twigs, fabric, and one bladelet covered about a square meter of the floor **(Figure 9:3)**.

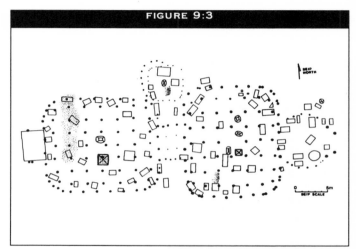

FIGURE 9:3

A range of deposit types associated with the Seip-Pricer Great House were recovered by the Ohio Historical Society excavations (Shetrone et al. 1925-1928, Shetrone and Greenman 1931). Some are located by the shaded areas here within an estimate of the floor plan of the great house (Greber 1983:Figure 10.1).

From Turner I have chosen as an illustration some of the burned areas found within the wall of the large enclosure. This type of cultural use has not been recorded for geometric enclosure walls in other regions. At Turner, the prepared floors were of limestones, a common construction material in the Little Miami region. The stones were placed on top of a low linear base composed of surface soils apparently collected in the immediate vicinity. All deposits were relatively shallow. Volk's 1890 field notes describe these features. "The soil in contact with the hearths is the blackest of all, apparently pulverized charcoal. Fragments of pottery, animal bone, a small fragment of turtle shell and bits of charcoal are found here." "Found more hearths...Found animal bones, mica, and fragments of pottery" (Putnam et al. 1882-1908). The profile section of the extreme end of Hearth Number 4 shown in **Figure 9:4** was copied from a drawing in Harvard Peabody Accession 1890-37. Large numbers of participants are not required for the activities which resulted in these shallow remains. They could of course have been there, but it seems reasonable to conclude that, in general, each deposit in this grouping represents a small scale event **(see Figure 9:2)**.

FIGURE 9:4

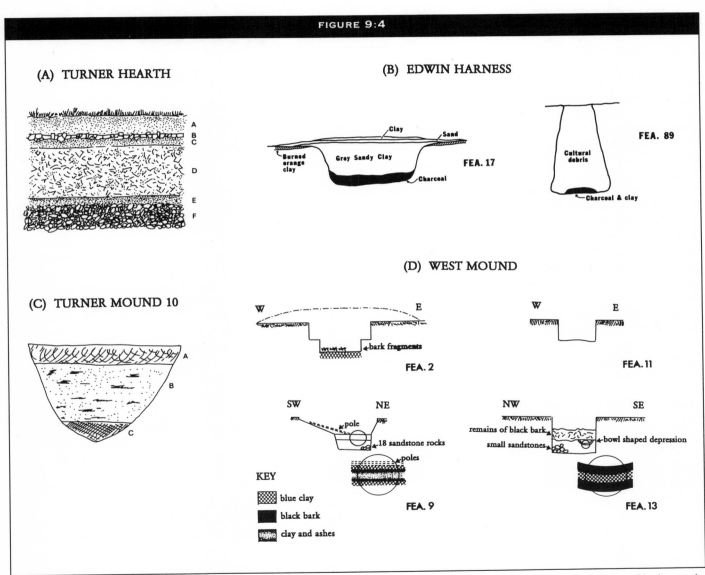

(A) TURNER HEARTH

(B) EDWIN HARNESS

(C) TURNER MOUND 10

(D) WEST MOUND

Smaller deposits. References in text. Turner Hearth No. 4: A: black soil; B: limestone hearth; C: black soil; D: black soil and clay, whole and broken snail shells; E: black soil containing bone, charcoal, and burnt limestone; F: undisturbed gravel. Edwin Harness: Depths, Feature 17: 45 cm; Feature 89: 71 cm. Turner Mound 10, Central Pit: A: black ashes (18 cm); B: gravel, sand, and ashes (41 cm); C: pure ashes (10 cm). West Mound: Width, pit base: Feature 2: 122 cm; Feature 9: 90 cm; Feature 11: 107 cm; Feature 13: 122 cm.

THE DESIGN AND CONTENTS OF PITS

In the records, pits are less common floor features than are the shallow burned areas. Pits vary in shape and contents but likely each represents remains from a single event. The distance between the pits and the locus of the activities from which the pit fill was accumulated is not clearly known. Not all pit fill contains man-made artifacts. Many features associated with Hopewell floors and spaces are found filled with natural stones or soils. This kind of fill has the characteristic of a "deposit" in the sense that the materials used were not merely convenient near-by soils, but were apparently sought out and brought to the floor. Cutting through a floor to make a pit can be a strenuous task as well as one likely subject to more cultural restrictions than the simpler act of making a single small fire on the floor. Such cutting is quite difficult on those floors made of clays and sands, a construction aptly named "Hopewell concrete". Pit construction varies. The more complex contents and/or design of some suggest that they were associated with relatively "complex" activities; that is, occasions of interest or importance to corporate groups larger than a single nuclear, or perhaps even an extended family. Examples of pits from several regions are shown in **Figure 9:4**.

The contents of simple pits overlap with those of the shallow floor deposits. For example, a pit which I consider to be a classic example of Hopewellian design was one of several cut through the floor at Edwin Harness. Feature 17, just outside the western side of the Great House, held much charred wood and seeds, two flint flakes, one bird bone, 112 mammal bone fragments, and 129 unidentifiable bone fragments **(Figure 9:4)**. Despite the quantities of burned materials inside the pit, there was no in situ burning. The remains of a fire, perhaps on the near-by floor, had been swept up and placed within the pit which was then carefully covered **(Figure 9:4** Feature 17, based on Greber 1983:Figure 3.6).

As an example from a much smaller scale bounded space, a pit under Turner Mound 10, held similar materials. Over a layer of pure ash (apparently white), were objects and charcoal mixed with gravel sand and ashes. These were capped by a layer of black ashes. A profile through the pit, copied from a drawing in Harvard Peabody Accession 1882-35, is shown in **Figure 9:4**. The Peabody Museum catalogue lists two pottery sherds, several fragments of mica, two flint chips, about 50 shell fragments, and about 30 broken mammal and bird bones from the pit (Accession 1882-35 Cat. Nos. 30064-70). The relatively fewer bone fragments in the Mound 10 listing most likely reflects differences in recovery techniques rather than a major difference in the type of items considered appropriate by the participants in the event that was the impetus for filling the pit. (This comment is not a complaint against the Peabody excavations; the records and documented collections of this work are a rare treasure.) With respect to the contents of the two pits, particularly the bone, both collections fit the description and conclusions written by Orrin Shane who patiently went through nearly 10,000 bone fragments recovered from the remnant of Edwin Harness Mound. "While animal parts may have been used as ornaments, certainly there is no evidence for mass offerings of animals, or for large-scale processing of foods for use on the mound floor." (Greber 1983:61). The larger pit through the floor beneath the Eagle Mound also fits this pattern. It contained large amounts of charcoal, one burned bone fragment, one chert fragment, and a lump of red burned clay. Like Edwin Harness Feature 17, this pit was at the edge of the main sets of apparently structural posts (Lepper 1989:124).

Another set of pits are different in profile, content, and likely the type of activities which they represent. Within this set, some pits have internal construction features which may indicate a more extensive set of activities than the sweeping up of fire debris and arranging it in a simple hole rather than on the floor. Others appear to have had a different use prior to becoming pits. For example, at Edwin Harness some are apparently reused post holes. Post Hole 216 within the southern circular room held a variety of burned woods in contrast to the single wood source more commonly identified in other, smaller post holes. This large post hole

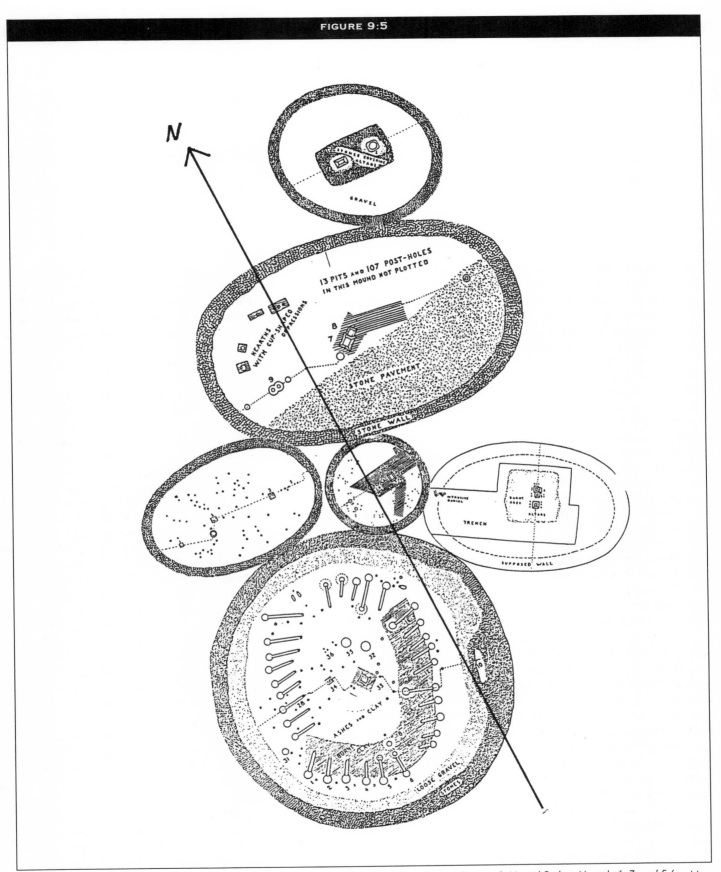

The major civic/ceremonial complex covered by the conjoined mounds at the Turner Site. From south to north Mound 3, then Mounds 6, 7, and 5 (west to east), Mounds 4 and 9. Various stratigraphic levels have been projected onto the plans (see Willoughby and Hooton 1922:33-81). No floor plan was published for Mound 14 which was adjacent to Mound 9. Mound 3 was approximately 100 feet (30 m) across at its base and about 14 feet (4 m) high when excavated.

also held ash, shell, bone, apparently fire cracked rock, and mica pieces mixed with a dark oily soil. The original large post was apparently removed before the deposit was made. Its size and position in the floor plan suggest that it was not intended to be an ordinary wall support (Greber 1983:Figure 3.2). Another probably refilled post hole contained cord marked and *Hopewellian Series* sherds from six to perhaps nine vessels, two bladelets, and the usual amount of burned and unburned bone, shell and mica fragments (**Figure 9:4** Feature 89, based on Greber 1983:Figure 3.6). One refilled post hole adjacent to the screen which was built about the Great House held a human skull (Greber 1983:31, Post Hole 25). This post also was not part of a building support. The range of burned woods or vessels, and other unusual contents suggest different levels of participation and/or different types of occasions as the impetus for the activities associated with the filling of these three features, than appears associated with Feature 17.

Additional examples of pits with distinctive shape and contents are found on the floor of Mound 2 at the Hopewell Site. This mound covered a deposit of large Wyandotte bifaces (**see Figure 9:1**). On the floor, a series of small conical shaped pits held chunks of yellow clay and red heavily burned clay fragments, apparently from a dismantled classic clay basin (Shetrone 1926:Figure 1). The adjoining pits at the eastern edge of the bounded space under Turner Mound 6 are examples of pits filled with a selected natural material. This small mound is a component of the major ceremonial/ritual area at Turner (**Figure 9:5**). The two pits (4 by 3.5 and 3 by 3 feet) were separated by a four inch thick clay wall. An internal oval pit had been dug in a corner of the floor of the smaller pit. After they had served some unknown use, they were all filled with "river sand" (Willoughby and Hooton 1922:76).

In sum, as a group, pit features are less common than the small layered floor deposits. They tend to fall into two sets. The first is distinguished by relatively simple construction and contents similar to that found in the small floor deposits. The other includes features with multiple use, or relatively complex architecture, and a differing range of contents. I interpret the whole pit grouping as associated with a wider range of activities than those associated with the small floor deposits, and, correspondingly, more social participants. The range in design and contents within the grouping may reflect a similar range in the number of participants in the associated rituals/ceremonies.

ABOVE THE FLOOR

Relatively few deposits are known to have been located above the floor. The thread that may tie this group together is pageantry, that is, some type of celebration or activity which includes the display of costumes and other paraphernalia. The location itself suggests activities associated with mound construction. Each mound on which a deposit was arranged was later mantled by a larger mound. The most spectacular deposit is fittingly from the most unique space, that covered by Mound 25, Hopewell Site. Here, apparently on the surface of a sub-mound, on a space defined by sheets of organic materials, more than 100 copper pieces were arranged together (Greber and Ruhl 1989:89; Moorehead 1922). Sheets of organic materials covered the deposit, and were possibly also interwoven. The various items appear to be dismantled elements of two costumes, one of which used motifs referring to a bear, plus parts of one or more standards or two-dimensional displays which used individual copper cutouts in a manner similar to that in which intertwined geometric and zoomorphic motifs form complex designs on carved bone. The use of such costumes and displays suggests a special public event that included great pageantry shared by a large number of participants.

A much smaller deposit, but one also with some evidence of pageantry comes from Mound 26 at the Hopewell Site. Due to prior grading of the mound, the excavators could not determine the origin of the lined cavity holding a copper plaque of unusual design that had been fastened to a 5/8 inch wooden backing (Shetrone 1922-1925: September 13, 1922; Shetrone 1926:Figure 112). The backing indicates that this object had been displayed by itself, perhaps as a standard. Also included were a pair of copper ear spools, at least a thousand shell beads, exquisite bladelets made from a fine red flint, and unknown organic remains.

A small deposit, without copper but one equally spectacular in its own form, comes from Tremper. It was located at a similar vertical height above the floor as others in this group and thus, I assume, on the surface of a sub-mound at a preliminary stage of the mound construction. This deposit contained nine pipes, a pair of napkin ring style ear ornaments, and a stone gorget. The outstanding craftsmanship seen in the "largest and finest pipe taken from the mound" (Mills 1916:Figure 77) and in the difficult to make ear ornaments, recalls the type of skill and care seen in the manufacture of the two unique pairs of ear ornaments from the Copper Deposit, Mound 25 (Ruhl 1992:Figure 3). These objects are also unusual in size and form. The brilliant red of the Ohio pipestone used for the Tremper pieces is reminiscent of copper red. The use of copper as a ritual material extends across the Hopewell core and beyond. However, the particular forms in which it appears differ (Greber 1991). I assume that color, which is clearly important in Hopewellian designs, was the symbolic element being emphasized in this case. Two tubular, one modified tubular, four other platform pipes, and a gorget of unknown design were also in the Tremper deposit. I interpret the range of pipe styles as reflecting the importance to the supporting society of the event that initiated the deposit, and the general character of all the objects as appropriate for special display.

The simplest deposit contents come from Edwin Harness. A "basin like depression", found by Putnam above a major ritual or ceremonial floor area located in the largest section of the Great House, contained much charred organic material and apparently only one artifact. This fragment of a small human effigy pipe is unique in design (Greber 1983: Figure 3.5).

In sum, this group of deposits occurs at a relatively consistent height above the floor. Unfortunately, the details of the contexts of these deposits are not presently well enough known to determine which, if any, features were included under the mound strata at that point. It does not appear to have been individual tombs. The deposits are few but clearly significant. They are recorded in some but not all regions. It is difficult to deal with negative evidence, particularly when the data base comes from widely different excavation methods. It is also difficult to correlate unique expressions, such as the Copper Deposit, with more general expressions. Overall, I expect that the number of participants associated with each deposit in this grouping was in general greater than that for pit deposits. The occasion which was the impetus for their arrangement was of major, but not the most major, importance.

I have not included the mica covered sub-mounds in this grouping of above-floor deposits. The occurrence of extensive mantles of sheets of mica that are found over sub-mounds or many areas of prepared floors I do not consider to be "deposits" in the same sense as the collections discussed above. Mica cutouts, as artifacts, are part of some deposits. The placing of mica books as a mantle, I believe, reflects a different aspect of the symbolic use of mica than that expressed in mica cutouts. In this aspect, mica is similar to the variety of culturally chosen sands, variously sized gravels, and other such materials used as mantles.

RITUAL CLAY BASINS

Formally constructed clay basins are a distinctive aspect of Ohio Hopewell bounded spaces. These features have been labeled both "altars" and "crematory basins". The variations found in both the morphology of the basins themselves, and in the bounded spaces with which they are associated, suggest that the physical and social uses of these features is similarly varied (Seeman and Greber 1991). Thus, I refer to them herein by more neutral terms as ritual basins or simply basins. The construction materials and final form no doubt had both practical and symbolic aspects. Functionally they were fireplaces, but of more formal design than normal domestic hearths. They were constructed of puddled clay on a prepared floor. They vary in size, final form, and orientation both within and across sites. For example, the mean size of basins at Mound City is significantly larger than that found at the Hopewell Site. Possibly this reflects a difference in functional use. (Konigsberg 1985; Seeman and Greber 1991). Some clearly stylistic attributes exist, for example, corner shapes. At Tremper these are sharp, trefoil forms

occur at Turner, and variously rounded ones appear elsewhere. Frequently, the basins themselves were eventually
covered by carefully designed small mounds. The majority
have been found "empty", at least of artifacts. Yet, almost
all the large artifact deposits for which Ohio Hopewell is
well known, were each within or adjacent to a ritual basin.

Small deposits also occur in the grouping associated with
these basins.   The volume of these deposits is of the same
magnitude as that from some of the pits or larger floor
deposits already mentioned, but the collections from basins
may include copper artifacts. "Altar 1" found under the
major embankment at Turner and "Crematory Basin 1"
found on the floor of Hopewell Mound 26 are examples.
"Altar 1" held amidst ashes and charred matter, perforated
small mammal canines, bone and copper beads, fragments
of copper ear ornaments, shark's teeth, a bladelet, mica,
and fragments of typical beautifully carved bone
(Willoughby and Hooton 1922:8). Hopewell Mound 26 covered a good example of a medium size bounded space. In a
ritual basin on the floor were four copper celts, several very
large marine shell beads, other badly burned shell objects,
and several thousand shell beads probably originally fastened to the "considerable quantity of woven cloth" identified
along with grass, twigs, and leaves as part of the charred
contents (Shetrone 1922-1925: September 14, 1922).
Smaller deposits, such as these two, are apparently more
numerous than the large ones.

Among the large deposits adjoining ritual basins, two are
unique. They are part of the set of features that make the
Hopewell Site so different from all other core sites as well as
from any other site in eastern North America. A deposit of
approximately 300 pounds of obsidian debitage was recorded on the floor of the relatively small Mound 11, located
south of the inner D-shaped enclosure that surrounded several small mounds and the great Mound 25. This deliberate
arrangement of debris certainly suggests that obsidian itself
was of special significance to a Hopewellian society. This
suggestion is corroborated by its major use, which was for
the chipping of large ceremonial bifaces, and by its limited
distribution among core sites, and within the Hopewell Site

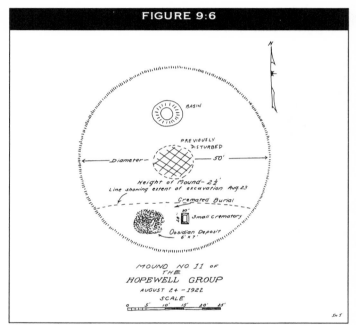

Floor plan of Mound 11, Hopewell Site. Estimates of the locations of findings attributed by Henry Shetrone to previous excavators are added to the
field map of the Ohio Historical Society excavations of the floor area undis-
trubed prior to 1922 (Shetrone 1926:39-43, Shetrone 1922-1925: August
22-29, 1922).

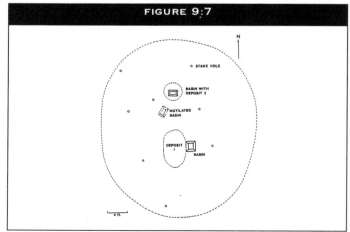

Example of paired symbolically complementary ritual basins under Shetrone
Mound 17, Hopewell Site. This pair contrasts in size, orientation, and the
arrangement of the associated deposits.

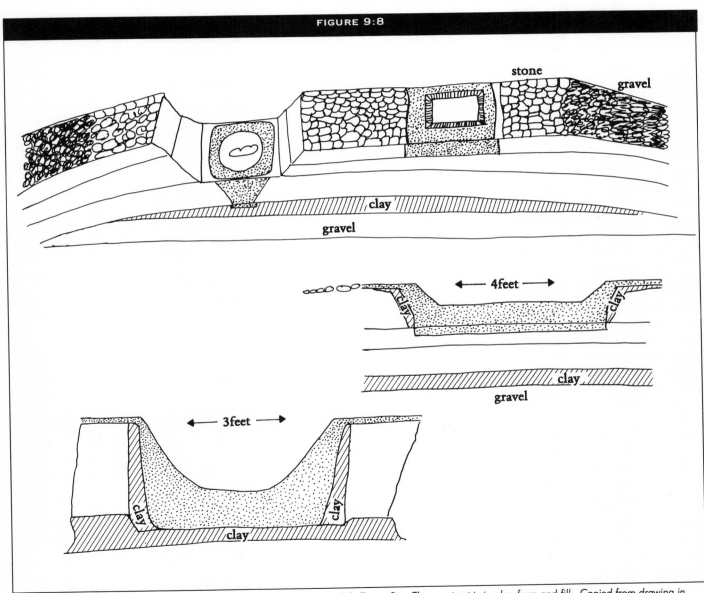

FIGURE 9:8

Example of paired, symbolically complementary ritual basins within Mound 9, Turner Site. The constrast is in plan form and fill. Copied from drawing in Harvard Peabody Accession 1882-35.

itself. Nearly one hundred bifaces have been restored from fragments found in a major deposit covered by Mound 25. A few true tools were also made and apparently used in limited circumstances (Greber and Ruhl 1989:191-194). It is most likely that the handling of this material was restricted to a small social group. Based on the field notes, I doubt the attribution of the debitage to a single individual's grave (see Figure 9:6).

The availability of a significant quantity of obsidian apparently coincides with the high point in availability and artistic craftsmanship seen in several other exotic materials including copper. The ties among those few privileged to handle the black glass could have been biological or social. The deposit of obsidian debitage signifies the end of the active use of the large quantity of raw obsidian from which it was flaked, whether one or several individuals did the flaking. The social group responsible was apparently small.

A third unique deposit at the Hopewell Site appears to warrant an interpretation different from that of both the Copper Deposit and the collection of obsidian debitage. This is the carefully designed two-tiered arrangement of over 8,000 Wyandotte bifaces found adjacent to a ritual basin on the floor under Mound 2 (see Figure 9:1). These are not dismantled parts, nor left over debris, but objects themselves. The physical appearance of some suggests that they were curated after manufacture. Although a small amount of raw material has been found at the site, a quantity of debitage to match the number of bifaces is not as yet known. A few isolated discs have been found in the general vicinity of the site, but again, no quantity of debitage. Thus, on the basis of present evidence, it appears that, at least a good number of these artifacts were brought to the site and not locally made. In contrast, I strongly suspect that the obsidian and copper items of the other two deposits were made relatively locally. Also, unlike the unique deposits of obsidian flakes and copper cutouts, relatively contemporaneous large deposits of flint discs have been found outside the Ohio Hopewell core. In the southwestern regions of the Ohio core, Wyandotte chert is a relatively common material for every day tools. A major aspect of the symbolic significance of the Mound 2 deposit may be the arrangement of the deposit itself. This point will be amplified later.

The remaining large deposits associated with basins contain a mix of assorted artifacts and raw materials. I will discuss these after the introduction of the next grouping of deposits.

PAIRS OF RITUAL BASINS

An apparent symbolic element of the design of a number of bounded spaces are paired features that show a pattern of complementary contrast. The pattern is seen in differences in size, shape, orientation, and when present, the contents of these features. The occurrence of such pairs suggests that each of the pair was used in complementary rituals associated with a single event. Examples of this pattern occur across regions. At the Hopewell Site, in several instances, two ritual basins, one larger than the other, were oriented at right angles to each other (Figure 9:7). Other examples come from Turner. At least four pairs of ritual basins occur under components of the conjoined mounds: Mounds 5, 7, and 9. The elements of each pair, consisting of a rounded and a quadrilateral basin, are superimposed (Figure 9:8). No artifacts are recorded. However, the fill of the lower basin is darker than that of the upper. The shape contrast is repeated outside the conjoined mounds. For example, a superimposed pair of basins was centered on the floor under Mound 12. The shape contrast also holds for features whose use was probably related to that of the ritual basins. Two simply constructed clay "hearth" features, one elliptical, one quadrilateral are paired under Mound 2 as are a large circular "fire place" and a nearby unusual rectangular platform under Mound 1 (Willoughby and Hooton 1922:Figures 13, 14).

A more detailed complementary contrast is seen in the contents of two pairs of deposits from the Hopewell Site. Each pair is associated with a pair of ritual basins. I have previously hypothesized that these complementary ritual remains reflect a corresponding dual ritual social organization (Greber and Ruhl 1989:75-88). I suggest here that the deposits from Mounds 3 and 4 at Turner are similarly complementary in nature, and likely associated with the same type of obviously important, relatively infrequent event as the Hopewell Site pairs.

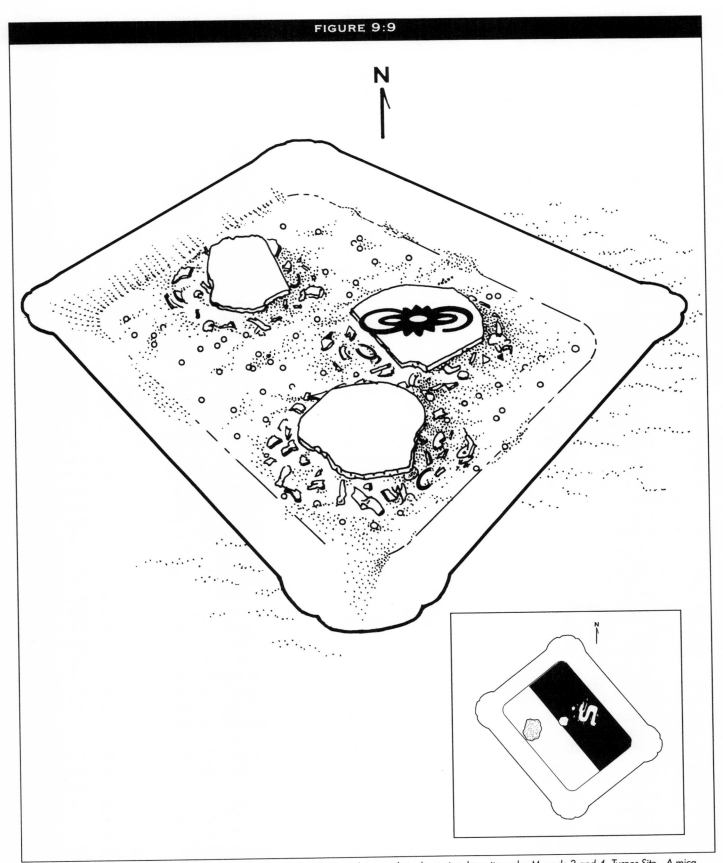

An estimate of one stratigraphic level from the arrangements of artifacts and materials in the major deposits under Mounds 3 and 4, Turner Site. A mica book covered each of three sets of objects within a ritual basin, Mound 3. A copper cutout lay on one sheet. Thousands of pearls were scattered about each pile (Willoughby and Hooton 1922:45). Layers of black and white ashes contrast within a basin of Mound 4. A large piece of cannel coal was placed on the southwest side. A copper nugget lay near the middle. Fragments of ceramic figurines and other objects were beneath the mica serpent effigy (Willoughby and Hooton 1922:63).

At Hopewell, one pair was associated with differently sized ritual basins, apparently built within separate rooms or sections of a Great House covered by the huge Mound 25. An almost unimaginable number of exotic and ordinary objects and materials were in these deposits (Greber and Ruhl 1989:Table 3.1). The other pair was arranged in a similar manner on a simple prepared floor covered by the small Shetrone Mound 17 (**Figure 9:7**). The Turner pair was within rooms or sections of the major ceremonial precinct. The two sections themselves show complementary contrast. The Mound 3 floor plan is circular, that of Mound 4 more nearly rectilinear (**Figure 9:5**). Other floor features suggest that related but not identical activities took place. For example, a limited number of clay covered pits under Mound 4 bear some similarities to the numerous unusual ones under Mound 3. The basins holding the deposits were differently sized and finished with rare trefoil shaped corners.

As would be expected, the details of the complementary pattern of the Southern Ohio pair differ from those of the Central Scioto. Very briefly, at the Hopewell Site, items from Shetrone Mound 17 contrast copper objects, pipes, and stone effigies with cut mica, bear claws, and bladelets. In Mound 25, copper and mica items occurred in both deposits, but in different form and in different numbers. Thousands of pearl beads and several ceramic vessels contrast with over 100 obsidian bifaces and five pipes (see Greber and Ruhl 1989:Tables 3.1, 3.2).

Space limits the amount of detail from Turner which can be considered here. As symbolic elements, the contrast between *dark and light* seen in the Mound 3 deposit, complements the mica mantled *three piles* surrounded by pearls in Mound 4 (**Figure 9:9**).

Both these sets of symbolic elements also occur across regions in architectural designs. At Turner, copper and mica occur in traditional forms as cutouts, but cannel coal is added as a significant raw material. The copper cutouts from the Mound 3 deposit were probably parts of some type of two dimensional display such as that suggested for the Copper Deposit. Only a few copper beads and tinklers and nuggets came from Mound 4. Unique objects, for the Ohio core, include the terra-cotta figurines restored from the fragments found beneath the mica cut-out seen in **Figure 9:9**.

My final comment concerns the number and types of animal remains recovered. In contrast with the floor deposits and pit contents, the number of animals represented here is mind boggling. In the Mound 4 deposit were 284 astragali of deer and elk, that is, the ankle bones of at least 142 different animals, and more than 1200 animal teeth and claws. On the floor of Mound 3 more than 2000 animal teeth, about 600 phalanges, and 48,000 pearls were within the arrangement. The acquisition of symbolic parts from the many animals represented in these *two* deposits required either many people, or some time, or more likely both. The missing bones of the animals, like the fragments of incomplete artifacts included in the deposits, were left elsewhere. Some parts were probably left at a hunting camp, others at home in the trash from dinner. All the animals could have lived in near-by areas. The total effort put into acquiring this ritual paraphernalia was significant, but could have been shared by many members of the sponsoring society.

In sum, pairs of ritual basins and basin-like features which were probably used in the same event, are found at least in the Central Scioto and Little Miami regions. Three major pairs of deposits are associated with three of the basin pairs. I interpret these deposits as associated with the most major Hopewellian celebration, held on the basis of a calendrical cycle. In honor of this occasion, all individuals of the sponsoring groups would have had a part in any given celebration, and probably quite a few visitors too (**Figure 9:2**).

HINTS OF A CALENDRIC CYCLE

The pieces of evidence which lead me to a possible two part, long term calendric cycle come from stratigraphy seen in architecture. This evidence should not be confused with either the many binary aspects of Hopewellian art style or the binary contrasts in the designs of horizontal ritual spaces. The stratigraphy examples are limited, but no more so than many attributes commonly attached to Ohio Hopewell. They come from across the core in mounds, wooden structures, enclosure walls and special features.

In a number of cases, the additions to mounds in the Central Scioto region can be divided into two major episodes (Greber 1991). The few large oblong mounds formed by placing unifying strata over primary conjoined mounds, follow this pattern: Edwin Harness and Seip-Pricer (e.g., Shetrone and Greenman 1931:Figure 5). The over-sized Hopewell Mound 25 likely contains evidence for more than one cycle (Greber and Ruhl 1989:Figure 2.14). At Mound City, at least two sets of two wooden structures and their associated features are superimposed. The two large Turner deposits were in the upper of two superimposed basins **(Figure 9:5)**. Also, at least two sets of the contrasting pairs of rounded and quadrilateral basins were superimposed; others may have been. Unfortunately, even at Turner we do not have the complete plan of a major ceremonial precinct.

Some enclosure walls show evidence of cyclic rebuilding. Two stages have been identified at Newark and possibly also at Pollock and High Bank (Lepper this volume, Riordan this volume, and Shane 1972, respectively). At Capitolium Mound, small excavations showed two prepared floors superimposed in two separate lobes (Greber 1990, Pickard this volume).

The existence of a cycle that is about two or three human generations long is known among many cultures. Allowing a society to plan and to accumulate the means for the celebrations reflected in the three pairs of large deposits over such a stretch of time, I believe, provides a realistic human time frame. The total effort in economic, social, and political terms is great. Many other events occurred during any given cycle, and the remains from some of these are recorded in other deposits.

BACK TO FLOORS, BASINS, AND OTHER FEATURES

Several well known large deposits remain for discussion. In what manner might these fit into the proposed deposit range extending from the shallow floor features to the paired great deposits? First, a few brief comments on deposits arranged near ritual basins at Mound City. Much

emphasis has rightly been placed on the mortuary aspects of Mound City (e.g., Brown 1979). It has even been described as a "City of the Dead." Yet, as at any ritual space, it is reasonable to consider the possibility that deposits were arranged during events that were not necessarily funereal. In ancient and present day churches, cathedrals or similar public structures, a burial crypt may share a floor and even be physically near, the locus of ceremonies or offerings associated with events in the life of an individual, family, or larger social group that are not funerals. As I handled the collection of many dozens of pipes excavated in the nineteenth century near a ritual basin on the floor under Mound 8, I saw the works of many craftsmen, far more than the eight individuals whose cremated remains were placed on that floor (Mills 1922). The event which was the impetus for placing the pipes was of importance to a relatively large social unit. It could have been death rites for individual(s), but equally well, it may have been in honor of other themes important in the Hopewellian world view.

A pair of deposits and an unusual ritual basin were possibly grouped on a floor under Mound 13. The larger of the two deposits contained, in a "mass of dark earth intermixed with much carbonaceous matter" objects of copper, obsidian, shark's teeth, crystal quartz, broken pipes, and pottery (Mills 1922:452). Just west of this deposit, more than 5000 large barrel shaped beads, likely from marine shell, had been placed in a mass of yellow clay. The basin did not have the usual flat bottom, but was v-shaped in cross-section. The east end of the basin was covered with light clay while the western half was "coated with a red pigment" (Mills 1922:454). This set of features contains the common dark-light complementary contrast. The shape of the basin suggests an activity different from the standard cremating of human remains, a use that could have been made of some other basins at Mound City. The occasion for arranging the deposits and coating the ritual basin likely involved more than one family unit.

The last two large deposits to be considered are from Tremper and Seip-Pricer. The major Tremper deposit was arranged adjacent to a ritual basin within the middle section

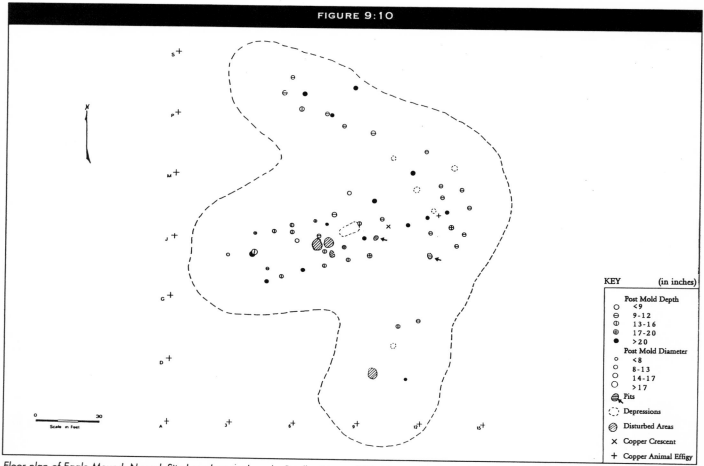

FIGURE 9:10

KEY   (in inches)

Post Mold Depth
○   <9
⊖   9-12
⊕   13-16
⊕   17-20
●   >20

Post Mold Diameter
○   <8
○   8-13
○   14-17
○   >17

⊕   Pits

⊙   Depressions

▨   Disturbed Areas

X   Copper Crescent

+   Copper Animal Effigy

0   30
Scale in Feet

Floor plan of Eagle Mound, Newark Site based on analyses by Bradley Lepper, Ohio Historical Society, of Society excavations under Emerson Greenman. The central depression is shown to scale. Other depressions are enlarged for visibility. The copper animal effigy had been placed on or in an upper level of the mound at the point marked (See also Lepper 1989).

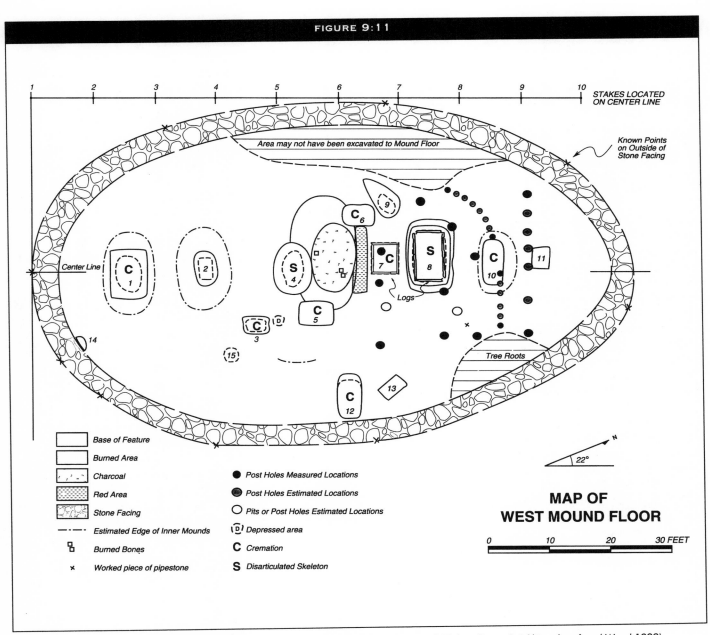

FIGURE 9:11

STAKES LOCATED ON CENTER LINE

Known Points on Outside of Stone Facing

Area may not have been excavated to Mound Floor

Center Line

Logs

Tree Roots

N
22°

MAP OF
WEST MOUND FLOOR

0   10   20   30 FEET

Base of Feature
Burned Area
Charcoal
Red Area
Stone Facing
Estimated Edge of Inner Mounds
Burned Bones
Worked piece of pipestone

● **Post Holes Measured Locations**
◉ **Post Holes Estimated Locations**
○ **Pits or Post Holes Estimated Locations**
⌐D⌐ **Depressed area**
C Cremation
S Disarticulated Skeleton

Floor plan of West Mound. Note the relative orientation and location of Features 2, 9, 11, and 13 (see Figure 9:4 [this volume] and Wood 1992).

of three rooms or sections at the eastern end of the Great House complex (Mills 1916:Figure 3). Attributes of the included artifacts and the arrangement itself have similarities to the larger Shetrone Mound 17 deposit (Greber 1987). Some artifacts were apparently grouped by type, but a full pattern is not available as yet. I do not, as did Mills, interpret the deposit as having accumulated over a long period of time. The total contents were probably viewed by those arranging them, as appropriate parts of a single, very major occasion. Perhaps, it was the same type of occasion as that I have proposed for the paired deposit, perhaps not.

The Seip-Pricer deposit has a different physical context from that of the other large deposits. Groups of artifacts were arranged, apparently on the burned floor of a large depression in the largest section of the Great House (**Figure 9:3**). The area was then capped with a clay cover. Later several log tombs, average in nature, were built on the cap. Clearly the placement of the deposit on the depression did not signal the end of the use of the Great House. It could have been part of the initiation of the structure, the cyclic major celebration I have proposed, or some other major event. There are two small wooden structures on the Seip-Pricer floor which share patterning with the paired basins. A collection of 12 copper plaques was arranged over a 20 inch copper celt on the floor of a small log structure in the largest section of the Great House (**Figure 9:3**). Fabric, several pearl beads, and three bear canines, each set with a pearl, were included. In a similar location in the adjoining room, a smaller log structure is recorded as holding only mica scraps. (Shetrone and Greenman 1931:Burial 68). Perhaps this is again a symbolic contrast of copper and mica, and a related dual ritual organization.

In sum, at Seip-Pricer the major deposit was likely associated with an event involving a large number of individuals. Because of the special nature of the deposit and its separate covering, these individuals may have in some manner represented all parts of the society sponsoring the Great House. If not, then the deposit represents the efforts of only that portion of the society holding the most prestigious ritual

position. The possible recognition of a two part ritual organization within the society sponsoring the Great House places another layer of organization upon the social groupings which I have previously suggested for the supporting population (Greber 1979a, 1979b, Greber 1983:86-89).

SPACES WITHOUT WITHOUT A LARGE DEPOSIT

The great and large Ohio Hopewell deposits represent rare events. There are many clearly Hopewellian bounded spaces that do not have such features. At a complex site like Newark, a bounded space such as Eagle Mound (**Figure 9:10**) may have been the location of only a part of the ceremonial/ritual activities occurring at the site. In other instances, a range of smaller deposits on the floor, in pits, or above the floor may represent all that should be expected. This is apparently the case at West Mound.

The activity remains at Eagle Mound have some similarities with those found at Seip-Pricer. The depression holding the major deposits at Seip-Pricer, perhaps 3 by 9 m, is at the large end of the range of depression types found on prepared floors. Under Eagle Mound, an apparently similar feature was located towards the northeastern end of the larger ritual area (Lepper 1989:124). This depression, which at about 3 m in length is in scale for this smaller bounded space, was found filled with sand, quite distinct from the general mound fill. A few fragments of burned flint were probably accidently left behind when the area was cleaned after its last use. The condition and disposition of the depression repeats that associated with ritual basins which were all used, but frequently cleaned of artifacts and fire debris after final use, and at times also refilled with materials such as "sand".

As pointed out to me by Bradley Lepper, another apparent similarity occurs in the disposition of mica and copper that resulted from activities on the floor (Bradley Lepper, personal communication, 1995). Two isolated copper objects, a modified crescent and an animal effigy, were recovered from Eagle Mound in an area which was likely a separate room or floor section (**Figure 9:10**). Lepper has tallied the occurrences of mica and found that the locations all fall outside the area in which the copper was found (**Figure 9:10**). Possibly this disjunction reflects a similar concept as that represented by the patterning seen at Seip-Pricer and the Hopewell Site.

The activities represented at West Mound are likely more self contained than those seen at Eagle Mound. Two radiocarbon dates place site use in the first to second centuries A.D. (Porter and McBeth 1957, 1958; Ruhl 1992; Wood 1992). The artifact collection consists only of three whole and three fragmentary copper ear spools, one worked fragment of pipestone, and several shell beads, but the features include floor deposits, depressions, specialized pits, tombs, and post holes. (**Figure 9:11**). The pipestone was in a thin deposit of charred material on the floor. Four pit features not associated with human remains were carefully constructed (**Figure 9:4** Features 2, 9, 11, 13 based on Wood 1992). Three were comparatively elaborate suggesting complex associated activities. The fourth, a simple pit, was located at the outer edge of a line of posts, as were simple pits at Edwin Harness and Eagle Mound (**Figure 9:11: Feature 11**). The relative location of Features 9 and 13 suggests a deliberate placement, perhaps a design idea similar to that seen in paired basins. Thus, the floor plan covered by West Mound shares some cross regional architectural canons in the design of ritual spaces, and possibly in the rituals themselves. The size of the associated social units probably reached only to the middle of the range found across all the valleys. In sum, no quantitatively significant deposits were placed on the floors under Eagle Mound or West Mound. The number of artifacts found with *all* the more common floor features on all known floors is only a fraction of that found in the rare great deposits. These features are none the less important for understanding the many activities associated with Hopewellian bounded spaces.

CODA

Hopewellian societies left behind remains of a landscape planned at many levels, from positioning clay basins on a simple floor to forming miles of complex enclosures. Objects representing both an aesthetic tradition and layers of symbolic meaning were used in this landscape and, at times, placed as part of it. The same general world view can be expressed by physically different symbols which have some quality deemed similar and appropriate by the users. I believe that Hopewellian objects and landscapes could share symbolic qualities that now, we can only estimate. To see the varied objects and architecture found in the Ohio Hopewell core in a light that may allow glimpses of a cultural unity based on an assumed shared world view, we need a framework that is flexible enough to cover variation without being over simplified. As I emphasized at the beginning of this essay, I consider the comments here a beginning approximation for such a framework.

As usual, any estimate of Ohio Hopewell activities is hampered by the lack of even a relative chronological yard stick. For example, do the known large deposits represent the entirety of the Ohio Hopewell era? Certainly they do not represent the entirety of the ceremonial/ritual/political/economic activities. What is the relative chronology of these deposits, particularly the paired deposits compared with those at Tremper and Seip? Are great artifact deposits and monumental structures coeval or spaced through time? What is the relative chronology of the construction of major mounds and large enclosures, especially at sites where both appear? Until there is a well documented time line for Ohio Hopewell, we will need to continue constructing our hypothetical cultural interpretations on very shifting sands of time.

Here is mine, for now. I believe a calendrical cycle paced a major portion of Hopewellian celebrations. The location of the Turner deposits in the upper of two basins suggests that the paired deposits mark the completion of a cycle or the beginning of a new one. Perhaps at the Hopewell Site, a focus for core events, the unique double layer of ceremonial bifaces is also a symbol of this cycle. At flat topped Capitolium Mound a pair of lobes joined to an unknown structure covered two superimposed floors. On top of the mantled upper floor the construction changed from horizontal layers to mounded, complex strata (Greber 1990, Pickard this volume). Perhaps these strata themselves were a recognition by celebrants of the same calendar event as that recognized by the paired object deposits at Turner and Hopewell. The ground plan of the circular and octagonal enclosures at Newark and High Bank are reminiscent of the complimentary design pattern seen in the basin pairs at Turner. Perhaps the construction of these enclosures celebrates the same event reflected in the pairs of great deposits. None of these celebrations need to have been in the same cycle. As I have noted elsewhere, separating the use and construction of the large bounded spaces marked by Seip-Pricer Mound and the extensive enclosure at Seip allows a more reasonable human time scale for the physical, economic, political, and social efforts involved in these pieces of the Hopewellian planned landscape (Greber n.d.). A calendar that spaces major events can provide the basis for organizing and justifying such a time scale. A cycle of time recognized by all Ohio Hopewell peoples would provide a strong cross-regional cultural bond. The basic characteristics of each event celebrated in the calendar gives unity while the particular activities and paraphernalia of any given celebration could have their local expression.

ACKNOWLEDGMENTS

This essay is based on a talk given in the plenary session of the 1992 meeting of the Midwest Archaeological Conference in Grand Rapids, Michigan. The text has been expanded although the illustrations, by necessity, have had to be limited. Bradley Lepper has made available to me his work with Emerson Greenman's field records from excavations for the Ohio Historical Society at Eagle Mound, and I thank him. I appreciate the comments of Katharine Ruhl who read drafts in process. Kathryn Wood most patiently assisted with editorial details as well as sharing her experience with the West Mound records; I am grateful for her help. As always, I thank those who curate the collections of Ohio Hopewell materials which form the foundation of knowledge for all research on the "Core".

REFERENCES CITED

Brown, J. A. 1979 Charnel Houses and Mortuary Crypts: Disposal of the Dead in the Middle Woodland Period. In *Hopewell Archaeology: The Chillicothe Conference*, edited by D. S. Brose and N. Greber, pp. 211-219. Kent State University Press, Kent, Ohio.

Greber, N. 1979a Variations in Social Structure Among Classic Ohio Hopewell Peoples. *Midcontinental Journal of Archaeology* 3(3):35-78.

1979b A Comparative Study of Site Morphology and Burial Patterns at Edwin Harness Mound and Seip Mounds 1 and 2. In *Hopewell Archaeology: The Chillicothe Conference*, edited by D. S. Brose and N. Greber, pp. 27-38. Kent State University Press, Kent, Ohio.

1983 *Recent Excavations at the Edwin Harness Mound, Liberty Works, Ross County, Ohio.* Midcontinental Journal of Archaeology, Special Paper No. 5, Kent State University Press, Kent, Ohio.

1987 Shetrone's Mound 17 at the Hopewell Site, Ross County Ohio: Excavated 1924; Studied 1986. Paper presented at the Annual Meeting of the Midwest Archaeological Conference, Milwaukee, Wisconsin.

1990 A Field Report on Excavations in Capitolium Mound, Marietta Earthworks, Washington County, Ohio. Paper presented at the 45th Annual Meeting of the Southeastern Archaeological Conference, Mobile, Alabama.

1991 A Study of Continuity and Contrast Between Central Scioto Adena and Hopewell Sites. *West Virginia Archaeologist* 43(1/2):1-26.

1992 Cultural Deposits: Consigned by Hopewellian Customs. Paper presented at Plenary Session, Annual Meeting of Midwest Archaeological Conference, Grand Rapids Michigan.

1993 Considering Some Possible Ecological, Social, and Political Boundaries Among Ohio Hopewell Peoples. Paper presented at Annual Meeting of the Society for American Archaeology, St. Louis, Missouri.

n.d. Two Geometric Enclosures in Paint Creek: An Estimate of Possible Changes in Community Patterns Through Time. In *Ohio Hopewell Community Organization*, edited by W. S. Dancey and P. J. Pacheco. Kent State University Press, Ohio "in press."

Greber, N. and K. C. Ruhl 1989 *The Hopewell Site: a Contemporary Analysis Based on the Work of Charles C. Willoughby.* Westview Press, Boulder, Colorado.

Konigsberg, L. W. 1985 Demography and Mortuary Practice at Seip Mound One. *Midcontinental Journal of Archaeology* 10(1):123-148.

Lepper, B. T. 1989 An Historical Review of Archaeological Research at the Newark Earthworks. *Journal of the Steward Anthropological Society* 18(1/2):118-140.

Mills, W. C. 1907 Explorations of the Edwin Harness Mound. *Ohio Archaeological and Historical Publications* 16:113-193. Reprinted 1907 in Mills, *Certain Mounds and Village Sites* 1(4).

1916 Exploration of the Tremper Mound. *Ohio Archaeological and Historical Publications* 25:262-398. Reprinted 1917 in Mills, *Certain Mounds and Village Sites* 2(3):105-240.

1922 Exploration of the Mound City Group. *Ohio Archaeological and Historical Quarterly* 31:423-584. Reprinted 1922 in Mills, *Certain Mounds and Village Sites* 3(4).

Moorehead, W. K. 1922 The Hopewell Mound Group of Ohio. *Field Museum of Natural History Anthropological Series*, Publication 211, 6(5):73-181. Reprinted 1968 by Kraus Reprint and Periodical Co., New York.

Porter, T. and D. McBeth 1957 Preliminary report on the West Mound. *Ohio Archaeologist* 7(3):106-110.

1958 Report on the West Mound, Ohio. *Ohio Archaeologist* 8(1):28-31.

Putnam, F. W. 1882 Notes on Copper Objects from North and South America. *Collections of the Peabody Museum 15th Annual Report* 3:83-148.

Putnam, F. W., C. L. Metz, E. Volk, and M. H. Saville 1882-1908 Field Notes of Excavations at the Turner Group. Ms. on file, Peabody Museum of Archaeology and Ethnology, Harvard University, Cambridge, Massachusetts.

Ruhl, K. 1992 Copper Earspools from Ohio Hopewell Sites. *Midcontinental Journal of Archaeology* 17(1):46-79.

Seeman, M. F. 1977 *The Hopewell Interaction Sphere: The Evidence for Interregional Trade and Structural Complexity.* Ph.D. dissertation, Department of Anthropology, Indiana University, Bloomington. University Microfilms, Ann Arbor.

Seeman, M. F. and N. Greber 1991 Flames of Reverence: Variations in the Use of Prepared Clay Basins Within Ohio Hopewell. Paper presented at Midwest Archaeological Conference, LaCrosse, Wisconsin.

Shane, O. and Field School Staff 1972 Field Notes from Work at High Bank, Ross County. Ms. on file, Department of Anthropology, Kent State University, Kent, Ohio.

Shetrone, H. C. 1926 Exploration of the Hopewell Group of Prehistoric Earthworks. *Ohio Archaeological and Historical Quarterly* 35:1-227.

Shetrone, H. C. and E. F. Greenman 1931 Exploration of the Seip Group of Prehistoric Earthworks. *Ohio State Archaeological and Historical Quarterly* 40:343-509.

Shetrone, H. C., F. Setzler, and R. Goslin 1925-1928 Field Notes of Ohio State Museum Archaeological Expedition at Seip-Pricer Mound (a.k.a. Seip Mound 2, Seip Mound 1). Ms. on file, Department of Archaeology, Ohio Historical Society, Columbus.

Willoughby, C. C. and E. A. Hooton 1922 The Turner Groups of Earthworks, Hamilton County, Ohio. *Papers of the Peabody Museum* 8(3).

Wood, K. M. 1992 Map of West Mound. *Ohio Archaeologist* 42(3):9-15.

TEN

SOCIAL STRUCTURE AND THE PRAGMATIC MEANING OF MATERIAL CULTURE: OHIO HOPEWELL AS ECCLESIASTIC-COMMUNAL CULT

A. MARTIN BYERS

ABSTRACT

This essay interprets the Ohio Hopewell earthworks as primarily sacred locales for performing world renewal ceremonies. This is based on an approach that treats material culture as the rule-based pragmatics of social practices. Although these earthworks were used for mortuary purposes, I interpret their primary function as the focus of emerging ecclesiastic-communal cults. I characterize these cults as a fusion of communal cults based on generational structure and shamanic cults producing a shamanic-priestly hierarchy. From my interpretation of the mortuary data, I postulate that the internal contradictions inherent in this fusion prevented mature stabilization of the structure and it collapsed.

A View From the Core a Synthesis of Ohio Hopewell Archaeology•edited by Paul J. Pacheco
© Copyright 1996 by The Ohio Archaeological Council• Columbus, Ohio
All Rights Reserved•ISBN 0-9626931-9-7

INTRODUCTION

Figure 10:1 is a "birds-eye" view of Seip, as depicted by Squier and Davis (1848) in their "magnum opus." Sadly, this monumental earthwork site, as with many similar ones, no longer exists in the form shown. Nevertheless, it remains among the best-known of the Hopewellian "geometrical" embankment earthworks of south central Ohio. This site will be the major focus of my essay.

Found within the larger of the two circular elements of Seip are two large earthen mounds, both of which covered the remains of a Hopewellian "Big House" (Greber 1976, 1979, 1983). Following the nomenclature established by Greber, I will refer to the central mound as Seip and the construction remains it covers as the Seip Big House. Just to the northeast of Seip is Seip-Pricer and the construction that it covers is the Seip-Pricer Big House. Greber has also demonstrated that the Edwin Harness Mound, situated in the largest circular element of Liberty Works **(Figure 10:2)**, covers another example of the same construction, which I will term the Harness Big House. Following her lead, I shall treat the embankment earthwork and its associated Big House(s) as constituting a complex system of monumental features which I shall term the Ohio Hopewellian Embankment Earthwork/Big House Complex.

The purpose of this essay is to interpret the sites of this monumental complex in terms of the socio-intentional meaning as this was collectively held and acted upon by the communities responsible. Intentions will be treated as those mental states humans have that are directed to the world and that we satisfy by performing actions. Such actions are defined as rule-based behaviors (Searle 1983). But all intentional acts are performed in social contexts, making our cultural understanding of these contexts a part of the content of material culture meaning. I will first give an outline of the social-structural approach I will follow, treating this as the complex set of positions and relations that constitute a society. I will follow this with a discussion of the action-constitutive or rule-based pragmatics of material culture. The term pragmatics is used here in its grammatical

sense, i.e., the rule-governed moment in which our behaviors are transformed into socio-intentional acts. A socio-intentionalist approach is particularly appropriate to interpreting monumental features, since almost by definition these cannot be coherently accounted for in strictly individualistic, utilitarian terms. Rather, as the outcome and context of social activities, they are better interpreted in terms of their action-constitutive meaning and strategic collective goals their construction and use were intended to achieve.

DEFINITION
Social Structure

I treat society as a complex of social positions and the reciprocal inter-connection of these I term social relations (Bhaskar 1979). A social position will be treated as a complex set of rights and duties activated by the agent or occupying party. This occupant can be an individual or a group, and by virtue of this position the agent becomes a person with social standing in the community. I find this definition useful because it leaves open the ontological status of the agent or party. Certain positions may be exclusively occupied by individuals, others by collectives. Furthermore, the agent may not even have a tangible existence, e.g., it could be an ancestor or a deity.

No position exists in a vacuum but always has one or more positions that complement it, e.g., clergy-laity, father-son, thereby constituting the relations in which occupants of positions participate actively. Action is always socially positioned (situated) in that a party behaves in terms of the rules that stipulate the range of rights and duties she/he has as an occupant of a position, and these rights and duties always exist relative to the rights and duties of the complementary positions. Social standing exists by virtue of the positions an agent occupies. The social standing of the agent is grounded upon, but not reducible to, the particular value attributed to the position(s) she/he occupies and this is based on the social value of the activities associated with position. Hence, the esteem of the occupant of a valued position is contingent on both the social value of the position's activities and the effectiveness with which a given

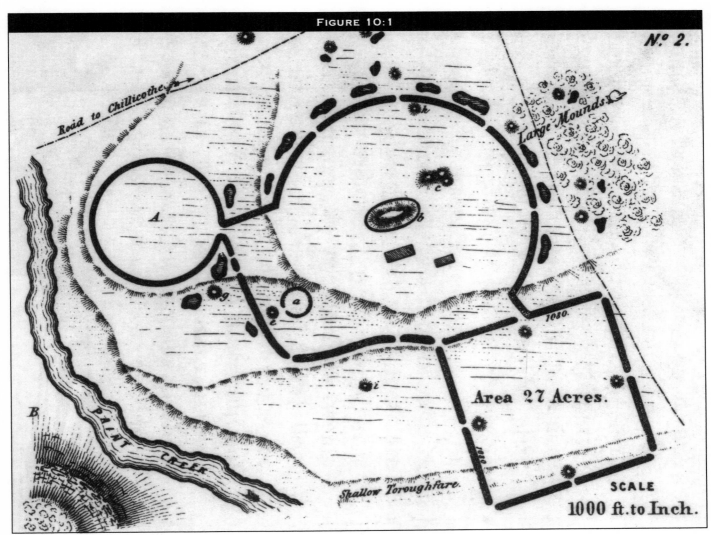

FIGURE 10:1

Seip Works (Squier and Davis 1848)

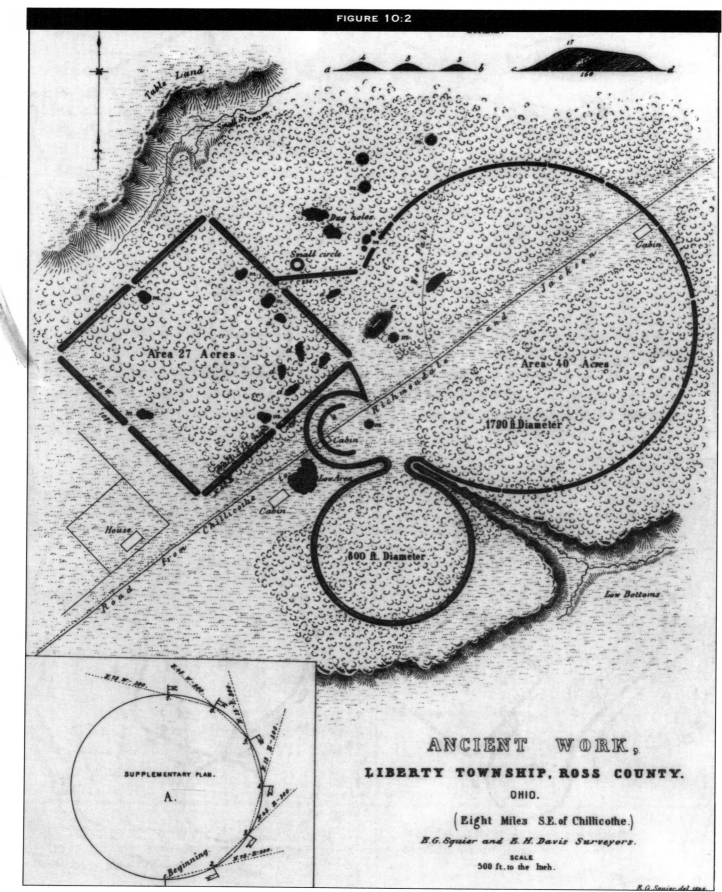

Liberty Works (Squier and Davis 1848)

occupant acted, thereby exercising these social powers (rights and duties). In this view social standing is unstable, something that must be continually worked for and worked upon (Harré 1979). The total standing of a person/party at any given moment is the result of an ongoing pursuit of respect and repute (and its corollary, avoiding shame and public disdain); and this is done by acting according to the powers of the positions a person occupies.

The temporal allocation of positions is constrained and directed by the career trajectories available in a society. These can be thought of as the temporal dimension of the social structures of a society as realized in the life cycles of the community members - from birth through youth, middle age, the position of elder to ancestor (Giddens 1976, 1979, 1984). And although we cannot speak about collective trajectories without becoming overly teleological, I believe that social reputation is always a significant dimension in organizing the strategies of collective parties, such as clans, military associations, or a total community with respect to other communities they perceive as highly relevant to themselves.

MATERIAL CULTURE MEANING

I define the meaning of things both in terms of the social positions with which they are identified and the content of the intentionality with which they are used. The content of our action intentions presupposes specific wants and beliefs and stipulates the forms that behaviors must have in order for them to be fully successful actions of the intended type (Searle 1983). I shall call this content the know-how rules and these rules are of the same order as pragmatic rules of grammar. In speech act terms, these rules govern the forms of utterances so that they are constituted as the types of speech acts we intend, such as uttering warnings, curses, promises, declarations, assertions, commands, and so on. In these terms, the rule-based pragmatics aspect of a material culture form will be termed its style and its pragmatic rule force is understood as transforming the material behavior it was used to perform into the intended material action (Searle 1969, 1979).

This can be illustrated directly by referencing Hopewell materials. It is well known that Hopewell manifests both bladelet and flake tools simultaneously. As Odell (1994:114) has recently pointed out, these two sets could be used to mediate the same objective range of material behaviors (scraping, slicing, gouging, graving, etc.), but that "...this information is insufficient to provide the social or ritual circumstances that caused a tool [bladelet rather than a flake] to be used..." He goes on to ground empirically his claim that the mortuary ceremony was mediated by the bladelets while the equivalent flake tools mediated mundane and domestic activities, even though both sets of actions required largely the same objective material behaviors. In rule-based pragmatics terms, the bladelet style used in ceremonial contexts transformed the behaviors it mediated into the intended ceremonial acts while the flake style used in domestic contexts transformed the objectively similar behaviors into mundane or domestic acts. To speak of context means that differently styled things are not only rule-based, but these rules are part of the make-up of social positions - those associated with for example, ceremonial and domestic actions respectively. Rules that govern material culture style, then, are part of the cultural or collective know-how that makes up the content of the intentionality of persons occupying the different social positions of the community.

MATERIAL CULTURE AS ACTION WARRANTS

I have used the term warrant (Douglas 1982) to characterize this rule-based pragmatics, action-constitutive, socio-intentional nature of material culture meaning. A warrant is a material document that endows its possessor with specific powers, constituting this person as a bailiff or police officer or some other court officer. Only someone who has the right to possess a warrant occupies one of these social positions and in exercising the rights and duties, i.e., social powers, embodied in and mediated by the warrant the court officer transforms her/his aggressive behaviors, e.g., physically restraining the free use of things or the free movements of others, into the legal acts of property seizure and person arrest. Literate societies are constituted by their rich documentary warrants - marriage licenses and gas coupons, residence visas and passports, and so on, and for individuals these make up their accumulated credentials of social life - the bases of their "curriculum vitae". I shall take the position that material warrants are intrinsic to all social life, regardless of the forms of material expression extant in a society. Hence, in non-literate societies, where documents - as such - are non-existent, the pragmatics view justifies treating the styles of material culture as having socio-cultural warranting powers. Since style pre-existed writing, it must be then that it was actually the original warranting medium of social activities, and documentation was a derivative (Byers 1991, 1992, 1994).

As Douglas (1966, 1970) has argued, social power in pre-industrial societies is usually associated with the powers of the cosmos which are embodied in natural categories (waters, trees, sun, moon, and animal species). Often the things derived from or associated with these categories of nature are themselves treated as sacred, thereby constituting the objects that humans make of these natural elements as participating in the sacred powers of that which they represent. Drawing on this cosmological theory which integrates the sacred and everyday material routines, I shall treat material cultural artifacts and features in non-literate societies as having sacred warranting powers.

In this way, I shall envision the exotic and even everyday things used by the Hopewell as endowing their users with differential warranting powers. These powers allowed them to perform actions which, in their understanding, had significant impact on the world around them and without which they could not perform effective actions of the intended type. In short, whose who used them did so as authoritative and constitutive action media by which they exercised the powers of the positions they occupied. As this authority is often taken to reside in the objects themselves as derived from the sacredness of nature, I will term them *icons of authority*. In these terms, material things will be treated as *iconic warrants* of the positioned actions they constitutively mediate (Byers 1991, 1992). It is useful to pair these warrants in contrasting complements, the most prominent being the license-coupon contrasting complement. I define a

license warrant as an item that mediates a prestigious or elite position - respected warrior, chief, priest, and shaman. The contrast to this is the coupon warrant, which mediates positions open to everyone of the same social category, thereby making their activities quite utilitarian and mundane in nature - those activities most closely associated with domestic and everyday obligations.

THE SOCIO-INTENTIONAL MEANING OF OHIO HOPEWELL
The Embankment Earthworks as Iconic Warrants

The Seip and Seip-Pricer Big Houses are situated within the large circular element of the Seip embankment earthworks. This is also the case with the Edwin Harness Big House at Liberty Works (Figure 10:3). Indeed these two earthworks and the Seip and Edwin Harness Big Houses that accompany them are almost mirror images of each other. In both cases, the large embankment circle is "bracketed" by a smaller circle and a large square. The latter I refer to as the Paint Creek Square and the former is what I generically refer to as a Hopeton Circle (Byers 1987). All three elements constitute a patterning that I term the C-R motif configuration. C stands for the Hopeton type circle, R stands for the rectilinear, which varies between a square, an octagon, sub-square, etc., and the hyphen (-) represents the juncturing link that connects the C (circle) and R (rectilinear) elements. In this case the infix element is the large inner circle which contains the Seip and Seip-Pricer Mounds.

Along with Seip and Liberty Works there are three other examples of this configuration within the Paint Creek drainage: Baum, Frankfort and Works East (Greber 1979). I have added to this list the Hopewell site itself - since it has both a Paint Creek Square and a Hopeton Circle. The infix element, however, is the large rectilinear embankment that surrounds the multiple burial mounds of the Hopewell site. Because of at least five, and if Hopewell is included, six examples of these same infix-type C-R motifs in this drainage, I have termed this the Paint Creek C-R motif variety.

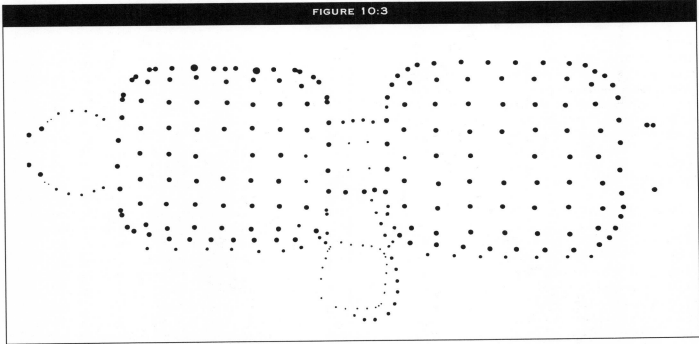

FIGURE 10:3

The Harness Big House Tripartite Layout (from Greber 1983:32, with permission from MCJA).

The C-R motif type has a complementary opposite, what I term the High Bank C-R motif. The latter is modeled on the circle-octagon of the High Bank Works **(Figure 10:4)**. In this case, the Hopeton Circle element is much larger than its Paint Creek equivalent. The rectilinear comes in more varieties also. At High Bank and Newark **(Figure 10:5)** it is an octagon. The juncturing element of this motif is usually a narrow neck, what I call the aggregation neck. The High Bank C-R motif is oriented along a single axis such that if a line were drawn parallel through the aggregation neck and extended on both ends, it would bifurcate the circle and rectilinear symmetrically, splitting the earthwork into almost two mirror image halves. In contrast, the Paint Creek C-R motif always has the C and R elements asymmetrically related, joined by the infix in a mutually skewed and off-centered manner.

This gives a formal description of these two variants of the C-R motif. The puzzling question might be why a prehistoric people should invest the material effort in building such monumental earthworks. In terms of the socio-intentional theory of the meaning of material culture given above, the sensibility of these earthworks was based on their action-constitutive power. As monumental iconic warrants they transformed the formal behaviors performed in their context so that they counted as and were socio-religious material actions. As I will argue below, the social position was occupied by the total community, constituted as living and ancestral generations, integrated in a complex cult. This cult would have as its complementary opposite, the total sacred powers of the cosmos, thereby constituting a human community which occupied a position in a sacred world society. Hence, the Hopewellian Embankment Earthwork/Big House Complex was the monumental iconic warrant of the living-ancestral social position. Both ances-

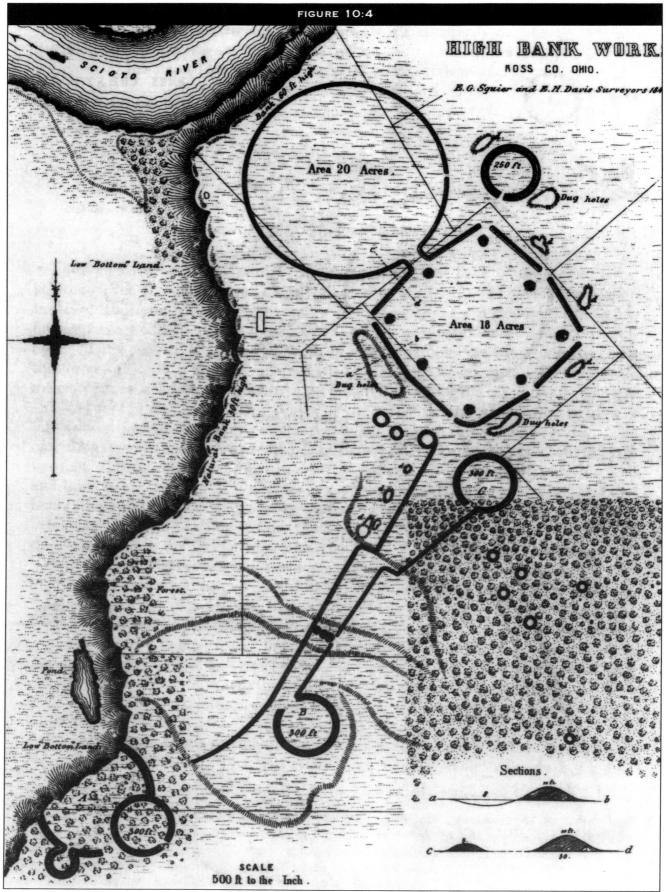

High Banks Works (Squier and Davis 1848)

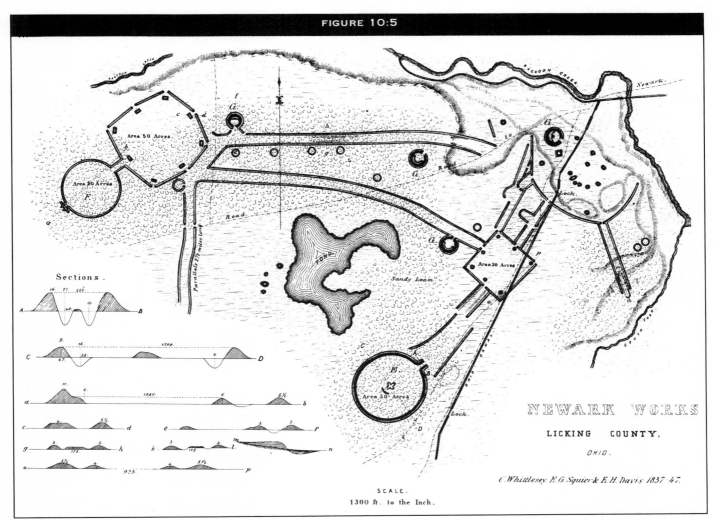

Newark Works (Squier and Davis 1848)

tral and world renewal ceremonies would have been the ongoing dynamic social activities by which the living realized their sacred duties to both their ancestors and to the sacred cosmos.

I will call this socio-cultural interpretation of the meaning of the earthwork complex the World Renewal Model. This paper is not the place to give a full empirical gounding to the claim that, indeed, the earthworks were iconic media (Byers 1987, 1992). Rather, I will simply summarize highlights of the empirical support I have marshaled so as to give confirmation of the theoretical position I have outlined above.

The earthworks represented and participated in the sacred powers that animated the world. This world was believed to be stratified into three levels, the Heavens, represented by the C element, the Middle World, represented by the (-) element, and the Underworld, represented by the R element. The Paint Creek C-R motif participates in and evokes the solar aspect of the universe and the High Bank C-R motif realizes the lunar aspect. Each motif, then, represents and participates in only one aspect of the total universe. For this reason, I have argued that we must treat the two varieties as working together, constituting for the builders a single mon-

umental expression of the world in its tri-partite vertical structuring of the Heavens-Middle World-Underworld stratification and its dual lunar and solar aspects. This model I have referred to as the Dual C-R motif, the best example being Newark itself. In my earlier work I argued that much (not all!) of the complexity of this site is the result of a strategy to integrate both motifs into one site, thereby generating a major physical feature that embodies the total structural nature of the world. In doing so, this would have had considerable prestige pay-off for the community.

It is reasonable to conclude from this that at Chillicothe the High Bank Works embody the lunar aspect of the Dual C-R motif and the Liberty Works, just south of High Bank, embody the solar aspect. The empirical grounds for claiming a lunar/solar dichotomy are the research findings of Hively and Horn (1982, 1984), for the lunar aspect, and both their work and Greber's work at Baum and Liberty Works for the solar aspect (Greber, personal communication, 1989). What this indicates is that the rectilinears were constructed so as to establish siting lines directed to horizon positions that mark the turning points of both the 18.6 year lunar cycle and the solstice and equinoxes of the solar cycle. Therefore, I take it as reasonable to treat these two sites as constituting a Dual C-R motif. The pragmatic socio-intentional meaning of the Dual C-R motif constituted it as the monumental medium for performing world renewal ceremonies by which the community actively discharged their collective sacred duties. These duties presupposed a social organization that I will characterize below as an ecclesiastic-communal cult. Therefore, the Big Houses that were founded within the Seip infix would have been the sacred center of this cult. Hence, the Hopewellian Embankment Earthwork/Big House Complex, including one or more associated lunar C-R motifs, constituted a civic-cult center.

THE GENERATION-CULT MODEL: TRIPARTITE PATTERN

Whereas the above sketches out the cultural content of the socio-intentional meaning of the Hopewellian Complex, a full interpretation also requires establishing the social structures that underwrote its construction and use. In terms of the World Renewal Model, this would be the community envisioned as the living and ancestral generations. But this is not sufficient by itself, for the notion that the living and the dead were socially bound by sacred duties surely would not be unique to the Ohio Hopewell. Indeed, we could easily envision this social structure underwriting the preceding (and in some cases possibly contemporary) Adena mortuary practices (Hall 1977, 1979). Hence, I wish to be more specific and stipulate and then empirically confirm the possible social structure transformations that would likely underwrite and account for the emergence of Ohio Hopewell earthworks. This requires a dynamic social model supplementary to the World Renewal Model. This I will term the Generation-Cult Model.

As Greber's excellent analyses have pointed out, all three Big Houses mentioned above share the same tripartite patterning, based on a Rectangle-Rectangle-Circle (R-R-C) configuration. She has suggested that the pattern is vertically structured into Upper and Lower Levels. At Edwin Harness, the Upper Level, supported on 48 posts for each rectangular room (Greber 1983:27), formed the floor of the Big House proper - where the activities of the living community

occurred, while the Lower Level consisted of the mound floor where most of the burial activities occurred. Greber referred to the individual units of the upper level as Rooms 1, 2 and 3 and the spaces below as (burial) Sections 1, 2 and 3. In her view the tripartite patternings of both the C-R motif of the embankment earthworks and the R-R-C configuration of the associated Big House possibly have a direct congruency of a socio structural nature. "I have suggested a possible social significance for the tripartite design of the earthwork as a reflection of the tripartite major division apparent within the burial population" (Greber 1979:27).

I agree that there is a connection between these two patterns, but not in the way Greber reads it. Rather, the C-R motif manifests the dominant belief structures and the Big House manifests the dominant social structures that, together, generated this Hopewellian Complex. The former was constituted as a monumental iconic warrant of the sacred world, and the Big House mediated and participated in constituting the social structure responsible for the world renewal ceremony. Situating the Big House in the C-R motif, reflects and constitutes the relation the community perceived itself to have in the world - as sacred and social - and the community's particular description is the basis of the Generation-Cult Model. These terms derive from my hypothesis that Ohio Hopewell was largely the historical conjunction of two dominant structural principles: generation and religious specialization. The former underwrites the dual structuring of the community into two aspects as living and ancestral generations. The latter specialization underwrites a new form of religious organization, which I postulate to be an Ecclesiastic-Communal Cult. This is a social organization based on an unstable clergy/laity structure. I will clarify the generational structure first and then elaborate the religious structure.

GENERATIONAL STRUCTURE

The Big House is found within the embankment earthworks, and as the latter were iconic in nature, in emic terms, it logically follows that the Big House, its spatial forms and their contents, were constituted as iconic also. This would suggest that the social structures that the Big House mediated were also treated as sacred, anchored in a sacred world (Douglas 1966, 1970). In these terms the Upper/Lower Levels, associated respectively with living and dead, manifested the living/ancestral social phases. Consistency and coherence leads to the conclusion that generational seniority would operate to structure both the ancestral/living phases and the living adult generations (e.g., retired/ active senior / active junior / pre-adult). Interpreting the Upper/Lower pattern as an iconic connection of the ancestors and the living leads to the conclusion that in their belief the dead continued both their pursuit of social standing and reputation and - to a lesser degree - their mundane pursuit of survival in the after life (Hall 1977, 1979). Hence the mortuary items, both those that were of an esteem producing nature, license warrants, and of a mundane nature, coupon warrants, would continue to warrant the dead to actively discharge their community duties in their new position as collective ancestors as they had in this life. This interpretation of mortuary artifacts suggests why these activities would also count as, and be opportunities for, gaining strategic political points and pursuing social prestige. Not all societies make mortuary activities media of political strategy, but in small scale societies that live according to an iconic world view, death was an opportunity to reproduce alliances and avoid or minimize enmities. In publicly displaying their commitment to ensuring that ancestors were active participants in ongoing community life, the living not only legitimized their own occupation of positions made vacant by death, but ensured allies of their commitment to pursuing the relations which these ancestors had themselves worked to sustain.

CULT STRUCTURE

I will draw on Wallace's (1966) cultic theory of religion to characterize the Hopewellian Embankment Earthwork/Big House Complex as a monumental civic-cult center for an emergent Ecclesiastic-Communal Cult. I have coined this term to speak hypothetically about an emergent social organization resulting from a fusion of pre-existing communal and shamanic cults. In Wallace's religious theory, communal cults are kinship or sodality-based with their religious and secular leadership occupied usually by the same persons. When the sodality goes into its religious posture, it constitutes a communal cult and its leadership shifts into the religious aspects of office. In Wallace's view, societies with communal cults also have shamans making up the shamanic cults. These are spiritually powerful individuals, usually in contact with strong animal or nature spirits, who act as part-time religious practitioners, conducting both curing seances and sometimes specialized rites for a communal cult, for which they are specifically contracted. Both the communal and shamanic cults guard their autonomy over discretionary control of the use and allocation of those iconic license warrants relevant to their respective cultic positions. Shamans cultivate youths who are drawn to such individual sacred pursuits much along the lines of a master-apprentice relation. Communal cults promote their own members into leadership positions and endow them with the right to use the license warrants of the lineage, military society, or other social grouping, in ceremonies when the spiritual resources of the group's authority are fused in the same office and there is no contradiction between religious and secular hierarchy.

As I mentioned above, communal cults contract a shaman to conduct special ceremonies. But the shaman does not challenge the cult's leadership since the role played by the shaman is quite severely limited. The question is, what happens when a fusion of the sort I am envisioning occurs in which shamanic and communal cults are integrated into a single community-wide ecclesiastic-communal cult? I postulate that the integration of communal and shamanic principles generates internal contradictions. This claim follows logically by extrapolating "backwards" from what Wallace argues is the characteristic structure of mature ecclesiastic-communal cults. These are based on usually full-time priestly specialization with equivalent and complementary "full-time" laity, together making up the congregation. Hence, at the heart of the ecclesiastic-communal cult is a clergy/laity congregational structure and these two groups have largely non-overlapping hierarchies, priestly and secular. The interaction of these two hierarchies of positions is highly variable and often stressful. In a mature ecclesiastic-communal cult, overall cult leadership responsibilities are distributed between laity and clergy hierarchies in different ways and relatively stable patterns of distribution constitute different types. The basis of what Wallace terms the episcopalian type is for the clergy to monopolize leadership of cult affairs by ascribing to themselves religious and, often, secular authority over the cult affairs - including the affairs of the laity, even in the non-religious positions of kinship and other group membership. And they sustain this by monopolizing the allocation of the licenses that go to make up and realize, both their own direct authority, and the authority of non-clergy positions. A theocracy can ensue. In extreme contrast, the congregationalist type centers authority on the laity hierarchy. Various between/betwixt possibilities ground the presbyterian types (Wallace 1966).

The Generation-Cult Model postulates a transformational historical process. Societies based on mutually autonomous communal and shamanic cult structures transform through a fusion of these structures into an Ecclesiastic-Communal Cult. I posit for the Ohio Hopewell that in the pre-fusion period, e.g., the Adena, the communal cults were based on the generation structure - primarily kinship-based sodalities, on the one hand, and military based sodalities, on the other. Hence tribal clan cult leaders and community peace chiefs were selected from the senior generation; military sodality leaders were selected from the junior generation. Local individuals would temporarily set aside their mundane responsibilities to take on their shamanic responsibilities and act as temporary sacred leaders of various ceremonies when circumstances required them; e.g., as curers, or to perform specialized ceremonies for and under the direction of the communal cult chiefs (lineage, clan, military, or artisan).

The emergence of a society-wide world renewal cult brought into one locale the pre-existing senior/junior generation-based communal cult organizations that previously had retained separate but related locales. This single locale, as the Hopewellian Embankment Earthwork/Big House Complex, became the monumental context of these pre-existing communal cults fusing into an Ecclesiastic-Communal Cult center. These two generational organizations would occupy the laity sectors of the Big House, while retaining the traditional leadership along junior/senior generational lines. The leadership hierarchy in each generation would probably be responsible for different but overlapping social tasks - as outlined above, namely, the senior adult generation leaders as peace chiefs and counselors responsible for alliance and long-distance exchange, and the junior cult leaders as responsible for military concerns, as well as, possibly, ritual construction of the sacred locales. Two different forms of valued social endeavor emerged in one context, and because of the generational and social task specialization, both the quantity and range of license warrant artifacts and features would vary systematically between these two groups (see Table 10:1).

TABLE 10:1		
SENIORITY	Senior	Junior
PHASE	Ancestral Phase	Living Phase
GENERATION	Senior Generation	Junior Generation

The Senority Princple

There would also be a third sphere of specialized license warrants generated in this same locale since this fusion would call for the creation of a space for the specialized shamans who, in their new duties as adjuncts to this complex communal cult, would emerge as part-time quasi-clergy, shamanic-priests. This new position would crystallize the senior/junior generational communal cults into a laity group dependent on an emergent clergy, constituting an unstable congregation based on a fragile laity/clergy structure. The shamanic-priestly clergy and their apprentice-acolytes would be partly independent of the generational structure, while struggling to form an autonomous college with its own responsibilities for conducting community-wide rites - an emergent clergy. Competition between the laity and clergy hierarchies would focus over control of allocating licenses and, thereby, control of the reputation-enhancing endeavor these warranted, such as quests for procuring potent raw materials for producing iconic warrants and the task of constructing embankment earthworks.

Hence, according to the Generation-Cult Model, two major factors constitute the central dynamics generating this Hopewellian complex: (1) The collapse into one locale of previously separated activities of communal cults based on a dual senior/junior generational structure creating overlapping jurisdictions; and (2) The competition between the leadership hierarchies of the unstable laity/clergy structure over control of the public modes of pursuing reputation. According to this model, Rooms 1 and 2 of the R-R-C Big House were the context of the laity organized according to senior/junior generations, respectively, and Room 3, as a sacred liminal vestibule into the Big House, would be the context of the shamanic-priestly clergy and their apprentice-like acolytes. I argue that this model most coherently accounts for the data. The interpretation of three archaeological categories empirically anchors the model:

(1) MORTUARY ARTIFACTUAL COUPONING AND LICENSING.

All the floor burials were cremated and placed on puddled clay platforms that were framed with low rectangular log cribs. This feature is consistent in all sections containing burials. This similarity of treatment contrasts with the accompanying mortuary artifacts. The latter were highly variable in form and in distribution. Hence, the mortuary record manifests the license/coupon duality. Couponing is expressed in the ubiquity both of (1) cremation, which eliminates the individuality of the dead, and (2) the rectangular log-cribs and puddled-clay platforms, through which, as iconic portals or "gateways" in the after world, passed all the dead in an equal manner. This invariant treatment contrasts with the highly variant forms and distribution of the mortuary artifacts, which both as license and coupon war-

rants emphasized the principle of inequality and social difference. I will define this particular license/coupon pattern, occurring with the very same burial population, as manifesting tokenism. I call tokenism any form of material expression which gives nominal or "lip-service" recognition to equality while actualizing inequality. This is done by juxtaposing licenses and coupons in the same context. In Ohio Hopewell mortuary contexts, couponing was expressed as cremation and log-cribbing while mortuary licensing crosscut and highlighted differentiation in social standing - elitism.

(2) CREMATORY BASIN DISTRIBUTION.

The distribution of the crematory basins also can be interpreted in couponing terms. However, the fact that crematory basins are not found in Room 3 suggests that this locale is treated as sacred liminal space, possessing a property that would be contradicted by crematory activity. Alternatively, it could suggest that the shamanic-priests of the Ecclesiastic-Communal Cult played a secondary role in mortuary activities, an interpretation which would be consistent with the Generation-Cult Model which postulated the Hopewellian Earthwork Embankment/Big House Complex to be more a world renewal than a mortuary locale. The exclusive locating of crematory basins in the rectangular sections suggests that the mortuary activities were dominated by laity leadership (see Table 10:2).

TABLE 10:2			
	SECTIONS		
MOUND	1	2	3
Seip	2 basins	2 basins	0
Seip-Pricer	1 basin	0	0

Distribution of Cremation Basins

(3) MORTUARY ARTIFACT PATTERNING.

Greber (1976, 1979, 1983) has demonstrated that the three burial populations under the Seip, Seip-Pricer and Edwin Harness Big Houses manifest similar patterning of the sectional rank-sum profiles. Those of Rooms 1 and 2 are similar to each other while radically differing from the patterning of Room 3. But the former two do mutually differ in terms of number of license holders and their relative degrees of achievement. This is particularly well illustrated by the copper artifacts. Room 1 had a significantly higher proportion of holders of copper plates and celts and other copper and non-copper exotic license warrants compared to Section 2. "In summary, the use of copper plates as a sociotechnic artifact mainly associated with one group of the society appears to be a consistent pattern for the three mounds" (Greber 1979:34).

This must be contrasted to both the overall scarcity of copper goods in Room 3 as well as the complete absence of copper plates and celts. In terms of the pragmatic, action-constitutive theory I have presented, such a radical difference is most reasonably interpreted as the result of basic structural relations and rules. Not only does this particular distribution reinforce the R-R-C distinction in terms of the laity/clergy structure, it suggests that these copper celts and plates were important license warrants of the laity hierarchy while being actively excluded from the clergy hierarchy. This interpretation is reinforced by the fact that most of those buried in Section 3 died with few if any of the license warrants dominant in Sections 1 and 2, reinforcing the conclusion that the copper celts and plates were, indeed, laity license warrants.

The radical skewing of the sectional rank profile of Room 3 compared to those of Rooms 1 and 2 is also consistent with the Generation-Cult Model as it suggests the view that those buried in Room 3 were constrained in their opportunities for accumulating such materials by career trajectory. This would be either (1) by being quite young at death, and/or (2) by being apprentice-acolytes at death, and/or (3) by pursuing shamanic-priestly position and responsibility

which probably systematically excluded them from competing for laity license warrants. This exclusion would have been a function of an ongoing struggle between laity and clergy elite for sustaining spheres of mutual autonomy in circumstances of an emergent Ecclesiastic-Communal Cult where overlapping responsibilities would necessarily occur.

In contrast, being structured as laity members in a competitive achievement, nominally egalitarian community, can account for the burials of Rooms 1 and 2 being significantly similar in rank profile patterns and spatial form. Similarly, being based on a generational structure can account for these two sections being significantly different in total number and quality of license warrants. In these terms the critical factor that accounts for the difference is age-at-death. Those individuals buried in the junior generation section would have died as relatively young adults compared to those buried in the senior generation section. Hence, compared to the latter, the former would have had much less time to pursue reputation and accumulate licenses by means of competitive pursuits. Hence, given the achievement-based pursuit of reputation suggested by the tokenism outlined above, and given the clergy-laity specialization, the two factors responsible for the differential accumulation and distribution of mortuary artifacts were: (1) age-at-death (generation); and (2) specialized career trajectory (laity/clergy).

THE SPLIT-GENERATION MORTUARY MODEL: EMPIRICAL CONFIRMATION

According to the stratigraphic evidence, the Seip Big House was constructed, used and abandoned before the Seip-Pricer Big House was even built (Greber 1976, 1979; Shetrone and Greenman 1931). According to the Generation-Cult Model, at the time of this transition it would be the survivors of Seip-Room 2 who would become the senior active adult generation and they would either actually undertake the construction of Seip-Pricer or direct and manage its construction. In fact, the abandoning of the Seip Big House and the construction of the Seip-Pricer Big House could be reasonably interpreted as part of community-wide rite of passage. If this were the case, the senior generation - survivors of Seip-Room 1 - would pass into retirement. The active junior adult generation would become the new active senior generation and it would collectively occupy the Seip-Pricer-Room 1 as its new cult space. Simultaneously, the pre-juniors would become the new active junior generation and would occupy Seip-Pricer-Room 2. If such a process were to continue indefinitely, then the buried members of each generation would be split between two Big House mortuary deposits: those buried in the equivalent of Room 2 of the older Big House would have died while in the junior generation and their generational mates who survived the rite of passage to the subsequent Big House would be buried in Room 1 of that house.

At Seip it is obvious that this process, initiated with the Seip Big House, was terminated with Seip-Pricer Big House. Indeed, given the much smaller burial population of the Seip-Pricer Big House in comparison to both the Seip and Harness Big Houses, not only does it appear that its active use was truncated before the normal transition period, but also the final mantle of earth that was required to complete the construction of its mound was never put in place, suggesting rapid social collapse, an interpretation that is consistent with the type of unstable situation postulated by the contradictions imminent in an emergent Ecclesiastic-Communal Cult. Greber (1976, 1979) has put forward an alternative interpretation, arguing that the three rooms and burial locations were identified with three separate, but ranked social groups having the same nature, e.g., clans. If this were the case, then the relative age-structure of burials in each section (Rooms 1, 2, and 3) would be equivalent. However, I believe that the available evidence gives the balance of support to the split-generation mortuary interpretive model.

Mills first excavated Edwin Harness at Liberty Works and later he excavated Seip-Pricer. He did not excavate the Seip Mound. Even though many of his field notes have been lost (Greber 1976, 1979) his published comments on the Seip-Pricer Mound are illuminating.

*As stated, the single graves in the first section (i.e., Seip-Pricer = Room 1) were similar in construction to those of the Harness Mound, **though the final burial ceremony must have been different**. In the Harness Mound, after the incinerated remains had been placed in the grave, objects of clothing, together with straw, bark, or twigs were placed over the remains and set on fire: while burning, clay was placed over the grave, thus preserving the cloth, the grass, and twigs in a charred state. This ceremony was dispensed with in this section of the (Seip-Pricer) Mound, and the incinerated remains were placed in the prepared grave, and a covering of wood, usually split pieces, was placed on the top and the grave covered with earth to a depth of a few inches [Mills 1909:24; emphasis added].*

In fact, this terminating fire ritual was never practiced at the Seip Big House - which we now know was built, used and abandoned before the Seip-Pricer Big House existed (Shetrone and Greenman 1931). Hence, Mills (1909:24) got it the wrong way around in saying that the fire "ceremony was dispensed with in this section of the [Seip-Pricer] Mound." The log covering ritual was used throughout the Seip Big House mortuaries. It was continued in the Seip-Pricer Big House - for all burials in Room 1 and for ten of the total nineteen burials in Room 2, the rest being completed with the fire ritual. In short, the fire ritual was introduced late at this site. "The final ceremony of burning straw, bark, and clothing over the remains, similar to the burial methods at the Harness Mound, was in evidence in 9 burials of the 19 found at the base of the section" (Mills 1909:26).

This line of reasoning leads to the conclusion that either all or most of those buried with the log ritual in Seip-Pricer died before those buried with the fire ritual. If the former occurred, then all those in Room 1 were buried before most of those in Room 2. If the latter occurred involving a period of overlap when both rituals were used, then still most of those in Section

1 would have pre-deceased most of those in Section 2. The simplest explanation in both cases is that burials of Locations 1 and 2 belonged to senior and junior generations, respectively. In warranting terms, the introduction of the fire ritual variation, partially breaking with local tradition, would not have occurred without contention. Its introduction would have involved considerable "discussion" and negotiation, possibly conflict between the surviving older occupants of Room 1 and the younger occupants of Room 2 of the Seip-Pricer Big House. Also, there were no burials in Room 3 of the Seip-Pricer Big House. However, Room 3 of both the Seip and the Edwin Harness Big Houses, effectively mirror images of each other, contained burials; nineteen in the former and twenty-one in the latter **(see Table 10:3)**. This suggests that - in normal circumstances - burials would be performed in each of the three locations. The complete absence of burials, from what I have characterized as the liminal locale of shamanic-priests and acolytes, should be viewed in conjunction with the wider conflict implicated by the introduction of new rituals and the possible displacement of older rituals. Likewise, the presence of only one crematory basin and a small number of overall burials under Seip-Pricer, indicates an emerging monopolization of powers by the senior generation leadership that were previously distributed across active generations.

TABLE 10:3				
	SECTIONS			TOTAL
MOUND	1	2	3	
Seip	53	38	19	110
Seip-Pricer	24	19	0	43

Distribution of Burials by section (after Greber 1979:34 Table 6.3).

This is strong presumptive support for a power struggle underwritten by the senior/junior generational structures and cross-cut by the laity/clergy structural contradiction as postulated by the Generation-Cult Model. This struggle would have been manifested as an event rupturing the ongoing activities of the community, possibly instigated as a conflict over what type of burial, and thereby cosmological rules would prevail in constituting material behaviors as fully felic-itous mortuary activities. Supporters of these two rituals would probably have stood opposed, each faction claiming its variety as the only proper burial But, a struggle over particular rules always presupposes a struggle over basic principles. These ground the totality of rules. The dispute over mortuary rules, then, would be merely the "tip of the iceberg" involving a profound disagreement among the leaders over clergy/laity and generational responsibilities.

SUMMARY

This interpretive analysis of Ohio Hopewell in terms of its socio-intentionalist meaning is far from complete, but it opens avenues to further interpretation and explanation of Ohio Hopewell in social and collective-intentional terms. For example, although I have not dealt with the mortuary events - both extended and cremated - that occurred above the mound floors, I think further work along these interpretive lines, building on the findings of this research, will both further confirm the model and extend our understanding of what actually brought the Ohio Hopewell termination. I have not attempted to place Seip historically and socially in its local context, e.g., Baum, Hopewell and the major sites in Chillicothe. But I believe that the Generation-Cult Model is sufficiently grounded and provocative in its implications that it can be used as a foundational model for interpreting these and other points.

Bhaskar, R. 1979 *The Possibility of Naturalism.* Humanities Press, New Jersey.

Byers, A.M. 1987 *The Earthwork Enclosures of the Central Ohio Valley: A Temporal and Structural Analysis of Woodland Society and Culture.* Ph.D. dissertation, Department of Anthropology, State University of New York at Albany. University Microfilms, Ann Arbor, Michigan.

1991 Structure, Meaning, Action and Things: The Duality of Material Cultural Mediation. *Journal for the Theory of Social Behaviour* 21(1):1-29.

1992 The Action-Constitutive Theory of Monuments: A Strong Pragmatist Version. *The Journal for the Theory of Social Behaviour* 22(4):403-446.

1994 Symboling and the Middle-Upper Palaeolithic Transition: A Theoretical and Methodological Critique. *Current Anthropology* 35(4): 369-399.

Douglas, M. 1966 *Purity and Danger.* Praeger, New York.

1970 *Natural Symbols.* Barrie and Jenkins, London.

1982 *In the Active Voice.* Routledge and Kegan Paul, London.

Giddens, A. 1976 *New Rules of Sociological Method.* Hutchinson, London.

1979 *Central Problems in Social Theory.* Macmillan Press, London.

1984 *The Constitution of Society.* University of California Press, Berkeley.

Greber, N. 1976 *Within Ohio Hopewell: Analyses of Burial Patterns from Several Classic Sites.* Ph.D. dissertation, Department of Anthropology, Case Western Reserve University, Cleveland. University Microfilms, Ann Arbor.

1979 A Comparative Study of Site Morphology and Burial Patterns at Edwin Harness Mound and Seip Mounds 1 and 2. In *Hopewell Archaeology: The Chillicothe Conference,* edited by D.S. Brose and N. Greber, pp. 27-38. Kent State University Press, Kent, Ohio.

1983 *Recent Excavations at the Edwin Harness Mound, Liberty Works, Ross County, Ohio.* Midcontinental Journal of Archaeology, Special Paper No. 5. Kent State University Press, Kent, Ohio.

Hall, R.L. 1977 An Anthropocentric Perspective for Eastern United States Prehistory. *American Antiquity* 42:499-518.

1979 In Search of the Ideology of the Adena-Hopewell Climax. In *Hopewell Archaeology: The Chillicothe Conference,* edited by D.S. Brose and N.B. Greber, pp. 258-265. Kent State University Press, Kent, Ohio.

Harré, R. 1979 *Social Being: A Theory for Social Psychology.* Basil Blackwell, Oxford.

Hively, R. and R. Horn 1982 Geometry and Astronomy in Prehistoric Ohio. *Journal for the History of Astronomy, Archaeoastronomy Supplement* 13(4):S1-S20.

1984 Hopewellian Geometry and Astronomy at High Bank. *Journal for the History of Astronomy, Archaeoastronomy Supplement* 15(7):S85-S100.

Mills, W.C. 1909 Exploration of the Seip Mound. *Ohio State Archaeological and Historical Publications* 10:269-321.

Odell, G.H. 1994 The Role of Stone Bladelets in Middle Woodland Society. *American Antiquity* 59(1):102-120.

Searle, J.R. 1969 *Speech Acts*. Cambridge University Press, Cambridge.

   1979 *Action and Meaning*. Cambridge University Press, Cambridge.

   1983 *Intentionality: An Essay in the Philosophy of Mind*. Cambridge University Press, Cambridge.

Shetrone, H.C. and E.F. Greenman 1931 Exploration of the Seip Group of Prehistoric Earthworks. *Ohio Archaeological and Historical Quarterly* 40(3):343-509.

Squier, E.G. and E.H. Davis 1848 *Ancient Monuments of the Mississippi Valley Comprising the Results of Extensive Original Surveys and Explorations*. Smithsonian Contributions to Knowledge. Volume 1. Smithsonian Institute, Washington, D.C.

Wallace, A.F.C. 1966 *Religion: An Anthropological View*. Random House, New York.

ELEVEN

HOPEWELLIAN GEOMETRY: FORMS AT THE INTERFACE OF TIME AND ETERNITY

WILLIAM F. ROMAIN

"Geometry existed before the creation. It is co-eternal with the mind of God...Geometry provided God with a model for the Creation...Geometry is God Himself."

- *Johannes Kepler (Imperial Mathematician to the Holy Roman Emperor, Rudolf II)*

"...our brains lack the capacity to take in the universe as a whole; we have to structure it in order to put little bits of it into our heads."

- *Ian Stewart and Martin Golubitsky 1992*

ABSTRACT

It has long been recognized that many of the large Hopewellian earthworks exhibit striking geometrical regularities in their design. Evidence for their interest in geometry is found in the dozens of parallel walls, squares, circles, ellipses, and octagonal earthworks found throughout central and southern Ohio. In this paper, the underlying principles of geometry that are expressed in these earthworks are explored. Recurrent patterns and relationships occurring between component parts of ' various earthworks are pointed out. And, it is shown how many of the earthworks are geometrically inter-related — even though they are often geographically separated from each other by many miles. Lastly, some of the broader implications of these findings are discussed.

WILLIAM F. ROMAIN

HOPEWELLIAN GEOMETRY: FORMS AT THE

INTRODUCTION

Overrun by civilization and now mostly destroyed, the ancient Hopewell earthworks hold the clues to a worldview more than two thousand years old. Interestingly enough, what we are beginning to find is that this worldview included a working knowledge of plane geometry, basic arithmetic, and observational astronomy.

In this paper these subjects will be briefly explored - with special emphasis on the geometry of the Ohio Hopewell earthworks. Evidence will be presented showing how individual components within each site are geometrically related to each other; and it will be shown how various sites are geometrically inter-related. Certain findings relevant to Hopewellian mensuration, calendrics, and astronomy will also be noted. And finally, a brief outline of an explanatory hypothesis for at least some of the enclosures will be offered.

For this study, the first task was to identify those Hopewell sites in Ohio, evidencing geometric symmetry. This was done by reference to Squier and Davis' (1848) magnum opus, *Ancient Monuments of the Mississippi Valley*. Although there are occasional errors in Squier and Davis' work, their volume is still the best source available in terms of maps and figures.

From the resulting list of geometrically-shaped earthworks, I selected for analysis those sites that were comprised of two or more geometric components, or otherwise seemed related to nearby sites. The next step was to redraw these sites in such a way as to reduce them to their most essential or idealized geometric shapes - while at the same time, standardizing their scale.

In this instance, all figures were re-drawn to a scale of one inch equals five hundred feet. (For publication purposes here, this scale has been further reduced and figures may appear at different scales.) Measurements are given in English units throughout the paper because of the preferred use of this system by surveyors, especially during the nineteenth century when most of the earthworks were first surveyed. Where measurement data had to be taken directly from Squier and Davis' figures, an engineer's scale was

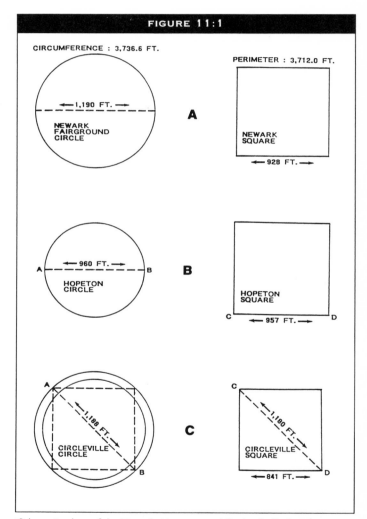

Schematic plans of the Newark, Hopeton, and Circleville Earthworks.

used. However, where possible, use of Squier and Davis' data was superseded by the use of more recent and more accurate information such as provided by Thomas (1894), Cowen (1892 [in Greber and Ruhl 1989]), Marshall (1987), Anderson (1980), and others. For reasons discussed elsewhere (Romain 1992c, 1993a), I consider Thomas', Cowen's, Anderson's, and Marshall's work to be accurate to within one or two percent of measured distances. Nevertheless, I make no claim that the dimensions for each and every earthwork given here are precise. Indeed, in many cases, because the earthworks have been so extensively destroyed, their true size will probably never be known.

The resultant set of drawings were then examined for geometric relationships between component parts and between sties. Recurrent patterns were grouped together and are presented here - generally from the simplest to the more complex.

THE DATA: FEARFUL SYMMETRY-IS GOD A GEOMETER ?

Intra-Site Relationships

The first set of relationships to be looked at are intra-site relationships found between component parts of individual earthwork complexes. The simplest of these concepts is expressed in the relationship between the Newark Fairground Circle and Square. As shown in **Figure 11:1a**, according to Thomas (1894:462, 466), the Fairground Circle has a diameter of about 1,190 feet, while the Newark Square has sides that are each about 929 feet in length. These dimensions are from midline to opposite midline of the embankments.

Given Thomas' data, it turns out that the perimeters of these two figures are almost equal to each other. More specifically, the circumference of the Fairground Circle is 3,736.6 feet, while the perimeter of the Newark Square is 3,712 feet - for a difference of only 24.6 feet. In terms of percentages, the circumference of the Fairground Circle and the perimeter of the Newark Square differ from each other by less than one percent:

$$(3712/3736.6 = .99357).$$

Given the nature of the geometric relationships found in other Hopewellian earthworks, it seems doubtful that the correspondence just noted for the perimeters of the Newark Square and Fairground Circle is coincidental. Most likely the creators of these two figures were intentionally engaged in a geometric exercise known as 'squaring the circle.'

Squaring the circle is the geometric practice of constructing a square which is equal in either perimeter or area to a given circle. It is a problem that has fascinated geometers for thousands of years. The difficulty is that because the circle is an incommensurable figure based in *pi*, it is impossible to draw a square that is exactly equal in area to a circle. Over the years, the problem has often taken on special importance because geometers frequently like to use the square and circle as fundamental cosmological symbols - representing for instance, opposing principles or realms such as the heavens and earth. In such instances, it is desirable that the dimensions of both symbols be equal.

The next concept to be discussed is found in the relationship between the circle and square enclosures of the Hopeton Earthwork. According to Thomas (1894:474), the north-south diameter of the Hopeton Circle is 960 feet. Correspondingly, the straightest side of the Hopeton Square has a length of 957 feet (Thomas 1894:474). As shown in **Figure 11:1b** therefore, the diameter of the Hopeton Circle is virtually the same length as any one side of the Hopeton Square.

What is especially fascinating about the Hopeton geometric construction is that a visual representation of two incommensurable ratios is expressed - without recourse to actual numbers or mathematics. What I mean is this: If we take a circle and square and give a value of one to both the diameter of the circle and any side of the square, then the circumference of the circle and the diagonal of the square will both be incommensurable or irrational numbers. In the case of the circle, this decimal is 3.1415..., or *pi*. In the case of the diagonal of the square, this number is 1.414. By making the diameter of the circle and the sides of the square the same length, a visual expression and comparison of the above ratios or incommensurable numbers becomes apparent.

The next four earthworks seem to demonstrate one underlying geometric concept - namely that of nested squares. In the case of the Circleville Earthwork I used Marshall's (1987) data. However, for the Milford, Works East, and Frankfort enclosures it was necessary to use data derived from Squier and Davis' figures. Unfortunately, because these three earthworks are totally obliterated it is not possible to confirm Squier and Davis' measurements.

According to data published by Marshall (1987:Figure 7), the diameter of the Circleville Large Circle is 1,188 feet; while the sides of the Circlevlle Square are each about 841 feet in length. As **Figure 11:1c** shows, this means that the diameter of the Circleville Large Circle is virtually the same length as the diagonal of the Circleville square. Also of interest is how the Circleville Square precisely fits into the Large Circle - thus dividing the Large Circle into quadrants.

At Milford, according to Squier and Davis' figure (1848:Plate 34, No. 1), the Large Circle has a diameter of about 1,400 feet; while the Milford Square has an almost equal diagonal of 1,350 feet. As **Figure 11:2a** shows, the Milford Square fits neatly within the perimeter of the idealized Milford Circle - and divides that Circle into quadrants. Similarly, at the Works East Earthwork we find that according to Squier and Davis' figure (1848:Plate 21, No. 3), the Large Circle has a diameter of 1,480 feet; while the Works East Square has a corresponding and equal diagonal of 1,480 feet. Again, as shown by **Figure 11:2b**, the Works East Square nests within the Large Circle and divides the Large Circle into quadrants. Also of interest is that the Works East Small Circle is close to one-half the size of the Works East Large Circle.

The Frankfort Earthwork is shown in **Figure 11:2c**. As can be seen, the dimensions of the tripartite components of this earthwork are almost the same as the Works East. Also, like Works East, what we find at Frankfort is that as per Squier and Davis' figure (1848:Plate 21, No. 4), the diameter of the Frankfort Large Circle and the diagonal of the Frankfort Square are virtually the same length. Again too, the Frankfort Square neatly fits within the Frankfort Large Circle and divides the Large

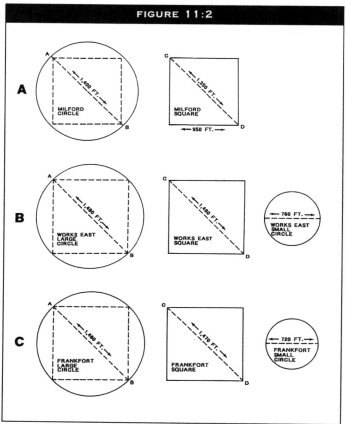

Schematic plans of the Milford, Works East, and Frankfort Earthworks.

Circle into quadrants. And, the Frankfort Small Circle is very close to one-half the size of the Frankfort Large Circle.

In a way, what seems expressed in the earthworks just discussed is reminiscent of *ad quadratum* geometry. This is especially true in the case of the Works East and Frankfort Earthworks. For example, a second square can be constructed within the Frankfort Square by joining the midpoints of the edges of the Frankfort Square. If any one side of this new square is used as the diameter for a new circle, then the new circle will be found to have the same diameter as the Frankfort Small Circle. The procedure of creating new

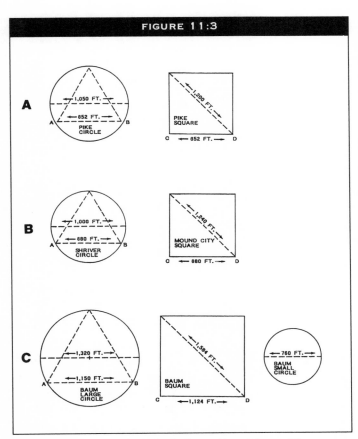

FIGURE 11:3

Schematic plans of the Pike (or Seal), Shriver, Mound City, and Baum Earthworks..

Perimeters (e.g., Newark Square and Fairground Circle); and 4) Square and Circle with Equal Areas (e.g., Marietta Large Square and Liberty Large Circle). Clearly, the Hopewell had a great interest in exploring the geometric relationships between circles and squares.

The next group of four earthworks seem related in that they can be explained by inscribed equilateral triangles. In this sense, the design of these earthworks is reminiscent of *ad triangulum* geometry. For example, as determined from Squier and Davis' figure (1848:Plate 24), the Pike (or Seal) circular enclosure has a diameter of about 1,500 feet, while according to Thomas (1894:491), the Pike Square has sides that are each about 852 feet in length. As shown by **Figure 11:3a**, if we divide the circumference of the idealized Pike Circle into three equal segments - and then connect the end points of these segments, what we find is that an equilateral triangle is thereby formed within the Circle. Notably, any one side of this inscribed triangle is almost equal in length to any one side of the Pike Square.

As shown by **Figure 11:3b**, the same geometric construct that is found at the Pike Earthworks also seems expressed between the Mound City and Shriver Earthworks - wherein any one side of the equilateral triangle inscribed within the Shriver Earthwork is equal in length to any one side of the idealized Mound City Square. For this analysis I used Marshall's (1987:Figure 6) data for Mound City and Squier and Davis' figure (1848:Plate 19) for Shriver.

For the Baum, Liberty, and Seip Earthworks, I used Squier and Davis' (1848:Plate 21, No. 1; Plate 20; Plate 21, No. 2) data for the dimensions of the circular enclosures, and Thomas' (1894:482-483, 488) data for the squares. Unfortunately, Thomas does not provide data for the circular features at these sites.

Like the Mound City-Shriver and Pike Earthworks, at Baum we find that if an equilateral triangle is inscribed within the Baum Large Circle, then any one side of this triangle will be almost equal in length to any one side of the Baum Square. This correspondence is shown in **Figure 11:3c**. Also note-

figures from a series of geometric progressions based on a square is the essence of *ad quadratum* geometry. While it is difficult to show that the Hopewell knowingly used *ad quadratum* geometry, it is on the other hand, very likely that the Hopewell recognized the four fundamental relationships between a circle and square. These relationships are: 1) Square containing a Circle - wherein the circle contained in a square has a diameter equal to the side of that square (e.g., Hopeton); 2) Square contained in a Circle - wherein the circle containing the square has a diameter equal to the square's diagonal (e.g., Circleville, Milford, Works East, and Frankfort); 3) Square and Circle with Equal

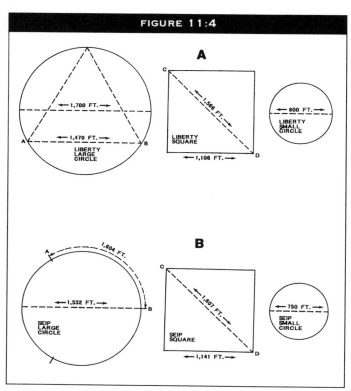

Schematic plans of the Liberty and Seip Earthworks.

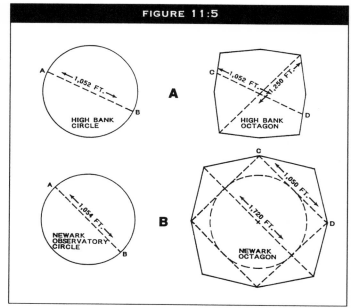

Schematic plans of the High Bank and Newark Earthworks.

worthy is that the Baum Small Circle is almost one-half the size of the Baum Large Circle. (There is also another way of constructing a square and circle having the same proportions as expressed in the Seal, Mound City-Shriver, and Baum Earthworks. First, a circle of any diameter is constructed. Next, a second circle having the same diameter as the first, is drawn using any point on the circumference of the first circle as the center of the second circle. The two overlapping circles will form a *Vesica Piscis*. The long axis of this *Vesica Piscis* is then used as one side of a new square. The first and second circles and the new square will have the same proportions as expressed in the earthworks just discussed.)

At the Liberty Earthwork, a slightly modified version of the equilateral triangle concept is evident. In this case, any one side of the equilateral triangle inscribed within the Liberty Large Circle is found to be close to the length of the diagonal of the Liberty Square. This correspondence is shown in **Figure 11:4a**.

The final tripartite concept to be discussed is found at the Seip Earthwork. As shown in **Figure 11:4b**, the diagonal of the Seip square is equal to one-third of the circumference of the Seip Large Circle.

The last intra-site concept to be discussed is found at the High Bank and Newark Earthworks. High Bank and Newark are unique in that both sites include octagons in their designs. Also fortunate is that for both High Bank and Newark we have the very accurate data of Thomas and Middleton (surveyor) to work with. At High Bank it happens that the apothem of the Octagon - shown in **Figure 11:5a** as line C-D, is equal in length to line A-B, which is the

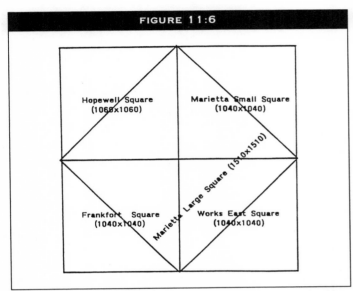

FIGURE 11:6

Schematic plan showing how the Marietta Large Square can be defined by the diagonals of the Hopewell, Frankfort, Marietta Small, and Works East Small Squares.

diameter of the High Bank Circle. Similarly, at Newark it happens that a line extending between the Octagon's alternate vertices - shown in **Figure 11:5b** as line C-D, for example, is virtually equal in length to line A-B, which is the diameter of the Observatory Circle. The correspondences just noted for High Bank and Newark were first pointed out by Hively and Horn (1982:S8, 1984:S92).

In addition to the similarities just noted, however, there are some further correspondences between High Bank and Newark. For example, the High Bank Circle and Newark Observatory Circle are almost exactly the same size - i.e., about 1,053 feet in diameter. Moreover, the length of the High Bank apothem and the length of a line extending between alternate vertices of the Newark Octagon are also both about 1,053 feet in length. Notably, this 1,053 foot unit of length is equal to a multiple of what may be a basic Hopewell unit of length. This proposed basic unit of length is equal to 2.106 feet, or 25.272 inches.

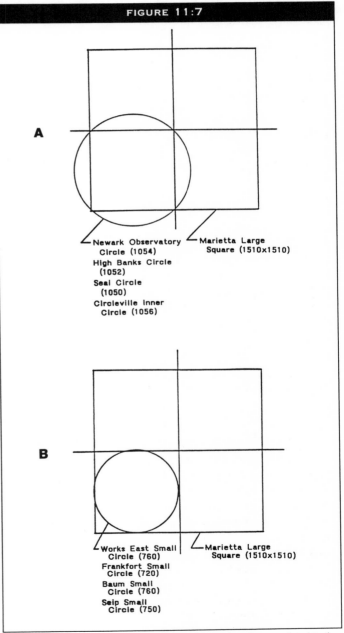

Schematic plans showing how various circular earthworks are related to the constructed squares within the Marietta Large Square.

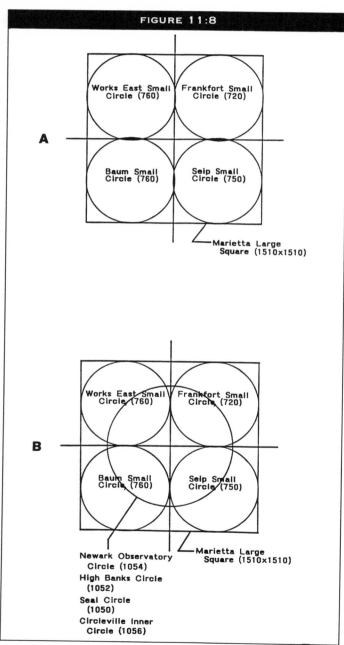

Further iterations of Figures 11:7a and 11:7b.

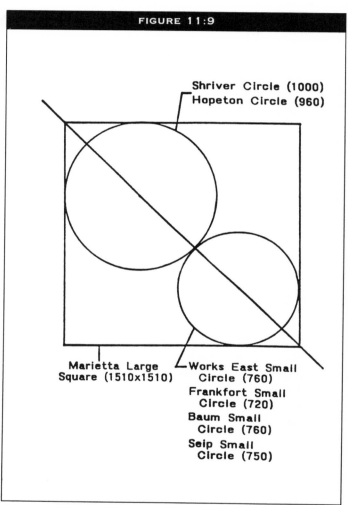

Schematic plan showing the Hopeton and Shriver Circles in relation to other circles and the Marietta Large Square.

In any event, octagons are related to squares in that octagons are truncated squares. By truncated I mean that the corners of the square are each progressively cut back so that an octagon is formed. In the Hopewellian earthworks therefore, the square and the octagon can be considered as symbolically interchangeable in their relationship to their opposite figure, which is a circle.

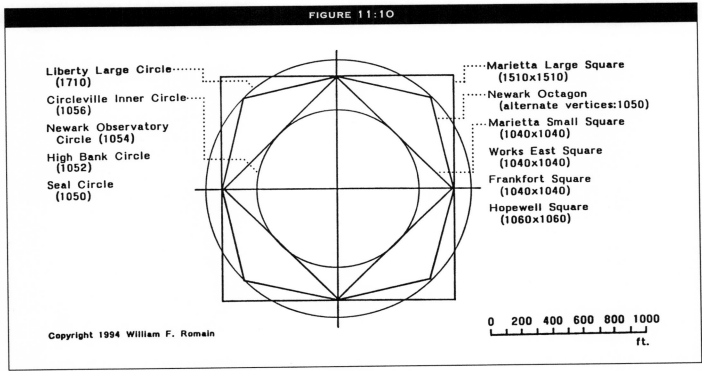

FIGURE 11:10

Liberty Large Circle
(1710)

Circleville Inner Circle
(1056)

Newark Observatory
Circle (1054)

High Bank Circle
(1052)

Seal Circle
(1050)

Marietta Large Square
(1510x1510)

Newark Octagon
(alternate vertices:1050)

Marietta Small Square
(1040x1040)

Works East Square
(1040x1040)

Frankfort Square
(1040x1040)

Hopewell Square
(1060x1060)

0   200   400   600   800   1000

ft.

Copyright 1994 William F. Romain

Scale drawing showing the geometrically inter-related nature of various Hopewell earthworks.

INTER-SITE RELATIONSHIPS

In the preceding section it was shown how various components within specific sites are related to each other. It also appears, however, that a series of geometric relationships is found between sites. **Figure 11:6**, for example, shows how the dimensions of the Marietta Large Square can be defined or established by the diagonals of the combined Hopewell, Frankfort, Marietta Small, and Works East Squares. Idealized shape and dimensions of the Marietta squares are based on Squier and Davis' figure (1848:Plate 26).

The geometric concept involved here is known as "doubling the square". Essentially, **Figure 11:6** provides a geometric solution to the following problem: given a square with sides that are of a given unit length, how can a second square be constructed that has twice the area of the first square?

Using only rational numbers the problem cannot be solved by arithmetic. By using the geometric solution shown in **Figure 11:6**, however, the problem is solved and the square is doubled. Continuing our analysis, if we take the Marietta Large Square and bisect its sides, the figure that results will be made up of four smaller squares. A circle drawn around any one of these four squares will, surprisingly enough, be equal in size to the Newark Observatory, High Bank, Circleville Inner, and Seal Circles. This correspondence is shown in **Figure 11:7a**.

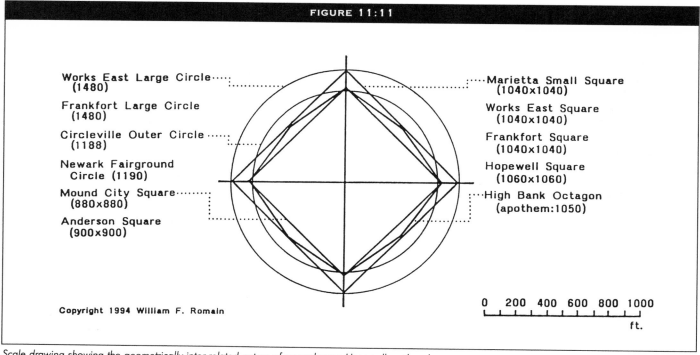

FIGURE 11:11

Works East Large Circle (1480)
Frankfort Large Circle (1480)
Circleville Outer Circle (1188)
Newark Fairground Circle (1190)
Mound City Square (880x880)
Anderson Square (900x900)

Marietta Small Square (1040x1040)
Works East Square (1040x1040)
Frankfort Square (1040x1040)
Hopewell Square (1060x1060)
High Bank Octagon (apothem:1050)

Copyright 1994 William F. Romain

0 200 400 600 800 1000 ft.

Scale drawing showing the geometrically inter-related nature of several more Hopewell earthworks.

Next we see how a circle drawn inside any one of the same four squares is equal in size to the Works East, Frankfort, Baum, and Seip Small Circles. This correspondence is shown in **Figure 11:7b**. It is one way to account for the peculiar size of the four circles just noted. **Figure 11:8a** is simply a further iteration of the small circle concept just discussed. However, if we take **Figure 11:8a** and draw a circle such that its circumference intersects the centers of the four small circles, then the resultant circle will be equal in size to the Circleville Inner, Newark Observatory, Seal, and High Bank Circles. This observation is shown in **Figure 11:8b**.

Figure 11:9 shows one way of accounting for the peculiar size of the Hopeton and Shriver Circles as well as a number of other circular earthworks - by reference to the Marietta Large Square and its diagonal.

In **Figures 11:10 - 11:12**, the incredible extent to which the Hopewellian earthworks are inter-related really becomes apparent. **Figure 11:10** shows how the idealized Newark Octagon nests within both the Marietta Large Square and the Liberty Large Circle. So too, the Marietta Small, Works East, Frankfort, and Hopewell Squares all fit within the Newark Octagon; while the Circleville Inner, Newark Observatory, High Bank, and Seal Circles all fit within the four squares just mentioned.

Interestingly enough, in connection with **Figure 11:10**, it happens that the area of the idealized Liberty Large Circle and the area of the idealized Marietta Large Square are equal to each other to within one percent. More specifically, the area of the Liberty Large Circle is 2,268,650 square feet, while the area of the Marietta Large Square is 2,280,100 square feet:

(2,268,650/2,280,100 = .9949)

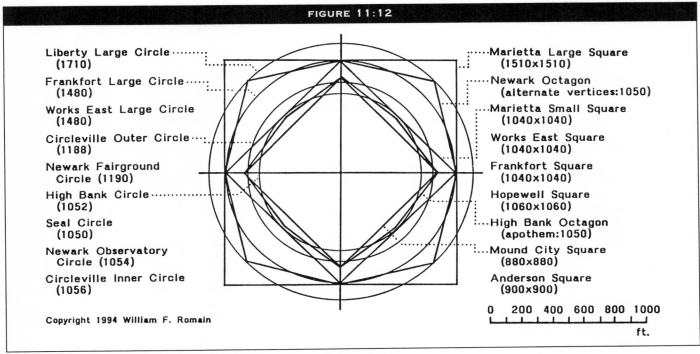

FIGURE 11:12

Liberty Large Circle (1710)
Frankfort Large Circle (1480)
Works East Large Circle (1480)
Circleville Outer Circle (1188)
Newark Fairground Circle (1190)
High Bank Circle (1052)
Seal Circle (1050)
Newark Observatory Circle (1054)
Circleville Inner Circle (1056)

Marietta Large Square (1510x1510)
Newark Octagon (alternate vertices:1050)
Marietta Small Square (1040x1040)
Works East Square (1040x1040)
Frankfort Square (1040x1040)
Hopewell Square (1060x1060)
High Bank Octagon (apothem:1050)
Mound City Square (880x880)
Anderson Square (900x900)

0 200 400 600 800 1000
ft.

Copyright 1994 William F. Romain

Composite scale drawing of the Hopewell earthworks shown in Figures 11:10 and 11:11.

Figure 11:11 shows how the High Bank Octagon defines the size difference between the Marietta Small, Works East, Frankfort, and Hopewell Squares - and the Mound City and Anderson Squares. **Figure 11:11** also shows how the Works East and Frankfort Large Circles are defined by the inscribed Marietta Small, Works East, Frankfort, and Hopewell Squares. And, **Figure 11:11** shows how the size of the Circleville Outer and Newark Fairground Circles are defined by the inscribed High Bank Octagon, and Mound City and Anderson Squares.

In **Figure 11:12**, we see how all the above earthworks nest together in one inter-related design. In fact, from the way the earthworks fit together it seems possible that the Hopewell were familiar with a class of figures known as icosatwists. An icosatwist is a figure that is made-up of pro- gressively smaller squares that are rotated within yet other

squares. The angular changes of the squares can vary from 2 to 45 degrees. In Figures 11:10 - 11:12, the squares have been rotated 45 degrees. Of course, without addi- tional evidence it is difficult to know if the Hopewell inten- tionally used the idea of icosatwists. But certainly, the way each earthwork neatly fits within other design shapes that may be miles and miles away is unique. And, the whole phenomenon is even more intriguing when we consider that many of these inter-nesting earthworks were built at different times over a period of hundreds of years.

MENSURATION, ALIGNMENTS, AND CALENDRICS

The geometric regularities just outlined are further discussed elsewhere (Romain 1992c, 1993b, 1993c). In addition to being geometrically interrelated though, it appears that the Hopewell enclosures are also mathematically and astronomically inter-related. More specifically, the geometrically-shaped earthworks appear mathematically inter-related in the sense that a common unit of measurement is found in the earthworks. This basic unit of length is equal to 2.106 feet, or 25.272 inches. This length, as well as small multiples of this length are found in the distances that separate the post holes that make-up the walls of various Hopewell charnel houses (see Romain 1991b, 1992c); while large multiples of this basic unit of length are found in the designs of the large geometrically-shaped enclosures. The 500 x 2.106 feet multiple, for example, is expressed in the diameters of the Seal, High Bank, Circleville Inner, and Newark Observatory Circles, and in the apothems of the High Bank and Newark Octagons. In each of these instances, the diameters or apothems of these earthworks are 1,053 feet in length - to within plus or minus 1.5 percent. So too, the sides of the Marietta Small, Works East, Frankfort, and Hopewell Squares are also 1,053 feet in length - to within plus or minus 1.2 percent. And, the diagonal of the Marietta Large Square is equal to 2 times the 1,053 feet unit of length - to within plus or minus 1.5 percent. All together, more than 24 large Hopewellian enclosures manifest the 500 x 2.106 feet multiple, or 1,053 feet unit of length in their designs.

Certainly, the use of a basic unit of length would have made the design and construction of the earthworks easier. In fact, it seems likely that before building something like the Newark Octagon, a smaller drawing, design plan, or model probably would have been made first. Use of a basic unit of measurement would have then facilitated the translation of the small-scale plan or model into a full-sized earthwork.

Interestingly enough, there is some reason to believe that the basic unit of measurement suggested here was based on the length of the typical adult male Hopewell arm - as measured from the shoulder joint, or proximal end of the humerus to the distal end of the metacarpal bones - where the fingers meet the palm of the hand. Data derived from an Illinois-based Hopewell population shows that this armspan is equal to 25.3 inches - or about 2.106 feet - which is the proposed basic unit of length (also see Romain 1991b). (No comparable database has been published for Ohio Hopewell populations.) By suspending a plumb-bob from between the fingers of a laterally outstretched arm, a very effective way of laying out accurate multiples of the basic unit of measure would have resulted. Through use of a basic unit of measure that was based on the dimensions of the human body, the Hopewell in effect, synthesized in their earthworks the measure of man with the cosmos.

A growing body of evidence (Essenpreis and Duszynski 1989; Greber 1986; Greber and Jargiello 1982; Hively and Horn 1982, 1984; Romain 1991c, 1992a, 1992d, 1992e, 1993b) also suggests that the Hopewell aligned many of their geometric earthworks and perhaps their char-nel houses to significant celestial events. My own opinion is that the evidence for specific solar and lunar alignments is compelling - especially for those sites where we have accurate orientation data - such as Newark, High Bank, Liberty, Baum, Circleville, and Anderson. Perhaps though, the significance of these alignments is not so much in their observational usefulness - but rather in their symbolic expression of the cyclic nature of Hopewellian time. Recall that in different alignments of the earthworks it has been argued that the Hopewell recognized the 18.6 year cycle of the moon, and the recurring, winter and summer solstices of the sun. As Suzuki and Knudtson have explained:

...the recurrent natural rhythms of circular time could quite legitimately be perceived as primary, life-affirming cycles. To many Native peoples, some of these cycles have always been sacred, worthy of the most profound veneration, and steeped in signs and significance for all humankind. Through ancient nature-honoring rituals, the primeval cycles of nature...are symbolically renewed...[Suzuki and Knudtson 1992:179].

With regard to these primeval cycles, there is also some intriguing evidence that the Adena and probably the Ohio Hopewell, employed a solar-lunar calendar that was particularly attuned to the phases of the moon - both on a monthly and annual basis. This information appears memorialized in the shape and markings of the Cincinnati and Wamsley tablets and also in several Hopewellian artifacts (see Romain 1991a, 1992b).

The idea that the Adena and Ohio Hopewell would keep track of time by some method such as a calendar device should not come as any great surprise. As Marshack (1991) has shown, humankind has kept track of time for thousands of years by marking its passage on stone, bone, and wood. And again, as Suzuki and Knudtson (1992:177) have noted, it is "[time] that binds together what might otherwise appear to be a chaos of cosmic elements and events." Ample reason indeed, for Hopewellians to keep track of times' passing.

SOME FURTHER OBSERVATIONS

Having briefly explored the world of Hopewellian geometry, the question still remains as to why the Hopewell would build such tremendous earthen structures. Earthen structures that in their very design incorporate, reveal, and even proclaim fundamental and universal geometric concepts. In response to such questions I am in agreement with John Michell who has proposed that:

The geometer's aim...is to imitate the universe symbolically, depicting its central paradox by bringing together shapes of different geometric orders, uniting them as simply and accurately as possible and thus creating a cosmic image which...most nearly resembles the original [Michell 1988:65].

Along these lines, I would suggest that the circle, square, and octagonal Hopewell enclosures were meant as ideological symbols. Within these symbols were performed rituals and ceremonies relating to passage from this world to the next, death and rebirth, world renewal, and creation. Underlying this interpretation is the recognition that many Native American peoples are found to have intentionally designed their ceremonial areas, ritual lodges, and even individual dwellings to reflect their beliefs about the structure of the universe. As explained by Nabokov and Easton:

The buildings of Native Americans encoded not only their social order but often their tribal view of the cosmos....Thereafter, Indian people held the ritual power to renew their cosmos through rebuilding, remodeling, or reconsecrating their architecture [Nabokov and Easton 1989:38].

Further discussion and supporting data for my hypothesis, is provided in a companion article (Romain 1994). In outline form, the most important elements of this hypothesis are as follows:

1) Square enclosures were meant as symbols of the sky or heavens. This is suggested by the occurrence of solar and lunar alignments within the square enclosures and by a statistical association between the general orientation of the square enclosures and the prevailing wind. Hence the association of the squares with the heavens and wind - or sky phenomenon. Further, ethnohistoric data shows that among many Indian peoples of the Southeast, the square was often used to represent the four world quarters, four winds, and four directions.

2) Circular enclosures were meant as symbols of the earth. This is suggested by the observation that as we look around us to the horizon, the figure that we trace between the edge of the earth and the sky is a circle. Further, many Native American peoples - including the Iroquois and Cherokee - believed the earth to be a flat circular island surrounded by water. This in turn is related to the "Earth-diver" myth and the frequent use of water-borne soils to cover Hopewell burials - which are often located within circular enclosures. It is proposed that the creation of the earth and life itself is symbolically recreated not only in the burial mounds of the Hopewell, as suggested by Hall (1979), but also in the design of the circular enclosures - with the earth being symbolically located within the circular enclosures, while the primeval waters are outside the circles.

3) Evidence for use of the earthworks for ceremonies relating to passage from this world to the next, death and rebirth, world renewal, and creation is found in the occurrence of numerous burials and symbols of transformation found within the enclosures. Proposed transformational symbols include cremation fires, smoking pipes, animal headdresses, and bird effigies. Indicators of ceremonies relating to world renewal and creation include passageways to nearby water, solar and lunar alignments, bear effigies, and floral remains found in ceremonial contexts.

CONCLUSION

It seems likely that the geometrically-shaped Hopewellian earthworks were used for a variety of purposes including social and community gatherings of various sorts and perhaps as trading or resource exchange centers. Most likely, each geometric earthwork served its own local constituency. In terms of ideology though, again my thought is that the geometric enclosures were primarily used for ceremonies relating to passage from this world to the next, death and rebirth, world renewal, and creation. Ultimately though, it was the geometric symbolism as discussed here, and as expressed in the earthworks, that gave these earthen creations their power. In essence, the geometric earthworks were models, or microcosms of the Hopewellian vision of the universe. By reconsecrating these monuments, or by adding layers to a central burial mound, or by performing sacred dances within such enclosures, the Ohio Hopewell reaffirmed their place in the universe, and at the same time, helped renew their cosmos, their universe, and their resources. Such world renewal ceremonies are still found today among many North American peoples. Indeed, if my explanation is correct, then we may, in the geometric enclosures of the Ohio Hopewell, be looking at further evidence for a continuity of belief and symbolism extending from historic times back into the Middle Woodland period - and probably earlier.

REFERENCES CITED

Anderson, J.C. 1980 A Recent Discovery - The Anderson Earthwork. *Ohio Archaeologist* 30(1):31-35.

Cowen, C. 1892 *Map of the Hopewell Site*. Map (N31722) on file, Peabody Museum, Harvard University Cambridge.

Essenpreis, P.S. and D.J. Duszynski 1989 Possible Astronomical Alignments at the Fort Ancient Monument. Paper presented at the Annual Meeting of the Society for American Archaeology, Atlanta.

Greber, N.B. 1986 Astronomy and the Patterns of Five Geometric Earthworks in Ross County, Ohio. Paper presented at the second Oxford Conference on Archaeoastronomy, Merida, Yucatan.

Greber, N.B. and D. Jargiello 1982 Possible Astronomical Orientations Used in Constructing Some Scioto Hopewell Earthwork Walls. Paper presented at the Annual Meeting of the Midwest Archaeological Conference, Cleveland.

Greber, N.B. and K.C. Ruhl 1989 *The Hopewell Site: A Contemporary Analysis Based on the Work of Charles C. Willoughby*. Westview Press, Boulder, Colorado.

Hall, R.L. 1979 In Search of the Ideology of the Adena-Hopewell Climax. In *Hopewell Archaeology: The Chillicothe Conference*, edited by D.S. Brose and N.B. Greber, pp. 258-265. Kent State University Press, Kent, Ohio.

Hively, R. and R. Horn 1982 Geometry and Astronomy in Prehistoric Ohio. *Archaeoastronomy* 4:S1-S20.

1984 Hopewellian Geometry and Astronomy at High Bank. *Archaeoastronomy* 7:S85-S100.

Marshack, A. 1991 *The Roots of Civilization*. (Revised and expanded.) Moyer Bell Ltd., Mt. Kisco, New York.

Marshall, J.A. 1987 An Atlas of American Indian Geometry. *Ohio Archaeologist* 37(2); 36-49.

Michell, J.A. 1988 *The Dimensions of Paradise*. Harper & Row, New York.

Nabokov, P. and R. Easton 1989 *Native American Architecture*. Oxford University Press, New York.

Romain, W.F. 1991a Calendric Information Evident in the Adena Tablets. *Ohio Archaeologist* 41(4):41-48.

1991b Evidence for a Basic Hopewell Unit of Measure. *Ohio Archaeologist* 41(4):28-37.

1991c Possible Astronomical Alignments at Hopewell Sites in Ohio. *Ohio Archaeologist* 41(3):4-16.

1992a Azimuths to the Otherworld: Astronomical Alignments of Hopewell Charnel Houses. *Ohio Archaeologist* 42(4):42-48.

1992b Further Evidence for a Calendar System Expressed in the Adena Tablets. *Ohio Archaeologist* 42(3):31-36.

1992c Hopewellian Concepts in Geometry. *Ohio Archaeologist* 42(2):35-50.

1992d More Astronomical Alignments at Hopewell Sites in Ohio. *Ohio Archaeologist* 42(1):38-47.

1992e Hopewell Inter-Site Relationships and Astronomical Alignments. *Ohio Archaeologist* 42(1):4-5.

1993a Early Aerial Photographs of the Ross County Hopewell Enclosures. *Ohio Archaeologist* 43(4):44-49.

1993b Further Notes on Hopewellian Astronomy and Geometry. *Ohio Archaeologist* 43(3):48-52.

1993c Hopewell Ceremonial Centers and Geomantic Influences. *Ohio Archaeologist* 43(1):35-44.

1994 Hopewell Geometric Enclosures: Symbols of an Ancient World View. *Ohio Archaeologist* 44(2):37-43.

Squier, E.G. and E.H. Davis 1848 *Ancient Monuments of the Mississippi Valley*. Smithsonian Contributions to Knowledge. Vol. 1. Smithsonian Institution, Washington, D.C.

Stewart, I. and M. Golubitsky 1992 *Fearful Symmetry: Is God a Geometer?* Blackwell Publishers, Oxford, England.

Suzuki, D. and P. Knudtson 1992 *Wisdom of the Elders: Honoring Sacred Native Visions of Nature*. Bantam Books, New York.

TWELVE

TOWARDS A DEFINITION OF THE OHIO HOPEWELL CORE AND PERIPHERY UTILIZING THE GEOMETRIC EARTHWORKS

JAMES A. MARSHALL

ABSTRACT

In this paper the results of precise instrumental surveys by the author of Hopewellian geometric and other earthwork sites are utilized to define the boundaries of the Ohio Hopewell core area based on the mathematical concepts embodied in the earthworks. Surveys are tied into state grid coordinate systems so that precise distances and directions can be determined between nearby earthworks, such as those in Ross and Licking Counties, Ohio. The data explored in this paper suggest a mathematical distinction between those earthworks in the Ohio Hopewell core area as compared to those in its periphery.

A View From the Core a Synthesis of Ohio Hopewell Archaeology•edited by Paul J. Pacheco
© Copyright 1996 by The Ohio Archaeological Council• Columbus, Ohio
All Rights Reserved•ISBN 0-9626931-9-7

J A M E S   A .   M A R S H A L L
T O W A R D S   A   D E F I N I T I O N   O F   T H E   O H I O   H O P E W E L L   C O R E   A N D

INTRODUCTION

The impetus for this research began in the early 1960s during conversations between the author and Dr. Stuart M. Struever, in Chicago. Struever argued that prevailing wisdom of the time believed either that the mathematical concepts embodied in Hopewellian earthworks developed first in the lower Illinois River Valley before spreading to Ohio, or were developed casually in place, on a case by case basis. Two objections to this view were raised. First, the number and complexity of Hopewellian earthworks in Illinois does not account for the number and complexity of Hopewellian earthworks in Ohio. Ohio is clearly the focal area for the development of Hopewellian earthworks. Secondly, mathematical learning is a step-by-step process, requiring individuals to learn and understand each step before proceeding to the next. The mathematics embodied in Hopewellian geometric earthworks is better explained as the culmination of many steps of learning. Conceptually, as this paper will attempt to demonstrate, it would be impossible to have created the knowledge necessary to build some works without knowledge of previously built works.

Taking this idea further, all earthworks are likely to be expressions of a single school of thought. In fact, some geometric expressions used in the ancient Old World probably have expression in the New World: one unit of measure, with small variations over space and time, one unit the side of a square and the other its diagonal. Likewise, a reality regularly observed in today's world - the "mathematics ceiling" - a step beyond which learners demonstrate a lack of willingness or an inability to progress, would also have been operative in ancient societies. Rather than representing an argument for transoceanic influences, the similarities between the Old World and the New World more likely point to the universality of geometric concepts (Critchlow 1976; Kline 1962, 1972; Menninger 1969). For this reason, it will be argued that the mathematical knowledge embodied in Hopewellian earthworks springs from one school of thought.

GEOMETRIC EARTHWORKS DATA

The Hopewellian geometric and other earthworks from which precise surveys are available have been placed into five classes. Geometric complexity increases in scale from class one to class five. However, classes two through five form a nested hierarchy, defined by the mathematical principles embodied in each earthwork, with complexity increasing in scale from class one to class five. Therefore, an earthwork of class five contains principles embodied in classes two through four, but not class one. The following section describes and discusses mathematical principles associated with each class, providing examples where appropriate (see also Marshall 1978, 1980, 1987). Note that most measurements are given in English units because of the preferred use of this system by surveyors, both in this century and the last, when most earthworks were first mapped.

Class One - No Mathematical Knowledge

This class covers the earthworks that display no mathematical knowledge in their plan and construction. This class therefore covers many earthworks that are not geometric, including several hilltop "forts" such as Glenford Fort (Whittlesey 1851:Plate V [No. 2]). Works in this class display no knowledge of precise units of measurements, circular arcs, right angles, cryptography, or concept of *pi*. Possibly some of these works were paced off. The Parker Works located in Ontario, Canada, demonstrate the widespread distribution of this earthwork class (Lee 1958:4).

Class Two - Basic Unit of Measurement

Rene Millon (1967) reported that the layout of Teotihuacan was based on a 57 m (approximately 197 feet) grid system. Grids of this unit, its diagonal (264 feet), half the unit (93.5 feet), and half the diagonal (132 feet), were placed over surveyed maps of Hopewellian earthworks. More than 100 mounded Hopewellian geometric earthworks from the eastern United States showed close agreement between one or another of these grids, indicating a shared basic unit of measurement that spans the ancient New World. Modular use of multiples of the basic unit is evident in several Hopewellian earthworks, especially those with large circles and squares. For example, the Baum Earthworks (Squier and Davis 1848:Plate XXI [No. 1]) large circle at 1,667 feet diameter is approximately nine times the basic unit, while the square has sides of 1,107 feet, 1,129 feet, 1,113 feet, and 1,118 feet, which are approximately six times the basic unit. The Eastern Citadel of the Pinson site in Tennessee also falls into this class (Mainfort 1986:7).

Class Three - Cryptographs

If one locates the center of a geometric earthwork, such as a square, circle, rectangle, octagon, or ellipse, then draws straight lines from it to the centers of nearby geometric earthworks, and then passes true north-south and true east-west lines through these centers, the resulting lines on some of those works will form geometric configurations that utilize the 57 m unit (187 feet) and also form simple right triangles. These purely abstract configurations are referred to here as cryptographs. The most commonly used right triangle is the 3-4-5 right triangle. Other right triangles found are base 1, altitude 1; base 2, altitude 1; a rare base 17, altitude 4; a unique 5-12-13 right triangle at Newark; a 7-24-25 right triangle at High Bank Octagon; and a 39-80-89 right triangle at the Newark Octagon. The presence of these latter right triangles is an indication that these people knew or understood the principles embodied in the Pythagorean Theorem.

Cryptographic Hopewellian earthworks in class three are concentrated geographically in southern Ohio, especially in Ross and Licking Counties. There are a few similar works from other areas of the eastern United States. The most distant of these class three Hopewellian works is found at Fort Center, Clades County, Florida (Marshall 1987:44). Closer to the Ohio area is the Mann Site, Posey County, Indiana (Kellar 1979:100).

Figure 12:1 shows the basic principle of cryptographic relationships in Hopewellian earthwork geometry as embodied in the Alexandersville Works, located in Montgomery

County, Ohio. This map was created by combining data from McBride's original survey (1847), this drawing in Squier and Davis (1848:Plate XXIX), a ground survey by the author, and aerial photographs. Other similar examples of class three works are found at the Liberty Township Works, and Baum Works, both located in Ross County, Ohio **(Figures 12:2 and 12:3)**. A larger version is represented at the Newark Earthworks, located in Licking County, Ohio **(Figure 12:4)**. All three of these maps (and all subsequent maps shown in this paper) were created by combining data from surveys conducted for Cyrus Thomas (1889a, 1889b, 1894), ground surveys by the author, and aerial photographs. Besides the apparent cryptographic triangles found in these works, there appears to be a corresponding mathematical interest in the bisection of angles. As discussed below, this fascination may be related to an interest in the concept of *pi*.

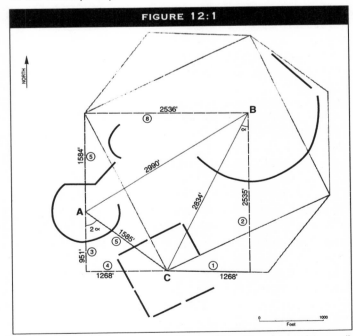

FIGURE 12:1

Alexandersville Works, Montgomery County, Ohio. The centers of the small and large circles are at A and B, with that of the square at C. The outlines of the suggested cryptograph, plus an octagonal cryptograph are shown as shaded lines. The proportions of the cryptographic triangles are shown in circled numbers.

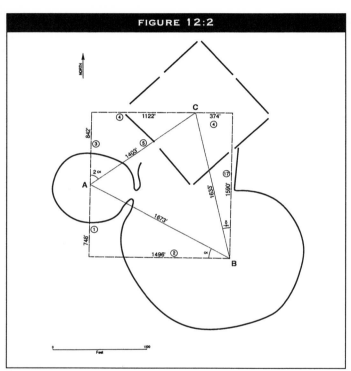

FIGURE 12:2

Liberty Township Works, Ross County, Ohio. The center of the ellipse is at A, the half circle at B, and the square at C. The dimensions of the suggested cryptograph are shown, as are the proportions of the cryptographic triangles.

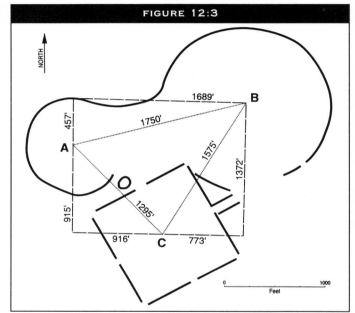

FIGURE 12:3

Baum Works, Ross County, Ohio. The centers of the small and large circles are at A and B, with the square at C. The dimensions of the suggested cryptograph are shown, forming an approximate 45/45/90 degree triangle, a 75/15/90 degree triangle, and a 30/60/90 degree triangle.

Class Four - Cryptographic Overlays

This class includes those earthworks that demonstrate the principle of cryptographic overlay, such that when the plan of one work is placed over another, so that centers of the geometric figures coincide or very closely agree, then straight walls of one work match or are parallel to their counterpart on the other earthwork. The situation where the circle on one earthwork is tangent to the circle on another earthwork is also considered a case of cryptographic overlay. The demonstration of cryptographic overlays between Hopewellian earthworks strongly argues that both works were drafted and laid out in the field by people who understood the relationships embodied in the corresponding work, enough so that they could even have been drafted by the same person(s).

The basic principle of cryptographic overlay is shown in **Figure 12:5**. In this figure, the Seip Works is overlaid on the Newark Octagon. The overlay indicates a strong correlation between the proximity of the openings in the Newark Octagon to those of the Seip Large Circle. There is also a parallelism between one side of the octagon and the near side of the Seip Square. **Figure 12:6** shows the strong correlation between the northeast corner of Ft. Ancient and the High Bank Works, after rotation. **Figure 12:7** documents the cryptographic overlay between the tangent circles of the Baum and Liberty Works. Some cases of cryptographic overlay are based on enlargements of one earthwork plan, using the standard 57 m unit of measurement. **Figure 12:8** places an enlarged version of the High Bank Works over the Baum Works cryptograph, which was presented earlier. There is a close agreement between interior lines of the octagon and the interior triangle of the Baum cryptograph.

FIGURE 12:4

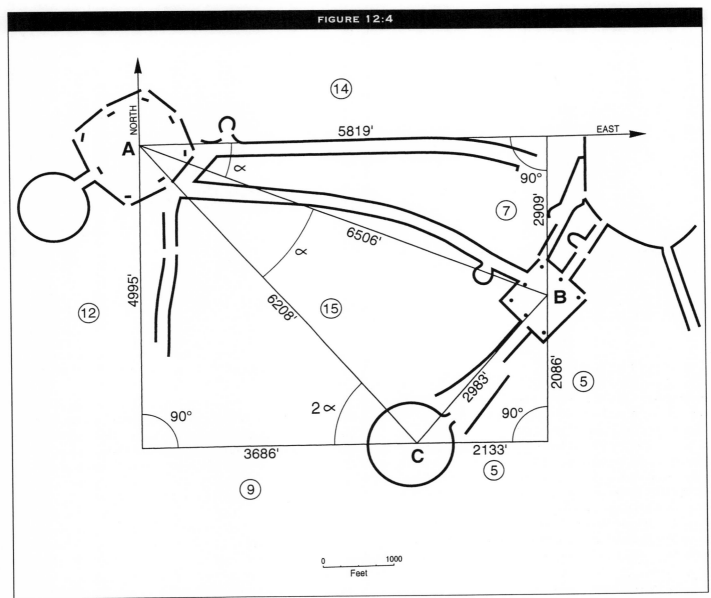

Newark Earthworks, Licking County, Ohio. The center of the octagon is at A, the square is at B, and the Moundbuilders Circle at C. The dimensions of the cryptograph are shown, as are the proportions of the cryptographic triangles.

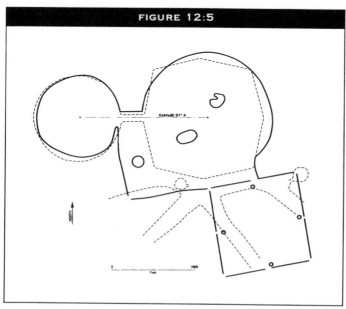

FIGURE 12:5

Newark Octagon rotated and placed over Seip Works, Ross County, Ohio.

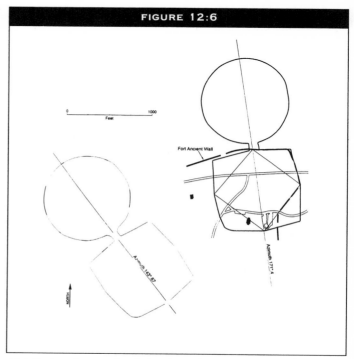

FIGURE 12:6

High Bank works rotated and placed over the northeast corner of Fort Ancient Earthwork.

Class Five - The Concept of Pi

Earthworks in this class demonstrate influence of the concept of *pi*; the relation of the circumference to the diameter of a circle. Today we approximate the value of *pi* = 3.1416. The ancient Hopewellian earthwork builders apparently created a nine unit square of 81 units total area, inscribed a nine unit diameter circle in it and drew the basic octagon as shown in **Figure 12:9**. The octagon interior area is easily calculated as 63 units. The octagon was presumed to approximate the area of the circle, meaning that the overlaps equaled the underlaps. This yielded a value for *pi*:

$$4.5^2 \cdot pi = 63$$

$$pi = \frac{63}{20.25} = 3.11+$$

However, there is also evidence that Ohio Hopewell people recognized (correctly) that the overlaps on this basic octagon diagram were greater than the underlaps, meaning that the actual area of the circle is between 63 units and 64 units:

$$4.5^2 \cdot pi = 64$$

$$pi = \frac{64}{20.25} = 3.160+$$

Therefore, the area of a circle nine units in diameter could be trapped between a square of 64 units area, and a rectangle of 63 units area.

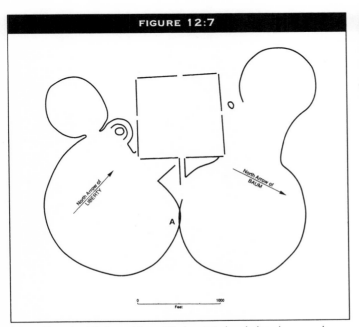

FIGURE 12:7

Liberty Township Works and Baum Works rotated and placed over each other, each to the same scale so that their respective squares coincide. When so alighned, the respective large circles become very nearly tangent at Point A, which is about 1,500 feet from the centers of the squares.

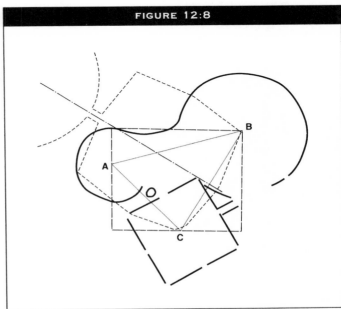

FIGURE 12:8

An enlargement of the High Banks Works placed on the cryptograph of the Baum Works.

Old World histories of the concept of *pi* (see Beckman 1970; Gillings 1972) parallel the results found in this study of Hopewellian earthwork geometry. Both Beckman (1970:23) and Gillings (1972:143-144) contain facsimiles of the template represented by **Figure 12:9**. These authors show that the geometric relationships embodied in **Figure 12:9** can be extended further by inscribing a circle onto the 64 unit square, which is then superimposed onto the basic octagon. A large number of Hopewellian geometric earth-works appear to have been built using the **Figure 12:9** template, or a variation of the template scaled by the ratio of the diagonal of a square to its side, or 1.414. **Figure 12:10** shows a template based on squares 132 feet on a side; which has a diagonal 187 feet on a side. The two concentric circles on the template fit those at Circleville, Ohio. Other possible templates of 264 feet and 93.5 feet on a side can be shown to fit additional earthwork plans.

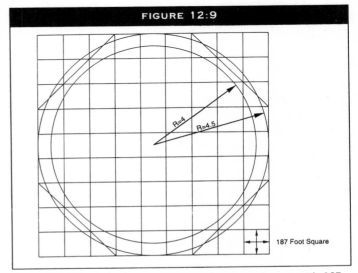

FIGURE 12:9

With each square in this basic octagon template measuring on a side 187 feet, circles of radius 4 times 187 feet (which equals 748 feet) and 4.5 times 187 (which equals 841.5 feet) were built.

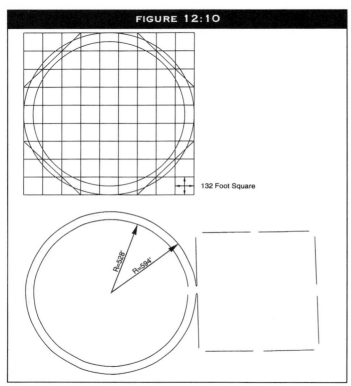

FIGURE 12:10

132 Foot Square

With each square in this basic octagon template measuring 132 feet on a side, circles of radius 4 times 132 feet (which equals 528 feet) and 4.5 times 132 feet (which equals 594 feet) were built. The diagonal of each square of 132 feet equals 187 feet.

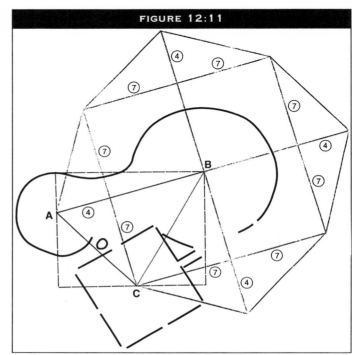

FIGURE 12:11

Shows unknown octagon of the proportions shown placed over the interior triangle of the Baum cryptograph.

CONCLUSION

The boundaries of the Ohio Hopewell core area can be distinguished from its periphery based on the distribution of the five mathematical classes of earthworks proposed in this paper. Earthworks from both classes one and two are widespread throughout the eastern United States, while classes three through five are very restrictive in their distribution, centering primarily in south central Ohio. The cryptographic overlays between geometrically related sites such as Seip and Newark, and High Bank and Fort Ancient, for instance, indicates the close relationships between earthworks within Ohio. The existence of these relationships suggests a mathematical definition to the Ohio Hopewell core, refined by

reference to the mathematical linkage between Liberty Township, Seip, Newark, High Bank, and Baum Works. Together, these works might be considered the *True Core* of Ohio Hopewell. The cryptographic overlays and projections between and within these earthworks indicates an attempt to develop octagons and polygons with greater number of sides that might yield more precise values of *pi*. As such it is argued that these works are evidence of the work of a residential school of Pythagoreans similarly preoccupied with mathematics. If there is an ultimate geometric center to the Ohio Hopewell core, it has to be the High Bank Works, with its strongly implied 22 sided figure.

The facts presented in this paper demonstrate stable use of closely related units of measure, specific mathematical principles and methods, the means of diffusing that knowledge over wide areas of eastern North America, and ability to transmit that knowledge through many generations. The geometric Hopewellian earthworks require a system of counting and tallying similar to Roman numerals or the bar-dot system of Mesoamerica. Use of standard drafting triangles, are implied also, presumably of wood similar to those used in Europe and America well into the twentieth century.

The extensive use of grids in these works indicates that the Hopewellian earthworks were planned on a sand table or drafting board as such facilities existed in those ancient times with the intent of replicating what was planned to a much larger grid out in the field, as is confirmed by the crypto-graphic overlays. Grids were clearly the means by which a figure, geometric or otherwise, was expanded from a draw-ing, at the very largest a meter on a side, to a layout in the field about 2,000 times that size. Precise surveying and mapping have indicated the specifics of Hopewellian mathe-matical principles and methods and demonstrated their diffu-sion over wide areas and across language boundaries.

ACKNOWLEDGMENTS

I acknowledge the assistance of Rick Pack, Monica Parrish, and John Morici, during the surveys of several of the earth-works presented in this study. I also thank Charles O'Connor and Joan Pintozzi, who helped computerize the High Bank data. I assume responsibility for any errors con-tained in this work.

REFERENCES CITED

Beckman, P. 1970 *A History of pi*. The Golem Press, Boulder, Colorado.

Critchlow, K. 1976 *Islamic Patterns: An Analytical and Cosmological Approach*. Schocken Books, New York.

Gillings, R.J. 1972 *Mathematics in the Time of the Pharaohs*. MIT Press, Cambridge, Massachusetts.

Kellar, J.E. 1979 The Mann Site and "Hopewell" in the Lower Wabash-Ohio Valley. In *Hopewell Archaeology: The Chillicothe Conference*, edited by D. S. Brose and N. B. Greber, pp. 100-107. Kent State University Press, Kent, Ohio.

Kline, M. 1962 *Mathematics: a Cultural Approach*. Addison-Wesley, Reading, Massachusetts.

  1972 *Mathematical Thought from Ancient to Modern Times*. Oxford University Press, New York.

Lee, T.E. 1958 The Parker Earthwork, Coronna, Ontario. *Pennsylvania Archaeologist* 38(1):3-30.

Mainfort, R.C. Jr. 1986 *Pinson Mounds: A Middle Woodland Ceremonial Center*. Tennessee Department of Conservation, Division of Archaeology, Research Series, No. 7, Memphis.

Marshall, J.A. 1978 American Indian Geometry. *Ohio Archaeologist* 28(1):29-33.

  1980 Geometry of the Hopewell Earthworks. *Ohio Archaeologist* 30(2):8-12.

  1987 An Atlas of American Indian Geometry. *Ohio Archaeologist* 37(2):36-49.

McBride, J. 1847 Survey Notes of Alexandersville Works. Ms. on file, Archives, Ohio Historical Society, Columbus.

Menninger, K. 1969 *Number Words and Number Symbols: A Cultural History of Numbers*. MIT Press, Cambridge, Massachusetts.

Millon, R. 1967 Teotihuacan. In *Archaeology, Myths, and Reality*, readings from *Scientific American*, pp. 85-95. W.H. Freeman, San Francisco.

Squier, E.G. and E.H. Davis 1848 *Ancient Monuments of the Mississippi Valley*. Smithsonian Contributions to Knowledge Vol. 1, Smithsonian Institution, Washington, D.C.

Thomas, C. 1889a *The Circular, Square and Octagonal Earthworks of Ohio*. Bureau of American Ethnology Bulletin No. 10, Smithsonian Institution, Washington, D.C.

  1889b Unpublished Notes from Ohio Earthwork Surveys. Ms. on file, Smithsonian Anthropological Archives, Washington, D.C.

  1894 *Report on the Mound Explorations of the Bureau of Ethnology*. Twelfth Annual Report of the Bureau of American Ethnology for the years 1890-1891, Washington, D.C.

Whittlesey, C. 1851 *Descriptions on Ancient Works in Ohio*. Smithsonian Contributions to Knowledge 3(7). Smithsonian Institution, Washington, D.C.

**PART TWO: RESEACH AT
EARTHWORKS AND MOUNDS**

THE NEWARK EARTHWORKS AND THE GEOMETRIC ENCLOSURES OF THE SCIOTO VALLEY: CONNECTIONS AND CONJECTURES

BRADLEY T. LEPPER

ABSTRACT

There are many similarities between elements of the Newark Earthworks and particular sites in the Scioto Valley. Moreover, there is evidence for a direct connection — a formal roadway — between Hopewellian Newark and Chillicothe. The Great Hopewell Road consisted of parallel walls of earth nearly 1m high and nearly 60m apart. It may have extended, in a perfectly straight line over a distance of 90 km, from Newark to Chillicothe. Such a connection implies a previously unrecognized degree of interaction between the groups living in the Raccoon Creek and Scioto River drainages. The paper will explore the nature of these connections.

A View From the Core a Synthesis of Ohio Hopewell Archaeology•edited by Paul J. Pacheco
© Copyright 1996 by The Ohio Archaeological Council• Columbus, Ohio
All Rights Reserved•ISBN 0-9626931-9-7

BRADLEY T. LEPPER

THE NEWARK EARTHWORKS AND THE GEOMETRIC ENCLOSURES OF

INTRODUCTION

The Newark Earthworks are extraordinary. This complex of geometric earthen enclosures is the largest in the Hopewell world (**Figures 13:1-13:4**). The Scioto River and Paint Creek Valleys around Chillicothe hold a greater number of earthworks of more diverse form, but these are dispersed widely up and down the valleys (**Figure 13:5**). In addition to being the largest complex of geometric enclosures, the Newark Works also are the northernmost of the great Hopewellian ceremonial centers.

Despite the exceptional nature of the Newark Earthworks, or, perhaps, because of it, they have been regarded as somewhat peripheral, in a geographic as well as cultural sense, to the mounds and earthworks of the Scioto drainage. Indeed, the area around Chillicothe usually is regarded as the defining core area of Ohio Hopewell (hence the name and venue of this conference).[1] But little archaeological research has been undertaken at the Newark Works, and the little that has been done has not been comprehensively reported. Therefore, it is premature, at best, to relegate Newark's earthen flamboyance to the status of a footnote to Hopewell archaeology in the Scioto drainage.

The hugeness of the Newark Earthworks and their situation at an archaeological, if not a prehistoric, frontier are factors which make it impossible to consider them as "typical" constructions of the Hopewell. Nevertheless, their preeminence makes them an interesting lens through which to view the entire Hopewellian achievement. And although it is true that relatively little is known about prehistoric Newark, thus making comparisons with Chillicothe problematic, enough has been learned to establish that Newark is not peripheral to the so-called Hopewell core area; although spatially separate, it is integrally connected to that core. One purpose of this paper is to consider the nature of that connection. A broader purpose is to discuss what is known about the form and function of Hopewell geometric earthworks using the Newark Earthworks as the preeminent exemplar of that class of phenomena.

GEOMETRIC EARTHWORKS

For the purposes of this paper I intend to confine the discussion to geometric earthworks. That is, only the earthen walls built in the shapes of circles, squares, octagons, parallel lines, and other simple geometric designs will be considered. Burial mounds, when they occur within a geometric enclosure, or are otherwise in clear association with a geometric earthwork, are included; but the phenomenon of hilltop enclosures, shaped to conform with the contour of the hill on which they are situated, will be reserved for others to consider (see, especially, Connolly and Riordan, both in this volume). Although this follows the general distinction drawn by Squier and Davis (1848:47-49) between "works of defense" and "sacred enclosures," I do not mean to suggest any necessary dichotomy in site function between these two classes of earthwork.

EARTHWORK FORM AND FUNCTION

There have been many attempts to unravel the meaning of the Hopewellian geometric earthworks. Interpretations have ranged from the arcane and romantic to the practical. A popular view among the earliest Euro-American observers was that the great earthen walls were ancient fortifications. For example, Atwater, foremost among the earliest investigators of the mounds, conjectured that "the larger works" of the Moundbuilders, such as the Newark Group, "...were really military ones of defense; that their authors lived within the walls; that the parallel walls were intended for...protecting persons in times of danger, from being assaulted while passing from one work to another..." (Atwater 1820:129). Atwater's commitment to the interpretation of the Newark Earthworks as defensive fortifications colored his graphical presentation of the site (**Figure 13:1**). Militaristic aspects of the works are exaggerated on his map, whereas features unrelated to defense, such as burial mounds, are not depicted.

This martial theme dominated scholarly interpretations for many years, but, whereas Atwater was not apparently bothered by the positioning of the ditch inside Newark's Great Circle, other more astute authors perceived a dilemma. Matthews (1839:6) conceded at least that structures such as

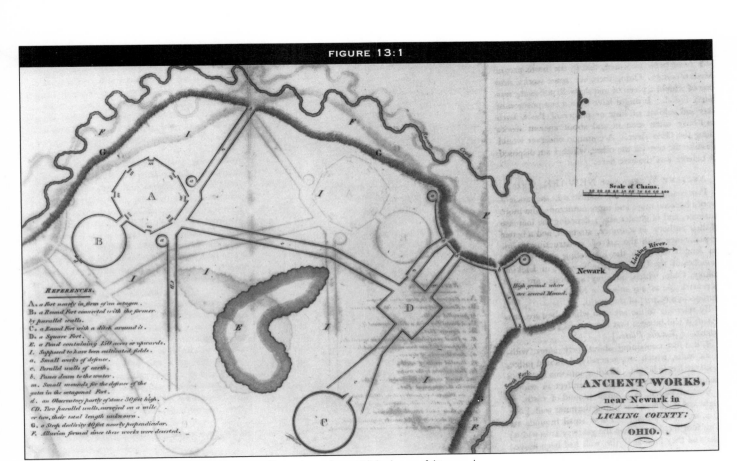

FIGURE 13:1

The Newark Earthworks according to Atwater (1820). This is the earliest published map of this complex.

the Great Circle were "constructed on principles of military science now lost or inexplicable." But not all early investigators were so obtusely committed to a military interpretation. Park (1870) wrote that "...to call such works military fortifications, is not only absurd, but supremely ridiculous, I care not what principle of warfare, you may assign to these mound builders" (1870:47). Park quipped that "*Col. Cognac, or Capt. Bourbon*, had more to do in arriving at this conclusion, than either Napoleon, Scott, or Hardee" (1870:45, emphasis in original).

Brown and Baby (1966) investigated the embankments at Mound City and considered the possibility that they might have served a defensive purpose. Inferring the original dimensions of the surrounding enclosure as "approximately 4 ft [1.2 m] high by 15 ft [4.6 m] wide" Brown and Baby concluded that "...the embankment is not designed to keep men either from getting out or getting inside" (1966:13).

In a more speculative vein, Brown and Baby noted that the shape of the Mound City embankment "resembles the outline of the ground plan of at least some of the structures in the mound group... the gaps or gateways occur in the same relative positions as the structures themselves" (1966:13).

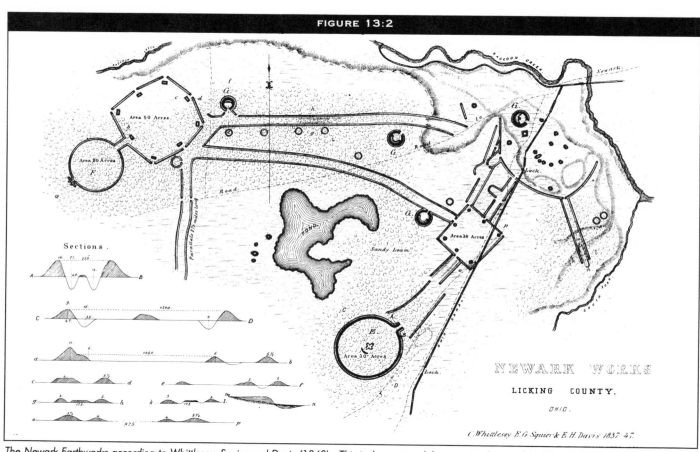

FIGURE 13:2

The Newark Earthworks according to Whittlesey, Squier and Davis (1848). This is the most widely recognized map of the Newark Works.

Therefore, "shape and position is [sic] highly charged with symbolic value" (1966:13). Coincidentally or not, the shape of the Mound City enclosure does have an apparent analog in a separate sphere of Hopewellian activity. It may symbolize some type of house structure. But the more abstract and precise geometrical forms are not so readily interpretable.

Byers (1987) conducted a structural analysis of Early and Middle Woodland earthwork enclosures in order to understand something about the symbolic meaning of these structures for their builders. The Newark Earthworks figures prominently in his research. In fact, Byers refers to Newark's

Observatory Circle and Octagon as "the `rosetta stone' of the enclosure traditions of the Central Ohio Valley" (Byers 1987:285, and this volume). Byers (1987) suggests that the Observatory Mound was constructed to block off the original entrance to the Observatory Circle when the design of the complex changed. Since the gateway was not simply re-excavated and filled in, Byers infers that there must have been some ritual prohibition against moving earth that had been excavated and deposited artificially as part of an earthwork. Byers calls this "the sacred earth principle" (1987:296) and concludes that the construction process, from the first basket-load of earth until the completion of the enclosure, was a "sacred enterprise" (Byers 1987:293).

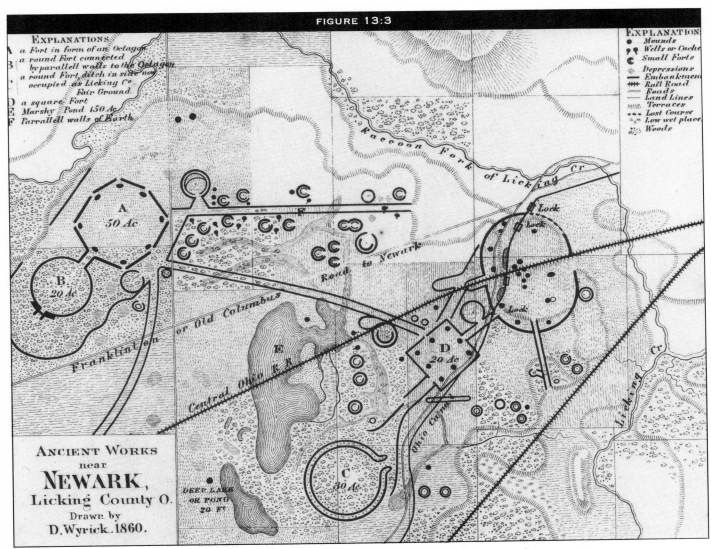

FIGURE 13:3

The Newark Earthworks according to David Wyrick (1866). This is an important but neglected map of the earthworks.

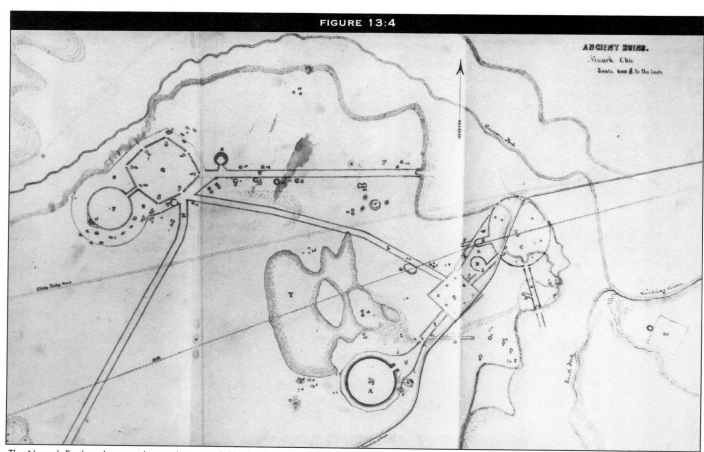

The Newark Earthworks according to James and Charles Salisbury (1862). Never before published, this map corroborates many of the features of Wyrick's map and adds details not documented previously, such as the additional square enclosure east of the main complex. Photograph courtesy of the American Antiquarian Society.

Byers' arguments are complicated and farfetched, but he has developed an intriguing and internally consistent model for the construction of the Newark Earthworks. Some aspects of the model can be tested by empirical observations. For example, Byers infers that the Observatory Circle was constructed with earth scraped from the surrounding surface of the ground whereas the Octagon was built with earth removed from deep borrow pits (1987:311). Byers bases this inference on the fact that Squier and Davis' (1848) map of the Newark Works shows borrow pits associ-

ated with the Octagon, but not with the Observatory Circle. Unfortunately, for Byers' model, other, more detailed surveys of the Newark complex (see also Holmes 1892:396) do indicate that extensive borrow pits also were associated with the circle (**compare Figure 13:2 with Figures 13:3 and 13:4**). Therefore, Byers' initial inference, and the intricate web of speculation he spins from it, are without foundation. But, regardless of where the Hopewell obtained the material with which to build the circle and the octagon, Byers' more extravagant claim that "the Octagon represents the under-

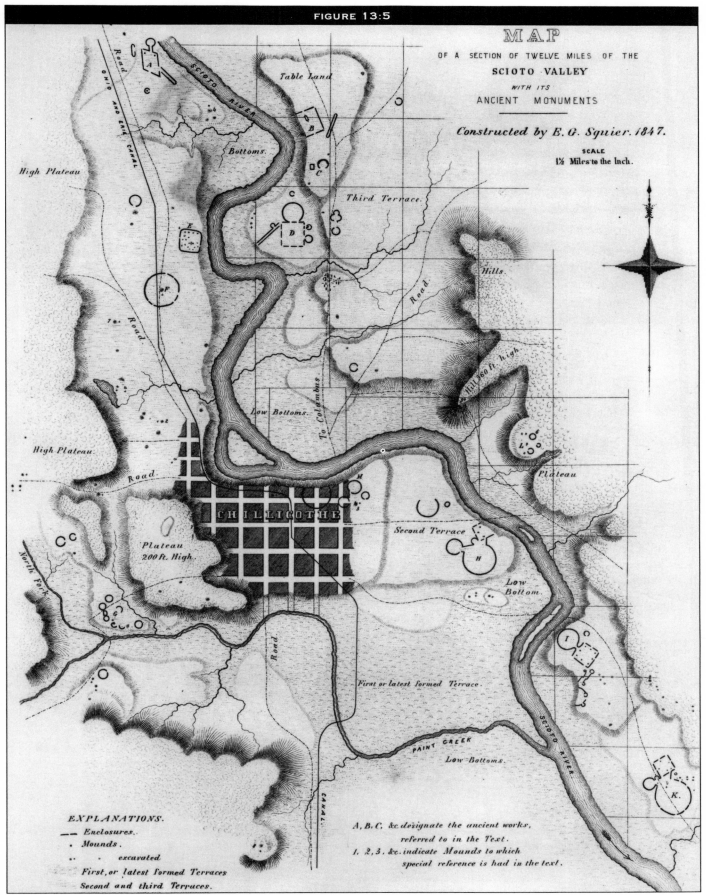

Map of a section of twelve miles of the Scioto Valley with its ancient monuments (Squier and Davis 1848).

world" (1987:332), goes beyond the present limits of our ability to interpret objectively the remains of preliterate societies. Nevertheless, Byers' research represents a brave attempt to increase our understanding of the earthwork enclosures of the Middle Ohio Valley.

Hively and Horn (1982) added a significant dimension to our appreciation of the Hopewellian achievement when they determined that the major rising and setting points of the moon, encompassing an 18.6 year cycle, are incorporated into the architecture of the Newark Earthworks. They speculate that this astronomical information is not just symbolically encoded into the site plan, but that the substantial earthen walls, with their long sight lines and a height that corresponds, more or less, to eye level, are massive (and therefore long-lived and tamper proof) fixed instruments for making astronomical observations.

In a second paper Hively and Horn (1984) demonstrate that High Bank Works in Chillicothe, the only other circle and octagon combination built by the Hopewell, also is aligned to the lunar cycle, but in a complementary fashion. The main axis of High Bank Works is aligned at 90 degrees to the main axis of the Newark circle and octagon.

INTERNAL STRUCTURE

In spite of the great intellectual efforts expended to interpret the form of the earthworks, there has been surprisingly little work directed at disclosing the internal structure of these embankments. Mills excavated a portion of the enclosure surrounding Harness Mound, but only to determine that "...the earth used in the construction of the ... earthworks was taken from the surface in close proximity to the earthworks" (Mills 1907:113).

Shetrone (1926:112) examined the embankment surrounding the Hopewell site, but he had little interest in the internal structure. He was searching for "burials or occupational evidence within or beneath the walls of the enclosures" and he found "nothing" (1926:112). He did note the occurrence of "several unimportant and not well defined fire-beds" on the

FIGURE 13:6

The Wray figurine depicting a Hopewell shaman. Height of figurine, 16 centimeters. Recovered from one of the principal burial mounds at the Newark Earthworks (Dragoo and Wray 1964).

original surface, but concluded that these were "only incidental to occupation previous to the erection of the wall" (Shetrone 1926:112).

Baby (1954) directed the excavation of the William Reynolds Earthwork, one of two circular enclosures in the valley below Fort Hill. The embankment covered the remains of two concentric rings of postmolds, 3 m apart, which Baby interpreted as the remains of an arbor, 53 m in diameter. "Flint chips and pottery and mica fragments were found on the floor of the structure..." (Baby 1954:86).

Brown and Baby (1966) investigated the remnants of the enclosure at Mound City. They observed that, in some areas, Hopewell borrow pits had intruded upon midden deposits and that some of this material was incidentally incorporated into the fill of the embankment (1966:12). They also sought, and did not find, evidence for "deep, load-bearing posts" (1966:13) which the Hopewell may have used in the construction of the earthworks.

Shane directed excavations at High Bank Works and concluded that the circle was constructed in four stages. First, the builders cleared the area and excavated a narrow, circular trench. Then, they set posts into the ground and piled earth up against the outside of the ring of posts. They added a stone facing onto the lower portion of the inside surface of the circular wall and finally, they covered this facing and raised the height of the embankment to approximately two meters. In contrast to the High Bank Works Circle, Shane determined that the Octagon was a series of simple earthen embankments with no evidence for multiple construction stages (Shane, personal communication, 1992).

Brose (1976) investigated the Hopeton Works and reported the results of avocational surveys as well as his own fieldwork. Observations made by Stanhope, while the walls of the square enclosure were being graded, indicate that the eastern and western walls "were composed of distinctly different soils" (1976:59). She also noted that large postmolds (35-40 cm in diameter) occurred within the western wall at intervals of 1.5 meters (1976:59). Within several of the gateways she observed small pits which contained "charcoal, ash, and unburned limestone boulders" (1976:59).

Quite recently, Greber and Pickard (personal communication, 1993) undertook salvage excavations at a remnant of the Anderson Works square enclosure. Their investigations revealed that the preserved portion of the embankment was composed of a distinctive reddish clayey silt and that substantial postmolds occurred beneath the earthwork.

Wymer, Lepper, and Pickard conducted a detailed investigation of the internal structure of the Great Circle at the Newark Earthworks (Wymer et al. 1992). We infer two principal phases of construction for the Great Circle. There was no evidence of any surface preparation prior to the beginning of construction. Pollen and phytoliths recovered from the buried A Horizon indicate that the environment, at the time of construction, was a mesic prairie (Linda Scott Cummings, personal communication, 1993). Preparatory to the first major construction stage, the Hopewell appear to have built a series of small mounds in a circle. Our trench bisected one small mound; we infer the existence of a circular pattern of additional mounds. (cf. MacLean, quoted in Fowke 1902:160-161). Next, the builders excavated a ditch well inside this circle of mounds, and piled the dark brown silt loam on top of the mounds, forming a low circular embankment. In the second major construction stage, the Hopewell obtained bright, yellow-brown silty clay loam and gravel from nearby deep borrow pits and added this material to the top and the inside of the embankment-filling in the gap left between the wall and the interior ditch. When complete, the embankment would have looked dark brown to persons approaching the enclosure. Upon entering the circle, the walls would have looked bright yellow-brown. It is likely that these colors played a symbolic role in the architectural presentation of the site.

HABITATION REMAINS

Fowke asserted, in his 1902 *Archaeological History of Ohio*, that "there are no surface indications of occupation within" any of Ohio's geometric enclosures (1902:154). Moorehead (1922:116) noted habitation remains surrounding the enclosure at the Hopewell site, but Shetrone (1926:112) claimed that there also was evidence for "limited occupancy" at two locations within the enclosure.

Baby directed investigations at Seip Mound which uncovered the presence of structures within the enclosure. Baby and Langlois (1979) interpreted these as specialized craft houses, but Griffin (in Brose and Greber 1979:64) notes that considerable "village debris" occurs in the fields surrounding the walls as well as from within the enclosure. Greber (n.d.:9) refers to "significant concentrations" of domestic debris outside the Seip enclosure and argues that there is no basis for the archaeologically convenient assumption that there was no overlap in Hopewellian domestic and ceremonial activities. She emphatically states that "the land at Seip and Baum was used by people performing ordinary domestic tasks" (n.d.:14).

Baby (1954) also directed the excavation of the remains of a large, 37 by 18 m, subrectangular structure a short distance south of the William Reynolds circular earthwork below Fort Hill. Based on the size of this structure, the "considerable" amounts of cultural material recovered, and the presence of subsurface features, Baby (1954:87) speculated that it, also, was some sort of specialized craft house. However, the above mentioned criteria are either insufficient or insufficiently reported to substantiate this interpretation. Prufer (1965:126) identified the area below Fort Hill as a possible exception to the claim that no Hopewell village sites were known.

Brose (1976) explored the area in and around the Hopeton Works and identified numerous domestic loci just outside the walls and "on the terrace immediately below the bluff" on which the enclosures are located (Brose and Greber 1979:65; see also Brose 1976). Within the square enclosure, near the site where a series of interior mounds once stood, Brose recovered artifacts of obvious ritual significance, such as "cut and polished wolf canines" and a "copper-covered wooden button" (1976:52-54). On a low rise "in the southwest corner of the square" he found a variety of more utilitarian items, such as broken projectile points and bits of pottery (1976:52). This low rise also yielded "abnormally high relative phosphate and calcium concentrations" (1976:52).

During archaeological investigations associated with the construction of State Route 79 in Newark, Ohio, Hale identified a small Hopewell habitation site which would have been located just outside the walls of the Newark Earthworks (Hale 1980; Lepper and Yerkes n.d.). Hale's

House site (33LI252) consists of the remains of a structure and several features. Yerkes' microwear analysis of the stone tools from the site, especially the bladelets, indicates that a variety of tasks were performed at the site; it was not a specialized activity area (Lepper and Yerkes n.d.).

Bernhardt (1976) investigated the DiGiondomenico site (33LI59) at the confluence of the South Fork of the Licking River and Ramp Creek. Bernhardt claimed that this habitation site was situated strategically to control access into the Newark Works from the southern "sacred way" (Bernhardt 1976:49). But, since this "sacred way" intersects Ramp Creek at a point nearly two kilometers west of the DiGiondomenico site it is difficult to imagine how the occupants could have served as gatekeepers.

James and Charles Salisbury uncovered other indications of habitation at the Newark Earthworks. In 1862 they reported to the American Antiquarian Society on their investigations which included excavations within several of the small circular enclosures east of the octagon (see Figure 13:4). They found "plates of mica generally much decayed, burnt stone, some arrow points and chips of flint, and many large fragments of pottery, marked on the outer surface as if the vessel was moulded in a sack of very coarse cloth of peculiar make" (Salisbury and Salisbury 1862:18).

DISCUSSION

Evidence from this meager handful of archaeological investigations suggests that geometric earthworks are quite variable. They can appear similar in form, but differ greatly in the details of construction and use. The selection of different colored sediment for different earthworks, or differing components of the same earthwork, is as pregnant with significance as Byers' (1987) structural analysis of earthwork form would suggest. Unfortunately, the meaning behind this variability may not be fully recoverable.

FIGURE 13:7

Black and white print from a color infrared aerial photograph showing parallel lineations in the soil which correspond to the predicted location of a segment of the Great Hopewell road 26 km south of Newark, Ohio (NAPP566-81, taken on 3-22-88).

Finally, there seems to be little justification for the notion that geometric earthworks were vacant ceremonial centers. Although these structures clearly are not the walls of large urban centers and the interiors of the earthworks sometimes appear to be vacant, when sought, domestic debris commonly is found both outside and inside the embankments. There is no evidence to support the claim that all of these domestic loci are merely ephemeral camp sites occupied either by laborers during the construction of the earthworks or ritual specialists during periodic visits to prepare the honored dead for burial. Since such sites are all that Prufer posits for the environs of earthworks (1964b:70-71), his "Vacant Ceremonial Center-Dispersed Agricultural Hamlet" model (Prufer 1965:127) may offer an incomplete view of Hopewell settlement.

BURIAL MOUNDS

Mortuary ceremonialism, in the form of burial mounds, often is regarded as the sine qua non of Hopewellian monumental architecture. And yet, actual burial mounds at the Newark Earthworks are restricted primarily to only one of the principal enclosures. Indeed, the lack of intact burial mounds to explore may, in part, account for the relative neglect of this gigantic earthwork complex by late nineteenth and twentieth century archaeologists.

Nevertheless, mortuary ceremonialism played a significant role in the Hopewellian occupation of the Newark Earthworks. Eagle Mound, at the center of the Great Circle, covers the remains of a structure which may have served as a charnel house (Lepper 1989). Although no human remains were encountered in Greenman's 1928 excavations, Smucker (1881) refers to earlier excavations which did encounter "...an altar built of stone, upon which were found ashes, charcoal and calcined bones..." (Smucker 1881:266).

There were true burial mounds at Newark which entombed the honored dead of the Hopewell, and cultural treasures every bit as spectacular as those recovered from Tremper, Seip, Harness, and the many mounds at Mound City, but the Newark mounds were largely obliterated by 1868 when a

local resident wrote "The group of ancient mounds that used to attract the attention and wonder of our early pioneers, when they visited the 'Old Fort' have at last been demolished, these beautiful monuments of antiquity that have been gazed upon and admired by thousands, have been at last destroyed by the iron shovel" (Wilson 1868:69).

The destruction of the mounds in the Cherry Valley Cluster (Lepper 1989) began as early as 1827 when the Ohio Canal was dug across this area and through at least one burial mound. Laborers digging the pit for Lock No. 2 went through a mound containing "ten or fifteen" burials covered by "eight or ten bushels" of mica plates "of various sizes and shapes, tho' generally triangular" (Newark Advocate, 29 March 1827).

The largest of the mounds in this cluster was a curiously shaped series of three or four conjoined mounds, comparable in size to Tremper or Harness. James and Charles Salisbury, in their unpublished descriptions of the Newark Works, claim that the outlines of this mound suggest, "with a little imagination,...the idea and form of a priest, clothed in a long gown, girded about the waist with head and arms extended forward towards the east, in the attitude and act of worshiping, perhaps the Sun" (Salisbury and Salisbury 1862:11-12). Actually, this description entails rather more than a "little" imagination, but it does convey something of the complexity of this conjoined group of mounds.

Much of this group was destroyed by the construction of the Central Ohio Railroad between 1852 and 1855, but the largest and northernmost segment survived until it "was leveled to form the site of a rolling mill" (Wilson 1868:69). Wilson (1868) recorded that the upper eight feet of the mound was composed of layers of "black loam" and included several "fine sheets of mica" although no skeletal remains were observed (Wilson 1868:69). The lower portion of the mound was composed of "layers of blue clay, then sand, and one layer of cobble stone, which was laid immediately over a very strong burning" (Wilson 1868:69). The base of the mound consisted of "disturbed earth four or more feet below the surrounding surface" (Wilson 1868:69).

According to the brothers Salisbury, near the base of this mound there was a "tier of skeletons" placed with their heads to the center and their "feet radiating towards the outside" (Salisbury and Salisbury 1862:12). Wilson noted numerous postmolds of varying sizes, some filled with sand, at least one filled with charcoal and ashes (Wilson 1868:69). No plan of the postmolds survives, but it is plausible to suggest the pattern might have revealed a structure similar to the "Great House" at Harness (Greber 1983:26-29). A partial list of the artifacts found with the human remains includes a copper "hatchet" and "quivers," mica sheets, a large shell, "beads and other trinkets" (Wilson 1868:69).

Charles Whittlesey (1868) viewed Wilson's artifact collection in 1868 and described several additional artifacts from the "mound at rolling mill." Whittlesey sketched a "copper axe," one of "3 copper fluted ornaments," and a drilled bear canine (1868:41-42). In addition, he referred to "numerous copper studs...copper beads...and whelks" (1868:43). He mentioned that the beads were "strung on hemp or nettles" (1868:43).

In 1881, the rolling mill was torn down and subsequent excavations revealed yet another burial four feet below the surface. A remarkable representation of a Hopewell shaman was found with the burial (Dragoo and Wray 1964). (**see Figure 13:6**).

THE GREAT HOPEWELL ROAD

Perhaps one of the most extraordinary aspects of the Newark Earthworks is the series of parallel walls which connects the enclosures in an intricate pattern. Note for example, that each circle is a cul de sac, whereas the square and octagon have multiple openings and are intersections for several roads defined by parallel walls (**see Figure 13:4**). And that, if one is prohibited from climbing over walls, there are only three routes of ingress into the Newark Earthworks complex: from the valley of Raccoon Creek, from the valley of the South Fork of the Licking River, and from the southwest along the road which extends beyond the border of every nineteenth century map of the Newark Works.

Atwater (1820:129) speculated that these walls extended more than thirty miles to another complex of earthworks along the Hocking River. Squier and Davis (1848) made no reference to Atwater's claim and stated that the walls were only two and a half miles (4 km) long (**Figure 13:2**). James and Charles Salisbury (1862) traced this roadway the two and a half miles to Ramp Creek. But, unlike Squier and Davis, the Salisburys crossed Ramp Creek, found that the walls continued, and followed them for about six miles (9.7 km) before turning back. They claimed that the walls continued beyond that an unknown distance, and likely went all the way to Chillicothe. If the Salisburys are correct, then the Ohio Hopewell built a roadway similar, in many respects, to the Anasazi roads of Chaco Canyon (Nials et al. 1987) and the Mayan sacbeob (Folan et al. 1983:81-87). It is difficult to test this idea since the land between Newark and Chillicothe has been cultivated since the early nineteenth century. Indeed, in 1870 Samuel Park attempted to trace the extent of these walls based on the testimony of early settlers. Park was unable to locate any traces of such a roadway and doubted that, given the "improved" state of the country in 1870, any extant traces could be found (Park 1870). In blithe disregard of Park's pessimism, I have, for the last three years, sought evidence for this roadway.

Extrapolating from the lines visible in 1930s aerial photographs (e.g., Reeves 1936; Shetrone 1937; Woolson 1931) and from the Salisbury data, I have projected the course of the Great Hopewell Road along the direct bearing of 31 degrees west of south. This bearing points directly to the heart of Chillicothe (**Figure 13:5**).

I have searched along this corridor for traces of road remnants using aerial reconnaissance and archival photography (both conventional and infrared). I have identified traces of parallel lineations in fields, at the expected locations, in several places. The most convincing segment, located 15 km southwest of the Newark Octagon, is visible in an infrared image (**Figure 13:7**). Another is located at the projected terminus of the Great Hopewell Road at Chillicothe (Lepper 1994).

Based on several interwoven lines of evidence, including the above mentioned data, paleoenvironmental reconstructions, archaeoastronomy, and ethnographic as well as archaeological analogy, I conclude that the Great Hopewell Road was a virtually straight set of parallel walls 60 m apart and extending a distance of 90 km from the Newark Earthworks to the cluster of earthworks in the Scioto Valley centered at modern Chillicothe. Near its terminus at Newark, the walls were nearly 1m in height. They may have been somewhat reduced in size, and hence more ephemeral, at increasing distances from the termini. This roadway was designed and laid out with great care and with intimate familiarity of the intervening landscape. The function of the Great Hopewell Road is unknown, but similar structures built by the Maya were monumental expressions of politico-religious connections between centers (e.g., Schele and Freidel 1990:353).

CONCLUSIONS AND CONJECTURES

What has this review of the Newark Earthworks contributed to our understanding of the Hopewellian achievement? First, since the Newark Works are the largest and most imposing example of Middle Woodland monumental architecture, it provides an indication of the upper limits of what the Hopewell could achieve in this sphere. It long has been recognized that the giant geometric enclosures built by the Hopewell, especially the Newark Earthworks, represent an unusual florescence of monumental architecture by a people without other obvious indications of a complex social system. This review has only exacerbated this paradox. When I began my investigation of the Great Hopewell Road, one prominent Midwestern archaeologist advised me that the Ohio Hopewell simply could not have built such a structure because they lacked the population, the subsistence base, and the political organization requisite for undertaking such long term public works projects. The high civilizations of Peru and Mesoamerica, and even the architecturally sophisticated Anasazi of the North American Southwest, might impose such marvels of engineering across the landscape, but not the humble Moundbuilders of the Eastern Woodlands. I submit that this is the fundamental mystery of the Hopewell: how were they able to achieve what, our theories suggest, was beyond their capabilities? I further submit that our theories are inadequate if they do not take into account the possibility that the Ohio Hopewell were building great roadways connecting widely separated centers of social and religious activity more than five centuries before the Anasazi erected their first pueblo.

In conclusion, although much of the Newark Earthworks complex has been destroyed, much remains (Lepper and Yerkes n.d.). Moreover, in spite of the pitifully small number of archaeological investigations undertaken at Newark, a surprising amount of information exists about what has been lost. In this short review I have been able only to outline the tip of this historical iceberg. I expect few readers of this work realized just how much data on the Newark Works are recoverable from archival sources. There is a critical lesson here for those engaged in research at other "lost" Hopewell sites.

ACKNOWLEDGMENTS

I extend my sincere thanks to Terry Cameron, Robert Fletcher, Jeff Gill, N'omi Greber, Paul Hooge, Roger Kennedy, Martha Potter Otto, William Pickard, Olaf Prufer, Orrin Shane, III, and Dee Anne Wymer for their help in understanding what the Hopewell were able to achieve in ancient America.

I thank the Ohio Archaeological Council for funding used to obtain infrared aerial photographs of the projected route of the Great Hopewell Road. In addition, many private individuals and institutions contributed funds to the Great Hopewell Road project. I thank the American Antiquarian Society, Worcester, Massachusetts, for permission to publish the Salisbury map of the Newark Earthworks.

Finally, I thank my family,
Karen, Benjamin, and Peter Lepper
for their support and understanding.

NOTES

[1]. As the ultimate in Hopewellian monumental architecture, Newark's earthworks frequently are illustrated in popular summaries of Hopewell archaeology (Forbis 1975:89; Jennings 1974:213; Prufer 1964a:92). Nevertheless, they are seldom mentioned in more technical treatments. Prufer's (1964b) scholarly review of Ohio Hopewell includes only a passing reference to Newark (1964b:49; see also McMichael [1964:130]) and the proceedings of the original Chillicothe conference (Brose and Greber 1979) include virtually no mention of the Newark Works.

REFERENCES CITED

Atwater, C. 1820 Descriptions of the Antiquities Discovered in the State of Ohio and Other Western States. *Archaeologia Americana* 1:105-267.

Baby, R. S. 1954 Archaeological Explorations at Fort Hill. *Museum Echoes* 27(11):86-87.

Baby, R. S. and S. M. Langlois 1979 Seip Mound State Memorial: Nonmortuary Aspects of Hopewell. In *Hopewell Archaeology: the Chillicothe Conference*, edited by D. S. Brose and N. B. Greber, pp. 16-18. Kent State University Press, Kent, Ohio.

Bernhardt, J. E. 1976 A Preliminary Survey of Middle Woodland Prehistory in Licking County, Ohio. *Pennsylvania Archaeologist* 46(1-2):39-54.

Brose, D. S. 1976 *An Historical and Archaeological Evaluation of the Hopeton Works, Ross County, Ohio.* Report on file, Mound City Group National Monument, Chillicothe, Ohio.

Brose, D. S. and N. B. Greber, editors 1979 *Hopewell Archaeology: the Chillicothe Conference.* Kent State University Press, Kent, Ohio.

Brown, J. A. and R. S. Baby 1966 *Mound City Revisited.* Report on file, Department of Archaeology, Ohio Historical Society, Columbus.

Byers, A. M. 1987 *The Earthwork Enclosures of the Central Ohio Valley: A Temporal and Structural Analysis of Woodland Society and Culture.* Ph.d. dissertation, Department of Anthropology, State University of New York at Albany. University Microfilms, Ann Arbor.

Dragoo, D. W. and C. F. Wray 1964 Hopewell Figurine Rediscovered. *American Antiquity* 30:195-199.

Folan, W. J., E. R. Kintz, and L. A. Fletcher 1983 *Coba: A Classic Maya Metropolis.* Academic Press, New York.

Forbis, R. G. 1975 Eastern North America. In *North America*, edited by S. Gorenstein, pp. 74-102. St. Martin's Press, New York.

Fowke, G. 1902 *Archaeological History of Ohio.* Ohio State Archaeological and Historical Society, Columbus.

Greber, N. B. 1983 Recent Excavations at the Edwin Harness Mound, Liberty Works, Ross County, Ohio. *Midcontinental Journal of Archaeology Special Paper* No. 5, Kent State University, Kent, Ohio.

n.d. Two Geometric Enclosures in Paint Creek Valley: An Estimate of Possible Changes in Community Patterns Through Time. In *Ohio Hopewell Community Organization*, edited by W. S. Dancey and P. J. Pacheco. Kent State University Press, Kent, Ohio "in press."

Hale, E. E., Jr. 1980 *Archaeological Survey Report, Phase III, LIC-79- 12.55, Licking County, Ohio.* Report on file, Ohio Historical Society, Department of Archaeology, Columbus.

Hively, R. and R. Horn 1982 Geometry and Astronomy in Prehistoric Ohio. *Archaeoastronomy* 4:S1-S20.

1984 Hopewellian Geometry and Astronomy at High Bank. *Archaeoastronomy* 7:S85-S100.

Holmes, W. H.1892 Notes Upon Some Geometric Earthworks, With Contour Maps. *American Anthropologist* 5:363-373.

Jennings, J. D. 1974 *Prehistory of North America*. McGraw-Hill, New York.

Lepper, B. T. 1989 An Historical Review of Archaeological Research at the Newark Earthworks. *Journal of the Steward Anthropological Society* 18(1&2):118-140.

     1994 The Great Hopewell Road: a Middle Woodland *Sacra Via* Across Central Ohio. Paper presented at the joint meeting of the Midwest Archaeological Conference and the Southeast Archaeological Conference, Lexington, Kentucky.

Lepper, B. T. and R. W. Yerkes n.d. Hopewellian occupations at the northern periphery of the Newark Earthworks: the Newark Expressway Sites Revisited. In *Ohio Hopewell Community Organization*, edited by W. S. Dancey and P. J. Pacheco. Kent State University Press, Kent, Ohio "in press."

Matthews, C. 1839 *Behemoth: A Legend of the Mound-Builders*. J. & H. G. Langley, New York.

McMichael, E. V. 1964 Veracruz, the Crystal River Complex, and the Hopewellian Climax. In *Hopewellian Studies*, edited by J. R. Caldwell and R. L. Hall, pp. 123-132, Illinois State Museum, Scientific Papers 12, Springfield, Illinois.

Mills, W. C. 1907 The Explorations of the Edwin Harness Mound. *Ohio Archaeological and Historical Society Publications* 16:113-193.

Moorehead, W. K. 1922 The Hopewell Mound Group in Ohio. *Field Museum of Natural History, Anthropological Series, Publication* 211, 6(5):73-181.

Newark Advocate 1827 Antiquities of Ohio. *The Advocate*, 29 March.

Nials, F., J. Stein, and J. Roney 1987 *Chacoan Roads in the Southern Periphery: Results of Phase II of the BLM Chaco Roads Project*. Report on file, Bureau of Land Management, Albuquerque District, New Mexico.

Park, S. 1870 American Antiquities. In *Notes of the Early History of Union Township, Licking County, Ohio*, pp. 35-56. O. J. Smith & Co., Terre Haute, Indiana.

Prufer, O. H. 1964a The Hopewell Cult. *Scientific American* 211(6):90-102.

     1964b The Hopewell Complex of Ohio. In *Hopewellian Studies*, edited by J. R. Caldwell and R. L. Hall, pp. 35-83. Illinois State Museum, Scientific Papers 12, Springfield, Illinois.

     1965 *The McGraw Site: A Study in Hopewellian Dynamics*. Cleveland Museum of Natural History, Scientific Publications 4(1), Cleveland.

Reeves, D. M. 1936 A Newly Discovered Extension of the Newark Works. *Ohio State Archaeological and Historical Quarterly* 45:187-193.

Salisbury, J. A. and C. B. Salisbury 1862 *Accurate Surveys & Descriptions of the Ancient Earthworks at Newark, Ohio*. Ms. on file, American Antiquarian Society, Worcester, Massachusetts.

Schele, L. and D. Freidel 1990 *A Forest of Kings*. William Morrow, New York.

Shetrone, H. C. 1926 Exploration of the Hopewell Group of Prehistoric Earthworks. *Ohio Archaeological and Historical Quarterly* 35:1-227.

     1937 Ancient the Newark Earthworks. *Museum Echoes* 10(1):1.

Smucker, I. 1881 Mound Builders' Works Near Newark, Ohio. *American Antiquarian* 3(4):261-270.

Squier, E.G. and E.H. Davis 1848 *Ancient Monuments of the Mississippi Valley*. Smithsonian Contributions to Knowledge 1, Washington, D.C.

Whittlesey, C. 1868 Field book, July 1, 1868. Ms. on file, Western Reserve Historical Society, MSS 2872.

Wilson, J. N. 1868 Mounds near Newark. In *Isaac Smucker Scrap Book*, pp. 69-71. Ms. on file, Granville Public Library, Granville, Ohio.

Woolson, B. 1931 Ancient Mounds Mark Landing Point on Newark's Intermediate Landing Field. *The Advocate*, 25 March.

Wymer, D. A., B. T. Lepper, and W. Pickard 1992 Recent Excavations at the Great Circle, Newark, Ohio: Hopewell Ritual in Context. Paper presented at the Midwest Archaeological Conference, Grand Rapids, Michigan.

Wyrick, D. 1866 Ancient Works near Newark, Licking County, Ohio. In *Atlas of Licking County, Ohio*, edited by F. W. Beers. Beers, Soule, & Co., New York.

FOURTEEN

THE ENCLOSED HILLTOPS
OF SOUTHERN OHIO

ROBERT V. RIORDAN

ABSTRACT

Excavation results from four southern Ohio hilltop enclosures
— Fort Ancient, Miami Fort, Foster's, and the Pollock Works —
as well as more limited information from others form the basis
of a discussion of enclosure chronology, construction and function. The sites are seen as having been constructed no later
than the first century A.D. and in use at least through the third
century, paralleling other Hopewellian phenomena. The recent
discovery of remains of a timber stockade at Pollock is viewed
as having been mirrored in results from Miami Fort and
Foster's. While the initial construction impulse is viewed as
having ritual/ceremonial roots, it is suggested that the Pollock
Works may have been hastily converted to military purposes for
a brief period.

A View From the Core a Synthesis of Ohio Hopewell Archaeology•edited by Paul J. Pacheco
© Copyright 1996 by The Ohio Archaeological Council• Columbus, Ohio
All Rights Reserved•ISBN 0-9626931-9-7

ROBERT V. RIORDAN

THE ENCLOSED HILLTOPS OF SOUTHERN OHIO

INTRODUCTION

The presence of earthworks atop certain Ohio hills and peninsular landforms has been a source of mystery for generations of scholarly antiquarians, members of the general public, and archaeologists alike. These several audiences have all asked the same core set of questions: why were these hilltops enclosed? Who did so, and when?

Nineteenth century answers, judging by published accounts, generally supported the notion that the hilltop sites had functioned defensively, hence the attachment of the appellation "fort" to several examples. It was surmised that they had been built at least hundreds of years previously, and for most of the century were viewed as the products of the vanished Moundbuilders. Late in the nineteenth century, the conventional wisdom conveyed by the antiquarian accounts and surveys of individuals such as Caleb Atwater, Ephraim Squier and J.P. MacLean began to be supplemented by the findings from the archaeological programs that investigated the Fort Ancient and Foster's enclosures, both located adjacent to the Little Miami River. These efforts sought to recover the skeletal remains of the builders, the artifacts and features they had left behind, and evidence of the construction techniques that had been employed in building the sites. Following this brief flurry of professional interest, the study of hilltop sites went into a long period of quiescence, broken only by the work of Mills in 1908 and Morgan and Ellis in 1939 and 1940 at Fort Ancient. In the 1960s research was conducted at Fort Hill, Miami Fort, and the Old Stone Fort in Tennessee, and beginning in the 1980s at the Pollock Works and again at Fort Ancient. In this paper, a number of assertions are made concerning hilltop enclosures that are based on interpretations of the findings and opinions of many current and past investigators. While recent efforts cannot be said to have constituted any sort of focus for Middle Woodland research in Ohio, their results have allowed us to view that which was discovered by investigators such as Moorehead and Putnam over a century ago with fresh regard, and also to propose some new answers to the old questions. Cumulatively, then, research old and new at southern Ohio hilltop enclosures indicates that the following propositions are likely to be true:

1. Hilltop enclosures had begun to be built early in the Middle Woodland period, by the first century A.D., and remained in use at least into the third century A.D.

2. Earth, stone and wood were the principal construction materials used at these sites.

3. Hilltop enclosures were typically built in two or more stages, in possible response to changing symbolic and/or functional requirements.

4. Hilltop enclosures were loci for activities that complemented, but were distinct from, those carried out at the mortuary/ceremonial earthwork and mound sites on the river terraces. The original impetus to their construction and their lasting use was the dedication of spaces wherein corporate secular and/or religious activities could be properly conducted.

5. Some hilltop enclosures were employed for military purposes during their histories.

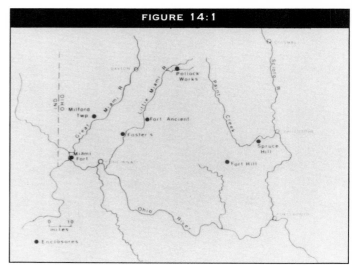

Locations of principal hilltop enclosure sites mentioned in text.

THE EXCAVATED SAMPLE

The most accessible excavation data have been used, from four of the sites noted above (Fort Ancient, Miami Fort, the Pollock Works, and Foster's) (**Figure 14:1**). This information supplies most of the support for the positions stated. Fort Ancient is the largest and most complex earthwork in the group, and it has been the beneficiary of by far the greatest amount of archaeological attention. The site includes three designated enclosures: the North, Middle and South Forts, which together contain about 50 ha, enclosed by walls that range from less than a meter in height to over seven, and run almost 6 km in total length (**Figure 14:2**). In addition to the unauthorized spades of a possible legion of unknown nineteenth century schoolboys and weekend adventurers, it has been professionally excavated on numerous occasions. This includes the work of Warren Moorehead between 1887 and 1891, William Mills in 1908, Richard Morgan and Holmes Ellis in 1939-1940, Patricia Essenpreis in the 1980s, and Robert Connolly since 1991. Occasional forays by others, generally from the Ohio Historical Society in response to requests for salvage assistance, have occurred but are essentially undocumented. These researchers have cut trenches through embankments, dug in the interior of the Fort, tested exterior loci, examined the parallel walls northeast of the enclosure, discovered stone pavements and other features, excavated in mounds located both inside and outside the enclosure, and examined the gateways and ditches. This is an incomplete listing of the research done, but is sufficient to establish the basis for the kind of interpretive results the site offers. Excavation results can be found in Moorehead's book (1890) and articles (1895, 1908), short works by more recent researchers (e.g., Morgan 1970, Essenpreis and Moseley 1984), technical reports (e.g., Essenpreis 1985), numerous conference papers, at least one thesis (Connolly 1991), and in archived field notes, plans, and photographs.

Miami Fort, located on high ground above the confluence of the Great Miami and Ohio Rivers, was excavated by the University of Cincinnati Field School under the direction of Fred Fischer in 1965 and 1966 (**Figure 14:3**). Essentially rectangular, its walls range up to about 3 m in height and enclose about 4 ha of space. Five excavation units were completed; three were situated in the interior of the enclosure and two were cut into the west and north walls (Fischer 1965, 1968).

Foster's, located on the Little Miami near Loveland, some 30 km downstream from Fort Ancient, was excavated in the summer of 1890 by a field crew supervised by Hilborne Cresson and George Dorsey under the overall direction of Frederick Ward Putnam, all of Harvard's Peabody Museum. Roughly 4.5 ha is enclosed within a wall of earth and stone that follows the rim of the hilltop; there is also a small protruding section on the north side with symmetrically-bulging lobes (**Figure 14:4**). The walls were between 1-2 m high, with about 700 m in total length. The only publication was a two-page article (Putnam 1891), but there are extensive and extant field notes, drawings and photographs. These and the materials collected from the site repose in Harvard's Peabody Museum. The artifacts and matrix samples collected in 1890 were never properly accessioned (S. Bond, personal communication to Michaeol Smolek, 1977) and apparently have never been closely studied.

The Pollock Works has been excavated by Wright State University Field Schools under my direction since 1981. Pollock is located on Massies's Creek, a Little Miami tributary, near Cedarville in Green County; the earthworks occupy only the western part of the circumference of a limestone mesa that was isolated from the surrounding topography by the waters of the creek (**Figure 14:5**). It is the lowest of the four sites with respect to its surroundings, and the only one of the four not employing embankments to completely encircle its hilltop or peninsula. The walls vary between less than a meter up to three in height, with a total length of approximately 350 m; the mesa contains about 5.5 ha of space. Excavations have been primarily located in or adjacent to embankments, with limited testing of the interior. Two reports (Riordan 1982, 1984) several conference papers (e.g., Riordan 1986, 1990, 1993), and a journal article (Riordan 1995) have communicated some of the results of this program.

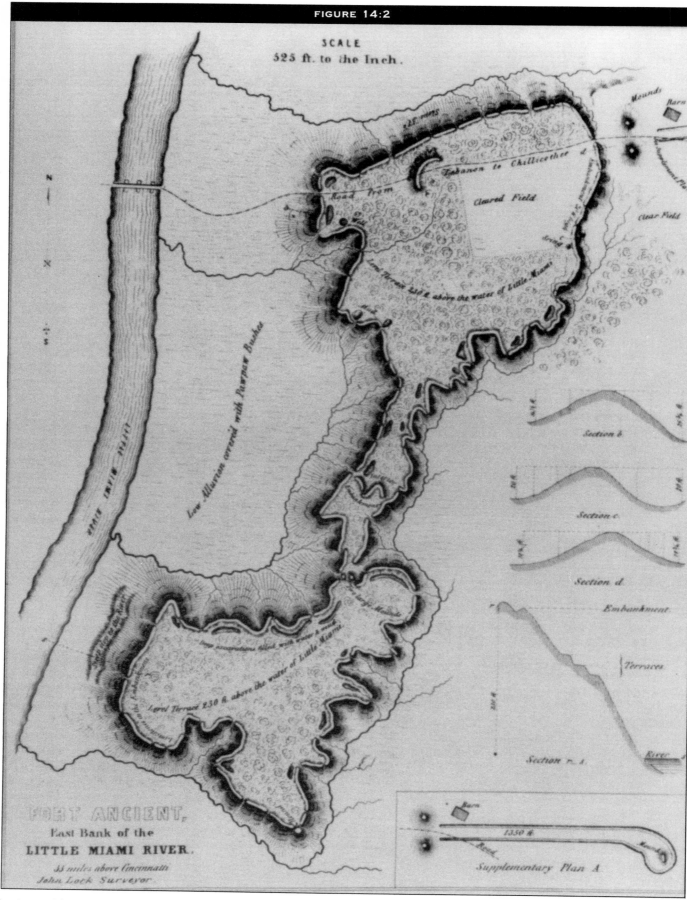

Fort Ancient (after Squier and Davis 1848:Plate VII).

A VIEW FROM THE CORE: A SYNTHESIS

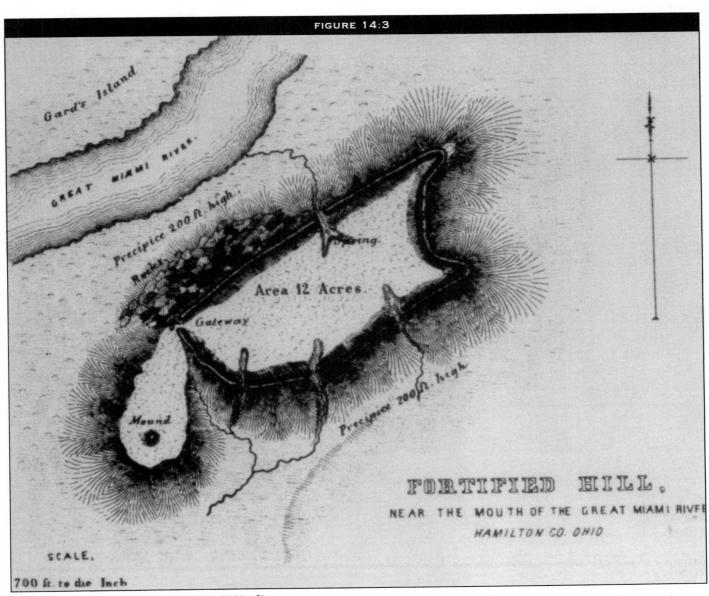

Miami Fort (after Squier and Davis 1848:Plate IX, No. 2).

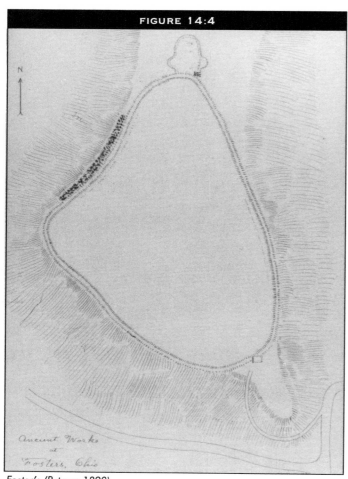

FIGURE 14:4

Foster's (Putnam 1890).

ENCLOSURE CHRONOLOGY

Three hilltop sites from southern Ohio have been radiocarbon dated: Fort Ancient, Miami Fort, and the Pollock Works. The single assay from Miami Fort yielded the date A.D. 270 ± 130 (M-1869). This date was obtained from wood charcoal found on the pre-earthwork surface which was believed to have been associated with features related to the wall's construction (Fischer 1968:20). This was the first carbon date obtained from an Ohio hilltop enclosure. Far from unambiguously defining the construction date of the earthwork, however, it can be used to suggest that the site's embankments do date to the latter half of the Middle Woodland period.

The first absolute dating done at Fort Ancient was by the late Patricia Essenpreis (1985, 1986), on charcoal from the fill in a ditch associated with the Twin Mounds, which are external to the earthwork. The date of 1960 ± 80 B.P., could, when calibrated, refer to either the first century A.D. or B.C. Essenpreis regarded the construction effort in this area as among the latest at the site, although this is still an untested argument.

Robert Connolly has directed work at locations in the Middle and North Forts during the 1992-1993 field seasons. His excavations in the Middle Fort have detected a significant amount of land modification prior to earthwork construction (Connolly 1992; Connolly and Sieg 1993). Radiocarbon dates have been obtained on wood charcoal from pit features on both sides of the walls that virtually duplicate Essenpreis's results (i.e., 1970 ± 100 and 1990 ± 90 B.P.). Construction activity therefore appears to have been underway on the Fort Ancient peninsula no later than the first century A.D., and quite possibly a century or so earlier. There are insufficient data available, however, to as yet refine or attach dates to the model of the site's development suggested by Essenpreis and Moseley (1984).

The Pollock Works is at this point the best-dated of the three sites, with 15 radiocarbon dates procured from material from under and within the embankments. Elsewhere I have detailed the basis for a construction scheme that involved at least five stages (Riordan 1995). Most of the dates come from features representing a fence built on intermediate stage surfaces of the walls spanning the distance between the creek-edge bluff and the outcropping cliff to the south, and others from the carbonized remains of a timber stockade that lay beneath the bluff-edge wall (**Figure 14:6**). The earliest construction stage is dated to the first century A.D., when a 90 m long wall between 1 m and 1.5 m high was built to connect the outcropping cliff on the south with the edge of the bluff above the creek on the north; this wall may have included a central gateway (**Figure 14:7**).

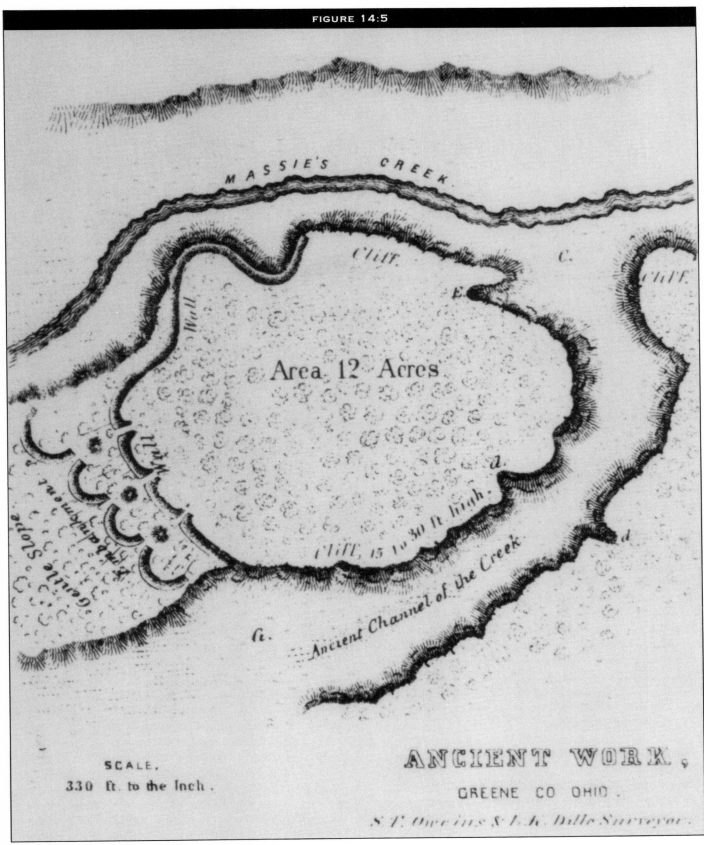

Pollock Works (after Squier and Davis 1848:Plate XII, No. 3).

While we have evidence that Pollock, and in all likelihood Fort Ancient, were both in use by the first century A.D., it will take directed research at other sites to obtain the necessary materials from the proper locations to determine their chronologies. When such dates are obtained, however, it is expected that all such sites will be found to have begun more recently than 100 B.C., with most probably after A.D. 1.

The dating results from these three sites tells us even less about how long they continued in use. At Pollock, the last construction stage is believed to date to the late second or early third century A.D. It is unclear whether the site plan was then considered complete, and was used for a time thereafter without major architectural modification, or whether abandonment followed soon after the final building boom. An important question that cannot presently be answered is whether the existence of both larger and smaller enclosures indicates a developmental trend. Does larger size perhaps indicate the gradual involvement of ever-larger populations that contributed to the maintenance and use of a site over a longer period of time? Does the large size of Fort Ancient signify the incorporation of ever-larger numbers into the using society, perhaps at the expense of (and involving the suppression of use of) a site like Pollock? Or were there functional differences between hilltop enclosures of different sizes, with both being present on the landscape at the same time? In any event, the limited available evidence supports the conclusion that the building of these enclosures began early in the Middle Woodland period, and that their use probably persisted as long as other Hopewellian phenomena.

ENCLOSURE CONSTRUCTION AND USE

The primary building materials, earth and stone, are present at all hilltop enclosures. Soil was generally scraped from enclosure interiors or drawn from interior ditches and heaped to form the walls. Basketloading has been noted at several sites, including Fort Ancient (Moorehead 1890:32) and Pollock (Riordan 1984). At the latter, loading was confined to the earliest two stages of construction. Later, broadcasting methods of distributing soil were used.

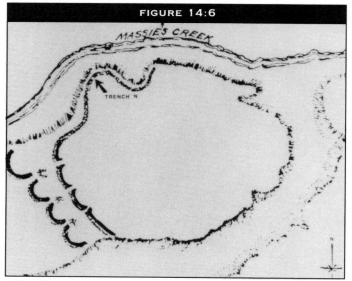

FIGURE 14:6

Pollock Works construction phase 5, showing location where timber stockade was found in 1992-93 (after Fowke 1902).

The use of stone is found at all the enclosures, but the way it was used can differ. At Miami Fort, Fowke observed that "very little stone" was employed (Fowke 1902:254), although Fischer states that limestone slabs were present as a capping on the interior slope of the west embankment (Fischer 1965:5). At Fort Hill, stone was quarried from the sandstone hilltop and used in the wall. The accounts of Spruce Hill state that the wall that surrounds it was composed entirely of sandstone (Squier and Davis 1848:11-12; Fowke 1902:242-244). In a recent article critical of including Spruce Hill within the ranks of enclosures, Pacheco (1988:13) notes (probably correctly) that the "walls" of the site may be a natural geological phenomenon; however, the scale and appearance of the main entrance, with its multiple gateways, does suggest the intentional (and considering the size of the space involved, perhaps expediently cost-effective) modification of the landform in such a way as to create a functional hilltop enclosure. At Foster's, stone was extensively used, and the fieldnotes and photographs suggest that at least at some points there was a double core of stone within the wall. At Fort Ancient, stone was used as an exterior facing, stacked as buttresses into exterior surfaces, and used as

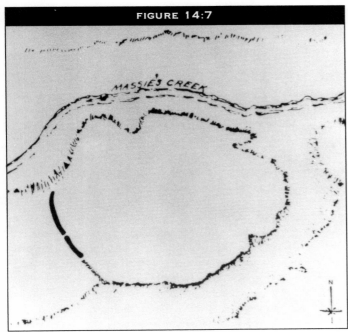

FIGURE 14:7

First construction phase of the Pollock Works (after Fowke 1902).

Putnam and his co-workers also uncovered very extensive quantities of burned soil at Foster's (Putnam 1891). This was generally found over loose limestone, which had also been burned. Field drawings from the project depict burned logs under the wall; one sketch depicts five of them side-by-side. Several postmolds are depicted in field drawings, as well as numerous ash-pits (Putnam 1890).

At the Pollock Works we have been finding burned soil since the start of work in 1981. It occurs as a distinct layer underneath the creek bluff embankment, usually with a layer of carbonized timbers sandwiched between it and the original surface. We suspected that this might be the remains of a mud-plastered stockade, but for a long time the postmolds that would have indisputably shown that the timbers and burned soil together constituted a feature that had once stood upright could not be located. This changed during the field seasons of 1992-1993, when thirteen postmolds were discovered along the bluff edge, fronted by piled limestones. Most of the postmolds had been heavily chinked with limestones set on end, jammed as many as three or four deep alongside the posts. The total weight of chinking stones found in 1993 ranged between 2.25 and 36 kg per post, with an 18 kg average. The post diameters ranged between 19 to over 40 cm, and most were found set between .50 and .75 m of each other.

At the location where these were found, the remains of the stockade's superstructure were also discovered, arrayed on the old surface where the stockade had collapsed into the interior of the enclosure. Approximately the lowest 2 m of the postmolds were found to have been mud-plastered, over a framework of branches interwoven across the vertical posts. The total height of the stockade was approximately 4 m, with the uppermost 2 m consisting of undaubed interlaced timbers. On the basis of this discovery, it is believed that the burned timbers and soil found elsewhere along the bluff edge in a similar stratigraphic position, were also remnants of this stockade. There is a corresponding structure on the portion of the earthwork that spans the gradual western slope, a woven fence, apparently never daubed, that stood about 1.5 m high on the surface of the third of four

a core material (Essenpreis and Moseley 1984:24). At Pollock, it was used to face embankment exteriors, as well as to pave gateway surfaces and face the ends of embankments adjacent to the gateways. Along the Massie's Creek bluff it constituted a piled exterior core that probably served to limit downslope erosion, helping to preserve the wall. Stone is generally absent from the interior surfaces of the walls.

The use of wood in embankments has been observed at three hilltop enclosures, although it may have been present in others. As a perishable material, it has generally been recognized in carbonized form. Fred Fischer (1965:5) found "horizontal logs" that lay parallel to the long axis and underneath the west wall of Miami Fort. While he stated that their function was unknown, he also described a massive deposit of burned clay at the base of the north wall. He suggested that this might be the remains of a "defensive structure of wood and clay daub," which "may have burned and fallen in place, leaving a mound of burned clay rubble" (Fischer 1965:5).

mantles of soil present there. These two features — the bluff edge stockade and the "fence" on the western embankment segments — together are considered to have been sections of the same structure. The calibrated average of ten radiocarbon dates from them (at one standard deviation) includes the range between A.D. 130 and 228 (with intercepts at 134, 153, 169, 201, 211) (Stuiver and Reimer 1986). The building of the stockade and fence is considered to have constituted the fourth of five stages in the site's construction sequence (Riordan 1995).

The Ohio climate is such that a wooden structure like the Pollock stockade could not have long survived without constant maintenance. We have not seen evidence of this; instead, the stockade seems to have had a single period of use, was then burned (accidentally or purposefully), and then was almost immediately covered over with the earthen embankment that replaced it. Destruction of the stockade and construction of the embankment had to have been concerted acts because the burned timbers lie essentially undisturbed beneath the wall. This action was therefore surely taken by the people who used the enclosure, and was not the work of a raiding party. It stretches the imagination to conceive of raiders who would not only burn a stockade during an attack, but then stop to also cover it with almost a meter of earth!

The existence of the Pollock stockade can be invoked as a probable explanation for the burned timbers and soil found at other sites. It seems likely that Fischer had it essentially right, and that in its first phase Miami Fort was bounded by a plastered timber structure. The same may also apply to Foster's, where Putnam's men found such overwhelming quantities of burned clay, charcoal, ashes and burned stone (Putnam 1891).

At the Four Mile Creek site (also known as the Milford Township Earthworks), an undated enclosure in Butler County, MacFarland observed in 1887 that burned limestone occurred along the former course of a wall in association with a band of dark earth containing charcoal. He supposed it to have been the remains of a row of "pickets"

that had been burned, and wondered "Whether or not this use of pickets was general among the mound builders" (MacFarland 1887:269).

While MacFarland never supported his intuitive assumption concerning the presence of pickets with fieldwork, the answer to his question is that their use was probably more frequent than we have realized. Besides the possible timber stockades noted at some locations, it is conceivable that stones may have been piled along the base of a stockade that were not subsequently covered by an earthen embankment. This would have created a line of stones that might now be barely detectable, especially if located slightly downslope from a hilltop (as a number of enclosure embankments are), which over time would have become partially covered by eroded soil. Carrying such speculation only a step farther, the possibility also exists that there were sites where a timber enclosure like the one at Pollock was built, but without any significant use of stone except perhaps to chink the posts; then, if such a feature went out of use without being covered by soil, its archaeological visibility would be virtually nil, its presence going unsuspected and undetected.

Building a hilltop enclosure involved massive quantities of stone and earth, and, it appears at least at some, great numbers of felled trees. Excavations in embankments have also demonstrated that most sites appear to have acquired their modern appearance over the course of a significant amount of time. The five state sequence proposed for Pollock is believed to have taken about a century to effect (Riordan 1995). At Fort Ancient, at least three stages have been observed in embankment excavations (Essenpreis 1986). At Foster's (Putnam 1890), Miami Fort (Fischer 1965) and Fort Hill (Prufer n.d.), two or more stages seem to be indicated. These sites grew by accretion, sometimes through modifications of original plans, at others possibly only gaining in size as successive soil layers were added. The real meaning of accretional growth is still to be understood, but it certainly signifies that these were dynamic places where change was part of the natural order of things.

It was stated earlier that hilltop enclosures were places where activities were conducted that were complementary to, but different from, those conducted at the geometric riverine enclosures. The underlying rationale for the earliest construction of hilltop enclosures is believed to have been rooted in Middle Woodland ritual/ceremonial requirements. The major alternative point of view regards them a refuge points or actual defensive forts (e.g., Prufer 1964; Fischer 1974).

This debate, long one of the major points of contention concerning hilltop enclosures, needs now to be considered against the backdrop of the Pollock construction sequence. There, as noted, we have found that the site began with the building of a wall of earth approximately 6 m wide and 1-1.5 m high across the 90 m wide western access slope to the plateau, possibly with a central gateway to provide a formal entrance. There is no sign of a stockade that preceded this wall, nor was there one built on its surface. I would submit that this simple wall, in its topographic setting, was then considered (along with the presence of such natural features as sheer rocky cliffs and steeply sloping banks) to have adequately completed the enclosing of the plateau, in the sense of setting it off as special, sacred, and perhaps taboo. It did not establish a fortified position, and could not have been useful either in protecting a population from warlike outsiders or in projecting a group's power into another's territory. When the developmental sequences of other sites as old as this are worked out, it is expected that some will exhibit very similar trajectories.

The fourth building stage at Pollock involved important new elements: the erection of the stockade on the bluff and the fence on the western walls. This is thought to have signaled a radical change, and it may indeed mark the temporary conversion of the plateau into a place of refuge. This explanation is suggested by several things. First, the earlier stages did not involve any construction on the bluff edge. The site seems to have originally been considered sufficiently "enclosed" there by the abrupt 7 m slope to the creek, and the site was presumably in use in this form for decades. Then, as we have reconstructed events, late in the second century A.D. the owning population suddenly felt the need

to build a 4 m high stockade on the creekside bluff. They went to a great deal of trouble to fell, haul, trim, and erect the timbers for an estimated 600+ vertical posts, to cut and collect much more wood that was horizontally woven through the uprights, to haul thousands of kilograms of rock up from the creek to chink posts and to face the stockade, and to plaster at least 2 m of its height with mud. It must be questioned whether this would have been expedient solution if the object was only to more emphatically symbolize the enclosing of the plateau. It would, on the other hand, have been a reasonable response to a perceived threat.

The burning of the stockade and its immediate replacement with the earth embankment may signal a return of the site to its former condition, perhaps symbolically completing the conversion of a military boundary with one more in keeping with the original purpose of the site. While a military use of the Pollock Works is now being entertained as a distinct possibility, no evidence has at this point been detected of any attack having been launched against the site.

Thus, on the basis of the Pollock data, a seemingly aberrant and probably brief period of unrest is hypothesized to have occurred in the southern Ohio woodlands around the beginning of the third century A.D. Support for this might be found if the radiocarbon ages of other burned and replaced stockades are eventually found to agree with the one at Pollock. This further raises the prospect that the first construction at some sites, possibly including Miami Fort, may have been initiated in response to such unrest. Perhaps the protracted debate over whether hilltop enclosures were built for defense or ceremony will end with both views in a sense being correct, but dependent upon the chronology of particular sites.

CONCLUSION

The archaeology of Middle Woodland hilltop enclosures, now spanning more than a century, can safely be said to be entering a new phase. Hopefully, new excavations will explore the internal chronologies of sites, search internally for features that may at last suggest the nature of the specific activities that were conducted within them, and more fully address the distributional and topographical relationships they possess with other sites of the period. When the hilltop sites are understood as integrated parts of the wider Middle Woodland world, we will know more of the people who lavished their labor on these monumental edifices.

ACKNOWLEDGMENTS

The Green County Recreation and Parks Department has graciously permitted Wright State's Field Schools to conduct research within the confines of Indian Mound Reserve, which it administers. The College of Liberal Arts of Wright State University has provided continuous support for the summer program of the Field School in Archaeology. The student and staff participants have been the willing workers who have made the finds that have secured a place for the Pollock Works on the map of Middle Woodland enclosure sites. Finally, the Peabody Museum of Harvard University has given permission for the reproduction of **Figure 14:4**, which comes from the field notes of the Putnam expedition of 1890 (accession number 90-37).

REFERENCES CITED

Connolly, R.P. 1991 *Prehistoric Site Structure at the Fort Ancient State Memorial: New Evidence from Lithic Analysis.* Master's thesis, Department of Anthropology, University of Cincinnati.

1992 Prehistoric Land Modification at the Fort Ancient Hilltop Enclosure, Warren County, Ohio. Paper presented at Midwest Archaeological Conference, Grand Rapids, Michigan.

Connolly, R.P. and L.E. Sieg 1993 Prehistoric Architecture and the Development of Public Space at the Fort Ancient Hilltop Enclosure. Paper presented at the 5th International and Interdisciplinary Forum on Built Form and Culture Research, 2nd CSPA Symposium on Architectural Practice, Cincinnati, Ohio.

Essenpreis, P.S. 1985 *Archaeological Excavations at the Fort Ancient State Memorial: Borrow Area and Gateway 44.* Report on file, Department of Archaeology, Ohio Historical Society, Columbus.

1986 An Architectural Examination of Fort Ancient. Paper presented at the Annual Meeting of the Society for American Archaeology, New Orleans, Louisiana.

Essenpreis, P.S. and M.E. Moseley 1984 Fort Ancient: Citadel or Coliseum? *Field Museum of Natural History Bulletin* 55:7.

Fischer, F. 1965 *Preliminary Report of 1965 Archaeological Investigations at Miami Fort.* Report on file, Wright State University, Laboratory of Anthropology, Dayton, Ohio.

1968 *A Survey of the Archaeological Remains of Shawnee Lookout Park.* Report on file, Wright State University, Laboratory of Anthropology, Dayton, Ohio.

1974 *Early and Middle Woodland Settlement, Subsistence and Population in the Central Ohio Valley.* Ph.D. dissertation, Department of Anthropology, Washington University, St. Louis, Missouri. University Microfilms, Ann Arbor.

Fowke, G. 1902 *Archaeological History of Ohio: The Mound Builders or Later Indians.* Ohio State Archaeological and Historical Society, Columbus, Ohio.

MacFarland, R.W. 1887 Ancient Work Near Oxford, Ohio. *Ohio Archaeological and Historical Publications* 1:265-271.

Moorehead, W.K. 1890 *Fort Ancient: the Great Prehistoric Earthwork of Warren County, Ohio.* Robert Clarke & Co., Cincinnati.

1895 A Description of Fort Ancient. *Ohio Archaeological and Historical Publications* 4:362-377.

1908 *Fort Ancient, Part II.* Phillips Academy, Andover, Massachusetts.

Morgan, R.G. 1970 *Fort Ancient.* The Ohio Historical Society, Columbus, Ohio.

Pacheco, P.J. 1988 Spruce Hill Revisted (33Ro43). *Ohio Archaeologist* 38(2):13-14.

Prufer, O.H. 1964 The Hopewell Complex of Ohio. In *Hopewellian Studies*, edited. by R.L. Hall and J.R. Caldwell pp. 37-83. Illinois State Museum, Scientific Papers 12, Springfield, Illinois.

n.d. Fort Hill 1964: New Data and Reflections on Hopewell Hilltop Enclosures in Southern Ohio. In *Ohio Hopewell Community Organization*, edited by W.S. Dancey and P.J. Pacheco. Kent State University Press, Kent, Ohio "in press."

Putnam, F.W. 1890 *Field notes, 1890 Excavations at Foster's.* Ms. on file, Peabody Museum, Harvard University, Cambridge, Massachusetts.

1891 A Singular Ancient Work. *American Antiquarian Society Proceedings*, 1890, n.s. 7(1):136-137.

Riordan, R.V. 1982 *The Pollock Works: Report on the 1981 Field Season*. Wright State University Laboratory of Anthropology Reports in Anthropology No. 6, Dayton, Ohio.

1984 *The Pollock Works: Report on the 1982 and 1983 Field Season*. Wright State University Laboratory of Anthropology Reports in Anthropology No. 7, Dayton, Ohio.

1986 The Pollock Works: Chronology and Construction of a Hilltop Enclosure. Paper presented at the Annual Meeting of the Society for American Archaeology, New Orleans, Louisiana.

1990 A Construction Sequence for a Hopewell Hilltop Enclosure. Paper presented at the Annual Meeting of the Society for American Archaeology, Las Vegas.

1993 A Timber Stockade at the Pollock Works. Paper presented at the Biannual Meeting of the Ohio Archaeological Council, Columbus, Ohio.

1995 A Construction Sequence for a Middle Woodland Hilltop Enclosure. *Midcontinental Journal of Archaeology* 20(1):62-104.

Squier, E.G. and E.H. Davis 1848 *Ancient Monuments of the Mississippi Valley*. Smithsonian Contributions to Knowledge Volume 1, Washington, D.C.

Stuiver, M. and P.J. Reimer 1986 A Computer Program for Radiocarbon Age Determination. *Radiocarbon* 28:1022-1030.

FIFTEEN

PREHISTORIC LAND MODIFICATION AT THE FORT ANCIENT HILLTOP ENCLOSURE: A MODEL OF FORMAL AND ACCRETIVE DEVELOPMENT

ROBERT P. CONNOLLY

ABSTRACT

Research at the Fort Ancient Site, Warren County, Ohio, revealed that considerable land modification to the central plateau of this Middle Woodland hilltop enclosure occurred during earthwork construction. Excavations showed that the Hopewell extended the plateau and filled erosional gullies to accommodate the placement of embankment walls, ponds and other architectural features. Initial radiocarbon dates suggest that the Woodland period occupation began on the plateau as early as 100 B.C. with subsequent architectural manifestations and occupation spanning at least the next 400 years. In addition, excavations showed that ponding areas and associated gateways were loci of activity and modified through time.

A View From the Core a Synthesis of Ohio Hopewell Archaeology•edited by Paul J. Pacheco
© Copyright 1996 by The Ohio Archaeological Council• Columbus, Ohio
All Rights Reserved•ISBN 0-9626931-9-7

ROBERT P. CONNOLLY

PREHISTORIC LAND MODIFICATION AT THE FORT ANCIENT HILLTOP ENCLOSURE:

INTRODUCTION

Fort Ancient is a Middle Woodland hilltop enclosure encompassing 51 ha at the edge of an escarpment 80 m above the Little Miami River in Warren County, Ohio **(Figure 15:1)**. The south and west sections of the enclosure overlook the Little Miami River that has cut a deep canyon through the wide plain flattened by Pleistocene glaciers. Except a small portion of the earthwork near the site's two large exterior mounds, the north and east sections of the enclosure overlook deep ravines cut by secondary streams.

Research conducted over the past 10 years at Fort Ancient examined areas providing evidence of Ohio Hopewell habitation. Excavations conducted between 1986 and 1990 revealed evidence of intensive prehistoric domestic activity on the plateau northeast of the earthwork, immediately east of the two large exterior mounds (Essenpreis and Connolly 1989; Connolly 1991, n.d.).

The 1992 and 1993 field work, reported here, is part of the ongoing attempt to develop a more holistic interpretation of the site area. The focus of these excavations was a ponding area and adjacent drainage system near Gateway 13 in the Middle Fort, similar features at Gateways 7 and 8 in the North Fort, and a reservoir feature located near Gateway 73 in the North Fort. A casual examination of the Fort Ancient enclosure shows that many gateways have associated interior ponds. When ponds are not present, metal drainage gratings often are, representing work of the Civilian Conservation Corps (CCC). The CCC drained and filled ponds, trenched through their associated gateways and laid drainage pipes to the exterior of the enclosure. **Figure 15:1** shows the locations of ponds mapped in 1848. The map's accuracy in delimiting the ponds is incomplete and erratic, necessitating verification through additional testing.

Although researchers in the past noted some pond locations (e.g., Moorehead 1890; Tichenor 1925) little evidence for the examination of these features is available. We chose the ponding area associated with Gateway 13 **(Figure 15:2)** for initial testing in 1992 because its general morphology matched that shown on maps dating to 1848 and initially we saw no evidence of CCC modification. Therefore, we began with the assumption that, excluding natural erosion and deposition processes, the Gateway 13 pond was not significantly altered in the historic period. In

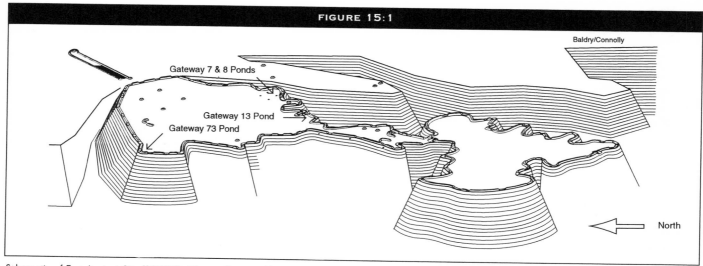

FIGURE 15:1

Gateway 7 & 8 Ponds
Gateway 13 Pond
Gateway 73 Pond
Baldry/Connolly
North

Schematic of Fort Ancient Site (33WA2), Warren County, Ohio. (200 Meters)

addition, **Figure 15:2** shows a contour map of the present ground surface indicating that the associated interior ditch drained into the central pond. In some of Moorehead's more informal field notes, he suggests the head of this ditch as the location of an underground spring.

During the 1993 field season we tested similar pond features at other locations within the enclosure. The space on the immediate interior of the earthwork adjacent to Gateways 7 and 8 and the reservoir feature near Gateway 73 were chosen because there was no immediate evidence of historic modification in their vicinities. We hoped to examine a gateway and pond in the South Fort but a lack of time forced the postponement of that investigation.

RESEARCH GOALS

Until recently, ponds and ditches at earthwork complexes were considered as related primarily to soil extraction for construction purposes with latent potential functions as defensive barriers. An examination of the ponds and ditches at Fort Ancient demonstrate the formality of these borrow pit features. Interestingly, in Moorehead's published accounts of Fort Ancient (1890, 1908) he describes these features as ditches. However in his field notes, he rarely uses the word "ditch", instead referring to the features as "ponds". For example, Moorehead's field notes state that the pond located at Gateway 45 in the South Fort would cover "½ acre and be 10 feet deep" had the feature not been drained by cutting through the embankment wall (1889). Current research demonstrates that relegating these features to the function of expedient linear borrow pits is overly simplistic. While these depressions certainly provided a portion of the soils used in construction of the embankment walls, they were not the sole source. Moorehead (1890) argued that the entire interior of the North Fort was leveled with the scraped soils providing construction material for embankment walls. Today, a nearly 2m drop in elevation is apparent between the interior and exterior plateau at the long stretch of linear embankment walls at the northeast end of the enclosure.

Byers (1987) argues for temporal, social, and spatial interpretations based on the type of ditch present at earthwork sites. While recognizing his contribution to the analysis of formal architectural elements at earthwork complexes, our research at Fort Ancient demonstrates that the system of pond and ditch features is far more complex. Further interpretations, as discussed below, that rely on a synchronic analysis of earthwork complexes are forced to not consider the evolution of architectural features through time.

Over the course of the past two field seasons we have examined the pond and ditch features from three separate locations at the Fort Ancient enclosure. This paper reports on two of these locations to illustrate the formality of the architectural elements, the land modification to the central plateau associated with their construction, and the accretive growth of the Fort Ancient earthwork complex.

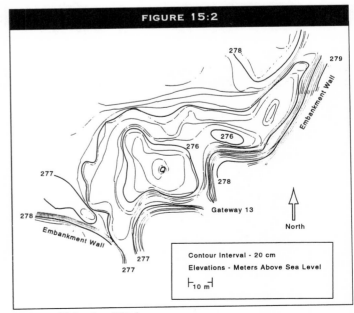

Gateway 13 Pond and Ditch.

The goal over the past two field seasons was to establish the original pond and ditch shapes and to assess associated natural and cultural features. We hypothesized that the location of an underground spring at the head of an interior ditch leading into a central pond would demonstrate that the features were not simply borrow pits but carefully constructed hydraulic systems. We noted that surface collections near remnant ponds in plowed fields immediately to the east of Fort Ancient produced more artifacts than in many surrounding areas. We further hypothesized that the type and density of artifacts recovered in association with the Gateway 13 pond would provide evidence on the function of the features. We used the investigations at Gateway 13 to form a baseline of expectations to guide research for similar features at other localities of the earthwork complex.

FIELD METODS

Our testing strategy was designed to achieve an expeditious examination of the study area while minimizing the amount of destruction to the archaeological record. **Figure 15:3** shows the placement of the excavation units, shovel test probes, and coring transects in the Gateway 13 pond. The 50 cm shovel test probes were dug to sterile subsoils and used to establish pond stratigraphy at 5m intervals. An Oakfield 5/8 inch soil tube was used at one meter intervals to fine tune the stratigraphy and detect anomalies. Although not shown in **Figure 15:3**, the pond periphery was cored at five meter intervals to delimit activity areas associated with the pond.

Excavation Units 1/92 and 4/92 were placed in an area that contained a gravel lens less than 10 cm below ground surface. Gravel and limestone paved areas at other portions of the site mark off discrete prehistoric activity areas (e.g., Connolly 1991; Moorehead 1890). Units 3/92 and 5/92 were excavated to expose limestone detected by cores 30-40 cm below the ground surface. We expected these units to yield a representative sample of artifacts and soils from the pond proper. Unit 6/92 was placed in front of Gateway 12. Gateways at Fort Ancient often are paved with limestone slab that overlay additional limestone used for structural support (Essenpreis and Moseley 1984). We expected Unit 6/92 to yield information on the construction sequence of the embankment wall and interior ditch. Unit 8/92 was excavated to establish a stratigraphic cross-section of the interior ditch. Unit 10/92 was placed in an area that coring showed to be the most likely location of a spring reported by Moorehead (1890). All units within the pond area were excavated to culturally sterile subsoils.

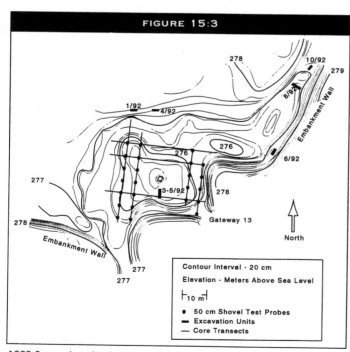

FIGURE 15:3

Contour Interval - 20 cm
Elevation - Meters Above Sea Level
⊢10 m⊣
● 50 cm Shovel Test Probes
▬ Excavation Units
— Core Transects

1992 Research at the Gateway 13 Pond and Ditch.

Overall, our research goals were achieved during the 1992 field season and laid the basis for the examination of similar features at other locations within the enclosure using less invasive field techniques. During the 1993 field season we completed the coring and excavation program to include those portions of the Gateway 13 ditch and pond flooded in 1992. Also in 1993 we employed a JVC environmental soil probe capable of retrieving and preserving intact soil samples (2.5 cm in diameter) to a depth of 5m below ground surface. As discussed below, this device was necessary to delimit cultural stratigraphy detected at a depth of greater than 1m below ground surface.

The relatively thorough examination of the Gateway 13 pond and ditch allowed for far less invasive investigations at the Gateway 73 reservoir and the Gateways 7 and 8 pond system. At these latter locations, both zones were cored at 3m intervals. A total of only three 1 x 1m test units were excavated at locations based on coring results. The purpose of the test units was to recover material for radiocarbon dating and representative artifact samples for comparison with other localities of the site.

Over the course of the two field seasons the ratio of cores to excavated units was in excess of 100:1. During the past five field seasons at Fort Ancient, an ongoing soil core program has provided invaluable research data using a relatively non-invasive technique. The reliance on soil probes supplemented by excavation units for the reconstruction of site stratigraphy and the selective examination of cultural features has provided a methodology that helps preserve the archaeological record while at the same time providing data that has validity and reliability for generating robust interpretations (Stein 1986).

GATE 13 RESEARCH

Although the formality of the Gateway 13 pond and ditch system is equal to, or even more apparent than the North Fort example, this discussion will focus on the significant prehistoric land modification evidenced at this portion of the site. The modification is best seen in unit profiles. An example is the east profile of Unit 6/92. **Figure 15:4** shows that this profile was located directly at the base of the embankment wall. The mottled yellow-brown and red-brown clays at the lowest level contained no artifacts and, based on fragipan development, are in situ soils. The uppermost level contained silt from embankment wall erosion. The intervening gray-brown silty clays represent cultural fill. Only occasional chert artifacts were recovered from the fill. Most notable was the

density and diversity of artifacts recovered at the interface of the cultural fill and the undisturbed substratum. Besides a gravel lens separating the two soils, quantities of charcoal, animal bone, chert and ceramics were recovered. At this interface in the west profile of Unit 6/92, three limestone slabs formed an arc that extended into the unit wall. The limestone area was the locus for most bone, charcoal, and ash recovered and represents a disturbed cooking feature extending west of the unit. Because of the current water table at the interface level, soils are saturated most of the time. The saturation allowed the preservation of small pieces of wood. Because no postmolds were observed in the unit, the wood may represent a stabilizing base for the cultural fill.

The interface between the gray clay fill and the lowest level shown in Unit 6/92 therefore represents an activity area that predates the construction of the embankment wall. The lowest level is the undisturbed substratum or culturally sterile soils. **Figure 15:4** shows that the substratum slopes down through the south end of the unit. By coring to a depth of 2m below ground surface we were able to trace the erosional gully through the ditch and onto the interior plateau. Cultural fill was added to close the gully as well as build up and extend this portion of the plateau to provide the desired surface for construction of the embankment wall.

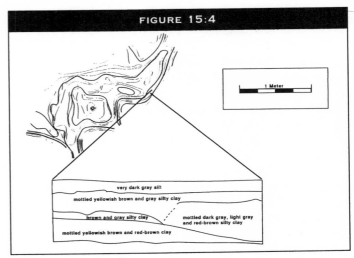

FIGURE 15:4

very dark gray silt

mottled yellowish brown and gray silty clay

brown and gray silty clay

mottled dark gray, light gray and red-brown silty clay

mottled yellowish brown and red-brown clay

1 Meter

Unit 6/92, east wall profile.

Two carbon samples recovered from within the cooking feature yielded radiocarbon determinations of 2340 $\pm$ 130 B.P. (Connolly 1995:Table 9.1), from the portion of the feature located in Unit 6/92 and 1620 $\pm$ 70 B.P. (Connolly 1995:Table 9.1), from the portion of the feature excavated in 1993. The early date is problematic given the Middle Woodland ceramics and the predominance of Harrison County (Wyandotte) and Ohio Flint Ridge chert varieties, some in the form of bladelet fragments and the presumed late Middle Woodland occupation of hilltop enclosures (Prufer 1964).

The obvious contradiction in the two assays is not readily explained. Both samples were taken from the opposite halves of the same feature. The earlier date from Unit 6/92 is supported by the unambiguous pre-embankment wall context of the feature. The later date from the 1993 excavation is problematic for precisely the same reason. In addition, the later range of radio-carbon years yielded by the 1993 sample does not accommo-date any known occupational sequence at the site. Contextually, the cooking feature appears relatively "sealed" with no apparent natural or historic disturbances compromising the integrity of the carbon samples. Probable causes of sample contamination (e.g., Aitken 1991; Taylor 1987) do not ade-quately account for the wide disparity in results. The two most likely explanations for the discrepancy are the following:

1)The potential of carbonates leaching from the surrounding limestone is considered likely given that the feature is below the water table level for at least 9 months out of the year. However, carbonate contamination alone should not cause the wide dis-parity noted (Taylor 1987:116-117).

2) The inherent problem of using unspecified wood char-coal in radiocarbon dating. The "old wood" concern is less an issue than that the 1993 sample result of 1620 $\pm$ 70 B.P. appears too late for a pre-embankment context.

For the purposes of this study, neither date is presumed valid, although it is tempting to accept the earlier of the two results as the closest approximation of the expectation based on context and diagnostic cultural materials recov-ered. Instead, context is given the overriding authority in generating interpretations.

Throughout the Gateway 13 pond vicinity, the yellow-brown and red-brown clays consistently encountered over the entire zone delimit the undisturbed substratum or culturally sterile soils. Core probes were extended to about one meter below this soil to detect buried "A Horizons" or irregularities in soil formation. In cores, shovel test probes, and excava-tions within the ponding area, the vertical artifact distribu-tion was strikingly similar to that discussed for Unit 6/92. That is, few artifacts were encountered in overlying dark gray silt. Only isolated artifacts, primarily flint debitage, were recovered from the underlying cultural fill of brown-gray silty clays. Only at the interface of the cultural fill and culturally sterile soils were significant quantities of artifacts and intact features encountered. No artifacts were recov-ered below the interface throughout the excavations. Further, a pea gravel lens was encountered at this interface throughout much of the pond, particularly in areas contain-ing the greatest density of artifacts. These gravels were judged culturally placed because of their widespread occur-rence in association with cultural activity throughout the pond area. Further, in typical Rossmoyne Series soil forma-tions, such gravels are not encountered for an additional 40-50 cm below ground surface (Garner et al. 1973).

Figure 15:5 illustrates that the culturally sterile interface con-tour, shown in the foreground, is markedly different from the pond shape as seen today, shown in the background. The dashed contours are based on interpolated elevations since water level prohibited direct examination in 1992. Particularly noteworthy are the drops in elevation on the west-central side of the pond and in the southeast corner. The depression on the west side suggests that prior to pond construction, an ero-sional feature was present extending west across the plateau. Also, the 275 m elevation in the southeast portion of the pond is nearly 2 m lower than the base of the overlying embankment wall. This finding is comparable to stratigraphy in Unit 6/92 and demonstrates again that portions of the plateau were extended and raised to accommodate the con-struction of embankment walls.

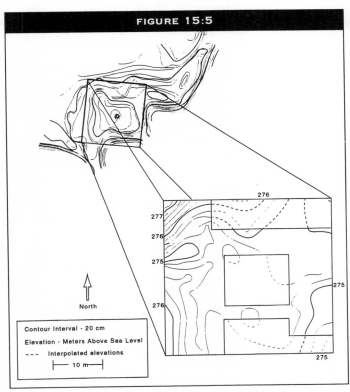

Pre-embankment wall ground surface at the Gateway13 Pond.

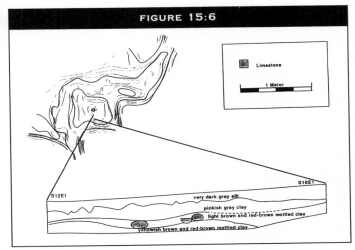

Units 3/92 and 5/92, west wall profiles.

During the 1993 field season, core samples were taken to a depth of up to three meters throughout the pond vicinity. As noted above, the erosional gully detected in Unit 6/92 was successfully followed to the central plateau. A second gully was detected in the ditch between Units 8/92 and 10/92 and was also successfully traced onto the interior plateau. Both of these gullies ranged in width from 3 to 6 m, at a depth of 2.5 m below the current ground surface.
Within the pond proper, Units 3/92 and 5/92 (**Figure 15:6**) contained an apparent cooking feature. Again, the feature was situated directly on the sterile interface. The limestone in the wall of the profile shows the location of the feature. Within and near the arc of limestone, animal bone, mica debris, bladelets, charcoal, burnt clay and a *Snyder's* projectile point base were recovered. Carbon from within the feature yielded a radiocarbon determination of 1970 ± 100 B.P.

(Connolly 1995:Table 9.1) calibrated to 100 B.C. - A.D. 120 (Stuiver and Reimer 1987), well within the first half of the Middle Woodland period.

The density of artifacts recovered from the shovel test probes was highest on the eastern most transect and in the four shovel tests in the southwest corner. Both locations are on the current pond edge. For example, the southwestern-most shovel test yielded eight bladelets, animal bone, pottery, fire-cracked rock and charcoal. In 1993, a 1 x 1 m test unit placed at this location revealed the corner of a pit feature containing faunal material, charcoal and burnt clay. The remainder of the unit produced flint bladelets, utilized flakes, and debitage along with Middle Woodland ceramics from a 5 cm level of mottled soil.

The northeastern-most shovel test produced a piece of worked mica, chert debitage, charcoal and animal bone. Smaller amounts of mica, chert, charcoal, pottery, and animal bone were recovered from most other shovel tests. Considering the limited area covered by the Gateway Pond excavations, and artifact analysis conducted to date, a meaningful discussion of the spatial distribution of artifact types recovered from the pond is premature.

In summarizing the Gateway 13 excavations reported thus far, the stratigraphy points to significant modification of the original plateau surface by Middle Woodland populations at Fort Ancient. The evidence is in the form of a consistent and sharply defined soil boundary between undisturbed substratum and cultural fill with cultural features and increased artifact densities at their interface. The sharply defined soil boundary indicates a lack of natural soil formation. The uniformity of the stratigraphic sequencing in the entire study area argues against the fill resulting from a single sheetwash event. However, the homogeneity of the fill does suggest that the deposition occurred over a brief period.

Unit 10/92 was excavated to the undisturbed substratum and unit profiles indicate that the plateau was likely built up and extended at this location in order to construct the embankment wall. The upper organic levels of the unit contained an abundance of ceramic sherds (n>400) and chert artifacts. These densities are typical of interior ditches at the North and Middle Fort portions of the earthwork. Evidence of Moorehead's spring was not conclusively demonstrated.

Finally Units 1/92 and 4/92 were excavated to examine the gravel lens located on the periphery of the pond. The lens was intermixed with a poor grade of asphalt suggesting an historic origin or minimally, historic disturbance of the lens. Above and immediately below the gravel and asphalt level few artifacts were recovered. However, at a depth of 35 cm below ground surface a well-defined buried "A Horizon" was encountered. Within and immediately below the horizon the density of artifacts increased dramatically. Ohio Flint Ridge, Harrison County (Wyandotte), and Knox chert varieties of Hopewell bladelets and lithic debitage were recovered. Charcoal flecks were evenly distributed throughout the unit at this depth.

The areas reported on above demonstrate that pond features centered on Gateways and adjacent to the embankment walls at Fort Ancient were the loci for activity conducted within the earthwork complex. This assertion is based on the wide range of artifacts recovered in and on the vicinity of the ponds and their associated features, including pavements, pits, and cooking areas. We suspect that such activities on the interior of the enclosure were not limited to the pond peripheries. At the Gateway 13 location, the distinct 5 - 10 cm level of mottled soils recorded from units excavated on the pond periphery were successfully traced toward the center of the enclosure with their margins terminating in areas historically disturbed. A review of field notes from excavations conducted over the past 100 years at the site indicates virtually no investigation of the open areas within the North and Middle Fort. The future investigation of these locations at Fort Ancient is long overdue and necessary for developing robust site interpretations.

GATEWAY 7 AND 8 RESEARCH

Figure 15:7 is a schematic of the current topography immediately interior to the Gateway 7 and 8 portion of the North Fort. The central plateau of the North Fort enclosure is west of the surveyed area. Immediately west of the surveyed area is an additional free-standing pond not associated with an embankment wall, three stone circles, and one stone mound. The mound was excavated by Mills in 1908. The stone circles are presumably associated with the Middle Woodland occupation of the site. Moorehead noted that the stone circles at Fort Ancient were sterile of any significant amount of artifacts or recognizable cultural activity (Moorehead 1890).

Figure 15:8 is a schematic of the same area that accounts for erosion and runoff from the adjacent plateau and embankment walls over the past 2000 years. Therefore, we presume this to be the approximate occupation level of the Middle Woodland populations. This Middle Woodland level was achieved through the analysis of core samples taken at 3 m intervals over the entire zone.

Topographically, the current elevation of the walkover between the two ponds at Gateway 8 represents the approximate unmodified prehistoric ground surface. Core samples taken from the walkover contained an upper humus band that graded quickly to sterile yellow-brown and orange clay. Similar soil profiles were obtained on the western margins of the area shown in Figure 15:8.

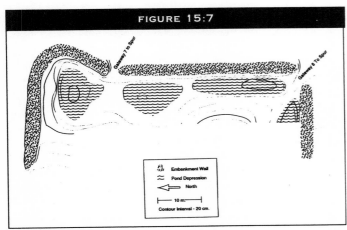

Gateway 7 and 8 ponds-current ground surface.

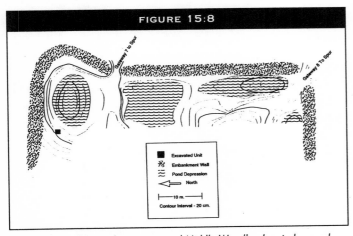

Gateway 7 and 8 ponds-reconstructed Middle Woodland period ground surface.

Therefore, at least a significant portion of the ground surface adjacent to the embankment walls, including surfaces peripheral to the ponds, were excavated from an elevation approximate to that of the Gateway 8 walkover. However, this interpretation is complicated by two factors. First, the elevated walkover, embankment walls, and interior plateau are the sources for much of the erosion deposits in the pond features and on their peripheries. Therefore, the

walkways and plateau today are somewhat lower than 2,000 years ago. Further detailed analysis of soil cores will allow reconciliation of this problem. A second complication is the assumption that the portion of the plateau illustrated in **Figure 15:8** was flat or regular in form prior to earthwork construction. For example, although intact culturally sterile soils were recorded within 1 m of the current ground surface along the eastern edge of the ponds, the same level was nearly 2 m below ground surface in the excavated unit shown. This finding suggests that Middle Woodland populations not only constructed the embankment walls and associated features but modified the land surface to accommodate the placement of architectural elements. This interpretation is tentatively proposed at two other areas in the North Fort, and as discussed above, conclusively demonstrated in a section of the Middle Fort.

The formal construction and nonrandom placement of pond and ditch features is recognized throughout the enclosure complex. The pattern of elements centered on Gateway 8 provides an example. At this location, the interior ponds or ditches are bridged by an elevated walkover at the gateway. Two ponds are located immediately north of the gateway and two ponds immediately west of the gateway (not shown). On entering or exiting the earthwork at this location, passage was through or over water. Numerous gateways at Fort Ancient consist of a break in the embankment wall, associated ponds, and an elevated earthen "bridge" across the ponds extending from the gateway opening to the interior plateau. Of the 67 gateway openings at Fort Ancient, 44 lead to exterior spurs or terraces as in the case of Gateway 8. This architectural pattern mimics the formation of the entire site, that is completely surrounded on all sides by water, with the exception of the space within the parallel walled pavement that extends northeast from the large twin mounds outside the North Fort. At this location, ditches were dug prehistorically to connect the mounds with their respective adjacent ravines (Atwater 1820; Essenpreis and Moseley 1984).

This juxtaposition of gateways with elevated pathways and water is not unique to the Fort Ancient Site. A cursory hike along the Fort Hill embankment walls in Highland County, Ohio, shows the presence of similar feature complexes. Bacon (1993:269) reports that 11 of Fort Hill's 33 gateway openings have "causeways" across the interior ditch. Bacon further discusses ethnographic material relating the Middle Woodland period Old Stone Fort enclosure's associated hydraulic system to mythological and cosmological concepts. A similar discussion focused on the Fort Ancient enclosure is presented elsewhere (Connolly and Sieg 1993).

The deliberate lining of pond floors with sand and gravel indicates the purposeful construction of these features as formal architectural elements. In the case of the northernmost pond in **Figure 15:8**, the pond contours shown represent the actual depths of the underlying gravel and sand lens. The nearby excavation unit uncovered a limestone pavement that abuts the gravel and sand lens at the edge of the pond. The total dimensions of the limestone pavement as recorded by soil probes is approximately 10 x 10 m with the northern edge paralleling the embankment wall and eastern side abutting the pond edge.

The limestone pavement associated with the Gateway 7 pond is virtually identical in composition to the lowest of three overlain pavements excavated northeast of the enclosure (Connolly 1991). Pavements at both localities were composed of small (10-20 cm) slabs of limestone set in a gravel and sand matrix. Also, like the northeast pavement, the Gateway 7 pond pavement is littered with faunal material, pottery sherds, chert debitage and tools, burnt clay and charcoal. The preliminary analysis of the ceramic and chert artifacts demonstrates the presence only of Middle Woodland materials.

Based on limited excavations, the northeast pavement is tentatively interpreted as a generalized multi-purpose activity area. This assessment is based on materials recovered, associated pit and cooking features, nearby house structures, and proximity to the habitation area noted by Prufer (1964) as the most likely spot for a true Hopewellian village. While tempting to argue for a similar interpretation of the Gateway 7 pond pavement, such an assessment is premature based solely on evi-

dence from coring and a single 1 x 1 m test unit. The materials recovered from the pavement may represent nothing more than refuse from activities conducted on the interior plateau or in association with the nearby stone circles or mound. A systematic examination of the adjacent section of the interior plateau has yet to be undertaken.

AN ACCRETIVE MODEL OF ARCHITECTURAL DEVELOPMENT AT FORT ANCIENT

Current research at Fort Ancient significantly expands the temporal framework for the multiple construction phases and occupation of the site. These findings can be extrapolated to several other Middle Woodland complexes in the region such as at Pollock (Riordan 1995), the Hopewell Site (Hatch et al. 1990) and Seip (Greber 1992). Evidence for accretive growth at Fort Ancient is seen in the development of architectural form, the multiple construction stages in embankment walls, radiocarbon assays, and in activity areas both within and on the periphery of the enclosure.

At Fort Ancient, Essenpreis and Moseley provide an analysis of embankment wall forms that explores the development of three architectural styles through time, occurring in spatially segregated areas of the earthwork complex:

> There are two types of segmented earthworks: contour embankments and straight embankments. The former type contours along the sinuous edge of the mesa and statistically speaking, comprises the longest embankments with the fewest passage segments. With the most passage segments, straight embankments are wider, higher, shorter and in layout only roughly approximate the sinuous mesa edge by making sharp, angular bends near ridges and gullies. The first embankment type was used to build the south and middle enclosures, and sections of the north enclosure, while the second type was employed in constructing the northernmost portion of the monument.

TABLE 15:1					
	Radiocarbon Age[a]		Calibrated Date[b]		
Lab Number	B.P.	B.C./A.D.		Material	Context
Beta 15161	1960 ± 80	10 B.C.	54 B.C. - A.D. 119	wood charcoal	Unit 1/85, Level 8, Feature 4/85
Beta 56269	2340 ± 130	390 B.C.	757 - 252 B.C.	wood charcoal	Unit 6/92, Level 4, Cooking Feature
Beta 56270	1970 ± 100	20 B.C.	100 B.C. - A.D. 120	wood charcoal	Unit 3-5/92, Level 4, Cooking Feature
Beta 56271	1990 ± 90	40 B.C.	105 B.C. - A.D. 88	wood charcoal	Unit 1/91, Level 6, Pit Feature

[a] All dates reported at one standard deviation (one sigma)
[b] Radiocarbon Ages calibrated using Stuiver and Reimer's (1987) Radiocarbon Calibration Program 1987, Rev. 1.3

Selected Radiocarbon Dates from Fort Ancient (33WA2), Warren County Ohio.

The contour embankments are more eroded and less well preserved than the straight structures. This supports Moorehead's observation that the southern enclosure . . . was built and used before construction of the northern. . . From its layout and outlying position, it is evident that the parallel-walled enclosure was erected after the north enclosure. Thus, Fort Ancient encapsulates three stages of an architectural history in which the layout of enclosures progressed from irregular contour embankments, through straight angular embankments, to linear geometric forms [Essenpreis and Moseley 1984:23].

Besides variation in embankment wall form, limited examination of both contour and straight embankments suggest that their construction methods were also different. These preliminary findings suggest that the contour embankment walls were primarily constructed of clay with exteriors reinforced by limestone footings and facings. The straight embankments contain large limestone and sandstone slab cores covered by clays. Both types of embankment walls contain at least three construction episodes separated by humus bands that indicate an interlude between building phases. Profiles of the South Fort contour walls show that besides an increase in height, embankments with flat-tops

and relatively vertical interior sides from the first construction stage were replaced by rounded forms in the second and third construction stages (Essenpreis 1986).

The radiocarbon dates from Fort Ancient (**see Table 15:1**, which does not include the 1620 ± 70 B.P. date) further preclude construction in one or immediately consecutive episodes. Current radiocarbon assays suggest a timespan of at least several hundred years for the occupation of the earthwork's plateau in contexts yielding artifacts diagnostic of the Woodland period (Connolly 1995). Thus, the Fort Ancient enclosure was built by many generations over a considerable period of time.

Essenpreis (1986) hypothesized the Fort Ancient earthworks are best explained as agglutinative and were sequentially built from south to north with the different enclosures drawing on architectural canons that shifted from irregular to standardized forms. The shift recognized by Essenpreis is the inevitable result of social growth and change through time. Similarly, Silverman notes the varying forms of construction at the Cahuachi complex in Peru (AD 1-750). She states. "...because these social groups change over time, agglutinative rather than a single-phase master plan would be characteristic. The site would grow as new groups came into existence, and individual mounds would undergo accretionary growth and diachronic abandonment" (Silverman 1990:235).

This accretive architectural development is also evident at Fort Ancient. Based on size alone, the site required a coordinated group effort to construct and maintain. The site was enlarged and expanded functionally according to changes in the architectural plan during the Middle Woodland period. A changing site plan suggests that social canons also shifted during the period of occupancy.

An unvarying plan would reflect a static, if not singular, social group. A single construction episode or even a series of construction episodes over a relatively short period time late in the Middle Woodland period is not supported by an analysis of the archaeological record at Fort Ancient. The assertion that the site served as a defensive fortification against invading populations provides the only basis for this interpretation. While not denying that the enclosure played any defensive role, investigations conducted over the past 100 years clearly demonstrate that a wide range of prehistoric activities were focused at the earthwork complex.

Pat Essenpreis, who conducted research at the site from 1982 until her death in 1991, argued that South Fort construction predated North and Middle Fort construction by about 200 years. This assertion was based on the shape of embankment walls and the sequence of construction episodes discussed above. Taking this into account, a plausible interpretation is that the space now within the Middle Fort was used for multiple activities during the period when the South Fort was the only portion of the site with embankment walls. When the enclosure was expanded to include the current study area, what was once outside the enclosure was brought within. Besides modifying the plateau, the type of activity permitted in the area likely changed. The assumption can be made that area within an enclosure is more restricted and controlled than exterior space.

Similarly, construction beyond the North Fort embankment walls in the form of the two parallel walls, caused a spatial and functional shift in the use of this area. The limestone pavements stratigraphically are later and overlay a portion of the original habitation zone of structures and pit features. The construction of the limestone pavements likely evolved

over several generations, based on the accumulation of soils between the pavements and the limited evidence of postmold patterns on individual layers of the pavement itself, suggesting rebuilding through time. The parallel walls that overlay a portion of the pavement and the original habitation zone marks the final building phase at this portion of the site (Connolly, n.d.).

The exact parameters of the temporal depth for the construction and Middle Woodland occupation at Fort Ancient is poorly known. At least the initial construction of all three sections of the enclosure are well within the first half of the Middle Woodland period. Despite the lack of absolute temporal control, the stage construction evident in all embankment walls examined, the shifting architectural canons as identified by Essenpreis, and the analysis of the Fort Ancient artifact assemblage demonstrate that the enclosure was constructed and occupied over an extended period.

DISCUSSION

The analysis of the research reported in this paper aids in assessing the placement and function of the prehistoric occupation at Fort Ancient during the Middle Woodland period. Assumptions that hilltop enclosures in Ohio were occupied only late in the Middle Woodland period (Prufer 1964; Fischer 1974) are not supported by research at Fort Ancient (Connolly 1995; Essenpreis and Connolly 1989) and at the Pollock Earthworks (Riordan 1995). Radiocarbon dates from both southwest Ohio sites show occupation as early as 100 B.C. and continuing to at least A.D. 300. These findings complement ongoing research at other Middle Woodland earthworks that suggest occupations at individual sites have greater temporal depth than previously thought. The obsidian hydration dates from the Hopewell Site (Hatch et al. 1990) and the reconstruction of the occupational history at Seip (Greber 1992) also suggest accretive architectural development. Therefore, greater contemporaneity existed among occupations at Ohio Hopewell centers, including hilltop enclosures, than previously perceived.

The research conducted over the past two field seasons provides extensive data for estimating the land modification and construction stages at hilltop enclosures. While recognizing hilltop locations did not allow for the same "open canvas" as flatland locales, the placement of embankment walls and hydraulic features at Fort Ancient demonstrate the extensive prehistoric modification and extension of the hilltop. Further, there is no evidence that local topography dictated the placement or occurrence of features within the earthwork such as stone circles, mounds, pavements, ditches, or ponding areas. Other New World earthwork complexes that pre-date the Middle Woodland period, such as at Poverty Point (Exnicios and Woodiel 1986: Gibson 1989; Woodiel 1986), San Lorenzo (Coe and Diehl 1980), and La Venta (Drucker et al. 1959) contain evidence of extensive land modification associated with earthwork construction. That Middle Woodland earthworks have not been previously noted for such modifications shows a lack of our understanding of specific earthwork site stratigraphic sequences.

The preliminary examination of earthwork construction at Fort Ancient shows that debates over accurate estimates of soil volume in mound and earthwork constructions (e.g., Jeter 1984; Shenkel 1986) provide limited gauges for estimates of labor expenditures. Instead, mound groups and enclosure complexes are more beneficially viewed as systems. Besides volume of earth moved, surface preparation, central planning, and the operation of the completed system must be considered. Further, Fort Ancient as a system expanded through time, not only in space, but in complexity. An analysis of the system will provide a basis for accurately gauging the social organization and complexity of the prehistoric architects. The current systematic architectural and hydraulic examination at Fort Ancient forms a base model for the evaluation and examination of other Middle Woodland hilltop enclosures.

CONCLUSION

Research conducted at Fort Ancient to date supports the following conclusions:

1) Ohio Hopewell populations modified the plateau on which the Fort Ancient enclosure is situated to accommodate the placement of embankment walls, interior ditches, and ponds.

If the amount of modification in the study areas proves typical for the site as a whole, then the volume of earth moved in leveling and extending the plateau may approach that used in the construction of embankment walls and mounds at the site.

2) Ponds associated with gateways were precisely crafted features that became loci of prehistoric activity during the Middle Woodland period. Reconstructed topography of the Gateway 13 pond and ditch system demonstrates that the complex effectively drained that portion of the Middle Fort plateau and may have served as a conduit for transporting water from a nearby spring.

3) The temporal depth of the area examined is not clear-cut. However, all lines of investigations support the hypothesis that construction began during the first half of the Middle Woodland period and expanded both spatially and functionally for a considerable period of time.

ACKNOWLEDGMENTS

I am deeply indebted to Lauren Sieg who served as co-director of field operations during the 1992 and 1993 seasons. I also wish to thank R. Barry Lewis, Tom Riley, David Grove, and Vern Scarborough for comments and advice on the research reported in this paper. The 1992 and 1993 field seasons at the Fort Ancient State Memorial were conducted as field schools of the University of Cincinnati with students participating from the University of Cincinnati, University of Illinois at Urbana-Champaign, John Hopkins University, along with numerous volunteers. Funding was provided in part by the Department of Anthropology, University of Cincinnati and a research grant from the Department of Anthropology, University of Illinois at Urbana-Champaign. Dr. Bruce Smith and the Ohio Archaeological Council generously provided funding for radiocarbon dates from the 1992-93 field seasons. Finally, I thank Jack Blosser, site manager at Fort Ancient, for his unwavering support of research at the earthwork.

REFERENCES CITED

Aitken, M.J. 1991 Principles of Radiocarbon Dating. In *Scientific Dating Methods*, edited by J.Y. Goksu, M. Oberhofer, A. Regulla, pp. 3-35. Kluwer Academic Publishers, Brussel.

Atwater, C. 1820 Description of the Antiquities Discovered in the State of Ohio and other Western States. *Transactions and Collections of the American Antiquarian Society*, Volume 1.

Bacon, W. S. 1993 Factors in Siting a Middle Woodland Enclosure in Middle Tennessee. *Midcontinental Journal of Archaeology* 18:245-281.

Byers, M. A. 1987 *The Earthwork Enclosures of the Central Ohio Valley: A Temporal and Structural Analysis of Woodland Society and Culture*. Ph.D. dissertation, Department of Anthropology, State University of New York at Albany. University Microfilms, Ann Arbor.

Coe, M. D. and R. A. Diehl 1980 *The Land of the Olmec, Volume 1: The Archaeology of San Lorenzo Tenochtitlan*. University of Texas Press, Austin.

Connolly, R. P. 1991 *Prehistoric Site Structure at the Fort Ancient State Memorial: New Evidence from Lithic Analysis*. Master's thesis, Department of Anthropology, University of Cincinnati.

1995 *The Built Environment of Middle Woodland Period Hilltop Enclosures: An Analysis of Development, Construction and Function*. Ph.D. dissertation, Department of Anthropology, University of Illinois at Urbana-Champaign. University Microfilms, Ann Arbor.

n.d. Hopewell Habitation at the Fort Ancient Site. In *Ohio Hopewell Community and Organization*, edited by W. S. Dancey and P. J. Pacheco. Kent State University Press, Kent, Ohio "in press."

Connolly, R. P. and L. E. Sieg 1993 Prehistoric Architecture and the Development of Public Space at the Fort Ancient Hilltop Enclosure. Paper presented at the Fifth International and Interdisciplinary Forum on Built Form & Culture Research, Second CSPA Symposium on Architectural Practice, Cincinnati, Ohio.

Drucker, P., R. F. Heizer and R. J. Squier 1959 *Excavations at La Venta Tabasco, 1955*. Bureau of American Ethnology, Bulletin 170, Washington D. C.

Essenpreis, P. S. 1986 An Architectural Examination of Fort Ancient. Paper presented at the Annual Meeting of the Society for American Archaeology, New Orleans.

Essenpreis, P. S. and R. P. Connolly 1989 Hopewellian Habitation at the Fort Ancient Site, Ohio. Paper presented at the Southeast Archaeological Conference, Tampa.

Essenpreis, P. S. and M. E. Moseley 1984 Fort Ancient: Citadel or Coliseum? *Field Museum of Natural History Bulletin*, June: 5-26.

Exnicios, J. and D. Woodiel 1986 Poverty Point Excavations, 1980 - 1982. In *Louisiana Archaeology*, Volume 13, edited by Kathleen M. Byrd, pp. 73-100. Louisiana Archaeological Society, Lafayette.

Fischer, F. W. 1974 *Early and Middle Woodland Settlement, Subsistence and Population in the Central Ohio Valley*. Ph.D. dissertation, Department of Anthropology, Washington University. University Microfilms, Ann Arbor.

Garner, D. E., N. E. Reeder and J. E. Ernst 1973 *Soil Survey of Warren County, Ohio*. United States Department of Agriculture, Washington, D.C.

Gibson, J. L. 1989 Louisiana Earthworks: Middle Woodland and Predecessors. In *Middle Woodland Settlement and Ceremonialism in the Mid-South and Lower Mississippi Valley*, edited by Robert C. Mainfort, pp. 7-18. Mississippi Department of Archives and History, Jackson.

Greber, N. B. 1992 The Seip Geometric Enclosures and Environs: An Estimate of Possible Changes in Community Patterns Through Time. Paper presented at the 57th Annual Meeting of the Society for American Archaeology, Pittsburgh.

Hatch, J. W., J. W. Michels, C. M. Stevenson, B. E. Scheetz and R. A. Geidel
    1990 Hopewell Obsidian Studies: Behavioral Implications of Recent Sourcing and Dating Research. *American Antiquity* 55:461-479.

Jeter, M. D. 1984 Mound Volumes, Energy Ratios, Exotic Materials, and Contingency Tables: Comments on Some Recent Analyses of Copena Burial Practices. *Midcontinental Journal of Archaeology* 9:91-104.

Moorehead, W. K. 1889 Field Notes of Excavations at the Fort Ancient Site. Ms. on file, Ohio Historical Society, Columbus, Ohio

    1890 *Fort Ancient: The Great Prehistoric Earthwork of Warren County, Ohio.* Robert Clarke and Co., Cincinnati.

    1908 *Part II - Fort Ancient: The Great Prehistoric Earthwork of Warren County, Ohio.* Phillips Academy, Andover.

Prufer, O. H. 1964 The Hopewell Complex of Ohio. In *Hopewellian Studies*, edited by Joseph R. Caldwell and Robert L. Hall, pp. 37-83. Illinois State Museum, Scientific Papers 12, Springfield, Illinois.

Riordan, R. V. 1995 A Construction Sequence for a Hopewell Hilltop Enclosure. *Midcontinental Journal of Archaeology* 20(1):62-104.

Shenkel, J. R. 1986 An Additional Comment on Volume Calculations and a Comparison of Formulae Using Several Southeastern Mounds. *Midcontinental Journal of Archaeology* 11:201-220.

Silverman, H. 1990 The Early Nasca Pilgrimage Center of Cahuachi and the Nazca Lines: Anthropological and Archaeological Perspectives. In *The Lines of Nazca*, edited by Anthony Aveni, pp. 207-304. The American Philosophical Society, Philadelphia.

Stein, J. K. 1986 Coring Archaeological Sites. *American Antiquity* 51:505-527.

Stuiver, M. and P. J. Reimer 1987 *User's Guide to CALIB and DISPLAY Rev. 2.1.* Quaternary Research Center, University of Washington, Seattle.

Taylor, R.E. 1987 *Radiocarbon Dating: An Archaeological Perspective.* Academic Press, New York.

Tichenor, W. C. 1925 *A Guide to Fort Ancient.* Self published, Lebanon, Ohio.

Woodiel, D. 1986 Investigations at the Visitor Center, Poverty Point State Commemorative Area, 1978. In *Louisiana Archaeology*, Volume 13, edited by Kathleen M. Byrd, pp. 41-71. Louisiana Archaeological Society, Lafayette.

SIXTEEN

1990 EXCAVATIONS AT CAPITOLIUM MOUND (33WN13), MARIETTA, WASHINGTON COUNTY, OHIO: A WORKING EVALUATION

ABSTRACT

Over the past century, a certain controversy has arisen concerning the presence at Marietta, Ohio of Mississippian-like platform mounds integrally situated within a set of Hopewellian earthen enclosures. Since 1915, the "truncated pyramid" known as Capitolium Mound has been the home of the Washington County Public Library. In 1990, controlled excavations in advance of a proposed library expansion were carried out by the Cleveland Museum of Natural History. A number of diagnostic Ohio Hopewell artifacts were recovered. The excavations further revealed a complex mound stratigraphy as well as evidence for a preference of specific materials and colors. The limited 1990 excavations strongly indicate that Capitolium Mound was indeed of Hopewell origin and was built, used, and abandoned centuries before the emergence of Mississippian culture.

A View From the Core a Synthesis of Ohio Hopewell Archaeology•edited by Paul J. Pacheco
© Copyright 1996 by The Ohio Archaeological Council• Columbus, Ohio
All Rights Reserved•ISBN 0-9626931-9-7

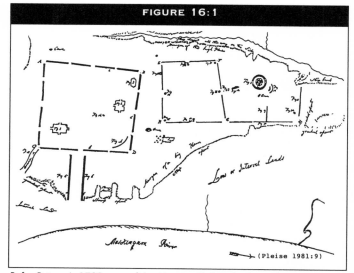

WILLIAM H. PICKARD

1990 EXCAVATIONS AT CAPITOLIUM MOUND (33WN13), MARIETTA,

INTRODUCTION

The enactment of the Northwest Ordinance of 1787 signaled the beginning of the systematic dispersal of those lands lying north and west of the Ohio River—lands the United States had gained as spoils of the Revolutionary War. After resolving the disputed claims on the northwest lands by the various eastern states, the Congress saw that it was in the nation's best interest to promptly open the territory to settlement by an eager citizenry. More importantly, in the face of a staggering war debt, land sales would be an immediate source of sorely needed revenue. The first major transaction under the terms of the 1787 Ordinance was with a group of New England land speculators known as the Ohio Company of Associates, headed by Rufus Putnam, Manasseh Cutler, and Winthrop Sargeant. The Ohio Company Purchase, as it would be called, consisted of nearly one million acres adjacent to the Ohio River in present day southeastern Ohio. The Ohio Company Purchase lands included the Northwest Territory's first permanent settlement at Marietta and first center of higher education at Athens.

When Putnam and his following of Ohio Company settlers landed at the mouth of the Muskingum River in April 1788, they were amazed to find the site of their future settlement already occupied by a remarkable set of mounds and geometric earthworks. As seen in Putnam's 1788 map **(Figure 16:1)**, these included a great conical mound, a pair of irregular squares that enclosed some 31 ha, and a finely constructed graded passageway that extended more than 200 m from the greater square toward the east bank of the Muskingum River. Located within the greater square were three raised earthen platforms or "truncated pyramids," each flanked on two or more sides by graded ascents. On July 2, 1788, in an extremely foresighted act, the directors of the Ohio Company voted to preserve for future generations a portion of Marietta's earthworks with some land attached to each for public use. Over the next few decades it became apparent to an enlightened few that progress was destroying many ancient monuments at an alarming rate. Few were as outspoken in their criticism as Caleb Atwater. While lauding the efforts of Putnam and Cutler as those of "truly intelligent men," he deplored the

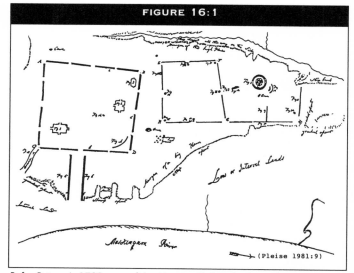

Rufus Putman's 1788 map of the Marietta Eathworks, from Pleise (1981:9).

seemingly wanton destruction of the magnificent tumuli found along the Scioto River near Chillicothe as the métier of "modern day barbarians" (Atwater 1833:37,85).

Today, the continued preservation of Marietta's Earthworks is overseen by the Marietta City Council, a charge that they hold in high esteem. Surviving to the present are the Conus Mound, the focal point of the town's oldest burial ground at Mound Cemetery, Quadranau Mound, the great rectangular raised platform in Camp Tucker Park, and Capitolium Mound, the site of the Washington County Public Library and the subject of this paper. Although it had originally been designated to be preserved, the grand graded way, known as the Sacra Via, has survived in a more diminished state. Where great walls once flanked the passage, rows of quaint Victorian houses now stand. In the mid 1800s, the walls of the Sacra Via were mined for their clay and recycled into building material for a local Protestant church. This apparently occurred shortly after a brickmaker was elected to the town council (MacLean 1903:38). As a pleasant, tree-lined parkway, however, it does seem to retain a certain suggestion of its original character.

HISTORY OF ARCHAEOLOGICAL INQUIRIES AT THE MARIETTA EARTHWORKS

As the most accessible to many early travelers, the Marietta Works were probably the most thoroughly mapped of any of Ohio's prehistoric earthworks. By 1850, nearly a dozen somewhat differing maps had been produced. The earliest published rendering, the Captain Heart map, closely conforms in detail to the Rufus Putnam map. It was drawn in 1787 while Heart was stationed at Fort Harmar, across the Muskingum River from the site of Marietta. Heart's map and a detailed description of the earthworks were published in *Columbian Magazine* in 1789. A slightly stylized and color tinted version of the Heart map was reproduced several years later in Paris, France to accompany J. Hector St. John de Crevecouer's published account of his travels in late 18th century America. The B. T. Putnam map (**Figure 16:2**), published by the American Antiquarian Society in 1820 and an 1822 drawing by Stephen DeWitte are unique in that they show a second graded passage extending from the greater square toward the Muskingum River. The 1820 B. T. Putnam map was republished in 1833 by Caleb Atwater in *Descriptions of the Antiquities Discovered in the Western Country* and again by Henry Howe in *Historical Collections of Ohio*. Perhaps the most familiar rendering is the map by Charles Whittlesey, published in the 1848 Squier and Davis volume *Ancient Monuments* (**Figure 16:3**). While in general agreement with most of its predecessors, this version shows that a fourth raised platform had suddenly appeared within the greater square. The stylized character of the platform mounds as published in *Ancient Monuments* as well as the words of the authors themselves that these mounds "cover no remains and seem obviously designated as the sites of temples...or as high places for the performance of certain ceremonies" (p. 173) influenced generations of archaeologists and laymen alike to associate these probable Middle Woodland period structures with the later Mississippian period temple mounds common to the lower Ohio and Mississippi River Valleys.

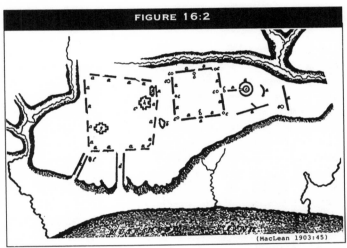

FIGURE 16:2

(MacLean 1903:45)

B.T. Putnam's 1820 map of the Marietta Earthworks, showing a second "Graded Passageway" extending from the lower left corner of the greater square, from MacLean (1903:45).

While both Middle Woodland and Mississippian period artifacts have, over the years, been recovered from the general vicinity of the Marietta Earthworks, prior to the 1990 project there had been no systematic survey relating to the inner structure or contents of any of Marietta's flat-topped mounds. But on the basis of data recovered from Capitolium in 1990, at least that portion of the mound that was investigated can be directly attributed to the Hopewell culture of Ohio's Middle Woodland period.

ARCHAEOLOGICAL INVESTIGATION OF CAPITOLIUM MOUND BY THE CLEVELAND MUSEUM OF NATURAL HISTORY

Capitolium Mound is situated on the second terrace above the east bank of the Muskingum River about 1.5 km above its confluence with the Ohio River. It is presently about 40 x 45 m at its base with the top of the mound approximately 2.5 m above street level. In 1916, Capitolium became the site of the Washington County Public Library, a project made possible through the generosity of Andrew Carnegie. Although there was some public opposition to the use of the mound in this manner, vivid memories of the 1913 flood that ravished much of Marietta influenced City Council to allow construction to proceed.

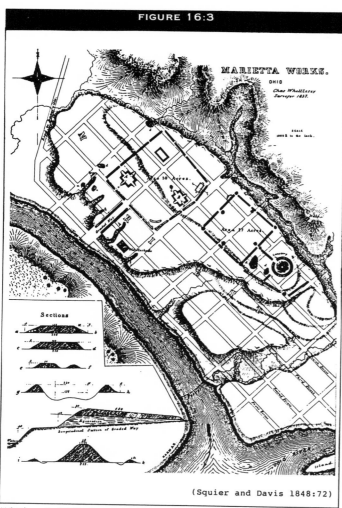

FIGURE 16:3

MARIETTA WORKS.

OHIO

Chas Whittlesey Surveyor 1837.

Sections

(Squier and Davis 1848:72)

Whittlesey's 1837 plan of the Marietta Earthworks as presented in Ancient Monuments (Squier and Davis 1848:72).

In 1988 the Washington County library board requested permission from the Marietta City Council to expand its present facility and to construct an external enclosed elevator to improve access for the physically challenged. Before granting its approval, however, the City Council required that an archaeological impact study be completed. In September 1989, coring operations under the direction of

N'omi Greber of the Cleveland Museum of Natural History confirmed that there were still extensive intact areas of the aboriginal mound within the proposed construction zones. Salvage excavations limited to the elevator shaft area were authorized in January 1990 and completed the following summer by students from the Marietta College Field School and selected local volunteers. The project was directed by Greber with the author as field supervisor and Kevin Gibbs as field assistant. Despite a number of practical and logistical problems, the goals of recording mound strata, the recovery of diagnostic artifacts and the obtaining of botanical samples for radiocarbon assays and flotation studies were successfully met.

The present configuration of Capitolium Mound shows a generally rectangular main section, trending SW to NE. Two of the three original ramps centered on this section are still visible in a 1990 contour drawing (Figure 16:4). The excavation site is marked by the shaded area at lower center. The driveway was original to library construction and placed to take advantage of the cleft between the lobes (a and b) . It allowed access to the library basement through a service door. Remnant ramps can be seen at top center (c) and along the left flank (d). The third ramp was apparently removed during the library construction period. Note that the ramps are centered on the main rectangular section and not on the mound as a whole, as shown on several early maps. Two separate lobe-like protrusions (see a and b, Figure 16:5) adjoin the mound along the southeast edge, giving Capitolium its unique configuration. Measurements made by Rufus Putnam and Samuel Hildreth also tend to confirm this general plan form.

For simplicity, our excavation grid was aligned parallel to the library building with the major axes designated grid north-south and grid east-west. Originally, our excavations were to be confined to the lobe at the south end of the excavation grid (Figure 16:4a), but were extended into the grid north lobe (Figure 16:4b) when the architect opted for an alternate elevator design about two-thirds of the way through our project. All things being equal, we were able to recover data from about 3 percent of the horizontal area covered by the mound.

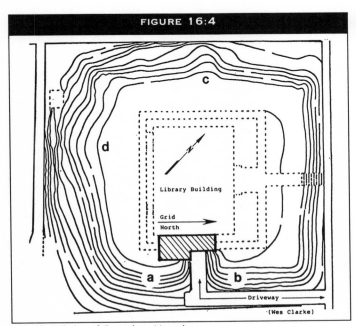

1990 Relief plan of Capitolium Mound.

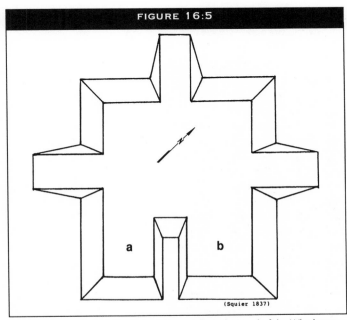

A stylized plan view of Capitolium Mound, based on a draft by Whittlesey, from Squier 1837.

Excavation began in mid June 1990 and, as expected, we found ample evidence of historic intrusion, especially immediately adjacent to the foundation of the library building. Over much of the excavation area there was a general covering of buried historic debris, such as broken bricks and concrete, from 20 cm to 1 m thick. Undoubtedly, this was construction residue covered during the landscaping of the library in 1916. The buried 1915 pre-library mound surface, as seen in a vintage photo owned by the Washington County Public Library, created a thin, dark, silty band that could be seen in the profile of nearly every excavation unit. This band, labeled Feature 4, was easily traced from the grid south lobe, across the driveway area between the lobes, and into the grid north lobe. The thicker dimension of Feature 4 as noted beneath the driveway probably represented an accumulation of slope wash between the lobes. The 1915 surface of each lobe could be seen to slope up and away from this point. In general, as demonstrated by our limited excavations, both the north and south lobes seem to have similar, although not identical, construction details.

The opposing outermost layer of each lobe consisted of a revetment of locally available heavy red clay soils. The stratigraphy within this outer clay revetment consisted of an intricate mix of superimposed prepared floors or activity levels. All major strata encountered extended beyond the limits of the excavation. In some instances, later aboriginal constructions intruded into and extensively damaged earlier ones and therefore a complete reconstruction of any single construction episode is not entirely possible. However, certain general observations can be made concerning the overall internal arrangement of the mound. Within the grid south lobe, for instance, the major upper strata seem to radiate from a point south and west of the excavation grid and could have been contained within the suggested outline of the lobe. Such stratigraphy is consistent with our pre-excavation interpretation of the general mound form, that is the lobes represent extensions added to a pre-existing structure.

Overall, in our 1990 excavations we were able to identify nearly 50 prehistoric features including significant mound strata, pottery concentrations, in-situ burnings, basin-like constructs, and miscellaneous lenses and stains. Because the grid south lobe contained a much better defined body of data, it will be the focus of discussion.

The construction sequence of the grid south lobe began with a prepared surface or floor that was formed by the simple removal of the vegetation covering and topsoil to expose the B Horizon subsoil **(Figure 16:6)**. This surface was covered, apparently after it had been used, by very thin layers of sandy soil, some no more than 5 mm thick. Discreet sections of the floor were demarcated by differing soils. No postholes or other features were found to originate on this floor. This arrangement of soil layers was in turn covered by a series of horizontal gravel layers up to 10 cm thick. Toward the center area of the lobe these gravel strata were themselves covered by a layer of mottled clayey sand to form another activity level. This floor was in turn covered over by the same pattern of sands and gravels seen on the lower floor. A small number of postholes and what appear to be short trenches originated at this upper level. However, the postholes were neither so numerous nor in a discernable pattern to suggest a major wooden structure. As is a common Hopewell trait, some posts had been prehistorically removed and the holes selectively refilled (Greber 1983:29). Vibrant colors were encountered here and elsewhere in the mound as bright red and yellow clays were often used as fills after the posts had been removed.

Above these two generally horizontal episodes the theme and manner of construction changed considerably. A major inner construction episode is illustrated by Feature 36 **(Figure 16:7)**. Feature 36 was an intricately constructed curving stratum of unusual design, the composition of which is the result of a multi-part construction sequence. The major material of choice used here was the same thick red, sandy clay used in the outer revetments of the lobes. The inner half of Feature 36 appears to have been deposited as a single continuous unit, while the outer half was comprised of superimposed layers of red clays 5 to 10 cm thick that were separated by thin layers of fine pea

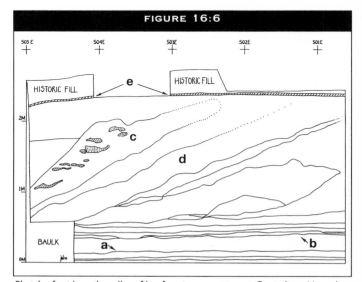

Sketch of grid-south wall profile of main excavation at Capitolium Mound showing key strata discussed in text: (a) primary activity floors; (b) second series of activity floors; (c) Feature 36; (d) Feature 51; (e) Feature 4.

gravels. In some areas the clay layers appear to have been slightly burned. The wall-like curving feature emerged from the southeast corner of the excavation and curved inward to the north and west, where it merged with the clay revetment near the north edge of the grid south lobe. To either side of Feature 36 was a fill of culturally sterile, coarse, brown sand.

Located within the limits of Feature 36, in a somewhat concentric arrangement, were a number of other distinctive strata. It might be suggested that due to the incomplete nature of these inner strata, Feature 36 may have acted as a preliminary internal cap to hold them in place. One of these inner strata, labeled Feature 51, was particularly interesting. Feature 51 was composed of a light, yellowish silty sand 25 to 35 cm thick, and its placement apparently mimicked the curvature of Feature 36. A number of postholes originated within the confines of Feature 51 and may represent a third platform or activity level. Additionally, integral to Feature 51 were what appeared to be at least one and possibly two pottery concentrations that together accounted for two-thirds of the nearly 600 recovered ceramics.

FIGURE 16:7

Cross section of Feature 36 illustrating its multi-part construction. Note the alternating layers of clay soils and fine gravels on the outer face of the feature. View is to the grid-south.

The primary concentration, labeled Feature 52, was located at the southerly end of the excavation where Feature 51 interfaced with the second series of horizontal activity floors and an irregular lens of fine gravels labeled Feature 20. Feature 52 produced a number of unique sherds **(Figure 16:8)**, including a local version of the traditional Hopewell zoned-incised motif, and a rim with crude but recognizable Hopewellian cross-hatching. There were also a number of distinctive cord marked body sherds and rims. Some exterior surfaces were deeply impressed while others were smoothed to the point of nearly erasing the cord marking. Most unusual was a rim sherd with deep "pie crust" notchings. It is interesting to note that upon casual inspection, some of the more unique specimens appear to have been made from a very similar construction paste. This is most evident on the inner surface. Most of the tempering used seem to be varieties of stone such as limestone and chert, as well as various sized grit. A projected detailed study of the pottery recovered from Capitolium Mound, including petrographic analyses of the tempering materials, should provide relevant data concerning the local ceramic variation and help verify impressionistic conclusions of contact, ties, and/or influences on Ohio Hopewell from the Southeast.

In addition to those already discussed, a number of other feature types were encountered during the excavations. Features 19 and 35 represent two levels of in-situ burning. Such features were most notable for the wide range of wood taxa represented. As identified by Dee Anne Wymer of Bloomsburg University, these included a number of locally and non-locally available taxa such as maple, walnut, ash, oak, elm, beech, pine, hickory, locust, red mulberry, and black cherry.

Feature 19 was located at the grid east edge of the excavation, outside of Feature 36 and immediately above the second series of horizontal activity floors. Feature 19 was a flat, irregularly shaped burned area, measuring more than a meter across and divided into two distinct thin strata. The soil above Feature 19 was slightly crusted but showed no extensive reddening or other evidence of intense heat. Wood taxa identified in Feature 19 include walnut, pine, red mulberry, oak, and beech.

Feature 5 was a shallow basin of fine clayey sands and gravels about 2 m in diameter and approximately 35 cm deep. It was located at the north edge of the grid south lobe. The surface of Feature 35 was burned a bright red that faded to a dull red-brown near the perimeter of the feature, indicating a more intense heat acting upon these soils. However, Feature 35 had apparently been prehistorically gleaned of most of its burned material and only a slight residue of charcoal remained. The feature was then covered over by a layer of fine grained soil. Wood taxa identified in the remnant charcoal include hickory and pine.

Typical Ohio Hopewell bladelets were the most common lithics recovered during excavations **(Figure 16:9)**. Some were isolated finds, but many were associated with the pottery concentrations. A total of 63 bladelets were recovered from the excavation and about 25 percent of these were of Flint Ridge material. The rest were either Upper Mercer or Zaleski cherts. Additionally, there was a single bladelet of Wyandotte chert. The microwear patterns on these items were examined by Richard Yerkes of The Ohio State

Selected ceramics from Feature 52.

University. Yerkes determined that the bladelets had been used for a variety of tasks such as hide and meat processing and bone and stone engraving **(Table 16:1)**. A bladelet found among the rim sherds in Feature 52 had been used exclusively to cut plant material.

In addition to bladelets, there was a small quantity of mica found with the pottery concentrations along with some core fragments. A few biface fragments were also found throughout the mound. A small, crude triangular biface found between lobes was the only item recovered that could even remotely be labeled post-Hopewell. A single stemmed projectile point was recovered from the gravel layers above the first activity floor.

As of this writing, only one charcoal sample has been processed for a radiocarbon determination. However, the initial results appear to be promising. An uncorrected date of 1880 ± 70 B.P. (Beta #67234) was obtained from charred honey locust (*Gleditsia tricanthos*) recovered from Feature 47, a charcoal concentration located on the top of the second activity floor sequence in the grid north lobe. As had been seen in a number of other features elsewhere in the excavation, the charcoal in Feature 7 was comprised of several different wood taxa. Considering the conditions noted in the surrounding soils, this may more accurately represent a depo-

sition of material as opposed to an in-situ burning. Although a date of 1880 ± 70 B.P. is slightly earlier than had been anticipated, it can only be considered a point of departure for a planned suite of radiocarbon dates that will allow a firm temporal placement of Capitolium Mound and the Marietta Earthworks within Ohio Hopewell.

CONCLUSION

It is apparent from the type and style of artifacts recovered as well as particular internal details, the activity floors found at Capitolium Mound were constructed, used and covered over by Ohio Hopewell peoples. The resulting flat-topped structure is rare but not unique in Ohio. The field notes from Henry Shetrone's excavations at Ginther Mound located across the Scioto River from Mound City in Ross County, Ohio indicate that there were inner structures possibly similar to those recorded at Capitolium (Shetrone 1922). Shetrone also recovered bladelets, mica and pottery sherds with Hopewellian designs (Shetrone 1925:154-163). The flat-topped Cedar Banks mound located just north of Ginther, is also a likely candidate for a Hopewell platform mound (Squier and Davis 1848:52). A third elevated square was situated in the extreme northeastern corner of the Newark Earthworks until it was destroyed by canal construction in the 1840's (Squier and Davis 1848:67).

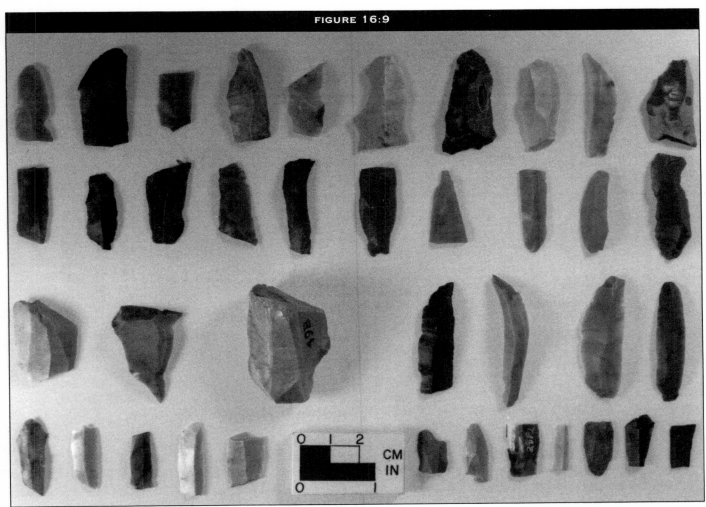

Bladelets and core fragments typical of those recovered in the 1990 Capitolium Mound excavation.

Outside Ohio, examples of platform mound constructions dating to Middle Woodland times occur at several well known sites, ranging from the Mann site in southern Indiana (Kellar 1979), to Pinson Mounds in western Tennessee (Mainfort 1986), to the Walling site in Alabama (Knight 1989). There are also certain similarities noted between the pottery concentrations found associated with the small circular embankment at Pinson called the Duck's Nest and pottery concentrations recorded at Capitolium (Mainfort 1986:27-46). Publications from the southeastern sites have clearly established for the larger audience that platform mounds were indeed constructed and used during Middle Woodland times. Therefore, it should come as no great shock to the archaeological community to find such structures well within the cultural limits of Ohio Hopewell. In time, it is expected that the 1990 excavations will add some new pieces to the Hopewell puzzle, particularly in an attempt to sort out the cultural dynamics within and among the politically separate Hopewell groups found in the several major river valleys in southern Ohio.

ACKNOWLEDGMENTS

Funds for the salvage excavations were provided by the National Geographic Society, the Ohio Archaeological Council, the Friends of the Washington County Library, and many private individuals and businesses in Washington County. Services in kind came from many sources including Marietta College, the Ohio Historical Society, the Cincinnati Museum of Natural History, and the Ohio University Archaeology Field School. Special thanks to Robert Mainfort, N'omi Greber, Dee Anne Wymer, Richard Yerkes, and to Jan Long for art work and technical assistance.

TABLE 16:1

CAT NO.	PLATFORM SCARS	HEAT TREATMENT	RAW MATERIAL	NOTES	MICROWEAR
1C			Upper Mercer		
3I1a	2 long, 1 short	luster, crazing	Flint Ridge		abrasion
3I1b	1 long, 3 short	luster	Flint Ridge	retouched	
3I1c	3 short	luster	Flint Ridge		
3I1d	1 long, 1 short	luster	Flint Ridge	retouched	
4I3	2 short	luster, crazing	Upper Mercer		
4J1		lus, craz, potld	Flint Ridge	retouched	cutting unknown material
5Ha		luster	Flint Ridge		
5Hb		lus, craz, potld	Flint Ridge		
5K1		luster, crazing	Flint Ridge	burned	edge damage (e.d.)
6I	1 long, 3 short	luster	Flint Ridge	burned	incising bone/antler (e.d.)
7A		luster	Flint Ridge		e.d.
14G	1 long	luster	Flint Ridge		e.d.
14Ha	3 long, 4 short	luster	Flint Ridge		e.d.
14Hb		luster	Flint Ridge		abrasion
19B	3 short	luster	Upper Mercer	retouched	cutting/scraping meat/fr. hide
20A		luster	Flint Ridge	retouched	cutting/scraping hide
21Ha	3 short	luster	Flint Ridge		
21Hb	4 short		Flint Ridge		
21Hc		crazing	Zaleski	burned	
21Hd	3 short	lus, craz, potld	Wyandotte	cortex	
23B	4 short		Upper Mercer	retouched	
24B3	2 long, 2 short	luster	Flint Ridge	crest/blade?	
24Ea		luster	Upper Mercer		edge damage
23Eb	2 short	luster	Flint Ridge		
24Ec		luster, potlids	Flint Ridge	burned	
24Ed		luster	Flint Ridge		
24F1a	1 long, 3 short	luster	Flint Ridge		
24F1b	2 short	luster	Flint Ridge		
24F1c	1 short		Zaleski	brkn. plat.	incising bone/ant.; hide awl
24F1d		luster, crazing	UM/FRF?		
24F1e		luster, potlids	Flint Ridge	burned	platform damage
24F1g		luster	Flint Ridge		
24F2a		luster	Flint Ridge		
24F2b	3 short (step)	luster, crazing	Flint Ridge		
24F2c		luster	Flint Ridge	burned	
24F3		luster	Flint Ridge		graving stone, abrasion
26A1a		luster	UM/Zaleski?		edge damage
26A1b		luster	UM/Zaleski?		
26B	1 short	luster	Flint Ridge		
26C	2 short		Upper Mercer	crystals	abrasion
26Ea		luster	Flint Ridge		platform snapped off
26Eb	1 long, 2 short	luster, potlids	Flint Ridge		edge damage
26Ec	3 short	luster	Flint Ridge		
28B1a		luster	Flint Ridge		edge damage
28B1b		luster	Flint Ridge		edge damage
35A1		luster	Flint Ridge		e.d., platform snapped off
36A		luster	Flint Ridge		
38A		luster	Upper Mercer		
40B2		luster	Upper Mercer	light use	scraping bone/antler
49..	2 short		Flint Ridge		
49Ba	2 short	luster	Flint Ridge	retouched	faceted platform
49Bb	1 long, 4 short		Flint Ridge		cutting plant material
49Bc	4 short	luster	Flint Ridge		
49Bd	2 short	luster	Flint Ridge	burned	faceted platform
52D1a		luster	Flint Ridge	brkn. plat.	abrasion (2 segments)
52D1b		luster, potlids	Flint Ridge	burned	platform damage
52D5		luster, crazing	Grey Chert	burned	
52D6		luster	Flint Ridge		
59..		luster	Flint Ridge		
TOTAL	14 long 69 short	51 luster 07 potlids 10 crazing	46 Flint Ridge 11 Upper Mercer 4 Zaleski 1 Wyandotte 1 Grey Chert	9 burned 1 cortex 7 retouch 1 crest 1 crystals 1 light use	5 abrasion 6 platform damaged 2 faceted platform 11 edge damage 1 cutting/scrape meat/fr. hide 1 cutting/scraping hide 1 hide awl 2 incising bone/antler 1 scraping bone/antler 1 engraving stone 1 cutting plant material 1 cutting unknown material

Yerkes' summary of the 33WN13 bladelets

A   V I E W   F R O M   T H E   C O R E :   A   S Y N T H E S I S

Atwater, C.1833 (republished) Descriptions of the Antiquities Discovered in the State of Ohio and Other Western States. *Archaeologia Americana* 1:105-267.

Greber, N. B.1983 *Recent Excavations at the Edwin Harness Mound; Liberty Works, Ross County, Ohio.* Midcontinental Journal of Archaeology Special Paper No. 5, Kent State University Press, Kent, Ohio.

Kellar, J. H.1979 The Mann Site and "Hopewell" in the Lower Wabash-Ohio Valley. In *Hopewell Archaeology: The Chillicothe Conference,* edited by D. S.Brose and N. B.Greber, pp. 100-107. Kent State University Press, Kent, Ohio.

Knight, V. J., Jr. 1989 *Excavation of the Truncated Mound at the Walling Site: Middle Woodland and Copena in the Tennessee Valley.* University of Alabama Press, Huntsville, Alabama.

MacLean, J. P. 1903 Ancient Works at Marietta, Ohio. *Ohio Archaeological and Historical Publications* 12:37-66.

Mainfort, R. C. Jr. 1986 *Pinson Mounds: A Middle Woodland Ceremonial Center.* Tennessee Department of Conservation, Nashville.

Pleise, R. B. ca1981 *Earthworks at Marietta, Ohio.* Ms. on file, Ohio Historic Preservation Office, Region 11A, Columbus, Ohio.

Shetrone, H. C. 1922 Ginther Mound excavation notes. Ms. on file, Ohio Historical Society, Columbus.

1925 Exploration of the Ginther Mound. *Ohio Archaeological and Historical Publications* 34:154-163.

Squier, E. G. 1837 *The Papers of Ephraim Squier.* Series IV, Volume 9. Ms. on file, Smithsonian Institution, Washington, D.C.

Squier, E.G., and E.H. Davis 1848 *Ancient Monuments of the Mississippi Valley.* Contributions to Knowledge Vol. 1. Smithsonian Institution, Washington, D.C.

SEVENTEEN

THE PURDOM MOUND GROUP: THE DAYTON MUSEUM OF NATURAL HISTORY'S EXCAVATION AND A SYNOPSIS OF THE EXCAVATIONS OF ADAMS AND BAILEY

J. M. HEILMAN AND LYNN M. MAHONEY

ABSTRACT

The Purdom Mound Group near Xenia, Ohio had its first recorded excavation in 1931 by Robert McCormick Adams, a student of Dr. Raymond Stites of Antioch College. In 1973 Douglas Bailey conducted a summer field school excavation at Purdom for Wright State University. Recent excavation by the Dayton Museum of Natural History (DMNH) concentrated on Mound 1-2, Mound 3/4, and the area between these mounds. Our excavation found significant divergences from Adams' recorded work on the site, but most importantly, we were able to document building techniques and date of construction.

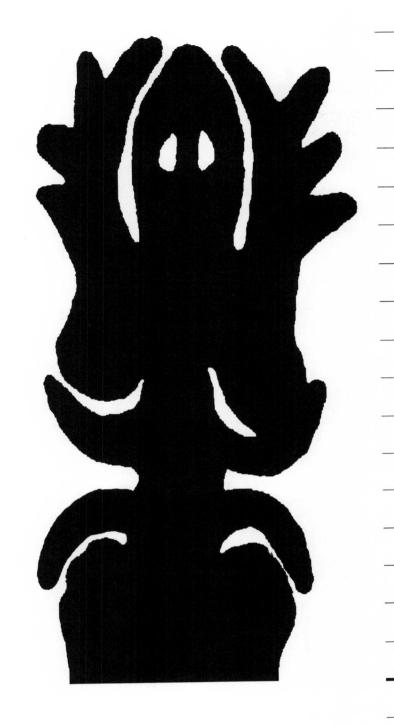

J. M. Heilman and Lynn M. Mahoney

THE PURDOM MOUND GROUP: THE DAYTON MUSEUM OF NATURAL HISTORY'S EXCAVATION

Introduction

The Purdom Mound Group (33GR12) is situated on a dissected plateau, 18 m above the west bank of the Little Miami River and 3 km northwest of Xenia, Ohio. The five to seven mounds which comprised the complex were located on a long ridge that parallels the Little Miami River in its northeast to southwest axis. The mounds are located 2.4 km west of Oldtown and an equal distance downstream from Massie's Creek and the Pollock Works. The geographic terrain of Purdom is reminiscent of Fort Ancient, which is less than 40 km south of the complex. The first documented excavation of the Purdom complex was in 1931 by Robert McCormick Adams, a student of Dr. Raymond Stites of Antioch College in Yellow Springs. According to newspaper articles in the *Dayton Daily News* in November of 1931, the two mounds excavated were carefully staked out and photographed prior to excavation, and copious field notes were recorded. Newspaper accounts of the excavation give a good deal of detail, although the exact location of the five mounds is not established and long-term residents in the area talk of seven mounds rather than five. Further, there is confusion as to which mound Adams called Mound 1, Mound 1-2, and Mound 3. Copies of Adams' original maps of Mound 1-2 and Mound 3, with an annotated listing of the various finds and their locations, are currently filed at the Dayton Museum of Natural History. Unfortunately neither of these maps has any directional axis or scale. We contacted Dr. Robert McCormick Adams in 1990 to see if he knew what had become of his notes or photos. He replied that he had no information pertaining to the excavation. There is a possibility that these notes may be with Dr. Raymond Stites' papers awaiting inventory at the Menninger Foundation in Topeka, Kansas. They are not with Dr. Stites' papers at the National Gallery of Art in Washington, D.C. or at Antioch College in Yellow Springs, Ohio.

The next excavation of the Purdom Mound Group was by Doug Bailey, who used the site for a field course in archaeology for Wright State University in 1973. He and his students removed the western half of the oval mound, which Adams' maps designate as Mound 1-2. Wright State has no

record of these excavations, but the few Purdom artifacts in their repository were kindly given to the Dayton Museum of Natural History (DMNH) to keep the collection together.

The DMNH became involved with the Purdom Mound Group in 1988, when Mrs. Jan Hutchison contacted the museum concerning remnants of some previously excavated mounds on the family's property. In conjunction with rebuilding an old log cabin, the Hutchisons planned to bulldoze the numerous backdirt piles into the configuration of the original mound, but were uncertain as to what was original and what was backdirt. They inquired if we would be interested in excavating the mounds prior to their rearrangement. We were interested in the prospect of extracting some good radiocarbon samples from the site, which could be used to more accurately date the artifacts from Adams' excavation which reside in the DMNH collection. Not much was left of Adams' Mound 1-2, as he had removed most of the central area of the mound, and Bailey's excavation had removed the remainder of the west side. According to our calculations, the original mound was approximately 15 m by 18 m, and a little over 2 m in height. The remainder of the east half of the mound had numerous scars, and Adams' maps showed that he had significantly cut into this section as well. We were particularly interested in excavation of the area surrounding the mound, as this upland ridge had never been plowed. We were given permission to excavate the area where the property owners planned to build, and to work on the remaining sections of Mound 1-2. The southwestern stake was used as the datum for each square in the museum's work.

Results of excavation
Adams' 1931 Excavation and Recovery of Artifacts from Mound 1-2

While neither of the Adams' maps has a north designation, it is possible to reconstruct the orientation of his excavation in Mound 1-2. Unfortunately we were not able to rediscover any of the features which Adams so dutifully marked with alphabetical designations on his maps. However in the newspaper account (Adams 1931a) Adams states that he

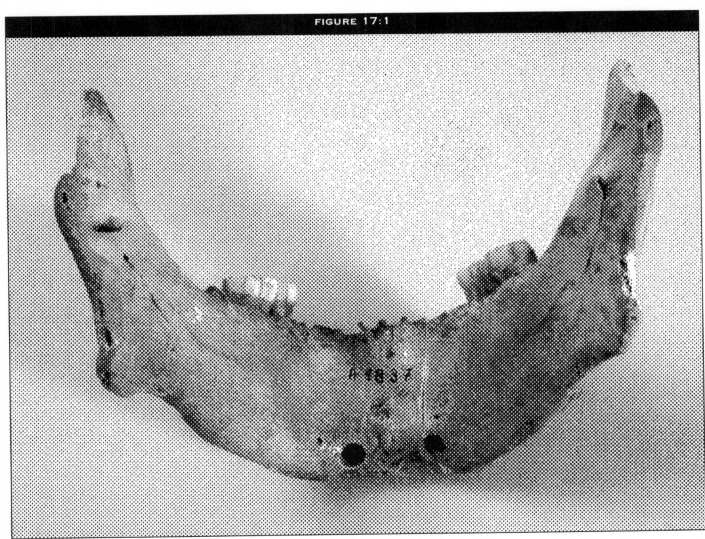

Cut, drilled, and polished male mandible recovered in Adams' 1931 excavation of Feature "I" of Mound 1-2.

began his excavation on the north side of the mound and worked to the south. This fits well with the alphabetical sequence in his allocation of pits, and we feel confident that Adams' two crematoria (C & D) are to the north end of the mound, and the burials indicated as L & N lie to the south end or later part of his excavation.

It is possible to trace the cut and drilled human mandible **(Figure 17:1)** to Burial I in Mound 1-2, as this is the only burial from Adams' excavation with the skull placed in the area of the knees. He mentions this specifically in the November 1, 1931 *Dayton Daily News* article (Adams 1931b). We are not positive if the skull that we think was in association with this burial is indeed the same one that

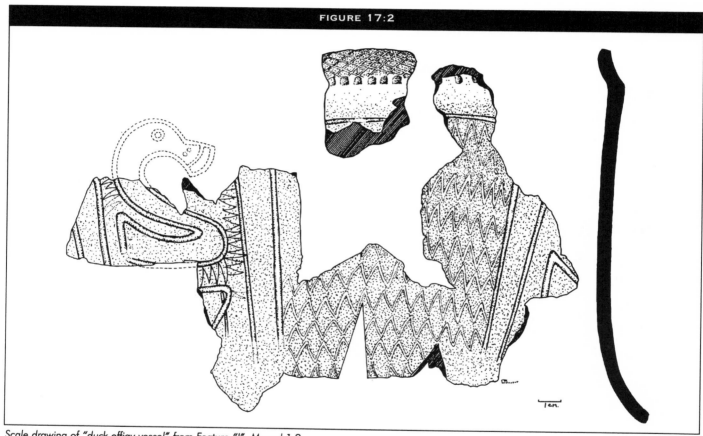

Scale drawing of "duck effigy vessel" from Feature "J", Mound 1-2.

Adams found in association with Burial I. Additional analysis by Paul Sciulli of The Ohio State University ultimately may be able to resolve this problem. He believes the "trophy" mandible is that of a male. The mandible has been bifacially drilled just below the canines. Each of the front drillings is 6 mm in diameter and is drilled toward the center of the mandible. The two drillings from the underside of the jaw are 5 and 7 mm in diameter and originate from below the second incisors. The condyles have been removed and the surface has been polished. The first and second premolars, incisors, and canines on both the right and left side of the mandible are not present. Whether they were present when Adams excavated the mandible or have subsequently become displaced is unknown.

Adams was most interested in the ceramics from the Purdom Mound 1-2. In the November newspaper article he states that "several of the potsherds...are identical in type of decoration to some found in the largest mound of the Hopewell Group" (Adams 1931a). The vessel was reconstructed for a DMNH display in 1931, with the separate pieces set in plaster of Paris to approximate the shape of the original vessel. The vessel was taken apart and reconstructed in 1970, with more bonds found than were recognized in the first reconstruction. Adams recovered this vessel from Mound 1-2 and labeled the Feature J, located between the burials he designates I and K.

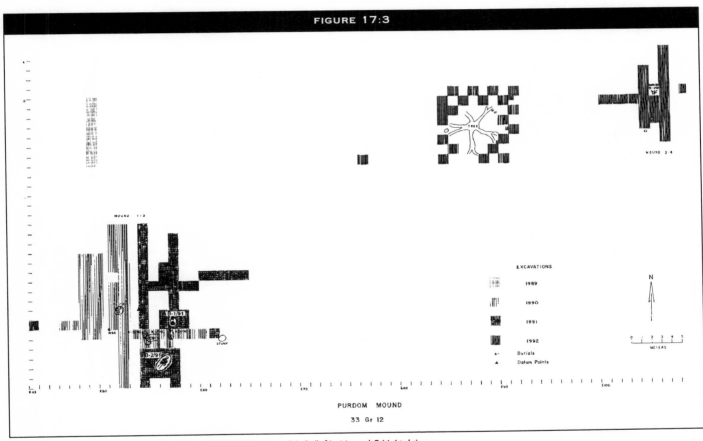

FIGURE 17:3

EXCAVATIONS

1989
1990
1991
1992
Burials
Datum Points

MOUND 1-2

MOUND 3-4

PURDOM MOUND

33 Gr 12

Overview of excavation areas and grid for 1989-1992, Mound 1-2 (left), Mound 3/4 (right).

This vessel (**Figure 17:2**) is most interesting as it is very similar in its motif to the "duck effigy" vessel recovered from Mound 2 of the Mound City Group. A bird effigy is portrayed, but on the Purdom vessel it makes its appearance on two of the four zoned panels, with the two intervening zoned panels decorated with rocker stamping, as in the type *Chillicothe Rocker Stamped* (Prufer and McKenzie 1965). The rim of the vessel exhibits an incised cross-hatching with punctates immediately beneath this flared rim. Unlike the Mound City vessel it has a rounded bottom rather than four projecting feet. The Purdom vessel is 15 cm tall and 13.3 cm in outside diameter. The tempering in this vessel is sparse and appears to be mixed grit and limestone. The vessel is well-potted and consistently 6 mm thick from the base to just below the rim where it thickens to 8 mm immediately behind the surrounding row of hemiconical punctates. Above the row of punctates the rim is classically decorated with fine cross-hatching. While the overall appearance of the vessel is that of a well-crafted ceramic, in actuality the design is not that well incised. The panels of rocker stamping are not particularly even, and the surface is unevenly burnished. These defects are not immediately apparent until one examines the surface in detail. In spite of the burnishing and light impression of the original rocker stamping, one can still make out vertical rows of rocker stamping behind some portions of the incised panel

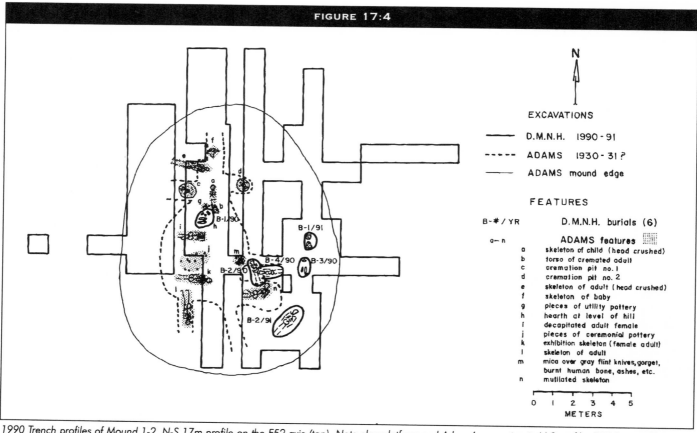

FIGURE 17:4

EXCAVATIONS

——— D.M.N.H. 1990-91

- - - ADAMS 1930-31?

——— ADAMS mound edge

FEATURES

B-#/YR   D.M.N.H. burials (6)

a—n   ADAMS features

a   skeleton of child (head crushed)
b   torso of cremated adult
c   cremation pit no. 1
d   cremation pit no. 2
e   skeleton of adult (head crushed)
f   skeleton of baby
g   pieces of utility pottery
h   hearth at level of hill
i   decapitated adult female
j   pieces of ceremonial pottery
k   exhibition skeleton (female adult)
l   skeleton of adult
m   mica over gray flint knives, gorget,
     burnt human bone, ashes, etc.
n   mutilated skeleton

0 1 2 3 4 5
METERS

1990 Trench profiles of Mound 1-2. N-S 17m profile on the E52 axis (top). Note clay platform and Adams' excavation in N-S profile. E-W 9 m profile on the E56 axis (bottom). Note intrusive (B2/90).

designs. The vessel's surface color ranges from a medium grey black to grey brown to a creamy buff. The core of the vessel ranges from a grey black to a red brown. It is apparent that various parts of the vessel were subjected to different intensities of heat after it had broken, as pieces which adjoin one another may be two distinctly different colors.

In Feature M of the 1931 excavation at least nine sheets of mica were recovered. The material was found as a burnt deposit on the "floor" of the mound in association with several chert knives, a gorget, and burnt human bone and ashes. The nine sheets of mica range in size from 4.5 x 18.5 cm to

18 x 23 cm, and from 1 to 5 mm thick. Another smaller piece was with this cache of mica, but it seems likely that this spalled from one of the other pieces. The mica does not appear to be all from the same geologic source, as both biotite and muscovite are represented. There is also a piece of pinkish mica, which could be lepidolite. However, the authors were unwilling to subject it to the flame test to be positive of its specific variety.

Two of the nine pieces of mica in this cache exhibit definite cut marks. One specimen, which is 17.5 x 2.5 cm, has a 3 x 1 cm cut. The 3 cm cut runs parallel to the long axis of the mica. The other piece of cut mica from this cache is 7.8 x 15 cm and has a 3.5 cm piece cut from one corner. The cut extends another 1.5 cm but did not completely penetrate the sheet of mica. The oval piece of mica found in this cache has an exceptionally small cut, 1 cm x 2 mm in size.

The pendant from Adams' Feature M is 10.5 cm long, 4.9 cm wide, and 1.3 cm thick. It is made from an iron-rich sandstone which may have been a concretion. The pendant is roughly rectangular with a smoothed missing corner, which may reflect the shape of the concretion from which it was crafted rather than an old break. Between the bifacially drilled hole and the indented corner is a patch of orange iron-rich oxide which may be part of the concretion's original surface color. The gray "flint" knives that were also reported to be a part of this feature are no longer present in the collection. The authors are of the opinion that these knives may be among the "no data" artifacts in the Museum's collection, but have no way of locating them as these items are not sufficiently described by Adams to allow a positive identification.

The only other identifiable piece from Adams' excavation of this mound is a single piece of *McGraw Cordmarked* pottery (Prufer and McKenzie 1965) found in the crematoria. Noteworthy by their absence are the pieces of "utility pottery" which Adams listed as Feature G. If the notes by Adams ever surface, it may be possible to find the missing ceramics among the museum's "no data" specimens.

THE DAYTON MUSEUM OF NATURAL HISTORY'S EXCAVATION OF MOUND 1-2

As a preliminary step to excavation at the Purdom Mound Group, in 1989 Chris Turnbow, formerly with the DMNH, excavated the area immediately north of Mound 1-2 where a log cabin was to be constructed (**Figure 17:3**). His excavation of a 7 m north-south trench revealed vestiges of the Hopewell occupation with finds of grit-tempered cord-marked ceramics, but the bulk of the material recovered was fire-cracked rock (FCR), along with the reworked wing of a banded slate bannerstone/atlatl weight that had been

drilled for reconnection with its other (missing) half. One posthole was recorded in square N73-E49. Numerous small ceramics were collected from squares N73, N74, and N75-E49. All of these 93 sherds were grit tempered, 27 of which were cordmarked, and 25 were plain. The 41 remaining sherds were too eroded or small to permit identification of their surface treatment.

Because of Adams' designation of Mound 1-2 for the large oval mound, we concluded that in his opinion a single mound had been constructed and then later extended, giving it its oval shape, or that two mounds had been conjoined. With this in mind, it was decided to excavate in 1990 the longest north-south profile of the mound to document construction, and to show any temporal differences in construction between the north and south ends of the mound.

We established a 17 m north-south profile along the E53 axis, and it was immediately obvious that Adams' excavation map was misleading. While signs of Adams' excavation were noted during our excavation (**Figure 17:4**), they suggest that he did not reach the floor of the mound on the west side. The uniform raised clay platform running along the north-south axis also indicated that the mound was raised as a single unit of construction with little or no variation in the time of building. This raised orange clay platform was covered by a secondary mantle of earth, which was then capped by an additional layer of humus.

Several interments were encountered during the 1990 excavation of Mound 1-2. We recovered Burial 1/90 in square N57-E52, on the floor of the mound. The individual was represented by skull fragments, postcranial remains and sections of long bones. Initial examination by Dr. Paul Sciulli indicates that the interment was an adult who died at less than 30 years of age. The skull exhibits blackening from being smoked, but it is not truly cremated. There were no associated artifacts with B1/90. One Flint Ridge bladelet fragment was recovered from the level below the burial.

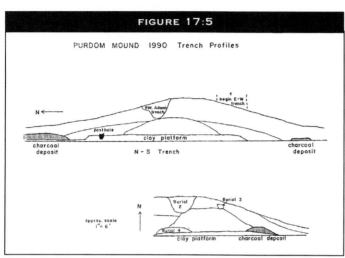

FIGURE 17:5

PURDOM MOUND 1990 Trench Profiles

1990-91 DMNH excavation overlaid on Adams' 1931 excavation map.

Burial 2/90 was an intrusive burial, located in squares N54-55 E54. Sciulli has reported the remains to be a female of 28 ± 5 years. The individual was intruded into the mound as a fully extended burial, which was then covered/backfilled with rotted limestone cobbles. She was accompanied by a large shell container (*Cassis madagascariensis* form spinella) which was interred to the west side of her left humerus with the cup facing east. This particular species of shell originates in the Florida Keys but extends as far north as North Carolina (Gary Coovert, personal communication, 1993). There were no other artifacts associated with B2/90. A bone collagen date on this individual, collected with the consent of the Indian Advisory Committee who work with the Museum, suggests that she was interred about 300 years after the mound had been constructed. This will be covered further in the section on Carbon-14 dating.

Burial 3/90 was represented by fragmentary remains in square N55-E57. Sciulli indicates from the study of the auricular surface that the individual was a female of 47 ± 5 years. Damage to this skeleton was extensive, both from rodent burrows and root penetration. The interment was well above the floor level, but was not intrusive into the mound. There were no associated artifacts with B3/90.

Burial 4/90 was a fully articulated extended burial that was located in squares N54-55 E54-55, situated below B2/90, the intrusive burial. Sciulli estimates from the auricular surface an age of 47 ± 5 years. This female is estimated to have been 149 cm tall. An unusual, unidentifiable white stain extended from just below the shoulders of the individual to the mid-thigh area, and may have been remnants of an underlying mortuary cloth. Samples of the stain were collected in hopes that a soil chemistry analysis may be able to identify its substance. The stain was about 100 x 80 cm, and occurred only under the bones of the interment. One local chert flake, located 6 cm south of the individual's right humerus, was recovered from this burial.

All flint/chert debris recovered from these excavations were visually examined. Artifacts were sorted out first, then waste flakes sorted according to horizontal and vertical location within the excavation. Chert flakes were also sorted according to two types: local and non-local material. Non-local material was then categorized: Flint Ridge, Upper Mercer, Harrison County (i.e., Wyandotte) (Vickery 1983). Artifacts were examined for diagnostics, i.e., established projectile point types (Justice 1987). The majority were identified as Archaic points, but a slate tube was also recovered during the 1990 excavation. Of the 802 waste flakes examined from the 1990 excavation of Mound 1-2, nearly two-thirds appear to be of local origin (64 percent, n=519). Non-local chert fell into three basic types: Flint Ridge, Upper Mercer, and Harrison County, Indiana. Of these three types, Flint Ridge appears by far the most prevalent, accounting for about 67 percent (n=191) of all the non-local chert material removed from Mound 1-2 in 1990.

The 1990 excavations of Mound 1-2 revealed that much of the east side of the mound was still intact. We were unable to identify specific features on Adams' map that allowed us to identify his earlier work (**Figure 17:5**). However, we could state unequivocally that Mound 1-2 was built as a single construction. We still wondered if the mound may have originally been built over a charnel house or other special activity area. However, few postholes were discovered. It was decided to continue the excavation of the site with another field season devoted to Mound 1-2, in hopes that we could identify some of the old features located by Adams, and to use these to match and clarify his map with our known proveniences.

Our 1991 excavations were two major north-south trenches along the E54 and E57 lines, with an east-west connecting trench along the N61 axis. The excavation was made exceptionally difficult by the many trees and tree roots encountered throughout the excavation and in profile cutting. Very little artifactual material was recovered from the north-south bearing E54 trench. The E57 trench contained Burial 1/91, which was the interment of a juvenile elk, possibly newborn. The elk was probably fully articulated when buried, but tree roots had penetrated all parts of the burial, and had caused shifting of the bones.

Burial 1/91 overlaid a feature of "varve-like" puddled clay. There were seven pairs of alternating dark and light bands that made up a rectangular pit with rounded corners. This feature was just over 2 m long and 1 m wide. Dr. Gail Wagner of the University of South Carolina (Gail Wagner, personal communication, 1993) identified the plant remains taken from flotation samples collected within two profiles in this feature. The first profile produced two burnt "wild" *Chenopodium* seeds and burnt wood which was dominantly hickory plus a little ash. The second profile included one hickory nut shell and four unidentifiable pieces of burnt wood.

Burial 2/91 was a female, estimated by Sciulli from the auricular surface to have been 47 years of age at time of death. She was interred in a pit measuring 263 x 188 cm, with the greatest depth of the pit at 35 to 40 cm below the mound floor. The individual had been re-articulated as a fully extended burial. However, the body must have been skeletonized prior to the time it was reassembled in the pit. A number of the bones were so placed that the positioning was anatomically impossible if she had been in the flesh. The bones of the individual's right hand, ulna and radius were missing. A fire had been placed along the left side of her body after she had been positioned in the grave. Charcoal samples were collected from the remains of this

fire and were used for Carbon-14 dating. A number of rotted limestone cobbles were clustered about the feet of this interment. There were several artifacts associated with B2/91. Three locally-derived chert flakes were located at the left side of the burial. One local flake was recovered 7 cm southeast of the individual's left hand. There were also two pieces of fire-cracked rock within the burial fill. In addition, two Harrison County, Indiana chert flakes were located just behind and to the west of the individual's skull.

Of the 17 pottery sherds collected during the Museum's excavation of Mound 1-2, all were grit tempered and nine were large enough to identify surface treatment. These nine sherds had plain surfaces and most were red-orange to red-brown in color, although two were tan and one was black. All were body sherds and ranged from 5 to 8 mm in thickness. These sherds were recovered from various locations within the mound fill, and were not clustered in one specific area.

Lithic material recovered from the 1991 excavation includes flint flakes, fire cracked rock (FCR), and one Archaic pestle. The chert debitage was analyzed in the same manner as 1990 debris. Similar results were obtained: of the 1,313 waste flakes examined, 940 (71 percent) were of local derivation. Flint Ridge chert represented the majority of non-local chert recovered (281 out of 373 or 75 percent).

While a few pieces of human bone were found loose in the mound fill, a number of small (1 cm) size pieces were found along the eastern and western perimeter of the mound. Their positioning was reminiscent of how debris accumulates adjacent to a wall or fence line. While no posthole defined walls were noted, the authors would not rule out a screened area around the periphery of the mound. It is hoped that future excavators of the remaining portions of the eastern edge will watch to see if this patterning of bone fragments continues to hold.

Mound 1-2 of the Purdom complex was rebuilt after the 1991 excavation season, and was restored to approximate its original appearance. There are substantial portions of the eastern side of the mound still intact, so great care was taken during the reconstruction of the mound to prevent compression of these unexcavated portions. The extensive notes from the DMNH's 1989-1992 excavations are on file at the museum, as well as the artifacts which were recovered.

CARBON-14 DATING OF MOUND 1-2

Four samples were processed for radiocarbon dating by Beta Analytic, Inc., and their results are shown below.

BETA #	CONTEXT	UNIT	AGE BP	MATERIAL SAMPLED
Beta-53457	Burial 2/91	N52-E56	1,850 + 80	Charcoal
Beta-53458	Burial 1/91	N57-E56	1,970 + 70	Charcoal
Beta-53459	126-135 cm b.d.	N60-E54	2,020 + 60	Charcoal
Beta-64221	Burial 2/90	N54-55 E54	1,630 + 90	Bone collagen

Beta 53457-53459 well represent the construction dates for Mound 1-2. The authors were somewhat surprised by the date on the intrusive burial (B2/90) as we expected it to be a little closer to the date of construction of the mound.

ADAMS' 1931 EXCAVATION AND RECOVERY OF ARTIFACTS FROM MOUND 3

While we were able to resolve a number of the issues relating to the excavation of Mound 1-2 by Robert McCormick Adams in 1931, we encountered more difficulty with another mound, described by Adams as Mound 3. We anticipated that it would be relatively easy to locate Mound 3 within the Purdom Mound Group, but its exact position still remains less than certain.

According to our calculations, Mound 3/4 is a small mound, only 1 m high and 13 m in diameter. It is the most southeastern mound on the ridge, overlooking the strong springs that flow into the Little Miami River. We referred to this mound as Mound 3/4 to resolve confusion as to whether this was Adams' old Mound 3. While the Museum retains a copy of the original Mound 3 map by Adams, many of the artifacts from this 1931 excavation are no longer present at the Museum. It is assumed that all the artifacts and burials listed

in the key to Mound 3 by Adams were donated to the Dayton Museum of Natural History by Elmer Purdom, but there are no accession records from this time to indicate exact listing of the donation. In the key to Mound 3 a number of artifacts are mentioned, and Adams specifically documents three interments: I, II, and III. Two and a half "flint knives" were recovered to the right of the skull of Burial I. Another "flint knife" was found about midway between the missing legs of Burial I but closer to the legs of Burial II. In his Dayton Daily News article Adams states that these were "flake knives".

Burial II from Mound 3 is depicted by Adams as a fully extended individual, interred with a ring of charcoal around the head. To the right side of the individual's skull a large quantity of charcoal was shown. Between the skull and the charcoal is a broken shell. Since this specimen cannot be documented in the collection it is not possible to know whether it was an imported marine or freshwater shell. At the feet of Burial II, a "loose" tooth of the individual was recovered. Small deposits of charcoal were located beyond the individual's feet.

Burial III is depicted as an extended burial, whose body is facing in the opposite direction from Burials I and II. An animal jaw and a bone ring were placed just below the left hand of this individual. At a point between this interment and the edge of the mound was a "small quantity [of] charcoal". This appears to be about the same distance as the charcoal deposit from Burial II.

Once again, we have no artifacts present in the museum collections that could be identified as the "bone ring". Likewise, none of the charcoal is present. Whether it was ever collected or brought to the museum is not known. The extended burials portrayed on the old maps of Mound 3 by Adams are represented by several cigar boxes of bone fragments from Burials I and III. Whether these are mis-marked fragments of other burials, or all that remains of these interments, is not known.

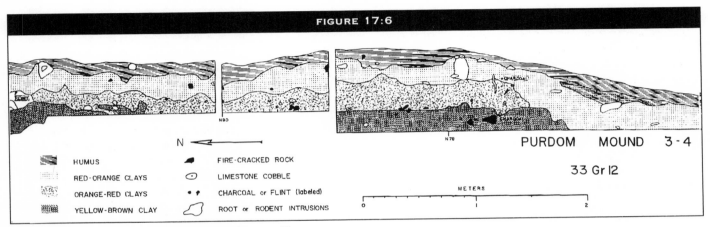

HUMUS

RED-ORANGE CLAYS

ORANGE-RED CLAYS

YELLOW-BROWN CLAY

FIRE-CRACKED ROCK

LIMESTONE COBBLE

CHARCOAL or FLINT (labeled)

ROOT or RODENT INTRUSIONS

PURDOM MOUND 3-4

33 Gr 12

METERS

Profile of Mound 3/4 showing clay platform and subsequent fill.

THE DAYTON MUSEUM OF NATURAL HISTORY'S EXCAVATION OF MOUND 3/4

We decided to excavate this previously excavated mound and the area between it and Mound 1-2 to its west, as the Hutchisons' plans for developing this area for their home would have a heavy impact on this eastern end of the Purdom Mound Group. We hoped to establish whether this was the old Mound 3 that Adams had excavated in 1931, and to recover some charcoal samples for Carbon 14 dating.

The mound had been previously bisected by a trench which began on the north-east side of the mound and progressed south toward the center. As it approached the center of the mound the trench turned 90 degrees to the west. At the southwestern edge of the center of the mound it turned 90 degrees back to the south until it exited the mound on its southwest margin, at the edge of the plateau. Our work mirrored that of the previous excavators as we created new profiles to ascertain the construction of the mound and to establish where features/burials had been recovered by the original excavators. We hoped that as we re-excavated the east-west trench through the central area of the mound, we might establish sufficient traces of the old burial pits/platforms to say with certainty that this was the old Adams' Mound 3.

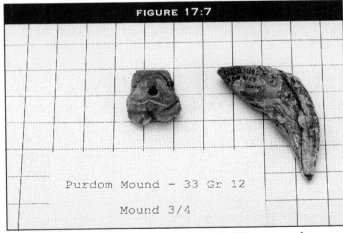

Purdom Mound - 33 Gr 12

Mound 3/4

Cut and drilled black bear molar and polished black bear canine from Mound 3/4, Burial 1/92.

Few features were encountered in this mound, although we did document where past excavators had been. In the east-west trench through the center of the mound we encountered fragments of human bone, some of which were in the backfill of the previously-excavated trench, and a few which were on the floor of the mound. Near the very center of their east-west trench in N80-E105 (the approximate area where Adams' Burial I was possibly interred - **Figure 17:6**) we did find a few bone fragments and a human tooth, which we designated as B1/92. In the area immediately above this burial we recovered a black bear (Ursus americanus) canine, with part of its root cut off (**Figure 17:7**). The canine, which is 2.7 cm across the cut root base, and 3.9 cm long, is cut and polished but not drilled. About 30 cm below B1/92, an upper right first molar of bear was recovered. It is 1.8 x 1.8 cm in size and has been severely modified. While its exterior or cheek surface has not been cut, virtually all other surfaces have been cut or ground. The molar was cut from the maxilla in such a manner that the interior surface of the tooth was sliced away, removing a portion of the enamel. This interior surface was ground flat, and the rear of the tooth was squared up. Parts of the maxilla still remain, and the tooth has been bifacially drilled with a heavily polished 1 cm boring. No other diagnostic Hopewell artifacts were recovered during the excavation of the burial or the remainder of the mound. While several charcoal concentrations were found, it could not be said with certainty that they were from the time of the Hopewellian building of the site, and may have originated from the Archaic-rich fill used in construction of the mound. Numerous fire-cracked rocks were found during the excavation, as well as Archaic points (Justice 1987).

The mound appears to have been constructed on a partially leveled surface that had been cut down to a yellow-brown clay, after the original humus was removed. Over this was an orange-red clay that was capped by a lighter red-orange clay. A rich humus developed on top of this clay cap. This sequence was frequently altered by rodent runs and the intrusion of hundreds of tree roots, plus the previous excavators' trenches (**Figure 17:6**). The only variant in this was the Hopewellian feature of limestone cobbles which was noted in square N79-E105. The heavy use of rotted limestone had also been noted on several occasions in the construction of Mound 1-2: as clusters of cobbles with no other association, as burial associations, and in the fill over the intrusive burial. In all instances these limestone cobbles were so rotted they left a chalky white residue on the hands.

In the fill of the excavated portion of Mound 3/4, 625 chert flakes were recovered. Of this number, 70 percent (n=438) appeared to be of local derivation. Of the non-local material (n=187), Flint Ridge was the most prevalent and accounted for 63 percent (n=118) of the "exotic" debitage recovered. Chert artifacts recovered from Mound 3/4 include scrapers and four projectile point fragments, all of which belong stylistically to the Archaic period (Justice 1987). There were no Hopewellian lithic artifacts recovered in the 1992 excavation of Mound 3/4.

THE LAND BETWEEN THE MOUNDS

The area between Mound 1-2 and Mound 3/4 was of particular interest to us, as historically, it had never been cultivated. An east-west line, linked with the grid on Mound 3/4, was our northern boundary at N80, and our southern-most squares were bounded by the N73 line. In this area, 22 one-meter squares were excavated arranged in a checker-board pattern (**Figure 17:3**). As this area is to be developed in the future as a home site for the landowners, it was dubbed the "House Site". All artifacts recovered from this area were kept separate from the objects recovered from Mound 3/4.

Since the 1989 excavation of the area to be impacted by the log cabin had revealed evidence of Hopewellian occupation in the form of a Flint Ridge bladelet and small grit-tempered cord-marked potsherds, we were hopeful of recovering evidence of Hopewell activity areas between the mounds. Excavation in the House area concentrated on the mid- to-southside area of the ridge, which the owners planned to develop. The north side of the ridge is bisected by an access road. No testing of this road was performed by the DMNH, as it was developed prior to our excavation of the mounds at Purdom.

We recovered few signs of the Hopewellian occupation from this area between the mounds. We did recover more Archaic artifacts, paralleling those taken from the 1989 trench and the mound fill. An Adena Leaf-Blade was recovered from a square just at the edge of the plateau. However, fire-cracked rock (FCR) and chert debris were the two most common varieties of objects recovered. Wood-snail shells were also noted in this area, although not in any abundance. No other type of shell was recovered from the House area.

One definite posthole was excavated in square N76-E91. The posthole was relatively small, 8 cm x 13 cm and only 9 cm deep, appearing first at 20 cm below datum, and bottoming out at 29 cm below datum. Two pieces of fire-cracked rock flanked the posthole, possibly as chinking, and there were several carbon chunks (in the 1-2.5 cm range) within and around the posthole. A limestone hammerstone was also recovered in proximity to the posthole.

The majority of occupation debris occurred between 10 and 20 cm below the surface. Waste flakes and fire-cracked rock were the most abundant artifacts recovered. Eight hundred sixty-eight waste chert flakes were analyzed, of which 61 percent (n=530) were of local derivation. Further analysis revealed that three squares in particular - N78-E85, N79-E86, and N80-E87 - accounted for over 30 percent (n=261) of all the chert debitage recovered from the House area (**Figure 17:3**). Additionally, they account for 34 percent (n=116) of all the non-local chert debitage recovered (n=338). Seventy percent (n=238) of all non-local chert recovered was of Flint Ridge derivation. The presence of "waste" chert flakes in such abundance and in three closely clustered squares points to the manufacture or re-working of tools in this area between the mounds.

Over 53 kg of FCR were removed from the twenty-two squares excavated in the House area. The majority of FCR was recovered from 10-20 cm below-surface level. Temporally recognizable artifacts taken from the House area were also recovered from this level (between 8 and 25 cm below surface). With the exception of scrapers which are demonstrably present in the artifact assemblages of many different time periods, all were Archaic (Justice 1987). A *McWhinney Stemmed* point base of local chert and a scraper fashioned from a broken *Kirk Corner-Notch* were only offset by the recovery of a black Upper Mercer bladelet.

The presence of Upper Mercer and other "exotic" chert types at the Purdom Mound Group were at their highest levels in the area between the mounds. Exotic chert material percentages ranged from nearly 21 percent (n=38) in the "log cabin" trench of 1989 to about 39 percent (n=338) in the "House" area. Decortication flakes were not well-represented in the assemblage from the House area, indicating that tool blanks were probably roughed-out at some other location, then transported to this area for final working. The appearance of black chert also took a decided up-swing in this area, accounting for over 10 percent (n=88) of all the chert debitage recovered in the House area in 1992. We cannot state conclusively that this cultural debris was made during a Hopewellian occupation. We can at least assert that this ridge overlooking the Little Miami River has been used since early Archaic times, and was later utilized by Hopewellian peoples to bury at least twenty of their dead.

SUMMARY: THE PURDOM MOUND GROUP AND ITS CARBON - 14 DATES

The Purdom Mound Group consisted of at least five mounds and possibly as many as seven. Mound 1-2 was excavated in 1931 by Robert McCormick Adams for Dr. Raymond Stites of Antioch College in Yellow Springs, Ohio. According to all conversations with residents in the area, what has been called Mound 1-2 was the largest of the mounds in this complex. While the Dayton Museum of Natural History curates many of the items recovered during the excavation by Adams, his original field notes, photographs, and most of his maps no longer seem to be extant. There are no records of Douglas Bailey's 1973 Wright State University Field School. It is interesting to note how little material was recovered from the area between the mounds on the Hutchison property that might relate to Hopewellian activities here. The only area where there was any concentration of material was that excavated by Chris Turnbow in 1989. In squares N73, N74, and N75-E49 (**Figure 17:3**), almost 100 sherds of Hopewellian ceramics were recovered as well as a single posthole. The area to the west and southwest of the log cabin would definitely merit further observation.

The authors feel that the three charcoal-derived 14C dates for Mound 1-2 are reasonable for the time of occupation of this mound complex. It is fascinating to note the presence of multiple types of mica (muscovite and biotite), both cut and in natural sheets; the drilled human mandible; the possible "bird effigy" zoned four-panel vessel; the large *Cassis* shell container; and the Indiana, and Flint Ridge chert materials. In light of the other imported items to this site it is intriguing that no copper has been recorded at Purdom.

The date on the bone collagen from the intrusive burial (B2/90) in Mound 1-2 is 300 years later than the dates for the construction of this mound. The soil that backfilled this intrusive burial was rich with rotted limestone cobbles, which made up at least 50 percent of the volume of the fill for this individual. This is a continuation of the extensive use of rotted limestone cobbles in association with burials and other features, suggesting that it at least had significance to the Hopewellian builders, even if it remains a mystery to us.

The significantly later intrusive burial suggests that this Ohio Hopewell complex continued to play a part in the Hopewell utilization of the valley for at least 300 years. It would be fascinating to know how many of these sites were maintained at any time. Over what period of time were the mounds being constructed at Purdom? Is Purdom the predecessor of Pollock Works, only to be abandoned as Pollock came into prominence?

ACKNOWLEDGMENTS

This paper would not be complete without extending special thanks to Mrs. Virginia Kettering and the Kettering Family Fund for making it possible for the Dayton Museum of Natural History to excavate these sites before they were rearranged, and to Joe and Jan Hutchison for their concern for the prehistoric works on their property. Thanks are also due to the Indian Advisory Committee members for their dedication and support of the DMNH's excavation at Purdom. Drs. Paul Sciulli and Myra Giesen of the Ohio State University volunteered their expertise in the non-invasive analysis of human remains. Chester Fannin and his bulldozing skills made possible the reconstruction of Mound 1-2. Dr. Robert Riordan kindly donated the Bailey Collection of artifacts from Purdom which were residing at Wright State University. Sandy Yee outdid herself by linking up all our 1 m profile maps into a coherent picture of the construction of Mounds 1-2 and 3/4. The Woodhull Corporation volunteered their time and skill to prepare the slides of Sandy Yee's maps. Dr. Gail Wagner of the University of South Carolina generously analyzed the float samples taken from the varve-like pit in Mound 1-2. Thanks are due to Holly Coovert for her accurate and attractive scale drawing of the reconstructed duck effigy vessel. Patterson Graphics, Inc. not only shot beautiful photographs of the artifacts from Purdom, but they developed them for us, too. Likewise, this work would not have been possible without all of the crew members and volunteers, who shared their muscles, brains, enthusiasm, and many special talents in the field, in the DMNH anthropology lab, and in the photographic studios. Special thanks to all of you who made this possible through your many contributions.

REFERENCES CITED

Adams, R. M. 1931a Antioch Student Tells Story of Mounds Found Near Xenia. *Dayton Daily News*, 21 November.

   1931b Museum Exhibition Reveals Culture of Mound Builders of this Vicinity. *Dayton Daily News*, 1 November.

Justice, N. D. 1987 *Stone Age Spear and Arrow Points of the Midcontinental and Eastern United States*. Indiana University Press, Bloomington.

Prufer, O. H. and D. H. McKenzie 1965 Ceramics. In *The McGraw Site: A Study in Hopewellian Dynamics*, by O. Prufer, Cleveland Museum of Natural History, Scientific Publications 4(1):16-57.

Vickery, K. D. 1983 The Flint Sources. In *Recent Excavations at the Edwin Harness Mound, Liberty Works, Ross County, Ohio*, edited by N.B. Greber, 73-85. Midcontinental Journal of Archaeology Special Paper No. 5. The Kent State University Press, Kent, Ohio.

SECTION TWO: THE PERIPHERY

EIGHTEEN

THE OHIO HOPEWELL CORE AND ITS MANY MARGINS: DECONSTRUCTING UPLAND AND HINTERLAND RELATIONS

MARK F. SEEMAN

ABSTRACT

Ohio Hopewell is a composition of many specific relationships of varying scope, intensity, and duration. As in all social exchanges, they were characterized by ambiguity, renegotiation, and unanticipated consequences. These themes will be explored by investigating Hopewell relations in the specific contexts of upland rockshelters and minor valleys.

A View From the Core a Synthesis of Ohio Hopewell Archaeology•edited by Paul J. Pacheco
© Copyright 1996 by The Ohio Archaeological Council• Columbus, Ohio
All Rights Reserved•ISBN 0-9626931-9-7

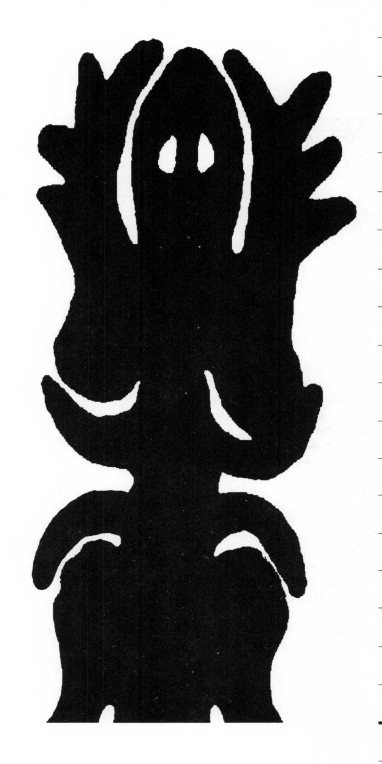

INTRODUCTION

The topic of this conference is a "view from the core". There is no reason to doubt that here, in Chillicothe, Ohio, we are situated within that core. All around us we see examples of unprecedented 2,000-year old "Hopewell" ceremonialism, involving elaborate ritual facilities, planned public monuments, various artifactual symbols, and evidence for long-distance encounters with Woodland societies throughout eastern North America. Here too, we have a model of regional settlement characterized by only modest population size, and by valley-based homesteads, clustered around integrating earthworks. These people exploited rich riverine resources, and practiced multi-crop agriculture (Smith 1992). In such "Ohio Hopewell" societies, we see a social complexity and an ideological commitment that is undeniable. Yet, if we look closer at this reconstruction, certain anomalies present themselves. Most fundamentally, and for purposes of this paper, it is clear that the Ohio Hopewell "core"—as either social or symbolic system— does not extend evenly across the Ohio region, and indeed, in some cases we may not have to go very far—perhaps to a mountain top, or into a secondary drainage, or across a river—to find that its limits are quite close at hand.

The distinctiveness of Ohio Hopewell has been recognized for many years. Originally, it was seen as a "mother culture" from which various concepts and beliefs emanated throughout eastern North America (e.g., Shetrone 1930). More recently, and with the growth of systems theory and ecological modeling, it is often regarded as one of several regional, and essentially equivalent, Middle Woodland complexes—bounded systems, often packaged in the tradition/phase systematics of Willey and Phillips (1958). Within Ohio Hopewell, it is common to see references to even more localized entities, for example, a *Hopewellian Phase* (Prufer 1965:18), a *Twin Mounds Phase* (Bennett 1986:214), or an *Esch Phase* (Stothers et al. 1979:55). This view has its limitations.

More specifically, the work of Hodder (1977, 1982), Wiessner (1983, 1990), DeBoer (1990), and others should cause us to question the utility of establishing and reifying "cultures" and

"phases"—the latter supposedly the archaeological analogue of historic societies and/or tribes (Willey and Phillips 1958:48-51, 53). Ethnoarchaeological observations suggest that many technological, social, and ideological relationships do not correspond with one another, nor with recognized political or ethnic boundaries; that "whether an artifact does or does not 'reflect' a particular type of interaction or information flow depends on how it comes to be used as part of the strategies and ideologies of particular groups" (Hodder 1982:85). Such ambiguities arise for the simple reason that social boundaries are negotiated, multi-faceted, and in no way "natural" (see Helms 1988; Waselkov 1989). They involve symbols and their meaning, and as such, are subject to constant manipulation, redefinition, and situational interpretation. In part, because of their own particular history, European archaeologists have been quicker to grasp this point; here we find comparatively less interest in taxonomy, and more in the careful examination of material culture in contexts of varying scope. Here too, such concepts as "diffusion", "migration" and "historical process" are not entirely shunned.

In sum, recent ethnoarchaeological studies permit the suggestion that both formal relationships and chance encounters within Ohio Hopewell must have transcended our typological "phase" constructions, while others never reached them at all. In order to further evaluate the implications of this premise, I would like to look at the seemingly different contexts of Hopewell involvement in extreme northeastern Ohio, and in upland rockshelters farther to the south. What these situations share is their seeming isolation—outward and upward—from developments at the Ohio Hopewell "core". What I hope to show is the differential scope and applicability of relationships commonly regarded as important in the interpretation of Ohio Hopewell.

"HINTERLAND OHIO HOPEWELL": THE YANT MOUND

The distribution of ceremonial centers in Ohio provides a useful starting point for examining Hopewell relations in the region. Undeniably, some sort(s) of ill-defined, "core" connections extended in Ohio southwest to Cincinnati, north to

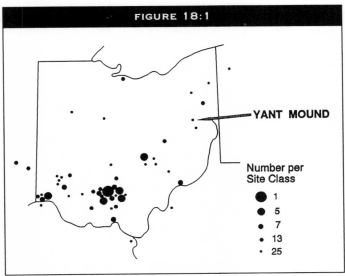

FIGURE 18:1

YANT MOUND

Number per
Site Class

● 1
● 5
· 7
· 13
· 25

Location of Yant Mound relative to other Ohio Hopewell ritual centers (site class data modified from Seeman 1979).

Circleville, east to Newark, and southeast to Marietta and Portsmouth. Throughout this region (ca. A.D. 1-A.D. 350), people were motivated to construct complex, similarly-styled earthwork enclosures. All across this area, I suspect that local lineages and their leaders were participating in local, regional, and interregional relationships of some complexity and importance (Braun 1987; Seeman 1995). However, within this area, and more especially as we move outward from it, inconsistencies of various sorts appear—clinal variation, selective involvement, and isolated participation. Thus, for example, at the eastern Indiana sites of Anderson and New Castle are found large "Ohio Hopewell" charnel structures and paired ceremonial floors, yet there is a lack of evidence for any associated "Ohio Hopewell" conspicuous consumption (Vickery 1979). To the northeast, "Ohio Hopewell" involvement along the Appalachian Plateau is even more ambiguous. Here small ceremonial sites exist, well-spaced along the stream valleys of the region. Their structure and content provide an important vantage point for examining the concept of a Hopewell core. A description of one such site, the Yant Mound, suffices for this paper.

The Yant Mound is located in southern Stark County, Ohio, on a low terrace of the Tuscarawas River (**Figure 18:1**). It was excavated in 1984 by local amateur archaeologists (Gramly et al. 1985). Although disturbed by plowing, it was composed of over three tons of sandstone slabs that had been dragged nearly a quarter of a mile. The slabs covered a prepared floor, which itself evidenced several subfloor pits and a central rock "altar". Few burials were represented. Artifacts consisted of 16 Flint Ridge bladelets, a mica sheet, several ground stone pestles, a celt, a copper panpipe, and a minimum of three ceramic vessels.

Several characteristics of this site are relevant to the discussion of Ohio Hopewell relations. First, the stone slabs, and the particular way they were used in construction, are part of a regional pattern in eastern Ohio (e.g., Magrath 1945). Second, the three pots from the site present an interesting, and eclectic combination. One is a small, limestone tempered, vertically cordmarked Watson Ware jar appropriate for the period, but more characteristic of drainages to the east. The second is a unique grit tempered, polished bowl with a thick, folded rim strip extending down the vessel wall about 10 cm. The third vessel is a zoned incised, grit tempered pot (**Figure 18:2**). The rim has been decorated with several bands of hemiconical punctates that are zoned from the neck by a poorly executed incised line. The body is divided into a series of geometric zones, some of which are filled with fine-line cordmarking and punctations. This is a poor local copy of Hopewell ware—not just poor in execution, but poor in replicating the pattern of decoration that is present at the "core" 120 km to the south. Ceramically, these vessels do not belong to three different phases, and despite their differences, there is no reason to suggest that they are anything other than local products.

In contrast to the ceramics, the bladelets recovered from the Yant Mound adhere to a narrow range of technological and stylistic conventions that make their identification with Ohio Hopewell quite clear (Greber et al. 1981). Thirteen of these were struck from a single core, and were found in a column of ashy fill extending below the floor. Regional surveys here in the hinterlands do occasionally identify bladelets and corner-

FIGURE 18:2

0 | | | | | 5
C M

Zoned Incised jar fragments, Yant Mound, Stark County, Ohio.

notched projectile points—generally of Flint Ridge flint—that indicate the existence of either a regular mechanism of supply, or the existence of other social conventions tied directly to the core (see Thomas 1986). Similar light densities of Hopewell lithic materials can be found all across northern Ohio, and northward into Ontario (Spence et al. 1990; Stothers et al. 1979).

Were the people that produced the Yant Mound participating in Ohio Hopewell? The available evidence suggests that many of the economic adaptations and social interactions of these Stark County folk were quite distinctive from those documented farther to the south. It suggests that they were largely outside the range of some "Hopewell" social and symbolic relationships, and yet at certain times, demonstrably well within the range of others. In fact, this sort of shifting and differential participation characterizes many of the drainages that are often viewed as "peripheral" to Ohio Hopewell (e.g., Adovasio et al. 1982; George 1992; Hemmings 1984; Vickery 1979). The Yant Mound data suggest that the boundaries or edges of a Hopewell "core" are more indistinct than our current conceptual schemes might imply.

UPLAND HOPEWELL: A ROCKSHELTER SUMMARY

The second portion of this paper focuses on data derived from upland rockshelters. Although the available evidence shows that southern Ohio Hopewell economies were focused on the grown-and-gathered resources of the major river valleys, it should not be forgotten that the bulk of the region is actually dissected, rugged country. In Ross County, for example, it is possible to climb more than 170 m in less than 600 meters. It can be assumed, therefore, that any Hopewell use of upland resources carried different scheduling and logistical considerations than in the lowlands. For these reasons, the kinds of Hopewell social and symbolic relationships that would have characterized the hilly uplands should once again contrast with current characterizations of the lowland "core".

For purposes of this paper, Ohio Hopewell rockshelter usage will serve as a measure of upland activity, although other types of upland Hopewell sites have been reported in the literature (e.g., Brown 1982; Carskadden and Morton n.d.; Smith 1985). Rockshelters, because they are fixed locations in space, and provide cheap shelter and dry fuel, tend to be utilized recurrently (Hall and Klippel 1988). Ohio area rockshelters have been investigated extensively, and have been interpreted variously as travel stops, hunting camps, permanent villages, ritual centers, barns...and even hideouts for horse thieves (e.g., Adovasio et al. 1982:177; Dragoo 1959:147; Prufer 1967, 1981; see also, Binford 1978:489-490; Flannery 1986). Rockshelter site formation is complex, and subject to a broad suite of cultural and natural processes that are beyond the specific scope of this study (see Brush 1990; Gremillion 1993:162; Klippel et al. 1987; Murphy 1975:310).

In the Ohio area, there is a long history of rockshelter investigation (e.g., Andrews 1877; Mercer 1896). The major issue that has characterized this work is that of upland-lowland relations. As early as 1905, William Mills excavated three Jackson County shelters in order to determine if they where occupied permanently, or if they were the temporary camps of people living elsewhere. He concluded that because of an absence of ornaments, the presence of only small quantities of pottery, and the fact that there were many bones present that could have been but were not used to make tools, that these sites were temporary camping stops (Mills 1912). It also should be noted that outside the Boone shelter, he found a few sherds of classic *Hopewellian Series* and *Southeastern Series* pottery.

In 1926 and 1927 Goslin and Shetrone re-investigated Ash Cave, and also worked in Kettle Hill Cave and Canter's Caves, where they found a number of uncarbonized, organic materials (Shetrone 1928). In contrast to Mills, they viewed these remains as those of a distinct "Rockshelter Culture" inhabiting the hinterlands of the Ohio Valley, a view later echoed in McMichael's (1968) interpretation of the Buck Garden Culture of West Virginia, and Prufer and Shane's (1970) of southern Ohio Late Woodland. Similarly, Cowan (1985:238-239) concluded that the rockshelters of eastern Kentucky were not seasonal encampments of the "Adena People" of the Bluegrass region, but rather, were sites in

locally-based settlement systems. This developing perspective of a distinct, rockshelter-using, upland-adapted, "hill folk" is important, and to some degree, supported by models of contemporary cultural dynamics in the region—at least prior to the easy availability of satellite dishes!

For purposes of the present study I have examined data from twelve Ohio area shelters (**Figure 18:3**). Collections from ten of these were available for direct study—White Rocks (Ormerod 1983), Dunham (Brush 1990), Eppley (Brush 1990), Knight Hollow (Felumlee 1983), Merry's Cave, Wheelabout (McKenzie n.d.), Chesser (Prufer 1967), Peters (Prufer and McKenzie 1966), Wise (Oplinger 1981), and Stanhope (Grunwald 1980). I also have included data on two others, Brady's Run (Church 1990) and Meadowcroft (Carlisle and Adovasio 1982), that are well described in the literature. These sites cover a fair amount of distance, and occur both in the "core" region and outside. In conjunction with recording information on Hopewell occupation, similar information on the preceding Early Woodland period also was collected for comparative purposes.

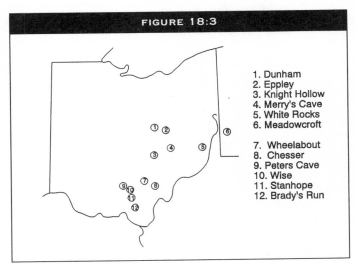

Selected rockshelter sites.

Sites in the sample vary considerably in size, but not in depth; with the exception of Meadowcroft where deposits reached depths of 3.2 m, the shelters in the study contained on average about a meter of accumulated fill. An investigation of artifact proveniences indicate that nine of the twelve sites are thoroughly mixed. Of the remaining three, Meadowcroft, White Rocks, and Merry's Cave show perceptible stylistic trends from top to bottom, but only Merry's Cave and Meadowcroft provide good geomorphological evidence of stratigraphic development (Carlisle and Adovasio 1982; Jeffery Carskadden, personal communication, 1993).

A total of 63 diagnostic Middle Woodland artifacts—mainly projectile points and bladelets—were recovered from the rockshelter sample (**Figure 18:4, Table 18:1**) . The majority of the points and nearly all of the bladelets were made of Flint Ridge flint. The ratio of projectile points to bladelets is considerably different than at habitation sites like McGraw or Murphy, where bladelets predominate. In the sample, only one site, Knight Hollow, yielded any diagnostic Middle Woodland pottery. Two vessels are represented—a small, thin, grit tempered, and finely executed *Turner Simple Stamped* pot, and a *McGraw Plain* rim. There is the possibility of a few more sherds at Stanhope, but they were much smaller than 4 cm, and thus difficult to type.

The rarity of recognizable Ohio Hopewell ceramics in these rockshelters is clear and consistent with the view that upland activities did not require much pottery. It is true that some of the later, flared-rim varieties of the Early Woodland type, *Adena Plain*, especially if they lack the "diagnostic" thickened rim, can be confused with *McGraw Plain*. On more solid ground, none of the varied rim forms, vessel shapes, and cordmarked vessels with smoothed necks that characterize sites such as McGraw, Twin Mounds Village, or Whitacre are present. Based on the present sample, there is not much Hopewell pottery in the rockshelters of southern Ohio.

A rank-ordering of the relative strength of the Middle Woodland components in the sample suggests three points. First, there is no apparent relationship between the relative strength of these components and shelter size; this suggests that

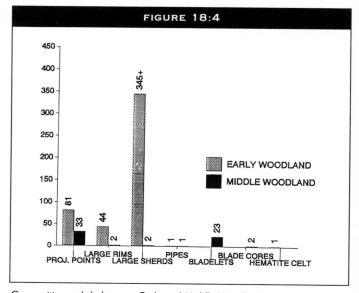

Comparitive rockshelter use, Early and Middle Woodland periods.

group size and/or the range of activities was sufficiently small that floor area was not a relevant consideration. Second, there is no obvious falloff in incidence with distance from the "core". For example, Dunham, White Rocks, and Eppley, sites that are in all cases at least several days travel time from Chilicothe or Newark, contained some of the strongest Hopewell components. This type of pattern certainly contrasts with the previously presented data on Yant Mound ceremonialism, and its inferred relationships to the Ohio Hopewell "core." Finally, it should be noted that Knight Hollow, the highest ranking component, is on a direct route and only about 11 km from Flint Ridge; it thus may relate to some type of specialized exploitation associated with this locality.

Middle Woodland activity in Ohio rockshelters was limited. To bring this into clearer focus, it is useful to compare the results of Middle Woodland usage with that of the preceding Early Woodland period. Early Woodland utilization is more intensive by any measure. Diagnostic projectile points are more than twice as frequent, and rim sherds are more than twenty times as frequent. Every site in the sample produced some Early Woodland material, and at some sites, notably Merry's

TABLE 18:1											
	Floor Area (m²)	Projectile Points		Large Rims ***		Large Body Sherds		Pipes		Bladelets	Blade Cores	Hematite Celts
		EW	MW	EW	MW	EW	MW	EW	MW	MW	MW	EW
1. Dunham	20	9	7	7	0	8	0	1	1	2	0	0
2. Eppley	80	16	6	9	0	200+	0	0	0	1	0	0
3. Knight Hollow	50	2	4	2	2	1+	2	0	0	6	1	0
4. Merry's Cave	140	18	1	6	0	51	0	0	0	2	1	0
5. White Rocks	380 *	0	6	1	0	0	0	0	0	4	0	0
6. Meadowcroft	80	4	0	0	0	Ind	Ind	0	0	0	0	0
7. Wheelabout	390	8	4	3	0	6	0	0	0	0	0	0
8. Chesser	330	7	1	1	0	12	0	0	0	1	0	1
9. Peters Cave	160	5	1	7	0	27	0	0	0	0	0	0
10. Wise	40	2	0	0	0	7	0	0	0	0	0	0
11. Stanhope	110	8	3	8	0	33	0	0	0	7	0	0
12. Brady's Bun	70 **	2	0	Ind	0	Ind	0	0	0	0	0	0
Totals		81	33	44	2	345+	2	1	1	23	2	1

* Approximately half excavated

** Approximately one-third excavated

*** Large = 4 cm +

Early Woodland types *Buck Creek Barbed* (N=6) & *Fulton Turkey-tail* (N=1) excluded from tabulation

Comparative Ohio rockshelter data

Cave and Brady's Run, the Early Woodland component is the dominant component at the site. Neither can be said for Hopewell rockshelter usage.

A rank-ordering of the Early Woodland sites reveal several patterns. Like Hopewell, occupation strength shows no regular relationship to shelter size. Unlike Hopewell, there are modest quantities of large rim and body sherds. A few of these are *Half Moon Cordmarked*, but the majority are plain surfaced, and relate to the types *Dominion Thick*, *Peters Plain*, and *Adena Plain*. Although a few of these shelters obviously are utilized late in the Early Woodland period—notably the upper strata at Merry's Cave—the impression is that much of the material in these shelters is somewhat earlier in the period. Also quite unlike Hopewell, there is a correspondence between the relative number of Early Woodland projectile points and the number of Early Woodland sherds at sites in the sample.

The Early Woodland projectile points in the sample require some additional discussion. Although many fit well into the defined types of *Adena Stemmed* and *Robbins Stemmed*, many do not; they are more "square-stemmed" than might be expected for Adena points, and sometimes exhibit moderately broad blades. I suspect such points may be fairly early in the Early Woodland period, and carry mixed attributes of the *Adena*, *Dickson*, and *Wade* clusters.

Another pattern relates to the size of the Early Woodland pots represented. Not only are they thick, but based on orifice diameter, they are large. A comparison of the 28 largest rims (all lips = 5+ cm) with the only good sample of later Woodland orifice data from the area—in this case Bennett's (1986) study of the Hopewell pottery from Miami Fort village—clearly shows a pattern of size reduction from Early to Middle Woodland times (**Figure 18:5**). Elsewhere, various authors have commented on the suitability of thick, Early Woodland wares for nut processing—a commodity certainly available in the uplands of southern Ohio (e.g., Ozker 1977). In sum, these data suggest a shift in vessel size (and shape) that goes beyond stylistic fancy.

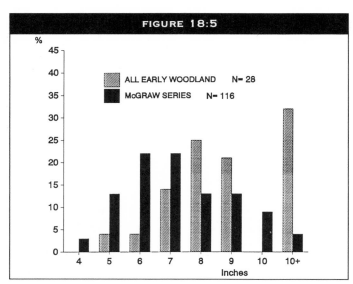

FIGURE 18:5

%

45 —
40 —
              ALL EARLY WOODLAND   N= 28
35 —
              McGRAW SERIES   N= 116
30 —
25 —
20 —
15 —
10 —
5 —
0 —

    4   5   6   7   8   9   10   10+

Inches

Early and Middle Woodland pottery, comparison of orifice diameters (McGraw Series data from Bennett 1986).

CONCLUSION

The notion of "core" implies edge or "periphery." In this study I have tried to show that several, only partially overlapping peripheries bear distinctive relationships to the Hopewell core. On the one hand, the Yant Mound in northeastern Ohio and its surrounding context suggests a selective involvement in those social and ideological relationships we identify with Ohio Hopewell. Flint Ridge bladelets are there, and both bladelets and catholic Flint Ridge flint "Hopewell" projectile points are found in the vicinity—yet the characteristics of local ceremonialism seem to bear mixed and poorly connected relationships to the south. I would resist calling the Yant site "reluctant" or "marginal", because such characterizations can mask a diversity of relationships of varying strength and reach. A lack of participation can not be used to infer simplicity, or vice versa. Active resistance and/or the presence of viable personal or local alternatives, for example, also are perfectly possible. The latter should not be confused with archaeological explanations that rely on the presence of "unknown" peoples to fill geographic voids where the evidence for Hopewell is scant (see Kinglsey 1981:157-163).

Based on a limited sample, Hopewell utilization of upland rock-shelters seems to be very similar across Ohio, regardless of proximity to the "core". Compared with Early Woodland, there is a marked decrease in the utilization—but not an abandonment—of the uplands. Such patterns are consistent with increased sedentism and settlement pattern simplification, the concentration of settlement in a few high-yield environmental localities, or both. In this article, however, I am less concerned with the notion of relative "abandonment" and more with the apparently broad pattern of similar usage within and without the Ohio Hopewell "core," and with the difference of this pattern from that posed by the seeming clinal variation suggested by some aspects of northeastern Ohio ceremonialism. In short, there is little correspondence.

What was Ohio Hopewell? I believe that to answer that ultimate question we must move somewhat away from a phase-constricted approach, and more toward the perspectives now developing in European, and especially British, archaeology. Much of this fits in the "post-processual" arena. I am not suggesting, however, that we all sit down in a circle and speculate about the "meaning" of Hopewell. We need to focus less on creating apparently integrated cultural systems, as implied by the notions of "phase" or "core", and more on context. I also think that large-scale distributional studies of basic diagnostics—if appropriately structured—will provide useful new perspectives, especially at a time when the development of massive, comparative data bases are possible for cooperating scholars. Such studies characterize European archaeology much more strongly than they do those in the Ohio Valley. In short, it is time for deconstruction to become a more significant part of Hopewell studies. By deconstruction, I mean more careful attention to the analysis and comparison of fairly specific patterns or contexts, rather than focusing on the description of hypothetical "tribal" systems.

ACKNOWLEDGMENTS

I would like to thank Nigel Brush, David Bush, Jeff Carskadden, Flora Church, Larry Morris, Charles Niquette, and Olaf Prufer for helping me with this study. Any errors are my responsibility.

REFERENCES CITED

Adovasio, J. M., R. C. Carlisle, W. C. Johnson, P. T. Fitzgibbons, J. D. Applegarth, J. Donahue, R. Drennan, and J. L. Yedlowski
1982 *The Prehistory of the Paintsville Reservoir, Johnson and Morgan Counties, Kentucky.* University of Pittsburgh, Ethnology Monographs No. 6, Pittsburgh.

Andrews, E. B. 1877 Report on Exploration of Ash Cave in Benton Township, Hocking County, Ohio. *Peabody Museum of American Archaeology and Ethnology, 10th Annual Report of the Trustees* 2:48-50.

Bennett, R. H. 1986 *The Twin Mounds Village and Hopewell in Southwestern Ohio: A Ceramic Identity Crisis.* Masters thesis, Department of Anthropology, University of Cincinnati.

Binford, L. R. 1978 *Nunamuit Ethnoarchaeology.* Academic Press, New York.

Braun, D. P. 1987 Coevolution of Sedentism, Pottery Technology, and Horticulture in the Central Midwest, 200 B.C.-A.D. 600. In *Emergent Horticultural Economies of the Eastern Woodlands* edited by W. Keegan, pp. 153-181. Center for Archaeological Research, Occasional Paper 7, Southern Illinois University, Carbondale.

Brown, J. D. 1982 *Archaeological Reconnaissance of Corps of Engineers Dams in the Muskingum River Basin.* Report on file, Corps of Engineers, Huntington District, Huntington, West Virginia.

Brush, N. R. 1990 *Developing an "Archaeology of Place": A Debitage Analysis of Rockshelter Utilization in the Lower Killbuck Valley of Holmes and Coshocton Counties, Ohio.* Ph.D. dissertation, Department of Anthropology, University of Southern California, Los Angeles. University Microfilms, Ann Arbor.

Carlisle, R. C., and J. M. Adovasio, editors 1982 *Meadowcroft: Collected Papers on the Archaeology of Meadowcroft Rockshelter and the Cross Creek Drainage.* Report on file, Department of Anthropology, University of Pittsburgh.

Carskadden, J., and J. Morton n.d. Living on the Edge: A Comparison of Adena and Hopewell Communities in the Central Muskingum Valley of Eastern Ohio. In *Ohio Hopewell Community Organization*, edited by W. S. Dancey and P. J. Pacheco. Kent State University Press, Kent, Ohio "in press."

Church, F. 1990 *Mitigation of the Brady Run Rockshelter 3: A Multi-Component Site in Washington Township, Lawrence County, Ohio.* Report on file, Ohio Historic Preservation Office, Columbus, Ohio.

Cowan, C. W. 1985 *From Foraging to Incipient Food Production: Subsistence Change and Continuity on the Cumberland Plateau of Eastern Kentucky.* Ph.D. dissertation, Department of Anthropology, University of Michigan, Ann Arbor. University Microfilms, Ann Arbor.

DeBoer, W. R. 1990 Interaction, Imitation, and Communication as Expressed in Style: the Ucayali Experience. In *The Uses of Style in Archaeology*, edited by M. Conkey and C. Hastorf, pp. 82-104. Cambridge University Press, Cambridge.

Dragoo, D. W. 1959 Archaic Hunters of the Upper Ohio Valley. *Annals of the Carnegie Museum, Anthropological Series* 3:139-246.

Felumlee, G. 1983 Report on the Knight Hollow Rockshelter. *Ohio Archaeologist* 33(4):22-28.

Flannery, K. V. 1986 *Guila Naquitz: Archaic Foraging and Early Archaic Agriculture in Oaxacan Mexico.* Academic Press, Orlando.

George, R. L. 1992 The Middle Woodland Occupation of the Sewickley Creek-Youghiogheny River Area and the Hopewell Interaction Sphere. *Pennsylvania Archaeologist* 62(2):1-44.

Gramly, R. M., E. Richards, and D. Lehberger 1985 Excavations at the Yant Mound, Stark County, Northeastern Ohio. *Ohio Archaeologist* 35(2):13-16.

Greber, N.B., R. S. Davis, and A. S. DuFresne 1981 The Micro Component of the Ohio Hopewell Lithic Technology: Bladelets. In *The Research Potential of Anthropological Museum Collections*, edited by A. Cantwell, J. Griffin, and N. Rothschild, pp. 489-528. Annals of the New York Academy of Sciences 376, New York.

Gremillion, K. J. 1993 Plant Husbandry at the Archaic/Woodland Transition: Evidence from the Cold Oak Shelter, Kentucky. *Midcontinental Journal of Archaeology* 18:161-189.

Grunwald, R. R. 1980 *Stanhope Cave: A Late Woodland Occupation in Jackson County, Ohio.* Master's thesis, Department of Sociology and Anthropology, Kent State University. Kent, Ohio.

Hall, C. L., and W. E. Klippel 1988 A Polythetic-Satisfier Approach to Prehistoric Natural Shelter Selection in Middle Tennessee. *Midcontinental Journal of Archaeology* 13:159-186.

Helms, M. W. 1988 *Ulysses' Sail: An Ethnographic Odyssey of Power, Knowledge, and Geographical Distance.* Princeton University Press, Princeton.

Hemmings, E. T. 1984 The Fairchance Mound and Village: An Early Middle Woodland Settlement in the Upper Ohio Valley. *West Virginia Archeologist* 36:3-51.

Hodder, I. 1977 Some New Directions in the Spatial Analysis of Archaeological Data at the Regional Scale (Macro). In *Spatial Archaeology,* edited by D. L. Clarke, pp. 223-351. Academic Press, New York.

    1982 *Symbols in Action.* Cambridge University Press, Cambridge.

Kingsley, R. G. 1981 Hopewell Middle Woodland Settlement Systems and Cultural Dynamics in Southern Michigan. *Midcontinental Journal of Archaeology* 6:131-178.

Klippel, W. E., L. M. Snyder, and P. W. Parmalee 1987 Taphonomy and Archaeologically Recovered Mammal Bone from Southeast Missouri. *Journal of Ethnobiology* 7(2):155-169.

Magrath, W.H. 1945 The North Benton Mound: A Hopewell Site in Ohio. *American Antiquity* 11:40-46.

McKenzie, D. H. n.d. *Wheelabout Cave: A Woodland Rockshelter in Vinton County, Ohio.* Report on file, Department of Anthropology, Kent State University, Kent, Ohio.

McMichael, E. V. 1968 *Introduction to West Virginia Archeology* (2nd edition). West Virginia Geological and Economic Survey, Morgantown.

Mercer, H. C. 1896 Cave Explorations in the Eastern United States in 1894. *American Antiquarian* 18(2):82-86.

Mills, W. C. 1912 Archaeological Remains of Jackson County. *Ohio Archaeological and Historical Society Publications* 21:175-214.

Murphy, J. L. 1975 *An Archeological History of the Hocking Valley.* Ohio University Press, Athens.

Oplinger, J. 1981 *Wise Rockshelter: A Multicomponent Site in Jackson County, Ohio.* Kent State Research Papers in Archaeology, No. 2, Kent, Ohio.

Ormerod, D. E. 1983 *White Rocks: A Woodland Rockshelter in Monroe County, Ohio.* Kent State Research Papers in Archaeology, No. 4, Kent, Ohio.

Ozker, D. B. 1977 *An Early Woodland Community at the Schultz Site 20SA2 in the Saginaw Valley and the Nature of the Early Woodland Adaptation in the Great Lakes Region.* Ph.D. dissertation, Department of Anthropology, University of Michigan, Ann Arbor. University Microfilms, Ann Arbor.

Prufer, O. H. 1965 *The McGraw Site: A Study in Hopewellian Dynamics.* Cleveland Museum of Natural History, Scientific Publications 4(1), Cleveland.

    1967 Chesser Cave: A Late Woodland Phase in Southeastern Ohio. In *Studies in Ohio Archaeology,* edited by O. Prufer and D. McKenzie, pp. 267-328. The Press of Western Reserve University, Cleveland.

1981 *Raven Rocks: A Specialized Late Woodland Rockshelter Occupation in Belmont County, Ohio.* Kent State Research Papers in Archaeology, No. 1, Kent, Ohio.

Prufer, O. H., and D. H. McKenzie 1966 Peters Cave: Two Woodland Occupations in Ross County, Ohio. *Ohio Journal of Science* 66:233-253.

Prufer, O. H., and O. C. Shane, III 1970 *Blain Village and the Fort Ancient Tradition in Ohio.* Kent State University Press, Kent, Ohio.

Seeman, M. F. 1979 *The Hopewell Interaction Sphere: The Evidence for Interregional Trade and Structural Complexity.* Indiana Historical Society, Prehistory Research Series 5(2), Indianapolis.

1995 When Words Are Not Enough: Hopewell Interregionalism and the Use of Material Symbols at the GE Mound. In *Native American Interactions: Multiscalar Analyses and Interpretations in the Eastern Woodlands,* edited by M. Nassaney and K. Sassaman. University of Tennessee Press, Knoxville "in press."

Shetrone, H. C. 1928 Some Ohio Caves and Rockshelters Bearing Evidence of Human Occupancy. *Ohio Archaeological and Historical Society Quarterly* 37:1-34.

1930 *The Mound Builders.* D. Appleton and Co., New York.

Smith, B. D. 1985 *Chenopodium Berlandieri* ssp. *Jonesianum:* Evidence for a Hopewellian Domesticate from Ash Cave, Ohio. *Southeastern Archaeology* 4:107-133.

1992 *Rivers of Change.* Smithsonian Institution Press, Washington, D.C.

Spence, M. W., R. H. Pihl, and C. R. Murphy 1990 Cultural Complexes of the Early and Middle Woodland Periods. In *The Archaeology of Southern Ontario to A.D. 1650.* Occasional Publication of the London Chapter, OAS Number 5, London, Ontario.

Stothers, D. M., G. M. Pratt, and O. C. Shane, III 1979 The Western Basin Middle Woodland: Non-Hopewellians in a Hopewellian World. In *Hopewell Archaeology: The Chillicothe Conference,* edited by D. Brose and N. Greber, pp. 47-58. Kent State University Press, Kent, Ohio.

Thomas, J. E. 1986 *An Archaeological Reconnaissance Survey in Portions of Jackson, Lake, and Plain Townships of Stark County, Ohio.* Report on file, Ohio Historic Preservation Office, Columbus, Ohio.

Vickery, K. D. 1979 "Reluctant" or "Avant-Garde" Hopewell? Suggestions of Middle Woodland Culture Change in East-central Indiana and South-central Ohio. In *Hopewell Archaeology: The Chillicothe Conference,* edited by D.S. Brose and N.B. Greber, pp. 59-63. Kent State University Press, Kent, Ohio.

Waselkov, G. 1989 Indian Maps of the Colonial Southeast. In *Powhatan's Mantle: Indians in the Colonial Southeast,* edited by P. Wood, G. Waselkov, and M. Hatley, pp. 292-343. University of Nebraska, Lincoln.

Wiessner, P. 1983 Style and Social Information in Kalahari San Projectile Points. *American Antiquity* 48:253-276.

1990 Is There A Unity to Style? In *The Uses of Style in Archaeology,* edited by M. Conkey and C. Hastorf, pp. 105-121. Cambridge University Press, Cambridge.

Willey, G. R., and P. Phillips 1958 *Method and Theory in American Archaeology.* University of Chicago Press, Chicago.

NINETEEN

THE MIDDLE WOODLAND - LATE WOODLAND TRANSITION IN THE CENTRAL MUSKINGUM VALLEY OF EASTERN OHIO: A VIEW FROM THE PHILO ARCHAEOLOGICAL DISTRICT

JEFF CARSKADDEN AND JAMES MORTON

ABSTRACT

The paper discusses changes in settlement patterns and mortuary practices occurring in a prehistoric community located along the Muskingum River in southern Muskingum County, eastern Ohio, during the period ca. A.D. 200-600. Settlement changes included the shift from hamlets to nucleated villages, and the occurrence of various improvements in village defense once nucleation had occurred. Changes in burial mode and mound construction included 1) possible cremations associated with earth covered clay platforms, 2) cremations associated with stone covered clay platforms, and finally 3) extended burials in stone covered stone box graves.

A View From the Core a Synthesis of Ohio Hopewell Archaeology•edited by Paul J. Pacheco
© Copyright 1996 by The Ohio Archaeological Council• Columbus, Ohio
All Rights Reserved•ISBN 0-9626931-9-7

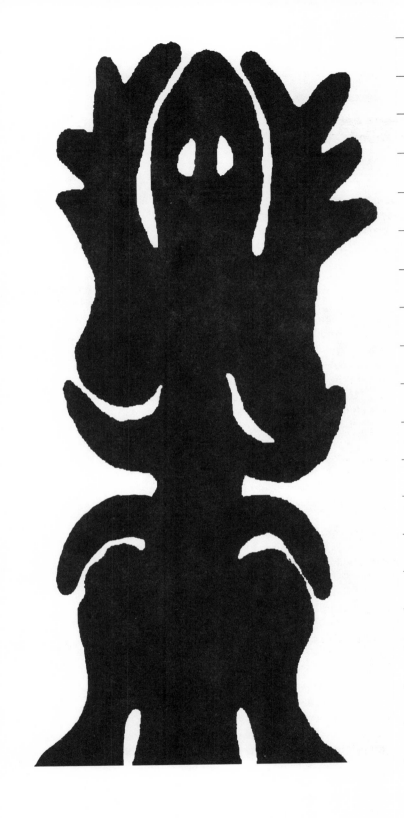

JEFF CARSKADDEN AND JAMES MORTON

THE MIDDLE WOODLAND - LATE WOODLAND TRANSITION IN THE CENTRAL MUSKINGUM VALLEY

INTRODUCTION

The Philo Archaeological District encompasses a 4 km stretch of bottoms and bordering ridge tops along the west side of the Muskingum River in Harrison Township, southern Muskingum County, eastern Ohio (**see Figure 19:1**). The river bottoms at Philo were continuously occupied from early Adena through Late Woodland and Fort Ancient, and as a result this is archaeologically one of the richest and, since the mid 1970s, the most extensively studied area in eastern Ohio. Among the more well known sites in the Philo Archaeological District include the 13th-century Fort Ancient Philo I, Philo II, and Richards sites, the protohistoric Bosman site, and relevant to this present study, a group of five early Late Woodland mounds known as the Philo Mound Group.

Recently excavated and previously unpublished sites in the Philo Archaeological District also relevant to this present discussion include the Tysinger site, a Hopewell hamlet excavated in 1993, the Linn 2 Site, a Hopewell logistical site also excavated in 1993 (Pacheco 1994), the Philo II "Lower Village", an early Late Woodland nucleated village partially excavated 1992-1993, and the early Late Woodland Black Dog Mound and Henderson Mounds 1 and 2, excavated in 1991.

In this paper we will first discuss the variety of settlement types found in the Philo Archaeological District that are believed to date between ca. A.D. 200 and ca. A.D. 600. These sites range from classic Hopewell hamlets to unfortified nucleated villages, and finally to nucleated villages fortified with wooden stockades and earthen embankments. The earth-walled village is believed to be the latest in the sequence. All of these sites are within 2 km of each other and presumably were inhabited by the same group of people. This local population was participating in a larger pattern of settlement change that was going on during this same period throughout much of the Muskingum Valley and elsewhere around the periphery of the Ohio Hopewell core area (e.g., Dancey 1992; Railey 1991).

Map of eastern Ohio showing the Muskingum River and the location of the Philo Archaeological District.

Also discussed in this paper are the mortuary practices and a possible sequence of burial mound construction during this same period, with emphasis on three previously unpublished mound excavations at Philo. We will also include comments on the diagnostic artifact traits recovered from the mounds and habitation sites, and contrast them with classic Hopewell material found elsewhere in the Muskingum Valley.

THE MUSKINGUM RIVER SETTING

The Muskingum River forms at Coshocton, at the juncture of the Tuscarawas and Walhonding Rivers. The Muskingum then follows a somewhat circuitous course southward for approximately 178 km through four Ohio counties (Coshocton, Muskingum, Morgan, and Washington), finally entering the Ohio River at Marietta. The entire course of the river is through the rugged unglaciated portion of the Allegheny Plateau physiographic province, which encompasses much of eastern and southeastern Ohio.

The river bottoms are widest in Coshocton and northern Muskingum counties, where the present-day Muskingum follows the abandoned 3.2 km wide channel of the pre-Illinoian Deep Stage "Newark River" (part of the Teays drainage system). At Dresden the modern river abruptly leaves the old Teays Valley and begins its southward course. The bottoms rarely reach more than .8 km in width below Dresden, and steep hills and occasionally cliffs border the river bottoms along much of the river's course to Marietta.

The Philo Archaeological District is located between river miles 63 and 66. The bottoms here reach a maximum of .5 km width. Illinoian and Late Wisconsinan terrace remnants can be found at the south end of these bottoms, and these features will become important later in the discussion. The otherwise low relief of the bottoms is broken by a .8 km long 2.1 m deep north-south running swale at the northern end. Prehistoric habitation sites can be found at various locations along either side of this swale, and immediately along the river. The mounds are situated on the 76 to 91 m high ridge tops overlooking the bottoms.

At the time of the first Euroamerican settlement (ca. A.D. 1800) the valley floor supported beech forests along the Muskingum River below Philo, and the bordering uplands were covered by mixed oak forests (Gordon 1966). Analysis of floral and faunal remains from the Philo II, Richards, and Bosman sites, however, indicate the presence of semi-open forest zones or old clearings in the bottoms. These could have resulted from Late Prehistoric agricultural

activities (Ericksen 1993; Murphy 1977; Shane and Barber 1976). Brush Creek chert outcrops occur in a ravine just 5.5 km down the Muskingum River from the Philo Archaeological District (Opossum Hollow at Eagleport) and river pebble chert was also readily available in the outwash gravels along the Muskingum in the Philo area. Artifacts of Flint Ridge chert, however, comprise the bulk of the sample from all of the sites discussed below.

SETTLEMENTS

In the pages that follow we will discuss the examples of the various types of habitation sites found in the Philo Archaeological District for the period under study. We will present them in the order that we believe the evidence suggests they occurred, starting with the Hopewell occupation.

STAGE 1: CLASSIC HOPEWELL HAMLETS

Hopewell settlements along the upper Muskingum River, in the nearby Licking Valley, and in southern Ohio generally have been characterized as dispersed clusters of sedentary farmsteads or hamlets, usually occurring in the vicinity of earthwork complexes (Pacheco 1989, 1993). It is probably not a coincidence that what is believed to be the densest concentration of Hopewellian habitation sites along the Muskingum River (outside the Marietta area) can be found in the upper portion of the valley between Dresden and Coshocton, where the bottoms are the widest. These Hopewell habitations along the upper Muskingum are associated with two large circular earthworks, one at Dresden in northern Muskingum County and the other just below Coshocton (Carskadden and Morton 1986, n.d.a.). Various researchers have pointed out the correlation between wide bottoms and the occurrence of Hopewell habitations and earthwork complexes along the Scioto (Seeman 1979) and elsewhere (Struever 1964).

TABLE 19:1

Site	Location	Component	Raw Date	Calibrated Date	Sample #	Reference
Triangle Site	Muskingum Co.	Intrusive Mound	A.D. 640 ± 80	A.D. 677	I-14819	Carskadden & Morton 1989
Triangle Site	Muskingum Co.	Intrusive Mound	A.D. 620 ± 80	A.D. 669	I-14890	Carskadden & Morton 1989
Hunter 1 Site	Muskingum Co.	E. Late Woodland	A.D. 450 ± 70	A.D. 561	Beta-37801	Church 1991
Black Dog Mound	Muskingum Co.	E. Late Woodland	A.D. 430 ± 80	A.D. 548	I-16553	Carskadden & Edmister 1992
Hunter 1 Site	Muskingum Co.	E. Late Woodland	A.D. 390 ± 60	A.D. 463, 478, 530	Beta-37356	Church 1991
Henderson Mound 2	Muskingum Co.	E. Late Woodland	A.D. 350 ± 80	A.D. 429	I-16860	Carskadden & Edmister 1992
Philo Mound B	Muskingum Co.	E. Late Woodland	A.D. 300 ± 60	A.D. 405	TX-2373	Morton 1977
Murphy Site	Licking Co.	Hopewell	A.D. 210 ± 60	A.D. 257, 296, 321	Beta-16621	Dancey 1991
Hunter 1 Site	Muskingum Co.	E. Late Woodland	A.D. 200 ± 60	A.D. 253, 304, 315	Beta-37800	Church 1991
Murphy Site	Licking Co.	Hopewell	A.D. 190 ± 60	A.D. 249	Beta-16620	Dancey 1991
Linn 7 Site	Muskingum Co.	Late Adena	A.D. 170 ± 80	A.D. 239	I-17127	Carskadden & Morton n.d.a.,
Locust Site	Muskingum Co.	Late Adena	A.D. 151 ± 118	A.D. 228	SMU-1868	Carr & Haas[a]
Locust Site	Muskingum Co.	Late Adena	A.D. 115 ± 80	A.D. 143	ETH-3070	Carr & Haas[a]
Route 79 Site	Licking Co.	Hopewell	A.D. 105 ± 60	A.D. 137	Beta-28062	Lepper 1989b
Linn 7 Site	Muskingum Co.	Late Adena	A.D. 100 ± 80	A.D. 134	I-17126	Carskadden & Morton n.d.a.
Miskimens Mound	Coshocton Co.	Hopewell	A.D. 90 ± 60	A.D. 128	TX-3287	Mortine & Randles 1981
Osborn Mound	Muskingum Co.	Late Adena	A.D. 80 ± 60	A.D. 123	Beta-71531	Carskadden & Morton n.d.b.
Murphy Site	Licking Co.	Hopewell	A.D. 60 ± 110	A.D. 113	Beta-16619	Dancey 1991
Mound F, Philo Mound Group	Muskingum Co.	Late Adena	A.D. 40 ± 80	A.D. 82	I-16519	Carskadden & Morton n.d.a.
Cox B Site	Muskingum Co.	Hopewell	A.D. 30 ± 80	A.D. 77	I-16023	Carskadden & Morton n.d.a.
Locust Site	Muskingum Co.	Late Adena	A.D. 20 ± 100	A.D. 72	ETH-3487	Carr & Haas[a]
Area C, Philo Mound Group	Muskingum Co.	Late Adena	A.D. 1 ± 80	A.D. 58	I-15979	Carskadden & Morton n.d.a.
Gerlack Mound	Morgan Co.	Late Adena	A.D. 1 ± 115	A.D. 58	GX-2537	Prufer & McKenzie 1975
Gerlack Mound	Morgan Co.	Late Adena	B.C. 10 ± 180	A.D. 28, 45, 51	GX-2536	Prufer & McKenzie 1975
Area E, Philo Mound Group	Muskingum Co.	Late Adena	B.C. 20 ± 80	A.D. 22	I-16521	Carskadden & Morton n.d.a.
Buckmeyer Site	Perry Co.	Late Adena	B.C. 25 ± 200	A.D. 18	GX-3305	Bush 1975

Note: Calibrations based on Stuiver and Reimer 1986
[a] Date provided by Christopher Carr, Arizona State University, and Herbert Hass, Southern Methodist University.

Selected Post A.D. 1 Radiocarbon Dates from Woodland Sites in the Muskingum Valley.

Classic Hopewell hamlet clusters also occur sporadically along the narrower sections of the river valley between Dresden and Marietta, and one such cluster can be found in the Philo Archaeological District. Classic Hopewell hamlets in the Philo bottoms are believed to date no earlier than A.D. 100, and probably not much earlier than A.D. 200. This assumption is based on a number of "late" radiocarbon dates from Adena sites in the Philo Archaeological District, as well as from sites in neighboring Perry and Morgan counties **(Table 19:1)**, which suggest that at least in portions of the Muskingum drainage what we call Late Adena (sites with *Robbins* points, *Adena Plain* ceramics, and no bladelets) may well have lasted into the first century A.D., perhaps even later. Equally plausible is the imprecise nature of radiocarbon dating, although the sheer number of Adena dates falling after A.D. 1 would suggest the former idea. Late Adena sites in the Hocking Valley have also produced similarly late dates (Abrams 1992; Skinner and Norris 1984; Norris and Skinner 1985). The calibrated radiocarbon date of A.D. 77 from the Hopewellian Cox B site near Dresden is considered the earliest acceptable date for Hopewell in the central Muskingum Valley (Carskadden and Morton n.d.a.). In any case, although none of the Hopewell sites in the Philo area have been radiocarbon dated, we would argue that by ca. A.D. 200 there were Hopewell hamlets in the Philo bottoms.

At least two and probably three classic Hopewell hamlets occur in the Philo bottoms **(see Figure 19:2, top)**, one of which has been excavated (Tysinger Area C). These sites appear to fit the typical definition of Hopewell hamlets as described by Pacheco (1989, 1993) and others. Hopewell logistical sites (such as Linn 2) are also present in the Philo bottoms (Pacheco 1994). Excavations at Tysinger produced a cluster of 16 thermal/cooking pit features, most of which occurred in an area measuring roughly 9 by 9 meters **(Figure 19:3)**. This appears to be the "food processing zone" identified at previously excavated Hopewell hamlets (Dancey 1991; Kozarek 1987; Pacheco 1993).

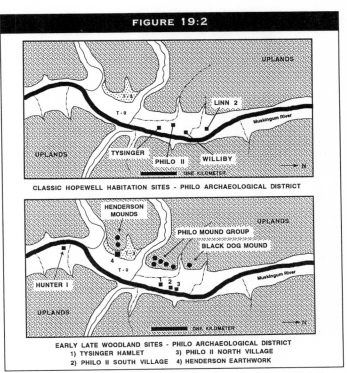

Maps of the Philo Archaeological District showing (top) the locations of Hopewell habitation sites, and (bottom) the locations of the early Late Woodland habitations and burial mounds.

Projectile points found at Tysinger Area C included typical *Affinis Snyders*, *Stueben*, and other generalized Middle Woodland corner-notched projectile point forms. Bladelets, blade cores, and mica were also found. At least one bladelet was fashioned from Wyandotte chert. Wyandotte chert has also been noted at the Linn 2 site (Pacheco 1994), and an obsidian flake was found in a Fort Ancient feature at Philo II, presumably originating from the Hopewellian component at this site. Ceramics from Tysinger are discussed in a later section of this paper.

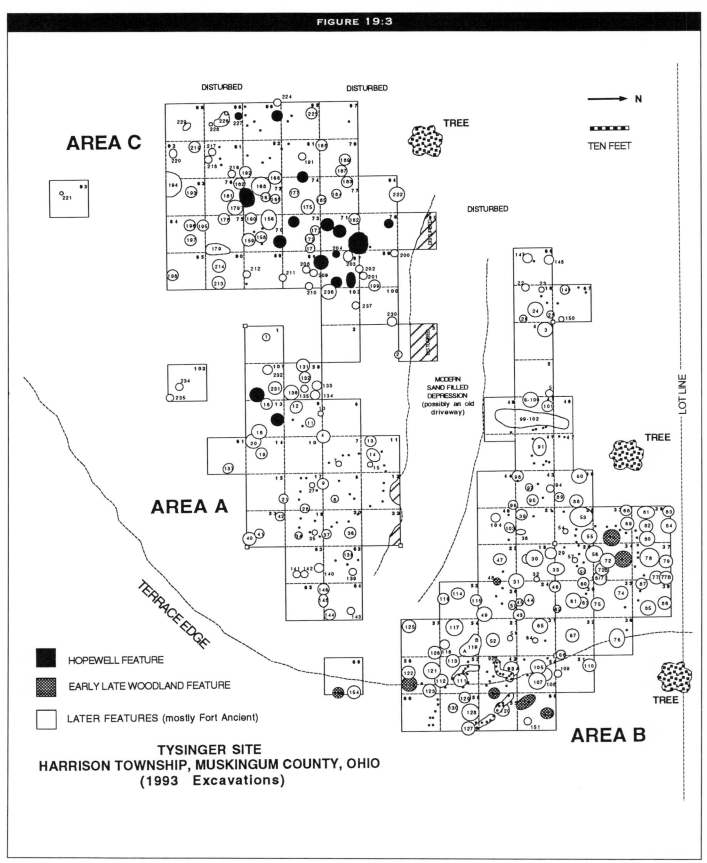

TYSINGER SITE
HARRISON TOWNSHIP, MUSKINGUM COUNTY, OHIO
(1993 Excavations)

Map of the 1993 excavations at the Tysinger Site, showing the cluster of Hopewellian features in Area C and early Late Woodland features in Area B.

STAGE 2: EARLY LATE WOODLAND HAMLETS (?)

A cluster of eight features excavated in Area B at Tysinger represents a separate and later component **(Figure 19:3)**. Flint Ridge debitage is still abundant in Area B, but there are fewer bladelets and the projectile points are of the *Lowe Flared Base* variety. (Two of the eight features at Tysinger Area B produced a total of three bladelets, whereas eight of the 16 features at Area C produced a total of 13 bladelets.) Ceramics are similar to that described later in this report for the early Late Woodland nucleated villages at the Philo II site, just 150 m upstream.

We believe Tysinger Area B represents a short-lived early Late Woodland hamlet that immediately post-dates classic Hopewell in the area. The abundance and variety of lithic refuse at Area B, the presence of ceramics, and the variety of feature types suggest that a full range of domestic/subsistence activities was being carried out at the site. Area B is the only possible early Late Woodland hamlet identified thus far in the Philo Archaeological District proper. However, across the river and 3km downstream, Church (1991) has recently described what she believed to be three feature clusters at the Hunter 1 site that possibly represent early Late Woodland households/hamlets. A series of calibrated radiocarbon dates from this component ranged from A.D. 253 to A.D. 561 **(see Table 19:1)**. For reasons discussed in the next section of this report, we would suggest that the A.D. 350 date most closely approximates the actual early Late Woodland occupation at Hunter 1, and Tysinger Area B. "Small" *Newtown Phase* sites have also been reported elsewhere in the Ohio Valley (Maslowski 1985; Ahler and Henderson 1988).

STAGE 3: EARLY NUCLEATION - PHILO II LOWER VILLAGE

By at least A.D. 400, and probably a little earlier, the scattered Hopewell or early Late Woodland hamlets in the Philo bottoms had been replaced by nucleated villages. Dates for the beginning of nucleation in the Philo area come not from the villages themselves but from nearby mounds associated with these villages, which are discussed in the next section of this paper. These dates **(Table 19:1)** include the

calibrated radiocarbon dates from Mound B at the Philo Mound Group (A.D. 405), from the nearby Henderson Mound 2 (A.D. 429), and from slightly earlier dates from elsewhere in the Ohio Valley (Dancey 1992; Railey 1984, 1991). The shift from the Hopewell dispersed hamlet style settlement to nucleated villages has been well documented for other areas of the Ohio Valley, and is believed to have occurred earliest around the periphery of the Hopewell core area (which would include the central Muskingum Valley). The reasons for this shift are not fully understood, although a number of possibilities have been suggested (Dancey 1992). For whatever reason, early Late Woodland inhabitants of the Muskingum Valley also shifted to nucleated villages, some fortified with earthen embankments and ditches. However, what we believe to be the earliest nucleated village in the Philo area (the Philo II Lower Village) was not fortified, suggesting that a perceived or real threat from outsiders was not the initial catalyst for village nucleation, at least in the Philo area.

Although best known for its Fort Ancient component, excavations at Philo (33MU76) also revealed evidence of one and probably two early Late Woodland nucleated villages **(Figure 19:4)**. What we believe to be the earliest of the two, the Philo II Lower Village, was exposed in 1992-1993 during excavations at the north end of the Fort Ancient village plaza, in an area not disrupted by many Fort Ancient pit features **(Figure 19:5)**. The Woodland features appear to occur in a 33 m diameter ring around an earlier plaza. An overall diameter of 60 m appears to include all of this Woodland village. Although there is a mix of Woodland and Fort Ancient postholes, portions of several possible Woodland structures were identified.

Lowe Flared Base projectile points are the typical projectile point form found at the Lower Village. Flint Ridge chert still comprised about 61 percent of the point sample, although the popularity of this material had dropped from the 74 percent represented at the local Hopewell hamlets. Very few true bladelets have been found at this site. Ceramics have early Late Woodland characteristics and are discussed below.

STAGE 4: FIRST FORTIFICATION - PHILO II UPPER VILLAGE

Limited excavations were undertaken in 1976 at the Philo II Upper Village, a probably nucleated early Late Woodland village located less than 30 m north of the Lower Village. Apparent in the site plan is a 18+ m long line of stone filled postholes, most measuring at least 25 cm in diameter and about 30 cm deep; many were also chinked with large early Late Woodland pottery sherds. The line of postholes is disrupted at the south end by Fort Ancient features and extended northward beyond the area we were allowed to excavate. We are certain that this feature is unrelated to the Fort Ancient component, and believe that these postholes may represent a stockade, the earliest known defense work erected in the valley. Local Fort Ancient sites are not stockaded, and the longest excavated Fort Ancient house wall at Philo II is only 10 m.

The Upper Village is still characterized by *Lowe Flared Base* projectile points, and some rudimentary bladelets and cores (Morton 1989), although these latter artifacts seem to occur with even less frequency than at the Lower Village. A polished slate disc and a spade-shaped pendant were also found at the Upper Village. Slate discs are a common artifact trait at Pyles and other Newtown sites, but are rare in the Philo area, even at these late sites. Ceramics are typical early Late Woodland (see below), and a ceramic seriation suggests that the Upper Village is later than the Lower Village. A radiocarbon date of A.D. 825±80 (uncalibrated) was obtained from one of the features at the Upper Village and reported by Morton (1989). From our present knowledge of Late Woodland chronology, however, we now know that this date is, at the very least, about 300 years too late.

STAGE 5: EARTH-WALLED VILLAGES - THOMAS EARTHWORK

What we believe to be the final stage in early Late Woodland village development in the Philo area was the selection of a more defensible location, and to fortify the site not just with a wooden stockade, but with an earthen embankment and ditch. This is represented by the Thomas

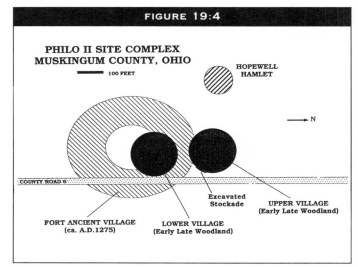

Map of the Philo II site complex showing the locations of the two early Late Woodland villages and a nearby Hopewellian hamlet.

Earthwork, situated at the south end of the Philo bottoms on the T-3 terrace. This terrace remnant, now a pasture, provided a relatively high bluff-like and easily defensible location.

The Thomas Earthwork does not show up on the ground today, but does show up plainly as a C-shaped stain on 1953 United States Department of Agriculture aerial photographs (USDA 10-17-50, CLZ-6G-53). The open end of the enclosed area measures 76 m along the edge of the terrace, and the apex of the crescent extends about 26 m back into the field. The open side was protected by a 9 m deep ravine which bisects the terrace remnant. This ravine was cut by a small creek which flows from the uplands past the earthwork and out into the floodplain, where it joins the Muskingum. The wall may have been visible in the mid 19th century, since this creek is referred to as "Fort Lick" in the 1866 Muskingum County Atlas (Beers 1866).

No testing has yet been undertaken within the earthwork, although several *Lowe Flared Base* projectile points have washed out along the creek bank below. We are confident that this is an early Late Woodland village, however, because it is situated directly below the Henderson Mounds.

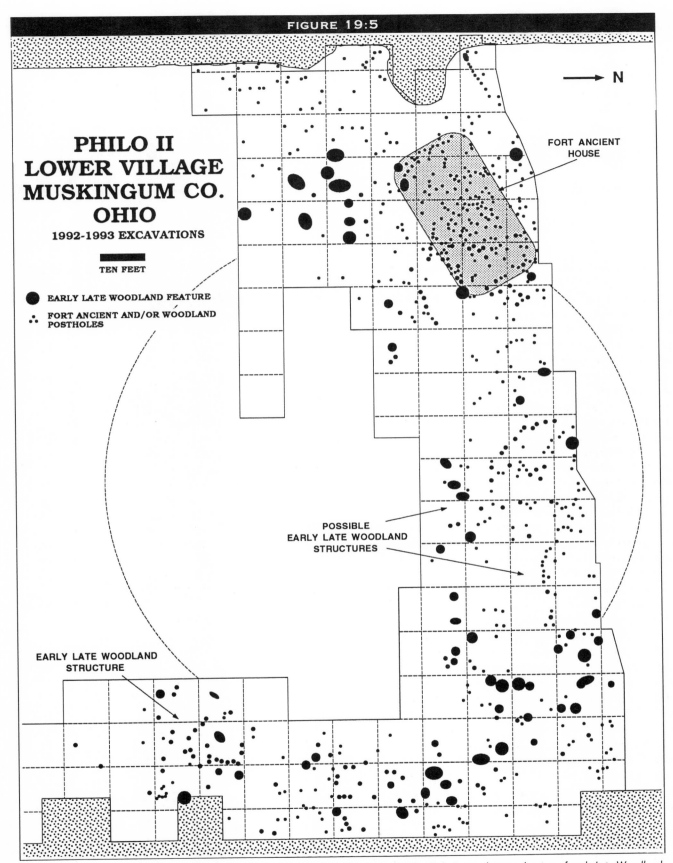

**PHILO II
LOWER VILLAGE
MUSKINGUM CO.
OHIO**

1992-1993 EXCAVATIONS

TEN FEET

● EARLY LATE WOODLAND FEATURE

FORT ANCIENT AND/OR WOODLAND
POSTHOLES

FORT ANCIENT
HOUSE

POSSIBLE
EARLY LATE WOODLAND
STRUCTURES

EARLY LATE WOODLAND
STRUCTURE

→ N

Map of the 1992-1993 excavations at the north end of the Fort Ancient village plaza at the Philo II site, showing the ring of early Late Woodland pit features that comprise the "Lower Village." Fort Ancient pit features are not shown. Some of the postholes may belong to the Fort Ancient component.

This ridge top mound group, known to be early Late Woodland, is discussed later in this paper. The location of the earthwork aptly fits Seeman's (1980:2) description of a typical *Newtown Phase* village: "There is an overwhelming locational preference for elevated situations often on high terraces adjacent to floodplains" (see also Dancey et al. 1987; Dancey 1992; Railey 1991).

CERAMICS

A detailed description of the ceramics from the Philo II Upper Village has already appeared in print (Morton 1989). Although a formal analysis of the ceramics from Tysinger Area B, Area C, and Philo II Lower Village await completion, it is possible to make some impressionistic distinctions between the earlier or classic Hopewell component at Tysinger Area C and the early Late Woodland components at Tysinger Area B and Philo II Lower and Upper villages. Vessels are entirely cordmarked at these three later sites, but both cordmarked and plain surfaced vessels are found at Tysinger Area C. Horizontal and oblique as well as vertical cordmarking can be seen on these Ohio Hopewell vessels, whereas vertical cordmarking predominates on the necks and rims of the completely cordmarked vessels at Tysinger Area B and the Philo II Lower and Upper villages. At all four sites, cord impressions can be quite fine and tightly twisted and wrapped. S-twist predominates at all four sites, but the percentage of Z-twist seems to increase through time (87 percent of the sherds from the Upper Village displayed S-twist and 13 percent Z-twist). Vessel walls seem to be somewhat thicker at Tysinger Area C, but all four sites produced exceedingly thin ware (2-3 mm). Lips on the Ohio Hopewell vessels at Tysinger Area C are more often smoothed and rounded and occasionally thickened. Lips on vessels from Tysinger Area B and the Philo II Upper and Lower villages tend to be flattened and cordmarked and do not display thickening.

One sherd displaying what seems to be a deep circular punctation was found at Philo II Lower Village. While resembling *"Newtown Punched"* (McMichael 1984), this particular example may be nothing more than an unfinished repair hole. Tysinger Area C produced sherds exhibiting fine line crisscross incising over a cordmarked surface. Lacking at Tysinger Area C, however, are vessels with fingernail impressions, rocker stamping, or simple stamping; these decorative motifs have been found, however, at classic Hopewell sites elsewhere in the central Muskingum Valley (Cox site cluster, Carskadden and Morton n.d.a.; Knight Hollow rockshelter, Felumlee 1983). In any case, these decorative motifs are not present at Tysinger Area B or the Philo II Lower and Upper villages. At the Upper Village, 79 percent of the sherds from the early Late Woodland features were limestone tempered, and the remaining 21 percent were grit tempered (crushed granitic material). Tempering is generally fine to medium in size and of medium density. A cursory examination of the sherds from the Hopewell component at Tysinger Area C suggests that the percentage of grit tempering may be higher than at the later sites.

Little can be said with regard to vessel shapes; typical elongate jars with subconical bottoms occur at both the Hopewell and early Late Woodland sites, but small globular shapes seem to be confined to Tysinger Area C. One sherd displaying an angular shoulder was found at the Philo II Upper Village; such angular shoulders distinguish the *Newtown Cordmarked* ware of southwestern Ohio (Ahler and Henderson 1988). Generally speaking, however, angular shouldered vessels are rare to absent on Muskingum Valley early Late Woodland sites.

MORTUARY CUSTOMS - BURIAL GROUNDS- CLASSIC HOPEWELL

In the Newark area and in southern Ohio generally, Hopewell hamlets cluster in the vicinity of earthwork complexes. Along the Muskingum above Marietta, however, Ohio Hopewell hamlets are associated with earthworks primarily in the wide bottoms between Dresden and Coshocton. Here is where the two large circular earthworks occurred. As Squier and Davis (1848:77) noted almost a century and a half ago, the narrow configuration of much of the central and lower Muskingum Valley below Dresden may be the reason for the lack of sprawling earthwork complexes until one gets to Marietta. On the other hand, the relatively narrow bottoms may have supported small populations, and there simply may not have been the work force to build large earthworks.

The lack of known Hopewell mounds and earthworks (with one possible exception) near the Ohio Hopewell hamlet clusters along the lower Licking River valley in western Muskingum County has been previously noted (Carskadden and Morton n.d.a.). The inhabitants of these local Hopewellian communities may have simply taken their dead 21 km up the Licking Valley to the earthwork complex at Newark.

The Hopewellian communities in the Philo area, however, are 64 km from the Newark Earthworks (and over 100 km from Marietta). While we suspect that the ceremonial focus of these outlying Hopewellian communities must have been centered around one or two small mounds near the habitations, we have yet to identify these mounds. It is possible that one or two of the mounds in the Philo Mound Group may date to the ca. A.D. 200-350 period of classic Hopewell occupation in the Philo bottoms. However, with the exception of mica, none of the mounds in the Philo group have what would be considered "classic" Hopewellian artifacts. This contrasts, for example, with the situation at the Martin Mound along the Walhonding River (Mortine and Randles 1978). The Martin Mound, which was also located many miles from a Hopewellian earthwork center, had been constructed over a typical subrectangular charnel house in which had been deposited a number of burials along with numerous classic Hopewell Interaction Sphere items (copper ear spools, copper inlaid bear canines, and a tetrapodal vessel; see Mortine and Randles 1978:Table 2). The presence of mica, Wyandotte Chert, and obsidian at the Hopewell hamlets at Philo, however, indicate participation in a regional trade network, and one should reasonably expect exotic items in local Ohio Hopewell mounds. There is the possibility that there were classic Hopewell mounds in the Philo area, but these may have been relatively small and located in the river bottoms near the habitations and have simply been destroyed by cultivation.

Based on artifact seriation, mound construction traits (such as the increased use of stone), and the proximity to the various habitation sites discussed above, we believe that the three mounds we will be discussing (Philo Mound C, Black Dog Mound, Henderson Mound 2), represent a sequence of moundbuilding starting about the time of Philo II Lower and Upper villages were occupied, and ending with the occupation of the Thomas Earthwork.

MOUND C- THE PHILO MOUND GROUP

The Philo Mound Group (33MU77) was located on a flat hilltop immediately overlooking the Philo II and Tysinger sites (see Figure 19:2 bottom). The group consisted of a large conical-shaped Late Adena mound (Mound F) towards the back of the hill, and a cluster of five smaller and later mounds near the front of the hill facing the river (Mounds A through E), separated from the Adena mound by about 90 meters. While the mound building activity at the Philo Mound Group may have centered around A.D. 400, based on the calibrated radiocarbon date for Mound B (Morton 1977), we suspect that the Philo Mound Group served as a mortuary center for many generations, and in fact several of the mounds appear to have been added to at various times (Carskadden 1989; Morton 1977).

Mound C produced three slate (Figure 19:6) and two cannel coal spade shaped pendants, also called shovel-pendants (Converse 1978, 1981). Complete and fragmentary spade-shaped pendants were also found during the 1960s and 1970s excavations at the Fairchance Mound and Village site near Moundsville, West Virginia (Hemmings 1978:97). One example of a spade-shaped pendant was found with Burial 17 under the Fairchance Mound. A charred log from the burial pit produced a calibrated radiocarbon date of A.D. 233. Charcoal from refuse pits at the nearby Fairchance Village site produced calibrated radiocarbon dates of A.D. 217 and A.D. 231. A submound fire pit produced a date of A.D. 420 (uncalibrated), a date more in line with an early Late Woodland placement for this pendant form. However, this date is discounted by some considering the clustering of the other three dates and the

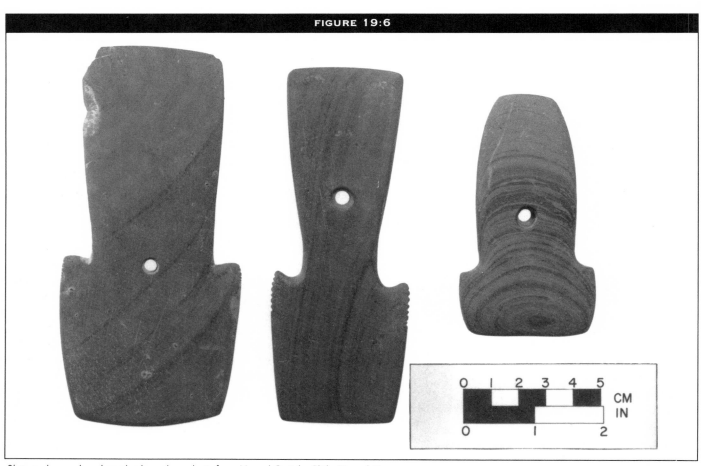

FIGURE 19:6

Slate and cannel coal spade-shaped pendants from Mound C at the Philo Mound Group.

imprecise location of the fire pit (possibly beyond the mound perimeter). Third century dates for this pendant form would place Mound C within the time frame of the classic Hopewell hamlets in the Philo Bottoms.

Outside of Fairchance, however, spade-shaped pendants have been radiocarbon dated one or two centuries later at various *Newtown* or *Watson Phase* sites. For example, an "anchor (barbed) pendant" (illustration indicates spade-shaped pendant) was reported from the Pyles site, a fourth century *Newtown Phase* site in northern Kentucky (Railey

1984: Plate 27). More recently, a spade-shaped pendant was found at the Dunsfort site near Wellsburgh, West Virginia, associated with radiocarbon dates (uncalibrated) of A.D. 300, A.D. 530, and A.D. 530 (Richard L. George, personal communication, 1994). Locally, a fragmentary spade-shaped pendant was recovered in a pit feature at the Philo II Upper Village (Morton 1989), which postdates the classic Hopewell occupation in the Philo area. Another example was found within the Krebbs/Little Earthwork, a known early Late Woodland fortified (earth-walled) village near Dresden in northern Muskingum County (Carskadden

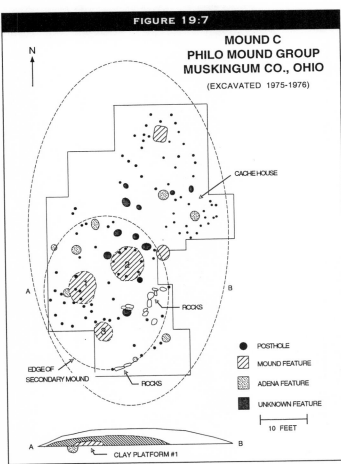

Excavation map of Mound C at the Philo Mound Group.

projectile points in Mound C and the lack of classic Hopewell Interaction Sphere goods in the mound (except mica) suggest that Mound C postdates classic Hopewell in the Philo area. However, we believe that Mound C is probably the earliest of the three mounds we will be discussing.

Mound C was the largest of the five late mounds at the Philo Mound Group, and was the only one that was oval shaped, measuring 22.8 m long, 11.3 m wide, and 90 cm high. The activities related to the mound site appear to have occurred in two functionally discrete areas on the mound floor. These two areas, which were separated by about 3 m of empty floor space, have been termed the "Burial Area" and the "Cache House" **(Figure 19:7)**.

The so-called "Burial Area" consisted of a roughly circular area measuring about 9.1 by 10.6 m in diameter, which was delineated by a few stones and probably some of the postholes. Within what we have termed the Burial Area were three clay primary mounds. These averaged between 1.2 and 2.4 m in diameter and from 20 to 47 cm high. Two of these were conical and the third was more platform-shaped. A few grams of minute incinerated human bone fragments were found at the base of one of these clay mounds; however all three are believed to have covered burials of some kind. Spade-shaped pendants had been place on top of two of these primary mounds, and one of these mounds was also covered with small slivers of mica. Prior to the construction of the clay primary mounds, there appears to have been two small circular areas delineated by upright posts, at or near the locations of two of the clay mounds. Perhaps these posts represented partitions or canopies. In both instances these posts were removed prior to the construction of the clay primary mounds. At some point the "Burial Area" under Mound C was covered by a low secondary earth mound. This secondary mound averaged not much more than 48 cm in height, barely covering the tops of the three clay primary mounds.

and Morton n.d.b.). Spade-shaped pendants were also found during the 1928 excavations at the Wells Mound Group near Newark (Lepper 1989a) and during the late 18th-century excavation at the Walter Davis Mound Group near Lowell (Murphy 1986). In both instances these were associated with *Lowe Flared Base* projectile points. Both mound groups appear to be early Late Woodland in origin.

Regardless of whether one accepts or rejects the third century dates for the Fairchance spade-shaped pendants, we believe that the presence of numerous *Lowe Flared Base*

The "Cache House" was outside the area covered by the secondary mound and consisted of a clustering of postholes which represented a rude subrectangular structure measuring roughly 7.6 by 3.6 m on a side. The caches of artifacts, including projectile points and slate ornaments, were placed on the mound floor within this structure, and a third cache was found just outside. The final construction episode at Mound C was the covering of both the cache house and the secondary mound covering the burial area with a single low oval earth mound - the tertiary mound.

Included here is the list of artifacts found in Cache 1 within the Cache House; the other caches had similar assortments (see Carskadden and Morton n.d.b.): a large undrilled banded slate bar, 20.9 cm long; a banded slate spade-shaped pendant; a banded slate anchor pendant; an irregularly-shaped flat sandstone abrader; and an irregular lump of faceted hematite. Chert artifacts include three small *Lowe Flared Base* projectile points (one Flint Ridge, two black Upper Mercer); a large square base cache blade and a matching *Lowe Flared Base* projectile point, both of tan Brush Creek chert; a crude square-base cache blade or preform fragment of black Upper Mercer chert; two projectile point tips and one projectile point mid-section of Flint Ridge chert, the base of a possible *Robbins* projectile point of Flint Ridge chert and 22 miscellaneous flint chips and shatter (eighteen Flint Ridge, two black Upper Mercer, one tan Brush Creek, and one unidentifiable tan). Additional items in Cache 1 included a round granitic pebble 3.8 cm in diameter, and 68 small quartz pebbles, the largest measuring 9 mm in diameter. The quartz pebbles were in a tightly compacted cluster and may have been in a bag or rattle. Most of the artifacts in Cache 1 had been placed on or around the large slate bar, except for the spade-shaped and anchor pendants, which were placed together about 20 cm from the slate bar.

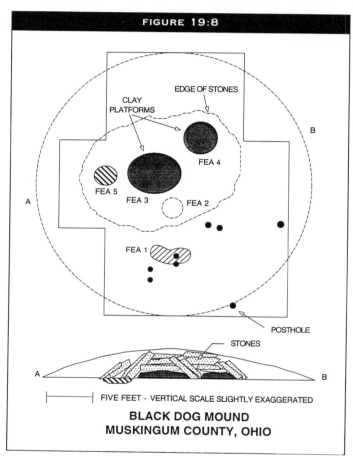

Excavation map of the Black Dog Mound.

BLACK DOG MOUND

In the Muskingum Valley, early Late Woodland mounds usually occur in pairs or groups; single early Late Woodland mounds are the exception rather than the norm, and when they occur, they are usually in the general vicinity of mound groups. The only single early Late Woodland mound in the Philo area is the Black Dog Mound (33MU540), located on the crest of a narrow ridge just across a ravine from the Philo Mound Group.

The Black Dog Mound produced a calibrated radiocarbon date of A.D. 548 **(Table 19:1)**. While this date suggest that the Black Dog Mound is later than Mound C and others mounds in the Philo Mound Group, we feel that the seriation of mound construction and burial traits also firmly place the Black Dog Mound later than Mound C, but earlier than the Henderson Mounds discussed below. The Black Dog Mound had two clay primary mounds or platforms like those found in Mound C **(Figure 19:8)**, but these clay mounds were covered by a stone cyst like that seen in Henderson Mound 2. Extended burials in stone box graves, which we believe to be the latest form of mound burial in the Philo area, are lacking at Mound C and at the Black Dog Mound, but one was found in Henderson Mound 2.

The Black Dog Mound measured a little over .6 m high and 9.1 m in diameter and covered the two clay primary mounds as well as a cremation in a subfloor pit. Three small sheets of mica placed on top of one of the clay mounds were the only artifacts found. The Black Dog Mound is different from any of the mounds in the Philo Mound Group, however, in that the clay platforms were covered with layers of large limestone slabs, the largest weighing 36.2 kg (80 pounds), which eventually formed a single stone cyst measuring 5.3 by 3.3 m in diameter and .6 m high. A mantle of earth was later placed over the top of this stone cyst, raising the height of the mound slightly and expanding the diameter. On the mound floor, outside the area covered by the stone cyst, was a large kidney-shaped area of bright red burnt earth, measuring about 1.2 m long and about 40 cm wide. This area of intense heat may have been where the cremation occurred.

CLASSIC NEWTOWN - HENDERSON MOUND 2

What we believe to be the final stage in mound building in the Philo area is represented by the Henderson Mounds (33MU538), two mounds situated 4.5 m apart on a ridge top directly overlooking the Thomas Earthwork. Henderson Mound 1 measured only 7.6 m in diameter and 60 cm high, and covered a crescent of stones and a cache of artifacts placed on the mound floor, consisting of a slate gorget and *Lowe Flared Base* projectile points (Carskadden and Edmister 1992).

Henderson Mound 2 was an oval structure, asymmetrical in profile, which measured 12.1 m long, 6 m wide, and 60 cm high at the highest point **(Figure 19:9)**. This mound is different from the previous ones just discussed because of the lack of cremations and the presence of extended burials, one of which was placed in a stone box grave under a stone cyst. Although this mound produced a calibrated radiocarbon date of A.D. 428 **(Table 19:1)**, we believe that the presence of the stone box grave indicates that this mound was built later than the Black Dog Mound, and represents the last stage of moundbuilding in the Philo area.

Poorly preserved remains of four individuals in three mound features were recovered under Henderson Mound 2, all clustered somewhat under the higher portion of the mound. The following age/sex determinations were provided by Paul Scuilli (personal communication, 1993).

Burial 1 was an adult, probably a male 20-30 years old, who had been placed in an extended position, lying on his back, directly on the mound floor. The body was then covered with a heap of flat stones, consisting of no more than two layers. A fingernail sized sliver of mica was found in the chest area of this individual; no other artifacts were found.

Burial 2 was also an adult, probably a male 25-35 years old, lying on its back in an extended position in the stone box grave. The body was placed directly on the mound floor and surrounded by large slabs of sandstone or siltstone. These stones were placed upright at the head and feet, and were simply laid flat and stacked two or three deep on the sides. The "box" thus measured a little over 1.2 m wide and 1.8 m long. After the body was placed in this box, layers of large slabs were placed over it, and other slabs were placed around the edge at varying angles, creating a stone cyst nearly 60 cm high.

This individual had his left arm extended along his side, but the right arm was drawn up to the middle of the chest. Around the hand area of the right arm were a number of wolf teeth, cut along the root. These were probably the disintegrated remains of a cut wolf jaw, which may have been

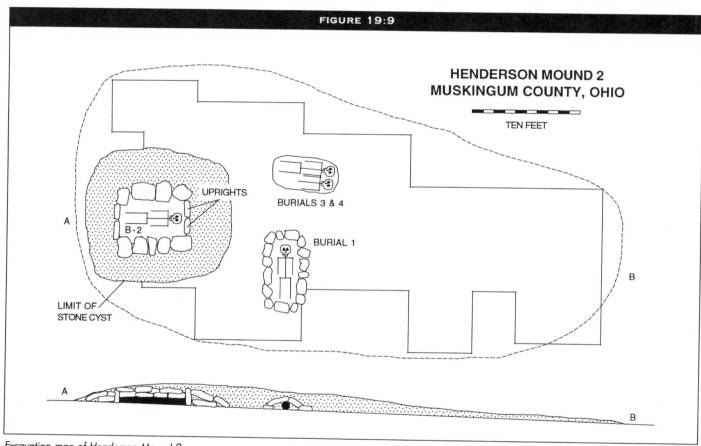

FIGURE 19:9

HENDERSON MOUND 2
MUSKINGUM COUNTY, OHIO

TEN FEET

UPRIGHTS

BURIALS 3 & 4

A

B-2

BURIAL 1

LIMIT OF
STONE CYST

A

B

B

Excavation map of Henderson Mound 2.

held in the hand. An oval bone disc, possibly a gorget, had been placed on the chest of this individual near the hand. No other artifacts were associated with this burial.

Burials 3 and 4 were male and female adults (20-30 years old) lying together in a shallow 10 cm deep pit dug into the mound floor. The bodies were covered with a sheet of bark. A *Lowe Flared Base* projectile point was found in the area of the left hip of the male, a badly preserved elk antler section was found near his feet, and a baseball-size sphere of white clay was placed near his mouth. Accompanying the female was a small irregular sheet of mica placed in the

chest area, and at her side was another *Lowe Flared Base* projectile point.

Stone box graves under earth mounds or earth covered stone cysts are relatively common along the lower Muskingum; many were encountered by Willard Davis while excavating in the Lowell area in the late 19th century. Coover (1908) illustrates a number of stone box graves excavated in 1907 under the Mary Dean Vincent Mound, a low earth mound located near Beverly in Washington County, just upstream from Lowell.

	SETTLEMENT TYPE	LOCATION	MOUND TRAITS
TABLE 19:2			
A.D. 600	Earth-walled Village	Bluff Edge	Stone Cyst Covering Stone Box Graves
	Stockaded Village	Flood Plain	Stone Cyst Covering Clay Platforms
A.D. 400	Unfortified Village	Flood Plain	Earth-covered Clay Platforms Spade-Shaped Pendants
A.D. 200	E. Late Woodland Hamlets	Flood Plain	Simple Cremations in the Subfloor Pits(?)
	Hopewell Hamlets	Flood Plain	No Known Local Examples

Proposed Evolution in Settlement Types and Mound Construction in the Philo Archaeological District ca. A.D. 200 - A.D. 600

Extended burials in stone box graves seem to be characteristic of "classic" *Newtown* or *Watson Phase* mounds elsewhere in the Ohio Valley (Applegarth and Cowin 1982; Hemmings 1978; Kellar 1960; Kreinbrink 1992). However, only one other stone box grave has been found in the Philo area. This example had been intruded into the top of Mound D at the Philo Mound Group (Carskadden 1989). With this partially flexed adult individual was a copper "dagger" or hair ornament, a large irregular sheet of mica, a small sandstone tablet, and a *Lowe Flared Base* projectile point. The copper ornament was the only copper artifact found in the Philo area mounds, although Willard Davis reported finding a few copper beads in early Late Woodland mounds at Lowell (Murphy 1986).

MUSKINGUM VALLEY OVERVIEW

Settlements

From a variety of sources we have documented that village nucleation was well established in the central Muskingum Valley after ca. A.D. 400, as it was elsewhere in the Ohio Valley about this time. Based on recent work in the Philo Archaeological District, we are able to offer the following possible development stages for Ohio Hopewell through early Late Woodland habitation sites in the Muskingum Valley. While this seems like a logical sequence, we must emphasize that this is tentative, and is based in part on as yet partially

analyzed collections and limited excavations at some sites. The suggested sequence, which is summarized in **Table 19:2**, includes the following, starting with the earliest:

1) Hamlets immediately along the Muskingum River in flood plain or low terrace localities, with "classic" Hopewell artifacts (examples: Tysinger Area C and Philo II Hopewell component).

2) Hamlets immediately along the Muskingum River in flood plain or low terrace localities, with early Late Woodland artifact traits predominating (examples: Tysinger Area B, Hunter 1).

3) Unfortified nucleated villages in flood plain or low terrace localities, with early Late Woodland ceramics and lithics (example: Philo II Lower Village).

4) Nucleated villages surrounded by wooden stockades situated along the river in otherwise indefensible flood plain or low terrace localities (example: Philo II Upper Village).

5) Earth-walled nucleated villages in the river valley but situated on the edge of high bluff-like defensible terraces (example: Thomas Earthwork).

TABLE 19:3					
	Late Adena Hamlets	Hopewell Hamlets	Early Late Woodland		
			Hamlets	Unfortified or Stockaded Villages	Earth-Walled Villages
River Bottoms	29	38	4	8	3
Hinterlands	20	24	0	1	1

Known Woodland Habitations, Muskingum County, Ohio.

The nucleated villages and their associated artifact traits (and burial mounds) relate the central Muskingum Valley sites, more or less, to the *Newtown Phase* of southwestern Ohio and northeastern Kentucky, and to the *Watson Phase* of the Upper Ohio Valley (e.g., Hemmings 1978; Kellar 1960; Railey 1984, 1991; Shott 1989, 1990).

The congregating of the Muskingum Valley populations into these nucleated communities resulted in a drastic drop on the number of habitation sites evident in the archaeological record for this early Late Woodland period. Along the 71 km of the Muskingum River and 30 km of the Licking River within Muskingum County that the authors have surveyed extensively, this change is marked by a decline from 38 Hopewell habitation sites to only 12 early Late Woodland nucleated villages **(Table 19:3)**. Actually the decline is even more dramatic when one considers that only three of these early Late Woodland sites are fortified with earth walls, presumably marking, as we have suggested, the last stage in the village formation sequence.

MOUNDS

Early Late Woodland mounds in the Muskingum Valley represent the last vestiges of burial mound building in eastern Ohio. While these mounds can be found all along the Muskingum River, they seem to cluster especially at two locations, one being Philo. Here could be found the Philo Mound Group (five mounds), the Henderson Mound Group (two mounds), and the Black Dog Mound. Associated with these mounds was the sequence of villages terminating, we believe, with the Thomas Earthwork.

From antiquarian Willard Davis' late 19th century excavations along the lower Muskingum, we know that another cluster of mounds occurred at Lowell, 22.5 km upstream from Marietta, where as many as three early Late Woodland mound groups (totaling eight mounds) and four single mounds occurred (Moorehead 1897:204-208; Murphy 1986). There were also one or two earthworks in the Lowell area that may represent fortified early Late Woodland villages, although information on these sites is very scanty.

Information on early Late Woodland mounds presented in this report is based primarily on the excavations by the authors of the eight mounds at Philo. Artifacts, burial traits, and radiocarbon dates from some of these sites, as well as information from some of Davis' excavations, have enabled us to propose the following as a possible developmental sequence of mound construction and burial mode for this period:

1) Classic Hopewell - no known local examples.

2) Very early Early Late Woodland - wooden structure built to house offerings, with burials (cremations ?) placed under small clay primary mounds elsewhere on the mound floor (examples: Mound C, Philo Mound Group).

3) Early Late Woodland-burials, possibly cremations, under clay primary mounds, which were in turn covered with stone cysts (examples: Black Dog Mound).

4) Classic Newtown/Watson - extended burials in stone box graves (examples: Henderson Mound 2, Philo Mound D upper level).

	SITE	L x W	SQUARE CENTIMETERS	THICKNESS
		TABLE 19:4		
e E T	Henderson Md. 2	15.2 x 7.6 cm	116.1	1 mm
	Philo Mound D (Stone Box Grave)	16.2 x 10.1 cm	167.7	3 mm
	Black Dog Mound	12.7 x 7.6 cm	96.7	1 mm
	Philo Mound C	21.5 x 15.2 cm 19.0 x 11.4 cm	329.0 270.9	3 mm 3 mm
	Philo Mound A	19.0 x 14.4 cm	277.4	4 mm

Mica Sheet Characteristics

In the Muskingum Valley, irregular sheets of mica and a few copper items (mostly beads) found in these early Late Woodland mounds are about the only carryovers from the Hopewell Interaction Sphere trade network. Caches of Flint Ridge debitage may indicate that some importance was still given to this material. However, for the central Muskingum Valley, Flint Ridge chert can be considered a local resource and would probably not have had to have been acquired through any elaborate trade network.

Mica was a rather ubiquitous trade item on Hopewell sites throughout southern Ohio, and has been called "basic exotica" (Greber and Ruhl 1989:84, 276). Greber and Ruhl have suggested that mica, along with copper, were probably the earliest exotic materials in Hopewell, and we would add that evidence from early Late Woodland mounds in the Muskingum Valley indicates that mica (and copper) may have also been the last of these exotic items available in the area. Mica has also been noted at *Newtown Phase* sites elsewhere in the Ohio Valley (e.g., Kreinbrink 1992). Whether this material was coming directly from outcrops in the Appalachians to early Late Woodland sites in the Muskingum Valley, or whether it was coming indirectly from some still active Hopewellian distribution center in southern Ohio, or if it had simply been curated locally for a number of generations, remains to be seen. It is interesting to note, however, that the mica sheets found in the sequence of

mounds in the Philo area were becoming fewer, smaller, and thinner as time went by (**Table 19:4**), if our suggested sequence of mounds is correct.

Although rectangular slate gorgets occur in both Ohio Hopewell and early Late Woodland contexts, the presence of certain other types of slate and cannel coal pendants and gorgets distinguish the Muskingum Valley early Late Woodland from classic Hopewell sites in the valley and elsewhere in southern Ohio. These ornaments include spade-shaped pendants and to a lesser degree anchor and pentagonal pendants. Slate ornaments in general did not seem to be held in high esteem in southern Ohio Hopewell, at least compared to items of a more exotic nature. For example, a "stone gorget" was found with only one individual out of a total of 301 individuals buried in Seip Mound 1 and Harness Mound in the Scioto Valley (Seip n = 123, Harness n = 178; Greber 1979, 1983).

Perhaps the increase in both the number and styles of slate ornaments seen in the early Late Woodland sites along the Muskingum River and elsewhere had something to do with the scarcity of copper and other exotic materials after the breakdown of the Hopewell Interaction Sphere. However, as just noted, the presence of mica may indicate that certain trade routes were still open.

REFERENCES CITED

Abrams, E.M. 1992 Archaeological Investigation of the Armitage Mound (33AT434), The Plains, Ohio. *Midcontinental Journal of Archaeology* 17(1):80-110.

Ahler, S.R. and G. Henderson 1988 Cultural Background for the Hansen Site. In *Excavations at the Hansen Site in Northeastern Kentucky*, edited by S.R. Ahler, pp. 19-41. University of Kentucky Archaeological Report 173, Lexington.

Applegarth, J.D. and V.L. Cowin 1982 *Excavations at Cross Creek Village (36WH293) and the Avella Mound (36WH415), Washington County, Southwestern Pennsylvania*. Prepared for The Meadowcroft Rockshelter Rolling Thunder Review: Last Act. Forty-Seventh Annual Meeting of the Society for American Archaeology, Minneapolis.

Beers, F.W. 1866 *Atlas of Muskingum County, Ohio*. Beers, Soule and Company, New York.

Bush, D. 1975 A Ceramic Analysis of the Late Adena Buckmeyer Site, Perry County, Ohio. *The Michigan Archaeologist* 21(1):9-23.

Carskadden, J. 1989 Excavations of Mound D at the Philo Mound Group, Muskingum County, Ohio. *Ohio Archaeologist* 39(1):4-8.

Carskadden, J. and L. Edmister 1992 Excavation of Henderson Mound 1, Muskingum County, Ohio. *Ohio Archaeologist* 42(1):6-9.

Carskadden, J. and J. Morton 1983 A Hopewell Mound, Dresden, Ohio. *Ohio Archaeologist* 33(1):44-47.

1986 "Sacred Circles" Along the Muskingum: A Preliminary Survey. *Ohio Archaeologist* 36(4):4-8.

1989 Excavations of Mound E at the Philo Mound Group, Muskingum County, Ohio. *West Virginia Archaeologist* 41(1):42-53.

n.d.a. Living on the Edge: A Comparison of Adena and Hopewell Communities in the Central Muskingum Valley of Eastern Ohio. In *Ohio Hopewell Community Organization*, edited by W.S. Dancey and P.J. Pacheco, Kent State University Press, Kent, Ohio, "in press."

n.d.b. *A Catalogue of Prehistoric Works in Muskingum County, Ohio*. Muskingum Valley Archaeological Survey, Zanesville, Ohio, "in press."

Church, F. 1991 *The Hunter 1 Site: Mitigation of a Multi-Component Late Woodland Site in Blue Rock Township, Muskingum County, Ohio*. Report on file, Ohio Historic Preservation Office, Columbus, Ohio.

Converse, R.N. 1978 *Ohio Slate Types*. The Archaeological Society of Ohio, Columbus.

1981 Caches of Hopewell Artifacts. *Ohio Archaeologist* 31(1):16-17.

Coover, A.B. 1908 Mary Dean Vincent Mound. *Ohio State Archaeological and Historical Publications* 17:36-43.

Dancey, W.S. 1991 A Middle Woodland Settlement in Central Ohio: A Preliminary Report on the Murphy Site (33LI212). *Pennsylvania Archaeologist* 61(2):37-72.

1992 Village Origins in Central Ohio: The Results and Implications of Recent Middle and Late Woodland Research. In *Cultural Variability in Context: Woodland Settlements of the Mid-Ohio Valley*, edited by Mark F. Seeman, pp. 24-29. MidContinental Journal of Archaeology Special Paper No. 7, the Kent State University Press, Kent, Ohio.

Dancey, W.S., M.L. Fricke and F. Church 1987 *The Water Plant Site and Other Sites in Southeastern Hamilton Township, Franklin County, Ohio*. Report on file, Ohio Historic Preservation Office, Columbus.

Ericksen, A.G. 1993 *Archaeobotanical Summary of the Bosman Site, Muskingum County, Ohio*. Report on file, Muskingum Valley Archaeological Survey, Zanesville, Ohio.

Felumlee, G. 1983 Report on the Knight Hollow Rock Shelter. *Ohio Archaeologist* 33(4):22-28.

Gordon, R.B. 1966 *Natural Vegetation of Ohio at the Time of the Earliest Land Surveys (map)*. Ohio Biological Survey, Columbus.

Greber, N.B. 1979 A Comparative Study of Site Morphology and Burial Patterns at Edwin Harness Mound and Seip Mounds 1 and 2. In *Hopewell Archaeology: The Chillicothe Conference*, edited by D. S. Brose and N. Greber, pp. 27-38. Kent State University Press, Kent, Ohio.

Greber, N.B. and K.C. Ruhl 1989 *The Hopewell Site: A Contemporary Analysis Based on the Work of Charles C. Willoughby*. Westview Press, Boulder, Colorado.

    1983 *Recent Excavations at the Edwin Harness Mound, Liberty Works, Ross County, Ohio*. Midcontinental Journal of Archaeology, Special Paper No. 5, Kent State University Press, Kent, Ohio.

Hemmings, T. 1978 *Fairchance Mound and Village: An Early Middle Woodland Settlement in the Upper Ohio Valley*. West Virginia Geological and Economic Survey, Morgantown.

Kellar, J.H. 1960 The C.L. Lewis Stone Mound and the Stone Mound Problem. *Prehistoric Research Series* 3(4):357-481. Indiana Historical Society, Indianapolis.

Kozarek, S.E. 1987 *A Hopewellian Homestead in the Ohio River Valley*. Masters thesis, Department of Anthropology, University of Cincinnati.

Kreinbrink, J. 1992 The Rogers Site Complex in Boone County, Kentucky. In *Current Archaeological Research in Kentucky 2*, edited by D. Pollack and A. G.Henderson, pp. 79-102. Kentucky Heritage Council, Lexington.

Lepper, B.T. 1989a An Historical Review of Archaeological Research at the Newark Earthworks. *Journal of the Steward Anthropological Society* 18(1-2):118-140.

    1989b A Radiocarbon Date from a Hopewellian Habitation Site Associated with the Newark Earthworks. *Ohio Archaeologist* 39(4):12-13.

Maslowski, R.1985 Woodland Settlement Patterns in the Mid and Upper Ohio Valley. *West Virginia Archeologist* 37(2):23-34.

McMichael, E. 1984 Type Description for Newtown Series Ceramics. In *The Pyles Site (15MS28): A Newtown Village in Mason County, Kentucky*, edited by A. Railey, Appendix A, pp. 132-135. Occasional Paper 1, William S. Webb Archaeological Society, Lexington.

Moorehead, W.K. 1897 Report of Field Work Carried Out in the Muskingum, Scioto, and Ohio Valley During the Season of 1896. *Ohio Archaeological and Historical Quarterly* 5:165-274.

Mortine, W.A. and D. Randles 1978 *The Martin Mound: an Extension of the Hopewell Interaction Sphere into the Walhonding Valley of Eastern Ohio*. The Muskingum Valley Archaeological Survey, Occasional Papers No. 10, Zanesville.

    1981 *Excavations of Two Mounds in Coshocton County, Ohio*. The Muskingum Valley Archaeological Survey, Occasional Papers No. 12, Zanesville.

Morton, J. 1977 Excavations of Mound B, a Hopewellian Site in the Muskingum Valley. *Ohio Archaeologist* 27(1):22-24.

    1989 Middle and Late Woodland Components at the Philo II Site, Muskingum County, Ohio. *Ohio Archaeologist* 39(2):61-69.

Murphy, J.L. 1977 *Vertebrate Remains from the Richards and Philo II Sites*. Occasional Papers in Muskingum Valley Archaeology 6, The Muskingum Valley Archaeological Survey, Zanesville, Ohio.

1986 Willard H. Davis: Nineteenth Century Archaeologist of the Lower Muskingum Valley. *Muskingum Annals* 2:59-76.

Norris, R. and S.M. Skinner 1985 Excavation of the Connett Mound 3. *Ohio Archaeologist* 35(1):21-26.

Pacheco, P.J. 1989 Ohio Middle Woodland Settlement Variability in the Upper Licking River Drainage. *Journal of the Steward Anthropological Society* 18(1-2):87-117.

1993 *Ohio Hopewell Settlement Patterns: An Application of the Vacant Center Model to Middle Woodland Period Intracommunity Settlement Variability in the Upper Licking River Valley*. Ph.D. dissertation, Department of Anthropology, The Ohio State University, University Microfilms, Ann Arbor.

1994 Recent Excavations at the Linn 2 Site (33MU611) in the Philo Archaeological District. Paper presented at the Spring Meeting of the Ohio Archaeological Council, Columbus, Ohio.

Prufer, O.H. and D.H. McKenzie 1975 *Studies in Ohio Archaeology*. The Kent State University Press, Kent, Ohio.

Railey, J.A., ed. 1984 *The Pyles Site (15MS28): a Newtown Village in Mason County, Kentucky*. Occasional Paper 1, William S. Webb Archaeological Society, Lexington.

Railey, J.A. 1991 Woodland Settlement Trends and Symbolic Architecture in the Kentucky Bluegrass. In *The Human Landscape in Kentucky's Past*, edited by C. Stout and C.K. Hensley, pp. 56-77. Kentucky Heritage Council, Lexington.

Seeman, M.F. 1979 *The Hopewell Interaction Sphere: the Evidence for Interregional Trade and Structural Complexity*. The Indiana Historical Society, Prehistory Research Series 5(2).

1980 A Taxonomic Review of Southern Ohio Late Woodland. Paper presented at the Midwest Archaeological Conference, Chicago.

Shane, O.C., III and M.B. Barber 1976 A Preliminary Analysis of Vertebrate Faunal Remains from the Philo II Site, Muskingum County, Ohio. *Pennsylvania Archaeologist* 46(3):1-6.

Shott, M.J. 1989 The Childers, Woods, and Late Woodland Chronology in the Upper Ohio Valley. *West Virginia Archeologist* 41(2):27-40.

1990 *Childers and Woods: Two Late Woodland Sites in the Upper Ohio Valley, Mason County, West Virginia*. University of Kentucky Archaeological Report 200, Lexington.

Skinner, S.M. and R. Norris 1984 Excavation of the Connett Mound 4, The Wolf Plains National Register District, The Plains, Ohio. *Ohio Archaeologist* 34(4):23-26.

Squier, E.G. and E.H. Davis 1848 *Ancient Monuments of the Mississippi Valley*. Smithsonian Contributions to Knowledge, Vol 1. Washington, D.C.

Struever, S. 1964 The Hopewell Interaction Sphere in Riverine - Western Great Lakes Culture History. In *Hopewellian Studies*, edited by J. Caldwell and R. Hall, pp.85-106. Illinois State Museum Scientific Papers 12, Springfield, Illinois.

Stuiver, M. and P.J. Reimer 1986 A Computer Program for Radiocarbon Age Calibration. *Radiocarbon* 28:1022-1030.

TWENTY

THE ADENA/HOPEWELL CONVERGENCE
IN EAST CENTRAL INDIANA

DONALD R. COCHRAN

ABSTRACT

Data from mounds and enclosures in east central Indiana have
consistently documented a late survival of Adena and an attenuated Hopewell expression. An appraisal of Adena and
Hopewell mound and enclosure sites in east central Indiana has
revealed: 1) that the sites represent a distinctive geographical
cluster, 2) that mound and enclosure sites are spatially connected, 3) that enclosure complexes and some mounds are built
sequentially, 4) that enclosure complex construction originated
with Adena and terminated with Hopewell, and 5) that the function of enclosure complexes changed through time. At least in
east central Indiana, archaeological concepts of Adena and
Hopewell converge into one ceremonial expression that are
inextricably linked, both chronologically and culturally.

A View From the Core a Synthesis of Ohio Hopewell Archaeology•edited by Paul J. Pacheco
© Copyright 1996 by The Ohio Archaeological Council• Columbus, Ohio
All Rights Reserved•ISBN 0-9626931-9-7

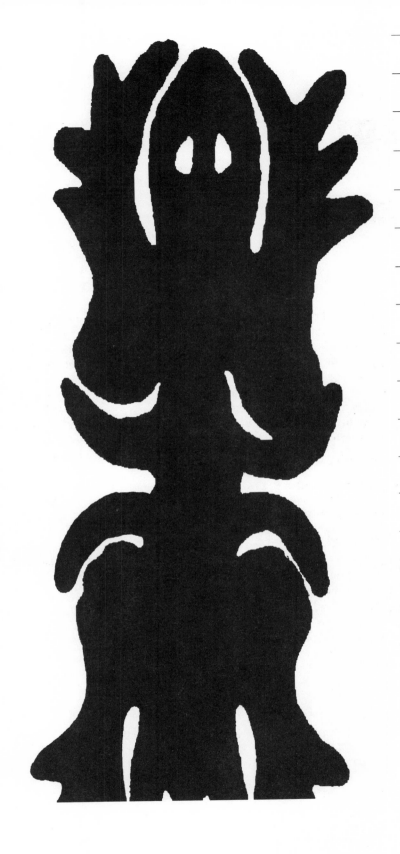

INTRODUCTION

*Why couldn't you take everything within
this time period in this one area and
assume it is a single system to start with,
instead of dealing out the cards into different regional traditions? See if you can
generate an internal pattern from your own
areas and from your own data here and
work outward from that [James Fitting in
"Discussion" following Kellar and Swartz
1971:132-133].*

For archaeologists working with the Adena and Hopewell
phenomena, one vexing problem has been the nature of the
relationship between them (Clay 1986:594; Dragoo
1963:259-260, 1977:27-34; Greber 1992; Griffin
1979:266; Otto 1979:13-14; Seeman 1986:566-567;
Webb and Snow 1945:335). Certainly there is little doubt
that early Adena predates late Hopewell but there are data
suggesting overlap between Late Adena and Early Hopewell
(Dragoo 1963; Griffin 1978; Otto 1979:13-14; Prufer
1964; Webb and Snow 1945). To date, no specific
instance that clearly demonstrates the relationship between
Adena and Hopewell has been reported.

In this paper I will argue that sites in the *New Castle Phase*
(Swartz 1976; Vickery 1970a, 1979) of east central Indiana
show a convergence of Adena and Hopewell ceremonialism
that is separate, clearly definable, and continuous. In addition, I will propose a model for the ceremonial relationships
between Adena and Hopewell sites in the region.

Given the variety of meanings associated with the terms
"Adena" and "Hopewell" (e.g., Struever 1964:87; Swartz
ed. 1971), for the purposes of this discussion I have used
the terms to represent complexes of artifacts with recognizable associations to Adena and Hopewell as defined in the
literature (Griffin 1978; Prufer 1964). The Adena Complex
is associated with dates of 500 B.C. to A.D. 1 (Seeman
1986:566). The Hopewell Complex dates from A.D. 1 to
A.D. 350 (Prufer 1965).

THE DATA SUPPORTING CONVERGENCE

The New Castle Phase

There is within the geographical confines of east central
Indiana a unique group of earthwork sites (**Figure 20:1**) that
have been of considerable interest to archaeologists for a
number of years (Kellar and Swartz 1971; Kellar 1983:46;
Lilly 1937; Setzler 1930, 1931; Swartz 1976; Vickery 1970a,
1979). Some of these sites have been incorporated into the
New Castle Phase defined as sites temporally "within the
Middle Woodland period; culturally, they are apparently transitional between Adena and Hopewell" (Vickery 1970a).
Griffin (1979:226) has called these sites "the best examples
of societies in transition from the archaeologists' Adena culture to the Hopewell development."

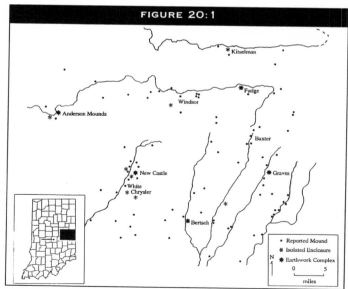

FIGURE 20:1

Mound and enclosure sites in east central Indiana.

Definition of the *New Castle Phase* was based on excavation data from two sites in east central Indiana: New Castle and Anderson Mounds. Both sites consisted of groupings of circular enclosures and associated mounds. Excavations produced both Adena and Hopewell artifacts and radiocarbon dates that suggested a Middle Woodland placement (Swartz 1976; Vickery 1970a, 1979). Sites were included in the *New Castle Phase* if they produced *New Castle Incised* ceramics, were associated with geometric earthworks and were in geographic proximity. Only four sites were included: Anderson Mounds, New Castle, Mound Camp in east central Indiana, and Spruce Run from central Ohio (Vickery 1970a:147).

Work at Anderson Mounds after Vickery's (1970a) excavations has shown that the enclosures within the site were constructed sequentially, that a longer time span than originally known was involved, and that an interpretation of sequential and continuous use for both Adena and Hopewell ceremonies was warranted (Buehrig and Hicks 1982; Cochran 1988, 1991, 1992; Cochran and Cree 1993; Hicks 1981; Kolbe 1992). In addition, an attempt has been made to include all the earthwork sites within east central Indiana into a coherent model which accounts for the similarities and differences between them (Cochran 1991).

In the next section of the paper I will argue that previous interpretations of a mixing of Adena and Hopewell materials at Anderson Mounds and the New Castle site (Swartz 1976; Vickery 1970a) are in error and that the materials are clearly separated, spatially defined and represent continuous, although different, activities. This hypothesis will be supported through a review of the locations of diagnostic Adena and Hopewell materials in the two sites and the relationships between them.

THE NEW CASTLE SITE

The New Castle site is the best example of continuity between Adena and Hopewell. The site was the focus of Ball State field school excavations in the late 1960s and early 1970s. Excavations were carried out in Mound 1, Earthwork 7, and Mound 4 **(Figure 20:2)**. Mound 1, a small earth mound not within an enclosure, contained human remains but no artifacts clearly distinctive of either Adena or Hopewell. Earthwork 7, a small circular enclosure, contained ceramics similar to *Adena Plain* (Cree 1990), but no burials. Mound 4 **(Figure 20:3)**, a panduriform mound surrounded by a ditch and embankment, contained both Adena and Hopewell artifacts, and was the focus of excavations (Swartz 1976). Primary among the features in Mound 4 were three areas labeled the Cremation Area, the Burial Area and the Ash Area. Distinctive artifacts recovered from each area included *New Castle Incised* ceramics from the Cremation Area, a plain platform pipe from the Burial Area and a partial vessel identified as *Hopewell Zoned Rocker Dentate Stamped* from the Ash Area (Swartz 1976).

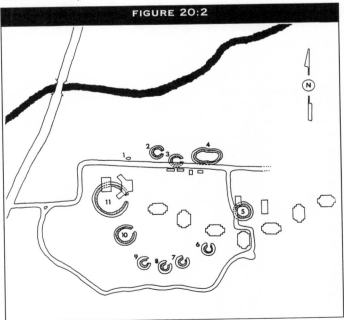

FIGURE 20:2

The New Castle site (after Lilly 1937).

The *New Castle Incised* ceramics are related to Late Adena *Montgomery Incised* ceramics from Ohio, West Virginia and Kentucky (Griffin 1978:259). Swartz (1976:58) obtained an associated radiocarbon date for *New Castle Incised* ceramics of 1940 ± 160 B.P. (M-1852), while a radiocarbon date of 2070 ± 70 B.P. (Beta-27170) was associated with *New Castle Incised* ceramics at Anderson Mounds (Kolbe 1992:61). The plain platform pipe from the Burial Area is similar to one recovered at Anderson Mounds (Swartz 1976; Vickery 1970a) and to forms dating to ca. A.D. 50 in Ohio Hopewell sites (Seeman 1977). This chronological placement is supported by a recent radiocarbon date of 1910 ± 80 B.P. (Beta-52612) associated with the platform pipe at Anderson Mounds. The partial Hopewell vessel from the Ash Area was identified by Griffin (Swartz 1971:4) as a late Middle Woodland type dated to around A.D. 200.

A review of the data from the mound shows no mixing of Adena and Hopewell artifacts within features or within burials. The diagnostic Adena artifacts, *New Castle Incised* ceramics, were restricted to the Cremation Area at the west end of the mound, while the diagnostic Hopewell artifacts were associated with burials in the remainder of the mound. The chronological placement of the *New Castle Incised* ceramics, the platform pipe and the Hopewell ceramics also indicate a chronological progression from west to east. The Adena ceramics were only recovered from the western end of the mound, while the most recent Hopewell ceramics were associated with the east lobe. The associated date for the Hopewell platform pipe in the center of the mound fell between the artifacts on either side. This sequence differs from that previously reported for the mound in which the west and east lobes were thought to be contemporaneous (Swartz 1976).

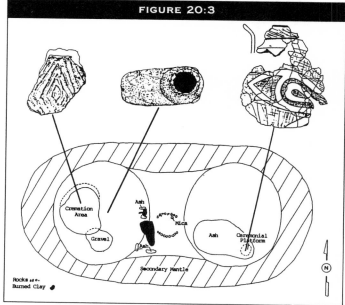

Distribution of diagnostic artifacts in Mound 4, New Castle Site.

In addition to the evidence for separation between the Adena and Hopewell materials in the mound, there was an apparent difference in the types of activities associated with the two components. No Adena burials were found in the mound, and the Cremation Area had no human remains associated with it (Swartz, personal communication, 1990). The Hopewell artifacts were clearly associated with human burials throughout the remainder of the mound. The two areas were "distinct and clearly separated" (Swartz 1976:12).

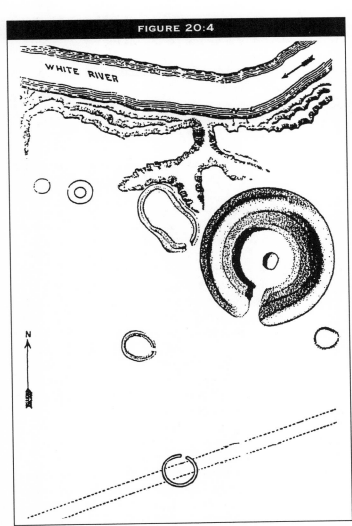

FIGURE 20:4

WHITE RIVER

N

Site map of Anderson Mounds (adapted from Cox 1878).

Mound 1 and Earthwork 7 contained no Hopewell artifacts, but instead appeared more closely related to Adena (Cree 1990). Thus, the New Castle site can more accurately be classified as a multicomponent ceremonial site containing both Adena and Hopewell materials and demonstrating continuing use through time. To classify the site as a "Hopewell Ceremonial Complex" (Swartz 1976) ignores the data for an equally important Adena component.

ANDERSON MOUNDS

A similar sequence of shifting activities and apparent continuity between Adena and Hopewell can be demonstrated at Anderson Mounds. The site consists of an assemblage of circular enclosures at the south end and three rectangular enclosures at the north end of the site. The two groups are about 800 m apart. The southern circular group contains one large enclosure (the Great Mound), a panduriform enclosure (Fiddleback Mound), and at least two smaller enclosures **(Figure 20:4)**. Although additional enclosures have been reported at the site (Cox 1878; Vickery 1970a), recent work has been unable to verify them (Cochran 1991).

The Great Mound had a small mound approximately 1 m high on the central platform **(Figure 20:5)**. This small mound was excavated by Indiana University in 1968 and 1969 (Vickery 1970a, 1970b; White 1968). Vickery's (1970a, 1970b) data has been used for this analysis, supplemented with additional data recovered since 1969 (Cochran 1991). Excavation of the mound revealed two distinctive sets of activities. The first set was associated with the construction of a primary mound. This mound contained a sequence of construction which included excavation and preparation of a submound pit, the erection of a number of posts, and construction of an initial clay platform. The posts were burned prior to the construction of the next clay platform. The first clay platform was sealed with a layer of white ash and two succeeding clay platforms, also covered with ash, were constructed over it. The primary mound was then capped with an earth mantle (Vickery 1970a).

Excavation of the primary mound revealed few associated artifacts, intrusive burials and scattered human bone in mound fill, but no burials in direct association with the clay platforms. Two sherds of *New Castle Incised* ceramics were found in disturbed fill and the mound capping (Vickery 1970a:91). Fragments of imitation bear canines were also found in disturbed fill and the mound capping. The only diagnostic artifact associated with features in the primary mound was one portion of an imitation bone bear canine found near the top of a posthole in the center of the mound. Bear canine ornaments have been considered important Hopewell Interaction Sphere artifacts (Seeman 1979), although black bear canine artifacts have also been reported from Adena sites (Webb and Baby 1957:17-18). The Anderson Mounds specimens were identified as imitations of black bear canines (Vickery 1970a:124).

Subsequent to the final earth capping of the primary mound, and representing the second set of activities, a log tomb was constructed adjacent to the mound and two burials were entombed. The log tomb and the primary mound were joined into one structure through a final earth capping (Vickery 1970a, 1970b).

The second set of activities associated with the mound included the construction of a log tomb adjacent to the primary mound. Two burials were in the tomb along with artifacts. The only diagnostic artifact in the tomb was a plain Hopewell platform pipe (Vickery 1970a). A recently obtained radiocarbon date of 1910 ± 80 B.P. (Beta-52612) for the log tomb suggested similar dating for the pipe as well. The log tomb and the primary mound were joined into one structure through a final earth covering (Vickery 1970a).

Further documentation for the sequence of activities and continuity between Adena and Hopewell at Anderson Mounds has been obtained through limited test excavations to obtain radiocarbon dates (Cochran 1988; Kolbe 1992). To date, a total of 12 radiocarbon dates have been recorded for the site. The radiocarbon dates from Anderson (Cochran 1992) suggest the following reconstruction of activities:

1) Construction of the post structure in the Great Mound occurred at ca. 2,200 B.P.

2) The embankment around the Great Mound was constructed ca. 2,110 B.P.

3) The embankment around the panduriform Fiddleback Mound was constructed ca. 2,090 B.P.

4) Construction of the mound in the center of the Great Mound was completed by ca. 1,910 B.P.

5) The focus of earthwork construction shifted to the northern part of the site and from circular to rectangular enclosures by ca. 1,955 B.P.

Comparison of the radiocarbon dates from Anderson Mounds with those from the New Castle site (Swartz 1976) shows overlap between them and suggests that Mound 4 at New Castle would be contemporary with later activities at Anderson. Drawing on the chronological data from both sites, it is suggested that activities at Anderson Mounds shifted from the Great Mound to the panduriform enclosure and ultimately to the rectangular enclosures at the north end of the site. Thus a pattern of shifting, but contemporary, interrelated activities were occurring at the site.

Except for two sherds of *New Castle Incised* ceramics in mound fill, Adena artifacts were lacking in the primary mound. The component association for the imitation bear canine found near the top of the post in the primary mound is ambiguous, but suggestive of Hopewell activities on the primary mound after the posts were burned. The radiocarbon dates, however, suggest construction of the post structure, the embankment and at least part of the primary mound by Adena followed by a shift in function to a Hopewell mortuary feature. While the activities associated with the clay platforms in the primary mound may be related to mortuary activities, they were different from those represented by the Hopewell burials placed in the log tomb. This situation is analogous to that documented previously in the Cremation Area and adjacent Burial Area at the New Castle site.

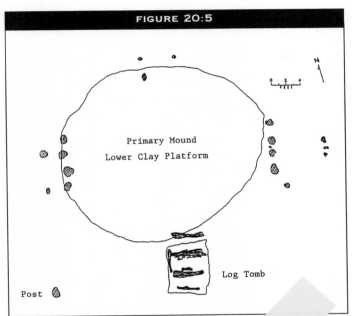

FIGURE 20:5

Relationship between the primary mound and the log to Great Mound, Anderson Mounds.

Thus, at both the New Castle site an son Mounds, Adena and Hopewell materials occu same mounds, although they are distinct and sepa. There is also a clear shift in activities associated with the two complexes. There is, however, no evidence that the shift is either abrupt or radical but, instead, appears to represent continuing use of a mound over a span of many years. The interpretation favored here is that what has been called Adena and what has been called Hopewell represent a continuum with Adena predating and ultimately being replaced by Hopewell. This argument has been anticipated by a number of investigators (e.g., discussion following Kellar and Swartz 1971; Prufer 1964; Webb and Snow 1945), but such clear evidence has not been previously documented.

These data indicate that the *New Castle Phase* as originally defined was correct in noting the transitional nature of the remains at the New Castle site and at Anderson Mound. However, the apparent mixing of components has not been

supported by more recent data and interpretations except that both Adena and Hopewell components are present within the sites. Further, previous interpretations based on comparisons of the two sites have been distorted, in that the contents of a panduriform mound have been assumed to be equivalent to the contents of a small mound within a different type of enclosure (Swartz 1976; Vickery 1970a, 1970b, 1979). The presence or absence of certain artifact and material types can only be compared between similar types of mounds. It is the opinion of this author that in order for the *New Castle Phase* to have validity, it must be redefined on a more inclusive level and it must account for other earthwork sites and ceramic types in the region. In working toward this goal, the following review of the other earthwork sites in the region is presented followed by a model of the relationships between them.

REGIONAL PERSPECTIVE

The sites involved in this review are located near the southern boundary of the Tipton Till Plain, a broad glacial plain with little relief (Schneider 1966). The White, Whitewater and Wabash Rivers head in this region. The sites are concentrated on the White and Whitewater Rivers, with few occurring in the Wabash drainage (**Figure 20:1**). Taken together, the sites, consisting of mounds, isolated circular enclosures and enclosure complexes (Cochran 1991), make up what can be identified as a ceremonial landscape (Clay 1991; Dillehay 1990). No similar regional grouping of earthwork sites occurs within Indiana (Kellar 1983:46-48), and they appear to represent the western periphery of Adena and Hopewell sites in the Middle Ohio Valley (Seeman 1979:259; Swartz 1981:18).

ENCLOSURE COMPLEXES

The enclosure complexes are the most distinctive regional sites. These are of two types: circular and rectangular. Three of these sites contain circular enclosures and two contain large rectangular enclosures. Anderson Mounds is the only site with both circular and rectangular enclosures although the two enclosure types are spatially separated within the site (Cochran 1991).

The circular enclosure complexes share common characteristics of geographic location and internal features. Geographic commonalities for these sites include location on the eastern bluff edge overlooking a river valley, and placement on different rivers (**Figure 20:1**). The sites also contain common earthwork features including a large circular enclosure ca. 90 m across, a panduriform enclosure and a number of smaller enclosures ca. 30 m across.[1] All enclosures in these complexes have internal ditches and external embankments. All three complexes are reported to have a small mound either within the complex or nearby (MacPherson 1878; Swartz 1976; Vickery 1970a).

Within the circular complex sites, excavated mounds within enclosures have both Adena artifacts and Hopewell artifacts and burials in them. A review of the stratigraphy of the sites shows clear separation and continuity between the Adena and Hopewell materials. The sites also show a change in activities between Adena and Hopewell (Cochran 1991).

Excavations of an enclosure without an interior mound within these sites revealed only plain ceramics which appeared most similar to *Adena Plain* (Cree 1990). The central platform of the large circular enclosure at the Bertsch site revealed a set of postholes and features comparable to some features in the central platform of the Great Mound at Anderson (Heilman 1976:93-103). The Bertsch site, however, contained a burial pit with the remains of three individuals (Heilman 1976) which has not been duplicated at Anderson. The large circle at the New Castle site was apparently destroyed by the construction of a building, and has not been excavated (Swartz 1976). No diagnostic Hopewell materials were recovered from Bertsch (Heilman 1976).

Rectangular enclosures only occur at three sites within the region: the three at the north end of Anderson Mounds, a large enclosure encompassing ca. 13 ha, called Fudge Mound (Setzler 1931), and a smaller rectangular enclosure, encompassing ca. 5 ha, called Graves Mound (Setzler 1930). Both Fudge and Graves enclosures are not of bank and ditch construction, but have embankments constructed of soil excavated elsewhere. Only Fudge has an associated mound (Setzler

1931). All of the rectangular enclosures are situated north of the circular enclosure complexes but they do not follow the same locational patterns evident in the circular enclosure complexes. The rectangular enclosures do not have associated radiocarbon dates except at Anderson Mounds where it appears that rectangular enclosures replaced circular enclosures by approximately A.D. 1.

MOUNDS AND OTHER ENCLOSURES

In spite of the evidence for Adena-Hopewell continuity in the New Castle and Anderson Mounds sites, other sites in the region do not reveal the same sequence. Excavated mounds not associated with circular enclosure complexes show a clear relationship to the Adena Complex (Cochran 1991; Kellar and Swartz 1971). Only two of these mounds have associated radiocarbon dates. A late series of dates from the White site is somewhat ambiguous due to large standard deviations and lack of specific provenience (Swartz 1973). A date of 2020 ± 70 B.P. (Beta-25224) obtained from an ash layer containing cremated human bone near the bottom of Windsor Mound shows contemporaneity with activities at Anderson Mounds (Cochran 1991). No Hopewell burials with associated artifacts have been excavated from mounds outside of circular enclosure complexes in the region. The unprovenienced base of a *Snyders* point is among the artifacts recovered from Windsor Mound (Kolbe 1992), a tantalizing suggestion of further connections between Adena and Hopewell within the region.

No isolated circular enclosures have been excavated within the region and, as currently known, only one still exists (Cochran 1991). This enclosure is located on a prominent hilltop and has a gateway oriented toward sunrise at the Winter Solstice. Combining the information from circular enclosure complexes, from burial mounds outside of enclosure complexes and from rectangular enclosures provides data to construct a model of the relationship between Adena and Hopewell ceremonial activities in the region.

A REGIONAL MODEL

The Adena and Hopewell ceremonial landscape in east central Indiana is a distinct regional grouping of mounds, isolated circular enclosures and enclosure complexes. Although the chronological data is limited, it is proposed that the region was initially defined by the construction of isolated circular enclosures and mounds by people with an Adena ceremonial complex.

By approximately 2,200 B.P., three locations were chosen within the region as the loci for particular ceremonial activites. The locations were chosen in reference to spatial divisions within the people occupying the area as suggested by the choices for sites on different river systems and to allow observations of astronomical events, particularly the setting sun (Cochran 1991). For approximately 200 years, the sites were the locus of activities related to tracking astr-nomical events and, in all likelinhood, mortuary activities and other undefined rituals. It is hypothesized that someone lived at the complex or nearby, a resident priest or priestess (cf. Hedges 1984:159-173), to keep track of astronomical events which were marked by group ceremonies.

Mounds continued to be built outside of the enclosure plexes as mortuary sites for subdivisions of the group people who were focused on the enclosure comple about 2,000 B.P. activities at the sites changed i tain people were buried within the enclosure c These people were interred with artifacts dia; Hopewell. Outside of the enclosure comple al mounds continued to be used and burials ir e mounds continued to be associated with Adena.

The function of the enclosure complexes apparently shifted from Adena activities that did not involve human burials to Hopewell activities that did. In addition, the region was fur-ther subdivided, after about 2,000 B.P., through the con-struction of two large rectangular enclosures. That one of these was constructed around an Adena burial mound demonstrates the ceremonial continuum. Given that burial mounds in the region contain only Adena artifacts, and that

radiocarbon dates suggest contemporaneity between the Adena acitivities in the enclosure complexes and the mounds, it is hypothesized that they represent two different components of the same ceremonial system.

CONCLUSION

One continuing plague on Adena and Hopewell archaeolo-gy has been the lack of chronological controls (Griffin 1978). Most of the larger Adena and Hopewell sites were excavated long before the development of radiocarbon dat-ing; field methods were not refined to current standards for sampling and stratigraphic control. Most of the sites in east central Indiana have been virtually destroyed, but Anderson Mounds remains relatively untouched, both from historic land use and early archaeology. Although the east central Indiana earthwork group is on the edge of the core areas for both Adena and Ohio Hopewell, it is also somewhat less complicated and may, therefore, offer an opportune research universe (Otto 1979). While the apparent conti-nuity between Adena and Hopewell ceremonialism within east central Indiana can be accounted for with the model proposed in this paper, it has not been tested against other data. It is hoped that the data and interpretations present-ed here will stimulate additional research into the relation-ships between these intriguing archaeological constructs.

NOTES

1. Bertsch site has been reported to consist of two large circular enclosures and five smaller circles (Heilman 1976; MacPherson 1878; Setzler 1930). An aerial photograph at the Indiana State Archives shows the site had a large circle, a panduriform enclosure and 14 small circles.

REFERENCES CITED

Buehrig, J.E. and R. Hicks 1982 *A Comprehensive Survey of the Archaeological Resources of Mounds State Park, Anderson, Indiana.* Archaeological Resources Management Service, Reports of Investigation 6, Ball State University, Muncie, Indiana.

Clay, R.B. 1986 Adena Ritual Spaces. In *Early Woodland Archaeology*, edited by K.B. Farnsworth and T.E. Emerson, pp. 581-595. Center for American Archaeology, Kampsville Seminars in Archaeology 2, Kampsville, Illinois.

   1991 *Essential Features of Adena Ritual: A Lecture Delivered at Angel Mounds National Historic Landmark, Evansville, Indiana on 3 April 1990.* Glenn A. Black Laboratory of Archaeology, Research Reports 13, Bloomington, Indiana.

Cochran, D.R. 1988 *1987 Excavations at Mounds State Park.* Archaeological Resources Management Service, Reports of Investigation 23, Ball State University, Muncie, Indiana.

   1991 Adena and Hopewell Cosmology: New Evidence from East Central Indiana. In *Native American Cultures in Indiana*, edited by Ronald Hicks. Proceedings of the First Minnetrista Council for Great Lakes Native American Studies, Minnetrista Cultural Center and Ball State University, Muncie, Indiana.

   1992 Anderson Mounds: Redefining the Stratigraphy of the Great Mound. Paper presented at the Annual Meeting of the Indiana Academy of Science, Ball State University, Muncie, Indiana.

Cochran, D.R. and B. Cree 1993 New Evidence from Anderson Mounds. In *Current Research in Indiana Archaeology and Prehistory: 1991 & 1992*, edited by B.G. Redmond. Glenn A. Black Laboratory of Archaeology, Research Reports 14, Indiana University, Bloomington, Indiana.

Cox, E.T. 1878 Antiquities. *Eighth, Ninth and Tenth Annual Reports.* Geological Survey of Indiana, Indianapolis.

Cree, B.A. 1990 Reanalysis of Collections: Anderson Mounds, Mounds Bluff, New Castle and White Site. Ms. on file, Archaeological Resources Management Service, Ball State University, Muncie, Indiana.

Dillehay, T.D. 1990 Mapuche Ceremonial Landscape, Social Recruitment and Resource Rights. *World Archaeology* 22(2):223-241.

Dragoo, D.W. 1963 *Mounds for the Dead.* Carnegie Museum, Annals 37, Pittsburgh, Pennsylvania.

   1977 The Development of Adena Culture and its Role in the Formation of Ohio Hopewell. In *Hopewellian Studies* (third printing), edited by J.R. Caldwell and R.L. Hall, pp. 1-34. Illinois State Museum, Scientific Papers 12, Springfield, Illinois.

Greber, N. 1992 A Study of Continuity and Contrast Between Central Scioto Adena and Hopewell Sites. *West Virginia Archeologist* 43(1&2):1-26.

Griffin, J.B. 1978 The Midlands. In *Ancient North Americans*, edited by Jesse Jennings, pp. 243-302. W.H. Freeman & Co., San Francisco.

   1979 An Overview of the Chillicothe Hopewell Conference. In *Hopewell Archaeology: The Chillicothe Conference*, edited by D.S. Brose and N.B. Greber, pp. 266-279. Kent State University Press, Kent, Ohio.

Hedges, J.W. 1984 *Tomb of the Eagles: Death and Life in a Stone Age Tribe.* New Amsterdam, New York.

Heilman, J.M. 1976 *Archaeological Survey of Wayne County, Indiana.* Masters thesis, Department of Anthropology, Kent State University, Kent, Ohio.

Hicks, R. 1981 *Final Report of an Archaeological Reconnaissance and Test Excavation, Mounds State Park, Madison County, Indiana, July-August 1979.* Report on file, Archaeological Resources Management Service, Ball State University, Muncie, Indiana.

Kellar, J.H. 1983 *An Introduction to the Prehistory of Indiana*. Indiana Historical Society, Indianapolis.

Kellar, J.H. and B.K. Swartz, Jr. 1971 Adena: The Western Periphery. In *Adena: The Seeking of an Identity*, edited by B.K. Swartz, Jr., pp. 122-137. Ball State University, Muncie, Indiana.

Kolbe, B. 1992 *Brookville Lake: An Archaeological Study in the Whitewater Drainage*. Archaeological Resources Management Service, Reports of Investigation 35. Ball State University, Muncie, Indiana.

Lilly, E. 1937 *Prehistoric Antiquities of Indiana*. Indiana Historical Society, Indianapolis.

MacPherson, J.C. 1878 Observations on the Pre-Historic Earthworks of Wayne County, Indiana. *Eighth, Ninth and Tenth Annual Reports*, Geological Survey of Indiana, Indianapolis, pp. 219-226.

Otto, M.P. 1979 Hopewell Antecedents in the Adena Heartland. In *Hopewell Archaeology: The Chillicothe Conference*, edited by D.S. Brose and N.B. Greber, pp. 9-14. Kent State University Press, Kent, Ohio.

Prufer, O.H. 1964 The Ohio Hopewell Complex of Ohio. In *Hopewellian Studies*, edited by J. Caldwell and R. Hall, pp. 35-83. Illinois State Museum, Scientific Papers 12, Springfield, Illinois.

1965 *The McGraw Site: a Study in Hopewellian Dynamics*. Cleveland Museum of Natural History, Scientific Publications (4), Cleveland, Ohio.

Schneider, A.F. 1966 Physiography. In *Natural Features of Indiana*, edited by Alton A. Lindsey. Indiana Academy of Science, Indianapolis, Indiana.

Seeman, M. 1977 Stylistic Variation in Middle Woodland Pipe Styles: the Chronological Implications. *Midcontinental Journal of Archaeology* 2:47-66.

1979 *The Hopewell Interaction Sphere: the Evidence for Interregional Trade and Structural Complexity*. Indiana Historical Society, Prehistory Research Series 5(2). Indianapolis.

1986 Adena "Houses" and the Implications for Early Woodland Settlement Models in the Ohio Valley. In *Early Woodland Archaeology*, edited by K.B. Farnsworth and T.E. Emerson, pp. 564-580. Center for American Archaeology, Kampsville Seminars in Archaeology 2, Kampsville, Illinois.

Setzler, F. 1930 The Archaeology of the Whitewater River Valley. *Indiana History Bulletin* 7(12):353-550.

1931 The Archaeology of Randolph County and the Fudge Mound. *Indiana History Bulletin* 9(1):1-51.

Struever, S. 1964 The Hopewell Interaction Sphere in Riverine-Western Great Lakes Culture History. In *Hopewellian Studies*, edited by J.R. Caldwell and R.L. Hall, pp. 85-106. Illinois State Museum, Scientific Papers 12, Springfield, Illinois.

Swartz, B.K,. Jr., ed. 1971 *Adena: The Seeking of an Identity*. Ball State University, Muncie, Indiana.

Swartz, B.K., Jr. 1971 *Comments on the Incomplete Pottery Vessel from East Mound, Earthwork Four, New Castle Site*. Archaeological Reports 8(4), Department of Anthropology, Ball State University, Muncie, Indiana.

1973 *Mound Three, White Site, Hn-10 (IAS-BSU): The Final Report on a Robbins Manifestation in East Central Indiana*. Ball State University, Contributions to Anthropological History 1. Muncie, Indiana.

1976 *The New Castle Site: A Hopewell Ceremonial Complex in East Central Indiana*. Ball State University, Contributions to Anthropological History 2. Muncie, Indiana.

1981 *Indiana's Prehistoric Past*. University Publications, Ball State University, Muncie, Indiana.

Vickery, K.D. 1970a *Excavations at Mounds State Park, 1969 Season*. Report on file, Archaeological Resources Management Service, Ball State University, Muncie, Indiana.

1970b Preliminary Report on the Excavation of the "Great Mound" in Madison County, Indiana. *Proceedings of the Indiana Academy of Science* 79:75-82.

1979 "Reluctant" or "Avant-Garde" Hopewell?: Suggestions of Middle Woodland Cultural Change in East Central Indiana and South-central Ohio. In *Hopewell Archaeology: The Chillicothe Conference*, edited by D.S. Brose and N.B. Greber, pp. 59-63. Kent State University Press, Kent, Ohio.

Webb, W.S. and R.S. Baby 1957 *The Adena People - No. 2*. The Ohio Historical Society, Columbus.

Webb, W.S. and C.E. Snow 1945 *The Adena People*. University of Kentucky, Reports in Anthropology and Archaeology 6, Lexington, Kentucky.

White, C.F. 1968 *Report on the 1968 Field Season at Mounds State Park*. Report on file, Archaeological Resources Management Service, Ball State University, Muncie, Indiana.

TWENTY-ONE

DECORATED LEATHER OBJECTS
FROM THE MOUNT VERNON SITE,
A HOPEWELL SITE IN POSEY COUNTY, INDIANA

CURTIS H. TOMAK AND FRANK N. BURKETT

ABSTRACT

The Mount Vernon site consists of a huge Hopewell mound located on General Electric property in Posey County, Indiana. It is a ceremonial/burial site of extraordinary magnitude which has strong ties with Ohio Hopewell. The site was found during borrow work for road construction in 1988, but unfortunately the discovery was not reported to highway personnel or to archaeologists before the mound had been largely destroyed by borrow work and by people digging for artifacts. A test excavation was conducted at the mound by the senior author in 1988. Thousands of Hopewell artifacts had been taken from the site by collectors prior to our excavation, and a variety of such artifacts were recovered by our work. The focus of this paper is the decorated leather objects from the site. The site has generated a precedent-setting ARPA case, and the material from the site has been reburied by Native Americans.

A View From the Core a Synthesis of Ohio Hopewell Archaeology•edited by Paul J. Pacheco
© Copyright 1996 by The Ohio Archaeological Council• Columbus, Ohio
All Rights Reserved•ISBN 0-9626931-9-7

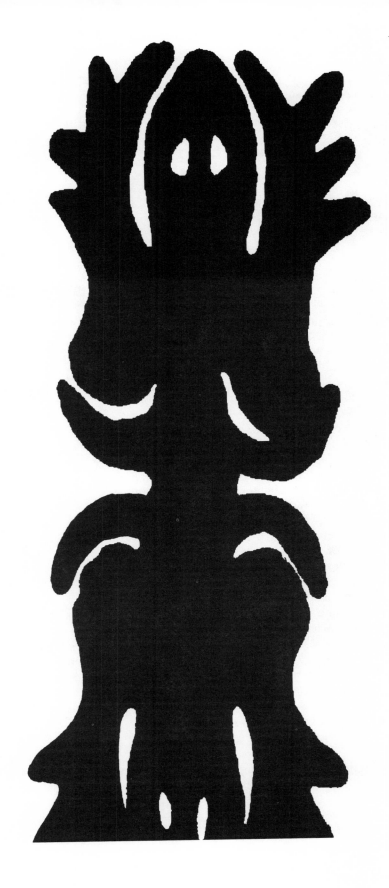

Curtis H. Tomak and Frank N. Burkett

D E C O R A T E D   L E A T H E R   O B J E C T S   F R O M   T H E   M O U N T   V E R N O N   S I T E ,

Introduction

As presently known, the Mount Vernon site (12PO885; Indiana Department of Highways [IDOH] site number 65-30) consists of one of the largest Hopewell mounds ever discovered. It is on General Electric property just southwest of the city of Mount Vernon in Posey County in the southwestern corner of Indiana (**Figure 21:1**). The mound is situated on a ridge immediately south of County Road (CR) 850S about 1.6 km northwest of the Ohio River and about 7 km east of the Wabash River.

The site was discovered during the construction of CR 850S, a project which was funded by the Federal Highway Administration (FHWA) and administered by IDOH. During construction the elevation constituting the site was selected as a source of borrow dirt for CR 850S. The evidence indicates that the site was discovered between April 11 and July 1, 1988, by employees of a construction company during borrow operations and that a great quantity of Hopewell archaeological material was found at that time. However, contrary to FHWA and IDOH regulations and the recommendations of the archaeological survey reports for the project (DeRegnaucourt 1986; Stafford 1988), the site was not reported to the proper agencies, i.e., the IDOH or the Division of Historic Preservation and Archaeology (DHPA) of the Indiana Department of Natural Resources. Numerous collectors found out about the site, and a great amount of collecting and digging for artifacts was done by them between April and August 1988.

The location of the site did not become known to archaeologists until Tomak found it in October 1988. At that time the site was covered with a heavy growth of grass, and the top of the remnant of the mound was concave as a result of a large, southwest to northeast, borrow trench which is over 30 m in width (**Figure 21:2**). The site had been severely disturbed, possibly essentially destroyed, by the borrow work and by people digging for artifacts.

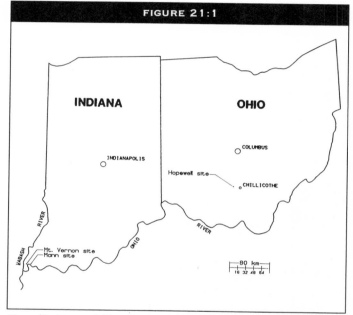

Map of Indiana and Ohio showing the location of the Mount Vernon site, the Mann site, and the Hopewell site.

After locating the site, discussions were immediately initiated between the IDOH and General Electric in regard to site protection and test excavation. An agreement was reached, and a test excavation was conducted at the site in October and November 1988 (Tomak 1990, 1994). Prior to testing the site, the IDOH coordinated with the FHWA, the DHPA, and the Miami Indians.

A good basic idea of the original character of the mound has been obtained by interviewing people who are familiar with the area and by utilizing aerial photographs and contour maps. Especially helpful are one foot contour maps prepared by the IDOH which are based upon aerial photographs taken in 1985 and 1989. Those two maps depict the mound before and after its disturbance by borrow work. They indicate that about 5.6 m have been removed from the highest point of the mound by borrow work and that our excavation units were in locations that vary from about 3.4 m to 5.8 m below the original surface.

FIGURE 21:2

The Mount Vernon site in 1988 from the east showing concave upper surface resulting from borrow work. The mound extends from the woods to the pole on the right.

We know that there was a large, prominent, elevation at the site and that most or all of that elevation was a large artificial mound (**Figure 21:3**). Part of the mound was composed of dark earth which had been carried to the site from a low lying wetland area. Measurements obtained from various aerial photographs indicate that the mound was about 122 m long, nearly 52 m wide, and approximately 6 m high. It was steep sided and loaf shaped. The top was flattened and is reported to have had sizeable depressions in it. The depressed areas on the top of the mound are interesting in that they could indicate the presence of collapsed tombs or structures. One informant gave evidence supporting that possibility by reporting that when the archaeological material was found during borrow operations, the bulldozer "just fell into it", indicating some kind of a hole or soft spot. Another individual has reported the possible existence of a

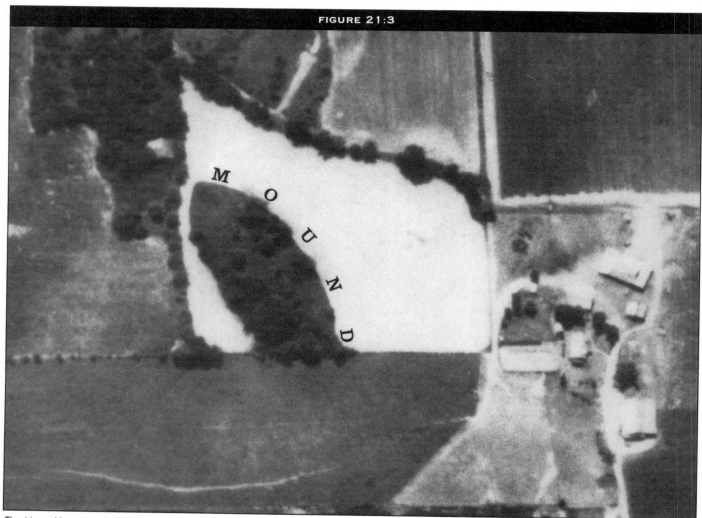

FIGURE 21:3

MOUND

The Mount Vernon site in 1966 prior to borrow work; aerial view.

wooden tomb at the site. The evidence indicates that a large quantity of artifacts and possibly a tomb or structure occurred on or near the base of the mound. The individual who found those artifacts estimated that the artifacts were found approximately 4.6 m below the original mound surface. It is not known just how high up in the mound artifacts occurred, but workers on the job have reported that arti-

facts, most noticeably chert bifaces, occurred well up in the mound. Human bone (burned, unburned, and some copper stained) was recovered from the site by the IDOH excavation, and it is thought that artifacts accompanied burials of important people and that separate caches of artifacts may also have been present.

FIGURE 21:4

Chert bifaces from the Mount Vernon site.

When the site was found by the IDOH investigation in October 1988, we named it the Mount Vernon site. That is its original and official name which has been used since 1988 in reports, records, and documents on file with the DHPA and the State Historic Preservation Officer (Tomak 1989, 1990, 1994). Later, other people referred to the site as the GE Mound, and as a result the site has unfortunately acquired two names.

ARTIFACTS FROM THE MOUNT VERNON SITE

Thousands of Hopewell artifacts had been taken from the mound by construction workers and collectors prior to our work, and a variety of such artifacts were recovered during our excavation. Among the materials from the site are thousands of chert bifaces, large points/blades of chert, obsidian, quartz crystal, and cannel coal, copper celts, copper and silver plates, panpipes, and earspools, copper covered wooden artifacts; silver covered hemispheres, mica, pearls, marine shell beads, bear canine teeth, worked human mandibles, and decorated leather objects (Tomak 1994). Examples of artifacts are pictured in **Figures 21:4-21:14**, and the decorated leather objects, which are the focus of this paper, are discussed below.

DECORATED LEATHER OBJECTS

As a result of an FBI investigation, about 3,000 artifacts were returned to General Electric by collectors. In the material returned by a group of eight people are two small, decorated, elongated leather objects which had been attached to a flat piece of copper (**Figure 21:11**). The objects are alike, but the designs are mirror images of each other. The objects are 41 mm long and 15 mm wide. One end is rounded, and the other end has two elongated projections. On the surface are grooves and larger recessed areas

FIGURE 21:5

Quartz crystal point from the Mount Vernon site.

which form a design or figure. There are four small perforations in the recessed surface of each of the objects. The perforations fit onto small projections extending from the surface of a flat piece of copper which is in the material which they returned to General Electric. Part of the outline of one of the leather objects is visible on one side of the piece of copper, and part of the outline of the other leather object is evident on the other side of the copper.

The figures on the leather objects (**Figure 21:13**) are like the raised and recessed figure on a copper artifact recovered by Moorehead from Mound 25 at the Hopewell site in Ohio (Greber and Ruhl 1989:123-124, Figure 4.45). In trying to determine what the figures on these objects might be, Frank Burkett (then archaeologist with IDOH) suggested that they may be representations of the human ear.

Morphologically the raised portions and the recessed portions of these artifacts conform to parts of the ear. Using a 1901 edition of *Gray's Anatomy*, the matching parts of the ear are the helix, fossa of the helix, antihelix with its bifurcation, fossa of the antihelix (fossa triangularis), concha, tragus, and the incisura intertragica (**Figure 21:14**). The copper artifact has more of the outline of an ear than the leather objects have, and instead of having two elongated projections, it has a rounded area which has a sizeable

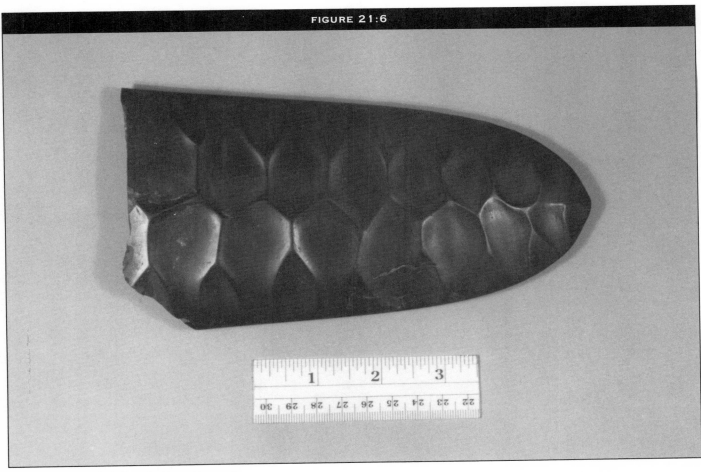

FIGURE 21:6

Cannel coal point/blade from the Mount Vernon site.

hole in it. The perforated rounded area may represent a pierced earlobe, and the projections on the leather objects may represent torn or cut earlobes. Since the designs on the leather objects are reversed, one would represent a right ear, and the other would be the left ear.

Further indication that the above objects represent ears is provided by the way the ear is depicted on a human effigy made from antler from the Hopewell site (Greber and Ruhl 1989:208, Figure 6.26; Moorehead 1922:167, Figure 66;

Figure 21:13 herein). All of the above mentioned parts of the ear are present on the ear of the effigy, and except for the elongated projections, the external outline of the leather objects is similar to that of the ear of the effigy.

Two other leather objects just like the ones described above have been returned by another collector. As with the previous pair, the design on each of them is the reverse of that on the other (**Figure 21:10**).

FIGURE 21:7

Copper celt with pearls, shell beads, and leather from the Mount Vernon site.

Another collector has returned a fragment of another of the decorated leather objects and a piece of copper onto which it fits (**Figure 21:12**). The piece of copper has a recessed area with a copper projection in it. The rounded part of the leather object fits into the recessed area, and the projection goes through a hole in the leather to hold it in place. There is a pearl on the piece of copper next to the recessed area.

DISCUSSION

The archaeological material recovered by the IDOH excavation and the items reported to have been found at the site by other people form a consistent assemblage. The artifacts, human remains, and the characteristics of the site clearly show that the Mount Vernon site is a Middle Woodland Hopewell ceremonial/burial site of extraordinary magnitude.

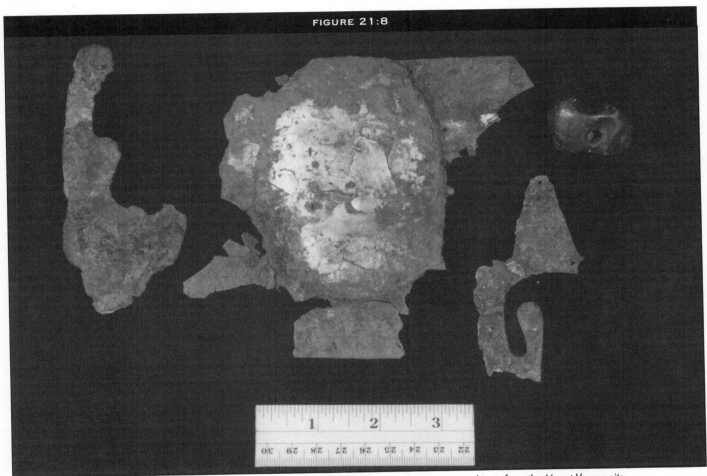

FIGURE 21:8

A large silver and copper plate, a silver covered bone (upper right), and two lobed, curvilinear, copper objects from the Mount Vernon site.

In terms of raw materials, artifacts, cremations, mound size, and concept, the site has strong ties to Ohio Hopewell. The items from the Mount Vernon site form a classic Hopewell assemblage and are well represented at major Ohio Hopewell sites such as Harness, Seip, Mound City, and the Hopewell site itself (Mills 1907, 1922; Moorehead 1922; Seeman 1979; Shetrone 1926; Shetrone and Greenman 1931). Obsidian artifacts, mica, copper objects (including plates and celts), earspools, silver, metal covered hemispheres or buttons, pearl beads, shell beads, and bear canine teeth are well known Hopewell items and were present at Harness, Seip, Mound City, and the Hopewell site. At least three of those sites produced quartz, and artificially modified human jaws and panpipes have been recovered from at least two of them. A cache of over 8,000 chert bifaces was found at the Hopewell site. The representation of the human ear on the decorated leather objects from Mount Vernon also matches that on a copper object from the Hopewell site. In fact, the Hopewell site (**Figure 21:1**) has produced practically everything that has been found at

FIGURE 21:9

Two silver panpipes from the Mount Vernon site.

or reported from the Mount Vernon site. In addition, the Turner site in Ohio (Willoughby and Hooton 1922) is the only other Hopewell site that we know of which has produced artifacts similar to the cannel coal point/blades (**Figure 21:6**) from Mount Vernon. Relationships with Illinois

Hopewell are indicated by the large quantity of Burlington/Crescent Quarry chert bifaces (Tomak 1994) and by the style of the worked human mandibles (Nawrocki 1994).

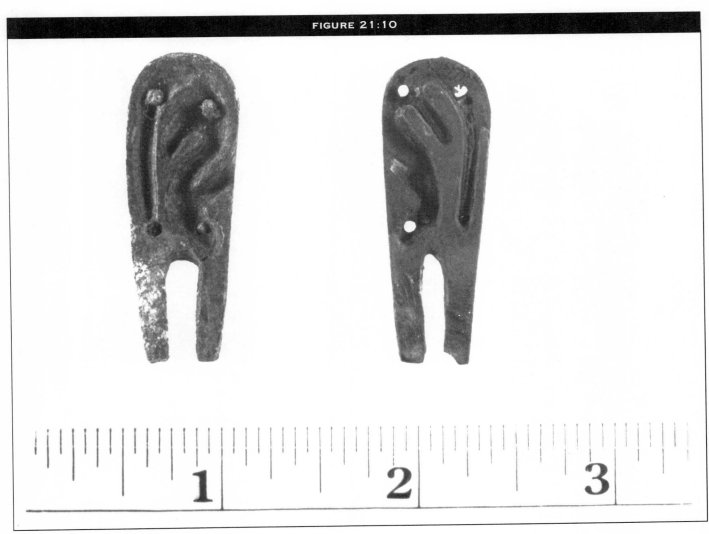

FIGURE 21:10

Two decorated leather objects from the Mount Vernon site.

The relationship of the Mount Vernon site to other sites in the area needs to be explored. Based upon our familiarity with Posey County and work that has been done there, we would not be surprised to find sites in the immediate area of the Mount Vernon site which produce a scattering or a limited amount of Middle Woodland material, i.e., points, lamellar blades, and potsherds. At present, however, the existence of substantial habitation sites or other burial sites of Middle Woodland affiliation in the immediate area of the Mount Vernon site is problematic, and we know of no such sites.

The major Middle Woodland site in Posey County is the Mann site which is about 8 km east of the Mount Vernon site (**Figure 21:1**). The Mann site is a very large and complex Hopewellian site which includes a large habitation area, 10 mounds, three rectanguloid enclosures, and a C-shaped enclosure (Kellar 1979). The largest mound is about 152 m long, 76 m wide, and over 4 m high (Kellar 1979), dimensions which are comparable with those of the mound at the Mount Vernon site. Some of the Mann site mounds have been excavated by non-professionals. Burials were found, and among the items reported are pearl beads, shell beads, copper earspools, other copper objects, mica, and bear canine teeth (Adams 1949; Kellar 1979). The habitation area has produced such Hopewellian materials as quartz crystal points, obsidian, mica, copper celts, shark teeth, clay human figurines, platform pipes, and pottery with Hopewell designs (Kellar 1979). Other material from Mann which is associated with the Middle Woodland occupation includes *Lowe Flared Base* points (Winters 1967), lamellar blades, cores, and cordmarked, plain, complicated stamped, simple stamped, and check stamped pottery. An outstanding Hopewell artifact which may be from the Mann site is discussed and pictured by Adams (1949). This artifact is a copper headdress with copper ears and holes that likely held antlers.

Based upon the nearness of the sites to one another, the size and complexity of the Mann site, and the presence of a wide variety of Hopewell materials, cremations, and large mounds at both sites, we would think that the Mann site and the Mount Vernon site likely pertain to the same occupation, i.e., a *Mann Phase* (Ruby 1993). Based upon the presence of such materials as obsidian and mica in the debris at the Mann site, it may be that some of the artifacts from the Mount Vernon site were manufactured at the Mann site. However, if everyday utilitarian objects had been recovered from the Mount Vernon site, there would be a better basis for comparing the two sites.

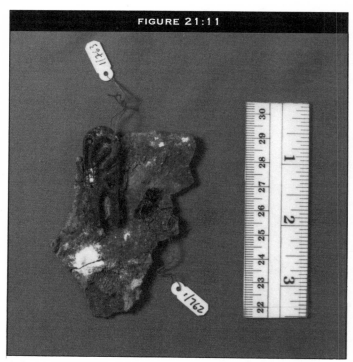

FIGURE 21:11

A decorated leather object attached to a flat piece of copper from the Mount Vernon site.

CONCLUDING REMARKS

In closing, something should be mentioned in regard to other issues connected with the Mount Vernon site. In addition to archaeological field work, the IDOH was quietly proceeding with an investigation of the disturbance of the site and of the unauthorized removal of artifacts from it. Subsequently, law enforcement agencies, including the FBI, began investigating the matter. The FBI became involved because there were indications that artifacts had been illegally taken from the site and had been transported across state lines. Five people were charged with violating the Archaeological Resources Protection Act (ARPA), Title 16, United States Code, Section 470ee(c). Those individuals pleaded guilty in the U.S. District Court, Southern District of Indiana, at Evansville and were sentenced. One of the

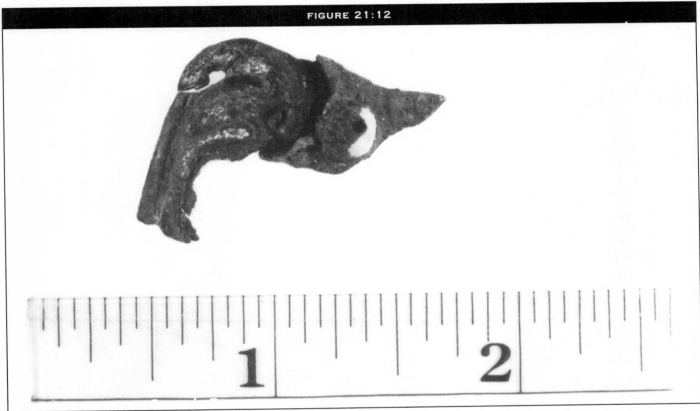

FIGURE 21:12

A decorated leather object attached to a recessed area in a piece of copper which has a pearl on it from the Mount Vernon site.

defendants appealed his case, taking the position that ARPA does not apply to private land. The Seventh Circuit Court of Appeals in Chicago upheld the conviction. The defendant submitted the case to the U.S. Supreme Court, and that court denied his petition, thus letting the judgements of the lower courts stand. This is a precedent setting case involving the applicability of ARPA to private land.

Approximately 3,000 artifacts were returned by collectors to General Electric via the FBI, and General Electric took possession of all of the items which were recovered by the IDOH excavation. General Electric had to decide what was to be done with the material, and that question caused much controversy and some heated differences of opinion.

Some individuals and groups wanted the material to be reburied, others wanted it to be permanently curated and available for research, and others took various middle positions. On May 9, 1994, the Native American Council of the State of Indiana (created in 1992 by executive order of Governor Evan Bayh and composed of Native Americans, archaeologists, and others) provided a public forum for discussion of this topic. Archaeologists, Native Americans, and other people presented their views to the Council and to the many people who attended the meeting. The artifacts and human remains from the Mount Vernon site were reburied with ceremony by Native Americans on General Electric property in Posey County on May 15, 1994.

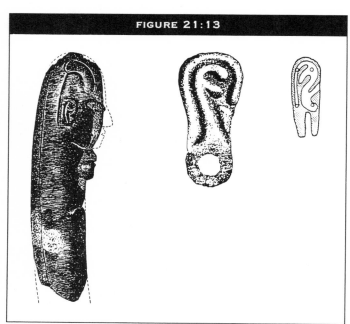

An antler human effigy (Greber and Ruhl 1989: 208, Figure 6.26) and a decorated copper object (Greber and Ruhl 1989: 124, Figure 4.45),both from the Hopewell site (with permission of N'omi Greber); at right, a decorated leather object from the Mount Vernon site.

ACKNOWLEDGMENTS

We want to thank the Indiana Department of Transportation (formerly IDOH) for being extremely considerate and for the great effort they put into the archaeology, particularly their handling of the Mount Vernon situation. In addition, General Electric was very agreeable and exceedingly cooperative during all phases of our archaeological investigation, and we are very grateful to them. A sincere thank you is extended to Larry Mackey and Scott Newman of the U.S. Department of Justice and to Jim Beck of the FBI for their consideration and assistance, in particular for kindly providing access to the artifacts from the Mount Vernon site which were returned by collectors. We are also very grateful to Brenda Fox (word processing), David Piepho (artifact photography), and Brad Steckler (computer graphics) for their talents and assistance with this paper. All of them are employees of the Indiana Department of Transportation.

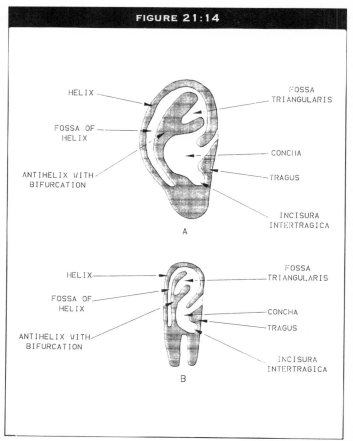

A comparison of the anatomy of the human ear (A), with a decorated leather object from the Mount Vernon site (B).

REFERENCES CITED

Adams, W. R. 1949 *Archaeological Notes on Posey County, Indiana.* Indiana Historical Bureau, Indianapolis.

DeRegnaucourt, R. A. 1986 *Archaeological Reconnaissance of Project RS-6665(1), Proposed Construction of a New Segment of County Road 850S between Old S.R. 69 and Relocated S.R. 69 near Mt. Vernon in Posey County, Indiana.* Report on file, Indiana Department of Transportation, Indianapolis.

Greber, N. B. and K. C. Ruhl 1989 *The Hopewell Site, a Contemporary Analysis Based on the Work of Charles C. Willoughby.* Westview Press, Boulder, Colorado.

Kellar, J. H. 1979 The Mann Site and "Hopewell" in the Lower Wabash-Ohio Valley. In *Hopewell Archaeology, the Chillicothe Conference,* edited by D.S. Brose and N.B. Greber, pp. 100-107. Kent State University Press, Kent, Ohio.

Mills, W. C. 1907 The Explorations of the Edwin Harness Mound. *Ohio Archaeological and Historical Publications* 16:113-193.

1922 Exploration of the Mound City Group. *Ohio Archaeological and Historical Quarterly* 31(4):422-584.

Moorehead, W. K. 1922 The Hopewell Mound Group of Ohio. *Field Museum of Natural History, Publication 211,* Anthropological Series 6(5):73-181.

Nawrocki, S. 1994 Human Remains from the Mt. Vernon (General Electric) Mound, Posey County, Indiana. Paper presented at the joint meeting of the Midwest Archaeological Conference and Southeastern Archaeological Conference, Lexington, Kentucky.

Ruby, B. J. 1993 Late Hopewell Settlement Patterns in Southwestern Indiana. In *Current Research in Indiana Archaeology and Prehistory: 1991 & 1992,* edited by B.G. Redmond, pp. 85-88. Glenn A. Black Laboratory of Archaeology Research Reports, No. 14. Indiana University, Bloomington.

Seeman, M. F. 1979 *The Hopewell Interaction Sphere: The Evidence for Interregional Trade and Structural Complexity.* Indiana Historical Society, Prehistory Research Series 5(2), Indianapolis.

Shetrone, H. C. 1926 Exploration of the Hopewell Group of Prehistoric Earthworks. *Ohio Archaeological and Historical Quarterly* 35(1):1-227.

Shetrone, H. C. and E. F. Greenman 1931 Explorations of the Seip Group of Prehistoric Earthworks. *Ohio Archaeological and Historical Quarterly* 40(3):343-509.

Stafford, C. R. 1988 *Archaeological Records Search, Reconnaissance, and Recommendations, Three Borrow Pit Areas on G. E. Property near Mt. Vernon, Posey County, Indiana.* Report on file, Anthropology Laboratory, Indiana State University, Terre Haute, Indiana.

Tomak, C. H. 1989 *The Mount Vernon Archaeological Site, Posey County, Indiana: A Synopsis.* Report on file, Indiana Department of Transportation, Indianapolis.

1990 *The Mount Vernon Site: A Hopewell Ceremonial/Burial Site in Posey County, Indiana.* Report on file, Indiana Department of Transportation, Indianapolis.

1994 The Mount Vernon Site: A Remarkable Hopewell Mound in Posey County, Indiana. *Archaeology of Eastern North America* 22:1-46.

Willoughby, C. C. and E. A. Hooton 1922 The Turner Group of Earthworks, Hamilton County, Ohio. *Papers of the Peabody Museum* 8(3).

Winters, H. D. 1967 *An Archaeological Survey of the Wabash Valley in Illinois.* Illinois State Museum, Reports of Investigations No. 10, Springfield, Illinois.

TWENTY-TWO

PINSON MOUNDS AND THE MIDDLE WOODLAND PERIOD IN THE MIDSOUTH AND LOWER MISSISSIPPI VALLEY

ROBERT C. MAINFORT JR.

ABSTRACT

In the Midsouth and Lower Mississippi Valley, the rich archaeological record of the Middle Woodland period is often overshadowed by the remains of the more recent Mississippian societies. Significant research and publications since 1980 have served to focus attention on the Middle Woodland legacy of this region. Data from a number of key sites are summarized here, with particular attention to site structure and mortuary programs.

A View From the Core a Synthesis of Ohio Hopewell Archaeology•edited by Paul J. Pacheco
© Copyright 1996 by The Ohio Archaeological Council• Columbus, Ohio
All Rights Reserved•ISBN 0-9626931-9-7

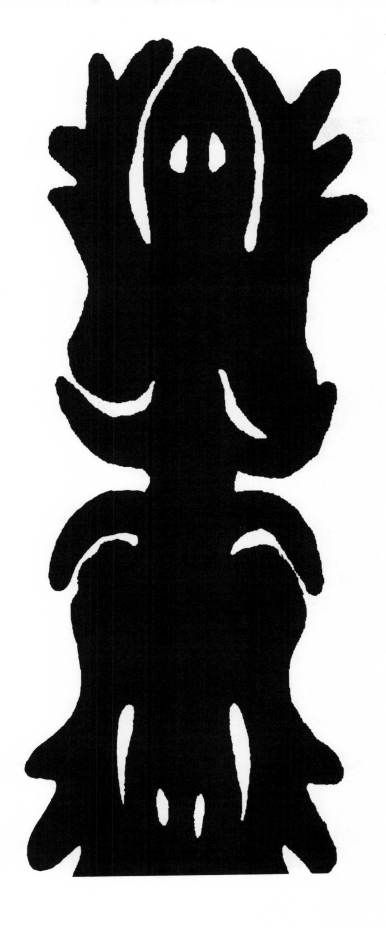

INTRODUCTION

Southern Ohio is without question central to understanding the phenomenon widely, and perhaps inappropriately, referred to as "Hopewell." The material remains, both arti-facts and earthen monuments, of Middle Woodland soci-eties in this region are virtually unparalleled elsewhere in eastern North America (Seeman 1977). Thus, when view-ing Hopewell from within its very heartland, the richness of the archaeological record is somewhat overwhelming, mak-ing it all too easy for researchers to overlook contemporary, related cultural developments in other regions. In this paper, I call attention to certain Middle Woodland sites in the Midsouth and Lower Mississippi Valley, some of which rival and even surpass their contemporaries in Ohio with regard to site size and complexity.

In the Midsouth and Lower Mississippi Valley, it has long been clear that the construction of mounds and embank-ments has a history that extends back in time well over 1,000 years prior to the beginning of the Middle Woodland period. Easily the most impressive, and certainly the least contentious, example is the impressive site of Poverty Point, located in northeastern Louisiana (**Figure 22:1**), which dates to circa 1000 to 1400 B.C. (Gibson and Shenkel 1988). The dominant feature of this mound and embank-ment complex is a series of six elevated, concentric earthen rings arranged to form a partial oval. The rings range in diameter from approximately 590 to 1,200 m, with a total length of about 11 km of embankments.

In addition to the embankments, the site complex includes two very large mounds, one of which stands over 21 m in height, the other about 15.5 m high. These constitute two of the largest recorded prehistoric mounds anywhere (and any time) in eastern North America (cf. Shenkel 1986). Yet, they were constructed over 3,000 years ago.

It stands to reason that Poverty Point did not suddenly appear out of a cultural vacuum and that the site does not repre-sent the sole example of pre-Woodland mound construction in the region, but additional convincing evidence has been

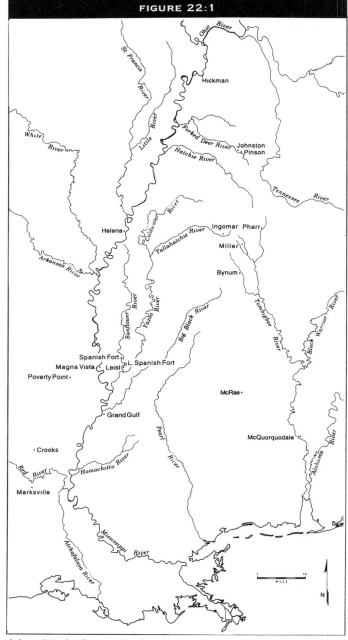

FIGURE 22:1

Selected Marksville period and earlier sites in the Midsouth and Lower Mississippi Valley.

slow to accumulate. This seems in no small part due to the past willingness of archaeologists to assume that virtually all conical mounds in the Lower Mississippi Valley were of Marksville (Middle Woodland) or more recent origin. However, studies by Gibson and Shenkel (1988) and, more recently, by Saunders and Allen (1993) make a strong case for the inception of mound construction as early as 4000 B.C. and continuing uninterrupted through the Tchula (Ford 1990) and Marksville periods.

MARKSVILLE AND CROOKS

The Marksville site, from which the Middle Woodland period in the Midsouth and Lower Mississippi Valley takes its name, is located in Avoyelles Parish, Louisiana, and occupies an upland area near the confluence of the Red and Mississippi Rivers (**Figures 22:1 and 22:2**). Three earthen enclosures and a number of mounds are present within the site limits as presently understood, although it must be stressed any attempt at interpretation is severely hampered by a paucity of archaeological research, much of which remains unpublished (see Toth 1974).

The largest enclosure, a C-form in Byers' (1987) terms, is approximately 520 m in diameter, with an external ditch (Gibson and Shenkel 1988; Toth 1974; cf. Williams and Brain 1983). Several openings (or hyphenations) are present and the northernmost section of the embankment terminates prior to intersecting the edge of the bluff. If Byers' (1987) interpretation of embankment profiles and relative chronology is applicable to southern Hopewellian manifestations, construction of the large enclosure at Marksville should constitute a fairly early event.

Within the enclosure are five mounds, ranging in height from 1 to 6 m, one of which (Mound 2) apparently represents a rectangular, flat-topped structure, while Mound 6 is a truncated, roughly circular earthwork. Despite the limited amount of available data, Toth's (1988:152) statement that "Until these features (i.e., the embankments at Marksville and Spanish Fort) are properly excavated the true cultural associations will never be known, and it is a waste of ink to

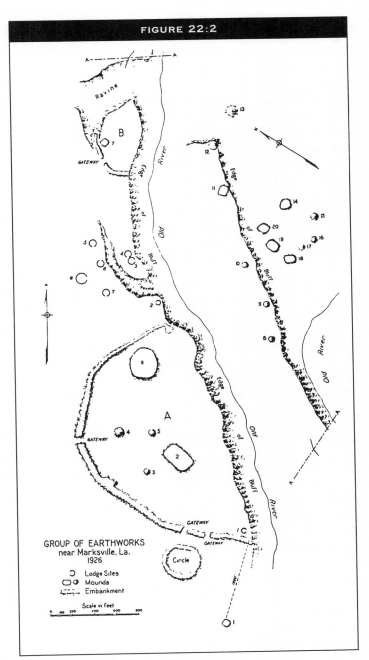

FIGURE 22:2

GROUP OF EARTHWORKS
near Marksville, La.
1926

   C   Lodge Sites
   ◖◖ Mounds
   ⟨⟨⟨ Embankment

Scale in feet

The Marksville site after Fowke (1928).

speculate any farther *[sic]* about a matter to which not a scrap of evidence can be applied" seems a bit foolish. If the *Marksville* site was located in southern Ohio, no one would question the age of its enclosures for a moment.

Immediately adjacent to the southern portion of the large enclosure is a small, roughly circular enclosure about 100 m in diameter. A third enclosure, consisting of a hyphenated linear embankment approximately 150 m long with an external ditch, defines a small, projecting section of the bluff top about 200 m north of the large enclosure. A rectangular platform mound of uncertain age and function (Mound 7) is situated within the northern enclosure.

The largest conical mound, Mound 4, was trenched by Gerard Fowke (1928), revealing a small rectangular (approximately 8 m on each side), 1.5 m tall, gray clay platform, on which a number of burials had been placed; as discussed below, earthen mortuary platforms occur throughout the study area. A roughly square pit, or "vault", was located in the central portion of the platform; several burials were located within. The pit was roofed over with relatively small saplings which, in turn, were covered by seven layers of bark and cane matting. Small upright support posts surrounded the pit (Toth 1974). An overlying mantle contained burials in pits. Interpretation of this structure is hindered by the lack of a published report, but it would appear to represent a form of charnel house.

Fowke also conducted excavations in the previously trenched Mound 8, a conical bluff top burial mound north of the enclosures. At the base of the mound, seven tombs excavated into subsoil and covered with cane matting were recorded. Four ceramic vessels were found, but the skeletal material was badly decomposed.

Extant collections from the Marksville site, which have been used as the basis for the *Marksville Phase* (Phillips 1970; Toth 1974, 1988), consist of 18 whole or largely complete ceramic vessels, approximately 1,500 decorated ceramic sherds, and a relatively small amount of diagnostic lithic material. Despite the small sample size, there is consider-

able diversity among ceramic vessel forms, including small "classic" tubby pots (including an example with a tapered pedestal base), small beakers, straight-sided jars, and several unusual forms. Both broad-billed and "raptorial" bird motifs are present. Among the projectile points are a number of fairly crude contracting stem forms that fall within the range of the *Gary* type. Three bladelets, probably of non-local chert, were collected on the surface of the site (Toth 1974, 1988).

There are no radiocarbon determinations for the Marksville site, in part, a consequence of the fact that no major archaeological work has been undertaken at the site since the 1930s. Hints of relative chronology within the site might be gleaned from variations in ceramic paste (e.g., Toth 1974), but without tight contextual controls, such inferences would be largely speculative. Based on ceramic vessel forms and design motifs, it can only be stated with any confidence that the Marksville site was utilized (including some mound construction) during the first two centuries A.D. (and perhaps a bit earlier).

Located about 35 km north of Marksville, the Crooks site (Ford and Willey 1940) is the best documented mortuary site within the *Marksville Phase* core area **(Figure 22:1)**. During a time period within which the extraordinary is to be expected, Crooks Mound A represents a mortuary situation unparalleled anywhere within the Hopewellian world. Initially, a low earthen platform with basal dimensions of approximately 12 m by 20 m was constructed. Within the upper portion of the platform, 168 burials were placed. This number of individuals is, of itself, without precedent in the Lower Mississippi Valley, but after an unknown period of time, during which the upper surface of the platform was slightly weathered, an additional group of 214 interments was placed on the platform. The platform was then covered by a primary mound in which 270 burials were included. A line of log steps extended up the eastern side of the primary mound. A secondary mantle containing an additional 503 burials was later added, bringing the total number of interments to over 1,150. The secondary mantle, however, contained both Marksville and post-Marksville artifacts, suggesting that more than a single construction episode is represented (cf. Ford and Willey 1940; cf. Griffin 1973; Gibson and Shenkel 1988). Deposits of ash and charcoal were found within the mound and on the burial platform; many of these seem to have been associated with burials.

Even accepting the premise that stratigraphic details indicative of numerous accretional and/or intrusive mortuary episodes within the secondary mantle were overlooked by the excavators, the fact remains that a very large number of individuals (minimally, over 650) were interred within Crooks Mound A during the Early part of the *Marksville Phase*. Forms of interment included 435 flexed, 223 isolated skulls (often placed adjacent to more complete skeletal remains), 137 bundle, 88 semiflexed, 55 partially disarticulated, and 5 extended; 216 were of indeterminate burial position. The bundle and partially articulated burials imply processing and curation in a charnel structure prior to interment. While it is not unreasonable to posit the existence of such a facility near Crooks Mound A (Brown 1979), the number of interred individuals strongly suggests they were brought to the site from numerous localities throughout the region, each with its own local charnel house.

Over 80 whole or partially restorable ceramic vessels were recovered from Crooks, including more than 40 decorated specimens. These constitute an important source of data on vessel form and decorative motifs. Most vessels exhibit a typical, chalky paste, although one example has a markedly sandy paste (Toth 1988). Vessel forms include tubby pots, beakers, and hemispherical bowls. At least one example exhibits tetrapodal feet and rim nodes seem to be present on two vessels; these attributes are characteristic of earlier Tchefuncte ceramics. Both broad-billed and "raptorial" birds are portrayed, and characteristic rim treatments are common (Canouts 1986; Ford and Willey 1940; Toth 1988).

Among the Hopewellian materials from Crooks are six copper earspools (of the single concave-convex disc style), cylindrical copper beads, a copper bracelet, several galena beads, freshwater pearl beads, and a number of complete and fragmentary quartz crystals.

Based on resemblances between several vessels from Crooks and Tchefuncte ceramics, Ford and Willey (1940) suggest that Crooks may slightly pre-date the Marksville site. This certainly seems plausible, but the dearth of published data from Marksville and the lack of radiocarbon determinations from the sites in question severely limit attempts at establishing relative chronologies.

THE YAZOO BASIN ENCLOSURES

Within and adjacent to the southern portion of the Yazoo basin in Mississippi are four intriguing (and under-investigated) sites characterized by the presence of semicircular enclosures. These include Spanish Fort, Little Spanish Fort, Leist Landing, and Magna Vista (see Phillips 1970; Thunen 1988:Figure 1).

Spanish Fort is the northernmost in a series of enclosures on the lower Sunflower River that are basically semicircular in form, with external ditches. Its name derives from a local tradition that attributes construction of the "fort" to the de Soto *entrada*. The Spanish Fort enclosure is somewhat larger than the C-form enclosure at Marksville, with a diameter of approximately 590 m (Phillips 1970; Walling and Roemer 1993). Phillips (1970) discusses a fairly large artifact sample obtained both from the surface, as well as a test unit in a restricted midden deposit, that includes specimens ranging in time from Poverty Point to Mississippian. A moderate number of sherds attributed to a Late Marksville *Issaquena Phase* occupation were recovered; a crosshatched rim was obtained from the same arbitrary excavation level that produced two "late" varieties of *Marksville Incised*.

A substantial portion of the artifact assemblage was obtained within or in proximity to the midden deposit. The presence of an actual occupation midden within and contemporary with a Middle Woodland enclosure would be most unusual, and it seems quite safe to assume that the Coles Creek and Mississippian material post-date the enclosure. For the same reason, there is no particular reason to associate the enclosure with the *Issaquena Phase* component. My own interpretation, while admittedly speculative in the absence of artifact samples from the embankment, is that the enclosure is of Early Marksville age. There is an

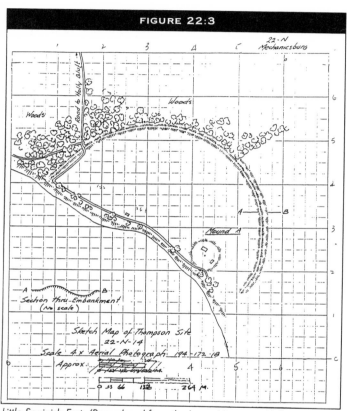

FIGURE 22:3

Little Spanish Fort. (Reproduced from the Lower Mississippi Valley Survey files housed at the Department of Anthropology, Memphis State University.

tion, 1993) of the University of Southern Mississippi has produced evidence of a Marksville component; additional field work is planned for the summer of 1994. At the very least, the presence of ceramics within the embankment fill clearly demonstrates that the earthwork is not of Poverty Point age (cf. Williams and Brain 1983).

Spanning a "narrows" between the Yazoo and Sunflower Rivers just south of Little Spanish Fort, the Leist Landing site consists of at least three mounds and a semicircular embankment approximately 470 m in diameter (Walling and Roemer 1993; cf. Phillips 1970; cf. Williams and Brain 1983). The open side of the enclosure, which was almost completely destroyed by levee construction in the early 1970s, faces the Yazoo River, while the impressive Mound C is situated to the west on a cut bank of the Sunflower River. Mound C is a rather large, but relatively low (approximately 2.5 m), flat-topped structure with a small conical mound located near the southern edge. Very limited testing of Mound C by the Lower Mississippi Valley Survey produced a variety of ceramic types ranging from Marksville to Late Mississippian in age (Phillips 1970). A small collection recently obtained by Pan-American Consultants from cultural deposits below Mound C includes a number of sherds compatible with an Early Marksville occupation (see Walling and Roemer 1993).

The last of the Yazoo Basin semicircular enclosures to be considered here is Magna Vista, which is located to the west of the other sites, near the present course of the Mississippi River. Within the embankment, which has a diameter of about 460 m (cf. Phillips 1970; see also Williams and Brain 1983:352) is a moderately large platform mound of irregular shape. A very small sample of ceramics (all shell tempered, including an example of the Late Mississippian type Barton Incised, *var. Arcola*) was obtained from an old humus zone about 75 cm above the base of the mound. No ceramics were obtained from the surrounding field, perhaps due to siltation (Phillips 1970). I attribute the enclosure, now virtually obliterated by plowing, to the Marksville period based on its resemblance and proximity to the sites discussed above, as well as the fact that semicircular embankments are not known to be associated with Late Mississippian sites in the Lower Mississippi Valley.

obvious need for additional research at this important site. Little Spanish Fort, located a few kilometers south of Spanish Fort, is actually larger than the latter earthwork, having a diameter of roughly 640 m (cf. Phillips 1970; cf. Williams and Brain 1983; **Figure 22:3**). A circular, flat-topped mound is located near the southern terminus of the embankment, but since little archaeological testing has been conducted, the temporal relationship between the mound and the enclosure is tenuous at best. The paltry (n=36) ceramic sample reported by Phillips (1970) represents usage of Little Spanish Fort during Coles Creek and Mississippian times, although several points may be provisionally considered to be evidence of a Marksville component. Recent testing by Ed Jackson (personal communica-

Apparently the upper 2 m of the mound is Late Mississippian in origin, but the presence of a probable old humus zone nearer to the base raises the possibility that a Middle Woodland earthwork was covered by later mound construction. Unfortunately no researchers have acted upon Phillips' (1970:515) statement that Magna Vista represents a "very pretty problem for future investigation."

In sum, it appears that something rather special transpired within the lower Yazoo basin during the Marksville period. No comparable sites have been recorded elsewhere within the Yazoo basin (Phillips 1970), nor, in fact, elsewhere in the Lower Mississippi Valley. While the artifactual data from several sites is both scant and unconvincing, the formal similarities between the four enclosures, as well as their tight spatial distribution, strongly suggests that these sites represent the efforts of a single Marksville period cultural entity.

HELENA CROSSING

The Helena Crossing site, located on the southeastern end of Crowley's Ridge in eastern Arkansas (**Figure 22:1**), was a group of five conical burial mounds occupying "a commanding position at the terminus of the ridge with fine view of the river and valley" (Ford 1963:5). The placement of the site ties in nicely with Chapman's (1981) notions about the construction of "monumental" mortuary facilities in prominent locations. All of the earthworks were between 4 and 6 m tall and approximately 30 m in diameter. Mounds B and C were excavated during the fall of 1960 under the direction of James Ford (1963), two other mounds having been destroyed a few years earlier.

Two features were exposed at the base of Mound B, one of which consisted of four large logs placed on the original ground surface near the center of the earthwork. A sub-mound mortuary crypt measuring 3 to 5 m was also disclosed. The top was covered with four large logs and the walls lined with split cane matting. Interred within this facility were the remains of a young male and a mature male.

Mound C was slightly larger and exhibited greater internal complexity (**Figure 22:4**). Four large mortuary crypts were exposed (one of which was intrusive through the primary mound that covered two earlier facilities), as were a log-covered individual tomb and a number of non-crypt burials. Structurally, the Helena Crossing mortuary facilities exhibit striking similarities with presumably contemporary structures in Illinois, notably Wilson Mound 6, at which a sub-pit extended below the floor of a mortuary crypt (Neumann and Fowler 1952). Importantly, it is apparent that the mortuary facilities at Helena Crossing continued to be maintained for at least 10 to 20 years after the completion of Mound C, as indicated by the repair of a collapsed area above Tomb B. Toth's (1988:40) suggestion that the Helena Crossing mortuary program represents the product of a "stratified" society is demonstrably incorrect (Mainfort 1988a).

Associated artifacts include a copper panpipe, copper earspools, several large conch shells, a mica sheet, a copper ferrule, bladelets of Harrison County, Indiana (Wyandotte) chert, and numerous *Marginella* beads. A number of whole and partial ceramic vessels were also recovered (virtually all from deposits within Mound C), including tubby pots, beakers, and hemispherical bowls. Two tetrapodal pots are more typical of (pre-Marksville) Tchefuncte vessels. The single four-lobed vessel represents a form relatively common in the Marksville core area of the Lower Red River. Decorative motifs include numerous examples of zoned stamping, rocker stamping, and crosshatched rims. The soft, chalky paste repeatedly noted by Ford (1963:31 *passim*) points to a relatively early date for the Helena Crossing Group (cf. Toth 1988).

Unfortunately, the four radiocarbon determinations obtained for the site are less informative than one might wish, as they span the period 150 B.C. to A.D. 335, all ± 75 radiocarbon years (Crane and Griffin [1963:240-241] note that the standard deviations published by Ford [1963] represent a doubling of the actual figures and that several of Ford's A.D. radiocarbon dates evidently were computed using A.D. 1960, rather than the customary A.D. 1950). The situation can be clarified a bit by evaluating the hypothesis that the two assays on Mound C, Tomb D (M-1198 and M-1199, which are

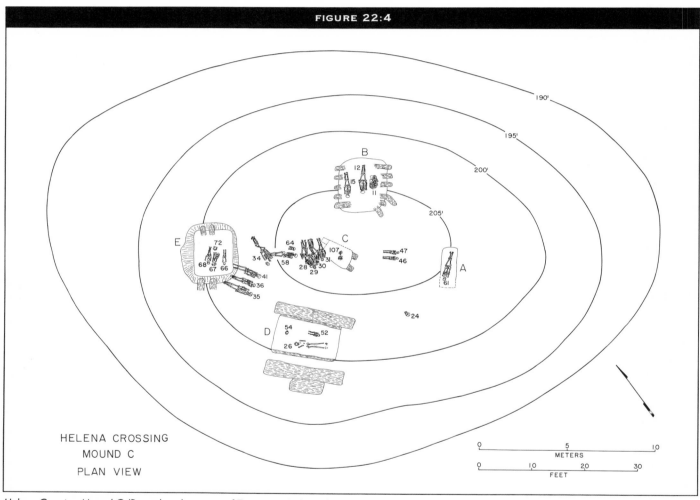

FIGURE 22:4

HELENA CROSSING
MOUND C
PLAN VIEW

Helena Crossing Mound C (Reproduced courtesy of Tennessee Anthropologist).

1625 ± 75 B.P. and 1930 ± 75 B.P., respectively) are synchronous. Using student's t-test, it can be demonstrated that these dates differ significantly (t=2.88, p=.01), allowing the more recent to be discarded. The remaining dates, especially the two earliest (150 B.C. and A.D. 20, both from Mound C contexts), are fairly compatible with the obviously early ceramic assemblage from Mound C.

INGOMAR AND THE TOMBIGBEE DRAINAGE

The Bynum Mound Group, located in the Pontotoc Hills of northeastern Mississippi near a minor tributary of the Tombigbee River (Cotter and Corbett 1951), is one of several important Middle Woodland mortuary sites in the upper Tombigbee drainage (**Figure 22:1**). Included within an area of roughly 8 ha were six conical burial mounds ranging in height from about 1.5 m to 4.2 m, as well as an extensive early Middle Woodland occupation area. Five mounds were excavated in the later 1940s, two of which (Mounds E and F) had been largely destroyed and yielded little information.

The remains of several ovoid bent-pole houses, as well as numerous postmolds and pits, were identified in the "village area" (Cotter and Corbett 1951), and it is obvious that many others were at least partially exposed. As pointed out by Bruce Smith (1992), the large size of these structures (diameters > 20 m), as well as the lack of associated hearths and storage pits, indicate that these represent specialized houses associated with ritual activities. Few non-local artifacts or raw materials were recovered in the occupation area, a small piece of copper, several lumps of galena, and a Marksville Stamped, var. *Marksville* vessel exhibiting a raptorial bird motif (see Toth 1988:134) being the only examples (Cotter and Corbett 1951:14-16).

Bynum Mound A, which measured slightly over 3 m in height, covered a low, earthen platform that had been substantially damaged by excavation of a modern house cellar. No artifacts or skeletal remains were recovered from the platform. At the base of the mound, below the platform, was an irregularly-shaped layer of clay that covered a thin habitation deposit and supported a mortuary feature consisting of two parallel burned oak logs lying about three meters apart. The remains of an extended adult female were located between the logs. A bicymbal copper earspool was found at each wrist, and a cluster of utilitarian pottery sherds was located near the feet. Also associated with this feature were three in situ cremations, including two slightly flexed adults and a child.

Mound B, with a height of 4.2 m and a diameter of approximately 20 m, was the largest of the Bynum earthworks. At the base, excavations disclosed the remains of a charnel house with a sunken floor and measuring approximately 11.5 m by 9.1 m (**Figure 22:5**). The exterior of the depressed floor was lined with small saplings. Sixteen large posts were identified within the depression; the relatively shallow depth of these (approximately 70 cm) makes it unlikely that these supported a

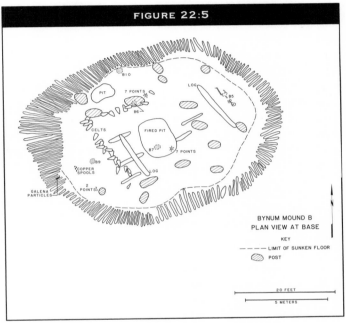

FIGURE 22:5

BYNUM MOUND B
PLAN VIEW AT BASE
KEY
– – – – LIMIT OF SUNKEN FLOOR
POST

20 FEET
5 METERS

Charnel house, Bynum Mound B.

heavy roof (Walling et al. 1991). Within the ashes on the pit floor were a series of horizontal log molds, interpreted by the excavators as a rectangular framework. A shallow pit exhibiting a burned interior, perhaps a crematory facility, was located near the center of the building (Cotter and Corbett 1951).

An L-shaped row of 29 greenstone celts and three secondary human cremations were located on top of the ash deposits above the floor, while the remains of an extended adult male were found near the eastern edge. Also associated with the structure floor were two pairs of copper bicymbal earspools, two fragments of *Busycon perversum* shell, and 19 *Gibson* or *Norton* projectile points that appear to be imports from the Illinois River Valley (Griffin 1979:270). All of the above were placed within the remains of the structure after it had burned. A piece of galena was uncovered below the exterior saplings, outside the sunken floor of the charnel house. Mound stratigraphy suggests that construction was completed as a single event.

Mound D, a small conical earthwork measuring about 1.8 m tall, was constructed over a small mortuary structure represented by a rectangular sunken floor with a fired circular pit near the center. Several fragments of human tooth enamel were found just below the rim of the pit, as were a rolled copper bead and a copper earspool. A greenstone celt was located on the floor of the building. About a meter outside the structure floor, four large posts were found and some small sapling or log molds were exposed on the western side of the floor. Cotter and Corbett (1951) interpret the structural remains as a rectangular canopy covering the fired pit.

Recently published radiocarbon evidence indicates that Bynum Mounds A and B were roughly contemporary and date to the second century B.C. (Walling et al. 1991), a bit earlier than suggested by Griffin (1979).

Located about 90 km northeast of Bynum in the headwaters of the Tombigbee River (**Figure 22:1**), the Pharr Mound Group includes eight conical mounds, ranging in height from 70 cm to 5.5 m, within an area of approximately 47 ha (**Figure 22:6**). Four mounds were excavated to varying degrees in the later 1960s (Bohannon 1972). Heavy equipment was utilized in the excavations, resulting in the loss of key data.

In contrast to Bynum, little evidence of an associated habitation area has been found, although the remains of one or more ovoid Middle Woodland houses, several burials, and some non-Woodland features were disclosed (Kardwesky 1980). Agricultural use and severe erosion may account for the apparent lack of additional non-mound Woodland features.

Unfortunately, all three acceptable radiocarbon assays for Pharr are from Mound E contexts; this earthwork probably was constructed between A.D. 50 and 150. Although the mounds probably are not strictly contemporary, the artifact assemblage and the internal structure of the earthworks suggest that all were constructed within a relatively short time period, perhaps over several generations (Walling et al. 1991).

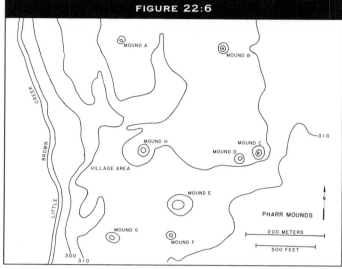

The Pharr site (Reproduced courtesy of Southeastern Archaeology).

Pharr Mound D stood about 4.6 m tall, and was 27 m in diameter. A rectangular burned area and an oval concentration of flat sandstone slabs were located on the mortuary platform. Associated with the latter feature were a broken copper earspool and some unidentified bone fragments. The platform was covered by a primary mound that apparently was not exposed to weathering. Some human skull fragments and a pair of copper earspools were found on the original ground surface slightly west of the primary mound. A final deposit of mound fill covered these remains and the primary mound.

Pharr Mound E, with a mean diameter of 52 m and a height of 2.4 m, was not completely excavated. Hence the exact size of the earthen platform covered by the mound and the precise stratigraphic association of several key features are unknown. Three probable mortuary features were associated with the platform. One was a shallow, fired depression on the platform surface; a small *Marksville Incised* vessel with a characteristic Lower Mississippi Valley paste (Toth 1988:134) was found near the edge. A pair of rectangular pits seem to have originated at the platform surface, but their exact stratigraphic position was not determined. Three stemmed points, four preforms, and two pieces of galena were found in the smaller pit. Adjacent to the sides of the larger pit, three logs had been placed on the platform surface, suggesting use as a mortuary crypt; no associated artifacts were found. Other material located on the platform surface included two small pottery vessels, the remains of a silver-plated panpipe, a rectangular piece of wood covered with copper, and some fragments of decayed bone (Bohannon 1972).

Near the eastern edge of the platform were three rectangular pits associated with initial construction of the mound. One yielded a cluster of utilitarian ceramic sherds and a sizable deposit of wood charcoal. A non-local, tetrapodal *Flint River Cordmarked* vessel was found in a slightly larger pit, while three deposits of unidentified calcined bone were found in the third pit.

A primary mound of uncertain dimensions covered the platform and the east side submound features. Two rectangular pits were excavated into the primary mound, one of which lacked associated cultural material. Two small pottery vessels (one a non-local tetrapodal *Flint River Brushed*, the other a compound *Alligator Bayou Stamped* vessel) were found in the other. The compound vessel is of interest because the only other recorded example was found at the Marksville site (see Jenkins 1979,1982: 75-76, 79; Toth 1974:49). Deposits of water-sorted soils were observed around the periphery of the primary mound, indicating that it had been exposed to weathering. The primary mound was covered by a final layer of fill. A large pit containing a sheet of mica, a greenstone labret, a sandstone grinding pallet, and a large lump of galena was intrusive through all three construction stages (Bohannon 1972).

A trench 18.3 m long (60 feet) and 6.1 m wide (20 feet) cut into the north side of the disturbed Pharr Mound H (Bohannon 1972). Within the original ground surface at the base of the earthwork was a fired depression containing a greenstone platform pipe. Nine posts surrounded the basin; these may represent the remains of a small structure similar to that beneath Bynum Mound D.

The mortuary platforms at Pharr and other Marksville period sites in the Midsouth and Lower Mississippi Valley required a relatively modest initial investment of time and energy and, unlike facilities that incorporated logs or saplings into their design, would have required very little maintenance. Even taking into account variables unfavorable to bone preservation, the paucity of skeletal material recovered at Pharr is striking. It would seem, therefore, that the mortuary facilities were primarily intended for processing the dead and that final interment was generally made elsewhere. This also suggests that the construction of the mounds themselves as monuments may have been of equal or greater importance than their mortuary function (Charles 1985).

Variation in the mortuary facilities at Pharr may reflect social distinctions, but diachronic variability cannot be ruled out. In the case of Mound E, however, there is fairly solid evidence for the contemporaneity of both platform and crypt processing. In contrast to Bynum, multiple use/construction episodes were observed in two mounds (A and E) and possibly a third (Mound D), indicating longer term use and maintenance of the mortuary features.

The type site of the *"Miller culture"* (cf. Jenkins 1982; Jennings 1941), the Miller site is located about 65 km north of Bynum (**Figure 22:1**) and consists of two conical burial mounds and a substantial habitation midden within an area of 3.5 ha (Jennings 1941). Radiocarbon assays from Mound B place its construction during the third century A.D. (Walling et al. 1991), and the two mounds are probably roughly contemporary.

Miller Mound A was a conical, accretional earthwork about 4.6 m tall and 26 m in diameter that was constructed directly on a humus layer containing habitational debris. At the base of the mound, near the center, were a pair of extended adult primary burials sandwiched between two layers of tan clay. The clay covered an area somewhat larger than that occupied by the two interments and may represent a low mortuary platform (Jennings 1941:194). Associated with one individual (an adult male?) were a crude limestone platform pipe and a conch shell cup. An estimated total of

30 individuals (all adults) was recovered from poorly-defined pits within the general mound fill. Due to poor bone preservation, burial position could not always be determined, but in addition to the extended burials at the base, there were 11 or 12 extended interments, three semi-flexed, and two multiple burials (Jennings 1941:194). Notably absent were bundle burials and cremations.

The internal structure of the slightly smaller Miller Mound B exhibited some important differences with Mound A. Three rectangular submound pits were exposed near the center of the earthwork; others may have been present to the north, as the area was not completely excavated (Jennings 1941:192). On the floor of one pit were a human skull and a utilitarian jar, while another contained a single tooth cap. Hence, the submound pits probably were burial crypts. Three flexed adults and a crushed *Baldwin Plain* vessel were found near the center of the earthwork, about 1.5 m above the base, suggesting that they were placed on the surface of a primary mound (cf. Jennings 1941:195).

Miller Mound B was constructed over habitation deposits, but the excavator's report provides intimations of the mortuary structure at the base of the mound in the southeastern quadrant. Identification as a mortuary structure, rather than a dwelling associated with the village, is based on the absence of a humic layer and Jennings' statement that "the house was abandoned a relatively short time before mound building began..." (1941:192). This typical Middle Woodland bent pole structure was approximately 6.7 m in diameter (Jennings 1941:205). Further supporting the case for a special function, this structure was larger than several formally similar houses disclosed in the village excavations. On the western side, much of the mound floor was covered by "an unusually high proportion of ash and charcoal and the clay beneath was reddened by fire" (Jennings 1941:192), presumably representing burned walls and/or a roof.

Mound burial at the Miller site appears to have been restricted to adults, perhaps due to their participation in subsistence activities of the group (cf. Charles and Buikstra 1983:136-139). Three burial programs are suggested by

the data. These include processing through a burial crypt or charnel house (Mound B) and primary interment (Mound A). Given the crypts and charnel house, the absence of disarticulated burials is unexpected and suggests that final interment was often made at another locality.

The Ingomar Mounds site, located west of Pharr in the Little Tallahatchie River drainage (**Figure 22:1**), several kilometers west of the Tombigbee/Mississippi River divide, was originally reported to include 14 mounds within an area of approximately 16 ha (Rafferty 1987, 1990). Many of these earthworks are no longer visible and some may simply have been small rises mistakenly inferred to be mounds. The largest extant earthwork is an 8 m tall ramped platform mound, very similar in appearance and size to the second largest structure in the Pinson Mounds complex (see below). As discussed below, two conical burial mounds were partially excavated in the late 1800s (Rafferty 1987; Thomas 1894). There is no evidence of a substantial habitation area. The meager ceramic assemblage includes a sherd of grog-tempered, red-filmed ware that is identical to specimens recovered from several localities at Pinson Mounds (Mainfort 1986; Rafferty 1987).

Although primitive excavation techniques and incomplete reporting limit interpretive potential, data from the two excavated burial mounds provide important documentation of mortuary activities (Thomas 1894). The most extensively excavated (four 2 m-wide trenches) of these, Ingomar Mound 1, was 4.3 m tall and 19.5 m in diameter. My interpretation of mound structure differs somewhat from that of Rafferty (1987).

At the base of Mound 1, near the center, was a small, fired area capped with a thin layer of red clay. To the north was a small pit from which a layer of ash approximately 2 m in diameter extended out. On the east side, a feature complex that may represent the remains of a small mortuary structure was partially uncovered. Here the excavators exposed part of a shallow, 3 m wide basin (Rafferty 1987: Feature 13). Adjacent to and within this depression were four large postholes filled with wet gray clay; one contained a fragment of human skull. Fill above these holes is described as "looser" than the surrounding soil, and profiles suggest that a collapsed portion of the mound had been repaired above the feature complex (Rafferty 1987; cf. Thomas 1894). On the mound floor, several meters northwest of the central fired area, was a shallow basin containing the lower skeleton of an adult male and a scapula.

At least three construction stages are evident from the published description and accompanying soil profiles (cf.Rafferty 1987; Thomas 1894). A low, asymmetrical primary mound composed of dark basket-loaded fill covered most of the submound features and may have partially covered the inferred structure on the east side. Rafferty's (1987) interpretation of two initial intersecting mounds seems to be based largely on an apparent editorial error in the published profile drawings (Thomas 1894: Figure 170). Alignment of the southeast profile of the northeast trench with the east profile of the south trench (cf. Thomas 1894) clearly reveals erroneous representation of the relevant soil zones.

The fragmentary remains of four individuals were found on or within the primary mound, as was an extended adult male with quartz pebbles under the skull. On the south side, a small, rectangular pit containing a group of disarticulated human bones (Rafferty's [1987] Burial 1) extended from the surface of the primary mound to the mound floor. Pit fill is described as "loose and cloddy," suggesting that the pit had originally been covered, although its size seems too small for a processing crypt. Within the secondary mantle were three small pits lined with puddled clay. Each was filled with loose soil, again suggesting coverings; one contained the incomplete, partially articulated remains of an adult, accompanied by over 400 shell beads that may have formed a bracelet. A portion of the secondary mantle in the eastern portion of the earthwork was capped by a thin layer of red clay, itself capped by a layer of puddled gray clay. This capping, reminiscent of Pinson Mound 6 (see below), quite clearly did not cover the western section of the mound, suggesting that the excavators failed to note some important construction details. The final major construction event was the addition of mottled fill to the east side of the mound, covering the depression and postholes described above.

Setting aside the possible mortuary building, which cannot be adequately assessed with the available data, several key points can be made about Ingomar Mound 1. First, it was an accretional earthwork, although the building process may have been continuous. Second, only adults were represented in the mound. Finally, with a single exception, all of the burials were disarticulated or consisted of incomplete remains. This, as well as the presence of several small, covered, crypt-like features, indicates that the interred individuals had first been processed through a mortuary facility, perhaps represented by one or more of the excavated features.

A 3 m wide trench was excavated through Ingomar Mound 5, yielding the remains of 13 individuals. Located some 800 m from the mound group proper, this small earthwork was approximately 1.2 m tall and 15 m in diameter. The brief description (Thomas 1894:275) suggests that Mound 5 was an accretional earthwork with burials at three distinct levels: the mound base, 60 cm above the base, and 120 cm above the base. All were located near the center of the earthwork. Thomas' statement that the "bones were put in without regard to position" implies that the interments were disarticulated (possibly bundle burials). Unlike Mound 1, the skeletal sample included "persons of different ages, from the child whose first teeth were beginning to appear, to the aged individual whose teeth were worn to the gums."

Ingomar provides clear evidence of at least two distinct burial programs, although it must be emphasized that the relative ages of the excavated burial mounds are unknown. Mound 1, yielded evidence of several features that may have served mortuary processing functions, an interpretation supported by the recovery of only a single primary inhumation from the earthwork. Access to Mound 1 apparently was limited to adults. The inclusion of both children and adults in Mound 5 suggests a less specialized function, but like most individuals from Mound 1, the interments had first been processed through a mortuary facility.

HICKMAN EARTHWORKS

At the northern extreme of the area under consideration here, the Hickman Earthworks are located on a bluff top overlooking the Mississippi River flood plain, northeast of Hickman, Kentucky (Mainfort and Carstens 1987:Figure 1). This mound and embankment complex includes an open-sided rectangular enclosure with a long aggregation element somewhat similar to the Turner site in southern Ohio (**Figure 22:7**). The remains of a conical mound are located at the southern end of the aggregation element, while a second mound lies within the larger enclosure. A third mound-like feature (cf. Mainfort and Carstens 1987) is actually a natural rise, but given its alignment with the two mounds, it was probably incorporated into the overall site design. Several additional conical mounds are located to the east of the enclosure; these are interpreted as Middle Woodland structures, although test excavations are required to conclusively demonstrate temporal affiliation.

Despite a lack of excavated data, the Hickman Earthworks complex is of considerable interest because of its close formal similarities to sites in southern Ohio. No comparable embankments have been recorded within the study area (Thunen 1990).

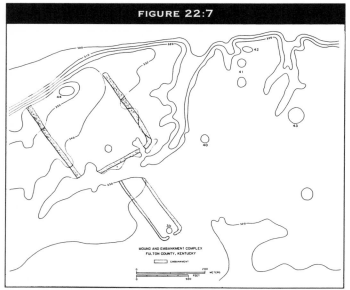

FIGURE 22:7

MOUND AND EMBANKMENT COMPLEX
FULTON COUNTY, KENTUCKY

Hickman Earthworks (reproduced courtesy of Southeastern Archaeology).

PINSON MOUNDS AND THE JOHNSTON SITE

The largest Middle Woodland site in the Southeast, Pinson Mounds is located about 20 km south of Jackson, Tennessee, on the South Fork of the Forked Deer River (Mainfort 1986, 1988b). Situated on a relatively level tableland on the bluffs above the river bottom land, the site includes at least 12 mounds, a geometric enclosure, and associated ritual activity loci within an area of approximately 160 ha (**Figures 22:1 and 22:8**). In addition to its large size and the immense volume of earthwork fill represented (>100,000 m^3), the presence of five large rectangular platform mounds, ranging in height from 2.5 to 22 m, of Middle Woodland age, underscores the unique nature of the Pinson Mounds site. Based on over 40 radiocarbon determinations (including multiple assays for all intensively investigated localities), primary use of the site, including construction of all of the large mounds and the enclosure, occurred between about 100 B.C. and 350 A.D. The site is preserved as a State Archaeological Area, and investigations have been accordingly conservative in extent and frequency.

Excavations on Ozier Mound (Mound 5) provided the first unequivocal evidence for the construction of rectangular platform mounds during the Middle Woodland period (Mainfort 1986, 1988b). This ramped earthwork, approximately 10 m tall, was constructed in at least six stages, with the summit of each stage covered with pale yellow sand. Mica, copper, and microblades of non-local chert were found in association with the uppermost summit, linking this locality with ritual activity areas elsewhere within the site. Features are sparse within the areas tested, but include several small hearths and a low, raised-clay platform.

Although no evidence of a building or other structural remains were encountered, the size of Ozier Mound and the recurrent renewal of the earthwork via additional construction clearly foreshadow later Mississippian substructural mounds. Current interpretations place construction of Ozier Mound within the first century B.C., and it is possible that it may have been the first earthwork constructed at Pinson Mounds (Mainfort and Walling 1992).

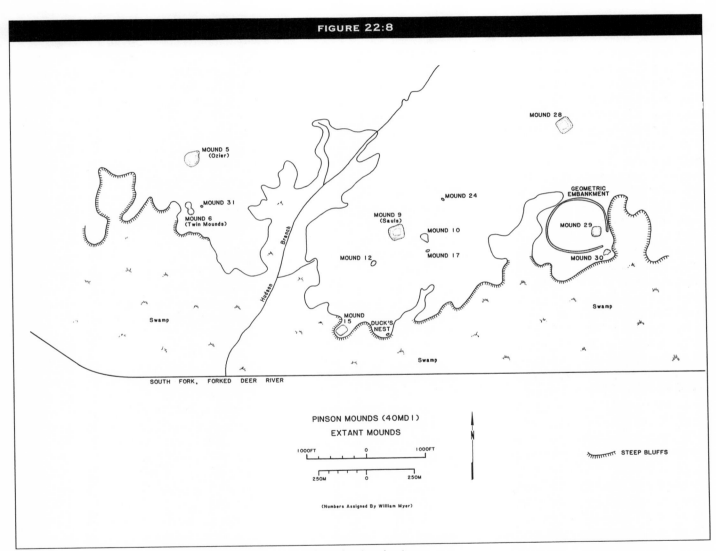

FIGURE 22:8

The Pinson Mound site (Reproduced courtesy of Midcontinental Journal of Archaeology).

Limited testing has also been conducted at a second flat-topped earthwork, Pinson Mound 10, a relatively small and somewhat polygonal structure located about 100 m east of Sauls Mound. Construction of this 1.5 m tall mound evidently was completed as a single event. The only recorded feature was a large hearth located immediately below the plowzone near the center of the earthwork. Three calibrated radiocarbon determinations place construction around A.D. 300 (Mainfort and Walling 1991), which, in addition to the anomalous shape of the earthwork, suggests that Pinson Mound 10 postdates the large rectangular earthworks at the site (e.g., Mainfort 1986).

The Twin Mounds (Mound 6) are a pair of intersecting conical mounds, each about 7 m tall and 25 m in diameter. Although few earthworks at Pinson Mounds were constructed specifically for burial of the dead, partial excavation of the northern Twin Mound provided a rare opportunity to view a large, undisturbed Middle Woodland burial mound. Excavation emphasized documentation of structural details, rather than simply the recovery of burials and associated artifacts (Mainfort 1986).

Approximately one quarter of the mound was excavated. At the base, four log and/or fabric covered tombs containing the remains of 16 individuals were excavated; two additional tombs were recorded but were not excavated. All burials were primary, fleshed inhumations; there is no evidence that the excavated tombs served as mortuary crypts. One tomb (Feature 48) contained the remains of at least eight relatively young women. A large quantity of *Marginella* beads covered this group of interments. Several individuals wore fiber headdresses decorated with copper ornaments, as well as freshwater pearl necklaces.

At the knees of an elderly male in an adjacent tomb, a pair of engraved rattles cut from human parietals and decorated in the classic Hopewellian artistic style (e.g., the Turner site) were found. Other items from mortuary contexts included a small mica mirror, a schist pendant, and a finely crafted boatstone of green speckled schist; the latter was associated with one of two interments placed in mound fill. No children are represented among the interred individuals.

The northern Twin Mound exhibits complex stratigraphy, reflecting the following construction sequence. Initially, all humus and topsoil were removed from the area planned for construction. A number of tombs were excavated into subsoil; various posts and other adjacent features are linked to preparation and/or use of the tombs. A layer of puddled clay was placed over the tombs and associated features. Bounding the area defined by the tombs, a circular, flat-topped primary mound cap with alternating bands of multi-colored sand and clay was then built. The uppermost cap is of reddish-brown subsoil and, thus, symbolically links the primary mound with the underlying subsoil.

Numerous sharpened wooden poles, represented archaeologically by pseudomorphs averaging about 1 m in length, were driven at intervals of about 50 cm into the surface of the primary mound. Neither the function, nor the significance, of these is known, but the poles would have presented annoying obstacles during subsequent mound construction.

A low, sand-covered platform that supported a number of large, outslanting posts (evidently used to support fill from a later stage of mound construction) encircled the primary mound, with a narrow walkway between the two structures. At this stage of construction, the mound would have resembled certain Adena earthwork complexes that consist of a mound surrounded by an embankment and ditch.

Several distinctive layers of fill, some apparently capped with gray clay, another including a number of large ferruginous sandstone boulders, were subsequently added to bring the northern Twin Mound to its final height. Four calibrated radiocarbon assays (one from each of the tombs) indicate that the mound was constructed around A.D. 100 (Mainfort and Walling 1991).

As was the case with other large Middle Woodland ceremonial sites, many of the earthworks at Pinson Mounds were not built by a single small corporate group. Ceramic evidence from virtually every tested locality suggests that individuals from as far away as southern Georgia and the Gulf Coast participated in rituals at the site. This is to be expected, since the size and importance of Pinson Mounds was undoubtedly known to groups throughout the Southeast.

Particularly strong evidence for this was obtained from a locality designated the Duck's Nest Sector, a ritual activity area dating to approximately A.D. 300 (Mainfort and Walling 1991). Of a minimum of 47 ceramic vessels recovered from this locus, at least ten are almost certainly of non-local origin. These include limestone tempered wares from the Tennessee River Valley, *Swift Creek Complicated Stamped* from southern Georgia, *McLeod Simple Stamped* from the Mobile Bay area, and several other types with no known local counterparts (Mainfort 1986, 1988b).

The function of the Duck's Nest Sector remains unclear; previous suggestions that this single-event deposit represents the remains of a "mortuary ceremony" (e.g., Mainfort 1986) might charitably be regarded as premature. The locality certainly was the focus of intensive, specialized activities that probably involved the corporate sphere.

Within the 72 m² excavation area, only a single identifiable feature was recorded. Artifact density was extraordinarily high for Pinson Mounds, including over 2,000 ceramic sherds, nearly 900 chert flakes, over 450 ferruginous siltstone flakes, and a large amount of ferruginous sandstone. Numerous very small, unidentifiable calcined bone fragments were present, as were eight microblades and three pieces of galena. The distribution of ceramics suggests that most of the vessels were "processed" through the single identified feature and subsequently dispersed throughout the deposit. Attention has previously been called to possible parallels with Feature 45 (Pottery Deposit 6) at Helena Crossing Mound C, which included fragments of 17 ceramic vessels and a quantity of calcined bone (Ford 1963; Mainfort 1986).

Off-mound excavations have documented several other ritual activity areas, characterized by the presence of large, ovoid, bent-pole structures and, in several instances, mortuary features. These include the "Cochran site" (west of Ozier Mound), the Twin Mounds sector (south of the Twin Mounds), and the Mound 12 sector (northeast of Mound 12). Various non-local materials, including copper, mica, galena, and Flint Ridge chert microblades, are associated with these localities, strengthening the case for use within the ritual sphere, rather than as domestic dwellings (Mainfort 1980, 1986; Smith 1992).

As one of the few Middle Woodland geometric embankments recorded in the Midsouth (Thunen 1988, 1990), the Pinson Enclosure warrants some mention. Although large expanses of virtually flat topography are present within the earthwork complex, the enclosure (particularly the western half) occupies some of the most precipitous terrain in the area. For approximately 140 degrees of its circumference,

the embankment describes a nearly perfect circle with a diameter of about 180 m, but the remainder lies well inside the projection of the implied circle. In this regard, the Pinson Enclosure somewhat resembles the embankment at Milford in Ohio (Squier and Davis 1848). A ramped platform mound, about 3 m tall and constructed in at least two stages, is located in the southeastern quadrant of the enclosure (Mainfort 1986; Thunen 1990). Its placement suggests the need to "rectify" the presence of a large erosion gully immediately to the south that existed during the Middle Woodland period.

Two smaller burial mounds apparently were built after the inferred peak usage of the Pinson Mounds site. Constructed roughly 100 m east of the Twin Mounds, Mound 31 is a low earthwork approximately 10 m in diameter. A basically rectangular tomb was excavated into subsoil near the center of the mound; an elderly adult male was interred within. Numerous deposits of unidentified calcined bone (possibly human cremations) were placed adjacent to the periphery of the pit, as were a number of ceramic sherds (some, including six limestone-tempered specimens, of probable non-local origin) and some small fragments of mica. This material was covered with a U-shaped ring of subsoil, open on the northeast side. Several burned areas and postholes were also identified on the mound floor. A human skull was recovered from a pit intrusive into the mound. Only two of the four radiocarbon assays on Pinson Mound 31 seem reasonable; these suggest that the earthwork was constructed during the sixth century A.D. (Mainfort and Walling 1991; cf. Mainfort 1986).

Pinson Mound 12, which also postdates construction of the largest earthworks, was constructed on a natural knoll that had initially been utilized for mortuary purposes as early as the first or second century B.C. (cf. Mainfort 1986, 1988b). This low, conical earthwork, with a height of about 1.5 m, was constructed over a low clay platform, in the center of which was an apparent crematory facility (Mainfort 1980). The calcined remains of one or two extended individuals were associated with this feature. Two nearly identical radiocarbon determinations on the crematory facility indicate usage during the sixth century A.D. (Mainfort and Walling 1991), considerably more recent than the similar mortuary platforms discussed above. To date, Pinson Mound 12 has produced evidence of both the earliest and most recent use of the site as a Middle Woodland ceremonial center.

Finally, mention should also be made here of the Johnston site, located about 4 km northwest of the Pinson Mounds complex (Kwas and Mainfort 1986). Within an area of approximately 30 ha are two rectangular platform mounds, a small conical burial mound, and associated occupation areas; several additional conical mounds may once have been present. No professional excavations have been conducted. Material obtained during several surface collections convincingly demonstrates that the Johnston site is roughly contemporary (perhaps antecedent) with the period of major earthwork construction at Pinson Mounds (ca. 50 B.C. - A.D. 300).

The largest earthwork at the site is a large platform mound, standing approximately 6 m tall and with a base measuring about 60 m on each side. Thus, this structure is larger than most of the earthworks at Pinson Mounds. A second rectangular, flat-topped mound, approximately 3 m in height, is located northwest of the largest earthwork. As at the Pinson Mounds site, artifact density is very light, but all identifiable ceramics collected from the Johnston site are early Middle Woodland utilitarian wares that are identical to specimens from the former locality.

CONCLUDING REMARKS

Although the Middle Woodland manifestations in the Midsouth and Lower Mississippi Valley do not, taken as a whole, match the exuberance of Ohio Hopewell, research conducted during the last 15 years makes it quite plain this region was not a cultural backwater (Mainfort 1989). Nowhere is this more clearly demonstrated than by the Pinson Mounds site, which represents Middle Woodland earthwork construction on a scale surpassed only by the enormous complex at Newark, while the structure and complexity of the Twin Mounds recalls Seip and other large Ohio mortuary earthworks. The unique regional "flavor" of Middle Woodland in the Midsouth is also brought into sharper focus by the Pinson Mounds data. Platform mounds, previously seen as Mississippian period structures, were integral to Middle Woodland ceremonialism in the Midsouth, with examples from Pinson Mounds, Johnston (Kwas and Mainfort 1986), Ingomar, and Marksville. Similar works have only recently been identified in Ohio (N'omi Greber, personal communication, 1990).

Low, earthen mortuary platforms are present at numerous sites throughout the region and may have considerable time depth (Gibson and Shenkel 1988). These may be structurally and symbolically related to platform mounds, but it seems clear that these small structures should not be considered the precursors of Mississippian substructural

mounds, since very large, multistage platform mounds were also constructed during the early Middle Woodland period (contra Rolingson 1990). Log-covered crypts similar to features frequently encountered in Havana-Hopewell occur, but do not seem to be common. Evidence of actual charnel houses has been found at Bynum, Miller, and possibly Marksville, while burial data from Crooks clearly implies the existence of such structures.

Finally, it seems necessary to address the "Hopewell Intrusion" scenario advocated by Toth (1988) in his valuable synthesis of Early Marksville. Briefly stated, Toth (1988:29) believes that the "widespread and apparently sudden presence of a number of good horizon markers" in the Lower Mississippi Valley was the result of "diffusion" and even direct contact with Hopewellian societies in Illinois. This model (using the term in its broadest sense) appears to be firmly rooted in the belief that not only is Marksville somehow "inferior" to Illinois Hopewell, but also that Early Woodland manifestations in the Illinois Valley were "more elaborate" than the "very generalized" Tchula/Tchefuncte to the south. Early Marksville burial mounds are viewed exhibiting specific traits that are traceable to the Illinois Valley, "but only in disjointed bits and pieces, not as a unified whole" (Toth 1988:41). Here the implication is that Hopewellian manifestations in Illinois exhibit minimal variation (which is not at all the case) and shared a universal belief system, while Marksville societies never reached such a level of development.

The evidence presented here demonstrates that such a view is seriously flawed. Mound construction apparently has a far longer history in the Lower Mississippi Valley than in more northerly areas, and conical burial mounds dating to the pre-Marksville Tchula horizon are now well-documented (e.g., Ford 1990). Large, rectangular Middle Woodland platform mounds are present at several sites in the Midsouth; none have been recorded to date in Illinois. Enclosures, virtually absent in Illinois, occur at a number of sites in the Lower Mississippi Valley. The widespread practice of burial platforms throughout the study area, further serves to distinguish the Middle Woodland societies of the Midsouth and Lower Mississippi Valley. This form of mortuary structure is not derivable from northern sources.

As additional research is conducted, it seems likely that the stature of the Midsouth and Lower Mississippi Valley within the Hopewellian world will continue to grow.

REFERENCES CITED

Bohannon, C. F. 1972 *Excavations at the Pharr Mounds, Prentiss and Itawamba Counties, Mississippi, and Excavations at the Bear Creek Site, Tishomingo County, Mississippi.* United States Department of the Interior, National Park Service. Washington, D.C.

Brown, J. A. 1979 Charnel Houses and Mortuary Crypts: Disposal of the Dead in the Middle Woodland Period. In *Hopewell Archaeology: The Chillicothe Conference*, edited by D.S. Brose and N.B. Greber, pp. 211-219. Kent State University Press, Kent, Ohio.

Byers, A. M. 1987 *The Earthwork Enclosures of the Central Ohio Valley: A Temporal and Structural Analysis of Woodland Society and Culture.* Ph.D. dissertation, Department of Anthropology, State University of New York at Albany, Albany. University Microfilms, Ann Arbor.

Canouts, V. 1986 *The Effects of Boundary Conditions on the Archaeological Record: A Stylistic Analysis of Havana Hopewell and Marksville.* Ph.D. dissertation, Department of Anthropology, Southern Illinois University, Carbondale. University Microfilms, Ann Arbor.

Chapman, R. 1981 The Emergence of Formal Disposal Areas and the "Problem" of Megalithic Tombs in Prehistoric Europe. In *The Archaeology of Death*, edited by R. Chapman, I. Kinnes, and K. Randsborg, pp. 71-81. Cambridge University Press, Cambridge.

Charles, D. K. 1985 *Corporate Symbols: An Interpretive Prehistory of Indian Burial Mounds in Westcentral Illinois.* Ph.D. dissertation, Department of Anthropology, Northwestern University, Evanston. University Microfilms, Ann Arbor.

Charles, D. K. and J. E. Buikstra 1983 Archaic Mortuary Sites in the Central Mississippi Drainage: Distribution, Structure, and Behavioral Implications. In *Archaic Hunters and Gatherers in the American Midwest*, edited by J. L. Phillips and J. A. Brown, pp. 117-145. Academic Press, New York.

Cotter, J. L. and J. M. Corbett 1951 *The Archaeology of the Bynum Mounds, Mississippi.* United States Department of the Interior, National Park Service, Archaeological Research Series, No. 1. Washington D. C.

Crane, H. R. and J. B. Griffin 1963 University of Michigan Radiocarbon Dates VIII. *Radiocarbon* 5:228-253.

Ford, J. A. 1963 *Hopewell Culture Burial Mounds Near Helena, Arkansas.* Anthropological Papers of the American Museum of Natural History 50(1). New York.

Ford, J. A. and G. Willey 1940 *Crooks Site, A Marksville Period Burial Mound in La Salle Parish, Louisiana.* Department of Conservation, Louisiana Geological Survey, Anthropological Study No. 3. New Orleans.

Ford, J. 1990 The Tchula Connection: Early Woodland Culture and Burial Mounds in North Mississippi. *Southeastern Archaeology* 9(2):103-115.

Fowke, G. 1928 Archaeological Excavations I- II: Explorations in the Red River Valley in Louisiana. In *Forty-Fourth Annual Report of the Bureau of American Ethnology*, pp. 399-436. Washington, D. C.

Gibson, J. L. and J. R. Shenkel 1988 Louisiana Earthworks: Middle Woodland and Predecessors. In *Middle Woodland Settlement and Ceremonialism in the Mid-South and the Lower Mississippi Valley*, edited by R. Mainfort, pp. 7-18. Mississippi Department of Archives and History, Archaeological Report No. 22. Jackson.

Griffin, J. B. 1973 Review of Archaeological Survey in the Lower Yazoo Basin, Mississippi, 1949-1955, by P. Phillips. *American Antiquity* 38(3):374-380.

1979 An Overview of the Chillicothe Hopewell Conference. In *Hopewell Archaeology: The Chillicothe Conference*, edited by D.S. Brose and N.B. Greber, pp. 266-279. Kent State University Press, Kent, Ohio.

Jenkins, N. J. 1979 Miller Hopewell of the Tombigbee Drainage. In *Hopewell Archaeology: The Chillicothe Conference,* edited by D.S. Brose and N.B. Greber, pp. 171-180. Kent State University Press, Kent, Ohio.

1982 *Archaeology of the Gainesville Lake Area: Synthesis.* University of Alabama, Office of Archaeological Research, Report of Investigations, No. 23. Tuscaloosa.

Jennings, J. D. 1941 Chickasaw and Earlier Indian Cultures of Northeast Mississippi. *Journal of Mississippi History* 3:155-226.

Kardwesky, R. A. 1980 *Archaeological Investigations at the Pharr Village and Mackey's Creek Sites in Northeast Mississippi.* Southeast Conservation Archaeological Center, Archaeological Research Report No. 6. Florida State University, Tallahassee.

Kwas, M. L. and R. C. Mainfort, Jr. 1986 The Johnston Site: Precursor to Pinson Mounds? *Tennessee Anthropologist* 11(1):29-41.

Mainfort, R. C., Jr., ed. 1980 *Archaeological Investigations at Pinson Mounds State Archaeological Area: 1974, 1975, and 1978 Field Seasons.* Tennessee Department of Conservation, Division of Archaeology, Research Series, No. 1. Nashville.

1989 *Middle Woodland Settlement and Ceremonialism in the Mid-South and Lower Mississippi Valley.* Mississippi Department of Archives and History, Archaeological Report No. 22. Jackson.

Mainfort, R. C., Jr. 1986 *Pinson Mounds: A Middle Woodland Ceremonial Center.* Tennessee Department of Conservation, Division of Archaeology, Research Series, No. 7. Nashville.

1988a Middle Woodland Mortuary Patterning at Helena Crossing, Arkansas. *Tennessee Anthropologist* 13(1):35-50.

1988b Middle Woodland Ceremonialism at Pinson Mounds, Tennessee. *American Antiquity* 53(1):158-173.

Mainfort, R. C. and K. C. Carstens 1987 A Middle Woodland Embankment and Mound Complex in Western Kentucky. *Southeastern Archaeology* 6(1):57-61.

Mainfort, R. C. and R. Walling 1991 Calibrated Radiocarbon Chronology for the Middle Woodland Period in the Midsouth. Paper presented at the Annual Meeting of the Society for American Archaeology, New Orleans, Louisiana.

1992 1989 Excavations at Pinson Mounds: Ozier Mound. *Midcontinental Journal of Archaeology* 17(1):112-136.

Neumann, G. K. and M. L. Fowler 1952 Hopewellian Sites in the Lower Wabash Valley. In *Hopewellian Communities in Illinois,* edited by T. Deuel, pp. 175-248. Illinois State Museum, Scientific Papers No. 5. Springfield, Illinois.

Phillips, P. 1970 *Archaeological Survey in the Lower Yazoo Basin, Mississippi: 1949-1955.* Papers of the Peabody Museum of Archaeology and Ethnology, Vol. 60, pts. 1 and 2. Harvard University, Cambridge.

Rafferty, J. 1987 The Ingomar Mounds site: Internal Structure and Chronology. *Midcontinental Journal of Archaeology* 12(2):147-173.

1990 Test Excavations at Ingomar Mounds, Mississippi. *Southeastern Archaeology* 9(2):93-102.

Rolingson, M.A. 1990 The Toltec Mounds Site. In *The Mississippian Emergence,* edited by B.D. Smith, pp. 27-49, Smithsonian Institution Press. Washington D.C.

Saunders, J. and T. Allen 1993 Archaic Mound Research in Northeastern Louisiana. Paper presented at the Midsouth Archaeological Conference, Memphis, Tennessee.

Seeman, M. F. 1977 *The Hopewell Interaction Sphere: The Evidence for Interregional Trade and Structural Complexity.* Ph.D. dissertation, Department of Anthropology, Indiana University, Bloomington. University Microfilms, Ann Arbor.

Shenkel, J. R. 1986 An Additional Comment on Volume Calculations and a Comparison of Formulae using Several Southeastern Mounds. *Midcontinental Journal of Archaeology* 11(2):201-220.

Smith, B. D. 1992 Hopewellian Farmers of Eastern North America. In *Rivers of Change*, by B. D. Smith, pp. 201-248. Smithsonian Institution Press, Washington, D.C.

Squier, E. G. and E. H. Davis 1848 *Ancient Monuments of the Mississippi Valley*. Smithsonian Contributions to Knowledge 1. Washington, D. C.

Thomas, C. 1894 *Report on the Mound Explorations of the Bureau of Ethnology*. Bureau of American Ethnology, 12th Annual Report. Washington, D.C.

Thunen, R. L. 1988 Geometric Enclosures in the Mid-South: An Analysis of Enclosure Form. In *Middle Woodland Settlement and Ceremonialism in the Mid-South and Lower Mississippi Valley*, edited by R. C. Mainfort, pp. 99-115. Mississippi Department of Archives and History, Archaeological Report No. 22. Jackson.

1990 *Planning Principles and Earthwork Architecture: The Pinson Mounds Enclosure*. Ph.D. dissertation, Department of Anthropology, Northwestern University, Evanston. University Microfilms, Ann Arbor.

Toth, E. A. 1974 *Archaeology and Ceramics at the Marksville Site*. Museum of Anthropology, Anthropological Papers, No. 56. University of Michigan, Ann Arbor.

1988 *Early Marksville Phases in the Lower Mississippi Valley: A Study of Culture Contact Dynamics*. Mississippi Department of Archives and History, Archaeological Report No. 21. Jackson.

Walling, R. and E. Roemer 1993 *A Cultural Resources Inventory Survey of Portions of the Big and Little Sunflower Rivers, Issaquena, Sharkey, and Yazoo Counties, Mississippi, Volume 1*. Panamerican Consultants, Report of Investigations No. 42-6. Tuscaloosa.

Walling, R., R. C. Mainfort, and J. R. Atkinson 1991 Radiocarbon Dates for the Bynum, Pharr, and Miller Sites, Northeast Mississippi. *Southeastern Archaeology* 10(1):54-62.

Williams, S. and J. P. Brain 1983 *Excavations at the Lake*

SECTION THREE: COMMENTARY

TWENTY-THREE

PUTTING AN END TO OHIO HOPEWELL

WILLIAM S. DANCEY

ABSTRACT

This paper presents an argument that the eclipse of
Hopewellian society can be best understood within an evolutionary framework based upon the Darwinian principle of
selection. This explanatory paradigm is explained briefly and
an example of its application to a similar problem in culture
history in the American Southwest is summarized. The
Southwestern case is used to construct a historical model for
the Middle Ohio Valley in which nucleated sedentary communities are seen as more reproductively successful than dispersed sedentary communities, including those of the Ohio
Hopewell tradition, in the practice of specialized strategies of
economic production based upon indigenous domesticates.

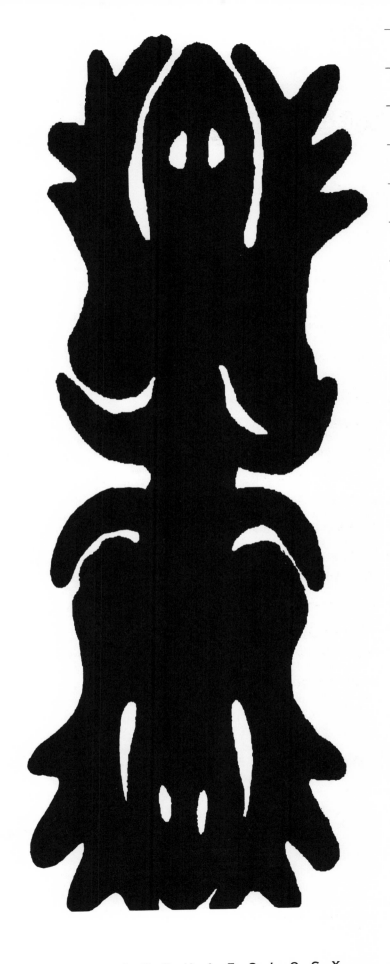

INTRODUCTION

Explaining the demise of the Ohio Hopewell is an old problem, as yet unsolved. This paper has the goal not of solving the problem, but of forcing hard thought about the question itself. It continues a line of reasoning advanced in an earlier paper on the culture history of the Middle Ohio Valley (Dancey 1992).

The problem is real enough. In A.D. 200 the Middle Ohio Valley was inhabited by people who constructed geometric earthworks and heaped dirt over the tombs and charnel houses of their dead. These people appear not to have lived in nucleated communities, but rather to have dispersed their households (hamlets) across the landscape. By A.D. 500, the archaeological record presents a dramatically different picture. At that time the area's communities were living in nucleated settlements (villages). While the burial mound complex remained alive in an attenuated form, earthworks were neither modified nor maintained. Importantly, the practice of adding expertly crafted artifacts of high value to graves, often in large numbers, ended. What happened?

THE OHIO HOPEWELL "COLLAPSE"

As well-known as the phenomenon itself are the many explanations for its disappearance from the archaeological record. Cultural fatigue, invasion, climate change, devolution, progressive evolution, and disease are among the many forces that have been invoked. While working on his own explanation in the late 1970s, Braun (1977) classified previous explanations as either univariate (prime mover) or multivariate. The former included migration, the loss or adoption of maize, adoption of bow hunting, and inter-regional warfare. Braun ruled out migration because no evidence for population movement had been found and analysis of skeletal remains produced strong evidence of epigenetic traits within local areas. The failure of maize agriculture or the increased importance of tropical cultigens was dismissed because maize does not become economically important, if even present, until the 9th century A.D.

He thought that introduction of a bow-and-arrow hunting technology in the early Late Woodland could not explain the shift because this also appeared not to have become common until later, possibly in the 8th or 9th century A.D. Warfare was rejected because in spite of evidence for homicides, he could find no cases dating to the Middle or Late Woodland. Furthermore, hostility appears to have been expressed on a personal, not societal level.

Explanations in Braun's multivariate category have survived somewhat better, although even here there is considerable controversy. To include more recent writing in this category we can turn to a paper written by Braun in the mid 1980s in which he (Braun 1986) identifies three "processual models": (1) conflict over unevenly accessible resources, as represented by Joseph Tainter, (2) development of more successful systems of cultivation, as sketched by Barbara Bender in her early writing, and (3) high risk associated with cultivation, Braun's own contribution. Multivariate explanations consider the interaction of several different dimensions of the social group, such as social structure, population, subsistence, and technology, in modeling the dynamics of change. Thus, Tainter (1977) relates population growth, horticultural intensification, and competition over access to resources to a collapse of the Middle Woodland social order and a lower scale of social complexity. Bender (1979, 1985), especially in more recent writing, links subsistence practice, demographic pressures, and tensions between the "social top and base" (Bender 1985:49) to the elite's loss of control over socially valued items and the subsequent breakdown of exchange networks. Braun and Plog (1982) examine the relationship of intensified subsistence practices to inter-community relations and social organization in coping with the higher risks associated with greater investment in cultivation.

The problem of inadequate data has contributed to the irresolute nature of these, and other explanations, especially in the Middle Ohio Valley, but paradigm failure is a more serious cause. The studies mentioned above combine elements of at least three current explanatory models: anthropological archaeology (also known as New Archaeology, or adaptationism), cultural evolution (a la White, Service, and Sahlins), and dialectical structuralism. According to recent critiques, including several by Braun himself (Braun 1990,1991; Dunnell 1980; Leonard and Jones 1987; O'Brien and Holland 1990, 1992) adaptationism is flawed by its inability to cope with systemic change, cultural evolution by its reliance on the concepts of stage, progress, and transformational change, and structuralism by ascribing causal power to human motives. In each case, the paradigm seems unable to encompass the complexity of real human populations embedded in the fabric of time. One possible alternative is a broader paradigm which has withstood the test of time, at least within biology as a whole: the Darwinian concept of evolution by natural selection. This paradigm, now favored by Braun, potentially can surmount the problems encountered by more narrowly conceived, and often anthropocentric, explanatory models. The remainder of the paper looks at this paradigm and whether it has any bearing on the problem of the Ohio Hopewell demise.

THE SELECTIONIST EVOLUTION PARADIGM IN ARCHAEOLOGY

As articulated by Robert Dunnell (1989, 1992) and others, a selectionist evolution paradigm has the virtue of making the central explanatory concept, natural selection, theoretical rather than empirical. Selection is a process, not a thing, and therefore can be universal. Furthermore, this approach separates the production of variation from the action of selection. Both features are central in the Darwinian theory of evolution and are favorable to its use in archaeology. By adopting this approach, as archaeologists, we need bicker no more about whether climate change, food choices, warfare, disease or any other particular event alone caused change. Nor do we need to apologize for not having genes or minds to analyze since biological and mental processes contribute to variation, but are not themselves selective in the Darwinian sense.

Another archaeologically attractive feature of the selectionist paradigm is its emphasis on inheritance. As Stephen J. Gould (1986) puts it: history matters! Thus while chronology

building has been derided by the New Archaeology and forced into a teleological mold by cultural evolution, a selectionist approach requires it. Selection acts upon individuals who are members of local groups (households and communities) whose biological and social interaction in regions over time creates the threads in the fabric of history. Archaeologists sore from the beating Culture History suffered at the hands of the New Archaeology might find solace in this feature of selectionist evolution.

Since first proposed by Darwin over 130 years ago, this approach has become highly elaborate and a coherent summary of it cannot be accomplished in a few pages. Furthermore, although controversies about its application in biology are peripheral, in anthropology they are central. A summary would have to grapple with the many debates about the application of selectionist theory to human populations. Expediency, then, forces me to jump from the tenets of the paradigm to some practical matters relating to its application in archaeology. Four in particular are pertinent to the present case.

1. Human populations function within regions and artifacts of their activities accumulate across the entire landscape.

2. Selection acts upon phenotypic variation, which among human populations includes artifacts along with behavior.

3. Classificatory devices such as the phase cannot be employed because they obscure variability.

4. Fine-grained local chronologies are important to mapping the histories of cultural traits and the populations in which they occur.

Selectionist evolution addresses the question of how regional population histories have been shaped by the differential persistence of functional behaviors. In the case at hand, this question might be phrased as follows: If there is a functional difference between what we think of as Ohio Hopewell compared to what we think of as early Late Woodland, what behaviors of the early Late Woodland have conferred upon the populations in which they occur a selective advantage over Ohio Hopewell populations? There is reason to believe that such functional differences exist, although no systematic functional analysis has yet been applied to the problem.

The evolution of specialized food producing economies and aggregated communities has been well documented in the American Southwest. This also is an area of North America famous for a dramatic cultural demise of its maize agriculturalists, the Anasazi of the Colorado Plateau. As with the Ohio Hopewell "collapse", the "Chacoan collapse" (Tainter 1988) of the 12th century A.D. is poorly understood despite decades of study. In an effort to solve that mystery, Robert Leonard (1989) and colleagues have been exploring use of the principles of selectionist evolution. His approach and findings potentially can provide a guiding light for solution of the Ohio Hopewell problem.

Leonard's model, as developed in a recent paper with Heidi Reed (Leonard and Reed 1993), unfolds as follows. In the Southwest, domesticates initially were incorporated in generalized procurement strategies as a means of extending diet breadth. The coevolutionary interaction of people and domesticates, by a process outlined by Rindos (1984), favored in some environments the reproductive success of subsistence strategies emphasizing domesticates. Gradually, systems of specialized food production became widespread within Puebloan communities living in dispersed settlements. Those groups inhabiting areas which experienced significant year to year perturbations in available moisture were challenged to adopt strategies and tactics which offset decreased available moisture (and possibly also less available arable land).

The solution to the ecological problem in the Colorado Plateau was to intensify labor in order to hold agricultural production constant. Intensifying labor resulted in the appearance of population aggregates, some of which were able to sustain occupation despite deteriorating climate. Aggregation appeared initially, but at different times, in the

most severely stressed habitats, and last in optimal areas. Populations unable to counter the inherent instability of specialized systems and the added burden of aggregation abandoned their territories and relocated in less severely stressed environments, thus producing the so-called Chacoan collapse.

In Leonard and Reed's analysis of the Puebloan case, aggregation is seen as linked to the action of selection on food-producing economies in which specialized strategies are favored because they offer (as do specialized procurement systems) an increased return for the effort and the potential for higher relative population density. Because specialized systems are unstable, however, the social groups practicing them, while increasing in number, become distributed differently than generalized systems. Furthermore, they contribute a dynamic quality to culture history through localized, irregularly timed population collapse and redistribution. Understanding the complexity of local culture histories does not require a search for prime movers, or construction of multivariate systems. Nor does it require creating ethnographic-like archaeological cultures or abstract cultural systems. It looks matter-of-factly at the interplay between aggregation, population size, specialized agricultural strategies and tactics, labor organization, and environment on the local level within fine-grained chronological control.

THE MIDDLE OHIO VALLEY

A similar scenario might be developed for the Middle Ohio Valley and help show the way to a solution of the Ohio Hopewell "collapse" and the subsequent emergence of aggregated social groups. This "selectionist history" unfolds as follows. Specialized production became common among dispersed, stable human groups during the first millennium B.C. (**Figure 23:1, Time 1-3**). These strategies developed around plants of the Eastern Agricultural Complex, which Smith (1989) and Wymer (1987) argue was a farming system, although the details of its strategy and tactics have not been explored. Stability is reflected in the development of fixed territories containing permanent facilities such as earthworks. Clay (1991) argues that such features become

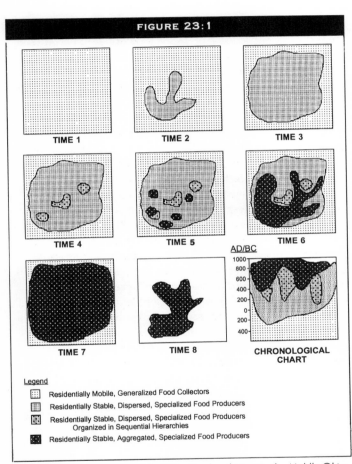

FIGURE 23:1

TIME 1   TIME 2   TIME 3

TIME 4   TIME 5   TIME 6

TIME 7   TIME 8   CHRONOLOGICAL CHART

AD/BC

Legend

- Residentially Mobile, Generalized Food Collectors
- Residentially Stable, Dispersed, Specialized Food Producers
- Residentially Stable, Dispersed, Specialized Food Producers Organized in Sequential Hierarchies
- Residentially Stable, Aggregated, Specialized Food Producers

Hypothetical time-space model of Woodland prehistory in the Middle Ohio Valley from ca. 1000 B.C. to A.D. 1000.

common by 500 B.C.. Alliances (possibly sequential hierarchies) formed in optimal areas (**Figure 23:1, Time 4**) as an alternative to labor intensification. Population growth resulting from the higher reproductive rates of the specialized production systems created competition for arable land, particularly in marginal habitats. Aggregation began earliest in the marginal areas and later in optimal areas.

Two periods are particularly significant in this historical model. The first is during the late Middle Woodland (Walthall 1985) when variation was at a maximum. Steve Ahler (1992:31) suggests that the earliest dates on Newtown villages are coeval with late Middle Woodland between A.D. 200 and 400 at the mouths of the Scioto and Great Miami Rivers, and in the Bluegrass. Henderson and Pollack (1985) argue the same point in their report on the Bentley site in Kentucky at the mouth of the Scioto River. This is the period (**Figure 23:1, Time 5-Time 6**) when the last uses are recorded for the classic earthwork sites in the Scioto-Paint Creek cluster of Hopewellian sites, an optimal area according to Maslowski and Seeman (1992:12). The second period is the early Late Woodland, between A.D. 600 and 800 (**Figure 23:1, Time 7**), when aggregated village communities come to dominate the landscape. Subsequently (**Figure 23:1, Time 8**), at variable rates and in unpredictable locations, the pattern of village life recedes, as Church (1987) has demonstrated for the central Scioto. Beginning around A.D. 900 nucleated sedentary communities again are found throughout the area, this time with specialized economies centered on maize (the Fort Ancient tradition).

How is the Ohio Hopewell demise explained in this selectionist scenario? In its early history Ohio Hopewell is seen as one of several kinds of residentially stable social groups, including those referred to as Late Adena. In its later history, when the lavish, public display of conspicuous consumption in burial ritual occurs, it is seen as a case of the late survival of a specialized production system within a non-aggregated settlement system. The investment of energy in burial ritual may in fact, as Dunnell (1989) has suggested, represent a population control mechanism, something suspected also for certain practices in the Southwest (Leonard and Reed 1993:657). The "collapse" is explained as the result of an eventual redirection of energy expenditure toward intensification of labor and community aggregation. As Rafferty (1985) has argued, nucleation of a community removes the need to aggregate for special ritual purposes, and this simple fact may account for the lapse in construction and maintenance of the earthwork centers.

This scenario assumes that the dispersed sedentary nature of Ohio Hopewell social groups has been demonstrated and is non-controversial. This is not the case, although Converse (1993) claims it has become unquestioned dogma. Opposing views have been expressed by Yerkes (1988), who seems to suggest that Ohio Hopewell populations are seasonally mobile. Converse (1993) champions an idea supported many years ago by Griffin (1967:183), and holds even today, that Ohio Hopewell lived in villages. Both extremes are reflected in a number of the papers in a book in progress edited by me and Paul Pacheco (Dancey and Pacheco n.d.) reporting results of habitation research conducted in Ohio during the last decade.

As I see it, residential seasonal mobility does not make sense for social groups investing time and energy in ritual precincts. Residential sites with Hopewellian artifacts that I know of are similar in structure from one to another. Differences in artifact proportions can be explained as a product of differing duration of occupation. If these places, such as the Murphy site (Dancey 1991) in Licking County and McGraw (Prufer 1965) in Ross County, represent seasonal utilization, where did the occupants go upon leaving these settlements? If the answer is into the canyon country of the Unglaciated Plateau, consider just this one implication. Rockshelters are not within the territories of very many of the Middle Woodland social groups. Therefore, the unlikely annual settlement system for most groups, especially in the Till Plain or the Glaciated Plateau, is to filter through alien territory at some season (winter?), passing the earthworks and burial grounds of their neighbors who most likely are competitors the rest of the year, on their way to rockshelter country.

What about villages adjacent to the earthworks? Where are they? Domestic trash has been recorded, as well as structures, but the record does not add up to villages, anywhere. Pacheco (1993) has argued that seasonal use of the ritual precincts will produce a variety of domestic archaeological remains and this seems the best explanation for the light scatter of debris, trash, and structural remains directly associated with the earthworks. Furthermore, all the reports of Middle Woodland villages spatially associated with earth-

works that I know of contain artifact styles post-dating the period of classic Ohio Hopewell. They appear to represent settlements formed after A.D. 400 when there is little if any evidence for maintenance, let alone new construction at the earthwork sites. In the period before A.D. 400, a more convincing case can be made for a pattern of dispersed sedentary household/hamlets distributed around the ritual precincts, which were visited seasonally for ceremonial activity, as argued by Prufer (1964, 1965) over 30 years ago.

CONCLUDING OBSERVATIONS

As a final topic, I would like to move from the local to the regional scale and view the distribution of earthwork sites within all of southern Ohio. **Figure 23:2** shows the distribution of nearly all recorded earthworks within central and southern Ohio, without distinguishing Adena or Hopewell and including partial representations. Excluded are sites which were disputed by knowledgeable individuals close to the time of a report and earthworks known to enclose Late Woodland villages. This data base has grown over nearly two centuries and while including some contested sites and being far from complete, I think it is a legitimate basis for drawing some general conclusions.

As far as the overall distribution is concerned, the highest density occurs between the Unglaciated Plateau and the Beech-Maple forest of the Till Plain. The Beech-Maple forest, historically a dark, wet area (Gordon 1969), appears to have been avoided, as was the more open, wet prairie south of and contiguous with this forest type. Enclosures are recorded within the dissected terrain of the Unglaciated Plateau, but at a very low density. Looking at the spacing of sites, it appears that regularity characterizes the entire data set, although the interval between enclosures is different in different places. In Ross County, for example, the average is 7 km while in the lower Little Miami it is 3 km, and in other segments of the two Miamis it is approximately 10 kilometers. Based upon the differential spacing, and on breaks in the distributions, Pacheco and I (Dancey and Pacheco 1992) postulated the existence of a series of peer polities.

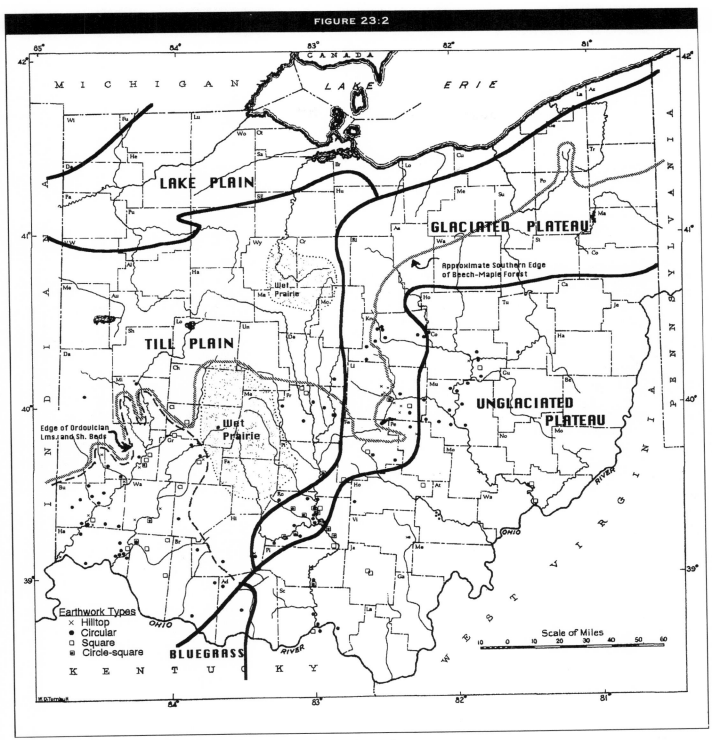

Earthwork distribution in central and southern Ohio in relation to select environmental parameters.

Although this proposition might easily be contested by filling in the gaps with unreported earthworks, the underlying observation is not new. A difference between the southwestern Ohio and Scioto-Paint earthwork sites has been recognized for many years.

Turning to the distribution of earthwork shapes, and distinguishing places with circular, square, circle-square combinations, and hilltop enclosures, some interesting, but not entirely unexpected, patterns emerge. Circles are ubiquitous and have the broadest distribution. Squares have almost as wide a distribution, but are fewer in number and do not always occur in areas containing circles. Circle-square combinations have a restricted distribution, with the majority located in Ross County. Hilltop enclosures occur predominantly in the margins of the total distribution, on the west and in the northeast.

As this mapping project continues, extending into adjacent states, uncovering more reported sites within Ohio, and accumulating descriptive data on each location, some elements of the patterning as generalized here may change. Overall, however, I think the basic patterning will persist. And if the enclosure data can be integrated with distributional data on burial mounds, added dimensions should be revealed. However the database might be expanded or enhanced, what we have before us appears to reinforce the general picture of population history sketched earlier. Two assumptions are invoked: that the enclosure locations represent community centers, and that the history of enclosure construction begins with circles, continues with squares, and finishes with the joining of earlier circles and squares. If these assumptions are correct, and excavation data appear to support them, the maps suggest the extension of a residentially stable adaptation to the limits of its applicability, the durability of this adaptation throughout most, but not all regions within southern Ohio, and the persistence of it in Ross County and possibly several other regions while marginal areas are experiencing challenges to the continued practice of traditional behaviors.

These data are far from what is required to construct tests of hypotheses drawn from selectionist evolution. Nevertheless, in my opinion, they are suggestive of the fruitfulness of this approach. And while Ohio Hopewell initially is sublimated to more general phenomena and processes in the application of this highly demanding paradigm, it may well emerge as a unique cultural entity. I cannot resist noting, in closing, that Seeman's (1979) examination of the distribution of Hopewell Interaction Sphere artifacts throughout eastern North America concluded that the greatest diversity and quantity centered on southern Ohio. If there was a Hopewell, perhaps it was only in southern Ohio, a point jokingly proclaimed by Dr. Griffin in Milwaukee at the 1993 Midwest Archeological Conference.

ACKNOWLEDGMENTS

This paper is the product of long discussions over many years with Paul Pacheco, whose comments on the manuscript have improved it immensely. It took its original form during the first of a two part graduate seminar on evolutionary ecology and Darwinian evolution in archaeology co-taught with Kristen Gremillion who critiqued the paper and helped sharpen the expression. In addition, a version of it was presented in a seminar at the University of New Mexico at the invitation of Ann Ramenofsky and Ana Steffan. At this event I had the opportunity to discuss the ideas with Bob Leonard. My thanks to Paul, Kris, Ann, Ana, and Bob for their support, and to the students whose feedback was influential in shaping the paper. Naturally, I shoulder full responsibility for the final product.

REFERENCES CITED

Ahler, S. R. 1992 The Hansen Site (15GP14): A Middle/Late Woodland Site Near the Confluence of the Ohio and Scioto Rivers. In *Cultural Variability in Context: Woodland Settlements of the Mid-Ohio Valley*, edited by M. Seeman, pp. 30-40. Midcontinental Journal of Archaeology Special Paper No. 7. Kent State University Press, Kent, Ohio.

Bender, B. 1979 Gatherer-Hunter to Farmer: A Social Perspective. *World Archaeology* 10:204-222.

    1985 Prehistoric Developments in the American Midcontinent and in Brittany, Northwest France. In *Prehistoric Hunter-Gatherers: the Emergence of Cultural Complexity*, edited by T. D. Price and J. A. Brown, pp. 21-57. Academic Press, Orlando.

Braun, D. P. 1977 *Middle Woodland-Early Late Woodland Social Change in the Prehistoric Central Midwestern U.S.* Ph.D. dissertation, Department of Anthropology, University of Michigan, Ann Arbor. University Microfilms, Ann Arbor.

    1986 Midwestern Hopewellian Exchange and Supralocal Interaction. In *Peer Polity Interaction and Socio-Political Change*, edited by C. Renfrew and J. Cherry, pp. 117-126. Cambridge University Press, Cambridge.

    1990 Selection and Evolution in Nonhierarchical Organization. In *The Evolution of Political Systems*, edited by S. Upham, pp. 62-86. Cambridge University Press, New York.

    1991 Are There Cross-Cultural Regularities in Tribal Social Practices? In *Between Bands and States*, edited by S. Gregg, pp. 423-444. Center for Archaeological Investigations, Occasional Paper No. 9. Southern Illinois University, Carbondale.

Braun, D. P., and S. Plog 1982 Evolution of Tribal Social Networks: Theory and Prehistoric North American Evidence. *American Antiquity* 47:504-525.

Church, F. 1987 *An Inquiry into the Transition from Late Woodland to Late Prehistoric Cultures in the Central Scioto Valley, Ohio circa A.D. 500 to A.D. 1250.* Ph.D. dissertation, Department of Anthropology, The Ohio State University, Columbus. University Microfilms, Ann Arbor.

Clay, R. B. 1991 Adena Ritual Development: An Organizational Type in a Temporal Perspective. In *The Human Landscape in Kentucky's Past: Site Structure and Settlement Patterns*, edited by C. Stout and C. K. Hensley, pp. 30-39. Kentucky Heritage Council, Lexington.

Converse, R. N. 1993 The Troyer Site: A Hopewell Habitation Site, and a Secular View of Hopewell Villages. *Ohio Archaeologist* 43(3):4-12.

Dancey, W. S. 1991 A Middle Woodland Settlement in Central Ohio: A Preliminary Report on the Murphy Site (33LI212). *Pennsylvania Archaeologist* 61(2):37-72.

    1992 Village Origins in Central Ohio: The Results and Implications of Recent Middle and Late Woodland Research. In *Cultural Variability in Context; Woodland Settlements of the Mid-Ohio Valley*, edited by M. Seeman, pp. 24-29. Midcontinental Journal of Archaeology Special Paper No. 7. Kent State University Press, Kent, Ohio.

Dancey, W. S., and P. J. Pacheco 1992 The Ohio Hopewell Settlement Pattern Problem in Historical Perspective. Paper presented at the Annual Meeting of the Society for American Archaeology, Pittsburgh.

Dancey, W. S., and P. J. Pacheco, eds. n.d. *Ohio Hopewell Community Organization.* Kent State University Press, Kent, Ohio "in press."

Dunnell, R. C. 1980 Evolutionary Theory and Archaeology. In *Advances in Archaeological Method and Theory, Vol. 3*, edited by M. B. Schiffer, pp. 35-99. Academic Press, New York.

    1989 Aspects of the Application of Evolutionary Theory in Archaeology. In *Archaeological Thought in America*, edited by C.C. Lamberg-Karlovsky, pp.35-49. Cambridge University Press, New York.

1992 Archaeology and Evolutionary Science. In *Quandaries and Quests: Visions of Archaeology's Future*, edited by L. Wandsnider, pp. 209-224. Center for Archaeological Investigations, Southern Illinois University, Carbondale.

Gordon, R. B. 1969 The Natural Vegetation of Ohio in Pioneer Days. *Bulletin of the Ohio Biological Society*, 3(2). The Ohio State University, Columbus.

Gould, S. J. 1986 Evolution and the Triumph of Homology, or Why History Matters. *American Scientist* 74(1):60-69.

Griffin, J. B. 1967 Eastern North American Archeology: A Summary. *Science* 156:175-191.

Henderson, A. G., and D. Pollack 1985 The Late Woodland Occupation of the Bentley Site. In *Woodland Period Research in Kentucky*, edited by D. Pollack, T. Sanders, and C. Hockensmith, pp. 140-164. Kentucky Heritage Council, Frankfort.

Leonard, R. D. 1989 Resource Specialization, Population Growth, and Agricultural Production in the American Southwest. *American Antiquity* 54(3):491-503.

Leonard, R. D., and G. T. Jones 1987 Elements of an Inclusive Evolutionary Model for Archaeology. *Journal of Anthropological Archaeology* 6(3):199-219.

Leonard, R. D., and H. E. Reed 1993 Population Aggregation in the Prehistoric American Southwest: A Selectionist Model. *American Antiquity* 58(4):648-661.

Maslowski, R. F., and M. F. Seeman 1992 Woodland Archaeology in the Mid-Ohio Valley: Setting Parameters for Ohio Main Stem/Tributary Comparisons. In *Cultural Variability in Context: Woodland Settlements of the Mid-Ohio Valley*, edited by M. Seeman, pp. 10-14. Midcontinental Journal of Archaeology Special Paper No. 7. Kent State University Press, Kent, Ohio.

O'Brien, M. J., and T. Holland 1990 Variation, Selection, and the Archaeological Record. In *Archaeological Method and Theory, Vol. 2*, edited by M. B. Schiffer, pp. 31-79. University of Arizona Press, Tucson.

1992 The Role of Adaptation in Archaeological Explanation. *American Antiquity* 57(1):36-59.

Pacheco, P. J. 1993 *Ohio Hopewell Settlement Patterns: An Application of the Vacant Center Model to Middle Woodland Period Intracommunity Settlement Variability in the Upper Licking River Valley.* Ph.D. dissertation, Department of Anthropology, The Ohio State University, Columbus. University Microfilms, Ann Arbor.

Prufer, O. H. 1964 The Hopewell Complex of Ohio. In *Hopewellian Studies*, edited by J. R. Caldwell and R. L. Hall pp. 35-83. Illinois State Museum, Scientific Papers 12, Springfield, Illinois.

1965 *The McGraw Site: A Study in Hopewellian Dynamics.* Cleveland Museum of Natural History, Scientific Publications, Vol. 4(1), Cleveland.

Rafferty, J. E. 1985 The Archaeological Record on Sedentariness: Recognition, Development, and Implications. In *Advances in Archaeological Method and Theory., Vol. 8*, edited by M. B. Schiffer, pp. 113-156. Academic Press, New York.

Rindos, D. 1984 *The Origins of Agriculture: An Evolutionary Perspective.* Academic Press, New York.

Seeman, M. F. 1979 *The Hopewell Interaction Sphere: The Evidence for Interregional Trade and Structural Complexity.* Indiana Historical Society, Prehistory Research Series, 5(2). Indianapolis.

Smith, B. D. 1989 Origins of Agriculture in Eastern North America. *Science* 246:1566-1571.

Tainter, J. A. 1977 Woodland Social Change in West-Central Illinois. *Midcontinental Journal of Archaeology* 2:67-98.

1988 *The Collapse of Complex Societies.* Cambridge University Press, New York.

Walthall, J. A. 1985 Early Hopewellian Ceremonial Encampments in the South Appalachian Highlands. In *Structure and*

Process in Southeastern Archaeology, edited by R. Dickens and H. Ward, pp. 243-362. The University of Alabama Press, Tuscaloosa.

Wymer, D. A. 1987 The Middle Woodland-Late Woodland Interface in Central Ohio: Subsistence Continuity Amid Cultural Change. In *Emergent Horticultural Economies of the Eastern Woodlands*, edited by W. Keegan, pp. 201-216. Center for Archaeological Investigations, Southern Illinois University, Carbondale.

Yerkes, R. W. 1988 The Woodland and Mississippian Traditions in the Prehistory of Midwestern North America. *Journal of World Prehistory* 2(3):307-358.

TWENTY-FOUR

CORE AND PERIPHERY:
THE FINAL CHAPTER
ON OHIO HOPEWELL

OLAF H. PRUFER

ABSTRACT

This paper is a solicited commentary and discussion of the 23
contributions to this volume. It reflects the personal opinions
and insights of the author, who has published extensively on
the subject of Ohio Hopewell archaeology. Each contribution
is discussed in turn.

A View From the Core a Synthesis of Ohio Hopewell Archaeology•edited by Paul J. Pacheco
© Copyright 1996 by The Ohio Archaeological Council• Columbus, Ohio
All Rights Reserved•ISBN 0-9626931-9-7

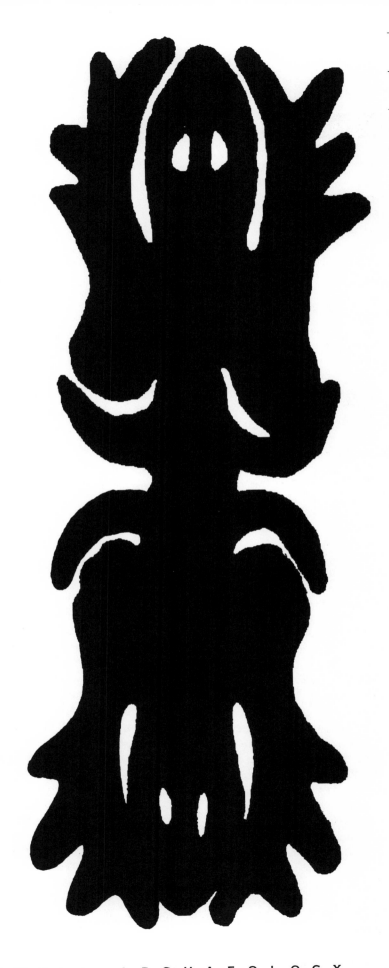

OLAF H. PRUFER

CORE AND PERIPHERY: THE FINAL CHAPTER

INTRODUCTION

Some 13 years ago (Prufer 1982), I wrote a fairly lengthy review article on Brose and Greber's landmark monograph of edited papers presented at the Chillicothe Hopewell Conference in 1978 (Brose and Greber 1979). At the time, this was the first attempt after 14 years (Caldwell and Hall 1964) at synthesizing accumulated information on the Hopewellian phenomenon in the eastern United States. Twelve years earlier, a similar collection of papers was published by Deuel (1952). In 1982 I predicted that "some ten years or so from now yet another volume on Hopewell will see the light of day" (Prufer 1982:15). As it happens, I was not so far off the mark. In fact, in addition to the present set of papers, we have a second such volume (Dancey and Pacheco n.d.) dedicated to Hopewellian studies, which is currently in press.

Having labored in the Ohio Hopewell vineyard in the 1960s, when little had been accomplished in this field since the venerable days of Moorehead, Mills, Shetrone, Greenman and, as an afterthought, Morgan, I am greatly impressed by these renewed efforts to shed light on Ohio Hopewell and its various relationships.

My friend Paul Pacheco, the editor of this volume, has asked me to discuss and critique the 23 papers that comprise this compendium. I have accepted this task, albeit with some minor trepidations, because I obviously carry with me the baggage of certain personal perspectives, perspectives that may not please all contributors to the cause. Rather obviously, I have no great sympathy for discussions that invoke either clearly untenable or scientifically untestable propositions. I was trained at a time when archaeology was considered to be an anthropological discipline ("Archaeology is nothing if it is not Anthropology"), based upon verifiable propositions grounded in solid data. This meant: a) that reconstructions and interpretations should never go beyond hard data; b) that philosophical and esoteric speculations should be avoided; and c) that archaeological practitioners should also be well grounded, beyond freshman level courses, in such anthropological areas as social organization, kinship, anthropological methodology, and so forth.

A few of the contributions in this volume do not, in my estimation, live up to these rigorous standards. This does not mean that I harbor any animus against their authors. It does show, however, that a fair amount of the recent (and sometimes marginal) literature in the field is devoted to this kind of writing. It is part of the times, the trendy thing to do. To deny its existence would be foolish. It is, in fact, part of the contemporary archaeological stage and should thus be heard and listened to.

I propose, in the following pages, to discuss seriatim each contribution. In many cases it was tempting to go into greater detail, but considerations of space prevented such a course. On the whole, and as noted, I am greatly impressed by the scope and content of these offerings. Having said all of this, let me proceed to the substance of these discussions.

COMMENTS AND DISCUSSSION-THE CORE

Settlement, Social Organization, and Symbolism

James B. Griffin's paper, somewhat facetiously entitled "The Hopewell Housing Shortage in Ohio, A.D. 1-350," provides the link between this volume and its predecessor, Dancey and Pacheco's collection of studies on Ohio Hopewell Community Organizations (n.d.). He is opposed to the notion that Ohio Hopewell domestic settlements were in the nature of small hamlets or farmsteads located beyond the great ceremonial centers. Instead he seems to argue for "real," i.e., substantial, nucleated villages. To this end, he had combed the literature for evidence in support of his position. He also adds some anecdotal material, such as an account of his experiences in 1937 with Moorehead, Lilly, and Morgan at Fort Ancient. Actually, this compilation does not really support his position. It is also quite incomplete.

Close inspection of the published data and the actual extant collections from the majority of his sites, shows that most of them are quite small and ephemeral. In the 1960s, I had numerous opportunities to inspect these collections. I found them to contain, by and large, minimal amounts of domestic debris, especially when compared to the huge ceremonial structures erected by the Hopewellians. Also fieldnotes and published accounts indicate that these domestic areas (if that's what they are) are shallow indeed, rather than densely packed with material, as is common in the case of Fort Ancient and (so-called) Whittlesey nucleated settlements. Even granted that some of the collections of past explorations have been curatorially somewhat decimated, the amounts of, say, pottery from any of these sites are unimpressive; the yield of other artifact categories, except for occasional cases of large numbers of Hopewell bladelets (Blank 1965; Prufer n.d.b.) is equally insubstantial.

Among other sites, Griffin tries to support his thesis with the evidence from the Turner Earthworks near Cincinnati, which were excavated over a period of many years, at the end of the last century, under the auspices of the Peabody Museum of Harvard University. The Turner collection is remarkably well provenienced, something one cannot say for the results of many of the later operations in Ohio conducted by the likes of Moorehead, Mills and Shetrone. I am concentrating here on Turner because, at first glance, it seems to have yielded considerable quantities of domestic debris. Using ceramic sherds as an index of domestic activities (and I agree with this assumption), Griffin notes that in 1943 he and Morgan examined a total of 6,185 well-provenienced sherds from this locality. For the following reasons I do not believe this to be as significant as it seems. 1) This material was collected over a period of about two decades. In this light the amount recovered is not impressive. 2) It derives from many different, discrete locations, amounting to quite separate localities within the orbit of the huge earthworks. 3) A very considerable number of these sherds was recovered in direct context of a redeposited burial mound, rather than true domestic contexts (Prufer 1968:96-139). Prior to the McGraw site excavations in 1963, at what was clearly a small hamlet (Prufer 1965), the Turner material constituted the largest sample of Ohio Hopewell ceramics, only in recent years exceeded by the assemblage from Twin Mounds Village (Hawkins, this volume).

In short, I do not see Turner as evidence for a large Hopewellian domestic settlement. Nevertheless, compared to this locality, the remaining major classic sites yielded minimal ceramics and other presumed domestic debris (Prufer 1968). Griffin expresses surprise that my sherd count from Turner (Prufer 1968:139) falls well short of his 1943 count based upon the shipment of this collection from the Peabody Museum to the Ohio State Museum. I have no idea why this should be so. In 1963 I spent about 10 days at the Peabody Museum, where I analyzed the complete Turner collection, cross-referenced to the accession catalogue, with the help of Karen Kerner, a student from Bennington College who later earned a Ph.D. in Anthropology from Columbia University, and who at the time was deputized by Bennington to help me as part of a program to gain practical, hands-on experience in the field. To the best of my knowledge, I saw all the extant material. I was, of course, aware of the fact that numerous sherds from this collection had been dispersed on loan; the Museum catalogue had notations to that effect. But these loan collections do not even remotely account for the discrepancy between my own and Griffin's counts. Even more curious is the fact that, at the time I prepared my Ohio Hopewell pottery monograph (Prufer 1968), Griffin never informed me of this problem. Yet he was deeply involved in the preparation of this study which was published in his own publication series, the *Anthropological Papers*, at the University of Michigan. At the time, I repeatedly visited Ann Arbor to consult with him, and he came at least once to Cleveland, where I taught at Case Institute of Technology, in order to sort out technical problems connected with this monograph.

Two final points in regard to the small size of Ohio Hopewell domestic settlements. First, beyond Griffin's list, there are records of numerous small, ephemeral Hopewellian settlements but, as yet, not a single nucleated village. Among these small localities are 22 sites I discussed in my Scioto Valley Survey (Prufer 1967). This operation covered the valley for some 32 km (20 miles) between Chillicothe and Waverly, i.e., the very heart of Ohio Hopewell. In addition, our crews located numerous similar sites in the Paint Creek and Salt Creek Valleys (fieldnotes on file, Kent State University). Second, for the sake of accuracy, I should like to note that the Brown's Bottom site #1 was not excavated by John Blank, but by me. At the time, John Blank was a student at Case Institute; I allowed him to publish this material as an exercise in professional training. While it is correct that the low ridges on which the Brown's Bottom sites were located measured roughly 91 m by 32 m (100 by 35 yards), the actual sites, specifically the one Blank reported upon, covered an area of no more than perhaps 23 m by 23 m (75 by 75 feet).

In sum, I cannot agree with Griffin's concluding remarks that his collection of past references to Ohio Hopewell domestic sites will "give pause to what I call the Columbus Circle Cabal conviction that the Hopewell earthwork sites were not occupied by the builders except on ceremonial occasions and that they were scattered in 'hamlets' the rest of the year."

Paul J. Pacheco's position regarding the thorny question of Ohio Hopewell settlement patterns and systems is opposed to Griffin's view of these matters. Although he grants that the case is not yet closed, Pacheco argues that the preponderance of presently available evidence argues in favor of what has been called the "Prufer Model" of vacant ceremonial centers and small dispersed hamlets, as opposed to domestically occupied centers and nucleated villages. While I (obviously) support his stance on my brain child, I applaud the fact that Pacheco does not view Ohio Hopewell as a monolithic sort of polity. On the basis of recent evidence, he suggests that the overall system should be further divided into geographically separate regions linked to the major drainage basins of the Ohio Hopewell core area. He further suggests that each of these regions, with its own local traditions, is linked to the others on a symbolic level. This is a refined version of what I had called in the 1960s the "double tradition" concept. For want of an adequate data base, this was a fairly crude construct implying that on a pan-eastern North American basis, Middle Woodland consisted of many local cultural traditions which were differentially linked to each other by what I then referred to as the "Hopewell Cult." This concept was akin to, but not identical with, Caldwell's "Hopewell Interaction Sphere," and

essentially identical with Pacheco's symbolic level of Hopewellian interaction. In fact, I would say that this symbolic level is, *sui generis*, Hopewell. At the time I viewed these "international" Hopewell manifestations in terms of the classic, internally homogeneous Hopewellian units established in the literature of the day: Ohio Hopewell, Havana Hopewell, Goodall, Santa Rosa-Swift Creek, Marksville, and others. The absence of any organized data base for Ohio prevented me from noticing that these units themselves were internally quite heterogeneous, as Pacheco now suggests.

I also agree with his notion that there are various degrees of Hopewellianization and that, indeed, there may be such a thing as cultural lag involved in this acculturation process, perhaps on the basis of geographically central and peripheral populations with all that this may imply on the cultural and economic levels. Looking at southern Ohio, sharply divided between lush, fertile valleys on the one hand, and the rugged Appalachian hinterland, the phenomenon of culture lag may well have been as real in Middle Woodland times as it is now. On a higher level of abstraction, I feel inclined to refer to this phenomenon, if it is real, as a case of transcultural continuity.

I am also glad to see that Pacheco sets the record straight on what I meant by "vacant" ceremonial center. Obviously, the "vacant" here does not mean that these places were devoid of domestic activities. Pacheco's point is well taken: the primary function of the earthworks was mortuary and ceremonial and not domestic; real, day-to-day domestic life, on a continuous basis, took place elsewhere.

Finally, I also agree with Pacheco's Mapuche analogy. These people seem to embody, and verifiably so, much of what I had in mind when I developed my "model." One could go a step further, just for fun, and take note that in some reasonably complex societies, such as the Ifugao of the northern Philippines, a dispersed hamlet (as opposed to a nucleated village) system can occur without the integrative symbolic glue of shared ceremonial centers. For the purpose of gaining some insight into the social organization of

Ohio Hopewell, it might be useful to compare Mapuche and Ifugao social (specifically kinship) organization. Perhaps it is possible to apply such insights to the Hopewellian archaeological record.

Dee Anne Wymer's contribution on human-land interaction in the Hopewell core area marshals powerful evidence for Hopewellian horticulture. I find her paper most impressive and persuasive. She states unequivocally that "I believe current research indicates *the Hopewell had been sophisticated farmers and managers of their environments.*" Wherever data were carefully and rigorously collected, the presence of large quantities of cultivated plants, referable to the Eastern Agricultural Complex, can be demonstrated. Wymer notes that literally thousands of seeds and achenes, mostly members of starchy taxa, have been recovered from site after site. Squash seeds and rinds are also virtually ubiquitous. Added to these cultigens is a bewildering variety of nuts, fruits and berries. She emphasizes - and I think this is singularly important - that the many cultigens recovered from Hopewellian sites reflect the use of gardens, and that cultigens were "a major, if not *the* major, portion of their diet." These garden products were not dietary supplements, but basic staples in the Hopewell economy. Wymer also notes that the occurrence of cultigens and second-growth plant genera in the same depositional contexts, implies the presence of deliberately cleared ground for garden plots in the vicinity of dispersed Hopewell hamlets. Last but not least, at some Hopewellian sites she relegates (although for reasons that I cannot quite understand) the use of corn to ceremonial rather than economic functions.

I think that Wymer's diligent and painstaking ethnobotanical labors will finally settle the issue of Hopewellian subsistence economics. Although maize is clearly present, the real core of Hopewellian farming was garden horticulture based upon the cultivation of native plants and cucurbits, something we surely did not anticipate thirty years ago, when the search for Hopewell maize was our primary concern.

I am less impressed with Wymer's discussion of the ceremonial use of plants in Hopewellian contexts. This discussion is mostly based upon the finds from the Capitolium Mound at the Marietta Earthworks. While I cannot explain the presence in the flotation samples, of such large numbers of different, often locally exotic, charred woods, I will reserve judgement on this matter, simply because the scope of the Capitolium excavations was so drastically limited to a very small area. I think Wymer's evidence is intriguing, but it is far from probative. On the other hand, it should be noted that plant offerings, in the form of clustered deposits, have been reported in the past from a number of Hopewellian ceremonial contexts, such as the Ginther Mound in Ross County, Ohio (Shetrone 1925).

Jack Blosser's contribution to this volume is a straightforward site report on the excavations carried out at the Jennison Guard (aka Whitacre) site in southeastern Indiana. The small dimensions of the two adjacent, stratified, Hopewellian midden areas excavated by Blosser, suggest a single household or farmstead. Two similar small site areas in the immediate vicinity of the excavated area would seem to indicate a cluster of such households. As I read the evidence, this cluster does not suggest the presence of a nucleated village. In fact, from the description I am reminded of the setting of the McGraw site in Ross County, Ohio, which exhibited what appears to be a similar situation (Prufer 1965:17, Figure 2.4, 1967:280-1).

It is clear that the principal occupation of the site represents a perennial, at least in part, domestic occupation of some duration. The presence of maize and domesticated *Chenopodium*, further supported by the presence of additional taxa (Wymer, this volume), implies a horticultural economic base.

The lithic assemblage is largely Hopewellian in nature, including 88 bladelets, *Snyders* and *Steuben* points. Flint Ridge chalcedony and Wyandotte cherts are well represented, as is Upper Mercer flint. Flint drills, scrapers, and numerous bone tools, as well as two ground stone tools attest to diversified domestic activities.

The extensive ceramic assemblage includes the local equivalent of the *McGraw Series* (Hawkins, this volume), cross-hatched rims, and tetrapodal supports. Faunal remains are abundant. The only odd note in this assemblage is struck by the unique occurrence of considerable quantities of cut mica. While small quantities of this exotic material have been found at other domestic Hopewell sites, the substantial presence of this material at Jennison Guard suggests, at first glance, that this site represents a specialized craft locus. On the other hand, the remainder of the assemblage clearly points to mundane household activities. Perhaps the presence of mica merely implies that a single individual resident of this locality engaged in the manufacture of mica products — after all, such objects, so prominent in ceremonial contexts, had to be made somewhere. The frequent occurrence of small quantities of mica in other living contexts suggests to me that the processing of this mineral was a widespread Hopewellian practice. Chronologically, Jennison Guard dates from Middle Hopewell times; four radiocarbon assays suggest a mean value of about A.D. 200, which I consider eminently acceptable.

As noted before, and apart from the slightly disconcerting presence of so much mica, the Jennison Guard site, in its setting and yield, strongly reminds me of the McGraw site and similar Ohio localities.

Since together with McKenzie I was the one who first systematized Ohio Hopewell ceramic typology (1965, 1968), I am particularly interested in Rebecca A. Hawkins' contribution to this symposium. I am impressed with the large ceramic sample she had available from the Twin Mounds West domestic site near Cincinnati. I am also glad that finally this material appears in published form; Hawkins' M.A. thesis (1986), the basis of her present paper is, after all, not an easily accessible source.

I agree with Hawkins that my old ceramic scheme - she refers to it as the "Four Series Approach" - is probably due for some revisions. Much more is known today than 30 years ago. I should emphasize, however, that what she refers to as my fourth ceramic series was merely an explicitly provisional catch-all category for a handful of sherds that seemed to relate to late Illinois Hopewellian manifestations. To the extent to which I used this *Miami Series* at all, I did so in order to underpin, in conjunction with "wild" rocker-stamping (of Illinoian *Pike* style), the apparently very late chronological position of the Turner site. As a "real" ceramic series it was never intended to have probative value. The sample was far too limited. I think Hawkins should not have used the term *"Miami Series"* for her own construct because, since I had never formally defined this material in the first place (Prufer 1968:7), her revision of my series is no revision at all.

I cannot agree with Hawkins' classification of what she now refers to as the *Miami Series*. I find her wholesale lumping of the common cordmarked and plain vessels that I have referred to as *McGraw Series* pottery, into a single category with assorted zoned, incised, rocker- stamped, and cross-hatched "rimmed" Hopewellian ware, and with clearly southeastern inspired, usually tetrapodal, stamped vessels, unacceptable. Nor do I, obviously, agree with the theoretical notions that underlie her reasoning, especially the *Principle of Analogous Pottery Types*. Whatever this may do in other ceramic situations, in the context of Middle Woodland Hopewell pottery such lumping merely obscures culture-historical realities. After all, what is so startling about Hopewell (and not only as far as pottery is concerned), is the fact that from the lower Mississippi Valley to Wisconsin, and from beyond the Mississippi to western New York and Pennsylvania, numerous, very different, local Middle Woodland cultures were intersected by the Hopewellian phenomenon and its material expressions. As I have frequently noted, the *McGraw Series* in Ohio, the *Havana Series* in Illinois, and other ceramic series are representative of local cultural traditions, whereas the *Hopewellian* and *Southeastern Series* are extraneous, and regionally overarching phenomena. Hopewellian ceramics occur in Ohio, Illinois, the lower Mississippi Valley, and the Southeast - *McGraw Series* ceramics do not; nor can Havana pottery be found in Ohio. This is a matter of culture and cultural processes, and not of formal classification schemes on the basis of hermetic technological criteria.

Again, I applaud the presentation of Hawkins' important ceramic material from the southwestern corner of the state. I also agree that, in the light of new data since 1965, the old Ohio ceramic scheme requires refinements, revision, and probably, additions. But, as far as I am concerned, the kind of lumping Hawkins proposes merely confuses the issue.

Robert A. Genheimer's discussion of Hopewellian bladelets as probably multipurpose tools is a well-focused and concise study of a rather unique category of Hopewellian artifacts. It is reassuring to note that Genheimer eschews, as did Pi-Sunyer a generation ago (1965), the many silly terms (ribbon flakes, lamellar flakes, flake knives, and so forth) that abounded, and still abound in the literature. The single most characteristic morphological aspect of these objects is that they are unifacial, parallel-sided blades in the Old World Palaeolithic sense of the word.

I concur with Genheimer that these artifacts are highly standardized objects that may have served many different functions which, in different cultural contexts, were assigned to other formal tools such as bifaces, scrapers, drills, supposed projectile points, and other defined tool types. I, too, have noted that with the massive appearance of Hopewell bladelets in Middle Woodland times, other tool categories markedly decrease in frequency. In short, the Hopewell bladelet was a kind of omnibus implement.

Before I became involved in New World archaeology, I had extensive experience with European Upper Palaeolithic and Mesolithic blade industries (Prufer n.d.a.). With this in mind, I am impressed by certain radically different attributes of Old World and Hopewellian blade assemblages. Palaeolithic and Mesolithic blades are not, by and large, tools in their own right; they are stages in the manufacture of a bewildering array of final products: endscrapers, burins, perforators, spoke-shaves, and so forth. The opposite is true of Hopewell blades. While they are, indeed true blades struck off specialized blade cores, few exhibit deliberate modifications into formal, readily recognizable tool categories. Hopewell blades are "raw" blades that were utilized for many purposes in many different contexts.

Thus, they are not specialized tools in and of themselves; they merely represent a basic, highly versatile, generalized, but nevertheless formal, morphological tool category. The evidence for their function(s) rests almost solely on traces of utilization. The efficiency of these tools is attested to by their great frequency. It is difficult to understand why, once invented, these bladelets disappear from the scene by Late Woodland times. I wonder if this may be partly related to the possibility that they largely functioned in the context of tool manufactures related to ceremonial activities, activities which also disappeared at the end of Middle Woodland times. The very consistent use of exotic flint varieties, notably Flint Ridge chalcedony and Wyandotte chert, in the manufacture of these objects, may argue in favor of this proposition. This would fit well into the general pattern of Hopewellian ceremonialism with its marked emphasis on exotica.

Kent D. Vickery's paper on the provenience and cultural function of flint raw materials used by Ohio Hopewellians testifies to the author's painstaking efforts to identify the flint sources of nearly 32,000 flint specimens from major sites located in three different drainage systems. Apart from unidentifiable material, Vickery identified 26 distinct flint varieties from six states: Ohio, Indiana, Kentucky, North Dakota, Tennessee and West Virginia. Some of these were found at all six sites, others have a more restricted and differential distribution. Some betoken long distance procurement, others could be defined as more or less "local" in origin.

Cutting across the issue of provenience is the well-known Hopewellian fascination with exotica, which is reflected in the frequent emphasis on high quality and colorful flint varieties, not to mention obsidian. Vickery cautions that not all of the flint types from far-distant sources need to have been procured by humans; a surprising number of such varieties was transported as gravel into the area by natural agencies such as glaciers and fossil river systems. Nevertheless, a considerable number of these materials involved elaborate and intensive procurement efforts that fall within the domain of what has been called the "Hopewell Interaction Sphere."

In order to explain this complex flint procurement network in terms of cultural dynamics, Vickery posits four models: a "political" model that should betoken relatively complex chiefdoms, a "ceremonial" model which presumes the need for exotica in ritual or ceremonial contexts; an "economic" model in which the flint exotica functioned as part of a complex procurement strategy based upon economic factors, and a "social" model which essentially suggests a non-systematic circulation of all kinds of odd goods within a loose, and not very complex, social system preoccupied with exotic raw materials and products.

My own inclination is to reject, as Vickery does, the political model, because there is no good evidence that Hopewell functioned on the complex level of chiefdoms. I would prefer a combination of the three other alternatives, with the ceremonial one being in the lead. Since there is more to Hopewell than its Ohio version, one should take into consideration, even in the domain of mere flint objects, the frequent, as it were international, recurrence of the same themes of raw materials and finished products over wide areas of the eastern United States. Thus, for instance, the great cache of more than 7,000 (by my count 8,285; Prufer 1961:281) large Wyandotte chert flint discs from the Hopewell site, Mound 2, can be duplicated by at least 63 similar caches from Ohio, Indiana and Illinois (Prufer 1961:282; Ellis 1940). This and similar, quite consistent occurrences of "fancy" flints and obsidian in clearly ceremonial contexts would seem to argue strongly in favor of Vickery's "ceremonial" model. In this event, the "economic" model, *exchange as a means of procurement*, would be a plausible secondary construct linked to the primary one. The "social" model, because of its flexibility, may also have some modest validity. All of which gets us back to the Hopewell Interaction Sphere.

C. Wesley Cowan's examination of the social implications of Ohio Hopewell art is an interesting, even fascinating, exercise in exploring the symbolic meaning of Hopewellian aesthetic products. I can agree with his theoretical proposition that symbols are means of communication that function within complex socio-cultural networks in an increasing order of intelligibility, ranging from purely private to publicly shared or, at least, shareable messages. The problem is that, as Cowan himself points out, the symbolic content of such Hopewell artistic expressions can never be known "from an emic standpoint," because whatever we may postulate on the basis of the material evidence can never be empirically tested. As the saying goes, dead men tell no tales. All I can suggest is, that to the extent to which the same general types of objects occur over and over again in the archaeological record, so the messages they contain must have been intelligible to large numbers of individuals in the social system. By the same token, idiosyncratic objects probably conveyed little more than private messages. Beyond this linear dimension of the problem, there is the added complication that Hopewellian *objets d'art* may well have functioned in other than purely symbolic domains. They may, for example, have represented wealth, especially when they were made from exotic, obviously scarce raw materials. Then again, they may have functioned in both the symbolically private and public domains, as well as being expressions of wealth. And so on. My point is this: since we will never be able to know, why bother with these kinds of speculations beyond keeping in mind that art, Hopewellian or otherwise, indeed held many complex symbolic and mundane meanings, aka messages.

N'omi B. Greber's contribution on the context of large and small Ohio Hopewell deposits provides a convenient analytical list of real and presumed ritual or symbolic deposits from a number of classic Ohio Hopewell ceremonial centers. I applaud her diligent search of the relevant literature and other data bases that made it possible to bring this material together in one place. Obviously, given the often very deficient older records, much of this information is likely to be quite unreliable; who knows what Moorehead, Mills, Shetrone, Metz, et al. really observed and thought fit to preserve for posterity. The incompetence of some of these individuals is legendary.

To the extent to which Greber presents these features and their content contextually, this compilation is useful indeed. Although in this paper she is much more restrained in her interpretations than in some of her past writings (see for example, Greber and Ruhl 1989:275, 295), I must still part company with her when it comes to what she reads into this material. All this talk about patterns of complementary contrast; the acquisition of symbolic parts of many animals from certain deposits; the symbolic contrast between dark and light as well as between copper and mica; calendrical cycles; dual ritual organization; and her belief that "a calendrical cycle paced a major portion of Hopewellian celebration," leaves me cold, because it is beyond empirical verification. Nevertheless, I do agree with her that there is a unity to the Ohio Hopewell core based upon a shared world view. But then, we have known this for a long time.

A. Martin Byers' paper is beyond the realm of what we normally understand to be formal, anthropological archaeology. It is, in fact, largely incomprehensible. Already its title, "Social Structure and the Pragmatic Meaning of Material Culture: Ohio Hopewell as Ecclesiastic-Communal Cult" conveys nothing particularly meaningful. The text is almost unreadable, a kind of archaeological metababble, laden with structuralist jargon and definitions that, to a large extent, the author has devised to suit his own obscure purposes. The spirit of Levi-Strauss hovers like a ghost over this contribution. I suspect that structuralists should not venture into archaeology. I am reminded of the Master's foray into the field of American Archaeology, specifically the Poverty Point site in Louisiana (Levi-Strauss 1963:142-3). In a critique of this excursion into our field, Rackerby (1968) pointed out that Levi-Strauss had neither sufficient knowledge of the field, nor an appropriate sense of how to use his own disciplinary canons for the interpretations of archaeological data. He notes (1968:390) that it "is desirous to develop interpretations of social organization from archaeological data, but the controls used in such arguments must be rigorously maintained." I feel the same way about Byers' contribution. Nothing in the Ohio Hopewell data, even to the extent to which they are reliable, warrants the many speculations he indulges in; none can be verified. All of this shows, I think, that essentially philosophical or speculative anthropology and scientific archaeology simply do not mix.

William F. Romain's contribution to this volume deals with the geometric attributes of the Ohio Hopewell earthworks. This paper is but one in a long series of similar studies published by the author in the domain of archaeoastronomy. It is replete with astronomical observations and alignments, measurements, correlations of measurements, and speculations on the units of Hopewellian measurements, including the startling observation that "there is some reason to believe that the basic unit of measurement here was based on the length of the typical adult male Hopewell arm - as measured from the shoulder joint...to the distal end of the metacarpal bones."

All of this apparatus is carted onto the field in order to interpret the meaning of Hopewellian geometric earthworks which, so Romain believes, "reveal, and even proclaim fundamental and universal geometric concepts." The geometric figures, such as circles, squares and octagons, are said to be ideologic symbols that reflect the structure of the universe. Squares, in this view, represent the heavens, circles, the earth. The earthworks are supposed to show evidence of purposeful solar and lunar alignments; archaeological records of ceremonial and mortuary ceremonies "relating to world renewal and creation." Ultimately, Romain believes, these architectural monuments were "models, or microcosms of the Hopewell's vision of the universe." I am unable to follow the author into this almost mystical and numerological interpretive jungle. In its obsession with geometric measurements it reminds me of Egyptian pyramidology, the endless cogitations as to the "deep" meaning of Stonehenge and the monuments on the Nazca Plain of Peru. All this is beyond the realm of verifiable archaeology. In these matters, I hold with the famed British archaeologist Glyn Daniel:

*Many people, no doubt bored by the pro-
saic account of megaliths to be got from
archaeological research...(accept) the
builders...not only as experts in
Pythagorean geometry and possessors of
accurate units of mensuration but also as
skilled astronomers who studied eclipses,
the movements of the moon and the positions of the stars. To me this is a kind of
refined academic version of astronaut
archaeology (Daniel 1980:78-90).*

I am equally baffled by James A. Marshall's paper dealing
with the geometry of Hopewellian earthworks and the nature
of Hopewellian mathematical knowledge. Apparently
Marshall is a diffusionist, suggesting that all this allegedly
complex mathematical knowledge did "spring from one
school of thought." Just as in Romain's papers there are
those endless measurements and units of measurement.
There is said to be a mathematical relationship between the
metrics of Teotihuacan in Mexico and those of more than
100 mounded (sic!) geometric earthworks in the eastern
United States. We also learn from Marshal that certain such
geometric earthworks, across space and time, demonstrate
the influence of the mathematical concept of *pi* upon the
(shall I use the hallowed term?) Mound Builders. In connection with the Newark, High Bank and Baum Earthworks
in Ohio, the "True Core of Ohio Hopewell," Marshall would
"argue that these works are evidence of the work of a
school of Pythagoreans similarly preoccupied with mathematics who resided nearby." Apparently it has never struck
the author that, in essence, the Hopewellian earthworks are
fairly simple geometric structures. Since, like probably all
other cultures, "primitive" or complex, the Hopewellians had
some basic units of measurement, the layout of any of their
known architectural structures could have been achieved
with the help of ropes and wooden pegs or poles. Any
moderately intelligent and mathematically untutored individual can do this.

COMMENTS AND DISCUSSION: THE CORE
Earthworks and Mounds-Recent Investigations

Bradley T. Lepper, in his discussion of the Newark
Earthworks in the context of the geometric enclosures in the
Scioto Valley takes cognizance of - and I am in agreement -
the exceptional nature of this truly gigantic structure of
clearly Hopewellian affiliation. I, too, have noted the geographic marginality of this site in relation to the Hopewell
core area in the Scioto Valley. I attribute the size and significance of this monument to its proximity to the Flint Ridge
chalcedony quarries which were the source of one of the
critical exotic raw materials of the Hopewell polity. Similarly,
I believe that the vast Portsmouth Earthworks at the confluence of the Scioto and Ohio Rivers, located on both banks
of the latter, and at a considerable distance from the site-
cluttered core area around Chillicothe, are located where
they are because of their proximity to the Ohio pipestone
quarries, another critical raw material within the Hopewell
Interaction Sphere. I also agree with Lepper that, while the
Newark Earthworks are indeed geographically peripheral to
the core area, they must surely be considered an integral
part of the Hopewellian landscape. It is therefore doubly
regrettable that, until recently, this site has received relatively
little archaeological attention. In this connection I also wel-
come Lepper's review of some of the older, not easily
accessible, reports on this site and its environs.

I do, however, part company with Lepper when it comes to
his discussion of the so-called Great Hopewell Road, 40 m
wide and flanked by earthen embankments which, so he
believes, ran over a straight distance of 90 km, o'er rugged
hills and through the glens, from Newark, Ohio, to the
Hopewellian heartland near Chillicothe. Apart from the
general unlikelihood that such a highway ever existed, there
is, as far as I know, no concrete evidence whatsoever in
support of such a line of communication.

Lepper is correct in noting that surprisingly little has been
done to investigate the internal structure of any of the great
Hopewellian geometric earthworks; and what has been
done in the past is frequently of little value because of the

limited nature and professional inadequacy of such operations. I might note in this context, that while Orrin C. Shane's 1972 excavations through the walls of the High Banks Earthworks demonstrate considerable architectural complexity, the extant fieldnotes of this operation (curated at Kent State University) do not confirm the orderly and neat construction sequence that Lepper elicited from Shane.

As far as Hopewellian habitation areas associated with the ceremonial centers are concerned, I shall not go and argue this matter in any detail. I have done so recently for Dancey and Pacheco's volume on Ohio Hopewell Community Organization (Prufer n.d.a.). However, I would like to make a couple of observations of some relevance. In the original draft version of his present paper, Lepper referred to a survey conducted (under my overall direction) below High Bank by Shane in 1968, which others have also cited (Smith 1992:242). According to Shane, he located "at least 21 small circular - I do not want to call them middens - but areas of refuse. These are 50 by 100 feet in diameter and produced cultural material typical of the *Hopewellian Phase*...This includes Hopewellian blades, *McGraw Cordmarked* and *McGraw Plain* pottery of the *Hopewellian Series*, corner- notched projectile points..." (Shane 1971:145). These sites do not exist. The actual survey produced six localities which yielded only two Hopewell tools. The remainder consists of modest amounts of Early and Late Woodland as well as other cultural debris. These materials are curated at Kent State University. Following a lengthy correspondence on this matter, Lepper decided to delete the relevant paragraph from his manuscript.

A further point regarding habitations associated with the great ceremonial centers should be noted. During Shane's fairly extensive 1972 excavations at High Bank, repeated surveys in and around this very large structure were conducted by a fairly sizable crew. The surviving polynomially arranged find register (High Bank fieldnotes, 1972, KSU archaeological archives) lists a total of 353 objects recovered from the surveys; the extensive excavations through the earthwork walls produced 800 objects. Most of this material consists of indifferent non-Hopewellian debitage, Flint

Ridge chalcedony is rare, and many of the identifiable tools are not Hopewellian either; interestingly, only 10 fire-cracked rocks were noted. A further 3-day survey at High Bank covering a total linear distance of 48 km (30 miles) and undertaken in 1988/89 under the direction of Jonathan Bowen, produced a total of 87 indifferent objects, mostly local chippage; except for two possible Hopewell bladelet fragments and a few fire-cracked rocks, there were no diagnostic artifacts of any kind. This sparse material does not look Hopewellian. These materials are also curated at Kent State University.

In support of his ideas on Hopewellian villages, Lepper also discusses Raymond S. Baby's 3-year long excavation stint at a site directly below the Fort Hill hilltop enclosure in Highland County, Ohio. According to Lepper, Baby here discovered a large specialized craft house, measuring 18 by 37 m, and great quantities of artifacts. Actually, Baby explicitly describes it as a large stockade or enclosure (1954:86) rather than a house. Lest I be thought picky, I analyzed this debris in the 1960s when I prepared my monograph on Ohio Hopewell ceramics (Prufer 1968). The actual amount of material found was quite negligible; three years of excavation yielded, among a few other items, no more than 154 small sherds representing perhaps half a dozen vessels. In 1964, when I conducted a brief excavation at the fort proper, I located Baby's site and found it to be but thinly strewn with chippage and other debris.

On the positive side, I hope that Lepper will continue to explore the archaeological potential of Newark before the site completely succumbs to urban destruction. He should be congratulated for having brought this greatest of all Ohio ceremonial centers back into our consciousness.

Robert V. Riordan's paper offers a useful overview of what is presently known about the hilltop enclosures (aka "forts") of southern Ohio. Of all the Hopewellian architectural monuments, the nature and function of these structures are least well known. Older fieldwork was sporadic and often inadequate. More recently, efforts at Fort Ancient, Fort Hill, Miami Fort, and Pollock clearly demonstrate that these structures, which are quite different from the classic Hopewell geometric earthworks, are complex indeed. They involve various (and variable) construction stages, a variety of building materials such as earth, stone and wood, they cover a considerable time span within the Middle Woodland period, and they seem to have served many purposes which, as Riordan puts it, "complemented but were distinct from those...[of] the mortuary/ceremonial earthwork and mound sites on the river terraces." He further believes that both secular and/or religious activities were conducted at these places. He also suggests that some of the enclosures did serve military purposes, a point that has been much debated for well over a century.

I concur with Riordan that the hilltop enclosures probably served multiple functions through time. Yet, as far as it goes, I can see clear-cut evidence for ceremonial activities only at Fort Ancient, unless the substantial residue of conflagrations at such sites as Miami Fort, Foster's Four Mile Creek, and Pollock be interpreted as evidence for ceremonial fires of some sort. I prefer to view these burnt areas as either the result of accidental fires or as the remains of military activities at sites that, by their very nature and locations, suggest some defensive functions (Prufer n.d.c.) — but I am willing to grant that this cannot be proven on the basis of present knowledge. It would be interesting to obtain radiocarbon dates on the conflagrations at each site, in order to determine whether they reflect a series of essentially related, regional events.

I do not think, as Riordan tentatively suggests, that the size differentials noted between the numerous hilltop "forts" reflect a chronological trend that might be correlated with increasing populations. It seems more realistic to view the dimensions of these structures to have been controlled by the topography of the "mesas" on which they were erected: small hilltops resulted in small enclosures, large ones in large circumvallations.

The complexity of hilltop enclosures is also attested to by Robert P. Connolly's extensive field operations at Fort Ancient, the largest and most famous "fort" in the Ohio

area. In one way or another, research of variable quality at this locality has been carried out for well over a century. Even in those early days the complexity of Fort Ancient was apparent, but the quality of the work by such individuals as Warren King Moorehead was such that it is virtually impossible to derive a coherent picture of the site from these labors. Only recently have endeavors been systematized by the late Patricia S. Essenpreis and Connolly. Especially the latter has done a great deal to arrive at what he calls a holistic interpretation of the site area.

In his present paper he effectively refutes my earlier notion that these enclosures were occupied only late within Ohio Hopewell. I agree. The radiometric and architectural evidence at Fort Ancient (and Pollock) clearly proves his point. I do share his notion, based upon a variety of seemingly reliable radiometric assays, that the temporal range of the Ohio hilltop enclosures covers a span from circa 100 B.C. to A.D. 300. If I had my druthers, I would place this range even later in time, from about A.D. 1 to A.D. 350.

Connolly adduces powerful evidence for some form of central architectural planning in the construction of Fort Ancient. The site locale was extensively modified in order to "accommodate the placement of embankment walls, interior ditches, and ponds." Ditches near gateways appear to have served drainage functions. The labors involved in these operations must have been prodigious, not to mention the efforts involved in erecting the actual circumvallation. The only thing that mars this splendid study in my view, is Connolly's notion that the ponds within Fort Ancient "provided an integral component to the earthwork's ability to serve as a symbol in the worldview of Middle Woodland populations." Why? There is no evidence whatsoever to support this thesis.

Pickard's preliminary report on N'omi Greber's excavations at the Capitolium Mound of the Marietta Earthworks brings to a close the long-standing argument as to the cultural affiliation of these platform mounds. They are Hopewellian and not Mississippian. I have long argued, with increasing conviction, in favor of this interpretation, because these mounds give the impression of being integral to the clearly Hopewellian Marietta Earthworks in which they are located (Prufer 1961). In the absence of any hard data, however, the issue was unprovable. In the course of several discussions, Griffin always opposed this view.

The recent, *per force*, very limited excavations at this structure document typical Hopewellian architectural features and stratigraphy, the presence of numerous Hopewell bladelets, some mica, and an appreciable amount of pottery. I fail to understand why Pickard did not present at least a preliminary description of these ceramics. From a cursory inspection of some of the sherds I conclude that they belong - not unexpectedly - in the *McGraw Series*. I agree with Pickard that the radiocarbon date of A.D. 70 ± 70 is too early for this mound. It should date from circa A.D. 200-300. For some of the interesting botanical remains from the Capitolium Mound, consult Wymer's paper in this volume.

Greber's work not only settles the issue of the affiliation of the Marietta platform mounds; it also casts a new light on some similar structures in the region, such as Ginther and the platform mounds at Newark. Incidentally, one such edifice in Ross County, the Cedar Bank Mound, appears to be no mound at all. Orrin C. Shane's field crews tested this locality during the 1972 field season and concluded that it was a natural feature (fieldnotes, High Bank file, KSU archaeological archives).

J.M. Heilman and Lynn M. Mahoney's report on the Purdom Mound Group near Xenia in southwestern Ohio demonstrates, among other things, how, in the absence of timely analysis and publication, attrition of poorly curated artifacts and fieldnotes can emasculate what clearly was an important local mortuary manifestation. Of the three explorations undertaken at this locality since 1931, only the most recent operations, undertaken by the authors in 1989-91, reflect appropriate professional standards.

The results of the older excavations had to be painstakingly reconstructed from newspaper records, some less than accurate site maps, and an annotated list of finds. Some of these finds are no longer extant. Alas, this is a non-too-uncommon tale in the history of Ohio archaeology.

It is clear that the five or seven (there is some uncertainty here) mounds of the Purdom Group are an excellent example of what Griffin once called the "High Church" aspects of Hopewell. Among other items, the burial associations include a perforated human "trophy" mandible, a classic Hopewellian zoned-incised, rocker-stamped vessel with a bird design, quantities of mica, a marine shell container, modified bear teeth, and a re-articulated extended burial. Some *McGraw Series* ceramic sherds were also recovered. Purdom obviously is a mound group of considerable importance.

In the light of the ongoing debate about Hopewell settlement systems, I find the most recent excavations in the previously uncultivated area between the mounds of more than passing interest. On the basis of the evidence from 22 one-meter squares, Heilman and Mahoney say they "recovered few signs of the Hopewellian occupation from this area." Most of the material found was Archaic, similar to other such finds derived from the fill of the mounds. Only a small area revealed a slight concentration of nearly 100 relevant sherds and a postmold; perhaps this is the remnant of a domestic dwelling.

COMMENTS AND DISCUSSION-THE PERIPHERY

Mark F. Seeman's elegant and closely reasoned discussion of the Ohio Hopewell Core and its many margins, argues persuasively for a highly complex set of interactions. He eschews the use of such terms and concepts as "reluctant" or "marginal" Hopewell. In order to assess the obviously different degrees of Hopewellianization in various areas of Ohio, Seeman pleads for the deconstruction of old interpretive models in favor of more emphasis on the "analysis and comparison of fairly specific patterns or contexts." Having been guilty of constructing some of the old models myself, I nevertheless heartily agree that we now must break through traditional interpretive constructs in order to gain deeper insights into the dynamics of the Ohio Hopewell phenomenon.

The questions of core versus margin, or periphery, can be viewed from many angles, ranging from geographic and culture-historic to ecological. Taking the region of Chillicothe, at the confluence of the Scioto River and Paint Creek, to be the epicenter of Hopewellian developments, it is immediately apparent, as Seeman notes, that this region is epicentral only in terms of the broad valleys and their rich flood plains. Sharply delineated from this environmental niche are the rugged Appalachian hills in which Ohio Hopewell is poorly represented, mostly in rockshelter contexts. Elsewhere in this paper I have argued that the situation in the mountainous hinterland may denote a form of ecologic and economic culture lag, rather than the presence of different peoples or tribes. Here, then, we have one kind of core versus periphery situation.

Casting further afield, beyond the classic Hopewellian core area, but still in the dissected Appalachian uplands, there are occasional, fairly isolated Ohio Hopewell mounds such as Seeman's Yant tumulus in Stark County, the Kohl Mound in Tuscarawas County (Whitman 1977), and the Martin Mound in Coshocton County (Mortine and Randles 1978). At least in the case of the Yant Mound, some of the Hopewellian elements appear to be poor imitations of the "High Church" materials from the core area. Some of these burial mounds, such as the Martin Mound in the Walhonding Valley which, because of the nearby Upper Mercer flint quarries, is one of the richest archaeological regions in the state, appear to be total isolates. Neither along the well-defined river bottoms and terraces, nor in the numerous rockshelters in the hills, are there any but the most minute traces of a Hopewellian presence. Thus it is difficult to relate these occasional funeral monuments to any Hopewellian settlement system.

Further north, on the glaciated till plain beyond the uplands, a few widely dispersed, but quite spectacular Ohio Hopewell mounds have been recorded. They are poorly understood. They include Esch in Erie County (Stothers et al. 1979), Everett Knoll in Cuyahoga County (Brose 1974), North Benton in Mahoning County (Magrath 1940, 1945), West Farmington (nee Byler) in Trumbull County (Zakucia

and Gunn 1974), and Towner Mound in Portage County (Shriver 1957, 1982). Again, these mounds stand out because of their isolated nature. Thus far, numerous archaeological site surveys in the region have produced virtually no Hopewellian artifacts; nor have such materials been noted in private and public collections. The extant mounds look as if they were intrusive to these northern cultural contexts.

My comments are meant to suggest the difficulties inherent in contrasting the Ohio Hopewell core area with the margin(s). I strongly believe that future work should take the direction suggested by Seeman in this paper.

For well over a decade, Jeff Carskadden and James Morton have been involved in the archaeology of the central Muskingum Valley of central Ohio. I think it is fair to say that, due to their systematic efforts, this is one of the most, if not the most, thoroughly and competently investigated areas of the state. In their contribution to this volume, Carskadden and Morton have attempted to define the Middle to early Late Woodland transition of this region which, certainly as far as Ohio Hopewell is concerned, appears to be somewhat marginal to the core area around Chillicothe. Much of the Middle Woodland material culture here, although clearly Hopewellian, lacks the "High Church" flavor of the great sites in the central Scioto Valley. In a sense this marginality is somewhat surprising, because of the proximity of the Newark Earthworks and Flint Ridge, the source of one of the classic raw materials cherished by the Hopewellians.

The authors use a two-pronged approach to tackle their problem. On the basis of massive and well-controlled data, they construct their archaeological sequence on the basis of settlement and mortuary customs, i.e., burial mounds. They have isolated, and I think with some success, five settlement stages involving a gradual shift from small domestic hamlets in Middle Woodland times, to nucleated and apparently fortified, stockaded villages in the Late Woodland period. This sequence is characterized by decreasing amount of Hopewellian artifacts through time.

Almost as an aside, the authors make the interesting observation, largely based upon radiocarbon dates that, compared to the core area, the appearance of Hopewellian elements in the region is rather late; no earlier than A.D. 100. By implication, Early Woodland Adena (if we must use this blanket term) elements here survive quite late. Again, radiocarbon assays seem to confirm this proposition.

Carskadden and Morton note that, throughout Stages 1-4, two of the Hopewell index fossils, bladelets and blade cores, were found in decreasing frequencies and declining quality. Ceramics and other trends seem to follow a similar pattern. By Stage 5 times, all Hopewellian elements appear to have disappeared. In short, the archaeological data from the central Muskingum Valley seem to demonstrate that Hopewellian cultural elements, rather than being abruptly replaced with the onset of the Late Woodland period, gradually fade out through time. The implications of these dynamics in terms of "real" culture processes are of great significance and warrant intensive further investigative efforts.

I like the authors' findings, because they parallel some of my own observations. I have always been puzzled as to why some southern Ohio rockshelters I am familiar with (e.g., Raven Rocks, White Rocks, Stanhope, Rais, and other shelters) have produced, in seemingly clear-cut Late Woodland contexts, a very few Hopewell bladelets, and on occasion, other isolated Hopewell elements. Apart from these items, the sites in question yielded no actual Middle Woodland occupations. Could this, too, be evidence of a gradual transition from Hopewell into Late Woodland?

While I am greatly impressed with Carskadden and Morton's settlement sequence, I am less convinced of their parallel burial mound seriations. Classic Hopewell mounds, although they exist in the region, are not part of their sample. Thus, their seriation pertains solely to Late Woodland tumuli. I am not at all sure that the rather impoverished data from these structures demonstrate an orderly chronological sequence within early Late Woodland. More work is needed before this issue can be settled.

Nevertheless, just as in the case of the Late Woodland settlements, the three mounds under discussion produced some typical Ohio Hopewell elements in the form of small amounts of mica. In line with the observations at settlements, this may also constitute evidence of some continuities from Hopewell into later times.

Donald R. Cochran's contribution deals with the problem of Adena-Hopewell continuities in east-central Indiana. As far as the theme of this volume is concerned, this area is on the very edge of the Ohio Hopewell periphery, truly marginal to the core. Essentially, Cochran demolishes the old notion of a *New Castle Phase* which supposedly consisted of a mixture of Adena and Hopewell traits in a presumably marginal situation. Cochran shows fairly conclusively that this phase, primarily based upon misinterpreted data from the New Castle and Anderson Earthworks and mounds, represents, in reality, continuous activities at culturally discrete and distinctive intra-site loci ranging from Early Woodland-Adena to Middle Woodland-Hopewell times. Additionally, his reinterpretation demonstrates the important fact that these localities represent no occupational break; they were clearly accretional, especially Mound 4 at New Castle and the Great Mound at Anderson. Failure to recognize that these tumuli originated in Adena times and were completed during the Hopewell period, in other words, the notion that they were "one-shot," unified monuments, was responsible for the creation of the spurious *New Castle Phase*.

I am glad that Cochran has resolved this problem. Over the years, I always felt uneasy about the New Castle construct, because of the apparently distinctive, and mutually exclusive, clusters of artifacts found at these places. However, from the point of view of Adena-Hopewell continuities in the Ohio core area, I suggest that there are indeed sites which reflect real acculturational transitions. The eponymous Adena Mound in Ross County (Mills 1902) and Tremper in Scioto County (Mills 1916) seem to be such monuments. The former, which is the type site for the Adena complex, produced the famous, stylistically, clearly Hopewellian human effigy pipe which represents a male dressed in a typical Hopewellian loin cloth and adorned with ear spools and a "helmet." Typologically, this human figure had been incorporated into a typical Adena tubular pipe. At Tremper, a variety of tubular Adena stone pipes and their derivatives occur in the context of characteristic Hopewell grave goods. Tremper is usually deemed to be one of the earliest Hopewell sites in Ohio. I would consider both of these localities representative of the Early to Middle Woodland transition in the very core area of the Hopewellian presence.

Even more marginal to the core than Cochran's paper, is Curtis H. Tomak and Frank N. Burkett's offering on decorated leather objects from the Mount Vernon Site, better known as the GE Mound, in Posey County, Indiana. This spectacular, unbelievably rich, Hopewell mound has recently gained a measure of sorry fame because of the appalling butchery and looting it was subjected to by the worst kind of pot hunters that feed on the margins of the archaeological profession. As is well known by now, the culprits involved were brought to justice in a federal trial that gained national attention (Munson et al. 1995). Although Tomak and Burkett sketchily deal with this matter, the true flavor of this affair had not yet appeared in print at the time they wrote their contribution to the present volume.

The five leather objects appear to have been part of a composite artifact. They are marked by grooved and recessed decorations which seem to form designs. Tomak and Burkett believe these curvilinear patterns to represent human ears. I am not convinced. If anything, they seem to resemble the highly stylized raptorial bird designs on a number of the famed engraved Adena tablets, as published by Webb and Baby (1957:82-94). Related designs have also been noted from classic Hopewell sites.

With Robert C. Mainfort's paper on the Pinson Mounds in Tennessee and on the Middle Woodland period in the Midsouth and Lower Mississippi Valley, we are no longer anywhere near the Ohio Hopewell periphery, let alone the core. We are beyond that culture area; on the outside as it were. Mainfort provides brief but useful summaries of several important sites and site clusters, with special emphasis on the cultural centrality of the Pinson Mounds. Using Poverty

Point in Louisiana as a point of chronological departure, he notes that in this macro-region, continuous mound and earthwork construction can boast considerably greater time depth than in the classic "mound building" belt between Illinois and Ohio. In terms of the flow of culture, this is an important observation. He also stresses that Middle Woodland in the South, although, in the aggregate, perhaps not as flamboyant as Hopewell in the core area, is nevertheless a resplendent manifestation with distinct regional characteristics. Neither observation is new.

Mainfort also emphasizes that, taken with other recent evidence in the South, Pinson, with its Middle Woodland platform mounds, demonstrates that such structures, usually considered of later Mississippian affiliation, are integral to the regional Middle Woodland scene. He also notes that "recently" similar platform mounds of Hopewellian affiliation have been identified in the Ohio core area.

Actually, Middle Woodland platform mounds with Hopewellian connections have been known from the South for quite some time. Mandeville in southeast Georgia is a good example (Kellar et al.1962). One might also add Kolomoki in Georgia (Sears 1953, 1964). For a summary discussion of the chronological and cultural issues in the debate between Sears contra Caldwell and Willey, see Prufer (1962). As far as Ohio Hopewell platform mounds are concerned, there is nothing "recent" about this matter either. Mainfort's reference here is to Greber's verification of the Hopewellian nature of the Capitolium Mound at Marietta (Pickard, this volume). As early as 1961, I argued for a Hopewellian affiliation of this and the other Marietta platform mounds (Prufer 1961). Ginther in Ross County is another demonstrable Hopewellian structure (Shetrone 1925), as are, most likely, the eight platform mounds strategically located interior to the "gateways" of the octagonal earthwork at Newark in Licking County (Squier and Davis 1848).

COMMENTS AND DISCUSSION-THE FINAL CHAPTER

William S. Dancey, in the final paper (bar my own synthetic effort) of this volume, tackles the perennial question of the Hopewellian demise. He notes correctly that virtually every possible cause has been invoked in the past to account for this very real phenomenon. They range from univariate to multivariate explanations. I confess that, in the proverbial old days, I was guilty of constructing an elaborate univariate scenario, involving warfare and population movements in order to account for the end of Ohio Hopewell (Prufer 1964:63-70). While in retrospect this scheme, like so many others at the time, looks labored and rather silly, I was at least aware of the fact that it was equally as hypothetical as the other schemes which I had rejected (Prufer 1964:66).

Dancey notes, I think correctly so, that neither univariate nor multivariate explanations are adequate to explain the transition from Hopewell into Late Woodland. Instead he invokes a Darwinian model of evolution by natural selection *a la* Dunnell, emphasizing regional population histories. He felici-tously compresses the issue into a question: "If there is a functional difference between what we think of as Hopewell compared to what we think of as Late Woodland, what *behaviors* [emphasis mine] of the early Late Woodland have conferred upon the populations in which they occur a selec-tive advantage over Hopewell populations?" This approach, which has been used with some success in the Southwest, would seem to promise better and more elegant results than previous, simple-minded efforts, especially when seen in the context of developing food production and all that such a "revolution" entails. In a wider, pan-Hopewellian perspective it might also be useful to explain the differential developments in, and interactions between, other regional Hopewellian developmental sequences.

CONCLUSION

And so I come to the conclusion of this lengthy and critical essay on the contributions to this symposium. As one might expect, these 23 papers vary in scope, significance and quality; but this does not matter, because they do indeed, reflect current concerns and trends in the broader perspec-tive of Hopewellian studies in general and Ohio in particu-lar. This is especially true if this volume is read in conjunc-tion with its companion, the collected papers of the sympo-sium on Ohio Hopewell Community Organization, held at the Annual Meeting of the Society for American Archaeology in 1992 (Dancey and Pacheco n.d.). We have come a long way since the 1950s, when Ohio Hopewellian studies were in the doldrums, although everyone in the pro-fession was fully aware of the pivotal significance of Ohio Hopewell to the prehistory of the eastern United States. On the other hand, we are still far from truly understanding the dynamics of this remarkable, multi-faceted cultural phenom-enon. I can only hope that efforts to gain ever greater insights will continue and intensify as they had done since the Chillicothe Conference in 1978. ***Good Luck!***

REFERENCES CITED

Baby, R.S. 1954 Archaeological Explorations at Fort Hill. *Museum Echoes* 27(11):86-7.

Blank, J.E. 1965 The Brown's Bottom Site, Ross County, Ohio. *Ohio Archaeologist* 15(1):16-21.

Brose, D.S. 1974 The Everett Knoll: A Late Hopewellian Site in Northeastern Ohio. *Ohio Journal of Science* 74(1):36-46.

Brose, D.S., and N.B. Greber, editors 1979 *Hopewell Archaeology: The Chillicothe Conference*. Kent State University Press, Kent, Ohio.

Caldwell, J.R., and R.L. Hall, editors 1964 *Hopewellian Studies*. Illinois State Museum, Scientific Papers 12. Springfield, Illinois.

Dancey, W.S., and P.J. Pacheco, editors n.d. *Ohio Hopewell Community Organization*. Kent State University Press, Kent, Ohio, "in press."

Daniel, G. 1980 Neolithic Monuments. *Scientific American* 243(1):78-90.

Deuel, T., editor 1952 *Hopewellian Communities in Illinois*. Illinois State Museum, Scientific Papers 5, Springfield, Illinois.

Ellis, H.H. 1940 The Possible Cultural Affiliation of Flint Disk Caches. *Ohio State Archaeological and Historical Quarterly* 49(2):111-20.

Greber, N.B., and K.C. Ruhl 1989 *The Hopewell Site: A Contemporary Analysis Based on the Work of Charles C. Willoughby*. Westview Press, Boulder, Colorado.

Hawkins, R.A. 1986 *The Twin Mounds Village in Southwestern Ohio: A Ceramic Identity Crisis*. Masters thesis, Department of Anthropology, University of Cincinnati.

Kellar, J.H., A.R. Kelly, and E.V. McMichael 1962 The Mandeville Site in Southeast Georgia. *American Antiquity* 26(3):336-55.

Levi-Strauss, C. 1963 Do Dual Organizations Exist? In *Structural Anthropology*, by C. Levi-Strauss. Basic Books, New York.

Magrath, W.H. 1940 The Temple of the Effigy. *Scientific American* 163:67-8.

　　　　1945 The North Benton Mound: A Hopewell Site in Ohio. *American Antiquity* 11(1)4:0-6.

Mills, W.C. 1902 Excavation of the Adena Mound. *Ohio State Archaeological and Historical Publications* 10:452-79.

　　　　1916 Exploration of the Tremper Mound. *Ohio State Archaeological and Historical Publications* 25:363-98.

Mortine, W.A., and D. Randles 1978 *The Martin Mound: An Extension of the Hopewell Interaction Sphere into the Walhonding Valley of Eastern Ohio*. Muskingum Valley Archaeological Survey, Occasional Papers in Muskingum Valley Archaeology 10, Zanesville.

Munson, C.A., M.M. Jones, and R.E. Fry 1995 The GE Mound: An ARPA Case Study. *American Antiquity* 60(1):131-59.

Pi-Sunyer, O. 1965 The Flint Industry. In *The McGraw Site: A Study in Hopewellian Dynamics*, by O.H. Prufer, pp. 60-89. Cleveland Museum of Natural History, Scientific Publications 4(1), Cleveland.

Prufer, O.H. 1961 *The Hopewell Complex of Ohio*. Ph.D. dissertation, Department of Anthropology, Harvard University, Cambridge.

　　　　1962 Prehistoric Hopewell Meteorite Collecting: Further Evidence. *Ohio Journal of Science* 62(6):314-16.

　　　　1964 The Hopewell Complex of Ohio. In *Hopewellian Studies*, edited by J.R. Caldwell and R.L. Hall, pp. 17-83. Illinois State Museum, Scientific Papers 12, Springfield, Illinois.

1965 *The McGraw Site: A Study in Hopewellian Dynamics.* Cleveland Museum of Natural History, Scientific Publications, 4(1), Cleveland.

1967 The Scioto Valley Archaeological Survey. In *Studies in Ohio Archaeology*, edited by O.H. Prufer and D.H. McKenzie, pp. 267-328. The Press of Western Reserve University, Cleveland.

1968 *Ohio Hopewell Ceramics: An Analysis of the Extant Collections.* Museum of Anthropology, Anthropological Papers 33, University of Michigan, Ann Arbor.

1982 Hopewell Archaeology. *Reviews in Anthropology* 9(1):7-16.

n.d.a. How to Construct a Model: A Personal Memoir. In *Ohio Hopewell Community Organization*, edited by W.S. Dancey and P.J. Pacheco. Kent State University, Kent, Ohio, "in press."

n.d.b. Appendix to "Beyond the Scioto Valley: Middle Woodland Occupations in the Salt Creek Drainage," by Flora Church. In *Ohio Hopewell Community Organization*, edited by W.S. Dancey and P.J. Pacheco. Kent State University, Kent, Ohio, "in press."

n.d.c. Fort Hill 1964: New Data and Reflections on Hopewell Hilltop Enclosures in Southern Ohio. In *Ohio Hopewell Community Organization*, edited by W.S. Dancey and P.J. Pacheco. Kent State University, Kent, Ohio, "in press."

Rackerby, F. 1968 Levi-Strauss, Poverty Point, and the Misuse of Archaeology. *American Antiquity* 33(3):388-90.

Sears, W.H. 1953 *Excavations at Kolomoki: Seasons III and IV: Mound D.* University of Georgia, Series in Anthropology, Athens.

1964 The Southeastern United States. In *Prehistoric Man in the New World*, edited by J.D. Jennings, pp. 259-87. University of Chicago Press, Chicago

Shane, O.C. III 1971 The Scioto Hopewell. In *Adena: The Seeking of an Identity*, edited by B.K. Swartz, Jr., pp. 142-5. Ball State University, Muncie, Indiana.

Shetrone, H.C. 1925 Exploration of the Ginther Mound: the Miesse Mound. *Ohio State Archaeological and Historical Quarterly* 34:154-68.

Shriver, P.R. 1957 Our First Citizens. In *Portage Heritage*, edited by J.B. Holm and L. Dudley, pp. 17-26. The Portage County Historical Society, Ravenna, Ohio.

1982 The Towner Mound of Pippin Lake: A Northern Ohio Hopewell Site. *Ohio Archaeologist* 32(2):40-1.

Smith, B.D. 1992 Hopewellian Farmers of Eastern North America. In *Rivers of Change: Essays on Early Agriculture in Eastern North America*, pp. 201-248. Smithsonian Institution Press, Washington, D.C.

Squier, E.G., and E.H. Davis 1848 *Ancient Monuments of the Mississippi Valley.* Smithsonian Contributions to Knowledge 1. Washington, D.C.

Stothers, D.M., M. Pratt, and O.C. Shane III 1977 The Western Basin Middle Woodland Tradition: Non-Hopewellians in a Hopewellian World. In *Hopewell Archaeology: The Chillicothe Conference*, edited by D.S. Brose and N.B. Greber, pp. 47-58. Kent State University Press, Kent, Ohio.

Webb, W.S., and R.S. Baby 1957 *The Adena People No. 2.* Ohio Historical Society, Columbus.

Whitman, J.K. 1977 Kohl Mound, A Hopewellian Mound in Tuscarawas County. *Ohio Archaeologist* 27(3):4-8.

Zakucia, J., and J. Gunn 1974 Appendix A: New Radiocarbon Dates from the Upper Ohio Valley, in "The Boarts Site: A Lithic Workshop in Lawrence County, Pennsylvania," by J.M. Adovasio, G.F. Fry, J. Zakucia and J. Gunn. *Pennsylvania Archaeologist* 44(1/2):100-102.

JACK K. BLOSSER
Ohio Historical Society
Fort Ancient State Memorial
6123 State Route 350
Oregonia, Ohio 45054

FRANK N. BURKETT
Burgess and Niple Limited
5085 Reed Road
Columbus, Ohio 43220

A. MARTIN BYERS
Department of Social and Cultural Sciences
Vanier College
821 Blvd. Ste. Croix
Montreal, Quebec
Canada H4L3X9

JEFF CARSKADDEN
Muskingum Valley Archaeological Survey
24 South 6th Street
Zanesville, Ohio 43701

DONALD R. COCHRAN
Archaeological Resources Management Service
Department of Anthropology
Ball State University
Muncie, Indiana 47306

ROBERT P. CONNOLLY
Poverty Point SCA
P.O. Box 276
Epps, Louisiana 71237

C. WESLEY COWAN
Cincinnati Museum Center
1720 Gilbert Avenue
Cincinnati, Ohio 45202

WILLIAM S. DANCEY
Department of Anthropology
Ohio State University
124 W. 17th Avenue
Columbus, Ohio 43210

ROBERT A. GENHEIMER
Cincinnati Museum Center
1720 Gilbert Avenue
Cincinnati, Ohio 45202

N'OMI B. GREBER
Cleveland Museum of Natural History
1 Wade Oval
University Circle
Cleveland, Ohio 44106-1767

JAMES B. GRIFFIN
Department of Anthropology
Smithsonian Institution
Washington, D.C. 20560

REBECCA HAWKINS
Algonquin Archaeological Consultants, Inc.
3327 Bishop Street
Cincinnati, Ohio 45220-2105

JAMES HEILMAN
Dayton Museum of Natural History
2600 DeWeese Parkway
Dayton, Ohio 45414

BRADLEY T. LEPPER
Ohio Historical Society
1982 Velma Avenue
Columbus, Ohio 43211-2497

LYNN M. MAHONEY
Dayton Museum of Natural History
2600 DeWeese Parkway
Dayton, Ohio 45414

ROBERT C. MAINFORT, JR.
Arkansas Archaeological Survey
Sponsored Research Program
P.O. Box 1249
Fayetteville, Arkansas 72702-1249

JAMES MARSHALL
1828 South Roselle Road
Schaumburg, Illinois 60172-5016

JAMES MORTON
Muskingum Valley Archaeological Survey
24 South 6th Street
Zanesville, Ohio 43701

PAUL J. PACHECO
Muskingum Valley Archaeological Survey
6185 Old Stagecoach Road
Frazeysburg, Ohio 43822

WILLIAM H. PICKARD
1003 Carlisle Avenue
Columbus, Ohio 43224

OLAF H. PRUFER
Department of Anthropology
Kent State University
Kent, Ohio 44242

ROBERT V. RIORDAN
Department of Anthropology
Wright State University
Dayton, Ohio 45435

WILLIAM F. ROMAIN
26933 Greenbrooke Drive
Olmstead Twp., Ohio 44138

MARK F. SEEMAN
Department of Anthropology
Kent State University
Kent, Ohio 44242

CURTIS H. TOMAK
Indiana Department of Transportation
100 North Senate Avenue
Room N755
Indianapolis, Indiana 46024-2249

KENT D. VICKERY
Department of Anthropology
University of Cincinnati
811 Swift Hall
Cincinnati, Ohio 45221-0380

DEE ANNE WYMER
Department of Anthropology
Bloomsburg University
Old Science Hall
Bloomsburg, Pennsylvania 17815

"A VIEW FROM THE CORE: A SYNTHESIS OF OHIO HOPEWELL ARCHAEOLOGY" ERRATA

	PAGE	LOCATION	CORRECTION
1	Page v	Table of Contents, entry 21	replace "Tomack" with "Tomak"
2	Page vi	column 2, paragraph 2, line 4	replace "Key-Note" with "Keynote"
3	Page vi	column 2, paragraph 2, line 8	replace "arrived to late" with "arrived too late"
4	Page 6	column 1, paragraph 3, line 11	replace "Peabody" with "the Peabody"
5	Page 6	column 2, line 8	replace "Willoughy" with "Willoughby"
6	Page 7	column 1, line 2	replace "aka Jennison Guard" with "Whitacre, aka Jennison Guard"
7	Page 8	column 2, line 5 from bottom	replace "aproximately" with "approximately"
8	Page 12	column 2, sentence 5	quotation mark after "sixty" should be struck
9	Page 14	Altick, second citation	replace "Boblett group"with "Boblett Group", "Writer's" with "Writers" & "Springfield, Ohio" with "Springfield, Ohio"
10	Page 18	column 1, paragraph 1, lines 9 & 10	replace all "n.d." with "1997"
11	Page 18	column 1, paragraph 2, line 10	strike "which is currently in press"
12	Page 18	column 1, paragraph 2, lines 11 & 12	replace "Ohio Hopewell Community Organization" with "that volume"
13	Page 18	column 2, line 5 from bottom	replace "n.d." with "1997"
14	Page 19	column 1, line 2	"intraregional" should read "interregional and intraregional"
15	Page 19	column 1, last paragraph, line 1	replace "Griffin (n.d." with "Griffin (1997" and
16	Page 19	column 2, last paragraph, line 4	replace "(Greber n.d.)" with "(Greber 1997)"
17	Page 19	column 2, paragraph 2, line 8	replace "Russel" with "Russell"
18	Page 20	column 1, paragraph 2, line 3	replace "(n.d.)" with "(1997)"
19	Page 20	column 2, paragraph 2, line 19	replace "n.d." with "1997"
		column 2, paragraph 3, line 2	replace "n.d." with "1997"
20	Page 21	column 1, full paragraph 2, line 3	replace "n.d." with "1997"
21	Page 21	column 2, full paragraph 1, lines 8 & 14	replace "n.d." with "1997"
22	Page 22	column 1, paragraph 1, lines 13 & 17	replace "n.d." with "1997"
23	Page 25	Table 2:1, column 7, data rows 10 & 11	replace "Jonathan" with "Jonathan Creek"
24	Page 25	column 2, paragraph 1, last line (19)	replace "n.d." with "1997"
25	Page 26	column 2, line 4	replace "n.d." with "1997"
26	Page 27	column 2, lines 6 & 12	replace "n.d." with "1997"
27	Page 28	Table 2:2, data column 2, total	replace "27" with "28"
28	Page 28	column 1, line 27 (last line)	replace "n.d." with "1997"
29	Page 28	column 2, paragraph 2, line 3-4	replace "north-west" with "north-east"
30	Page 29	column 1, line 3	replace "n.d." with "1997"
31	Page 30	column 1, paragraph 1, quote last line	replace "emphasis added" with "figure citation added"
32	Page 30	Table 2:3, footnote	replace "Johnathan Creek" with "Upper Jonathan Creek"
33	Page 31	Figure 2:11, footnote	replace "Upper Johnathan Creek" with "Upper Jonathan Creek"
34	Page 32	column 1, full paragraph 1, line 22	replace "n.d." with "1997"
35	Page 33	Carskadden & Morton citation	replace "n.d." with "1997", strike "in press"
		Church & Ericksen citation	replace "n.d." with "1997", strike "in press"
36	Page 34	Dancy citation & Greber citation	replace "n.d." with "1997", strike "in press"
		Griffin citation & Kazarek citation	replace "n.d." with "1997", strike "in press"
		Lepper & Yerkes citation	replace "n.d." with "1997", strike "in press"
37	Page 34	Deboer citation and Dillehay citation	insert line space between "Deboer" citation and "Dillehay" citation
38	Page 35	Pacheco citation & Wymer citation	replace "n.d." with "1997", strike "in press"
39	Page 38	column 1, paragraph 2, line 1	hyphenate "paleoethnobotany" after the second "o"
40	Page 38	column 1, paragraph 3, line 7	hyphenate "paleoethnobotanical" after the first "o"
41	Page 41	column 1, paragraph 2, line 4	hyphenate "paleoethnobotanical" after the second "o"
42	Page 45	column 2, line 3	replace "was" with "were"
43	Page 46	column 1, title	replace "CERMONIAL" with "CEREMONIAL"

44	Page 47	column 1, full paragraph 1, line 3	replace "the Plains" with "The Plains"
45	Page 60	column 2, Figure 4:8, data row 5	replace "Cormarked-Limestone" with "Cordmarked -Limestone"
46	Page 60	column 2, Figure 4:8, footnote	replace "Traits: Unit" with "Traits: Units"
47	Page 60	column 2, full paragraph 1, line 1	insert a line space before this new paragraph
48	Page 65	column 2, paragraph 1, line 9	replace "occupants " with "occupants' " (add apostrophe)
49	Page 76	column 2, line 2	replace "sheds" with "sherds"
50	Page 76	column 2, line 7	replace "inter-site" with "intersite" (strike hyphen)
51	Page 78	column 2, paragraph 2, line 18	hyphenate "participation" after second "i"
52	Page 82	column 1, full paragraph 1, line 9	replace "seven unknown series" with "seven Unknown Series"
53	Page 84	column 2, second paragraph, line 16	replace "to" with "too"
54	Page 85	column 1, paragraph 2, line 13	replace "seven unknown series" with "seven Unknown Series"
55	Page 86	column 1, last paragraph, line 5	replace "Westt" with "West"
56	Page 87	column 1, Figure 5:7, footnote, line 1	replace "throught time" with "through time"
57	Page 87	column 2, last paragraph, line 12	replace "that" with "than'"
58	Page 126	Appendix, entry 6 B	replace "PLUMBROOK" with "PLUM BROOK"
59	Page 130	column 2, paragraph 2, line 3	replace "it's" with "its"
		column 2, paragraph 3, line 2	replace "it's" with "its"
60	Page 144	Figure 8:10, footnote	replace "bears's " with "bears' "
61	Page 153	column 1, Figure 9:2	replace original figure with insert
62	Page 168	column 2, first full paragraph, title	replace "SPACES WITHOUT WITHOUT" with "SPACES WITHOUT"
63	Page 170	column 1, line 26	replace "n.d." with "1997"
64	Page 171	Greber reference, ninth from top	replace "n.d." with "1997", strike "in press"
65	Page 176	column 1, paragraph 2, lines 5, 6 & 7	replace "Seip" with "Seip-Pricer"
66	Page 177	column 1, paragraph 2, line 7	replace "is Seip-Pricer and" with "is Seip-Conjoined and"
67	Page 176	column 1, paragraph 2, line 8	replace "Seip-Pricer" with "Seip-Conjoined"
68	Page 176	column 2, line 8	replace "and strategic" with "and the strategic"
69	Page 180	column 1, paragraph 3, line 7	replace "whose" with "those"
70	Page 180	column 2, full paragraph 1, lines 1 & 17	"Seip" should be "Seip-Conjoined"
71	Page 187	column 1, last paragraph, lines 1 & 2	replace "All" with "Most of" and strike "puddled clay"
72	Page 187	column 2, Table 10:2, data row 1	replace "Seip" with "Seip-Pricer" and "2 basins" with "3 basins"
73	Page 187	column 2, Table 10:2, data row 2	replace "Seip-Pricer" with "Seip-Conjoined"
74	Page 188	column 1, line 2	replace "Seip" with "Seip-Conjoined"
75	Page 188	column 2, paragraph 3, lines 1, 6 & 10	replace "Seip" with "Seip-Pricer"
76	Page 188	column 2, paragraph 3, lines 2, 3, 8 & 10	replace "Seip-Pricer" with "Seip-Conjoined"
77	Page 189	column 1, line 1	replace "Seip" with "Seip-Pricer"
		column 1, full paragraph 1, lines 1 & 4	replace "Seip" with "Seip-Pricer"
		column 1, paragraph 2, line 3	replace "Seip" with "Seip-Pricer"
		column 2, paragraph 1 after quote, line 2	replace "Seip" with "Seip-Pricer"
		column 2, paragraph 1, line 8	replace "Seip" with "Seip-Pricer"
78	Page 189	column 1, lines 4 & 6	replace "Seip-Pricer" with "Seip-Conjoined"
		column 1, full paragraph 1, lines 2, 3 & 4	replace "Seip-Pricer" with "Seip-Conjoined"
		column 1, paragraph 2, line 2	replace "Seip-Pricer" with "Seip-Conjoined"
		column 1, paragraph 2, line 5 (last)	replace "Seip-Pricer" with "Seip-Conjoined"
		column 2, quotation, lines 2 & 14	replace "Seip-Pricer" with "Seip-Conjoined"
		column 2, paragraph 1, lines 3 & 6	replace "Seip-Pricer" with "Seip-Conjoined"
		column 2, paragraph 1, line 6	replace "Seip-Pricer" with "Seip-Conjoined"
		column 2, paragraph 1, lines 8 & 9	replace "Seip-Pricer" with "Seip-Conjoined"
		column 2, paragraph 2, line 2	replace "Seip-Pricer" with "Seip-Conjoined"
79	Page 190	column 1, line 9 & 10	replace "Seip-Pricer" with "Seip-Conjoined"
80	Page 190	column 1, line 11	replace "Seip" with "Seip-Pricer"
81	Page 190	column 1, line 21	replace "small" with "smaller"

82	Page 190	column 1, line 22	replace "Seip-Pricer" with "Seip-Conjoined"
83	Page 190	column 1, Table 10:3, data row 1	replace "Seip" with "Seip-Pricer"
84	Page 190	column 1, Table 10:3, data row 2	replace "Seip-Pricer" with "Seip-Conjoined"
85	Page 197	column 1, line 2	insert space after "Nevertheless," and before "I"
86	Page 197	column 1, full paragraph 1, line 2	replace "sties" with "sites"
87	Page 197	column 1, paragraph 3, line 5	replace "Figure 11:1a" with "Figure 11:1A"
88	Page 197	column 2, paragraph 3, line 6	replace "Figure 11:1b" with "Figure 11:1B"
89	Page 198	column 1, paragraph 2, line 4	replace "11:1c" with "11:1C"
90	Page 198	column 1, paragraph 3, line 4	replace "11:2a" with "11:2A"
91	Page 198	column 1, paragraph 3, line 11	replace "11:2b" with "11:2B"
92	Page 198	column 1, paragraph 4, line 1	replace "11:2c" with "11:2C"
93	Page 199	column 2, full paragraph 1, line 6	replace "1,500" with "1,050"
94	Page 199	column 2, full paragraph 1, line 9	replace "11:3a" with "11:3A"
95	Page 199	column 2, full paragraph 2, line 1	replace "11:3b" with "11:3B"
96	Page 199	column 2, last line	replace "11:3c" with "11:3C"
97	Page 200	column 2, paragraph 1, line 6	replace "11:4a" with "11:4A"
98	Page 200	column 2, paragraph 2, line 2	replace "11:4b" with "11:4B"
99	Page 200	column 2, paragraph 3, line 7	replace "11:5a" with "11:5A"
100	Page 201	column 1, line 3	replace "11:5b" with "11:5B"
101	Page 203	column 2, last line	replace "11:7a" with "11:7A"
102	Page 204	column 1, line 4	replace "11:7b" with "11:7B"
103	Page 204	column 1, line 5	replace "11:8a" with "11:8A"
104	Page 204	column 1, line 7	replace "11:8A" with "11:8A"
105	Page 204	column 1, line 11	replace "11:8b" with "11:8B"
106	Page 207	column 2, paragraph 1, line 4	strike "that"
107	Page 208	column 1, line 1	strike the comma following "hypothesis"
108	Page 212	column 2, last paragraph, line 2	replace "197" with "187"
109	Page 217	Figure 12:7 caption, line 3	replace "alighned" with "aligned"
110	Page 234	column 1, lines 2, 8 & last line	replace "n.d." with "1997"
		column 2, line 5	replace "n.d." with "1997"
111	Page 238	column 2, paragraph 2, line 3	replace "n.d." with "1997"
112	Page 239	Greber citation	replace "n.d." with "1997", strike "in press"
113	Page 240	Lepper & Yerkes citation	replace "n.d." with "1997", strike "in press"
114	Page 240	between McMichael and Mills citations	remove one space/line
115	Page 245	column 1, paragraph 1, line 9	strike the space between "ha" and the ff. comma
116	Page 245	column 2, full paragraph 2, line 4	replace "Green" with "Greene"
117	Page 252	column 2, full paragraph 2, line 6	replace "state" with "stage"
118	Page 252	column 2, full paragraph 2, line 11	replace "n.d." with "1997"
119	Page 253	column 1, line 7	replace "a refuge points" with "as refuge points"
120	Page 253	column 2, line 8	replace "been expedient" with "been an expedient"
121	Page 254	column 1, last paragraph, line 1	replace "Green" with "Greene"
122	Page 255	Prufer citation	replace "n.d." with "1997", strike "in press"
123	Page 260	column 2, last paragraph, line 2	comma and space should follow "....1925)"
124	Page 262	column 2, section heading "METODS"	replace "METODS" with "METHODS"
125	Page 262	column 2, paragraph 2, line 11	replace "limestone slab" with "limestone slabs"
126	Page 265	column 2, full paragraph 1, line 2	replace 'eastern most' with 'easternmost'
127	Page 270	column 1, paragraph 3, line 14	replace "that area" with "that an area"
128	Page 270	column 2, paragraph 1, line 6	replace "marks" with "mark"
129	Page 272	Connolly citation	replace "n.d." with "1997", strike "in press"
130	Page 285	Pleise citation	insert period and space after "ca" and before "1981"
131	Page 299	column 2, paragraph 3, line 8	replace "imported items" with "items imported"
132	Page 310	column 2, line 5	replace "Chilicothe" with "Chillicothe"
133	Page 309	column 1, line 2	replace "n.d." with "1997"
134	Page 313	Carskadden citation	replace "n.d." with "1997", strike "in press"
135	Page 319	column 2, last paragraph, line 14	replace "n.d.a." with "1997a"
136	Page 321	column 1, line 23	replace "n.d.a." with "1997a"
137	Page 326	column 2, line 5	replace "n.d.a." with "1997a"

138	Page 327	column 1, line 5	replace "n.d.a." with "1997a"
139	Page 328	Figure 19:6 caption	strike "and cannel coal"
140	Page 329	column 1, line 1	replace "n.d.b." with "1997b"
141	Page 329	column 2, paragraph 3, line 12	replace "place" with "placed"
142	Page 330	column 1, paragraph 2, line 3	replace "n.d.b." with "n.d."
143	Page 331	column 1, lines 2 and 3	replace "suggest" with "suggests" and "others" with "other"
144	Page 334	column 1, paragraph 2, line 2	replace "drop on" with "drop in"
145	Page 336	Carskadden & Morton citation	replace "n.d.a." with "1997a", strike "in press" replace "n.d.b." with "n.d."
146	Page 358	Figure 21:3, footnote	replace "aerial view" with "aerial view; buildings to the north'
147	Page 372	column 1, paragraph 3, line 5	strike "cf" abbreviation
148	Page 373	column 1, paragraph 3, line 3	strike "cf" abbreviation
149	Page 375	column 1, paragraph 1, line 2	strike the 2 "cf" abbreviations
150	Page 376	column 1, line 4	strike "cf" abbreviation
		column 2, paragraph 1, line 6	strike "cf" abbreviation
		column 2, paragraph 2, line 5	strike "cf" abbreviation
151	Page 376	column 2, paragraph 2, line 18	strike "see"
152	Page 376	column 2, paragraph 3, line 5	strike "cf" abbreviation & "see also"
153	Page 377	column 2, paragraph 2, line 15	strike "cf" abbreviation
154	Page 379	column 1, full paragraph 1, line 6	">" should read "approx."
155	Page 381	column 1, full paragraph 2, line 9	strike "see"
156	Page 381	column 2, paragraph 3, line 1	strike "cf' abbreviation
157	Page 382	column 1, paragraph 2, line 12	strike "cf" abbreviation
		column 1, last paragr, line 3	strike "cf" abbreviation
158	Page 383	column 1, line 4	strike "cf" abbreviation
		column 1, full paragraph 1, lines 2 & 11	strike "cf" abbreviation
159	Page 384	column 1, paragraph 1, line 10	strike "cf" abbreviation
160	Page 384	column 2, paragraph 1, line 17	"350 A.D." should read "A.D. 350."
161	Page 385	column 2, line 5 (last line)	strike "e.g."
162	Page 387	column 1, line 3	strike "e.g."
163	Page 387	column 2, paragraph 2, line 19	strike "cf" abbreviation
		column 2, paragraph 3, line 4	strike "cf" abbreviation
164	Page 391	Williams & Brain, last reference	reference was truncated: should continue *Excavations at the Lake George Site, Yazoo County, Mississippi, 1958-1960, Peabody Museum of Archaeology and Ethnology, Harvard, University, Cambridge.*
165	Page 400	column 1, lines 10 and 11	"a book" should read "the book", strike "in progress"
166	Page 400	column 1, line 12	"n.d." should read "1997"
167	Page 403	Dancy & Pacheco, third ref from bottom	replace "n.d." with "1997", strike "in press"
168	Page 408	column 1, lines 14 & 15	replace "n.d." with "1997", strike "which is currently in press"
169	Page 408	column 2, paragraph 3, line 5	replace "n.d." with "1997"
170	Page 409	column 1, line 11	replace "n.d.b." with "1997b"
171	Page 413	column 1, paragraph 4, line 3	replace "n.d.a." with "1997a"
172	Page 416	column 1, paragraph 1, line 11	"Marshal" should read "Marshall"
173	Page 417	column 1, paragraph 2, line 5	replace "n.d.a." with "1997a"
174	Page 418	column 1, paragraph 2, line 10	replace "n.d." with "1997"
175	Page 423	column 2, line 11	replace "n.d." with "1997"
176	Page 424	Dancy & Pacheco, sixth ref from top	replace "n.d." with "1997", strike "in press"
177	Page 425	Prufer, fifth, sixth, & seventh refs from top	replace "n.d.a." with "1997a", strike "in press", replace "n.d.b." with "1997b", strike "in press", replace "n.d.c." with "1997c", strike "in press"